'This book is a must-read for both those troubled by the basis of CBT's dominance in the field of psychotherapy, and also those who are persuaded by the rhetoric put out by CBT's supporters. The critique found in this collection of essays is broad ranging, deep and utterly convincing.'
Farhad Dalal, psychotherapist and group analyst, and author of *CBT: the cognitive behavioural tsunami*

'Perhaps there is no discussion where the fault line between modernity and what's next is more starkly revealed than in the ongoing debate between promoters of CBT and those who champion humanistic, person-centered and meaning-focused psychotherapies. I can think of no other single book that gives practitioners of any persuasion a compass by which to navigate the liquid cultural moment.'
Maureen O'Hara PhD, Professor of Psychology, National University, US, and Director, International Futures Forum-US

'This book provides an interesting range of viewpoints on the prevalence of CBT in the NHS today. The brief, protocol-driven IAPT curriculum training omits complex philosophical and theoretical CBT underpinnings. CBT is at great risk of being watered down to the point of disintegration. This book goes some way toward discussing the commercialisation of CBT at the cost of its integrity.'
Rhena Branch, CBT practitioner/psychologist and co-author of *The Cognitive Behavioural Counselling Primer* (PCCS Books)

I went to an excellent workshop a few years ago led by Professor Aaron Beck. Talking therapies balance relationship and structure: too much structure can lose the individual; too little structure perhaps misses out on helping people learn effective ways of changing; Without relationship, no amount of structure – whether evidence based or not – will help. There is often too much criticism in our wider society. We can see the 'opponent' not the person – or practitioner. It's good to ask questions of each other. CBT emphasises Socratic questions – powerful questions that aid understanding. As someone who loves questions, I welcome this book for its varied and challenging perspectives. None of us should be afraid to stop, think and reflect on our ways of working. I hope that these different perspectives lead to reflection and improved understanding across therapies. Perhaps achieving balances between relationship and structure points to a way forward.
Professor Chris Williams MBChB, BSc, MMedSc, MD, FRCPsych,
President of the British Association for Behavioural and Cognitive Psychotherapies

Why Not **CBT?**

AGAINST *and* FOR CBT
REVISITED

EDITED BY
DEL LOEWENTHAL & GILLIAN PROCTOR

An updated second edition of
Against and For CBT: towards a constructive dialogue?

First edition published 2008
This second edition 2018

PCCS Books Ltd
Wyastone Business Park
Wyastone Leys
Monmouth
NP25 3SR
contact@pccs-books.co.uk
www.pccs-books.co.uk

Why Not CBT?
Against and for CBT revisited

British Library Cataloguing in Publication data: a catalogue record for this book is available from the British Library.

ISBN 978 1 910919 34 7

Cover design by Jason Anscomb
Front cover illustration © Roz Woodward (Thinkstock)
Typeset in-house by PCCS Books using Minion Pro and Myriad Pro
Printed by Short Run Press, Exeter, UK

Contents

THE FOLLOWING ARE REPRODUCED WITH THE KIND PERMISSION OF THE PUBLISHERS.

AMERICAN PSYCHOLOGICAL ASSOCIATION

Woolfolk R, Richardson F (1984). Behavior therapy and the ideology of modernity. *American Psychologist 39*(7): 777–786.

TAYLOR AND FRANCIS, UK

Bracken P, Thomas P (1999). Cognitive therapy, Cartesianism and the moral order. *European Journal of Psychotherapy and Counselling 2*(3): 525–544.

Guilfoyle M (2008). CBT's integration into societal networks of power. *European Journal of Psychotherapy and Counselling 10*(3): 197–205.

Hemmings A (2008). Critiques of CBT. *European Journal of Psychotherapy and Counselling 10*(3): 271.

Lees J (2008). Cognitive behavioural therapy and evidence-based practice; past, present and future. *European Journal of Psychotherapy and Counselling 10*(3): 187–196.

Mansell W (2008). Commentary on contexts of CBT: a weak case against a straw man but a strong case for an informed debate about how to improve access to effective psychological therapies. *European Journal of Psychotherapy and Counselling 10*(3): 261–269.

Pilgrim D (2008). Reading *Happiness*: CBT and the Layard thesis. *European Journal of Psychotherapy and Counselling 10*(3): 247–260.

Proctor G (2008). CBT: the obscuring of power in the name of science. *European Journal of Psychotherapy and Counselling 10*(3): 231–245.

Snell R (2007). Book review. *European Journal of Psychotherapy and Counselling 9*(2): 231–239.

Strong T, Lysack M, Sutherland O (2008). Considering the dialogic potentials of cognitive therapy. *European Journal of Psychotherapy and Counselling 10*(3): 207–219

Winter, D. (2008) 'Cognitive behavior therapy: from rationalism to constructivism?' *European Journal of Psychotherapy and Counselling 10*(3): 221–229.

TAYLOR AND FRANCIS, USA

Bryceland C, Stam H (2005). Empirical validation and professional codes of ethics: description or prescription? *Journal of Constructivist Psychology 18*: 131–155.

WILEY, UK

Milton J (2001). Psychoanalysis and cognitive behavioural therapy: rival paradigms or common ground? *International Journal of Psychoanalysis 82*: 431–447.

Acknowledgements

First, we would like to thank Richard House, co-author of the first edition, who managed to both encourage this second edition and not be a co-editor! We would in particular like to thank the following contributors who revised, and in many cases rewrote, their chapters for the first edition, with both enthusiasm and timeliness: Arthur C Bohart, Patrick Bracken, David Brazier, Christy Bryceland, Konstantinos Chondros, Isabel Clark, Michael Guilfoyle, Adrian Hemmings, Richard House, John D Kaye, Paul Kelly, John Lees, Mishka Lysack, Warren Mansell, Jane Milton, Fred Newman, Paul Moloney, Stephen Palmer, David Pilgrim, Frank C Richardson, Andrew Samuels, Robert Snell, Henderikus Stam, Tom Strong, Olga Sutherland, Philip Thomas, Keith Tudor, David A Winter and Robert L Woolfolk. Many thanks also to Andrew Samuels and Stephen Palmer for their forewords. Further thanks to Jay Watts, who accepted our invitation to write a new chapter for this second edition.

We particularly also want to thank Trudy Meehan for her help following the sad and sudden death of her husband, Michael Guilfoyle, whose insightful critical thinking was and is so important to so many.

Once again, Del would like to acknowledge staff and students at the Research Centre for Therapeutic Education in the Department of Psychology, Roehampton University, UK, who are associated with the UKCP existential-analytic psychotherapy training through the Southern Association for Psychotherapy and Counselling (SAFPAC). Also, thanks to the Critical Psychotherapy Network for their help in reviewing some of the chapters. Particular thanks to Elizabeth Nicholl, again of the Research Centre for Therapeutic Education, for so ably keeping the project on track. Gillian would like to thank Del and Richard for inviting her to co-edit this edition, and the team for the MA in counselling and psychotherapy programme at the University of Leeds (Jane Cahill, Stuart Gore, John Lees and Netalie Shloim) for ongoing support and debate and constructive dialogue among diverse approaches.

We also very much wish to acknowledge and thank Catherine Jackson of PCCS Books, who has been so ably there for us throughout the evolution of this second edition.

Finally, thanks also to Taylor and Francis, publishers of the European Journal of Psychotherapy and Counselling (in which several of the book's chapters originally first appeared) for their co-operation, and also to the American Psychological Association and Wiley.

Abbreviations

ACT	Acceptance and commitment therapy
ADD/ADHD	Attention deficit (hyperactivity) disorder
AI	Artificial intelligence
APA	American Psychological Association
BABCP	British Association for Behavioural & Cognitive Therapies
BACP	British Association for Counselling & Psychotherapy
BPS	British Psychological Society
CAT	Cognitive analytic therapy
CBT	Cognitive behaviour/al therapy
CBCT	Cognitive-based compassion training
CCT	Client-centred therapy
CfD	Counselling for depression
CFT	Compassion-focused therapy
CMT	Compassionate mind therapy
CT	Cognitive therapy
DBT	Dialectical behaviour therapy
DIT	Dynamic interpersonal therapy
DSM	*Diagnostic and Statistical Manual of Mental Disorders*
EBM	Evidence-based medicine
EBMWG	Evidence-Based Medical Working Group
EBP	Evidence-based practice
EST	Empirically supported treatments
ESVT	Empirically supported/validated treatments
IAPT	Improving Access to Psychological Therapies
ICS	Interacting cognitive subsystems
IPT	Interpersonal psychological therapy
MBCT	Mindfulness-based cognitive therapy
MiBCT	Mindfulness-integrated cognitive behaviour therapy
NHS	National Health Service
NICE	National Institute for Health and Clinical/Care Excellence
OCD	Obsessive compulsive disorder
PCSR	Psychotherapists and Counsellors for Social Responsibility
PCT	Person-centred therapy *or* personal construct therapy *or* perceptual control theory
PTSD	Post-traumatic stress disorder
PWP	Psychological wellbeing practitioner
RCT	Randomised controlled trial
RET	Rational-emotive therapy
TCC	*Les therapies cognitivo-comportementales*
TEACCH	Treatment and Education of Autistic and Related Communication-handicapped Children
UKCP	UK Council for Psychotherapy

Foreword

Andrew Samuels

I very much welcome the second edition of this book. Its arguments are no less needed than they were 10 years ago. The government is continuing to support the expansion of the Improving Access to Psychological Therapies (IAPT) programme in England. Psychotherapists have failed, in my view, to express our concerns about it with sufficient force. We have allowed the proponents of CBT to caricature all other psychotherapies as delving unendingly into the patient's past and lacking any scientific validity as regards efficacy. Yet CBT's science is clearly inadequate, the methods naïve and manipulative, and the reluctance to engage with the deep and complex relationship between client and therapist is very inappropriate. Hence the urgent need for this revised edition.

What are we actually referring to when we speak of against or for CBT? There have been some robust and enlivening engagements in the psychotherapy world between those favouring a major shift in the balance of available therapeutic help towards CBT, and those, like me, who have long championed the importance of pluralism and diversity in the field. I take it as axiomatic that competition and bargaining are, in some sense, unavoidable and even valuable between approaches to psychotherapy, or any other praxis (my book *The Plural Psyche* (Routledge, 1989) was all about this). If such pluralism is cancelled out by professional putsch or government fiat, then the contribution psychotherapy can make to social justice and social policy will be muted.

It is therefore hardly surprising that what I (and many others) have objected to is the expectation that we will take CBT's allegedly scientific status as incontrovertible; that we will accept without murmur that it need not be exposed to the kind of pluralistic competition to which all other therapy modalities are, continuously and rightly, subject. One of the main strengths of this welcome updated collection is that it provides us with many cogent and convincing arguments for, at the very least, questioning the epistemological underpinnings and the methodological validity of the 'evidence-based' ideology in which CBT and its supporters have become accustomed to basking.

We have long needed a systematic and incisive taking-apart of the case for positivistic randomised controlled trial and related methodologies. For too long, these have been uncritically accepted as the 'gold standard' by which therapeutic experience should be measured. This book presents compelling arguments for a more reflective and considered methodological exploration.

Nearly all therapists agree that the relationship formed with the client or clients is at the core of what they do. CBT has recently begun to take a more concerted, creative, and non-mechanistic interest in the therapeutic relationship, and some have spotted an opportunity for an alliance between CBT and other therapies therein. But there is still little in the CBT literature about the power dynamics of the therapy relationship. Moreover, the crucial, often decisive part played by the therapist's subjectivity is dangerously under-recognised. In CBT, the therapist and patient/client tend to be seen as what the jargon calls 'unified subjects' – monolithic agents with all that we know about external and internal difference and diversity smoothed out. A number of the chapters in this book shine a very revealing light on these lacunae.

It is also refreshing that many of the book's chapters face head on the linked political and ethical questions that arise when psychotherapy is given – and slavishly accepts – a social-engineering or economistic mission (getting clients back into the workforce, off benefits, and so on). Certainly, a close reading of this book will decisively undermine any remaining claim that the inexorable rise of an allegedly value-free CBT in modern Western societies has nothing to do with political and economic interests. I am reminded here of the mediaeval notion of *trahison des clercs*, resurrected in the 1920s to describe the betrayal by intellectuals and professionals of their ideals and calling in pursuit of material gain.

Of the many other critical themes highlighted and skilfully developed in the book, I would like to mention just two that have special resonance with my own interests and practice. First, there is what I perceive to be the silence of CBT around questions of meaning and purpose that are absolutely central to the contemporary clinical project of psychotherapy. I do not think the situation is changed much when an attempt is made to bolt on a bit of 'meaning', as in the case of mindfulness-based cognitive therapy. It is sometimes difficult to imagine how on earth CBT's 'model of the person' and the kinds of spiritual practices entailed in mindfulness could conceivably sit together – and sceptics like me can easily find ourselves wondering whether this reversal on the part of CBT is not, in fact, driven by insuperable problems within its mainstream application. Jung, following Heraclitus, wrote of *enantiodromia* – the way things swing to their opposite when they have become too one-sided, in order to survive unaltered. Sometimes this leads to fruitful fusion; sometimes to an ersatz outcome; sometimes to the secret dominance of one of the elements in the equation, appearances to the contrary notwithstanding. *Enantiodromia* always requires penetrating analysis.

Another – and somewhat predictable – concern is CBT's lack of any perspective on, or consideration of, the unconscious, especially the creative unconscious. This in turn touches on quite fundamental questions about the possibilities and limitations of agency and autonomy. To address these questions, we need to locate

CBT and its model of the person in terms of the evolving history of ideas. A claim is made for the success of conscious and realistic control of 'thought' at the very moment when the *zeitgeist* is redolent with a ubiquitous sense of perpetual and unmanageable risk and the consequent inevitability of political failure. We should invoke the Trade Descriptions Act. This book provides the reader with ample food for thought in addressing these questions.

In closing, I want to say, as a pluralist, that I am again delighted to know of another competing foreword to my own from a major figure in the field, Stephen Palmer, who I believe is far more favourably disposed towards CBT than I am. I also greatly welcome the three substantial chapters in this book that make a case for CBT. I believe there needs to be a great deal more of such engagement before we can begin to assess just what common ground, if any, the different therapy approaches are able to inhabit.

But I welcome most of all this splendid new book in itself. It promises to open up a crucial and long-overdue dialogue and introduce the associated 'battle for the soul' of therapy work itself. Battles over praxis naturally involve polemic, and here, once again, I turn to Heraclitus, who told us that Polemos (war, strife, conflict) is 'the Father of all and the King of all'. How this battle unfolds – including its possible truces, armistices, treaties and subsequent alliances – is an essential prerequisite for our work reaching the kind of maturity to which we individually and collectively aspire.

Foreword

Stephen Palmer

A decade has passed since the first edition of this book was published. It certainly was thought-provoking then, and the revised edition is no different. The majority of the contributors still hold strong views. Of course, this is understandable.

My colleagues and I set up the Centre for Stress Management in 1987, and I am still working there as a trainer, therapist, coach, supervisor and researcher. Based on our practice, we have found that the cognitive behavioural approach is generally effective with the stressed clients we see in London. Our approach focuses on both the psychological and practical aspects of a presenting issue, whether it is a clinical disorder and/or life event the client is having to address. This solution-seeking, dual-systems model is particularly effective for tackling both stress-related emotional and practical problems. My experience undoubtedly influences my perspective in any argument for or against CBT. Recently, a workshop delegate suggested that I was 'evangelical' as a CBT trainer – I would prefer to view myself as an enthusiastic pracademic (that is, an academic and practitioner) who is informed by my experience and knowledge of the research.

I had hoped that in this book that there would be a gradual shift in opinions towards a consensus. Some of the criticisms of CBT in this book still do not accurately reflect modern practice. As a number of the contributors have commented, there is a difference between first-, second- and third-wave CBT. In my own practice, I still believe there is a place for all three waves of CBT, and this is reflected in my published work (for example, Palmer, 2015; Curwen, Palmer & Ruddell, 2018). For a specific phobia, a simple, first-wave behaviour therapy intervention, such as exposure therapy, is effective, and a client can overcome a phobia they have had for decades in one extended therapy session. There is no need to allocate time to cognitive interventions in these particular cases. On the other hand, examining beliefs is important for some presenting issues. I meet CBT therapists who are aligned to third-wave therapies and seldom use thought records, as apparently they 'don't work'. Yet, in my practice, clients have found them really helpful. So, even within CBT, there can be divergences of opinion, although these are not major issues. A key factor is that CBT practitioners have generally been influenced by research findings. I realise that some authors in this book have questioned the validity of these findings. However, as a therapy, CBT's outcomes are easier to measure, because it is goal-focused.

Perhaps the real issue is whether or not we can establish the truth through reasoned arguments and debate. It's doubtful, as whatever arguments are put forward, it is nearly always possible to undermine them from a particular angle. At times it seems CBT has been demonised, and this can even over-generalise to its advocates.

CBT will continue to evolve, develop and adapt. If a technique or strategy is effective, CBT practitioners are likely to incorporate it into their practice, while still using a cognitive behavioural theoretical framework. Innovation has been embraced by the CBT community. For example, CBT has easily adapted to online environments and computers, which some clients prefer. A free CBT system, 'Woebot' (*https://woebot.io*), can be accessed online via Facebook messenger. It is educational and users can self-refer, starting CBT within 60 seconds. It undertakes a brief assessment to check the user's mood, asks questions, engages in a conversation, and also uses informative videos. You can have a daily appointment. According to Woebot, 'clients' start to feel better after two weeks. After a short chat, it does remind you it is a 'robot' and states that it is 'not capable of really understanding the nuances of what you say or need'. It advises that, in emergencies, the user can type 'SOS' and Woebot will send some resources. This is a giant leap forward from ELIZA, developed by Joseph Weizenbaum in 1966, which was a simple computer programme that emulated a Rogerian client-centred therapist. Weizenbaum did find that some people believed that ELIZA was a real therapist. Of course, his computer programme was still revolutionary in its time.

It is likely that, in another decade or two, we will have the fourth wave of CBT. Will it be influenced by the positive psychology field and/or futuristic online or phone app technology? Perhaps, with the technological innovations, we have just entered the fourth wave and we haven't noticed. I am really interested to see what it will be like, and hope that Del Loewenthal and Gillian Proctor will assist in continuing the dialogue. My thanks go to all the contributors who have given their time in sharing their views with us in this book.

References

Curwen B, Palmer S, Ruddell P (2018). *Brief Cognitive Behaviour Therapy* (2nd ed). London: Sage.

Palmer S (2015). *The Beginner's Guide to Counselling and Psychotherapy*. London: Sage.

Weizenbaum J (1966). ELIZA – a computer program for the study of natural language communication between man and machine. *Communications of the ACM* 9(1): 36–45. See http://psych.fullerton.edu/mbirnbaum/psych101/Eliza.htm (accessed 4 February 2018).

Introduction to the second edition

Del Loewenthal and Gillian Proctor

It is now 10 years since the first edition of *Against and for CBT* was published. Judging by sales, it is still very relevant to those involved in the psy fields. Much has changed in that period, where CBT has become increasingly dominant. However, much has also remained unchanged, or magnified. This is in part due to the state's ever-expanding interest in mental health. Here, increasingly, therapy is provided to help growing numbers of clients take their minds off their problems, in preference to attempting to help work their difficulties through or providing the social and economic environment to minimise their occurrence. We think all approaches have their place, but no one therapeutic approach can claim to be 'the only game in town'.

This domination by CBT, in turn, is having enormous effects on the provision and training of all psychological therapists and the responses of their professional bodies. Thus the need, we think, for this second, updated edition.

Some of the original chapters have been almost completely rewritten – for example, those by Michael Guilfoyle; Paul Kelly and Paul Moloney; Tom Strong, Olga Sutherland, Mishka Lysack and Konstantinos Chondros; David Winter, and Jane Milton. Other chapters have been updated significantly, such as those by Christy Bryceland and Henderikus Stam; Pat Bracken and Phil Thomas; Keith Tudor and David Pilgrim. There are only two chapters that have not seen any changes. One is the seminal work by Robert Woolfolk and Frank Richardson, and the other the important work by the sadly departed Fred Newman. We also commissioned Jay Watts to write a new chapter, bringing us up to date with what is happening out there, in the field, in the way CBT is being delivered.

Richard House, one of the founding editors of *Against and for CBT*, was keen to have a second edition. So too was PCCS Books. However, Richard's interests were focused elsewhere, and he persuaded Del to take the reins. He, in turn, was delighted when Gillian agreed to co-edit this edition. Gillian has spent the last 10 years experiencing first hand the vagaries of CBT-dominated IAPT from within, and then training counsellors working in IAPT, with ever-increasing concerns about the impact on clients and therapists alike (see Proctor & Hayes, 2017).

There was the question, too, of this book's title, which we felt could do with a refresh: this is more than a tweaked second edition, and, as Warren Mansell points out in his chapter, very few of the contributors have engaged in this second edition with what other contributors wrote in the first. If anything, the 'against' arguments have become louder. We are left therefore with the embarrassing question as to whether most of us would rather stay on our own hobby horses than dismount to engage in a dialogue with others that might leave us open to change ourselves. Are we too much caught up with attempting to change others? In the end, we decided on *Why not CBT? Against and for CBT revisited,* which we felt captured the essence of this second edition and reminds readers that it isn't the first.

In asking why CBT is not the solution to mental distress, most of the chapters in this book offer critiques and warnings of the dangers of the CBT model – literally, reasons 'why not' CBT. Conversely, the chapters by proponents of the model (Clarke, Hemmings and Mansell) ask, why not offer CBT as one approach among many that can be helpful, apply the critiques to other models of therapy too, and promote an approach to CBT that places the client and the therapy relationship at the centre? Here our CBT colleagues offer us fine examples of taking critiques seriously and offering another perspective. Indeed, this book offers a fine example to students of therapy wanting to learn about critical analysis.

The chapters

In this second edition, we have changed the order of the sections, bringing forward Political and Cultural Perspectives to the start of the book and repositioning the CBT Perspectives and Responses to the end, which seemed to make more sense, as they are answering many of the critiques in the earlier sections.

Political and cultural perspectives

Our first chapter in this section is Michael Guilfoyle's chapter, 'CBT's integration into societal networks of power'. Here, Michael argues that, like any clinical practice, CBT is a participant in societal networks of power relations. He explores how the success and widespread recognition of CBT may be a function, not of its effectiveness *per se*, but of its comfortable integration with, and in, certain circumscribed fields (for example, clinical psychology), and its assignation of an authoritative role within existing cultural and institutional power arrangements and common-sense discourse. For Michael, the danger of its institutional success is the establishment and legitimisation of a therapeutic hegemony, in which therapists are ranked, therapeutic activities prescribed, and clients required to shape their identities in line with particular normalising discourses and practices. All of this, in his view, contributes not only to the diminishment of a once rich landscape of therapeutic possibilities, but also to a curbing of the people, communities and ways of living to which our practices can speak.

In the second chapter, 'CBT: the obscuring of power in the name of science', Gillian Proctor explores how CBT addresses power in therapy, and suggests that CBT therapists need to give this some serious consideration. She considers the concept of 'collaboration' in CBT and proposes that this is more accurately described as 'compliance', with the aim to encourage the client to internalise the therapist's approach. She then points to the power of the appeal to science by CBT, and questions the notion of the therapist's objectivity, noting the lack of the ethical principle of respect for client autonomy in the BABCP ethical framework (2009, 2016). Gillian suggests that the focus on beneficence, along with the claim for objectivity and expertise of the therapist, leads to paternalism and the disempowerment of the client. She concludes by proposing that it is necessary for CBT to look realistically and honestly at the dynamics of power in therapy relationships, for without such an inquiry, CBT therapists are in danger of obscuring their power, and not taking an ethical stance to avoid domination and abuse.

In Chapter 3, 'Happiness: CBT and the Layard thesis', David Pilgrim argues that, in the past 10 years, the economist Professor Lord Richard Layard has applied his particular form of naïve British empiricism to the challenge of curing mental illness and understanding wellbeing in society. David expands on this assessment of Layard's contribution. He argues that Layard's summary of upstream factors that affect mental health has not been without merit. However, for David, Layard's reliance on psychiatric knowledge as an indicator of psychological distress and dysfunction has been reductionist and unilluminating. David argues that this problem has been compounded by Layard's assumption that 'mental illness' can be cured with a few sessions of CBT. David concludes by elaborating on the implications of this appraisal.

In Chapter 4 we again reproduce Robert Snell's excellent chapter '*L'Anti-Livre Noir de la Psychanalyse*: CBT from a French/Lacanian perspective'. Here, Robert considers considers the 'invasion' of France by Anglo Saxon-dominated CBT, and the attack on the 'irony, scepticism, and disrespect, definitively anti-modern' nature of French psychoanalysis. A new marketing onslaught is outlined – 'TCC', which is being presented to health administrators and insurance companies as 'a fully developed product, meeting European and international standards and offering rapid and low-cost solutions to the majority of psychological problems'. Psychoanalysis in France 'finds itself under new and fierce attack', Robert writes. In summarising *L'Anti-Livre Noir de la Psychanalyse*, Robert illustrates how the struggle so eloquently dramatised in the book has a far wider relevance. There is a political and ideological battle going on in the UK, as in France and elsewhere: 'Psychotherapists of whatever persuasion, if they are concerned to oppose the technologising of the human spirit, need to take its arguments very seriously indeed'.

Chapter 5 is Paul Kelly and Paul Moloney's 'CBT is the method: the object is to change heart and soul'. In this much-revised chapter, Kelly and Moloney provide a critical exploration of CBT in relation to three main issues: first, how CBT practitioners claim to ease distress, while simultaneously supporting the outlook of neo-liberalism and entrenching some of its main socio-political causes; second, a critical analysis of outcome evidence for the effectiveness of CBT, particularly in relation to the IAPT programme in England; and third, a brief critical evaluation of so-called third-wave CBT, which has incorporated the South-East Asian meditative practice of 'mindfulness'. They conclude with the argument that CBT is a neo-liberal therapy, designed to support the ideal of the enterprising, flexible, competitive, individualistic self. Kelly and Moloney argue that, in doing so, this therapeutic approach deflects attention from how psychological damage is inflicted, above all, by the world in which people live.

Chapter 6, Jay Watts' contribution, 'The social construction of CBT', was specially commissioned for this second edition. For Jay, CBT is referred to in policy, research and, increasingly, the public domain as if it were a thing. Yet, as she discusses in this chapter, CBT refers to an umbrella of approaches with little, if anything, in common. For Jay, its 'thingness' can be unpacked easily, as she illustrates. She argues that maintaining the idea that CBT is a thing is a powerful act, and one that serves the vested interests of key stakeholders. But, Jay questions, is this really in the interests of service users? She argues that CBT's 'We do this too' approach to anything that works in the psychotherapy world gets in the way of real progress by inserting a brand name, and accompanying ideology, unnecessarily into the therapeutic encounter, squeezing the opportunity for choice away from service users.

Paradigmatic perspectives

The first chapter in the Paradigmatic Perspectives section is Robert Woolfolk and Frank Richardson's 'Behaviour therapy and the ideology of modernity'. In this classic text, they analyse the moral and epistemological underpinnings of behaviour therapy from a socio-historical, hermeneutic perspective. For Woolfolk and Richardson, the *Weltanschauung* of behaviour therapy is closely linked with the values and patterns of thought characteristic of modernity. Readers may also be interested in Woolfolk's further exploration (Woolfolk, 2015) of the major problems with research on CBT, given that he considers that it relies on the randomised controlled trial as crafted by the pharmaceutical industry. Woolfolk considers this critique not so much to reveal the disguised ideology of CBT, but rather to highlight problems in the research methodology (in the form of a logical muddle) that lead to an overstatement of its benefits. Here, for Woolfolk, even when applying its own standards, CBT fails as a rigorous scientific practice.

Our next chapter in this section (Chapter 8) is David Brazier's 'CBT in historico-cultural perspectives'. Against a backdrop of awareness of the fundamental problem of how humankind is to learn to live in peace and wellbeing on an increasingly crowded planet, David offers an intriguing, long-term perspective on the main currents of thought in psychology and Western culture. Here, David argues that 'romantic', 'classical' and 'utilitarian' tendencies, deriving from our Judeo-Christian and Greek heritage, take turns to dominate in the history of Western ideas. Furthermore, these trends are manifest in the different forms taken by therapeutic psychology, not only in ideals, but also in methodologies, and even in the professional rivalries that they spawn. David suggests that the dominance of any one tendency can only ever be a transient phenomenon, thus offering perspective on the relative popularity of particular contemporary methods.

Chapter 9 concerns 'Cognitive behaviour therapy and evidence-based practice', by John Lees. Here, John explores how CBT and evidence-based practice are currently favoured by the government and healthcare authorities in England, and how this is a cause for anxiety and concern among some therapists. John argues that, if we take a broader view of the current debates about these approaches to clinical practice in the counselling and psychotherapy profession, based on the evolution of consciousness, we can develop a different view about the current state of affairs. John concludes by outlining his view that our understanding of such developments can be transformed if we adopt a broader, evolutionary perspective.

Our last chapter in this section is 'Cognitive therapy, Cartesianism, and the moral order', by Pat Bracken and Phil Thomas. In a reworking of their original chapter, they accept that cognitive therapy is one of the best known and most often prescribed interventions currently available in the field of mental health. They seek to show that this form of therapy is based on a cognitivist understanding of mind, which ultimately derives from a rationalist, Cartesian philosophy. Bracken and Thomas argue that this understanding is consonant with the values endorsed by consumer capitalism, and so this form of therapy is neither politically nor ethically neutral, nor objective.

Clinical perspectives

In the first chapter in this next section (Chapter 11), Jane Milton considers 'Psychoanalysis and cognitive behaviour therapy: rival paradigms or common ground?' She compares the psychoanalytic and cognitive behavioural paradigms. The psychoanalytic participant-observer stance, focusing on unconscious communication taking place within the therapeutic relationship, allows access to deeper layers of the mind than the cognitive approach. This, Jane argues, makes psychoanalysis both more radical and more intrusive: the more socially ordinary stance of the CBT therapist may be more immediately acceptable and comfortable than the psychoanalytic one, to both patients and therapists. Jane traces how cognitive therapy split from psychoanalysis, using Beck's biography. She argues that CBT is steadily altering as it rediscovers the phenomena known to analysts: transference, countertransference and resistance. She further argues why attempts to 'integrate' CBT and psychoanalytic therapy will result in an essentially cognitive approach. Finally, Jane examines the empirical research base that seeks to compare these very different paradigms. She points to recent evidence that medium-term psychoanalytic treatments have something additional and substantial to offer.

In his intriguingly-titled Chapter 12, 'Person-centred therapy – a cognitive and behavioural therapy', Keith Tudor questions, this time from a person-centred perspective, some of the politics surrounding CBT, including the trend toward short-termism. In the first edition of this book, Tudor also examined some of the research evidence on CBT in comparison with other therapies, and especially person-centred therapy (PCT). As that argument has been well made, in this edition he has replaced it with new material that locates PCT as a process-centred therapy and delineates its ontology, epistemology, methodology and method. This serves as an introduction to and philosophical grounding for the second part of his chapter, in which, as a counterpoint to the apparent dominance of CBT in the psychology of cognition and behaviour, he elaborates the less-known or less-considered cognitive and behavioural aspects of PCT.

David Winter's Chapter 13 is on 'Cognitive behaviour therapy: from rationalism to constructivism?' David points out that, in current treatment guidelines, the treatment of choice for most psychological problems is stated to be cognitive behaviour therapy. In this chapter, David takes a critical view of the evidence base from which this recommendation is drawn and reviews an alternative evidence base that considers the relationship between clients' and therapists' philosophical beliefs, 'personal styles', and treatment preferences. David focuses in particular on the distinction between rationalist and constructivist epistemological positions, the reflections of which in therapeutic practice are illustrated by approaches to the client who is considered to be resistant. Implications of constructivist trends apparent in the diversification of cognitive behaviour therapy are discussed.

Del Loewenthal's Chapter 14, 'Post-existentialism as a reaction to CBT?,' then seeks to describe a place for exploring notions of wellbeing at the start of the 21st century that is in contrast to the increasing cultural dominance of CBT, and to offer an alternative, post-postmodern place where we might still be able to think about how alienated we are through valuing existential notions such as experience and meaning. In proposing post-existentialism in part as a reaction to CBT, Del is not doubting that some clients will benefit more from CBT, nor that, in terms of conventional costings, it can be more cost effective. But he is concerned about *any* therapy approach being a 'totalising move', warning that we need to beware of 'making CBT culturally dominant in a way such that we can no longer recognise ourselves and are too frightened at any possibility of doing so'.

In their new chapter for the second edition, Chapter 15, 'Considering the dialogic potentials of cognitive therapy', Tom Strong, Mishka Lysack, Olga Sutherland and Konstantinos Chondros argue that there has emerged a distorted version of CBT, where therapists alone (not clients and therapists together) judge what correct thinking is or should be in clients' lives. Encouraged by collaborative and social constructionist developments inCBT, they propose dialogic and discursive (that is, social constructionist) ideas as collaborative resources for how CBT might yet develop. Adapting these ideas, they critically examine how CBT might be narrowly practised in monologic or ideological ways that obscure and negate client preferences and resourcefulness. They then turn a Bakhtinian and discursive lens on therapeutic dialogue itself to consider a CBT practised in ways that are collaborative, critically reflective, and generative.

Epistemological and research perspectives

John Kaye opens this section with his chapter on 'Thinking thoughtfully about cognitive behaviour therapy'. Here, John explores the ongoing evolution of CBT theory and methodology towards an enriched cognito/emotive process model. He critiques what he terms a first-order therapeutic model, governed by a foundational paradigm with its codified assessment and associated manualised interventive techniques. Arguing that this model is limiting and potentially iatrogenic, Kaye then traces the emergence of a second-order model, incorporating concepts and techniques from outside the dominant paradigm – for example, visualisations, acceptance of experience, mindful observation, interoceptive imaging, and narrative, discursive and existential exploration. John argues that engagement in such processes that are inimical to the maintenance of embedded patterns enables an alternative stance toward experience, disruption of established emotionally troubling patterns and formation of transfigured interpretive pathways.

In the next chapter, Chapter 17, 'CBT and empirically validated therapies: infiltrating codes of ethics', Christy Bryceland and Henderikus Stam argue that codes of ethics have begun to refer to preferences that interventions be 'empirically supported'. They start by examining how the movement towards empirically supported treatments (ESTs) is based on a medical model of intervention that uses randomised controlled trials as the prime method, and presumes standardised, 'objective' procedures that demonstrate interventions in an unambiguous manner. For Bryceland and Stam, this methodology limits the demonstrable efficacy of alternative forms of psychotherapy. They then consider the historical context of the professionalisation of psychotherapy, the development of modes of outcome research, and the role of institutional texts, such as ethics codes. They argue that the latter can act as regulatory tools, guarding the autonomy of the psychology profession and responding to the pressures of the market to maintain psychology's self-regulatory role. The move toward placing ESTs within codes of ethics is premised on limited conceptions of therapy that, they argue, fail to grasp the moral nature of the therapeutic relationship.

In Chapter 18, 'Empirically supported/validated treatments as modernist ideology, part I: the dodo, manualisation and the paradigm question', Bohart and House first examine the so-called dodo bird verdict in psychotherapy and its paradigmatic significance. They then outline the implicit logic of the paradigm underlying the empirically-supported/validated treatments (ESVT) approach (of which CBT is a prominent exemplar), along with the implicit logic of an alternative plausible paradigm – a relational one. They maintain that the latter can convincingly be argued to underlie, and make sense of, psychotherapy experience and practice, of which the ESVT criteria seem to make at best only limited sense. Bohart and House argue that the research and practice of psychotherapy need to remain open to a rich diversity of alternative paradigms until, through the slow, steady accumulation of results and by emerging common consent, one or another paradigm begins to take prominence. Finally, they maintain that there exist 'evidence-based' and demonstrably effective ways of practising therapy that do not depend upon the ESVT world-view.

In the next chapter, Chapter 19, 'Empirically supported/validated treatments as modernist ideology, part II: alternative perspectives on research and practice', House and Bohart look at phenomena central to an alternative paradigmatic world-view and its associated research undertaking, paying particular attention to phenomenological qualities like subtlety, intuition, discernment and 'the tacit', which rarely, if ever, figure in scientistic therapy research and practice. They discuss the role of science and human relational experience and follow this with an exploration of 'tacit knowledge' (Polanyi), the role of the therapy practitioner, and the place of subtlety and intuition in therapy work, where 'intuitive practitioners' openly and unapologetically acknowledge that we often don't know what we are doing. House and Bohart advocate moving from a *competency*-centred to a *being*-centred conception of therapy work, concluding that a 'trans-modern' world-view entails moving far beyond therapy as mere technology and the medical-model 'diagnosis/treatment' approach envisaged by cognitively biased CBT and positivistic evidence-based practice. Instead, they advocate embracing the reality that therapy as healing practice entails many practitioner qualities that are in principle beyond rational modernist specification.

Chapter 20 is Fred Newman's 'Where is the magic in cognitive therapy? A philo/psychological investigation', which is unchanged from the first edition, where it was described by House and Loewenthal as exploring the connection between cognitive therapy and common sense, the relationship between common sense and science, and the inter-relationships between the cognitive, the linguistic and the post-modern turn. We are treated to an engagingly discursive, philosophical *tour de force* that incorporates such philosophical giants as Quine, Davidson, Wittgenstein, Vygotsky and Searle – and, of course, Fred Newman and Lois Holzman's own distinctive brand of 'social therapy'. As always with Newman's writings, the reader is in for a journey of many fascinating philosophical twists and turns –not least, the post-modern one.

CBT perspectives and responses

The next chapter, which opens this final section of responses to the 'against' arguments, asks, 'What is CBT *really* and how can we enhance the impact of effective psychotherapies such as CBT?' Here, Warren Mansell notes what he sees as the unfortunate lack of dialogue between the contributors following the first edition of this book. He then brings this in as part of a wider critique of the 'silos' of therapeutic disciplines and psychological theory that are more generally holding back discoveries and innovations in mental health. Warren systematically describes and rebuts the criticisms of CBT, both through considering the historical, philosophical and conceptual origins of CBT and through identifying the essential criteria of adherence to CBT. Warren agrees that CBT is subject to criticisms that are shared with other forms of counselling and psychotherapy – namely, that they are inefficient, not sufficiently client-led, and their components of delivery and practice are not informed by a single, unified theory. For Warren, the therapist typically makes untested assumptions about the nature of the client's problems and the number of sessions of therapy required. In contrast, Warren argues, method of levels therapy, based directly on perceptual control theory, allows the client to control the timing, duration and pace of therapy and, by asking questions to sustain awareness on chronic goal conflicts, aims to help the client regain control of their lives as a whole.

The next chapter, chapter 22, by Isabel Clarke, is entitled 'The case for CBT: a practical perspective from the NHS frontline'. Isabel starts by agreeing, as she sees it, with other contributors that issues of power are central, and links these with successive efforts to reign in medical power. Isabel identifies evidence-based medicine as the latest to attempt an external standard. She acknowledges the limitations of the Layard analysis, but welcomes the unprecedented injection of funds into talking therapies provided through IAPT. Isabel defends CBT as being collaborative and respectful and safe for working with people with severe and acute problems. She cites recent, mindfulness-based developments in CBT as introducing a broader philosophical base. She further cites a CBT founded in interacting cognitive subsystems and dialectical behaviour therapy as providing a sophisticated model of the person, combined with an easily grasped therapeutic rationale. She concludes her chapter with developments since the first edition of this book, including a movement to re-envisage mental health beyond diagnosis, and more pluralism of modality within IAPT.

In the last chapter in this section, Chapter 23, Adrian Hemmings writes 'A response to the chapters in *Why Not CBT?*'. Here, Adrian responds to some of the criticisms of CBT made by other authors in the book. He starts by examining the research evidence for CBT, which he considers makes a strong case for the usefulness of CBT. However, Adrian also acknowledges the flaws in the research methodology – particularly the preponderance of randomised controlled trials and efficacy studies, and the lack of acknowledgement of therapist effects. He goes on to describe what he considers to be the almost exclusive use of CBT in IAPT, and reviews opportunities to integrate CBT with other models. Adrian then challenges the notion of CBT being a single entity and highlights the danger of focusing on specific aspects of some schools of CBT in order to criticise CBT as a whole. Next, he evaluates the pros and cons of CBT's relationship with powerful institutions, before concluding with an examination of the therapeutic relationship in CBT that challenges the view that the potential abuse of power is unique to this model.

Finally, the original conclusion to the first edition, Del Loewenthal and Richard House's 'Contesting therapy paradigms and what it means to be human' is followed by Del Loewenthal and Gillian Proctor's conclusion to this second edition, 'No single therapy should be the only game in town'. In the conclusion to the first edition we stated our hope that the book would lead to more of a 'constructive dialogue' between the different psychotherapeutic schisms. In the conclusion to this second edition, we also consider why this original aim has at best been only partially achieved.

References

BABCP (2009, revised 2016). *Standards of Conduct, Performance and Ethics.* [Online]. www.babcp.com/files/About/BABCP-Standards-of-Conduct-Performance-and-Ethics-0917.pdf (accessed 4 February 2018).

Proctor G, Hayes C (2017). Counselling for Depression: a response to counselling education in the twenty-first century. Ethical conflicts for a counselling approach operating within a medicalised bureaucratic health service. *British Journal of Guidance & Counselling* 45(4): 417–426.

Woolfolk RL (2015). *The Value of Psychotherapy: the talking cure in an age of clinical science.* New York, NY: Guilford Press.

Introduction to the first edition: an exploration of the criticisms of CBT

Richard House and Del Loewenthal

In the UK, at the start of the 21st century, critical reflection on the place of cognitive behaviour therapy (CBT) in current therapeutic practice, and in the prevalent cultural discourse around wellbeing and 'happiness' (Layard, 2005), has garnered substantial (and not always flattering) media attention (eg. Hope, 2008). These developments have dominated the kinds of impromptu discussions in which therapists commonly engage with each other about 'developments in the field'.

In other European countries, such as France (see Miller, 2006; Snell, Chapter 4, this volume), and even further afield – for example, Australia (see Kaye, Chapter 16, this volume), there is also a developing critical discourse around CBT. Yet what is the precise nature of these criticisms, and are they any more than the defensive arguments of vested interest groups whose over-long-held privileges are being threatened? Or even the envious attacks of the displaced and the superseded in therapy's 'free' market?

We are being somewhat provocative here, of course. Yet, in our experience, CBT has certainly tended to become the unwilling target – a convenient kind of cultural whipping boy, even – upon which disgruntled therapists of each and every hue have tended to project their current dissatisfactions, whatever their origin, and we certainly do not excuse ourselves from having occasionally 'used' CBT in such a less-than-mature way.

In some senses, we do believe that CBT has received an unfair press, and, to date, there has been little systematic and concerted attempt within the specifically academic therapy literature to engage thoughtfully with the controversies around it. In this book, then, we aim to address this previous lack by initiating a robust, yet (as we hope and intend) constructive dialogue about CBT's place on the modern therapy landscape and within the wider culture.

As co-editors of *Against and for CBT*, we of course have our own views about CBT, which are located toward the critical end of the spectrum. For DL, CBT is fine as one approach among many within a rich plurality of different approaches, particularly for those who cannot bear the thought of thoughts coming to them, but disastrous as the main approach for a whole society. RH fundamentally questions the assumptive (modernist) world-view that underpins CBT's foundational theory and practice. Yet, we would like to think that we are both also committed to embracing a questioning, deconstructive sensibility in our work – and not least toward our own, cherished and taken-for-granted assumptions and prejudices. So, in this book, we have actively welcomed an open and mutually respectful dialogue between some of CBT's most articulate critics and several of CBT's able theorists and practitioners. It will not serve either 'side' if each merely snipes at the other from deeply entrenched positions and defences, without each, at the very least, making a genuine effort to understand the other's position.

'Normal schism' in the psychotherapy world?

The psychotherapy world has historically been riven by schism and, at worst, scarcely containable internecine warfare (eg. King & Steiner, 1992; see also, Dryden & Feltham, 1992; Feltham, 1999), and it seems to us that recent struggles in and around CBT are merely the latest manifestation of such conflicts. This leads us in turn to say a few words about our chosen book title [for the first edition]. Some colleagues have expressed surprise at *Against and for CBT*, in that it suggests 'sides' and schism, and is potentially divisive. Our own view is that, for some years, there has indeed been an all-too-real, eminently tangible 'paradigm war' going on in the therapy field, and we certainly don't wish to hide behind any 'mom-'n-apple-pie' political correctness in somehow denying that reality, or pretending everything is fine and that 'we all love each other really'. Such a position would be to deny the very real conflicts over power, resources and (professional) identity that many of our contributors illuminatingly write about in this book. Moreover, our question mark in the book's subtitle [*Towards a constructive dialogue?]* is also telling, for we believe it to be very much an open question, given the scale of the vested interests and competitive resource issues at stake in what is an environment of comparative scarcity, whether any such rapprochement and shared understanding will ultimately be possible. In our view, we would not be doing the field any service at all to pretend that real-world schism and bad feeling doesn't exist, when they quite demonstrably do. Take the highly topical issue of research, for example.

CBT has recently and very rapidly become the battleground upon which a veritable 'paradigm war' (Kuhn, 1962) is playing itself out between 'modernist' and 'postmodernist' views on what legitimate and appropriate research into the psychological therapies might look like. From our own quasi-postmodernist position (which-is-not-one), for example, we believe that randomised controlled trial (RCT) methodology is open to a range of compelling challenges that, in our view, have never been satisfactorily responded to – namely, that (see Bohart & House, Chapter 18, this volume):

- its statistical methodology hides, through the comparison of means, what actually happens to individuals in the trial – meaning, for example, that there may easily be some people in both groups who are worse off after 'treatment'
- RCT methodology therefore ignores the different responses of different individuals to the same treatment, so that, as Heron argues, it 'cannot help with the everyday question, "What is the treatment of choice for this individual patient?"' (1996: 198; see Hemmings, Chapter 23)
- it tends to ignore the powerful effect of mind on body, and the latent phenomenon of self-healing
- RCT methodology simply assumes the validity of its univariate approach, which separates out the single treatment variable from all other influences to assess its causal impact (as if real, lived life were like that); thus, for example, the interplay of differences in the extent and quality of therapist experience, the nature and extent of their supervision etc, etc are not 'variables' that are able to be fully considered
- it objectifies suffering as a 'thingified' process, reifying 'external' causal influence and ignoring subjective illness categories experienced and made sense of by the patient/client, and ignoring too the meaning or tacit intentionality of the illness
- RCT methodology ignores the possibility that its so-called 'statements of fact' (including variable specification and measurement) may inevitably be theory and value laden, and can only be formulated within a pre-existing (and self-fulfilling) set of theoretical assumptions, which can then so easily become a circular proving of what was assumed to exist at the outset (see Parker et al, 1995)
- the populations studied through RCTs are different to the ones that present for therapy, and, finally
- the methodology usually assumes fixed treatment goals, which are only applicable to some modalities.

Hemmings (Chapter 23) and others in this book add further to the fascinating debate about the place of RCT and other 'positivist' methodologies in psychotherapy research. This can be seen as part of a wider discussion that is only starting to re-emerge on 'What is research?' (see, for example, Loewenthal & Winter, 2006; Loewenthal, 2007). We would tend to follow Lees' approach (Chapter 9) in advocating a paradigmatic meta-view that attempts to locate and account for our historically and culturally specific methodological procedures within the context of the evolution of consciousness (Crook, 1980; Tarnas, 1991), if we are to gain a reflexive purchase on those methods and, hopefully, deepen and widen them (see also House & Bohart, Chapter 19).

Research methodology is just one of the central themes with which the chapters in this book grapple in attempting to identify and clarify the various points of difference that exist between CBT and its critics and just what might be at stake in legislating or choosing between those different positions.

Opening up a dialogue?

As a way into opening up a long overdue dialogue – which included a conference on CBT held at Roehampton University in November 2008 – we offer some contextualising questions under several key headings – questions that are variously addressed in the following chapters. It is the full engagement with these questions that we regard as essential if we are to make collective progress beyond the rather unhelpfully polarised positions that the 'pro' and 'anti' CBT camps have commonly occupied to date. As we will see, there are also some significant reservations from within the CBT field itself, such as the claim that it was never intended as just a short-term approach. On the other hand, it is claimed by some CBT proponents that developments within CBT have more than answered what they assert to be increasingly caricatured and outdated concerns. We have therefore organised below what are some, hopefully, evocative and pertinent questions from the following perspectives: paradigmatic, clinical, epistemological and research, and political and cultural.

Paradigmatic perspectives

- Is it helpful to attempt to locate CBT within wider paradigmatic perspectives on 'modernity' and 'post-modernity'? (for example, Lees, Chapter 9, and Woolfolk & Richardson, Chapter 7, this volume).
- To what extent is it possible to get to the root of the foundational/metaphysical differences between the world-views of CBT and other therapy approaches – and can we at least respectfully 'agree to differ' about those metaphysical assumptions, and then track through what the implications are for therapy practice that necessarily stem from those paradigmatic differences?
- To what degree, if at all, can 'modernist' CBT, on the one hand, and therapies influenced by postmodern thinking on the other, be commensurable and able to converse with one another – and, if a 'good-enough' degree of commensurability is not achievable, then what is to be done?

Clinical perspectives

- First, as a relatively unified approach to therapy practice, to what extent is the category 'CBT' a coherent, valid category – or is there greater diversity within the category than its assumed unitary status implies?
- To what extent might critics of CBT be setting up a 'straw man' category?
- What model of therapeutic change underpins CBT, and to what extent does that model of change differ from that of other modalities?

- What does it mean to say that CBT 'works' – and to the extent that it does, can we say how much this is down to CBT-specific characteristics, and how much to the kinds of relational 'common factors' across all modalities that some researchers have identified (eg. Hubble, Duncan & Miller, 1999; van Kalmthout et al, 1985), or to its being a culturally sanctioned vehicle for healing in 'late modernity' (eg. Frank & Frank, 1991)?

Epistemological and research perspectives

- What counts as valid research in reaching a view about CBT's efficacy? And how do we legislate or discriminate between different research ontologies and methodologies?
- Can we reach some kind of agreed consensus across the field about what an appropriate methodology researching into therapy experience and efficacy might look like? And what are the implications if such a consensus proves to be impossible to reach?
- How can we appropriately include clients' voices in our discussions about CBT and how it is experienced by clients?
- How do we satisfactorily approach any possible trade-off that might exist between effectiveness, cost and diversity in therapy practice?

This latter question then leads naturally on to...

Political and cultural perspectives

- To what extent, if at all, is it fair to cast CBT as a 'quick-fix' therapy approach that is being pushed for wider economic, Treasury-driven motivations (the so-called happiness agenda (Layard, 2005; see Pilgrim, Chapter 3)?
- What is the balance of responsibility between policymakers, the CBT field itself, and the 'modernist' zeitgeist for the way in which CBT has increasingly been made into the prevailing therapy of 'choice' in modern Western societies?
- What understanding of power as a social and political process does CBT subscribe to, if any? And how does CBT respond to its critics around questions of power?
- Can and should the influence of economics and a political agenda be kept out of the consulting room? And what are the implications of this for practitioners, clients and for society more generally?

These various questions only begin to scratch the surface of the issues thrown up by the CBT question – and a close reading of the following chapters will doubtless throw up a long list of further questions that should surely be exercising a critically minded psychotherapy world at this key moment in the evolution of the field.

Towards a conversation, rather than none at all?

We hope the following chapters succeed in opening up a long-overdue conversation about the place of CBT within the evolving field of psychotherapy and counselling. This is a conversation that, to date, has been conducted via disgruntled snatches and polemical broadsides rather than in anything like the kind of systematic and respectfully open way that would be needed for light and insight (rather than heat and prejudice) to be generated and reflectively thought about.

The kinds of questions raised in this book are ones that we all surely need to face and reflect upon if the unpleasantness of current schisms in the field are to lose at least some of their divisiveness. Our hope is that this can take us towards the engaged and constructive, mutually respectful dialogue and tolerance of difference that we believe are important values of the work we do in this peculiar activity of ours.

References

Crook J (1980). *The Evolution of Human Consciousness.* Oxford: Oxford University Press.

Dryden W, Feltham C (eds) (1992). *Psychotherapy and its Discontents.* Milton Keynes: Open University Press.

Feltham C (ed) (1999). *Controversies in Psychotherapy and Counselling.* London: Sage.

Frank JD, Frank JB (1991). *Persuasion and Healing: a comparative study of psychotherapy* (3rd ed). Baltimore, MD: Johns Hopkins University Press.

Heron J (1996). *Co-operative Inquiry: research into the human condition.* London: Sage.

Hope J (2008). Talk therapy for the depressed 'could be wasting millions'. *Daily Mail*, 7 July: 25.

Hubble MA, Duncan BL, Miller SD (1999). *The Heart and Soul of Change: what works in therapy.* Washington, DC: American Psychological Association.

King P, Steiner R (eds) (1992). *The Freud–Klein Controversies, 1941–45.* London: Routledge.

Kuhn TS (1962). *The Structure of Scientific Revolutions.* Chicago, IL: Chicago University Press.

Layard R (2005). *Happiness: lessons from a new science.* London: Allen Lane.

Loewenthal D (2007). *Case Studies in Relational Research.* Basingstoke: Palgrave Macmillan.

Loewenthal D, Winter D (2006). *What is Psychotherapeutic Research?* London: Karnac Books.

Miller J-A (ed) (2006). *L'Anti-Livre Noir de la Psychanalyse.* Paris: Editions de Seuil.

Parker I, Georgaca E, Harper D, McLaughlin T (1995). *Deconstructing Psychopathology.* London: Sage.

Tarnas R (1991). *The Passion of the Western Mind: understanding the ideas that have shaped our world view.* London: Pimlico.

Van Kalmthout MA, Schaap C, Wojciechowski FL (eds) (1985). Common Factors in Psychotherapy. Lisse: Swets & Zeitlinger.

POLITICAL AND CULTURAL PERSPECTIVES

1 CBT's integration into societal networks of power*

Michael Guilfoyle

Like any clinical practice, CBT is a participant in societal networks of power relations. This chapter explores one aspect of this and considers how the success and widespread recognition of this approach may be a function not of its effectiveness per se, but of its comfortable integration with, and, in certain circumscribed fields (for example, clinical psychology), its assignation of an authoritative role within existing cultural and institutional power arrangements and commonsense discourse. Our Enlightenment heritage calls for a rationalist ordering of the therapies, in accordance with narrow and preconstructed values and knowledges that correspond with and can take forward those of society's most powerful institutions. I suggest that it is within this context that we should understand CBT's overwhelming emergence as 'the therapy of choice'. The danger of its institutional success is the establishment and legitimisation of a therapeutic hegemony, in which therapists are ranked, therapeutic activities prescribed, and clients required to shape their identities in line with particular normalising discourses and practices. All of this, in my view, contributes not only to the diminishment of a once rich landscape of therapeutic possibilities, but also to a curbing of the people, communities, and ways of living to which our practices can speak.

My argument is that CBT's success as a therapeutic form owes much to its strategic success in the domains of institutional and political power. I suggest that its discourses and practices are both aligned with and subject to many of the dominant *political* requirements of a modern therapy: it *looks* – perhaps more than other therapies – scientific; it has a reasonable – though far from exemplary – 'empirical evidence base'; it sits comfortably with existing dominant mental health and medical discourses, policies and practices; it is apparently time-efficient and therefore economically justifiable, and its language is close enough to that of

*An earlier version of this chapter appeared in the *European Journal of Psychotherapy and Counselling* 2008; 10(3): 197–206.

Western commonsense discourse (for example, consider the popular binaries of positive/negative, rational/irrational) to make its relevance immediately visible to large sectors of the lay public. This is not an approach that will cause too much trouble for existing power structures and ways of coordinating institutional practices. It is a politically convenient technology, whose theoretical tools are not designed to help us critique the political, social, and cultural practices of persons' lives, except to the extent that these practices seem unscientific, irrational or lacking in evidence. It tends to stick to solving problems within psychiatrically and medically accepted terms. It changes people's thoughts so that they can get back to an *a priori*, taken-for-granted political landscape, hence adapting their lives to this apparently 'real' world. CBT has managed to manoeuvre itself, more successfully than any other approach, into the policies and decision-making structures of professional psychological bodies and mental health systems internationally.

In this landscape, in order for a therapy to even be in the race – to be in contention for the title 'therapy of choice' – it must satisfy a few simple criteria: it must be amenable to measurement, standardisation and manualisation. If it is not, it cannot hope to be a serious contender. This immediately and substantially reduces the field, barring entry to a host (perhaps the majority) of therapeutic approaches. However, we should be clear that their exclusion is *not in any way* a comment on their effectiveness or lack thereof. All we can say is that excluded therapies do not comply with a particular way of playing the game and deciding on winners. Interestingly, CBT practitioners do not always adhere to the 'science' or the manual in practice. Waller, Stringer and Meyer (2012) have noted that practitioners tend to 'drift' theoretically and practically (p171). What I found most intriguing in these authors' paper is their belief that this is a problem to be resolved. They were less interested in the possibility that 'drift' might *aid* effectiveness and focused more on calling on practitioners to fall back into line – to stick to the script. After all, it is only in this way that these practitioners can really participate in the scientifically and politically sanctioned race. It seems to me that effectiveness, as such, has become less important than scientific compliance.

CBT's complicity with contemporary power arrangements – in, for example, legal, educational, psychiatric, psychological, political, even commonsense institutions – is surely a comfort to its practitioners. This complicity reassures the practitioner of continued support and approval, and permits its alignment with broader social, political, medical, economic and cultural aims and objectives. But what continues to strike me is the extraordinary difficulty of challenging with any effectiveness the taken-for-granted belief that this approach is superior – in almost all scientific respects – to other therapies. It is worth dwelling on this for a moment, because it tells us much about how the therapeutic landscape has evolved and is evolving.

Impotent critiques of CBT

A series of critiques have been articulated in relation to CBT itself and its alleged superiority over other approaches. But it seems to me they have been largely ineffective in shifting the discourse about how therapies are evaluated.

The first difficulty in effectively critiquing CBT lies in the apparent refusal of its promoters to recognise the enormous complexity of the requirement that our therapies be ranked according to evidence. Certainly, its scientifically 'proven' status – its success in 'the race' – has been challenged on many fronts (see the many relevant chapters in this volume): its selective use of scientific principles; its blurring of efficacy and effectiveness; its skewed research populations and simplistic categorical view of the person; its mechanistic and objectivist orientation to research, despite the availability of alternative models of science that might enable more nuanced accounts of persons (cf. Clarkson, 2003), and there is even much contradictory 'scientific' evidence. A considerable amount of research, for example, supports the notion that common factors contribute more to therapeutic change than specific factors associated with (for example) CBT (Andrews, 2000; Messer & Wampold, 2002; Bohart & House, Chapter 18, this volume).

It has been argued that much of the 'evidence' for CBT is actually nothing of the sort. For instance, Wampold and colleagues (2017), who recently conducted an examination of meta-analyses that concluded in favour of CBT over other approaches, found that these studies were built on the foundations of problematic primary studies, and yielded only small, non-significant effects. Similarly, Shedler (2011) reported that some studies found no advantage for CBT (his focus was on psychodynamic therapies in particular), but, as he put it: 'No one took notice' (p152). His argument is that this selectivity indicates that some practitioners (and academics) 'value only evidence that supports an *a priori* agenda, while ignoring, dismissing, or attacking evidence that does not'. He goes on to say: 'This is not science, but ideology masquerading as science' (p154). So problematic is the reading of the 'evidence' – particularly in the UK – that Bolsover (2002) has described CBT's promotion as 'a marketing rather than a research strategy' (p294). On these accounts, CBT's success is more to do with its marketing prowess and with its ideological situation. I refer to such related ways of thinking about CBT's success in terms of its integration with networks of power.

Wampold and colleagues (2017) also raise the issue of *which* CBT is being spoken of when it is advanced as what Tarrier (2002) has termed 'the treatment of choice' (p291). It is by no means one single approach, and different studies incorporate certain techniques and therapies into their definition of CBT (eg. dialectical behaviour therapy, mindfulness, schema therapy), while others do not. It is also evident that many experienced CBT practitioners do not strictly adhere to the manuals supported by the 'science' (Waller, Stringer & Meyer, 2012). Waller and colleagues call for practitioners to look out for this apparently dangerous drifting tendency – as if it were the product of laziness or a lack of rigorous reflection, or worse, of their seduction by other approaches – and to move back to adherence to the manual. Does this not effectively call on experienced practitioners, who might have otherwise learned to practise in ways that attend to the nuances and complexities of their clients' lives – a level of complexity that CBT itself is not designed to notice (Bolsover, 2002) – to act more like novices? For me, this is the worst use of science. It reduces the practitioner to a technician – one who is expected to rigidly, uncritically, and without contextual sensitivity or deviation, apply approved principles and techniques. To their credit, however, Waller and colleagues do at least acknowledge the possibility that deviations from the approved script might not necessarily lead to a compromise in therapeutic effectiveness.

Challenges to CBTs scientific claims have done little to tame the bold, sometimes arrogant and dismissive claims of this approach's superiority. When Jeremy Holmes (2002) argued that CBT's superiority 'may be more apparent than real' (p288) – a view expressed by numerous other scholars, as we have seen – Tarrier (2002) responded that Holmes was simply 'unhappy that those who make policy in the NHS... have become wise' to CBT's 'evidence base' and have begun to 'act on it' (p291). To my mind, this is far from the spirit of questioning, fallibility and openness to critique that I associate with the sciences more broadly.

If the science seems invulnerable to critique, then perhaps we can focus on some of the ethical limitations of this approach. For example, we might argue that CBT focuses on problems instead of people, in its own language rather than that of the client; that it patronises in its educative stance, and that it only works to the extent that the therapeutic common factors are actively put into practice (eg. Castonguay et al, 1996). One possible response to such critiques is the oft-touted claim that CBT is collaborative (eg. Chadwick, Birchwood & Trower, 1996), and that its practitioners are open to the views and experiences of clients. Often, what is meant by 'collaboration' is unclear to me, and certainly does not tally with the way the term is understood in some other approaches. For example, Harlene Anderson (eg. 1997) situates her postmodern, collaborative approach very carefully at a theoretical level. She draws on the theoretical linkage between power and knowledge, on Bakhtin's distinction between monologue and dialogue, and on Shotter's notion of 'joint action' to build a deep understanding of what collaboration can mean. Similarly, for the narrative therapist, collaboration might be thought of in terms of an honouring of the client's values, hopes and beliefs, and of his or her very way of making sense of self and the world. In other words, in such approaches, the term 'collaboration' has a particular meaning and entails far more than paying attention to the client's experience, getting agreement on a procedure, or allowing the client to have a say.

Precisely what does 'collaboration' mean in CBT? I wonder, sometimes, when I read CBT literature and case studies, is collaboration here anything more than a belated recognition that *any* interpersonal situation is inevitably a two-way street, and that a client should be consulted on what happens in the room? The practitioner hears a client's account, and – *influenced* by her stories, and attending to her hopes – goes on to formulate it in terms of negative automatic thoughts, schemas etc. So too, the medical doctor listens to our list of symptoms and uses them to come to a diagnosis or obtains agreement from us to pursue a particular medicinal or surgical strategy. Is this what is meant by collaboration? It seems to me that this approach has a rather minimalistic and misleading take on the term.

Consider the idea of 'collaborative empiricism', intended to combine the empiricism of CBT with a collaborative therapeutic spirit. Merali and Lynch (1997) explain it thus:

> ... client perceptions of the etiological and maintaining factors underlying their presenting problems may be impoverished or erroneous... If a counsellor relies exclusively on the client's self-reports of his/her situation, the wrong intervention may be implemented, thus compromising therapeutic efficacy. In order to prevent such errors, the counsellor must guide the client in collecting data surrounding the presenting problem and the counsellor and client must work together in examining the data. This technique is called collaborative empiricism. (pp287–288)

Where is the collaboration here? Well, from the authors' perspective, it seems to lie in the fact that the client's report on his or her situation is considered, but not trusted, as it 'may be impoverished or erroneous', and so the therapist must 'guide' the person to yield error-free data before they 'together' examine what emerges. The authors go on to argue that part of this collaboration entails the therapist 'explaining' to the person why this or that intervention is appropriate and how it should be done (eg. homework exercises), clarifying 'instructions' for these tasks to prevent 'errors', and 'giving praise for homework completion' (p290). Aside from the patronising tone – in a paper designed *specifically* to show off CBT's collaborative credentials – it seems that there is only a minimalist, certainly hardly persuasive, understanding of collaboration.

Merali and Lynch's (1997) account takes me to the views of Proctor (2002, 2017), who has argued that CBT practices tend to confuse collaboration with client compliance and docility, and that this effectively conceals power and what she considers to be the 'paternalism' of its practices (p79). She notes that this paternalism is underscored by the educative style associated with the approach. Here, on the one hand, we have the 'well-motivated intentions' (Allison, 1996: 156) of the therapist posing as a naïve guarantee of the practice's ethical standing, and, on the other, a client 'relegated to the role of the ignorant pupil' (Proctor, 2002: 77).

In a defence of CBT, Kazantis and colleagues (2013) say that collaboration is evidenced by 'balanced decision-making, balanced contributions to the session, and the extent to which client and therapist are respectful, interested, and responsive to each other's contributions' (p458). What 'balance' means is unexplained. Does it mean each person has equal time? Or that they take turns making decisions? Indeed, can CBT even function if the client's way of looking at self and world – which may *not* be in terms of CBT discourse of rationality, the primacy of cognitions etc – has an 'equal' chance of shaping the therapy process? To what extent can the client's words count as truth?

Still, the term persists. Tarrier (2002) insists that CBT is 'collaborative – the patient is an equal, and information is shared' (p292). He goes on to quote South in this respect: the practitioner must 'produce evidence and... share their knowledge with their patients' (p292). But such claims ring hollow. One wonders how much 'sharing' (balance, equality, collaboration) is really possible when it is scientific knowledge that is most highly valued, and yet it is the practitioner – *not* the client – who invariably holds this knowledge. It requires that clients accept not only the science paradigm as the best way to approach their lives, but also the therapist's claims to represent such truths.

This defensive self-labelling – CBT is collaborative – could possibly be symptomatic of a broader dishonesty in the therapeutic professions, as Goldberg (2001) once argued. But perhaps this criticism is too harsh. Perhaps it is associated more with simplistic conceptualisations of issues like collaboration, ethics and power. Perhaps the lack of nuanced explorations into such concerns can blind practitioners to the ways in which we exercise our expert knowledge, minimise that of our clients, and use this imbalance to shape people's visions of how they should think about themselves and their problems. Under such circumstances, one wonders how nuanced ethical questions concerning the subtleties of power operations and the constructive power of language can be appropriately addressed.

The troubling science issue persists, as does the collaboration claim. We might then turn to examine CBT's collusion with psychiatric power structures, and the manner in which it has, in the process, summarily dismissed decades of meticulous attempts by psychologists and others to question these very systems. Well-known critiques of this power network – of which the CBT practitioner cannot in good conscience claim ignorance – include the concern that forms of subjectivity are imposed upon clients (and related 'labelling' critiques), that clinical categories can have self-fulfilling effects, that clinical interactions lean toward monologue rather than dialogue, and that there is a press for normative and cultural compliance rather than resistance (eg. Kirk & Kutchins, 1997). Considering that CBT functions within this network, what more can be said on these issues? What benefits might accrue from a reiteration of such concerns, or from the production of new ones? Indeed, is there any real sense of compulsion within the CBT community to seriously engage with these challenges, and will such dialogue make any difference?

It seems that challenges against CBT on scientific, ethical, or political grounds are likely to be fruitless. This relative impotence is itself already an indication that something very significant – and very troubling – has happened in the therapeutic world. It seems that the title of 'most important' therapy – or, more medically, the 'first-line treatment of choice' (Wilson, 1996: 197) – can be awarded without any serious consideration of the numerous philosophical, ethical and political formulations that have been designed to give us pause in how we think about therapy. I do not argue with the claim that CBT can sometimes be an effective approach. But even its scientific basis, apparently the biggest weapon in its armoury, is unconvincing to many academics and practitioners. Our best objections and cautions, which include some of the issues already touched on, are more easily dismissed out of hand than ever before. Indeed, what is most alarming is that they do not even have to be addressed.

This did not matter so much when therapists were given space to practise in any number of ways, and toward a range of different ends; to make choices about how to work instead of having practices prescribed by professional bodies and other crystallisations of power. But it matters a great deal now, as many therapists find their approaches delegitimised to the extent that they are not represented on centralised lists of approved therapies. The voice of the dissenting therapist, or even that of the client who might not appreciate CBT discourses and practices, can be ignored. In at least one study, drop-out from CBT interventions was a major feature (Leff et al, 2000). To be acknowledged, one must learn to speak in the prescribed language, act in accordance with pre-constructed and independently developed priorities and measure one's work using prescribed methods. The psychoanalyst's concerns about CBT's inattention to unconscious forces (see Milton's Chapter 11, this volume) need not be heard unless there is a specific sort of evidence to support his claims; the feminist therapist's questions about the role of subtle forms of gender discrimination in producing distress can be ignored if they are based only on case studies, or if there aren't enough meta-analytic studies to justify her claims. It has become legitimate to dismiss critique that is not couched in the discourse of science, or even to disregard critique altogether. Thus, we might challenge CBT's narrow version of science, its complicity with psychiatry, and so on, but these critiques are, in any case, no longer on the agenda for dialogue over what shall be counted as a valid therapy.

I aim here to develop some ideas about how this agenda is constructed and maintained. In the process, I discuss CBT's institutionalisation as the 'most important' therapy, and the marginalisation of its competitors.

Managing the therapeutic horizon

In order to understand CBT's political situation, I think it is useful to situate it briefly in relation to its strategic competitors: the full range of therapies aiming for recognition, circulation and reproduction. This aggregate, comprising hundreds of approaches, can be seen as a therapeutic discursive horizon in that they constitute a kind of store of culturally available ideas and practices from which therapists are, in principle, able to draw. In what is sometimes described as a postmodern age (see Lyotard, 1984), in which difference and choice are celebrated (eg. Sampson, 1993) and essentialism and grand narratives are treated with suspicion, some might have hoped to find in the therapeutic industry a proliferation of creative ideas and practices. Different therapies speak to different people, to different concerns and values, to different ways of life.

Indeed, Safran and Messer (1997) noted precisely such a multiplication of therapeutic approaches in the second half of the 20th century, broadly enabled by the pluralism and contextualism of post-modernism. In recent years, however, many Western societies have begun to aim once more, with renewed vigour, to fulfil a more convergent, consensually orientated, rationalist vision of the world that is our Enlightenment heritage (eg. Habermas, 1972/1987; cf. Brazier's and Lees' chapters xx and xx respectively, in this volume), and from which we have been unable to escape. Difference and diversity in the therapeutic landscape have become constructed as a danger, as a threat to the wellbeing of the broader populace.

Safran and Messer (1997) have noted in the therapeutic domain a move toward convergence in the last few decades (which they see approvingly as integrationism), as attempts are made to organise and manage this seemingly unwieldy therapeutic diversity. Under the influence of this privileging of agreement, consensus, unification and convergence, and perhaps out of a fear of the alterations of power that a truly inclusive, postmodern social system – which embraces a range of values, religions, hopes, and ways of living – might bring, certain ideas have become entrenched as absolutes, despite the avowed respect for difference and choice so intrinsic to the rhetoric of modern societies. All societies must adopt specific versions of democracy; consensus must overcome difference at a fundamental level; consensus is to be established around objective, absolute truths, and we should not be satisfied with diverse opinions/perspectives; science is the only proper means for knowing the truth, and scientists are the only valid truth tellers. With such assumptions in place, a normative, closely regulated, and ultimately authoritarian system is created, posing as a protector of our rights and promising to rescue us from charlatans by steering us to the approved therapeutic 'officer' (Hook, 2003) – that person deemed qualified, and awarded the authority, to diagnose our thoughts and guide us on what is in our best interests, and how we should think, act, interact and live our lives.

It is in such circumstances that the proliferation of therapeutic approaches seems to be grinding to a halt and pulled into reverse. Under the influence of Enlightenment principles of rationalism and consensus, it appears that we feel the need to suppress this therapeutic variation in order to discover the objectively 'best' treatments. This, our Enlightenment principles inform us, is the most responsible and ethical thing to do. Exemplifying this stance, King and Ollendick (1998), for example, make the often-cited twin assertions that the identification of empirically validated treatments facilitates protection of clients and ensures the survival of the profession. It was originally rationalised in the National Institute for Health and Clinical Excellence (NICE) system of guidelines as a way of overcoming the 'lottery' model of healthcare provision. In these terms, the quest for the 'best' and most scientific therapy is easily constructed as a noble undertaking. Thus, each approach must be evaluated according to absolute scientific methods and principles, and once those principles are in place, a kind of consensus can be generated.

Under the influence of such consensus – and the positive valuation placed on consensus as such, in contrast to difference – the critical therapist starts to doubt his or her own ideas, as the impression is created that 'right-thinking' practitioners recognise the importance of having therapeutic work monitored and legislated, of evidence-based practice, of meeting economic needs, insurance company demands, and psychiatric and forensic requirements of clear diagnoses, categorical interventions and unequivocal recommendations. Not all therapies satisfy these demands, and so the multitude of approaches – of *choices,* for clinician and client alike – that we might have expected begins to dwindle as the therapeutic landscape is gradually overtaken by a few selected approaches, of which CBT is the most salient example. A therapeutic hegemony sets in.

What I have referred to as the therapeutic horizon has already begun to take on a new shape, although it is noteworthy that alternative views continue to be expressed, and new practices continue to be developed. Still, the shape of the therapeutic world is strongly influenced by forces inside and outside the therapeutic industry itself. The American Psychological Association (APA) has drawn up lists of approved therapies and is joined by insurance companies in expecting psychologist practitioners to use psychiatry-like diagnostic categories, and to match these up with their corresponding validated interventions. The APA is a world leader among psychological bodies, moreover, and so others are closely following suit. Training courses in the Western world, in clinical psychology in particular, are increasingly advocating the use of such 'evidence-based' practice, drawing from such lists (usually headed by CBT) to inform training and practice.

Clearly, many therapies are not represented on such lists because they do not play the 'games of power' (Foucault, 1980: 298) at which CBT has proven itself so adept. Many therapies are simply not amenable to standardisation and manualisation, and they might conceptualise problems, measure change and construct objectives in ways that do not suit the criteria laid out by the APA and other governing bodies. Narrative therapy, psychoanalysis, systemic therapy, collaborative therapy, and many others, tend to be scientifically awkward. This does not mean they are therapeutically ineffective, only that their ways of working, and the concerns of the people they aim to assist, are more nuanced than the hard sciences are able to assess. But their awkwardness is potentially costly. It may have the longer-term effect of their delegitimisation and eventual disqualification as reputable therapies. It is these approaches, adjudged to be unscientific and based on conjecture rather than fact, whose opinions can be ignored, and whose concerns are increasingly absent from the agenda of the dialogue on valid therapies. Under the force of such pressures, the training of clinical psychologists is increasingly dominated by CBT, with other therapeutic approaches relegated to the periphery (Lloyd, 2009). Indeed, the profession of clinical psychology itself seems to be increasingly conflated with CBT, confusingly implying that cognition can stand alone in representing the breadth and depth of human psychological processes (Gilbert, 2009).

Further, CBT has been prescribed at government level in the UK (see Pilgrim's Chapter 3, this volume). Economist and former prime ministerial advisor Lord Richard Layard (2005) called for the training of 10,000 CBT specialists for the UK health services. This call received support from different sources (eg. the Body Dysmorphic Foundation (2017); the Centre for Mental Health (2006)). CBT continues to be recommended for use in the UK's national health service (NHS) by NICE and the Department of Health for numerous designated problem 'types'. CBT – above all other approaches – is systematically being called forth as the Western world's 'therapy of choice', and this is beginning to give the therapeutic landscape a decidedly skewed appearance.

The therapeutic horizon, in other words, is managed, ostensibly, in the name of truth, but it would be more accurate to say that it is in the service of prevailing power arrangements. Political and economic forces are dictating that only certain therapies will be allowed to remain in place – therapies that are, for instance, time-limited and 'scientific', but which more fundamentally speak into, rather than away from, the linguistic and practice contexts of relevant institutions. Therapies are to be arranged in terms of their capacity to meet the needs of societal systems of power.

Thus, the plethora of available approaches is given an order, and each therapy assigned a place along a narrowly constructed continuum of proven effectiveness. This ordering is then advertised directly or indirectly by such bodies as NICE, the American Psychological Association (APA), and other psychological and therapeutic governing bodies, by government departments of health and other interested officials, by media talk show hosts, and sometimes by those therapists who find their favoured approach catalogued on the approved therapies list, and who are thereby given permission – it seems one is merely telling the objective truths of science, after all – to express disapproval of other therapies in their writing, in their engagements with other professionals, and of course very persuasively (given the power imbalance) in sessions with clients. With all of this public activity, CBT now finds its name and its ideas entering into mainstream commonsense discourse.

Therapeutic dominance and political serviceability

In any society that values consensus and absolute truth, competition will inevitably involve a differentiated 'natural' selection of participants. At present, as I have argued, this is moving toward a situation of therapeutic hegemony and a reduction of available therapies. This may not be the final result, and we may not be witnessing an end to therapeutic history, since we cannot know what new developments might be ushered in by changes in politics (for example, reduced intervention in the therapeutic industry), or in the 'science' of therapy (for example, via an acknowledgement of the limitations of scientific methods in answering questions of how people should live or think about themselves or their lives, or a growing respect for research into the so-called 'common factors', which might once more open up the field – see Bohart and House, Chapter 18, this volume). But at present, various forms of government – from public officials, to insurance and mental health industries, to therapy's governing bodies – seem to have converged to promote specific therapeutic practices (of which CBT is the exemplar), and to demote others. But then, we must ask, if CBT has been selected from the universe of therapeutic possibilities as 'the single most important… approach' (Salkovskis, 1996: xiii), what has it been selected to do?

If we consider the range of forces that have converged to establish a broad-based (though not universal) consensus on the issue, then we cannot simply assume that therapies are chosen on the basis of their scientific merits or their capacity to improve happiness, minimise distress, or even advance mental health. This is not to suggest that CBT practitioners do not strive at precisely these goals. Rather, my question concerns CBT's institutionalised selection as the best therapy – the status it is granted by powerful bodies of public, economic, and professional governance. It is surely reasonable to suspect that there are likely factors involved in CBT's success that transcend those that therapists and clients tend to value the most.

To take an obvious instance, Professor Lord Layard advocates CBT in the UK at least in part because it will aid the economy: it will get people back to work more quickly than other therapies, and thereby reduce strain on the benefit system (see Pilgrim's Chapter 3, this volume). This call has even been followed up by attempts to integrate into CBT practices what Wesson and Gould (2010) call a 'return-to-work' agenda. These authors argue that the 'RtW' (return-to-work) component of therapy should not be 'a hidden agenda item' but brought into the open and included as part of the therapeutic goals (p32). And if the client does not raise this issue as an explicit concern, then the authors suggest that – in order to avoid imposition and to protect CBT's 'collaborative spirit' – it should be integrated into 'the social domain of a client's formulation' (p33). It is stunning how easily economic arguments can come to shape therapeutic practices and objectives; how easily therapeutic practices become tools for the promotion of political and economic objectives. It seems to me naïve to believe that economists, governments, insurance companies and so on – primary shapers of the therapeutic landscape – are more invested in the population's happiness than in its productivity and its maintenance of societal institutions. And yet many practitioners continue to find ways to align their activities with the interests of those forces.

On the question of CBT's serviceability to society's institutions, let us consider a hypothetical scenario. If science is the defining criterion for a selected therapy, then what would happen if it emerged – scientifically – that the most effective therapies were those that *challenged* many of society's institutions: those that proactively put on hold the drive for economic growth in order to prioritise psychological wellbeing; that challenged psychiatry's centrality in mental health practice, or that pointed toward unjust economic, educational and foreign policies, rather than cognitive distortions, as key factors in maintaining distress? One wonders if such a therapy would be afforded the same marketing and promotion avenues that we have witnessed in the case of CBT over the last couple of decades.

As it is, such therapies (for example, narrative, feminist, and some psychoanalytic approaches) do not, in any event, fit the shape desired by official society, although numerous efforts are under way to reshape them so that they lose their critical edge and become more serviceable to existing power arrangements (Guilfoyle, 2005).

Different therapies do different things. They embody different visions, not just of the narrow tasks that have been assigned to professional therapists: diagnose, understand what facilitates 'mental health', formulate and solve problems in the domains of private thoughts and emotions. The range of therapies also speaks to a range of visions of what is important in life, of how life should or could be lived. Diversity in the therapies enables us to make space for multiple ways of being a person and positions us – as a body of therapists – so that we are better able to speak to diverse cultural and societal values and practices, not all of which assume the primacy of science, rationality and testable and measurable thoughts. It seems to me that such questions are not high on the agenda for bodies such as NICE. We are given a narrowly defined job to do: a job that intersects with and contributes just so to social, political and economic institutions. The suppression of its variation might mean that it becomes accomplished at a narrow range of practices that are authored, ultimately, by external forces. It is the significance of these external influences that we should question, more, perhaps, even than the fact that CBT is winning the race they want us to run. The more pertinent question is how the rules for competition are constructed, and which institutions stand to gain.

As therapists, we must be alert to being reduced to government agents. CBT practitioners face this quandary imminently. It is not our job to reproduce existing power arrangements, or to satisfy the needs of society's most powerful institutions. Yet the political reality is that therapies that perform such a reproductive function are useful institutional partners, and thereby more likely than others to become successful, popular, and recognised, and even to become part of commonsense discourse (which itself then enhances the likelihood of effectiveness). All therapists risk becoming inadvertent agents of 'social control' (Hare-Mustin, 1994: 20) – a position that we should surely resist. But CBT's popularity is such that we practitioners – especially at the point of training – are inundated with very tempting invitations to become part of the fold – to find a place in the havens that such belonging provides. One would like to think these invitations will be in some way refused. Very often they are. But that is a risky strategy for the practitioner. It not only calls on us to critique the games of power to which CBT's technologies are so well suited; it also puts us in a position of being subject to the normalising judgments of our colleagues, the professional bodies of which we are a part, our referral networks, and perhaps even our clients.

Have a look at the NICE guidelines: being something other than a CBT practitioner might not be a good career move.

References

Allison A (1996). A framework for good practice: ethical issues in cognitive behavioural therapy. In: Marshall S, Turnbull J (eds). *Cognitive behaviour therapy*. London: Balliere Tindall (pp155–180).

Anderson H (1997). *Conversation, Language and Possibilities: a postmodern approach to therapy*. New York, NY: Basic Books.

Andrews HB (2000). The myth of the scientist-practitioner: a reply to R King (1998) and N King and Ollendick (1998). *Australian Psychologist 35*(1): 60–63.

Body Dysmorphic Foundation (2017). Getting help. [Online]. http://bddfoundation.org/helping-you/getting-help-in-the-uk/ (accessed 8 February 2017).

Bolsover N (2002). Commentary: The 'evidence' is weaker than claimed. *British Medical Journal* 324(7332): 288–294.

Castonguay LG, Goldfried MR, Wiser S, Raue PJ, Hayes AM (1996). Predicting the effect of cognitive therapy for depression: a study of unique and common factors. *Journal of Consulting and Clinical Psychology 64*(3): 497–504.

Centre for Mental Health (2006). We need to talk. [Online]. www.centreformentalhealth.org.uk/we-need-to-talk (accessed 8 February 2017).

Chadwick PD, Birchwood MJ, Trower P (1996). *Cognitive Therapy for Delusions, Voices and Paranoia*. Chichester: Wiley.

Clarkson P (2003). *Citrinitas* – therapy in a new paradigm world. In: Bates Y, House R (eds). *Ethically Challenged Professions: enabling innovation and diversity in psychotherapy and Counselling*. Ross-on-Wye: PCCS Books (pp60–74).

Foucault M (1980). *Power/Knowledge: selected interviews and other writings 1971–1977* (C Gordon ed). New York, NY: Harvester Wheatsheaf.

Gilbert P (2009). Moving beyond cognitive behaviour therapy. T*he Psychologist 22*(5): 400-403.

Goldberg C (2001). Influence and moral agency in psychotherapy. *International Journal of Psychotherapy* 6(2): 107–115.

Guilfoyle M (2005). From therapeutic power to resistance? Therapy and cultural hegemony. *Theory & Psychology 15*(1): 101–124.

Habermas J (1972/1987) *Knowledge and Human Interests* (J Shapiro trans). Oxford: Polity Press.

Hare-Mustin RT (1994). Discourses in the mirrored room: a postmodern analysis of therapy. *Family Process 33*(1): 19–35.

Holmes J (2002). All you need is cognitive behaviour therapy? *British Medical Journal 324*(7332): 288–294.

Hook D (2003). Analogues of power: reading psychotherapy through the sovereignty–discipline–government complex. *Theory & Psychology 13*(5): 605–628.

Kazantzis N, Tee JM, Dattilio FM (2013). How to develop collaborative empiricism in cognitive behavior therapy: conclusions from the *C&BP* special series. *Cognitive and Behavioral Practice 20*(4): 455–460.

King NJ, Ollendick TH (1998). Empirically validated treatments in clinical psychology. *Australian Psychologist 33*(2): 89–95.

Kirk H, Kutchins S (1997). *Making Us Crazy – DSM: the psychiatric bible and the creation of mental disorders*. New York, NY: Free Press.

Layard R (2005). Mental health: Britain's biggest social problem? Paper presented at No 10 Strategy Unit seminar on mental health, 20 January 2005. London: London School of Economics. http://eprints.lse.ac.uk/47428 (accessed 4 February 2018).

Leff J, Vearnals S, Wolff G, Alexander B, Chisholm D, Everitt B, Asen E, Jones E, Brewin CR, Dayson D (2000). The London depression intervention trial. *The British Journal of Psychiatry 177*(2): 95–100.

Lloyd J (2009). Threats to clinical psychology from the CBT stranglehold. *Reformulation 33(Winter)*: 8–9.

Lyotard JF (1984). *The Postmodern Condition: a report on knowledge*. Minneapolis, MN: University of Minnesota Press.

Merali N, Lynch P (1997). Collaboration in cognitive behavioural counselling: a case example. *Canadian Journal of Counselling 31*(4): 287–293.

Messer SB, Wampold BE (2002). Let's face facts: common factors are more potent than specific therapy factors. *Clinical Psychology: Science and Practice 9*(1): 21–25.

Proctor G (2002/2017). *The Dynamics of Power in Counselling and Psychotherapy: ethics, politics and practice*. Ross-on-Wye: PCCS Books.

Safran JD, Messer SB (1997). Psychotherapy integration: a postmodern critique. *Clinical Psychology: Science and Practice 4*(2): 140–152.

Salkovskis PM (1996). Preface. In: Salkovskis PM (ed). *Frontiers of Cognitive Therapy*. London: Guilford Press (ppxi–xiv).

Sampson EE (1993). *Celebrating the Other: a dialogic account of human nature*. San Francisco, CA: Westview Press.

Shedler J (2011). Science or ideology? *American Psychologist 66*(2): 152–154.

Tarrier N (2002). Commentary: yes, cognitive behaviour therapy may well be all you need. *British Medical Journal 324*: 291–292.

Waller G, Stringer H, Meyer C (2012). What cognitive behavioral techniques do therapists report using when delivering cognitive behavioral therapy for the eating disorders? *Journal of Consulting and Clinical Psychology 80*(1): 171–175.

Wampold BE, Fluckiger C, Del Re AC, Yulish NE, Frost ND, Pace BT, Goldberg SB, Miller SD, Baardseth TP, Laska KM, Hilsenroth MJ (2017). In pursuit of truth: a critical examination of meta-analyses of cognitive behavior therapy. *Psychotherapy Research 27*(1): 14–32.

Wesson M, Gould M (2010). Can a 'return-to-work' agenda fit within the theory and practice of CBT for depression and anxiety disorders? *The Cognitive Behaviour Therapist 3*: 27–42.

Wilson GT (1996). Treatment of bulimia nervosa: when CBT fails. *Behaviour Research and Therapy 34*(3): 197–212.

2 CBT: the obscuring of power in the name of science

Gillian Proctor

In this chapter, I suggest that the most important factor that may determine whether or not the client deems a therapy relationship successful is the dynamics of power within it.

If therapists take control, and do not think carefully about how to avoid domination during therapy, how can we expect clients to walk away feeling more in control? Here, I explore how cognitive behaviour therapy (CBT) addresses the issue of power in therapy and suggest there are some problems with the CBT model, and that CBT therapists need to give this issue some serious consideration. Hemmings (Chapter 23, this volume) suggests that my critique applies equally to other therapists and not just CBT, and I agree: indeed, all therapists need to consider the dynamics of power with their clients and the risks of taking power-over their clients (see Proctor 2002, 2017). However, particular modalities have particular issues to consider, depending on how the therapy relationship is conceptualised, so this chapter focuses specifically on the implications of how the CBT literature discusses the role of the therapist with respect to power.

Powerlessness and distress

I maintain that the experience of powerlessness is one of the most significant causal factors contributing to the experience of psychological distress (Proctor, 2002, 2017). There is much more evidence for environmental causes of distress than, for example, biological or genetic causes (for example, Bentall, 2004). Common factors associated with distress are poverty, deprivation, and abuse (see Pilgrim, 1997). I would argue that underlying all these factors is the experience of powerlessness.

The experience of sexual, physical and emotional abuse and neglect is a significant causal factor in all types of psychological distress. The numbers of survivors of abuse are notably high among survivors of the psychiatric system (for example, Williams

& Watson (1994) suggest a figure of at least 50% for sexual abuse specifically). Surviving experiences of abuse is likely to involve regaining power and control (Kelly, Burton & Regan, 1998). Power, control and the experience of powerlessness are strongly associated with all kinds of psychological distress. Clearly, the way to deal with difficulties that stem from abuse, deprivation and powerlessness is not to impose further power and control. Yet the dynamics of power in therapy certainly make it easy for the therapist to have power over the client. As Dorothy Rowe points out in her review on the book jacket of Proctor (2002): 'When we enter into therapy we give enormous power to the therapist because we want to see that person as someone who can take our pain away. Such power can be abused.' The power that society affords us as therapists leaves us with a large burden of responsibility to do what we can to try and ensure that we do not abuse this position.

There are clear values in the foundation of the practice of therapy, the most obvious general aim being to help the client and help improve the client's quality of life. How each therapy model, and indeed each therapist, believes the client's life will be improved is a matter of ethics and value judgments. Given the association of distress with powerlessness, having a sense of agency or control over one's life is likely to be important to clients. How do therapists assist clients with this aim, given the power in the therapy relationship? The notion of empowerment was advocated as a laudable goal for helping professionals, and still is at times. This notion has been critiqued, however, due to the betrayal of its underlying notions of patronage. Parker criticises the rhetoric of 'empowerment' often used in speaking about therapy. He explains:

> Even the word 'empowerment' betrays something of the position of the expert who thinks that they have been able to move an enlightened step beyond 'helping' people but cannot give up the idea that it is possible to bend down to lift someone lesser than themselves up a step, to give them a little empowerment. (1999: 9–10)

However, Read and Wallcraft (1992) define empowerment as follows: 'No one can give power to another person but they can stop taking their power away. They can also help people to regain their own power.'

Fish (1999: 67) cites Foucault (1980: 298) in suggesting a way forward in dealing with relations of power:

> I do not think that a society could exist without power relations, if by that one means the strategies by which individuals try to direct and control the conduct of others. The problem, then, is not to try to dissolve them in the utopia of completely transparent communication but to acquire the rules of law, the management techniques, and also the morality, the *ethos,* the practice of the self, that will allow us to play these games of power with as little domination as possible. (Original emphasis)

Power in therapy

I identify three aspects of power in the therapy relationship (Proctor, 2002, 2017). The first is *role power*: the power inherent in the roles of therapist and client due to the authority given to the therapist to define the client's problem, and the power the therapist has in the organisation and institutions of her/his work. The second aspect of power is *societal power*: the power due to the social structural positions of the therapist and client, with respect to aspects of identity such as gender, age, and so on. The final aspect of power in the therapy relationship is *historical power*: the power due to the personal histories of the therapist and client, and their experiences of power and powerlessness. These personal histories and experiences will affect, and to some extent determine, how individuals are in relationships, and how they behave, think, and feel with respect to the power in the relationship.

Psychotherapy outcome research demonstrates that the most important key to successful therapy is the quality of the therapy relationship (Bozarth, 1998; Lambert & Ogles, 2004; Paley & Lawton, 2001). The most consistent relationship variables related to effectiveness are the therapeutic alliance, goal agreement and empathy (Norcross, 2002). Cooper (2008) summarises the evidence for the importance of the therapy relationship and qualities such as empathy. Sparks, Duncan and Miller (2008) demonstrate that the most effective therapists are those who seek and learn from feedback from their clients – a practice that is founded on humility, not the arrogance of expertise. I suggest that each of these variables could perhaps better be explained by an over-arching variable, described by the dynamics of power in the therapy relationship. A therapy relationship characterised by empathy, goal agreement and an effective alliance would be a relationship where the therapist is not taking power-over the client but is encouraging the client's power-from-within: that is, a mutual, respectful relationship. In contrast, an unhelpful therapy relationship would be one in which the therapist uses power-over the client and diminishes the client's sense of power-from-within.

Much of the literature on power in therapy has taken a structural approach. This approach sees power as a possession wielded by a therapist over a client in a negative way. Writers such as Masson (1989) argue that therapists have authority, with which comes power that is necessarily negative, and even abusive. Structural perspectives emphasise the importance of structures and roles but leave little room for individual agency. In contrast, post-structural ideas (in particular, those of Foucault) emphasise the individual in dynamic social relation to others, and also incorporate the notion of individual agency, which widens the scope of analysis from a radical environmental behaviourism to considering the internal life and histories of individuals and their relationships.

There are longstanding debates about the primacy of structure or agency. More recently, various theorists have argued that both are important and irreducible to the other and have proposed ways to investigate power while holding both in mind. More detail of structural and post-structural approaches to power can be found in Proctor (2002, 2017).

CBT and power

Appeal to science

Broadly speaking, cognitive behaviour therapy (CBT) is based on the claim that the cause of distress lies in the individual's maladaptive thinking or cognitive processes. Recent adaptations of, or additions to, CBT theory (such as compassionate mind therapy or acceptance and commitment therapy) tend to consider emotions in more detail, while still focusing on the cognitive processes. While CBT is claimed to be a collaborative endeavour with the client, the therapist has the knowledge about how to think in a more helpful way, and this knowledge is said to derive from research evidence. Thus, the authority of the therapist rests on an appeal to science.

The whole basis of the model, then, is strongly founded on principles of modernism and the rationality of science, as described at some length in a number of chapters in this book. 'Knowledge' and research 'evidence' are not questioned, but are presented as fact, and the therapist is assumed to be in an objective position to present this knowledge. CBT is presented as a 'psychoeducational approach', albeit with the call for an active and involved student. However, more recent, so-called 'third-wave' departures from classic CBT theory, such as compassionate mind therapy (Gilbert, 2004) do focus more on the importance of the therapy relationship. From a Foucaultian perspective, traditional CBT (eg. Beck, 1976/1991; Beck et al, 1979) is rife with 'regimes of truth' – normalising principles on which the 'right' or 'helpful' way to think are based. The focus on 'realism' can be used to discount or challenge the feelings or views of the client, who can then be accused of being prey to 'cognitive distortions'. Rationality is a clear value behind CBT, and what is defined as irrational is discounted or challenged.

The 'evidence base' for CBT is marketed consistently, and yet the evidence for the importance of the therapy relationship is minimised in favour of 'evidence' for techniques. Even in Gilbert and Leahy (2007), who explore the therapy relationship in CBT, the focus on the evidence base is foundational. They try to distinguish this from the idea of the objective application of scientific principles, by saying (p17): 'CBT has a range of techniques at its disposal for helping people change and these are increasingly evidence-based, but this in no way means that we become psychological mechanics.' However, Hardy, Cahill & Barkham (2007), in the same volume, emphasise that the therapeutic relationship is associated far more strongly with treatment outcome than specific therapy techniques. They discuss the debates within CBT of the importance of techniques or relationship and suggest the distinction is artificial, as the two cannot be separated. They point particularly to the evidence that early ratings by the client of the therapeutic alliance are highly associated with outcome.

The objectivity of the CBT therapist

Alongside the appeal to science to justify CBT principles is the position of the therapist as objective. As with the authority that comes with the role of the therapist, this expert stance and idea of objectivity brings a great deal of role power for the CBT therapist. Starhawk suggests the dangers inherent in the therapist's authority:

> Healing that empowers and liberates springs from a mutual struggle with the forces that hurt us all. When we start believing we are 'more together' than someone else, we use our healing power as another way to establish our own superiority. (1987: 147)

Within traditional CBT literature, there is some caution about the objectivity of the therapist. Marshall (1996), for example, points out that the therapist's authority leads to ethical implications that therapists have a duty to consider. She also emphasises the importance of supervision to ensure ethical practice and that the therapist's agenda does not impinge on the therapeutic relationship. She emphasises the danger of the therapist using their power to fulfil their own needs in the therapy relationship, when the aim should be to use this power to help the client.

However, the assumption in the CBT model is that the therapist can be in an objective position to decide scientifically what is best for the client. Thus, the aim of supervision here is to ensure that the therapist is acting from this neutral position, rather than from a position in the therapy relationship where the client could be used to fulfil the therapist's needs. Given the philosophy of the CBT model, however, it is not apparent how a focus on self-awareness in supervision could be accommodated (and it is certainly not theorised as being part of the model). This would be particularly so if supervision were a process by which the therapist and supervisor joined forces to decide what is in the best interests of the client.

The possibility of being in a neutral objective position is not problematised. It is clear that the concept of power referred to here is one in which the therapist is assumed to possess the power, and power is assumed to be unidirectional – characteristics of a structural model of power. However, unlike structural models of power, it is not assumed that this imbalance of power is necessarily negative. Instead, the power imbalance is justified and legitimised, again with the appeal to the rationality of science and the expert knowledge of the therapist.

Telford and Farrington (1996: 149) suggest that the therapist is not in a neutral position but is part of the therapy relationship: 'Cognitive behaviourists must wake up to the fact that the notion of the therapist as a neutral onlooker is no longer acceptable within therapy.'

Here, there is some acknowledgement that 'objectivity' has been questioned, and that the possibility of a therapist being a neutral scientist whose values are not involved is dangerous. However, despite some focus on the importance of the therapy relationship, the full implications of this problematising of objectivity are not explored with respect to the knowledge base of CBT, or the therapist's position in the relationship. Inconsistencies remain in the questioning and acceptance of the authority of the therapist.

The client's acceptance of the therapist's authority is seen as a necessary prerequisite for CBT, and when a client disagrees with the model or does not comply with requests, this is seen as a 'set back' – or, indeed, an opportunity to challenge the client's thoughts and beliefs. There are many examples in the CBT literature of how therapists should handle a rupture in the alliance, a 'set back', or a disagreement with the client. Most suggest using the opportunity for the therapist to correct the client's misunderstanding – for example, Beck (1995: 73) and Padesky and Greenberger (1995: 8–9). These examples again follow the idea of the CBT expert educating the client.

There are also clear examples of where a therapist persuades the client to agree with the therapist's perspective. Marcinko (2003), for example, discusses the 'problem' of clients not wanting to take medication, and how this can be dealt with by saying:

> ... however, if the patient wants the therapist to work on other goals with him or her or to help him or her pursue his or her values, the therapist would be more motivated to do so if the patient agreed to work on medications as well. (p328)

However, there are also examples where the therapist does take responsibility for their behaviour and how it has affected the client, and takes on board the client's perception, rather than challenges it (eg. Padesky & Greenberger, 1995: 54–56). Indeed, 'woebot' (the robot offering CBT via Facebook) as discussed by Palmer (Foreword, this volume) is programmed to regularly ask for feedback from the user about the helpfulness of particular techniques, to improve its own approach. Stevens and colleagues (2003) point out the dangers in the traditional CBT approach, writing:

> When such significant ruptures in the alliance occur, the faith that cognitive behaviour therapists have in technique and the belief that ruptures in the alliance are roadblocks to be overcome can work to the detriment of treatment. (p278)

Instead, they suggest that, at such points of disagreement, the therapist should focus on the alliance.

From the beginning, CBT is presented as the right way to think, and success is when the client thinks and behaves in accordance with the CBT model. The danger here is that, if therapy fails, it is because the client has not followed the therapist's suggestions well enough; the responsibility lies with the client. As Spinelli (1994: 244) explains, due to the therapist's unquestioning belief in the principles and assumptions underlying the CBT model, therapeutic failure can 'be blamed on… the client's misapplication of (or unwillingness to apply) the specified instructions presented by the therapist'.

Social control

Spinelli points out that the therapist makes judgments about what is rational or desirable, and that, rather than this being a scientific appraisal, these judgments are culturally influenced. Furthermore, the appeal to the rationality of science itself is clearly a value held by mainstream culture. Spinelli explains: 'In this way, the therapist becomes a broadly libertarian representative of the norms and codes of conduct of society in which both the therapist and client are members' (1994: 249). However, he argues that these cultural norms are not 'objective', and that, in pretending to be objective, cognitive behaviour therapists 'run the risk of imposing a socially conformist ideology on the client'. Pilgrim and Treacher (1992: 30) similarly explain that 'psychologists… could play out a highly political role in terms of the management of the population, whilst at the same time disowning such a role by pointing to their "disinterested" scientific training and credentials'.

Spinelli (1994: 248) discusses the notion of the 'objectivity' of the therapist, and casts doubt on the validity of this claim: 'The problem with this view, however, is that the notion of a truly scientific investigator, observer, or experimenter has been sufficiently cast into doubt by developments within science itself.' Spinelli's critique is from a structural framework of power (see Proctor, 2002, 2017). It is assumed that objectivity gives authority and power to the therapist; authority and power are seen as synonymous, as though power were *a possession*, and power is seen to be unidirectional and oppressive.

His critique of science, however, fits in much more with a Foucaultian perspective on power. Foucault's analyses of the human sciences (1973), of the history of madness (1977a), and of the history of sexuality (1979) all provide an analysis of the context in which therapy takes place. He describes the idea of the 'confession' as a disciplinary technique and questions the objectivity of 'madness' as a category entailing treatment. Foucault's analyses encourage us to investigate the way in which psychotherapy can be a context for surveillance and disciplinary techniques of the self – techniques of normalisation. He describes the ways in which power can be observed in the practices in psychiatry and psychotherapy that attempt to normalise people. This has been played out more explicitly with the advent of the Increasing Access to Psychological Therapies programme (IAPT) in the UK, which explicitly ties an economic agenda to mental health and promotes the use of CBT techniques to move as many clients to 'recovery' as possible in as short a time as possible, in order to restore them to economic productivity (see Proctor 2015, 2017; Proctor & Hayes, 2017).

Foucault's notion of the stylisation of the self is particularly relevant to issues of power in therapy, as therapy explicitly sets out to reconstitute the self according to normalising rules (particularly in CBT). However, Foucault does not place a value judgment on these practices of power, and also emphasises the productive aspects of power (explained by Butler (1990: 98) as 'the way in which regulative practices produce the subjects they come to subjugate'). He also emphasises the resistances that will always be present wherever there is power.

Here, Foucault's ideas about the relationship between power and knowledge, and the role of normative rules in constituting subjects, are both relevant (see Proctor, 2002, 2017). It is clear that the explicit aim in CBT is to reconstitute the subjectivity of the client: to change the way the client thinks about the world. Thus, it seems that Foucault's 'practices of the self' are an integral part of what happens in therapy. Theory in CBT is a normalising discourse. From Foucault's later work, this describes the dynamic nature of power, where individuals constitute themselves within the context of the normative rules – the disciplinary techniques of the self. These regulative practices are explicit in CBT, where the normative rules of how a client should reconstitute him/herself are spelled out. Beck (1995: 26), for example, explains that the goals of the initial session include 'socializing the patient into cognitive therapy'.

It is also clear from Foucault's consideration of the practices of the self that the client also has a role in resisting and constituting themselves within the context of these normative rules. However, as McNay (1992) points out in her critique of Foucault, by not acknowledging the way different techniques of the self are imposed at different levels, Foucault's notion of the subject's agency, and the idea of aesthetic stylisation of the self, hide the force of cultural norms. There is an issue here concerning how much the therapist uses his/her authority to enforce the norms established by CBT, how much the client is able to constitute themselves in their own way, or whether their only choice is to take on the idea and norms of CBT wholeheartedly or leave therapy. Given also that clients who seek therapy are generally in a state of distress, their choices or resistance to the norms communicated by the therapist are likely to be very limited. Thus, it may be more realistic to talk about Foucault's concept of disciplinary power as he applied it to the human sciences, while also acknowledging a limited role for the client in terms of resistance.

The 'collaborative' relationship

Beck emphasises that the therapy relationship needs to be 'collaborative' (1991: 220; Beck et al, 1979), meaning that the therapist and client must agree on the problem, the goal of therapy and the means to reach the goal. The ultimate goal in cognitive therapy is to teach the patient how to solve their own problems, which the therapist does by teaching the patient certain principles of rational thinking. The style of therapy is described as 'collaborative empiricism' (Beck et al, 1979). Westbrook, Kennerley & Kirk (2012: 23–24) explain the nature of this collaboration, saying:

> CBT is fundamentally a *collaborative* project between therapist and client. Both are active participants, with their own areas of expertise: the therapist has knowledge about effective ways to solve problems, and the client has expertise in his own experience of his problems.

The therapist is expected to structure sessions and use reinforcement selectively to encourage the patient to talk more about what the therapist considers most relevant and most likely to promote change. This would refer to a power process (Cromwell & Olson, 1975) — an interactional technique to take control over an aspect of the relationship (see Proctor 2002, 2017). Therapists are to explain to their patients that talking about how problems are now is most useful, according to the 'here and now principle' (Westbrook, Kennerley & Kirk, 2012).

Westbrook, Kennerley & Kirk (2012: 24) emphasise that the client is expected to take more responsibility as therapy progresses, and the therapist is expected to facilitate this by 'fostering the sense that he is becoming his own therapist'. Thus, it is clear that the 'collaborative' relationship emphasises the therapist's expectations of the client that they will contribute to the therapist's ideas and plans for treatment (within the CBT model). Padesky and Greenberger (1995: 6) explain:

> Collaboration requires an active stance on the part of both therapist and client to work together as a team. Since many clients enter therapy expecting to play a more passive role ('Fix me'), the therapist often needs to socialise the client to expectations for mutual collaboration.

What seems to be described here is more the expectation on the client to take responsibility for the therapy. The danger here is that the client is made responsible if therapy does not work.

An often-discussed example in the CBT literature to illustrate the notion of collaboration is the expectation that the client will complete homework. Tompkins (2003: 63) suggests that therapists reinforce homework compliance and 'similarly avoid reinforcing homework noncompliance'. Padesky and Greenberger (1995) discuss the expectation of clients to complete homework as part of the idea of collaboration. Here, the notion of collaboration is used interchangeably with 'compliance with assignments' (1995: 35). They suggest that a therapist may increase compliance/collaboration by saying: 'Clients who do assignments tend to get better faster. This explanation is often sufficient to increase compliance. It is best to provide a thorough rationale for active therapy participation along with or before the first assignment' (1995: 35).

Tompkins (2003: 63) describes further the nature of collaboration in relation to homework, writing that:

> ... clients usually understand more fully than the therapists do what is or is not a useful homework assignment and what difficulties may arise... At times, a client may suggest a homework assignment that seems tangential to the focus of the therapy session. Rather than dismissing the assignment out of hand, therapists can explore the client's rationale for the assignment (be curious), perhaps soliciting the advantages and disadvantages of this assignment over another one the therapist might suggest.

So, the client may suggest homework tasks that seem unlikely to prove better than the therapist's suggestions (given their superior knowledge of CBT) and the idea of completing homework is a given.

While some things are perhaps negotiable, there are clearly some aspects of CBT that the patient must agree to for the therapy to go ahead. It is clear that the therapist structures the sessions and decides what is useful for the client to talk about. Thus, the idea of collaboration seems to incorporate a demand that the client will conform to and welcome the therapist's approach and will agree to various forms of activity that the therapist suggests.

'Collaboration' but different roles

Turnbull (1996: 20) suggests that this is not collaboration between equals:

> It is better to see the client and therapist occupying different roles but collaborating on a joint enterprise. The therapist's role in the relationship is to make decisions concerning therapy and the client's role is to take decisions about how this can be applied to his or her lifestyle. In order to work properly, this collaboration needs to be based on a mutual respect for each other's role.

He cites Rogers' core conditions (1957) as key qualities of a therapist that will help develop trust and encourage collaboration. He suggests that these conditions should be used to encourage compliance in the client. Here again, the notion of collaboration and compliance are used interchangeably. Turnbull also points out an aspect of the cognitive behaviour therapist's power with respect to the client: that of the therapist's authority and of their 'superior knowledge' (1996: 20). He contends that the client must accept the therapist's superior knowledge, although not to the extent where the client's ability to self-manage is compromised. How to achieve this balance is not explained any further. In short: 'There are times when the authority of a therapist's knowledge must be exercised and accepted by the client.' Thus, for Turnbull it is important that the client accepts the role of the cognitive behaviour therapist as the one with the knowledge and hence the decision-maker with regard to therapy. Here the connection between power and knowledge is explicit.

Critique of notion of 'collaboration'

Lowe (1999) critiques the notion of 'collaboration' as an appeal to promote equality, which he argues is impossible in the context of therapy and the power embedded in the institutional role of the therapist. He explains (1999: 82):

> How collaborative can collaboration be... if they are institutionalised within a particular mode of practice? It is one thing to offer clients a voice within a professional therapeutic discourse, but it might be quite another thing to allow them a discourse of their own.

He further points to the effects of these discourses with respect to power, which are to increase the power of the therapist, by concealing it (1999: 83).

Though the declarative intent of these ideas may be to empower clients, the constitutive effects might be quite the opposite, being not so much disempowering but what Potter (1996) calls *mis*-empowering: adding new tools to the armoury of the already powerful.

Thus he demonstrates how the rhetoric of 'collaboration' can actually increase the power of the therapist and hide the power imbalance between therapist and client.

Telford and Farrington (1996) usefully point to the dangers in CBT that the rhetoric of 'collaboration' and 'equality' in the therapy relationship obscure the power differential between client and therapist that remains. They also suggest ways in which the therapeutic relationship can be used to help clients take more control over their own therapy. They give an example where the therapist avoids suggesting solutions to the client, but instead 'guides' the client to find their own solutions. As with the idea of the therapist reinforcing matters when the client talks about issues that the therapist believes are most relevant to change, this seems to reflect a one-dimensional understanding of power (as described by Lukes, 1974, see Proctor 2002, 2017) – a level of the therapist's power is still being missed here. The therapist 'guiding' the client to what they (the therapist) believe will be a good solution means that the therapist is shaping the outcome of the client's decisions, and is using power-over the client, as described by Lukes' (1974) second dimension of power. Ultimately, it seems that the client is encouraged to take control over their own therapy, as long as they follow the therapist's model and ideas: 'You can make the decision, as long as you decide what I think is good for you.' At the same time, the therapist is encouraged to use their power to increase the client's compliance with CBT. Thus, the therapist's authority is not really questioned or problematised.

The notion of 'collaboration' seems to appeal to a notion of reducing power imbalances in therapy. However, the notion of power implied by this is a one-dimensional view of power. Collaboration is seen to have been achieved when the client agrees and complies with the therapist's world-view. The notion of collaboration is very muddled with the idea of compliance in CBT. However, as Gramsci points out (Ransome, 1992), there is a distinction between coercive and consensual control, and power is still involved in consensual control. There are further dimensions of power (as suggested by Lukes, 1974) that are missed from the account of collaboration. The extent to which the therapist determines what can be put on the agenda to discuss, or how much the client has been shaped to know what the therapist does not want to hear about, is not considered. It is also clear that the therapist is seen to have authority about what is best for the client – authority that is legitimised by the therapist's knowledge of science.

It would be more honest and accurate to refer to compliance, instead of 'collaboration', and thus be explicit about the nature of the power relations involved.

Autonomy or beneficence?

Issues of power raise ethical questions, and values are an inescapable part of the consideration of power. In ethical guidelines for therapists (eg. those of the British Association for Counselling and Psychotherapy (BACP, 2018)), the traditional approach to ethics has been to consider the balance of the ethical principles, which together comprise the ethics of justice (see Keys & Proctor, 2007; Proctor, 2014). These principles are doing good (beneficence), avoiding harm (non-maleficence), and respecting autonomy and justice. The balance between the ethical principles of doing good (beneficence) and respecting autonomy has been unclear and left to decisions by individual therapists, depending on whether they see the therapist or client as the expert.

The professional body specifically for CBT practitioners is the British Association for Behavioural and Cognitive Psychotherapies (BABCP). It has its own ethical framework and it is notable that the standards of conduct, performance and ethics makes no mention of client autonomy, focusing instead on the responsibility of the therapist to act in the best interests of the client, and the rationality with which the therapist makes these decisions. The standards of conduct (BABCP, 2009, revised 2016) are clear in their use of medical language that CBT is a medical model. In CBT, therapy is referred to as treatment; the model is clearly of a therapist who has expertise on how to best treat the patient's problems, and the first standard refers to beneficence. The competence of the therapist to make these decisions is crucial. Informed consent is clearly a matter of explaining clearly to the patient the therapist's suggested intervention.

The main ethical principle that underlies the practice of CBT is beneficence. The therapist is believed to be in a better position than the client to decide what the client needs, and the authority of the therapist is justified by the principle of beneficence, or paternalism. There has been little consideration given to the dangers of the power inherent in the beneficent CBT therapist's position. It is suggested that an aspect of CBT is to give the client the information about the model to enable self-understanding and autonomous decision-making.

However, it is not clear at what point the client's autonomy is considered, particularly if the client does not agree with what the therapist believes to be best. Respecting the client's autonomy is directly contradicted by the belief that the therapist has rationality and science on their side, and therefore knows what is best for the client, whatever they may believe. Ultimately, the client's views can be dismissed as 'irrational' within the model of the therapist as superior, with an appeal to science that could be difficult for a client to argue with, given the authority that science still has in this culture. Allison (1996: 160) does raise a question about therapists making these decisions with regard to the threat to the client's autonomy:

> Basing decisions on the foundation that you are exercising your judgement in order to bring about a better outcome for the client may well be a paternalistic way of working and may subjugate the client's autonomy to the therapist's power.

However, there are no suggestions for how to avoid subjugating the client's autonomy in CBT.

Blease (2015) suggests a further danger of unethical practice for CBT therapists – a lack of evidence-based information giving, which also leaves therapists in danger of not following the principle of beneficence. She investigates the evidence that it is the common (namely, relationship, therapist and client factors) rather than specific (technical) factors that are responsible for the therapeutic effects of CBT (as proposed by Hardy, Cahill & Barkham, 2007). Blease argues that this evidence is continually ignored in processes for gaining informed consent in CBT, with therapists giving explanations of how CBT works from technical rationales. Her view is that CBT therapists should give the client information about the common factors that research tells us make all therapies effective: specifically, the client agreeing the goals and aims of treatment, therapist attributes such as empathy, and that the client is the best judge of the quality of the alliance. She argues that therapists who don't do this are failing ethically, both with respect to the principle of respecting client autonomy and on the grounds of beneficence, as there are no grounds to believe that withholding this information is better for clients.

Paternalism

Turnbull (1996) discusses in more detail paternalism in the therapy relationship in CBT. He supports the view that the therapy relationship can indeed display aspects of paternalism. He also agrees that CBT can be paternalistic in the early stages of a relationship, when the therapist 'may sometimes need to coerce the client into carrying out actions which he or she will find unpleasant in order that progress can ultimately be made. This is something that may often be required early in therapy when the client may not be in a position to make choices' (1996: 19).

Turnbull defends this type of coercion by stating that it should be based on the ethical principles of beneficence, but he does admit that this should be acknowledged as an example of paternalism. He does not explain why, at the start of therapy, a client may not be in a position to make choices and does not seem to consider the alternative of providing the client with the necessary information to be able to make a choice. Compliance seems to be sought in preference to informed consent, and no comments are made about the dangers of the therapist justifying coercion by beneficence, or the possibility of the therapist being in a position to know the client's best interests. There seems to be no question that the therapist's knowledge of the model and the scientific principles behind CBT place them in a position to know what is best for the client.

Paternalism or autonomy?

Searle (1993) discusses ethical dilemmas in therapy and the competing values of paternalism or autonomy. She suggests that moral justification for the teleological principle of beneficence is sought from the outcome, arguing that this ethical principle is often used to defend paternalism. Beneficence is used to protect the client from autonomy when this could result in harm, or even just when the therapist does not agree with a client's decision and believes they know best. She describes the competing deontological principle of autonomy, which suggests that the therapist has a duty to respect the integrity and individuality of their client and must therefore respect autonomy. Searle asserts that the values of the therapist influence therapy in many ways, particularly because of the power difference in the therapy relationship.

She suggests that it is essential that clients should make their own choices regarding values, and that being exposed to the therapist's value system should be an issue for informed consent. In CBT, therapists are encouraged to describe the cognitive model as the 'right' one, according to their values and beliefs. Informed consent is often ignored in favour of coercion, and autonomy rejected in favour of beneficence, thus increasing the power of the therapist. The principle of beneficence also seems to be justified again by the belief that the outcome of a client changing their thinking in accordance with CBT principles is inevitably good and beneficial to the client. The risk of whether a particular client may not believe that the ends justify the means is not considered, again as a result of the appeal to research and science, which then concludes that CBT is right for everybody, despite the research demonstrating that this is very far from the case. This insistence that one way of thinking is the answer for everyone is in direct contradiction to respect for the autonomy of the individual client.

Power-within of the client

The rhetoric of 'collaboration' in CBT seems to imply the importance of the increasing agency or 'power-within' of the client. Telford and Farrington refer to the client's power:

> ... if therapy is successful, it must help the client to assume his/her own power, in other words to become his/her own therapist. Thus, if the client is to generalise his/her gains and self-maintain, the balance of perceived power must shift from being invested (by the client) in the therapist to being invested in the client him/herself. (1996: 125)

Here the concept of power is implicitly one in which power is seen as a possession, ideally to be passed from the therapist to the client, although the power is always over the client's life. There seems to be a conflation of two models of power here. One is about domination and power over someone ('power-over'), which the therapist initially holds over the client. Then the client should take power over their own lives from the therapist, which seems to be an internal, individual notion of power, or the feminist notion of 'power-within' (see Proctor, 2002, 2017). The idea of passing power from the therapist to the client also seems to suggest the notion of the therapist initially having power over the client, and gradually the client resisting this power, the goal of therapy being the abolition of the therapist's domination. It is not clear, however, how this resistance or process is supported or encouraged by the behaviour of the therapist. The goal of therapy to encourage the client's 'power-from-within' is not consistent with the means of 'collaboration', which hardly challenges the therapist's 'power-over' the client.

Self-regulation

This concept of power assumes a behavioural, one-dimensional concept of power, visible only when the therapist dominates and controls the therapy by their instructions. Implicit in the writing about CBT is the notion that therapy is successful when the client takes on the CBT model and the world-view of the therapist: that is, when the client begins to regulate and discipline themselves in line with how the therapist would do this. Thus, even when the client begins to make their own decisions and is seen to be taking her/his own power, it could be argued that this reflects the client's internalisation of the norms suggested by the therapist, and the client has begun to regulate themselves, with no further need for the therapist to encourage this. This idea is reminiscent of Foucault's reference to Bentham's Panopticon (Foucault, 1977b), when surveillance starts to be carried out individually by those being surveyed. Here, clients take over the therapist's role and become surveyors and regulators of their own thoughts. However, this does not remove the power in the norms internalised by the client, or the power of the therapist in communicating and encouraging these norms to be internalised.

Power in personal histories

It could be claimed that the intention behind CBT – to change the negative automatic thoughts and negative schemata of the client – could be to increase the internal feeling of 'power-from-within' in the client and reduce the power of clients' personal histories of powerlessness. However, the means by which CBT attempts to achieve this are not consistent with the ends. It is difficult to argue that the aim of CBT is to increase the power of the client by the therapist using 'power-over', or their authority. Hardy, Cahill and Barkham (2007) briefly discuss historical power with respect to the personal histories of the therapist and client in relation to 'contextual factors' that can affect the therapy relationship. They give the example of the client feeling shame due to a feeling of inferiority to the therapist. It is not clear how the therapist's use of their authority could help to change this.

Structural social power

CBT theory takes no account of issues of power due to social-structural positions. There is a danger that, in challenging the 'realism' of a client's thoughts, the material realities of power are ignored and deemed 'unrealistic'. The focus in CBT is on changing the thinking of the individual, which entails the danger of ignoring the social-structural positions and the material realities of oppression and power in people's lives (see Proctor, 2006; Kearney, 2018).

Conclusion

Very little attention is paid to the issue of power in most of the CBT literature. Yet CBT invests much authority in therapists who, according to the model, know what is best for their client. There are few considerations of the dangers of this position, or even a questioning of the assumptions underlying this position. A belief in the importance of cognitive processes does not have to lead to a belief in an authoritative CBT therapist who educates the client in the right way to live their life. I maintain that it is necessary for CBT to look realistically and honestly at the dynamics of power in therapy relationships. For, without such an inquiry, CBT therapists are in danger of obscuring their power, and of not taking an ethical stance to avoid domination and abuse.

Given the association of distress with the experience of powerlessness, should the ultimate aim of therapy be to try to help clients take more control of their lives? If so, then CBT therapists surely need to consider carefully how their practice helps or hinders this aim, particularly with respect to the internal consistency of the means and the end. If therapists take control and do not think carefully about how to avoid domination during therapy, how can we expect clients to walk away feeling more in control?

References

Allison A (1996). A framework for good practice: ethical issues in cognitive behaviour therapy. In: Marshall S, Turnbull J (eds). *Cognitive Behaviour Therapy.* London: Balliere Tindall (pp155–180).

BABCP (2009, revised 2016). Standards of Conduct, Performance and Ethics. [Online]. www.babcp.com/files/About/BABCP-Standards-of-Conduct-Performance-and-Ethics-0917.pdf (accessed 4 February 2018).

Beck AT (1976/1991). *Cognitive Therapy and the Emotional Disorders.* London: Penguin.

Beck AT, Rush AT, Shaw BF, Emery G (1979). *Cognitive Therapy of Depression.* New York, NY: Guilford Press.

Beck JS (1995). *Cognitive Therapy: basics and beyond.* New York: Guilford Press.

Bentall R (2004). *Madness Explained: psychosis and human nature.* London: Penguin.

Blease CR (2015). Talking more about talking cures: cognitive behavioural therapy and informed consent. *Journal of Medical Ethics 41*: 750–755.

Bozarth J (1998). *Person-Centered Therapy: a revolutionary paradigm.* Ross-on-Wye: PCCS Books.

British Association for Counselling and Psychotherapy (BACP) (2018). *Ethical Framework for Good Practice in Counselling and Psychotherapy.* Lutterworth: BACP.

Butler J (1990). Gender trouble, feminist theory, and psychoanalytic discourse. In: Nicholson LJ (ed). *Feminism/Postmodernism.* London: Routledge (pp324–340).

Cooper M (2008) Essential Research Findings in Counselling and Psychotherapy: the facts are friendly. London: Sage.

Cromwell RE, Olson DH (1975). *Power in Families.* New York, NY: John Wiley.

Fish V (1999). Clementis's hat: Foucault and the politics of psychotherapy. In: Parker I (ed). *Deconstructing Psychotherapy.* London: Sage (pp54–70).

Foucault M (1980). *Power/Knowledge: selected interviews and other writings 1972–1977.* Brighton: Harvester Press.

Foucault M (1979). *The History of Sexuality, vol 1: an introduction.* London: Penguin Press.

Foucault M (1977a). *Madness and Civilisation.* London: Tavistock.

Foucault M (1977b). *Discipline and Punish.* London: Penguin Press.

Foucault M (1973). *The Order of Things: an archaeology of the human sciences.* New York, NY: Vintage Books.

Gilbert P (2004). Evolutionary approaches to psychopathology and cognitive therapy. In:

Gilbert P (ed). *Evolutionary Theory and Cognitive Therapy.* New York, NY: Springer (pp3–44).

Gilbert P, Leahy R (2007). Introduction. In: Gilbert P, Leahy RL (eds). *The Therapeutic Relationship in the Cognitive Behavioral Psychotherapies.* London: Routledge.

Hardy G, Cahill J, Barkham M (2007). Active ingredients of the therapeutic relationship that promote client change: a research perspective. In: Gilbert P, Leahy RL (eds). *The Therapeutic Relationship in the Cognitive Behavioral Psychotherapies.* London: Routledge (pp24–42).

Kearney A (2018). *Counselling, Class and Politics: undeclared influences in therapy* (2nd ed) (G Proctor ed). Monmouth: PCCS Books.

Kelly L, Burton S, Regan L (1998). *Legacies of Abuse – 'It's more complicated than that': a qualitative study of the meaning and impacts of sexual abuse in childhood.* London: Child and Woman Abuse Studies Unit, University of North London.

Keys S, Proctor G (2007). Ethics in practice in person-centred therapy. In: Cooper M, O'Hara M, Schmid P, Wyatt G (eds). *The Handbook of Person-centred Psychotherapy and Counselling*. Basingstoke: Palgrave Macmillan (pp353–365).

Lambert MJ, Ogles BM (2004). The efficacy and effectiveness of psychotherapy. In: Lambert M (ed). *Bergin and Garfield's Handbook of Psychotherapy and Behavior Change* (5th ed). New York, NY: John Wiley (pp139–193).

Lowe R (1999). Between the 'No Longer' and the 'Not Yet': postmodernism as a context for critical therapeutic work. In: Parker I (ed). *Deconstructing Psychotherapy*. London: Sage (pp71–85).

Lukes S (1974). *Power: a radical view*. London: Macmillan Press.

McNay L (1992). *Foucault and Feminism: power, gender and the self*. Cambridge: Polity Press.

Marcinko L (2003). Medication compliance with difficult patients. In: Leahy RL (ed). *Roadblocks in CBT: transforming challenges into opportunities to change*. London: Guilford Press (pp318–340).

Marshall S (1996). The characteristics of cognitive behaviour therapy. In: Marshall S, Turnbull J (eds). *Cognitive Behaviour Therapy*. London: Balliere Tindall (pp29–54).

Masson JM (1989). *Against Therapy*. London: Fontana.

Norcross JC (ed) (2002). *Psychotherapy Relationships that Work: therapists' contributions and responsiveness to patients*. New York, NY: Oxford University Press.

Padesky CA, Greenberger D (1995). *Clinician's Guide to Mind over Mood*. London: Guilford Press.

Paley G, Lawton D (2001). Evidence-based practice: accounting for the importance of the therapeutic relationship in UK National Health Service therapy provision. *Counselling and Psychotherapy Research 1*(1): 12–17.

Parker I (1999). Deconstruction and psychotherapy. In: Parker I (ed). *Deconstructing Psychotherapy*. London: Sage (pp1–18).

Pilgrim D (1997). *Psychotherapy and Society*. London: Sage.

Pilgrim D, Treacher A (1992). *Clinical Psychology Observed*. London: Routledge.

Potter J (1996). *Representing Reality: discourse, rhetoric and social construction*. Sage: London.

Proctor G (2017). *The Dynamics of Power in Counselling and Psychotherapy: ethics, politics and practice* (2nd ed). Monmouth: PCCS Books.

Proctor G (2015). The NHS in 2015. *Therapy Today 26*(9): 18–25.

Proctor G (2014). *Ethics and Values in Counselling and Psychotherapy*. London: Sage.

Proctor G (2006) Therapy: opium for the masses or help for those who least need it? In: Proctor G, Cooper M, Sanders P, Malcolm B (eds). *Politicising the Person-centred Approach: an agenda for social change*. Ross-on-Wye: PCCS Books.

Proctor G (2002). *The Dynamics of Power in Counselling and Psychotherapy: ethics, politics and practice*. Ross-on-Wye: PCCS Books.

Proctor G, Hayes C (2017). Counselling for Depression: a response to counselling education in the twenty-first century – ethical conflicts between a counselling approach operating within a medicalised bureaucratic health service. *British Journal of Guidance and Counselling* 45(4): 417–426.

Ransome P (1992). *Antonio Gramsci: a new introduction*. London: Harvester Wheatsheaf.

Read J, Wallcraft J (1992). Guidelines for empowering users of mental health services. London: Confederation of Health Service Employees.

Rogers C (1957). The necessary and sufficient conditions of therapeutic personality change. *Journal of Consulting Psychology 21*(2): 95–103.

Searle Y (1993). Ethical issues within the therapeutic relationship: autonomy or paternalism? *Clinical Psychology Forum 63:* 31–36.

Sparks JA, Duncan BL, Miller SD (2008). Common factors in psychotherapy. In: Lebow JL (ed). *Twenty-first Century Psychotherapies: contemporary approaches to theory and practice.* Hoboken, NJ: John Wiley & Sons (pp453–497).

Spinelli E (1994). *Demystifying Therapy*. Ross-on-Wye: PCCS Books.

Starhawk (1987). *Truth or Dare: encounters with power, authority and mystery*. San Francisco, CA: Harper & Row.

Stevens C L, Muran C, Safran JD (2003). Obstacles or opportunities? A relational approach to negotiating alliance ruptures. In: Leahy RL (ed). *Roadblocks in CBT: transforming challenges into opportunities to change*. London: Guilford Press (pp274–294).

Telford A, Farrington A (1996). Handing over: generalisation and maintenance of self-management skills. In: Marshall S, Turnbull J (eds). *Cognitive Behaviour Therapy*. London: Balliere Tindall (pp121–152).

Tompkins MA (2003). Effective homework. In: Leahy RL (ed). *Roadblocks in CBT: transforming challenges into opportunities to change*. London: Guilford Press (pp49–68).

Turnbull J (1996). The context of therapy. In: Marshall S, Turnbull J (eds). *Cognitive Behaviour Therapy*. London: Balliere Tindall (pp11–28).

Westbrook D, Kennerley H, Kirk J (2012). *An Introduction to Cognitive Behaviour Therapy: skills and applications* (2nd ed). London: Sage.

Williams J, Watson G (1994). Mental health services that empower women: the challenge to clinical psychology. *Clinical Psychology Forum 64*: 11–17.

3 Happiness: CBT and the Layard thesis*

David Pilgrim

'Money can't buy me love.'
(Lennon & McCartney, 1964)

In this chapter, I examine an important contribution from an economist, Richard Layard, to debates about the social and economic sources of mental distress and ways of responding to the latter. Layard's book *Happiness: lessons from a new science* (Layard: 2005) is one of many contributions from him about these topics. It provides a persuasive case for 'upstream' causes of mental health problems, which includes a critique of modern consumerism. A much less persuasive case is made, though, for therapeutic social engineering in response to psychological casualties of these socioeconomic forces.

Layard's work has been a very useful stimulus for debates about mental health in society. Many of these have been around for a long time in disciplines outside of economics, and so it may be relevant that it has taken an economist to encourage discussion about mental health in the political class. It confirms one of Layard's key points that, currently, when measuring social progress, finance is privileged over the subjective lives of ordinary citizens.

Layard uses a range of evidence from genetics, neuroscience, medicine, philosophy, psychology and sociology (as well as drawing heavily on his own discipline of economics) to make his case. The latter starts with the claim that, while absolute poverty certainly leads to misery, for those not in that state, happiness does not increase with more wealth. Setting out this stall in the opening paragraph of the first chapter of *Happiness* is this clear-enough statement:

---

* An earlier version of this chapter appeared in the *European Journal of Psychotherapy and Counselling 2008; 10*(3): 247–260.

> There is a paradox at the heart of our lives. Most people want income and strive for it. Yet as Western societies have got richer, their people have become no happier. (2005: 3)

Layard goes on to marshal evidence, not just to support this claim but also to suggest causal mechanisms and corrective interventions. To use a medical metaphor here, he provides us with a diagnosis and some thoughts on aetiology or pathogenesis, as well as a treatment plan. However, he goes beyond medical metaphor – he also literally accepts medical categories and authority. Indeed, an academic feature of his book is that, while Layard is highly logical and detailed in his curiosity about empirical claims from all the disciplines on which he draws, he gives little time or interest to interrogating the concepts and theories favoured by them.

The exception to this is that he does make small detours of conceptual clarification in response to philosophy and economics. Thus, for example, he challenges Kant with MRI scans to show that the philosopher was wrong to claim that doing the right thing should give no pleasure. Similarly, he shows that the reductionist emphasis of Hobbes on punishment to maintain moral order was flawed. The broad sweep of Layard's thesis is very sound. In economies in which real income levels have risen steadily, the cultural expectation is to want more money. Consequently, there is an unending game of catch-up – more money is given, but more is wanted. The gap between actual income and that deemed appropriate for happiness and satisfaction of need inevitably leads to chronic dissatisfaction. Moreover, that restless and grasping focus on work and its riches has created economies fraught with other consequent problems of venal materialism and 'rampant individualism' (a favoured phrase of Layard). At the heart of this dissatisfaction is 'The Hedonic Treadmill'. As he puts it, succinctly:

> … living standards are like alcohol and drugs. Once you have a new experience, you need to keep having more of it if you want to sustain your happiness… you have to keep running in order that your happiness stands still... (2005: 48)

The news gets worse, however. It is not merely that modern consumerism is a false god promising happiness but not delivering; the social and cultural arrangements around that idol bring pain and suffering to many. Most of us have a distressing work–life balance (especially in the US and the UK). The idealisation of the ultra-rich legitimises large discrepancies in wealth and de-legitimises redistributive economic policies, such as high taxation. Not only have authoritarian socialist experiments in the East (rejected by Layard) been displaced by anarchic 'wild west' capitalism, to the further detriment of its long-suffering citizens, but social democracy in northern Europe (highly favoured by Layard) has been in retreat. In Scandinavia, for example, the stable emergence of social democracy has now broken down, and, further south, it has been captured by neo-liberal economics and conservative social policies.

According to Layard, socio-economic arrangements that focus singularly on the pursuit of personal financial advantage divert us from understanding the factors that might illuminate a more important type of wealth. He argues that 'the aim of politics is to make the world a friendlier place, not an assault course' (2005: 232). I presume that he means here that the aim of politics ought to be this, as clearly, by his own argument, it is currently failing.

Layard identifies seven main factors that create a synergy for happiness: good family relationships; enough money to avoid absolute poverty; enjoyable work; community engagement and friendships; good health; personal freedom, and a clear personal value system. By implication, people may lose the level of happiness achieved in life by any negative aspects of the seven factors. Thus, happiness and its opposite are shaped and maintained dynamically by an interaction of these factors in a person's life. By the end of the book, he lays out a range of policies to support this shift of emphasis to happiness, and away from the rat race of money-chasing.

By focusing on chasing more money, individualism in the capitalist economy creates lifestyles at odds with this synergy for happiness. Family relationships are undermined; work becomes an obsessive vehicle for wealth and status; social bonds in the community and with friends are weakened by individualism, and health is affected negatively. Personal freedom is intrinsic to rampant individualism, but it is expressed at the cost of all the above when only expressed egotistically. As for personal value systems, these are individualised and secularised, so the advantages of collective political and religious meaning systems are lost.

Layard talks of a 'moral vacuum' created by this collapse of mutuality and social solidarity. Moreover, the aggregate loss of trust and respect for others arising from materialistic egotism brings with it high crime and suicide rates. The predictions of post-Second World War economists that increasing overall wealth in a society would bring lower crime rates has proved to be wrong, as is evident in western Europe and North America.

The limits of Layard's reasoning

Having summarised Layard's thesis and broadly endorsed it, I now want to highlight what I consider to be some substantial shortcomings. Layard is an economist, not a psychologist or sociologist, and so he has either been brave and erudite, or unwise and arrogant, to take on such a huge topic about the nature of wellbeing in its social context. Human happiness is surely a huge topic by anyone's estimation. Poking around curiously with a stick in the arcane world of other disciplines will lead to some bits of uni-disciplinary knowledge emerging, but others remaining hidden.

The point I am making here, then, is not *ad hominem* about Layard but a more general one about the challenge of interdisciplinarity. The other general point I want to make, before critiquing Layard's *Happiness*, is that, whatever Layard's personal take on his topic, all of us, but especially those in and around the therapy trade, need to reflect long and hard on the relationship between upstream causes and downstream solutions.

Some of Layard's empirical claims about social differences in happiness are questionable. For example, he minimises gender and age differences in happiness, arguing that the seven factors noted above generate degrees of wellbeing in all of us. However, there are clear differences in gender and age. Far more women than men present with 'common mental health problems', and medical sociologists have not resolved the reasons for this gender gap (Pilgrim, 2016). As for age, a predictable inverted 'U'-shaped curve characterises the lifespan in relation to misery: basically, the young and the very old are disproportionately worse off.

As an economist, Layard is predictably stronger on the link between labour market position and happiness. He points out, correctly, that unemployment and insecure employment impact negatively. However, he endorses the picture offered by Helliwell (2003) that unemployment has the greatest negative impact – a conclusion that is challengeable. Other studies indicate that global mental health scores for the unemployed lie between secure employment and insecure employment, with the latter actually creating the greatest distress and existential uncertainty (Rogers & Pilgrim, 2003).

Taken overall, these are important points of academic hygiene, but they do not alter the validity of Layard's basic argument. The greater doubt arises not from his empirical claims, but that he approaches the academy and the clinic, with all their relevant disciplines and associated vested interests, with such enthusiastic and artless trust. The whole spirit of Layard's work is one of bullish empiricism, and the latter is naïve, not critical (see Bhaskar, 1989; Pilgrim, 2015a).

This naïve realism in turn creates an uncritical trust in pre-existing bodies of knowledge. And, because the latter are bound up with disciplinary interests, there is no interrogation of the power relationships they contain. These interests and quests for power from academic disciplines – and especially their applied wings, the professions – readily tip into rhetoric and strategies to gain the privileges of epistemological control, occupational autonomy, dominance over others, political influence and improved income. The elaborate facts so favoured by Layard's style of argumentation are theory laden, and they also reflect preferred concepts. Human science cannot proceed properly unless these are interrogated – it is not just a matter of methodological rigour about knowledge claims, although this is still important.

This caution is not limited to Layard's work. A range of post-Popperian philosophers, such as Feyerabend, Lakatos, Bhaskar, Kuhn and others, have highlighted the argument that empirical claims need to be understood in relation to concepts and theories. Sociologists of science have reinforced this necessity when they have investigated the way in which scientific knowledge emerges, is contested and changes. Layard's retained faith in a post-Enlightenment approach to all matters in the world, including the conventional wisdoms of modernist human science, is both a strength and a weakness. The advantage is that he has no postmodern doubts. Consequently, this faith in the contemporary scientific academy saves his readers the interminable intellectual fiddling on the spot of the post-structuralism that has infected social science in the last 20 years.

But between the modern and the postmodern, as the philosophers I list above indicate, there remains a serious case to 'check our facts': not in the sense of their accuracy (an empirical question of methodology), but in relation to their pre-empirical or non-empirical character. There are two good reasons for this sort of cautious or critical inquiry. The first is that taken-for-granted factualism, as positivist disciplinary knowledge prefers to present itself, could lead to mystification, not clarification. Experts, applied and academic, often present their currently preferred reality as superior to that of colleagues in the past and in other disciplines. But experts may be wrong in how they theorise the world, and they may generate misleading data and truth claims by testing those theories.

Second, naïve empiricism means that concepts preferred at a moment in time may be poor, so we need a method to check this possibility. Theories and concepts are pregnant with values and interests – they are not merely simple springboards for logical and empirical inquiry. Thus, pre-empirical critique is just as important as empirical inquiry in the human sciences. Instead of exercising caution on these two fronts, Layard is simply seduced by the certainties of naïve empiricism.

It is important to distinguish my line of caution and criticism of Layard's naïve realism here from that of postmodernists who argue that 'everything is socially constructed' so we can never make stable knowledge claims about reality. It is not reality that is socially constructed, but our understanding of reality. This is why we should approach knowledge claims in human science and their underpinning interests sceptically. Layard fails in this task; indeed, he does not even make a start on it in his book.

The technological fix of CBT and the faith in psychiatric knowledge

Most forms of psychological intervention to ameliorate distress are derived not from the academic discipline of psychology but from medicine. For example, medical practitioners, not psychologists, first championed psychoanalysis and existential analysis. Many of the early members of the British Psychological Society were medical practitioners, and, significantly, the first separate section of the Society was formed in 1919 – the Medical Section. The flow of 'shell-shock doctors' from the 'Great War' swelled its ranks (Stone, 1985).

When psychodynamic therapy was superseded in legitimacy by behavioural, and then cognitive behavioural treatments in the late 20th century, clinical problems were clearly the main 'pull from the front'. The morphing of behaviour therapy into the seemingly contradictory model of cognitive behaviour therapy had no coherent 'ism' as a 'push from behind' in the academy. Indeed, very few forms of therapy have emerged purely from academic psychology. Kelly's personal-construct therapy

(PCT) is an exception here. But PCT was then quickly incorporated into 'cognitive-analytical therapy' by a pragmatic general medical practitioner (Ryle, 1990).

As for the bigger players in the cognitive therapy field, these were pragmatic psychologists and psychiatrists in the clinic (Beck, 1976; Ellis, 1994). They were seeking accessible and efficient treatments, which avoided the time-consuming past–present focus of the psychodynamic tradition. Their primary interest was not about researching ordinary cognitive functioning (the norm in academic departments of psychology during the 1980s), but about altering dysfunctional conduct. Thus, 'cognitive therapy' in its various guises has been driven, by and large, not by academic psychology but by practical concerns in clinical settings.

The above historical reality testing is relevant, given that, in *Happiness*, Layard makes much use of psychology as a discipline that offers a corrective to the economic reductionism of his own profession. He also suggests that applied psychology today carries similar helpful wisdoms to that of ancient cosmologies like Buddhism. He is enamoured by what he calls the 'new psychology', and implies, or assumes, that it is a unitary body of knowledge waiting to be tapped for human betterment.

However, in the light of the previous discussion, he focuses on clinical innovations, not academic psychology, and it is not clear from the text whether he is aware of conflating the syncretism of CBT with the 'new psychology'. He rejects the historical determinism of the old. Freud is mentioned episodically to demonstrate how daft you can get. He also rejects historical determinism of a different kind – Skinner's radical behaviourism. His love of the academic new is reflected in contestable comments like: 'Fortunately psychology has returned to the study of feelings' (2005: 128).

However, there are problems with his infatuation with the new. For example – and this may reflect Layard's belief in scientific incrementalism – psychology has not progressed in a linear fashion, with outmoded models being cast aside. Instead, we find layers of approach co-existing, which wax and wane in fashion. For example, there are plenty of psychologists (academic and applied) who remain attached to both behaviourism and psychoanalysis. Moreover, Layard does not mention social constructionism. His academic psychology advisors, acknowledged generously at the end of the book, seem to have emphasised inner events rather than social representations and discursive practices. The latter are now studied as often by social psychologists as by sociologists, and they have particular points to make about therapy (McNamee & Gergen, 1992; Parker, 1999).

Moreover, there is no clear evidence that psychology has, by and large, returned to feelings *per se*, but it has (for now) accepted the need to study internal events. The latter in the main are represented in undergraduate courses in psychology, not in their affective form, but in their cognitive form. Feeling states are studied, but less often than verbalised cognitions. Thinking is now studied systematically. We now have 'cognitive science', but 'affective science' is fairly well hidden.

Moreover, as has been noted, the interest by some applied (not academic) psychologists in the relationship between thought, action and affect has not been driven by academic innovations, but by the interests of clinical psychiatrists. This may seem a trivial point, but it is not. Unless it is made, then a superficial reading is that psychological science has marched resolutely forward to advise clinical practitioners about how to conduct their work, state-of-the-science fashion. CBT may be the current orthodoxy in clinical psychology, but it is essentially a form of psychiatric treatment, the roots of which are not in cognitive science (Pilgrim, 2011).

Any resemblance to cognitivism in cognitive therapy is superficial; when it occurs genuinely, it has been a *post hoc* cultivation. Layard alludes frequently to psychiatry – or, more often, its by-product, mental illness – in his work. The term 'by-product' is used here to point up that Layard's naïve acceptance of psychiatric representation is at work. I do not mean that people are not frightened, or profoundly sad or crazy. What I am emphasising, *contra* Layard, is that the medical codifications of 'anxiety disorders' or 'depression' or 'schizophrenia' add little or nothing to ordinary-language representations of misery and madness. Consequently, we need to understand the variety of interests that maintain categories that are scientifically dubious and are often experienced as stigmatising and unhelpful by their recipients (Pilgrim, 2007).

Moreover, psychiatric diagnoses are not straightforward facts but representations that are conceptually weak and tautological. Symptoms are used to warrant a diagnosis, and the symptoms are explained by the diagnosis (Pilgrim, 2005):

> Q: How do we know this patient is depressed?
> A: Because they are low in mood and feel unable to face work.
> Q: Why are they low in mood and cannot face work?
> A: Because they are suffering from depression.

Layard's confidence in psychiatric diagnosis and his love of the new suggest that he takes current expert claims at face value. This leads to his own version of naïve tautology. For example, he asks, 'Which causes more misery: depression or poverty? The answer is depression… mental illness is probably the largest cause (sic) of misery in Western society' (2005: 181). But depression is misery: the former is a medical codification of the latter. If we say that misery is the largest cause of misery, it is absurdly circular. So how can Layard use the same logic persuasively when substituting the word 'depression' at the start of the formula?

The answer probably rests in his pre-empirical assumption, offered to him by psychiatrists (and, by the way, many psychologists), that depression has a non-problematic facticity that separates it clearly from ordinary misery. Not only is this position empirically challengeable, but the social and political implications are enormous. Thus, for example, it means that depression-as-illness is located in individuals. Our whole focus risks shifting, in a blinkered fashion, to their medical problem, rather than the very upstream factors Layard is so keen to emphasise. It also assumes that discontinuous emotional states exist in nature. While this is logically possible, where is the evidence?

What we do know about emotions is that misery is ubiquitous and fluctuating between and within individuals, and across time and place. People, over time, move up and down a continuum of misery and happiness. Indeed, Layard himself endorses this assumption when discussing Buddhism, which accepts suffering as a regular part of the emotional flux of living and dying. Moreover, the diagnosis of depression not only diverts us from socio-political relationships to the diseased person; it renders the latter a passive victim of their putative disease. It thereby risks robbing them of their agency and their opportunity for existential reflection.

Elsewhere, with colleagues, I have explored this problem with psychiatric diagnosis in general (Pilgrim, 2007), and the diagnosis of depression in particular (Pilgrim & Bentall, 1999; Pilgrim & Dowrick, 2006). Here I will simply note that Layard compounds the epistemic fallacy common in psychiatric and other forms of expert knowledge – the confusion of the map with the territory. Because psychiatrists reify 'major depression', it becomes for them a real, natural category, rather than a point on an existential continuum. This claim of naturalism is premature, as philosophers interrogating psychiatric nomenclature have demonstrated (Cooper, 2004). The latter author demonstrates how commercial and professional interests have shaped premature claims of psychiatric success about categorising misery and madness.

Depression, like other functional psychiatric diagnoses, is not readily distinguished from normality. This is a crucial test of a diagnostic category, because medicine operates the binary principle of present/absent. Nor is 'clinical depression' readily distinguished from other common distress, such as anxiety. Nor are the causes of depression definitely known (it lacks aetiological specificity). Nor is a medical treatment specified for it and not applied to other conditions (it lacks treatment specificity). When we take all of these shortcomings together, depression is a very poor medical concept, yet it has entered the vernacular. It has widespread legitimacy, but it is a mystification that obscures a range of necessary moral, political and intellectual explorations implied by ordinary-language accounts of 'distress', 'misery', or 'unhappiness'.

Because Layard accepts the psychiatric reification of 'depression', he also accepts the currently preferred expert technical fix for the putative condition – CBT and antidepressants. It should be emphasised, though, that Layard does not argue that the cure for misery can ever be a total technological fix. For example, early on he endorses both psychological and pharmacological successes, but asks sceptically, '… how much further can this process go in the relief of misery?' (2005: 9). His wider preference is for upstream prevention by the construction of social and economic policies implied by the seven factors he highlights (listed earlier).

Thus, my criticism here is not of Layard's wholesale psychological or psychiatric reductionism, as he makes a clear case for socioeconomic determinism. Rather, it is the contradiction he creates for himself when he invests too much faith in the technological fix. He also implies that the mechanisms of extreme misery are being increasingly explicated by modern therapeutic technologies, when they are not.

It is as though he cannot carry through the full implications of his own reasoning about upstream factors.

So, despite his lack of crude reductionism, Layard still falls into the traps of the illusory technological fix and of psychiatric reification. Under the heading 'disorders of the mind', he argues, with typical enthusiasm for what is for him the factually obvious, that:

> What drug you need depends on what kind of problem you have. If we consider only serious mental problems, about a third of us will experience one of them some time in our life. They include schizophrenia (1% of us), depression (15%), manic-depression (1%)… [He goes on to list more psychiatric categories] (2005: 208)

In case the reader is in doubt about Layard's faith in medical categories, he then describes the pros and cons of drugs for relief of suffering and says this: 'We all become what we would call depressed at some time in our lives. But a major depression is something quite different' (2005: 209).

The final phrase signals his commitment to the digital logic of psychiatric diagnosis – you are either depressed, or not. But the words before it indicate that Layard nearly had an insight about the human condition: people are more or less miserable across time and space.

In his enthusiasm for antidepressants, Layard then goes further by accepting that depression is 'associated' with serotonin depletion, but he does not interrogate the uncertainty about the direction of causality. For example, is a headache caused by a lack of aspirin in the brain? (The answer is 'no'.) And could suffering a saddening loss or insult to the self then lead to changes in the brain? (The answer, by Layard's own arguments earlier in his book, is 'yes'.) Moreover, the putative pharmacological rationale for the selective seratonin reuptake inhibitors (SSRIs) is weak, given that randomised controlled trials (RCTs) show a narrow gap of results in the drug and placebo arms (Dowrick, 2004; Moncrieff & Kirsch, 2005).

Layard does not limit his confidence in a therapeutic regime for depression to pharmacology. He advocates the optimal combined use of drugs and talk. By implication, we need more therapists, and more and better drugs. Music to the ears is consequently offered to his psychiatric colleagues:

> We should spend more on tackling the problem of mental illness. This is the greatest source of misery in the West, and the fortunate should ensure a better deal for those who suffer. Psychiatry should be a top branch of medicine, not one of the least prestigious. (2005: 233)

This conclusion is well intentioned. Who can argue with wanting to ameliorate misery? But it is without reference to the contestation that surrounds psychiatry, and has done so for so long. Not only has that profession, in the main, opted for a categorical view of human functioning that does not hold scientific water and has dehumanising consequences; it has been a source of recurring criticism from insiders and outsiders alike. The enlightened biopsychosocial model favoured by Layard is not typically applied in psychiatric practice (Rogers & Pilgrim, 2015), and it tends to default, in practice, to psychosomatic reasoning, thus ignoring and obscuring the social (Pilgrim, 2015b).

Finally, Layard's commitment to the technological fix of CBT reinforces the view that the model of intervention to ameliorate human distress is all that matters. In fact, over 30 years of process-outcome research in psychotherapy tells us that it is the therapeutic alliance, not other variables (like the model used, therapist background, gender, age etc) that is the best predictor of success (Lambert, 2007; see many of the chapters in this volume). Thus, the seduction of technology diverts our attention from the centrality of relationality. Layard makes his particular contribution to this mystifying techno-centric discourse about how people change and how they might feel better about themselves and the world.

In the first part of his book, Layard lets us know that we are being short-changed over happiness. He has got all the upstream factors in place to make his case, except one. He emphasises the general role of the family as a stable point of reference for mental health in the growing child. However, no mention is made of high rates of childhood sexual abuse among those receiving treatment in psychiatric facilities. Also, physical abuse in childhood predicts both violence and revictimisation in adulthood. A consequent omission, then, is that an effective child protection policy would be an important building block of a public policy aimed at raising the average level of happiness in the population. Thus, Layard is particularly weak in truly understanding the mediating factors about relationality, support, and attachment in the emergence and amelioration of mental health problems.

Moreover, there is an implication here for the therapy trade. We know that a minority of therapists surveyed anonymously admit to boundary violations about sexual contact (Pilgrim & Guinan, 1999). We also know that this is a source of iatrogenic distress for clients, with some of them experiencing revictimisation. Layard flags up the adverse effects of drug treatment, but does not mention this risk from talking therapies (save that people might be offered ineffective forms). He writes as if therapy is always benign, when we know that bad therapists create deterioration effects, and that many clients gain no benefit while being exposed to its risks.

In line with his confidence in therapy, Layard believes there are now experts in misery. As we know, there is a counterargument to this assumption, with some vociferously rejecting therapeutic expertise (Masson, 1989), or damning it with faint praise (Smail, 1996). Whatever stance we take on either side of these arguments, therapy has to be viewed as a problematic form of social engineering. It contains risks as well as potential benefits. It is not just a good news story.

The weaknesses of CBT

I want to return at this point to the weaknesses of CBT (liked by Layard) and the remaining strengths of the older traditions, such as psychoanalysis and existentialism (disliked by Layard). CBT is a technology without a true theory. Moreover, it has taken much of its advocates in nursing and clinical psychology (who should know better) in a direction that reinforces the irrationalities of psychiatric diagnosis. The latter leads to a nomothetic rather than idiographic approach to therapeutic work, with patients being fitted into *a priori* categories, which are then 'treated' – hence we find CBT 'for' depression, generalised anxiety disorder, schizophrenia and so on (eg. Tarrier et al, 1998).

The tendency for clinical psychologists to use rather than reject psychiatric categories has been evident since behaviour therapy, and then cognitive behaviour therapy, became medicalised (Pilgrim, 2011). Behaviour therapy and CBT have become part of the psychiatric treatment armamentarium, taught to and delivered by nurses, cookbook style. These clinical techniques have simply become forms of treatment for mental illness. The medicalisation trend has been reflected in the work of Aaron Beck and his colleagues. As they had no theoretical allegiance to behaviourism *per se*, but did want to extend the applicability of behaviour therapy to inner events, Beck's atheoretical psychiatric pragmatism prevailed. Hence, there was the eventual dominance of the current orthodoxy of cognitive behaviour therapy and its emphasis on treating diagnostic categories. Psychiatric knowledge and medical dominance were thereby left intact, neither scrutinised nor criticised. In his book, Layard simply accepts this inheritance and its epistemological assumptions.

But does any of this matter? After all, those on the outside of these professional concerns may understandably be left cold by the history and the arguments. I would argue that it does matter, because of questions of reflexivity and comprehensiveness. Whatever we think of the behaviourists of the 1960s, they were trying to develop a general psychological frame of reference that didn't just enable and test behavioural change, but also provided the basis for context-specific formulations. As such, it could be applied to the therapist themselves in accounting for their own current behaviour in relation to their peculiar reinforcement history, and it was linked to general psychological theorising.

But, because of the medicalisation of behaviour therapy and, subsequently, CBT, we are left in a paradoxical position 40 years on. Some CBT practitioners now special-plead for formulation in the face of diagnostic imperialism (Bruch & Bond, 1998; Butler, 1999), but many others simply accept the advantages of medical orthodoxy without question, and at their peril (Pilgrim & Carey, 2012; Scott & Sembi, 2006). Psychologists outside of this allegiance to a narrow CBT orthodoxy argue that formulation must now displace a reliance on diagnostic psychiatry (Johnstone & Dallos, 2013).

In the latter regard, clinical psychologists in the thrall of CBT have now often become part of the problem, rather than the solution. Under pressure to obtain research grants allocated by medical committees that are committed to diagnostic-related groups (DRGs), clinical psychologists' research on, for example, 'CBT for schizophrenia' reinforces the idea that madness and misery are carved at the joints of nature, when they are not. Being a contested discipline, with biology at one end and sociology at the other, we also find psychology containing biodeterminists, who can operate comfortably within a biomedical paradigm. The epistemic fallacy (confusing reality with what we consider to be reality) and the ontic fallacy (naïvely considering reality to be the immediate surface of what we see) are reinforced, then, not by psychiatrists but by psychologists (Pilgrim, 2007).

If CBT has little to say theoretically about general human functioning, and reinforces questionable medical categories, what are the implications of Layard rejecting older and, in his view, outmoded psychological models? The first is that, given his commitment to understanding the subjective elements of 'human nature' – both its rational and its non-rational character – Layard may be throwing the baby out with the bathwater. Although Eysenck was the first in the queue to attack the therapeutic effectiveness of psychoanalysis (Eysenck, 1952) when putting forward a bid for legitimacy for behaviour therapy, it should be remembered that the focus of his disdain was never primarily intended as a form of treatment for mental illness. Its main goal was to understand the unconscious – Freud did therapy out of the necessity to earn a living (Freud, 1959).

If judged by the standards of treatment effectiveness, psychoanalysis is indeed poor. It is, however, a reflexive theory (applicable to therapist and client alike), and is elaborately theoretical. Moreover, some variants of it have had useful hermeneutic potential in social science – a value that can also be found in existentialism. The latter is reflexive, and it enables us to understand people as agents in their social context. It thereby allows us to take the personal accounts of people seriously to illuminate both their context and their view of that context. This, in turn, allows us to listen to misery without necessarily turning its narrators into patients who 'suffer from depression' (Pilgrim & Dowrick, 2006).

Ironically, Layard at points endorses the need for this existential sensibility (2005: 8) when citing Frankl (1985). Can we seriously imagine CBT illuminating and shaping investigations of such general importance to social science in ways that have flowed from psychoanalysis and existentialism? Theoretically confused and pragmatically inflected CBT has no such obvious prospects.

Thus, both psychoanalysis and existentialism can give a voice to misery in social science without necessarily being co-opted narrowly as 'treatment methods'. This cannot be said for CBT or drug treatments. Accordingly, these socially mute technologies risk individualising distress and disconnecting it from its biographical and social origins. This point about the older traditions being pathways into social understanding has another connection with Layard's thesis. He is keen to argue on moral grounds that the acceptance of suffering is wrong. He makes this response to those who have argued against the widespread use of drugs like Prozac: 'The most puritanical of them argue that misery is a part of human experience. We should accept misery rather than fight it. This view is simply immoral' (2005: 218).

The apocryphal graffiti, 'You are born, it's horrible, and then you die' is rather nihilistic, but it is also true for many people. For example, try being poor, female, suffering sexual abuse in childhood and being revictimised in adulthood, and see how happy you can become by learning to reverse your 'faulty' thinking about these facts of your life. And Layard is content to endorse Buddhism, without conceding that it takes a version of the above graffiti seriously. However, it then offers forms of mental discipline and Stoicism to transcend the dire implications of ubiquitous suffering.

Some of this dispute here with Layard may be semantic. Surely it is possible to accept that suffering is indeed intrinsic to the human condition, without being accused of being cruel or puritanical in response? Life really is tough and that struggle is not spread evenly over time and space: what chance the mental health of Syrian children at present, or the combatants of Vietnam and the Somme from the past?

When focusing on civil society in developed societies in conditions of peace, Layard himself argues that our consumerist culture ensures a high prevalence of misery. So why can we not raise political expectations in line with Layard's upstream arguments, and yet still accept that suffering is not necessarily pathology requiring treatment? The pathologisation of individual victims risks diverting us from the upstream arguments Layard himself makes so very well.

Moreover, the adoption of Layard's commitment to CBT in social policies about getting 'mentally ill' people back to work began in the UK under Gordon Brown's premiership. and continues as a trend to the time of writing. The *Pathways to Work* policy of 2007 soon began to look absurd following the crash of international capitalism in 2008 and the rise of unemployment. Nonetheless, the subsequent UK Conservative government has pushed on to punish the poor by insisting that CBT should be accepted by unemployed claimants or they risk losing their benefits. This is a consequence, in part, of the contradictions of Layard's reasoning and political lobbying. If he had stuck to his good points about socio-economic determinism and eschewed the absurdities of diagnostic psychiatry and an undeserved faith in the technological fix of CBT, he was offering us a form of wisdom. Unwittingly, he subverted his own case by stepping unwisely into the world of therapy. That is why now, with hindsight, we can see that *Happiness*, written before 2008 and the global financial crisis, was ill-judged.

Conclusion

In this chapter, I have outlined the case made by Richard Layard in *Happiness* and offered a view about its strong and weak points. I was left supporting his upstream analysis and proposals, but I suggest that child protection should also be incorporated into this frame of reference. I was less convinced, though, by Layard's faith in the technological fix, when we try to pull struggling people out downstream. Yes, some are drowning, but others are just getting by, fairly browned off, even though they aren't waving either. Should they all be assessed ('diagnosed') and offered therapy to turn them into patients? There is after all, 'a lot of it about', as they say about human misery.

The contradictions and limitations of Layard's work invite us to think critically about the limits of forms of therapeutic social engineering. Instead of more CBT for the masses, we might imagine and seek to create other possibilities. These could include ordinary forms of social solidarity, mutual support for the survivors of childhood adversity, and political initiatives to reverse the effects in the UK of nearly 30 years of neo-liberal governance by political parties of both political hues, which has atomised communities and encouraged the 'rampant individualism' Layard understandably laments.

References

Beck A T (1976). *Cognitive Therapy and the Emotional Disorders.* New York, NY: Meridian.

Bhaskar R (1989). *Reclaiming Reality.* London: Verso.

Bruch M, Bond FW (1998). *Beyond Diagnosis: case formulation approaches in CBT.* Chichester: Wiley.

Butler G (1999). Clinical formulation. *Comprehensive Clinical Psychology 6*: 1–24.

Cooper R (2004). What is wrong with DSM? *History of Psychiatry 15*(1): 1–25.

Dowrick C (2004). *Beyond Depression: a new approach to understanding and management.* Oxford: Oxford University Press.

Ellis A (1994). *Reason and Emotion in Psychotherapy* (revised and updated). New York, NY: Birch Lane Press.

Eysenck HJ (1952). The effects of psychotherapy: an evaluation. *Journal of Consulting Psychology 16*: 319–324.

Frankl V (1985). *Man's Search for Meaning.* New York, NY: Basic Books.

Freud S (1959). The question of lay analysis. In: Freud S. *The Complete Works of Sigmund Freud.* London: Hogarth.

Helliwell J (2003). How's life? Combining individual variables to explain subjective well-being. *Economic Modelling 20*: 331–360.

Johnstone L, Dallos R (2013). *Formulation in Psychology and Psychotherapy.* London: Routledge.

Lambert M (2007). What we have learned from a decade of research aimed at improving psychotherapy outcome in routine care. *Psychotherapy Research 17*: 1–14.

Layard R (2005). *Happiness: lessons from a new science.* London: Allen Lane.

McNamee S, Gergen K (eds) (1992). *Therapy as Social Construction.* London: Sage.

Masson JM (1989). *Against Therapy: warning – psychotherapy may be hazardous to your mental health.* London: HarperCollins.

Moncrieff J, Kirsch I (2005). Efficacy of antidepressants in adults. *British Medical Journal 331*: 155–157.

Parker I (ed.) (1999). *Deconstructing Psychotherapy.* London: Sage.

Pilgrim D (2016). *Common Mental Disorders*, vol 3. London: Sage.

Pilgrim D (2015a). *Understanding Mental Health: a critical realist exploration*. London: Routledge.

Pilgrim D (2015b). The biopsychosocial model in health research: its strength and limitations for critical realists. *Journal of Critical Realism 14*(2): 164–180.

Pilgrim D (2011). The hegemony of cognitive-behaviour therapy in modern mental health care. *Health Sociology Review 20*(2): 120–132.

Pilgrim D (2007). The survival of psychiatric diagnosis. *Social Science & Medicine 65*(3): 536–544.

Pilgrim D (2005). Defining mental disorder: tautology in the service of sanity in British mental health legislation. *Journal of Mental Health* 14(5): 435–443.

Pilgrim D, Bentall RP (1999). The medicalisation of misery: a critical realist analysis of the concept of depression. *Journal of Mental Health 8*(3): 261–274.

Pilgrim D, Carey T (2012). Improving access to psychological therapies: an account of recent policy aspirations in the UK and Australia. *Advances in Mental Health 10*(2): 117–27.

Pilgrim D, Dowrick C (2006). From a diagnostic-therapeutic to a social-existential response to 'depression'. *Journal of Public Mental Health 5*(2): 6–12.

Pilgrim D, Guinan P (1999). From mitigation to culpability: rethinking the evidence about therapist sexual abuse. *European Journal of Counselling, Psychotherapy and Health 2*(2): 153–168.

Rogers A, Pilgrim D (2015). *A Sociology of Mental Health and Illness* (4th ed). Milton Keynes: Open University Press.

Rogers A, Pilgrim D (2003). *Mental Health and Inequality*. Basingstoke: Palgrave.

Ryle A (1990). *Cognitive-Analytic Therapy: active participation in change*. London: Wiley.

Scott MJ, Sembi S (2006). Cognitive behaviour therapy treatment failures in practice: the neglected role of diagnostic inaccuracy. *Behavioural and Cognitive Psychotherapy 34*: 491–495.

Smail D (1996). *Getting by Without Psychotherapy*. London: Constable.

Stone M (1985). Shellshock and the psychologists. In: Bynum W, Shepherd M, Porter R (eds). *The Anatomy of Madness*, vol 2. London: Tavistock (pp242–271).

Tarrier N, Yusupoff L, Kinner C, McCarthy A, Gladhill G, Haddock G, Morris J (1998). A randomised control trial of intense cognitive behaviour therapy for chronic schizophrenia. *British Medical Journal 317*: 303–307.

4 *L'Anti-Livre Noir de la Psychanalyse*: CBT from a French/Lacanian perspective*

Robert Snell

France is facing an Anglo-Saxon invasion – by les Thérapies Cognitivo-Comportementales ('les TCC'), better known in Britain as cognitive behavioural therapy (CBT). Developed out of the ideas of the American behaviourists JB Watson and BF Skinner, and cognitive psychologists from the US and Canada such as Albert Ellis, Albert Bandura and Aaron Beck, CBT/TCC has in fact been part of the therapeutic landscape in France for several decades – the Association Française de Thérapie Comportementale et Cognitive was founded as long ago as 1971, and there is a significant home-grown literature.

What has been taking place over the last few years, as Jacques-Alain Miller writes in his book *L'Anti-Livre Noir de la Psychanalyse* (2006), is a new marketing onslaught: 'les TCC' relaunched and presented to health administrators and insurance companies as 'a fully developed product, meeting European and international standards, and offering rapid and low-cost solutions to the majority of psychological problems'. In the process, psychoanalysis in France, 'a school of irony, scepticism, and disrespect, definitively anti-modern', finds itself under new and fierce attack.

This attack comes from two main directions. On the one hand is a campaign launched in 2001 by INSERM – the Institut National de la Santé et de la Recherche Médicale, the equivalent of the British NICE (the National Institute for Health and Care Excellence). The report that INSERM published in February 2004 claimed to be a scientific evaluation of three approaches to psychotherapy: the psychoanalytic,

* Apart from a few minor alterations, this chapter is as it first appeared, as a review of the book *L'Anti-Livre Noir de la Psychanalyse*, published in the *European Journal of Psychotherapy and Counselling* 2007; 9(2): 231–239. It is followed by a brief update from the continuing French 'psy' wars.

the cognitive behavioural, and family and couples therapy. Its research aimed to ascertain the most up-to-date, 'effective', 'evidence-based' treatment for mental health problems; the public, it proclaimed, had a right to nothing less. Psychoanalysis came out last (INSERM, 2004). The INSERM campaign was backed up on TV, on the internet (including, for a time, on a government website), and in the periodical and popular press – for example, in the glossy magazine *Psychologies,* with its questionnaires and surveys and its focus on 'lifestyle' and 'wellbeing'.

On the other hand, there is a book that appeared in September 2005. Barely registered in the UK (although it did receive a weary rebuttal by a French psychoanalyst in the *International Journal of Psychoanalysis* (Kipman, 2006)), *Le Livre Noir de la Psychanalyse* (Van Rillaer et al, 2005) was a publishing sensation in France. *The Black Book of Psychoanalysis* – in English the title sounds like something dreamt up by the late Ivor Cutler – is a compilation of often-rehearsed anti-Freud arguments penned by some familiar enthusiasts (Borch-Jacobsen, Crews, Ellis, Sulloway and Swales, among others). It was heavily promoted by the weekly news magazine *Le Nouvel Observateur,* and it seeks, in the process of debunking psychoanalysis, to advance the claims of 'les TCC'.

L'Anti-Livre Noir de la Psychanalyse

Commentators sympathetic to psychoanalysis, such as the analyst and historian Elisabeth Roudinesco, were quick to point out the conspiracy-like feel of these various initiatives (Roudinesco, 2005). *L'Anti-Livre Noir de la Psychanalyse* is the most concerted counter-attack so far, mounted by the impassioned cohorts of Lacanian psychoanalysis and their allies, under the generalship of Lacan's son-in-law and leading heir, Jacques-Alain Miller. *L'Anti-Livre Noir* contains contributions by some 44 analysts and academics. In best Napoleonic tradition, it calls to its aid the spirits of the great national departed, from Cyrano de Bergerac to the poet Baudelaire, and (to the delight of this writer) the flamboyant Théophile Gautier. One contributor cites Maréchal Foch, architect of the allied victory in Europe in 1918: 'My centre's collapsing, my right flank's retreating – excellent conditions! I shall attack!' As Miller states at the outset, the book is not a defence against an 'enemy we did not even know we had... [and] a potpourri of complaints as booming as they are ineffectual'; *L'Anti-Livre Noir* is an attack, and it is a blistering one.

For where the UK psychoanalytic establishment has, for the most part, been anxious to go along with the challenge to produce 'evidence' and demonstrate 'treatment efficacy', the francophone world – as represented in Miller's book, at least – will have none of it. In a detailed and tightly argued essay at the very heart of the book, Yves Cartuyvels, a professor of law from Belgium who has spent his professional life examining the nature of evidence, refutes the claims of cognitive behavioural therapy to be founded – 'objectively' and 'scientifically' – in solid evidence. Such claims, he writes, are mere scientism; they rest on 'a superannuated conception of science as the measure of ultimate truth' and a naïve, 19th-century scientific positivism: '... the epistemology of science might as well not have bothered underlining, as it has been doing for many years, the social construction of science, or describing the interplay of its actors, and the interests and values behind the practice of science.' These claims also necessitate a refusal to accept that a patient might choose 'a rationality other than scientific rationality in response to psychic malaise'. In any case, what is 'effective' in the field of mental health, Cartuyvels asks: 'The suppression of a symptom? Help with living with a symptom? Who fixes and defines the thresholds of effectiveness? Science? The therapist? The subject? Are these thresholds the same from one individual to another, from one kind of suffering to another?'

Cartuyvels brings his lawyer's eye to *Le Livre Noir*'s methods of argument. In 1997, two science academics, Alan Sokal and Jean Bricmont, published a book called *Impostures Intellectuelles,* which took various important thinkers to task – Derrida, Lacan, Baudrillard, and Deleuze, for example – for, the authors claimed, misappropriating scientific and mathematical concepts in order to lend cheap credibility to their theorising. The *Livre Noir*'s procedure, for Cartuyvels, is the same: attack the authors' good faith, the better to disqualify their works (the book's main thrust is that Freud and several generations of his followers, not least Jacques Lacan, perpetrated a money-making fraud). But the result, Cartuyvels continues, does not even begin to refute an underlying philosophical position; what it does do is to combine a powerful impact in the media with an absence of in-depth discussion. Indeed, its media impact precisely depends on an absence of demanding, in-depth discussion. Such a project also allows for, or requires, misapprehensions of its own: Cartuyvels cites a work by one of *Le Livre Noir*'s lead contributors, Jacques van Rillaer, which writes off Lacan as 'an apostle of pleasure and egotism'. Such readings are, for Cartuyvels, merely evidence of breathtaking epistemological feebleness.

While Cartuyvels argues for a plurality of therapeutic approaches, for him 'the Freudian "tool-box" is, heuristically, incomparably richer than the terms of reference of a "scientific" psychology whose arguments are regularly linked to staggering truisms'. He has fun listing some of these: in cases of depression, it is better to have a family, and access to pleasant social activities; those with eating disorders should not have too much food in the house – and so on. If, as Cartuyvels writes, the cognitive behaviourists' 'neo-positivist stance is, to the mind of a jurist... rather surreal', it also has more disturbing, political, and ethical implications. For 'behind the war of the "Psys" is a fundamentally political question': can one ever seriously attempt to separate – as these claimants to 'scientific objectivity' would have us do – psychic from social suffering? To break this conceptual link is to try to wave goodbye to questions of 'normality and deviance, exclusion and increasing inequality'.

Cartuyvels' conviction is that 'the human being is specifically a being of meanings and language... and psychic suffering calls to this dimension'. This is a conviction shared by all the contributors to *L'Anti-Livre Noir*. The first of its four sections is entitled '*Coups d'Épingle*' – the English translation, 'pin pricks', does not do justice to the sense of something over-inflated being punctured or the voodoo-like quality of the pricking enacted in the 39 short essays that follow. Most were written by psychoanalyst members of Lacan's École de la Cause Freudienne. Gérard Miller early on explodes the INSERM authors' claim that their report is a response to 'public demand'. INSERM cites two organisations representing patients and their families; the only 'demand' Miller can discern is that these organisations were indeed founded to demand a public voice, one of them 40 years ago. The INSERM experts, Miller discovered, had only the most cursory meetings with these organisations, in order to inform them, it seems, that their task was to read the extensive Anglo-Saxon CBT literature, since it was only this – they ignored the mass of French clinical writing, from all orientations, except some of their own – that they considered 'scientifically' based. The results of their exhaustive endeavours were a foregone conclusion.

Gérard Miller's bitter wit is echoed in other brief contributions. So too is a dark sense of something very sinister unfolding. Jean-Claude Maleval explores another facet of INSERM's *expertise collective* ('collective assessment') – the researchers' commitment to 'psychological autopsy' (INSERM, 2005). This is a means of determining, in the most 'objective' way possible – that is, without the interfering presence of a living, if suicidal, person – the reasons and risk factors behind suicide. Maleval traces some of the historical antecedents for such thinking in the nascent materialist psychiatry of the mid-19th century in France; in the ideology of the early behaviour modifiers, with their electric shocks, in the First World War; in Watson and Rayner's notorious experiment with 'phobic' Little Albert in the 1920s, and in French publications of the 1960s and 1970s – translations of Eysenck and works by Joseph Wolpe and Jean Cottraux, who is an editor of *Le Livre Noir*. 'Les TCC', writes Maleval, 'are the avatar in the health domain of techniques of control and domination'.

What a godsend is suicide for neuro-biological psychiatry, muses Pierre Sidon: 'psychological autopsy' allows full play to the quantifiable. With the requirement for the clinical interview out of the way, and thus 'disconnected from the Real, biological psychiatry can take to dreaming limitlessly' about (this is a quotation from the INSERM team) 'neurobiological determinants, independent of psychiatric pathologies'.

Child and adolescent mental health is also well within the INSERM researchers' purview; they propose, as Sophie Bialek demonstrates, a national programme of tests and measures within the education and health systems. The particular report to which Bialek refers (*Troubles Mentaux: dépistage et prévention chez l'infant et l'adolescent* (INSERM, 2002)) is by a collective of unnamed experts. It fails to mention that three more relational-minded paediatricians from the original team had withdrawn, disquieted no doubt by a sense of where the work was going: one of the report's concluding recommendations is to 'develop animal models of developmental anomaly'.

Who, indeed, are the INSERM experts? They are, as Catherine Lazus-Matet shows, drawn from a small world of academic psychologists and therapeutic practitioners with more than a passing interest in the cognitive. They include a psychoanalyst, Daniel Widlocher – President of the International Psychoanalytic Association, no less – who is also, hardly incidentally, a member of the Association Française de Thérapie Comportementale et Cognitive. Ivy Blackburn (University of Newcastle) has written two books with Jean Cottraux on cognitive therapy for depression and personality disorder. David Servan-Schreiber is a cognitivist from the US. Mardjane Teherani was a student of Widlocher. Others are on the INSERM staff. And so on. The experts' collective claim to be 'independent' is unsustainable.

The 'psychoanalysis' of the INSERM research is a medicalised version, its aims consistent with those of the World Health Organization ('the promotion of wellbeing') – in other words, psychoanalysis adapted so as to be measurable. Thus, it can be shown 'objectively' not to perform very well. Jacques-Alain Miller, with whom Widlocher collaborated in 2004 on a book on the future of psychoanalysis, takes him to task later in *L'Anti-Livre* for the particular manner in which he has 'cognivitised' psychoanalysis (unconscious 'drive', for example, becomes domesticated 'instinct'). As Herbert Wachsberger points out, what the experts call psychoanalysis's 'ethic' is far removed from what Lacan meant when he spoke of the 'ethics of psychoanalysis' – its ability to render the subject to himself. For 'les TCC', of course, reject the unconscious in favour of 'maladaptive behaviour' (Hélène Deltombe); it is the genetically founded 'biosocial symptom' that is the 'keystone in the INSERM report's vault'.

'So-called mental health is the capacity to conform to the dominant values of the society:' this is neo- Darwinian pseudo-science, which, in Agnes Aflalo's analysis, points toward a racist *neohygiènisme,* a kind of born-again eugenics. Mental pathologies are defined in relation to religious and national norms; poverty, divorce, and immigration become factors in the definition of mental deviance.

The further tenet that the maladaptive symptom is something localised in the brain, rather than something that requires the therapist to listen to the patient, inexorably becomes a justification for psycho-surgery. Valérie Pera-Guillot examines this with respect to obsessive compulsive disorder (*le trouble obsessionel compulsif*) and the horrible circularity with which the diagnosis – made, like that of attention deficit disorder, on the premise that it is a cerebral, neuronal dysfunction – indicates the pharmaceutical or surgical nature of the cure. Hervé Castanet remarks on the slippage that occurs in the INSERM report between the words 'official' and 'scientific', fearing a utilitarian utopia based on a principle-free 'official science'. Philippe La Sagna likens the social vision of 'les TCC' to that of scientology, noting a shared language of 'scientific management' and 'biofeedback', both of which envisage a techno-totalitarianism in which man is reduced to machine.

For, built into this techno-totalitarian vision, as François Leguil shows, is a 'premeditated suppression of the question of the subject'. To undergo cognitive behavioural treatment, the patient must first tacitly submit to the paradigm of measure and engage in self-evaluation. Henceforth, treatment success is guaranteed: the self-evaluative questionnaire is conceived so that everything that cannot be measured is excluded from the clinical field, since only that which can be measured can be taken care of. The measurable comes before the measure; a fantasy of universal curability and expert clinical mastery flourishes; the enigma of the subject – that which, according to Baudelaire, is loathed by lazy believers in progress – disappears.

What all this can mean in practice is illustrated in a collection of case studies, all published by 'les TCC' practitioners and summarised in *L'Anti-Livre*. There is Aline, a patient of Dr Jean Cottraux himself, a description of whose treatment he published in a book in 2004 (Cottraux, 2004). The overriding aim seems to be to get the patient back to work. Aline, a bus driver in the deprived suburbs, is threatened and abused by her passengers. She is indeed helped back to work through the self-affirmations Cottraux teaches her: 'I am intact, I have survived,' she intones, as Cottraux helps her relive her trauma by making the gesture of drawing a knife blade across his throat. Aline has a family history of alcoholism and violence and was raped at knifepoint aged 18. In Cottraux's expert view, these are predisposing life events that make it difficult for her to manage her present working conditions. He draws attention to an additional aggravating factor: 'It is often hard to work if trauma has taken place in the workplace itself.' Carole Dewambrechies-La Sagna, who gives us this account in a laudably deadpan manner, notes in passing how the compulsion to repeat, a Freudian concept *par excellence*, is tacitly commandeered by Cottraux and emptied of meaning. Meanwhile, Aline, who has gone back to work several times in the course of a single year, is no doubt swelling the statistics that show the efficacy of 'les TCC'. Dewambrechies-La Sagna suggests Dr Cottraux might like to present his theses to the bus drivers' union next time they are on strike.

Roberta's treatment for the obsessive compulsive disorder with which she has been diagnosed consists in the substitution of one ritual for another: she is now condemned to write, for hours daily, about the terrible thoughts she has been struggling to keep at bay, involving awful accidents that might befall her little boy. Estela Solano Suárez offers a rather more compelling psychoanalytic way of thinking about Roberta's difficulties – one that might indeed offer some eventual relief.

Monique Amirault retells the story of a treatment by proxy, published in a specialist journal under the title 'Cognitive and behavioural management of a case of erotomania'. This has echoes of *Les Liaisons Dangereuses*. A middle-aged male professor seeks therapy for a young female student with whom he is sexually involved. The 'treatment' culminates in the therapist, who never meets the young woman, advising the professor to introduce her to a substitute. The abuse of civil and human rights inherent in this procedure is, as Amirault says, nothing less than scandalous.

Another patient, Clara, attracted to violence and seeking rejection, finds a TCC therapist who, like a ferocious super-ego, tells her to think positively, and then abandons her when the treatment, in the therapist's terms, has come to a successful conclusion (reported in *L'Anti-Livre* by Hélène Bonnaud). Two troubled children have become highly adept at 'speaking "TCC"' and self-therapising. One responds to self-evaluating questionnaires in her nightmares: 'My dog bites the ears of the other dogs. I have to answer if I love him (1) in spite of this, (2) very much, (3) not at all' (reported by Véronique Mariage). The husband of an alcoholic woman is instructed by her therapist to practise paradoxical intention and encourage his wife to drink even more (reported by Anne-Marie Lemercier).

By this point in the book, the reader may be experiencing symptoms of mild delirium. As if further to reinforce the feeling that we have stepped into a caricature parallel universe, Jean-Pierre Klotz, and later Pierre Streliski and Jasmine Grasser, tease out links between BF Skinner's 1948 science fantasy novel *Walden 2* and dreams of a 'scientific utopia' closer to the INSERM home page. Even closer to home is the pervasiveness of 'les TCC' on television, in particular in programmes like *Super Nanny*, a huge success in France (as reported in *L'Anti-Livre* by Catherine Lacaze-Paule, Marlène Belilos). The TCC model of child rearing, of 'normalised happiness, happiness by rote' – key words are 'punishment, behaviour, distraction, order, participation, by-pass refusals, explanation, family meeting, objective, gain the attention' – has its counterparts in the world of relationships, work, and leisure (Rose-Paule Vinciguerra offers a reading of the magazine *Psychologies*), and in 'techno-scientific' sport, with its requirement for participants to engage in 'mental preparation, coaching, sophrology, neuro-linguistic programming, mental imaging, rational emotive therapy, cognitive and affective stress management' (reported by Françoise Labridy).

The apotheosis of TCC thinking on learning and education is the TEACCH programme (Treatment and Education of Autistic and Related Communication Handicapped Children, founded under psychoanalytic auspices at the University of North Carolina in 1960). Alexandre Stevens explores some wider implications of its 'brutal imperative: Communicate!': 'Autists must communicate. But does anyone wonder for an instant what there might be to say to them? No. It is enough to describe the way in which you would need to communicate if you did have something to say!... the cognitive behavioural approach denies the subjectivity and desire at work in the fact of communicating.'

Similarly, for Marga Mendelenko-Kars, while the TEACCH programme, founded in Skinner's 'operative conditioning' of the 1930s, aims at a reduction or elimination of disturbances supposedly caused by a faulty genetic set-up, the disappearance of the subject is anticipated too, as the INSERM report makes clear. Jean-Pierre Rouillon adds a further important and pregnant thought: '[In TEACCH] signal and conditioning take... the place of the Real, that which produces an encounter with autism in us all.'

Six short essays spell out the different ways in which 'les TCC' have colonised Western European countries – Italy, Belgium, Greece, Spain, Great Britain and France, each with their differing health legislation and institutions – and the extent of this colonisation. What about the fertile breeding grounds that must surely be provided by former communist bloc members of the European Economic Community? The third-from-last *coup d'épingle* reminds us of how

Lacan demonstrated, in 1967 (*Seminar*, book XV), that the great Soviet scientist Ivan Petrovich Pavlov was in fact a Lacanian, in so far as Pavlov proved the theory according to which a signifier represents a subject for another signifier. In Pavlov's most famous experiment, writes Marie-Claude Sureau, 'the sound of the trumpet is the signifier which represents the subject Pavlov for another signifier, the gastric secretion produced by the dog at the sound of said trumpet... [T]he dog... is conditioned to salivate not at the approach of the plate but at the sound of the trumpet' (ie. Pavlov). The experimenter, in Lacan's subtle and mischievous thesis, is fundamentally implicated in his experiment. Furthermore, unlike modern neuro-cognitivists and behaviourists, who are concerned only with the biological, real behaviourists like Pavlov are obliged to consider the centrality of the structure of language. Marie-Hélène Brousse argues, alongside Lacan, that psychoanalysis itself, with its recognition of the autonomy of the signifier and of human symbolic memory, is an authentically cognitive discipline, which behaviourist therapies are absolutely not. On the contrary, 'the expression "TCC" is a stolen label, a mendacious piece of advertising, a smoke screen for an attempt to eradicate the signifier in the human being'.

The *coups d'épingle* close with an imaginary dialogue (first published in the newspaper *Libération*) in which Jacques-Alain Miller takes up the theme with which *L'Anti-Livre Noir* set out: that the TCC project is, above all, an exercise in marketing, 'merchandising the mental'.

'What is at stake in society' (*L'Enjeu de Société),* a topic already widely opened up by the pin-prickers, is the title of the next section, which contains Cartuyvels' seminal essay. A third section, *Ponctuations,* offers further pauses for thought. Alain Abelhauser, Professor of Psychopathology at the University of Rennes II, addresses an open letter ('*Cette frase contient quatres ereurs*' – 'This sentance contains for erors' – there are only three, but that makes four, since the whole sentence is wrong. Is it three or is it four?) to the Director of INSERM, in which he argues for the undecidable against the reductionist certainties of the *expertise collective.* A clinical psychologist, Michel Normand, examines the sheer scale of 'les TCC's' ambition, to shape and embody national policy on mental health. Philippe La Sagna publishes an open letter to Philippe Pignarre, author of *La Sorcellerie Capitaliste* (2005) (*Capitalist Witchcraft*), denouncing the dark witch of scientism. Eric Laurent, a Lacanian analyst who will be known to many in the UK as a speaker at analytic conferences, takes up in greater depth and detail Marie-Helene Brousse's theme: 'les TCC' are not part of the cognitive project.

A final section, 'Reflections of a Philosopher', offers two essays by philosopher and psychologist Clotilde Leguil-Badal. The first, '*Être ou ne pas Être?*', pits Sartre against a neuroscientific view that claims to hold the key to the resolution of all our difficulties. Scanning techniques now mean we can see brain activity – what, though, of the voice of the brain's owner? There is what Leguil-Badal calls a 'new Empire' of cognitive neuroscience: its special domain, its object, is spirit, soul, subject. In the new 'biologisation' of spirit, 'brain' becomes a kind of politically correct version of 'unconscious'. Neuroscience, with its seductive pull toward a theory of cerebral determinism, invites us to forget our freedom. Her second essay, 'On cognitivism', is a powerful argument for why an analytic cure cannot be a measurable thing. It speaks of Lacan's other use of mathematics, *le mathème*: his little fractions 'recount something of the logic of the illogical symptom... and the singularity of the subject... they are of a couple with poetry.'

Discussion

It has felt important to try to summarise *L'Anti-Livre Noir de la Psychanalyse* in some detail, if only to convey an idea of the quality of its thinking to non-French readers. A concluding attempt to contextualise might also be helpful. While standing up for the inalienable right of the speaking subject to his and her idiosyncratic unconscious and unique subjectivity, psychoanalysis in France has also been more firmly established as part of a medical and health hegemony than has British psychoanalysis, which had probably lost any equivalent position by the late 1960s. Broadly speaking, psychoanalytic groupings within the UK seem either to want to regard themselves as part of an establishment (the British Psychoanalytic Council trainings, whose members are, incidentally, often very interested in neuroscience), or to relish a position on the oppositional margins (the College of Psychoanalysis, The Site, some UKCP trainings).

French psychoanalysis as a whole seems to manage to be both official *and* oppositional (particularly its Lacanian branch). This, together with the new, aggressively marketed profile of 'les TCC', needs to be appreciated if we are to understand how much the Lacanian practitioners represented in this book feel is at stake, and the vehemence and the theoretical rigour and force of their collective and individual responses. Such has been the energy of the psychoanalytic response, and the official clout psychoanalysis still has in France, that in February 2005 the Minister of Health, Philippe Douste-Blazy, publicly declared psychic suffering to be 'neither measurable nor open to evaluation', and withdrew the INSERM report from his ministry's website. A war of words continues to be waged on the internet between analysts and affronted cognitive behaviourists.

The struggle so eloquently dramatised in *L'Anti-Livre Noir de la Psychanalyse* is, of course, far from merely a local one. For example, CBT has made huge political advances in the UK in recent years, thanks particularly to IAPT. Meanwhile, those of us who assert ourselves as psychoanalytic practitioners in the UK often tend to view CBT in a collegiate spirit, or else to see it as just part of the climate, to be lived with, made the most of even, like the British weather. Historically, intellectual and ideological debates in France have tended to be highly polarised, with few holds barred: think, for example, of the bloody wars between the Freudians and the Lacanians. One might wish that Jacques-Alain Miller and his colleagues had addressed, as a fair-minded British commentator might, patients' documented claims that CBT has helped them gain a sense of control and mastery over unmanageable feelings, and has made daily life feel a bit more livable. One might have wished their response could have been a little more nuanced and less political. But this might also have been to gloss over the sheer grotesqueness of some of the practices they report (students of French literature might be reminded of certain *Contes Cruels* by Villiers de l'Isle Adam) and the brutality of the thinking behind them. There is a political and ideological battle going on, in the UK as in France and elsewhere. In France, where the conflict has only relatively recently flared into a full-scale battle, the lines are now starkly drawn. *L'Anti-Livre Noir* offers a breadth and vigour of argument that has to date been missing from debates in Britain. Psychoanalysts, and psychotherapists of whatever persuasion, if they are concerned to oppose the technologising of the human spirit, need to take its arguments very seriously indeed.

Livre versus *Anti-Livre* – an update

What has happened since 2005/2006 and the publication of *Le Livre* and *L'Anti-Livre Noir de la Psychanalyse*? *Le Livre Noir*, published in September 2005, has clearly been a publishing success. By as early as November 2005, if Frederick Crews is to be believed, it had been reprinted three times and sold about 30,000 copies (Crews, 2005). It was reprinted again in 2006, and a further edition appeared in 2010, with an expanded version in 2013. The book has been translated into Spanish, Chinese, and other languages, and it receives 4.5 stars on Amazon.fr. The *Anti-Livre*'s fortunes have been more modest. Published in February 2006, it re-appeared in a new paperback edition in 2008, in French and English, and it scores 2.5 on Amazon.fr (September 2016).

The war of words declared in France over a decade ago might indeed seem to have led to little more than point scoring – to renewed attack and counter-attack, and ever-deeper entrenchment, each side mounting critical sorties from the security of its therapeutic position, with the greatest explosion of polemical activity in the first couple of years.

A prompt response to *L'Anti-Livre* from the authors of *Le Livre Noir* appeared online in March 2006 (Meyer et al, 2006). '*L'Anti-Livre Noir de la Psychanalyse: tromperie sur la merchandise*' ('a swindle') took Miller and colleagues' volume to task for being in no way a response to the critical questions about psychoanalysis raised in *Le Livre Noir*. It was, rather, just a recycling of material presented at a day conference, the 'Forum Anti-TCC', that had been held in Paris under the auspices of the Lacanian École de la Cause Freudienne on 9 April 2005, five months *before* the publication of *Le Livre Noir* (contributors to this conference had included well-known figures from the analytic world such as Catherine Clément and Eric Laurent). Among *Le Livre Noir* authors' allegations against psychoanalysis – Freud's mendacity, psychoanalysis as pseudo-science, its failure to treat psychosis, its attitudes to women and homosexuality – was a reminder of its relative hegemony in France: thanks to the '*exception française*', in contrast to the situation in most of the rest of the world, where, the authors claimed, Freudianism was in steep decline, psychoanalysis was the dominant paradigm in French pedagogy, social work and psychology (and this, to repeat a point made in my original review, has no doubt been a major factor in the ferocity of the ongoing debate). The authors lamented the psychoanalysts' refusal to take up their challenge to refute and debate the charges against them and write a real *Anti-Livre*.

Among analytic ripostes to *Le Livre Noir* (a fuller compendium of responses and counter-responses can be found on fr.wikipedia.org/wiki/Le-Livre-noir-de-la-psychanalyse) was the airily dismissive observation that its polemical tone had an anachronistic, old-world feel, and that, while this was not without its charm, it could probably be accounted for by the fact that the authors were quite incapable of following psychoanalytic debates and developments (Kipman, 2006, whose review in the *International Journal of Psychoanalysis* has already been mentioned). The psychoanalyst Bernard Brusset described the book as an encyclopaedia of bad temper and bad faith ('*cette encyclopédie de la mauvaise humeur et de la mauvaise foi*'. (Brusset, 2006)). Another commentator, Thierry Trémine, head of the psychiatric hospital at Aulnay-sous-Bois, noted that *Le Livre Noir de la Psychanalyse* came out in the same week as *Le Livre Noir de Saddam Hussein*, and that the choice of such a title, historically associated with crimes against humanity, was merely opportunistic marketing that foreclosed on any possibility of debate. He sincerely hoped that things would not descend to gutter level (Trémine, 2005).

For the other side, Jacques Van Rillaer, one of *Le Livre Noir*'s key contributors, used similar terms. He condemned Elisabeth Roudinesco's criticisms – on which more below – as polemical, in bad faith, and mendacious (Van Rillaer, 2006). Jean Cottraux, another co-author, was asked by a journalist if he thought calling Freud every name under the sun was really the best way to launch a debate. He responded: 'Perhaps we exaggerated a little… a debate needs to be polemical… Freud was… a political leader… and we have explored his dark side. It was a democratic exercise, the public has a right to know' (Favereau, 2005). Others (Union Rationaliste, 2006) deplored the power of the psychoanalytical caucus to intervene in government policy, as it had successfully done in the original representations to the Minister of Health when it objected to the INSERM findings. The left-wing journalist Laurent Joffrin (former editor of *Le Nouvel Observateur*, managing co-editor of *Libération* in 2016) maintained that a little group of psychoanalysts was determined to characterise the adherents of a 'psychology without Freud' as 'fascists', 'ultra-liberals', and 'agents of Big Pharma'. He claimed Roudinesco had told him that the *Livre Noir* bordered on anti-semitism (Joffrin, 2005). Meanwhile, the anthropologist and journalist Nicolas Journet has listed the book among the 200 most important works of social science (Journet, 2014).

A carefully constructed response to *L'Anti-Livre*, '*Le livre blanc et le livre noir de la psychanalyse*', appeared in 2006 on the website of the Union Rationaliste (2006), a generally well-respected body founded in 1930 to promote the role of reason in intellectual debate. Its final verdict struck a familiar note: *L'Anti-Livre* was 'a pamphlet, superficial, scathing and slapdash'. But it came to this conclusion in terms that were refreshingly consistent with ordinary academic discourse; its arguments ask to be taken seriously. The anonymous author(s) set out to defend *Le Livre Noir* against *L'Anti-Livre's* two major strictures against 'les TCC': adherence to a paradigm of measure, and appeal to neuroscience for legitimacy. What is wrong with the idea of measures in psychology, the essay asks? Piaget's theories of development, for example, relied on identifying quantitative changes, as did Freud himself, in the 'Project for a Scientific Psychology'. Nor did Freud ever reject the idea that the neuroses had neurological bases: the superstructure of psychoanalysis, he more than once iterated, would eventually be found to rest on an organic substructure. The essay invokes Wittgenstein in order to critique Clotilde Leguil-Badal's conception, as voiced in the last two chapters of *L'Anti-Livre*, of psychoanalysis as uniquely positioned to address a 'subject able to say "I"'. For Wittgenstein, the essay argues, words do not so much give us privileged insight into some interior world as require us to question the circumstances surrounding their usage: 'It is not some sort of internal counterpoint but rather its surrounding context that gives a declaration meaning.' If psychoanalysis is also out of step with medical standards of verification for the efficacy of treatment, one reason may be – here the essay follows Thomas Szasz – that it cannot make up its mind whether it is a branch of medicine or a sort of moral conversation.

The essay repeats the argument that psychoanalysis is not a science, according to Karl Popper's criteria of falsifiability and experimental repeatability. But, in presenting this argument as if it were decisive, it falls into a category confusion of its own – one that *L' Anti-Livre* had been at particular pains to expose. It ignores the philosophical and ethical problems involved in reducing the human being to a system of stimuli and responses, where psychoanalysis, with its patient, mutual exploration of relationship, history, ideas, feelings, and of course language, is in a position to do rather more justice to human complexity and recalcitrance.

Generally speaking, and in the best, or worst, traditions of French intellectual controversy, there has been little or no attempt by either side to meet the other on its terms – for example, the psychoanalysts to acknowledge the part played by cognitive processes within psychoanalysis, the cognito-behaviouralists to address the possibility of unconscious processes as factors in CBT. Have there been *any* moments of rapprochement between psychoanalysis and 'les TCC'? 2007 saw the publication of a book by the cognitive psychologist and psychotherapist Jacques Montangero called *Comprendre ses Rêves pour Mieux se Connaître* (*Get to Know Yourself Better by Understanding your Dreams*) (Montangero, 2007). The book's promise, however, to reject 'simplistic or fantastical explanations that make dreams say what they don't mean', hints not so much at a new collegiality as at unremitting belligerence. There is no doubt as to the continuing relevance and conceptual and philosophical persuasiveness of *L'Anti-Livre*'s arguments. But the writers of *Le Livre Noir* had a point when they said they awaited a proper *Anti-Livre*: that is, one that would stoop to refute, article by article, the attacks made on psychoanalysis, laughable to analytic 'insiders' as they might seem. In this refusal, and in their insistence on going on the attack instead, the Lacanian camp left themselves exposed to accusations of arrogance and being out of touch. And this was to do no service either to psychoanalytic or TCC patients.

Not that some attempts at such refutations had not already been made. In a short book published in 1999, the historian and psychoanalyst Elisabeth Roudinesco had roundly challenged the claims of pharmacology and cognitive science to have made psychoanalysis redundant (Roudinesco, 1999). As early as September 2005, Roudinesco, who was not among *L'Anti-Livre*'s contributors, published a riposte to *Le Livre Noir*, in collaboration with four colleagues, *Pourquoi Tant de Haine? Anatomie du Livre Noir de la Psychanalyse* (*Why So Much Hatred? Anatomising the Livre Noir de la Psychanalyse*) (Roudinesco, 2005) – a book that sought to understand why psychoanalysis was still able to stir up so much hatred. More recently, in 2013, the playwright and commentator on psychoanalysis Michel Mogniat has carried on the project of anatomising the opposition by publishing an *Anti-Livre* of his own, *Pour Freud! Le petit livre noir de l'anti-freudisme* (Mogniat, 2013). But it seems to have taken yet another fierce attack on Freud and his legacy to elicit the more considered and direct kinds of refutation that seemed to be missing in 2005/06. In 2010, the controversial 'post-anarchist' philosopher Michel Onfray, who had already been a vociferous defender of *Le Livre Noir*, published *Le Crépiscule d'une Idole* (*The Twilight of an Idol*) (Onfray, 2010), a book that once more treated Freud as an unscrupulous charlatan, but this time as a perverse and even anti-semitic one. Roudinesco responded with a new book, *Mais **Pourquoi** Tant de Haine?* (*But **Why** so Much Hatred?*) (Roudinesco, 2010), which set out to address and deconstruct historically some of Onfray's allegations. The philosopher and psychoanalyst Julia Kristeva was among other high-profile intellectuals to join the fight (Onfray & Kristeva, 2010, and see Malaguarnera, 2010). But if the Onfray affair has been the latest really major battle in the French couch wars, it seems extremely unlikely that it will be the last.

Acknowledgements

All translations are by the author. With warm thanks to George Craig for his linguistic and editorial help with the original review.

References

Brusset B (2006). Une lecture du Livre Noir de la Psychanalyse. *Revue Française de Psychanalyse 70*(2): 571–582.

Cottraux J (2004). *Les Visiteurs du Soi.* Paris: Odile Jacob.

Crews F (2005). *A Zero Theory.* [Online]. Butterflies and Wheels, 5 November. www.butterfliesandwheels.org/2005/a-zero-theory (accessed 23 September 2016).

Favereau E (2005). Interview: La psychanalyse n'est en rien démontrée. [Online]. *Libération,* 17 September. www.liberation.fr/evenement/2005/09/17/la-psychanalyse-n-est-en-rien-demontree_532653 (accessed 23 September 2016).

INSERM (2005). Suicide : Autopsie psychologique, outil de recherche en prévention. Paris: INSERM.

INSERM (2004). *Psychothérapie: trois approches evaluées. Une expertise collective de l'Inserm.* Paris: Les Editions INSERM.

INSERM (2002). *Troubles Mentaux: dépistage et prévention chez l'infant et l'adolescent.* Paris: Les Editions INSERM.

Joffrin L (2005). Retour sur 'Faut-il en finir avec la psychanalyse?', L'Obs a-t-il trahi les psys? *Le Nouvel Observateur.* Le 9 Septembre 2005.

Journet N (2014). La bibliothèque des idées d'aujourd'hui: 200 livres qui comptent. *Sciences Humaines (numéro special)* 255s(January).

Kipman SD (2006). Review *of L'Anti-Livre Noir de la Psychanalyse. International Journal of Psychoanalysis 87*(5): 1425–1428.

Lacan J (1967–1968). Séminaire XV : l'acte psychanalytique : 1967-1968. (Unpublished papers.) Available in translation as: The Seminar of Jacques Lacan. Book XV: the psychoanalytic act – 1967–1968 (Gallagher C trans). [Online.] Jacques Lacan in Ireland. www.lacaninireland.com/web (accessed 26 January 2018).

Malaguarnera S (2010). [Online.] Serafino Malaguarnera. http://malaguarnera-psy.wifeo.com/interventions-onfray-freud.php (accessed 20 September 2016).

Meyer C, Borch-Jacobsen M, Cottraux J, Pleux D, Van Rillaer J (2006). *L'Anti-Livre Noir de la Psychanalyse: tromperie sur la marchandise.* [Online]. Science... & Pseudo Sciences. www.pseudo-sciences.org/spip.php?article486 (accessed 14 September 2016).

Miller J-A (ed) (2008). *L'Anti-Livre Noir de la Psychanalyse.* (Mass-market paperback; English and French edition.) Paris: Points Essais.

Miller J-A (ed) (2006). *L'Anti-Livre Noir de la Psychanalyse.* Paris: Editions du Seuil.

Mogniat M (2013). *Pour Freud!: le petit livre noir de l'anti-freudisme.* Paris: Editions L'Harmattan.

Montangero J (2007). *Comprendre ses Rêves pour Mieux se Connaître.* Paris: Odile Jacob.

Onfray M (2010). *Le Crépiscule d'une Idole.* Paris: Grasset.

Onfray M, Kristeva J (2010). Freud : le débat Onfray-Kristeva. [Blog.] Bibliobs. http://bibliobs.nouvelobs.com/essais/20100422.BIB5255/freud-le-debat-onfray-kristeva.html (accessed 21 September 2016).

Roudinesco E (2010). *Mais Pourquoi tant de Haine?* Paris: Editions du Seuil.

Roudinesco E (2005). *Pourquoi Tant de Haine? anatomie du livre noir de la psychanalyse.* Paris: Navarin.

Roudinesco E (1999). *Pourquoi la Psychanalyse?* Paris: Fayard.

Snell R (2007). Review of Miller J-A (ed) (2006) *L'Anti-Livre Noir de la Psychanalyse. European Journal of Psychotherapy and Counselling. 9*(2): 231–239.

Sokal A, Bricmont J (1997). *Impostures Intellectuelles.* Paris : Odile Jacob.

Trémine T (2005). Série noire. Editorial. *L'Information Psychiatrique 81*(8):679–681.

Union Rationaliste (2006). *Le Livre Blanc et le Livre Noir de la Psychanalyse.* [Online.] Union Rationaliste. www.union-rationaliste.org/index.php/rationalismescientifique/publications/articles-des-cahiers-rationalistes/112-le-livre-blanc-et-le-livre-noir-de-la-psychanalyse (accessed 21 September 2016).

Van Rillaer J, Pleux D, Cottraux J, Borch-Jacobsen M, Meyer C (eds) (2005). *Le Livre Noir de la Psychanalyse: vivre, penser et aller mieux sans Freud.* Paris: Les Arènes.

Van Rillaer J (2006). *Réponse du professeur Jacques Van Rillaer à Madame Elisabeth Roudinesco.* [Online.] http://esteve.freixa.pagesperso-orange.fr/reponse_jvr_a_roudinesco_vd.pdf (accessed 19 September 2016).

5 CBT is the method: the object is to change the heart and soul

Paul Kelly and Paul Moloney

Since publication of the first edition of this book in 2008, the availability of cognitive behavioural therapy (CBT) has been greatly expanded via the national rollout of the government-sponsored Improving Access to Psychological Therapies (IAPT) programme (Department of Health, 2010; Clark, 2011). Despite serious questions about the 'effectiveness' of CBT (eg. Dalal, 2015; Johnsen & Friborg, 2015; Shedler, 2015), it appears that an alliance of political and professional interests has served to create a 'carry-on-regardless' approach to the expansion of the CBT empire. Fancher (1995) argues that when a profession such as psychiatry continues to flourish despite any evidence for its theories, it must be because it provides important social functions other than those professed. It is ironic (but not surprising) that the profession of clinical psychology has recently published a position statement challenging the diagnostic system of psychiatry on conceptual and empirical grounds (BPS Division of Clinical Psychology, 2013), yet has remained largely silent when similar criticisms have been levelled at the conceptual and empirical grounds of CBT (Fancher, 1995; Moloney, 2013; Moloney & Kelly, 2008; Newnes, 2014; Pilgrim, 2008). Our aim in this chapter is to contribute to the exposure of some of the possible hidden 'social functions' played by CBT in society.

In our original chapter in 2008, we articulated a number of challenges to CBT (Moloney & Kelly, 2008). These included research within psychology that conflicts with some of the core theoretical foundations of CBT; problems with the claimed evidence-base for CBT, and a robust research literature showing that social factors, such as economic inequality and poverty, for example, are among the most important and enduring determinants of psychological distress. This literature challenges the core claim on which CBT is based (drawn from ancient stoic philosophers) that 'Men are disturbed not by things, but by the views which they take of them' (Robertson, 2010: 5).

In this chapter we will expand and develop our original critique in the light of ongoing developments in the theories and practices of CBT. Our critique will focus on three main issues: first, a discussion of how CBT both reflects and supports the ideology of neoliberalism and, in doing so, serves to entrench some of its main socio-political causes, while claiming to alleviate distress; second, an updated examination of some of the outcome evidence for the effectiveness of CBT, particularly in relation to IAPT, and third, a brief critical evaluation of so-called third-wave CBT, which has incorporated the South East Asian meditative practice of 'mindfulness' (eg. Segal, Williams & Teasdale, 2013). Our conclusion remains the same as that of our original chapter: it is the world in which we live that is the most important cause of psychological distress, and if we want to make any real progress in easing our troubles, then the only lasting way to do so is to make that world a less damaging place.

A neo-liberal therapy for a neo-liberal era

In his cultural history of psychotherapy, Philip Cushman provides a critical exploration of the socio-political contexts in which different psychotherapies have arisen and flourished (Cushman, 1995). He argues that each historical era produces a characteristic subjectivity or 'self', with attendant psychological ills and modes of psychotherapy aimed at alleviating them. However, in agreement with others writing from a 'critical psychology' perspective (eg. Fox, Prilleltensky & Austin, 2009), Cushman contends that many modes of psychotherapy are not the value-neutral, scientific practices portrayed in textbooks and professional journals. Rather, they represent cultural artefacts that transmit the values of the dominant socio-political contexts in which they arise, and in doing so 'inevitably reproduce the very causes of the ills they treat' (p7).

Cushman's thesis focuses primarily on what may be termed 'psychodynamic' therapies. We intend to apply this same kind of critical analysis to CBT, as the therapy that most accurately reflects and supports the values and ideology of the modern neoliberal era, and, in this sense, *is* a neoliberal form of therapy. To do so we will briefly outline some of the core features of neoliberalism and the characteristic sense of self that it fosters. This will be followed by a discussion of the types of psychological ills that predominate in a neoliberal society and how CBT operates ideologically as the dominant therapy for such ills.

Neoliberalism

Harvey (2005) describes neoliberalism as:

> ... a theory of political economic practices that proposes that human well-being can best be advanced by liberating individual entrepreneurial freedoms and skills within an international framework characterized by strong private property rights, free markets and free trade. (p2)

As a form of political-economic governance, neoliberalism replaces the role of the welfare state in the provision of social goods (such as healthcare, education and social welfare) with competitive market mechanisms through processes of deregulation, market liberalisation and privatisation (Allen, 2003; 2007; Judt, 2005). Dardot and Laval (2013) describe neoliberalism as a mode of governance structured on a 'universal principle of competition', in which society is made up of competitive enterprises that have largely replaced the previous workplace and welfare state institutions. Boltanski and Chiapello (2005) analyse how this transition from hierarchical institutions to network-oriented enterprises has blurred work and personal life, to the detriment of both: a process that has been accelerated by the introduction of computers and mobile communication devices that make us instantly available, and trackable (Fleming, 2015). Bourdieu (1998) argues that, for neoliberalism to achieve its aim of achieving pure market logic, it must destroy any collective structures that challenge its core ideology, including nations, unions and families. Other critics have argued that neoliberalism fundamentally undermines democracy and replaces active political citizenship with transactions in the market, or consumption as a new form of citizenship (Giroux, 2014).

All of these critics point to the power of the seemingly far-removed socio-political domain to shape our immediate family life, friendships, workplace and community, with profound implications for our experience of who and what we are, whether we recognise these distal influences or not (see Smail (2005) for a detailed discussion).

Neoliberal subjectivity

One of the key political figures associated with the rise of neoliberalism in the early 1980s, the then UK Prime Minister Margaret Thatcher, identified the need to actively shape the subjectivity of citizens as a way of neutralising potential dissent to the creation of a new society structured along neoliberal lines (Dardot & Laval, 2013). In a now infamous interview in the Sunday Times newspaper in 1981, she neatly summed this up, stating, 'Economics are the method. The object is to change the heart and soul' (Butt, 1981).

A number of writers have traced the outlines of this new, changed 'heart and soul'. In their discussion of what they term the 'neo-subject', Dardot and Laval (2013) identify it as an efficient, competitive self, constantly seeking to invest in self-improvement projects, aspiring to reach a state of perfection in relation to measurable life outcomes and high-performance standards. Such a self becomes akin to a business enterprise, the so-called 'entrepreneurial self', with investment in personal gain or fulfilment becoming the measure of a successful life (Cederstrom & Fleming, 2012; Rose & Miller, 1992; Verhaeghe, 2014). In common with the way the ideology and practices of capitalist business enterprises have been wholeheartedly imposed on public institutions through mechanisms of new managerialism (Lynch, Grummel & Devine, 2012), using technologies of audit (see Power, 1999), the individual begins to view and organise themselves along the lines of a business enterprise. Success or failure of the neo-self as enterprise is evaluated through a constant process of self-inspection and self-evaluation in relation to external 'measures', including social status indicators, such as career advancement, and psychological and personal measures, including intelligence, personality measures, ratings of attractiveness etc. Many of these are created within the discipline of psychology and endlessly circulated via the mass media (Rose, 1996; 1999).

Giroux (2014) refers to the neo-subject as one that is immersed in notions of individual responsibility and self-help, is blind to inequalities in power, wealth and income, and scornful of compassion and concern for the welfare of others, which he contends is based on the core neoliberal 'ethic' of 'survival of the fittest'. Nafstad (2002) also describes the ideal person of the neoliberal age as one with little interest in values such as empathy, solidarity or the common good. This can clearly be seen in contexts such as the education system, which has often been at the forefront of neoliberal reforms (Apple, 2004; 2007; Jonathan, 1997; Lynch, 2006). Critics have written about how the student's identity has been fundamentally transformed from that of an active citizen engaged in the development of the capacity to critically reflect on and engage in cultural and political pursuits for the greater good, to one based on a competitive entrepreneurial investor in the self, making self-interested, calculated, 'rational' decisions for individual enhancement in career and social status (Allen, 2007; Lynch, Crean & Moran, 2010; Peters, 2005). In this environment, neoliberal education ceases to be a human right or a public good in the service of societal interest, but rather, a personal investment towards 'acquiring marketable skills, acceptable attitudes, a set of personal tastes, and, if fortunate, an advantageous position in the social structure' (Jonathan, 1997: 7). Similar analyses can be applied to other previously considered public goods, such as healthcare, which under neoliberal rule is rapidly being privatised (Pollock, 2005).

In summary, too many of us have fallen in love with our captors. We have swallowed the ideas and values of the neoliberal enterprise as the 'common sense' that must govern our hopes and fears, and indeed, our lives. The social scientist Richard Sennett (2006) summarises the new kind of self that goes with this 'new culture of capitalism'. This is an individual who is enterprising, flexible, competitive, individualistic, perfectionistic and constantly working to improve themselves via psychological techniques in the scramble for whatever security and control the fast-changing social environment can offer (see also Boltanski & Chiapello, 2005; Fitzsimons, 2002; Fleming, 2015).

The psychological ills of neoliberalism

Although there are widely differing views about its causes, it is generally agreed that there has been a significant rise in the diagnoses of psychological distress in Western society in recent years (see, for example, Whitaker, 2010). A number of researchers have convincingly demonstrated a causal relationship between this rise and the exponential growth in socioeconomic inequalities that have resulted from almost 40 years of neoliberal 'reforms' (Rogers & Pilgrim, 2002; Stuckler & Basu, 2013; Wilkinson, 2005; Wilkinson & Pickett, 2010). One of the key 'psychological' effects of such inequality is the constant sense of negative social comparison, which has a severe impact on physical and psychological wellbeing (Sapolsky, 2004). For example, Sayer (2005) analyses how relative social class position is associated with judgments of moral worth and resulting feelings of failure for those who find themselves in positions of low social status. From a clinical perspective, Smail (1984) and Gilbert (1992) have shown how low social status leads to feelings of anxiety and depression.

Cushman (1995) contends that, in order to make sense of the complexity of the relationships between broad social factors such as inequality and psychological distress, it is important to analyse the specific types of distress that arise in different historical epochs. So, what are the dominant ills of our neoliberal epoch?

Verhaeghe (2014) describes 'an avalanche of depression and anxiety disorders among adults, and ADHD and autism among children' (p193). He also refers to a huge increase in social anxiety in particular, along with alcoholism. In their analysis of the 'clinical diagnoses of the neo-subject', Dardot & Laval (2013) focus on depression, the erosion of personality, demoralisation, and the 'imaginary illusion of total pleasure' (p295).

Ehrenberg (2010, cited in Dardot & Laval, 2013) finds a sevenfold increase in diagnoses of depression between 1979 (the year that Margaret Thatcher came to power), and 1996, by which time neoliberalism had become the dominant mode of political-economic governance in the Western world. Dardot & Laval (2013) show how depression is all but inevitable when there is constant pressure on individuals to perform and compete, leaving many feeling inadequate, exhausted and defeated. They also link the increase in suicides related to the workplace with the individualisation of responsibility to perform and achieve objectives. This, they argue, cuts workers off from previous collegial solidarity and jeopardises their ability to maintain the respect and recognition of bosses and co-workers, who are pitted against each other in a toxic work environment (see also Sennett, 2006).

Dardot & Laval (2013) discuss how the substitution of the social institutions of the welfare state (which served to provide social solidarity and a framework of values and identity) with neoliberal competitive enterprises has had profoundly negative effects on social solidarity and security. The German sociologist Ulrick Beck has written extensively about the phenomenon of 'individualisation': how people can no longer rely on traditional identity categories such as social class, ethnicity or gender and have had to become the authors of their own lives (Beck, 1992). Richard Sennett (1999) identifies drastic changes in the lives of working Americans in recent decades. In a series of interviews, workers described how, whereas skills and experience had once been valued in the workplace, employers now reward those who display the ability to forget and adjust quickly to ever-changing demands. The insidious result is what Sennett calls the 'corrosion of character' – the destruction of any notion of oneself as a set of stable identities, relationships and ethical values. Sennett observes that this is inherently stressful for most people, who 'are not like this; they need a sustaining life narrative, and they take pride in being good at something specific, and they value the experiences they've lived through' (Sennett, 2006: 5). It is not surprising, then, that Cushman (1995) likewise describes the resulting self of the neoliberal age as an 'empty self':

> a self that experiences a significant absence of community, tradition, and shared meaning – a self that experiences these social absences and their consequences "interiorly" as a lack of personal conviction and worth. (p79)

It is easy to see how the individual often attempts to deal with the resulting feelings of 'emptiness' through the consumption of goods, experiences and substances, readily available for purchase in the neoliberal marketplace, and how this has led to a rise in compulsive and addictive behaviours (Orford, 2015).

The growing incidence of 'anxiety disorders' has also been linked to the pressures on the neo-self to 'perform' – having to constantly engage in competitive, short-term, insecure projects. A number of writers have referred to a profound sense of ontological insecurity that is fostered by the aggressively competitive nature of the modern neoliberal world, whereby individuals are constantly seeking to measure up to frequently changing standards (Ball, 2003; 2009; Lynch 2006). Verhaeghe (2013) focuses on social anxiety in relation to the constant evaluation of the self through mechanisms such as workplace audit interviews and performance reviews, along with the erosion of previous social sources of trust and authority. This is also likely to be linked to the explosion in social media, via which manufactured images of success and achievement are endlessly circulated.

Timimi and Leo (2009) comment that the 'diagnosis of Attention Deficit Hyperactivity Disorder (ADHD) has reached epidemic proportions, particularly amongst boys in North America' (p1). They link this to the promotion by the drug industry of stimulants such as Ritalin, which in turn has been linked to the desire among parents to enhance their children's 'performance' (for example, in exams). One of the contributors to their book, Simon Sobo, further discusses how the phenomenon of ADHD links with our transition from a society based on moral expectations to one characterised by pleasure and seeking stimulus, whereby boredom and associated inattention become the norm (Sobo, 2009). In a similar vein, it could be argued that the increase in diagnoses of 'autistic spectrum disorders' is not a reflection of an improved ability to detect incidences of a diagnosable entity, but rather that the individuals so diagnosed fail to live up to the neoliberal norms of the performative, fluid, flexible self, and are therefore deemed dysfunctional (Moloney, 2010; Timimi, Gardner & McCabe, 2011).

CBT and neoliberalism

In his book *Governing the Soul*, Nikolas Rose (1999) uses Foucault's concept of 'governmentality' to take a searching look at the role of psy professions in modern forms of liberal governance. He describes governmentality as 'the conduct of conduct': programmes, strategies, techniques for 'acting upon the action of others towards certain ends' (pxxi). He views psychotherapy as one of the key techniques for the governance of subjectivity in a post-welfare state society through its espousal of liberal notions of freedom, autonomy and fulfilment. While Rose provides a broad analysis of psychotherapy in advanced liberal society, it is our view that the dominance of CBT as a specific mode of therapeutic technology reflects its particular ideological alignment with neoliberalism – it *is*, therefore, a neoliberal therapy for a neoliberal age.

Dahlstedt and colleagues (2011) critically analyse the introduction of CBT programmes in schools in Sweden and identify how these programmes – with an eye to the requirements of the modern labour market – engender a mode of neoliberal governance. This is achieved through promoting the ideals of flexibility, individual responsibility and activity, and that change and success mean working on the self to manage emotions, rather than looking to the world on which that self ultimately depends. The injustice of this approach is well captured by Pilgrim (2008):

> ... try being poor, female, suffering sexual abuse in childhood and being re-victimised in adulthood and see how happy you can become by learning to reverse your 'faulty' thinking about these facts of your life. (p258)

In picturing both the causes and the solutions to distress as private rather than public issues, CBT is complicit in promoting the ideal of the neo-self: an autonomous, private, individualised entity, separate from social context (Pilgrim, 2011; Proctor, 2008). CBT therefore reinforces the idea of the neoliberal self as both the cause of the problem of psychological distress, via irrational thoughts, and the solution – a self that must help itself by continually investing in self-improvements (Illouz, 2007).

Ferguson (2007) discusses the close relationship between the promotion of CBT via IAPT and the government's aim to equip individuals to survive in a globalised neoliberal workplace. He argues that the CBT 'therapeutic' mechanism of changing thinking as a way of addressing distress fits perfectly with the core themes of neoliberal governments, including health as an individual responsibility; a rejection of social/structural causes of mental health issues, and an abhorrence of dependency in any form, leading to the policy of attempting to save billions of pounds by removing one million people from incapacity benefit. This abhorrence of dependency and vulnerability is also highlighted by Rizq (2012). She views the neoliberalisation of mental healthcare in the NHS (via programmes such as IAPT) as constructing a 'virtual reality' of human experience based on targets, outcomes, protocols and policies, which serves to conceal or deny the emotional realities of the real and complex suffering of individuals. The illusion of control created by the collection of statistics forms a core element in the armoury of CBT practitioners, who regularly administer so-called 'measures' of psychological distress, such as the PHQ-9 and GAD-7 scales, despite serious reservations about whether such measures demonstrate any validity whatsoever, or that human experience can even be measured or quantified in these ways (Epstein, 2006; Midlands Psychology Group, 2017; Moloney, 2017). However, it appears that any such serious scientific concerns are routinely ignored in the service of an ideological alignment between the neo-self as a measurable, performative self and the use of clinical measures used within the CBT framework.

In a powerful critique of the IAPT programme, based on her personal experience of having supervised a number of IAPT workers, Watts (2016) concludes that it is no coincidence that CBT is the dominant approach, due to its ideological alignment with neoliberalism. She sums this up in her statement: 'CBT fits well in an era which combines a competitive, economic focus with an "audit explosion"' (p87). She identifies a number of neoliberal governance themes evident in the CBT approach, including the focus on performativity, measurement and surveillance; the selling of CBT as a progressive, forward-looking approach; the attribution of individual responsibility for change, and the downplaying of social causes of distress. She argues that this leads to the CBT patient not being enabled to explore and critically evaluate their own values, but instead having an implicit set of social values or norms – such as work performativity as a measure of the good citizen – imposed on them. This process occurs perniciously, as often neither the patient nor the worker may be aware that the choice of, for example, individualising outcome measures creates an invisible standard of how one should be feeling or thinking: that, in Watts words, wellbeing is a case of thinking 'correctly' and that 'the self is a project that can be molded and chipped away at so as to become attractive to the market' (p97).

In summary, we contend that the dominance of CBT (in all its guises), as supported by central government funding and government agencies such as NICE, reflects its close ideological alliance with the dominant mode of neoliberal governance. We view CBT as a fundamental part of the technology of the neoliberal state in its mission to replace the care and equality ethic of the welfare state with a socially corrosive ethic of survival of the fittest (Lynch, Grummell & Devine, 2012).

Improving Access to Psychological Therapies – outcome evidence

This section aims to provide a brief but critical summary of some of the main arguments around the UK government's programme for Improving Access to Psychological Therapies, or IAPT, as it is commonly known: an unprecedented attempt by the state to introduce standardised psychological treatments and techniques to the population of England and Wales, on demand and free at the point of delivery. This programme has very broad aims: to improve the treatment and prevention of psychological disturbance; to coax the long-term mentally distressed into swapping their dependency on sickness and disability benefits for paid work, and to boost national wellbeing. Of particular relevance to the focus of this book is that the treatment on offer has been primarily CBT, and even the non-CBT treatments have been 'delivered' to their recipients in a way that mimics CBT.

The programme began in 2006, at two relatively small 'demonstration sites', in Newham, in east London, and Doncaster, in South Yorkshire. With the aid of Department of Health funding, from 2008 it was rolled out across all 10 strategic health authority areas in England, with each local IAPT service designed to a similar structure: a call centre to deal with initial self-referrals, including people needing straightforward, basic mental health advice; followed by more complex, personalised, face-to-face therapy services, dispensed at mounting levels of 'intensity' to clients deemed to have more severe problems (Richards & Suckling, 2008). In its early years, the scheme was entirely CBT-based, and, while this remains the primary therapeutic approach, it has since diversified to include interpersonal and psychodynamic therapies, albeit in highly manualised forms.

In line with a technological approach, IAPT uses a 'stepped care' model: referrals and self-referrals go through stages, 'stepping up' if each approach fails to deliver the expected positive results. At Step One, they get advice, psycho-education and referral onto other services that might help (housing, for example); at Step Two, they get psycho-education, group therapy and guided self-help and information from a 'psychological wellbeing practitioner' (PWP). At Step Three, they finally get to see a trained and qualified counsellor or psychotherapist, in the main a CBT-trained practitioner. The IAPT practitioners are thus divided into two skill echelons: the PWPs, who are in the main psychology graduates, give advice and information and guided self-help in personal problem-solving methods, via telephone, online and groupwork. Above all, they teach sufferers to frame their difficulties and hopes of cure in the language of cognitive-behaviourism. The 'high intensity practitioners', the qualified counsellors/CBT therapists, seek to help those with more severe and longstanding problems, who have in most cases already been through a course of guided self-help with a PWP before being 'stepped up' to this level, unless identified at initial assessment as needed to go straight to Step Three. Step Three therapists offer traditional face-to-face individual therapy, although in a form that is highly codified, in accordance with the latest National Institute of Health and Care Excellence (NICE) guidelines.

Despite its seemingly flawless clinical and scientific credentials, IAPT was not a virgin birth. Its parent was Richard Layard, economist, UK 'happiness czar', and founder and Director of the Centre for Economic Performance – a free market-oriented 'thinktank', based at the London School of Economics. At the dawn of the new century, he was asked by the then New Labour administration to coin fresh ideas for a more efficient NHS adult mental health service – a request that resulted in *The Depression Report* (Centre for Economic Performance's Mental Health Policy Group, 2006). The report carried the signatures of an elite metropolitan group mainly comprising psychiatrists and NHS chief executives, and Layard himself. Intended for a lay readership, it was largely welcomed by the liberal social-democratic press and commentators, although few of them seemed to notice the contradiction at the heart of its thesis. On the one hand, it condensed a large body of research into the alleged genesis of 'happiness' – based largely on the ideas of the conservative American psychologist Martin Seligman. A key exponent of 'positive psychology', Seligman and colleagues argued that situational influences – and, in particular, economic and social deprivation – had only a limited significance for personal wellbeing and happiness. For governments, it might be legitimate from a mental health point of view to protect the citizen from utter destitution, but beyond that point, there was little to be gained from taking any further steps to redress longstanding economic inequalities. It was considered far better to teach as many people as possible the techniques of positive thought.

By contrast, Layard and his associates acknowledged that childhood experiences are crucial to wellbeing and to the ability to flourish across the lifespan. Improved detection and prevention of the misery and mistreatment of children would do much to improve the health of the whole population, and, although *The Depression Report* did not dwell on the subject, it is clear that such measures would be expensive and complicated to carry out. In the end, Layard plumped decisively for an expanded cadre of government-funded psychologists and therapists as the best way to improve happiness, reduce malaise, get the mentally unwell back into employment, and rebalance the public purse. By Layard's calculations, the cost of a course of CBT would be precisely repaid by the savings in one month in sickness benefits when the subject was restored, happy again, to the labour market. In his subsequent writings and work as a parliamentary advisor and consultant, Layard has tirelessly repeated this theme, just as he has kept his attention firmly on the latest developments in the field of psychological treatment.

While Layard has always admitted his naïvety in matters 'psychological' (despite being the child of two Jungian analysts), he took heart from his readings of the NICE treatment guidelines for anxiety and depression (which have tended to favour CBT) (2004, 2009, 2017), and from the advice of a select group of clinical psychologists and psychiatrists at the University of Oxford and the Institute of Psychiatry, respectively. In common with New Labour and with subsequent UK governments, all of these parties shared an identification with the world of managed healthcare, and Layard's speeches and writings sought to make a strong clinical *and* fiscal case for his proposals. *The Depression Report* emphasised the ubiquity and the expense of emotional disturbance – a burden carried by one in every six adults in the UK population, equating to more than a million people claiming incapacity benefit, at an annual cost of £12.5 billion to the Exchequer – or two per cent of the UK's Gross Domestic Product.

> We now have a million people on Incapacity Benefits because of mental illness – more than the total number of unemployed people receiving unemployment benefits. (CEP, 2006: 1)

And yet 'work is a major route to recovery. And, as taxpayers who pay for Invalidity Benefits, we can all say amen to this' (Layard, 2005). Prayers could be answered, because there was little difference between the cost of a month's Incapacity Benefit, and the typical course of CBT. Should each claimant return to work for merely one month, then their therapy would have paid for itself. The whole scheme would be a kind of perpetual-motion machine for good mental hygiene.

Outcomes of IAPT

Right from the beginning, the official story of IAPT has been one of unmitigated success –evaluated according to measures that include rates of referral, treatment, improvement, and client satisfaction (Anekwe, 2008). In the words of Dr Alan Cohen, national primary care lead for IAPT, at the end of its first three years, the programme had 'made psychological therapies practical and available to primary care patients, which [was] fantastic. The finding that 49% of patients no longer have a clinical diagnosis after treatment is the sort you see in randomised controlled trials. To be able to duplicate that in practice is extraordinary' (Cohen, cited in Anekwe, 2008).

While the original proposals had strictly insisted that the first test sites must prove themselves before further expansion would be permitted, the Department of Health approved stage two for funding well before all of the data from Doncaster and Newham were in. Far from asking pertinent questions about this quiet slippage in official policy, most of the UK news media meekly accepted it, often with jubilation (BBC News, 2007). In 2008, the Doncaster pilot project bagged a National Health and Social Care Award for its 'breakthrough ideas' in 'the improvement of frontline services' (Richards & Suckling, 2008). By 2011, IAPT had recruited and trained a workforce of 3,600 practitioners. They had delivered therapy to 400,000 individuals and had achieved an overall client recovery rate of 40%. This was well below the official target of 50%, but for supporters it was still an encouraging outcome, given that this was a new scheme and therefore likely to suffer from teething problems. Moreover, almost 14,000 of these improved clients had come off sick pay or other state benefits to pursue training or employment, in most instances (Clark, 2011). The Conservative-Liberal coalition government that replaced New Labour pledged an additional £400 million to the scheme in 2011. This boosted its ability to reach out to new groups of patients – children and adolescents, older people, and those suffering from long-term physical health problems and medically unexplained conditions (Department of Health, 2010). In 2015, there were proposals to place 350 IAPT therapists in job centres as a means to help unemployed people experiencing depression to return to work, through online and telephone CBT.

On paper, IAPT in England has delivered on its promises of efficient growth and treatment. It appears to have achieved many of its main targets, and to have missed others only by a sliver – a rare achievement for any UK public health programme. The official outcome data for the period 2015/16 report this seeming story of success. The scheme appears close to attaining its main long-term goal, of having treated more than 900,000 individuals – or 15% of everyone in England classed as having a 'mental disorder'. Furthermore, of the 490,395 referrals who finished a course of treatment in 2015/2016, having met the criteria for 'caseness', 226,850 (46.3%) were deemed to have moved to recovery (NHS Digital, 2016) – the target is 50%, if Layard's cost-benefit projection is to add up.

Supporters and champions of the project attribute this apparent success to its rationalised structure. They see the stepped care approach as an intrepid attempt to bring mental health care firmly into the 21st century, melding the principles of humane treatment with the smooth efficiency and precision of the automated production line (Layard & Clark, 2015). The supporters claim that it marks the biggest improvement in mental health services since the inception of community care in the 1980s. Even some of its critics concede that it is a 'bold attempt to expand psychological therapies and to link that expansion to the use of effective therapies' and hail it as an end to the chronic cash starvation of mental health services (Marzillier & Hall, 2009: 396).

But how valid is this official view of IAPT?

From the start, this project has encountered a mixed reception from mental health practitioners and researchers. In large part, this is because of the sizeable gap between the publicity generated for the scheme and the reality of what seems to be happening on the ground. For example, an official report by the North East Public Health Observatory (Glover, Webb & Evison, 2010) examined the first year of full operation, or 'roll out', of 34 IAPT sites, from October 2008. The report confirmed that 'NHS psychological therapists enable four in 10 [clients] to recover', according to the Department of Health (McInnes, 2011). However, a more careful reading of the report reveals a more complicated picture: little more than half of those introduced to the service turned up for their first assessment, and half again of this group were judged to have completed their contact with it. Of this latter subgroup, just a third had successfully finished their treatment – the rest were deemed unsuitable, or had simply dropped out or declined to participate. The widely proclaimed success rates – 'four out of ten recovered' – held only for the 12,000 or so people who had completed their course of 'CBT-based intervention': nine per cent of those originally assessed. This was not a headline-worthy cure rate, especially for a scheme that was steadily displacing extant local NHS therapy services, many of them with a far better performance record and offering a much wider choice of therapies (see McInnes, 2011).

In the following years, independent evaluations have revealed a similar story. In 2013, researchers led by Steve Griffiths at the University of Chester's Centre for Psychological Therapies in Primary Care (CPTCP) published two analyses of the IAPT's performance, based on IAPT outcome data obtained from the NHS Information Centre for 2011–2012. NHS England had proclaimed an official recovery rate of 44%, based on those clients who were deemed to have been at 'caseness' at first contact and had gone on to complete their treatment. However, when the CPTCP researchers considered *everyone* who had entered the scheme and had attended at least one therapy session, the figure dropped to 22%. When all the patients referred to IAPT were included, the percentage of recovered patients sank lower still – to just 12% of the total (Griffiths & Steen, 2013).

In their second analysis, the CPTCP team used a Freedom of Information request to secure data from primary care trusts (PCTs) on the actual cost of each low- and high-intensity IAPT session. They found the overall figure exceeded the government estimates by a factor of three, and they concluded that GPs and commissioners should scrutinise more carefully 'the optimistic message' of high and sustainable patient recovery rates (Griffiths et al, 2013).

When health practitioners are asked to comment on their own clinical experience, they will often echo this sceptical message. According to Dr Henk Parmier, a west London GP and a primary care lead in the UK Mental Health Research Network:

> Only a minority of patients [referred to IAPT] will 'recover' – my clinical estimate around 15–20%. Most patients will not be accepted, or will drop out, due to long waiting times before they can get some counselling. (Quoted in Price, 2013).

As the programme has continued to expand, with the overall level of new referrals rising steadily year on year, the proportion of clients who are considered recovered has not improved, contrary to what we might expect of a proclaimed quality-controlled therapy service. Instead, the ratio has remained stubbornly at around one in every four of those who enter treatment (NHS Digital, 2016). In other words, the programme is still underperforming in its own terms. Furthermore, a recent evaluation of low-intensity CBT for depression and anxiety (Ali et al, 2017) found that 53% of cases relapsed within one year. On top of this, there are big variations – up to threefold – in the apparent effectiveness between services (NHS Digital, 2016). While this variability might plausibly reflect population characteristics, such as rates of deprivation (see Davies, 1997; Rogers & Pilgrim, 2002), it also suggests the variable quality of the IAPT services themselves. It certainly undermines Layard's bland claims about the automatic potency of CBT and the ability of highly rationalised therapy services to deliver predicted outcomes, regardless of local populations' culture and context.

Proponents of the programme, such as Professor David Clark, its National Clinical Advisor at the Department of Health and a professor of psychology at the University of Oxford, hold that critiques like these are flawed: '... it was always intended that a substantial number of people [referred to IAPT] will receive a one-off assessment and advice and will not need to enter a formal course of therapy' (Price, 2013). However, such arguments distract from the fact that, right from the start, its proponents have avoided public discussion of the only valid way of assessing the scheme's performance – by comparing how it stands up against alternative (but comparable) local counselling services. Others *have* looked at this question, however, and the results have not been encouraging. Thus, for the early IAPT demonstration projects, a (decidedly) modest lead in clinical outcome scores over traditional provision in neighbouring boroughs had evaporated eight months after completion of treatment, and IAPT was more costly (Price, 2013). For sites developed in the subsequent national roll out, analyses conducted by the Artemis Trust (Barnes, Hall & Evans, 2008; Evans, 2011) found that the mean number of patients achieving recovery for a fixed outlay of £1,000 was far below the attainment of the voluntary sector counselling services that IAPT had engulfed or supplanted. Notably, recovery rates, as a proportion of patients referred, were low for IAPT when compared, for example, with the university and employee assistance and GP counselling services that had preceded it (Timimi, 2014). As the child and adolescent psychiatrist Sami Timimi notes, this situation represents 'a truly remarkable achievement. The government has spent large amounts of taxpayers' money creating an expensive service that provides little choice and has poorer outcomes than cheaper alternatives that were already in existence' (Timimi, 2014: 2). This poor record is in line with that of many other large-scale monopoly contracts awarded by the UK government in recent years – including those for NHS computer systems and for buildings and infrastructure, which have become bywords for poor quality, bureaucratic muddle, and exorbitant expenditure (see Meeks, 2014; Pollock, 2005).

The same desultory analysis applies to IAPT's ability to tackle malaise in the general population. One of the explicit aims of the scheme was to create a climate in which everyone, and especially doctors and their patients, would cease to view personal problems as medical ones, needing diagnosis and then correction with pills. Prescriptions of antidepressants have risen during IAPT's lifetime (Gruet, 2016; Timimi, 2014). Likewise, there are few signs that IAPT has lightened the burden of societal distress. Within its lifetime, the number of people claiming disability benefits because of depression and anxiety (the main target conditions for the programme) has risen, while reported job-related stress and the absenteeism linked to it are now at record levels in the UK (Jones, 2016; Trades Union Congress, 2015). Community psychiatric surveys indicate rising malaise in comparison with 20 years ago, especially for the impoverished elderly (Age UK, 2016) and the young (Dorling, 2016). Suicide rates for young men have risen dramatically since the 2008 financial crash (McVeigh, 2015).

But none of this should be a surprise. No thoughtful person would expect IAPT to succeed, even on its own terms. The IAPT programme is, in fact, nothing like the rigorous 'experiment' that its architects claimed. One of the longstanding criticisms of CBT is that it is no more than a label of convenience: a disparate collection of theories and techniques aimed at changing aspects of mind, behaviour and feeling – but lacking any unified theory of the origins of distress, let alone what it means to be a person (Fancher, 1995; Moloney & Kelly, 2008; Moloney, 2013; Newnes, 2014; Wampold & Imel, 2015). This criticism applies in full force to IAPT, where none of the treatments, from the 'demonstration' stage onwards, have been as tightly regulated as the publicity for the scheme might suggest. Rather, practitioners choose from a menu of micro-interventions, which include the provision of advice, cognitive therapy, behavioural interventions, psycho-education, interpersonal therapy and counselling, based on the uneducated guesses of PWPs, who mostly conduct the initial assessments and assign patients a 'diagnosis' picked from a list.

The question arises, just what form of treatment was being tested within the scheme at the demonstration stage? Indeed, a scientific assessment of any kind of treatment must include a reliable specification of the problem that it is designed to treat. However, 'moderate depression', for example, is a vague diagnostic category that says little about the history, causes or nature of the sufferer's problems, and still less about the best ways to treat it. Two people described as 'depressed' can display very different 'symptoms', and might be regarded as not suffering from the same putative 'disease' at all. Moreover, when it comes to the symptoms manifested by the patient, the diagnosis overlaps with (is sometimes indistinguishable from) other problems, such as obsessional states, anxiety and psychosis (Horwitz & Wakefield, 2007; Pilgrim & Bentall, 1999). These are just some of the reasons why the full version of the NICE 2004 guidelines for the treatment of moderate depression was ambivalent about the effectiveness of CBT for this condition, but this was ignored by Layard and other enthusiasts for the programme.

Perhaps the most dubious feature of the programme, however, is the powerful demands that it imposes on its employees – not unlike the forms of mandatory personal commitment and enthusiasm required by Japanese car manufacturers and, increasingly, within the public sector (Davies, 2015). This issue assumes even greater importance in any assessment of the helpfulness of psychological interventions, because of the powerful cultural demand characteristics that *already* permeate the therapeutic encounter. There are good reasons for believing that most clients will assume a heavy moral burden of responsibility for their own ability to profit from their therapy, and therefore have every reason to dissemble about the helpfulness or otherwise of their treatment – as much to themselves, as to their therapist (Epstein, 2006; Millard, 2016). And yet the IAPT programme appears to be designed to inculcate positive endorsements from everyone involved, beginning with the practitioners themselves. Governed by stringent performance targets linked to payment by results, they are often younger people – especially at the low intensity levels – on the bottom rungs of their professional ladder, and keen to show their ability to achieve good results to their superiors and funders. They also have very high caseloads of 75 or more clients, and they are intensively monitored and supervised – conditions that are likely to make for anxiety and a habit of demonstrating full compliance with managerial expectations (Fleming, 2015). The clinical psychologist Jay Watts writes of her own experience of working in an east London IAPT site, which she describes as corporate, and grinding, in contrast with Layard's glossy and evangelical version. Watts implies that this urge to impress management undermines each practitioner's ability to be fully present to their clients, and this is borne out by descriptions of recorded therapy sessions (used in the supervision of IAPT workers), in which the client's viewpoint is downplayed to favour the approved answers (Watts, 2016).

And what goes for the practitioners surely goes for those they treat. The scheme is a widely publicised flagship service, billed as offering the newest technologies in mental health care. Any intervention that carries such an aura is likely to generate high expectations for recipients, and to be judged by them as more effective than its competitors, all else being equal. To the extent that the practice of therapy embodies widely shared beliefs about the sovereign autonomy of the self, then to sit before a therapist is akin to sitting before a moral judge, and the more that subtle forms of moralising are built into the treatment and the context in which it is delivered, the more clients are likely to distort their reports of how they experience their therapy. In IAPT, such inducements are legion. The guiding assumption for the scheme is that distress for the most part is internally generated and the solution is the responsibility of the individual sufferer, with a little help from a suitably trained expert. This view is fast becoming the common sense of mental health care – most clients are likely to adopt it, and to feel that they are personally at fault if they report a failure to benefit. That they are required to report their mental health status at the end of each IAPT session, via two standardised psychiatric questionnaires (PHQ-9 and GAD-7), can only add to these expectancy effects. Repeated use of 'measuring instruments' like these has been shown to school clients into giving the 'right' answers – answers that are indicative of improvement – even when they are receiving a bogus or 'pure placebo' therapy (Epstein, 2006; 1995). As if this were not enough, IAPT patients are also required to report their employment status at the end of each session. This cannot be a neutral question, given that neoliberal societies regard the workless with suspicion, if not contempt (Seabrook, 2016). For those clients who are claiming benefit, and perhaps for many who are not, this question alone would ensure that each session would represent a tightrope walk across a chasm of judgment and shame, giving the client every incentive to exaggerate their symptoms at the outset (in order to deflect accusations of malingering), and to then demonstrate their mettle for improvement as the treatment progresses (see Epstein, 2006; Moloney, 2013).

In addition to all of the above empirical and ideological issues, the growth of IAPT can be seen to have wider, pernicious social effects. Mental health organisations formerly known for their campaigning and dissent have forced themselves into the bland mould of IAPT in order to follow the money and have been rebranded as 'excellent IAPT organisations'. The whole IAPT programme shrinks the spectrum of acceptable or 'normal' mental health, and its publicity makes people question their own wellbeing and demand more from the NHS (Watts, 2016). In its equation of good mental health with the cheerful, well-balanced and compliant worker (or jobseeker), IAPT is a pure expression of the neoliberal view of the self as a project, to be relentlessly shaped, but in the interests of the marketplace, above all (Fleming, 2015; Sennett, 2006).

Third-wave CBT

IAPT is not the only recent innovation in the CBT field. No discussion of this subject would be complete without at least touching on the growth of 'mindfulness-based' or 'third-wave CBT': a set of approaches that trade heavily on the ancient contemplative traditions of Asia. Rather than relying exclusively on an attempt to challenge unhelpful beliefs, third-wave CBT practitioners regard such cognitive exercises as supplementary to traditional meditational techniques, such as *vipassana* – 'watching of the breath' – and other physical and visualisation exercises designed to soothe and foster compassion toward self and others (Gaudiano, 2014; Gilbert, 2009; Kabat-Zinn, 2001; Roemer & Orisillo, 2009). Our critique of CBT could be accused of attacking a 'straw man', given these more recent developments, which, for their proponents, represent a radical break with traditional CBT's reliance on 'mind over matter' in the form of rational argument or therapeutic 'self-talk' (see for example, Gilbert, 2009).

Mindfulness is certainly popular. Over 500 peer-reviewed academic papers on the subject appear every year (Barker, 2014), and GPs cannot keep up with patient demand (Mindfulness All-Party Parliamentary Group (MAPPG), 2015). In 2015, under the leadership of Richard Layard, a cross-party group of MPs issued an official report, entitled *Mindful Nation UK* (Mindfulness All-Party Parliamentary Group (MAPPG), 2015), urging the deployment of these techniques throughout the public sector. This document stakes much of its credibility on clinical research into mindfulness, on the scientific credentials of CBT, and on what its authors regard as the unmitigated success of the IAPT programme (see Layard & Clark, 2015).

Limited space prevents a full discussion of this latest brand, which the interested reader can find elsewhere (Farias & Wikholm, 2015; Moloney, 2016). However, it is worth noting that mindfulness-based CBT (MBCT) retains the familiar and fundamental assumption that, in the end, the individual sufferer can transcend their own misery and the circumstances that engender it, via the application of therapeutic techniques. This approach thereby rejects one form of problematic dualism – that between mind and body – and promptly replaces it with another: namely, the traditional Western dualism of self, on the one hand, and of world, on the other (see Fuchs, 2013; Throop, 2009). Moreover, when examined carefully, the most widely cited evidence for the effectiveness of MBCT and its variants – whether applied as clinical tools, or as crucibles for happy communities and productive workplaces, schools and prisons – is entirely equivocal (Barker,

2014; Booth, 2014; Database Abstract of Reviews of Effects (DARE), 2015; Davies, 2015; Felver et al, 2015; Gaynor, 2014; Goyal et al, 2014; Moloney, 2016; 2013; Stanley & Longdon, 2016).

Clearly, the success of third-wave CBT cannot be attributed to an avalanche of scientific evidence in its favour. Rather, we view the proliferation of this approach as a reflection of the changing nature of capitalism: particularly in relation to how elements of neoliberalism have intensified during the so called 'information age' (Castells, 2010). In their analysis of the history of capitalism, Boltanski and Chiapello (2005), identify an evolution from the big industrial companies of the mid- to late-20th century towards the 'network'-oriented firms of the 1980s onwards. A parallel can be seen in the ways in which CBT has developed: from the first-wave behaviourism dominant during the age of the big hierarchical firm, reflecting the central external authority directing the individual, to second-wave cognitive-behavioural therapy dominant during the early phases of network capitalism, where the individual becomes the locus of self-control but is still guided by the force of 'reason', to the latest, third-wave iterations of CBT, which reflect the intensification of the loss of any identifiable central, controlling authority in the fully-formed, neoliberal, project-oriented 'network'. The 'neo-self' has become a corresponding type of internal networked self – a 'mindful self' that operates as both subject and object of its own temporary projects.

Conclusion

Despite a lack of any convincing evidence for its theoretical underpinnings or its clinical effectiveness, CBT, like a virus, has continued to evolve and dominate the therapy ecosystem. By any stretch of the imagination, this can surely only represent 'bad science' (see Goldacre, 2009). Its core ideology that distress is primarily caused by internal psychological processes conflicts with the robust scientific evidence for social causation, structured by growing socioeconomic inequality. We can only conclude, therefore, that its success serves the interests of those who have the power and influence to create the ideological agenda. In our era of post-truth, Orwell's successors have a lot of work to do.

In concluding that CBT is a neoliberal therapy for a neoliberal era, we return to our core question: what social functions (other than those professed) does it serve? Some clues to the answer may be found in the following statement from the *Mindful Nation UK* government report on mindfulness:

> We have been impressed by the quality and range of evidence for the benefits of mindfulness and believe it has the potential to help many people to better health and flourishing. On a number of issues, ranging from improving mental health and boosting productivity and creativity in the economy through to helping people with long-term conditions such as diabetes and obesity, mindfulness appears to have an impact. This is a reason

> for government to take notice and we urge serious consideration of our report. (Mindfulness All-Party Parliamentary Group (MAPPG), 2015: 4).

A heart and soul that can be productive and creative in the neoliberal economy is indeed one that has been changed!

References

Age UK (2016). *Mental Health Services are Failing Older People*. [Online]. London: Age UK. www.ageuk.org.uk/latest-press/archive/new-report-from-age-uk-shows-mental-health-services-are-letting-older-people-down (accessed 4 February 2018).

Ali S, Rhodes L, Moreea O, McMillan D, Gilbody S, Leach C, Lucock M, Lutz W, Delgadillo J (2017). How durable is the effect of low intensity CBT for depression and anxiety? Remission and relapse in a longitudinal cohort study. *Behaviour Research and Therapy 94*: 1–8.

Allen K (2007). *The Corporate Takeover of Ireland*. Dublin: Irish Academic Press.

Allen K (2003). Neither Boston nor Berlin: class polarisation and neo-liberalism in the Irish Republic. In: Coulter C, Coleman S (eds). *The End of Irish History: critical reflections on the Celtic Tiger*. Manchester: Manchester University Press.

Anekwe L (2008). Plan for major talking therapies expansion revealed. [Online]. *Pulse Today;* 3 March. www.pulsetoday.co.uk/plan-for-major-talking-therapies-expansion-revealed/10973079.article (accessed 4 February 2018).

Apple MW (2007). Ideological success, educational failure? On the politics of no child left behind. *Journal of Teacher Education 58*: 108–116.

Apple MW (2004). Creating difference: neo-liberalism, neo-conservatism and the politics of educational reform. *Educational Policy 18*(1): 12–44.

Ball SJ (2009). Privatising education: privatising education policy, privatising educational research: network governance and the competition state. *Journal of Education Policy 24*(1): 83–99.

Ball SJ (2003). The teacher's soul and the terrors of performativity. *Journal of Education Policy 18*(2): 215–228.

Barnes D, Hall J, Evans R (2008). *Survey of the Current Provision of Psychological Therapy Services in Primary Care in the UK*. Chichester: Artemis Trust.

Barker KS (2014). Mindfulness meditation: do-it-yourself medicalization of every moment. *Social Science and Medicine 106*: 168–176.

BBC News (2007). More funds for talking therapies. [Online.] *BBC News*, 10 October. http://news.bbc.co.uk/1/hi/health/7037400.stm (accessed 18 February 2018).

Beck U (1992*). Risk Society: towards a new modernity*. London: Sage.

Booth R (2014). Mindfulness therapy comes at a high price for some, say experts. [Online.] *The Guardian*; 25 August.

Boltanski L, Chiapello E (2005). *The New Spirit of Capitalism*. London: Verso.

Bourdieu P (1998). The essence of neoliberalism. *Le Monde Diplomatique,* December. http://mondediplo.com/1998/12/08bourdieu (accessed 23 March 2018).

BPS Division of Clinical Psychology. *Classification of behaviour and experience in relation to functional psychiatric diagnoses: time for a paradigm shift.* DCP position statement. Leicester: British Psychological Society.

Butt R (1981). Mrs Thatcher: the first two years. Sunday Times, 3 May. www.margaretthatcher.org/document/104475 (accessed 4 February 2018).

Castells M (2010). *The Information Age: economy, society and culture, volume 1. The rise of the network society* (2nd ed). Oxford: Wiley Blackwell.

Cederstrom C, Fleming P (2012). *Dead Man Working.* Alresford: Zero Books.

Centre for Economic Performance's Mental Health Group (2006). *The Depression Report: a new deal for depression and anxiety disorders.* London: London School of Economics.

Clark DM (2011). Implementing NICE guidelines for the psychological treatment of depression and anxiety: the IAPT experience. *International Review of Psychiatry 23:* 318–327.

Cushman P (1995). *Constructing the Self, Constructing America: a cultural history of psychotherapy.* Boston, MA: Da Capo Press.

Dahlstedt M, Fejesb A, Schönninga E (2011). The will to (de)liberate: shaping governable citizens through cognitive behavioural programmes in school. *Journal of Education Policy 26*(3): 399–414.

Dalal F (2015). Statistical Spin: linguistic obfuscation – the art of overselling the CBT evidence base. *The Journal of Psychological Therapies in Primary Care 4:* 1–25.

Dardot P, Laval C (2013). *The New Way of the World: on neoliberal society.* London: Verso.

Database of Abstracts of Reviews of Effects (DARE) (2015). [Online]. www.ncbi.nlm.nih.gov/pubmedhealth/about/DARE (accessed 4 February 2018).

Davies D (1997). *Counselling in Psychological Services.* Milton Keynes: Open University.

Davies W (2015). *The Happiness Industry: how the government and big business sold us well-being.* London/New York, NY: Verso.

Department of Health (2010). *Realising the Benefits: IAPT at full roll-out.* London: Department of Health.

Dorling D (2016). *A Better Politics: how government can make us happier.* London: London Publishing Partnership.

Ehrenberg A (2010). *The Weariness of the Self* (D Homel trans). Montreal: McGill-Queens University Press.

Epstein WM (2006). *Psychotherapy as Religion: the civil divine in America.* Reno, NV: University of Nevada Press.

Epstein WM (1995). *The Illusion of Psychotherapy.* New York, NY: Transaction.

Evans R (2011). *Comparing the Quality of Psychological Therapy Services on the Basis of Number of Recovered Patients for a Fixed Expenditure.* Chichester: The Artemis Trust.

Fancher RT (1995). *Cultures of Healing: correcting the image of American mental health care.* New York, NY: WH Freeman & Company.

Farias M, Wikholm C (2015). *The Buddha Pill: can meditation change you?* London: Watkins.

Felver JC, Celis-de Hoyos CE, Tezanos K, Singh NN (2015). A systematic review of mindfulness-based interventions for youth in school settings. *Mindfulness 7*(1): 34–45.

Ferguson I (2007). Neoliberalism, happiness and wellbeing. [Online]. *International Socialism: A quarterly review of socialist theory 117.* http://isj.org.uk/neoliberalism-happiness-and-wellbeing (accessed 4 February 2018).

Fitzsimons P (2002). Neo-liberalism and education: the autonomous chooser. *Radical Pedagogy 4*(2): 1–10.

Fleming P (2015). *The Mythology of Work: how Capitalism persists despite itself.* London: Pluto.

Fox D, Prilleltensky I, Austin S (2009). *Critical Psychology: an introduction* (2nd ed). London: Sage.

Fuchs T (2013). Depression, intercorporeality and interaffectivity. *Journal of Consciousness Studies 20*(7–8): 219–238.

Gaudiano B (ed) (2014). *Incorporating Acceptance and Mindfulness into the Treatment of Psychosis: current trends and future directions.* New York, NY: Guilford Press.

Gaynor KJ (2014). A critical review of mindfulness-based psychological treatments for worry and rumination. *Open Access Behavioural Medicine 2*(1): 2.

Gilbert P (2009). Moving beyond cognitive behaviour therapy. *The Psychologist 22*(5): 400–403.

Gilbert P (1992). *Depression: the evolution of powerlessness.* Hove: Lawrence Erlbaum Associates.

Giroux H (2014). *Neoliberalism's War on Higher Education.* Chicago, IL: Haymarket Books.

Glover G, Webb M, Evison F (2010). *Improving Access to Psychological Therapies: a review of the progress made by sites in the first rollout year.* Newcastle-upon-Tyne: North East Public Health Observatory.

Goldacre B (2009). *Bad Science.* London: Harper Perennial.

Goyal M, Singh S, Sibinga EM, Gould NF, Rowland-Seymour A, Sharma R, Berger Z, Sleicher D, Maron DD, Shihab HM, Ranasinghe PD, Linn S, Saha S, Bass EB, Haythornthwaite JA (2014). Meditation programs for psychological stress and well-being: a systematic review and meta-analysis. *JAMA Internal Medicine 174*(3) : 357–368.

Griffiths S, Steen S (2013). Improving Access to Psychological Therapies (IAPT) programme: setting key performance indicators in a more robust context: a new perspective. *The Journal of Psychological Therapies in Primary Care 2*: 133–141.

Griffiths S, Foster J, Steen S, Pietroni P (2013). Mental health's market experiment: commissioning psychological therapies through any qualified provider. Centre for Psychological Therapies in Primary Care. Chester: University of Chester Press.

Gruet J (2016). Antidepressant prescribing has more than doubled in ten years. [Online]. *Pulse;* 6 July. www.pulsetoday.co.uk/clinical/prescribing/antidepressant-prescribing-has-more-than-doubled-in-ten-years/20032240.article (accessed 4 February 2018).

Harvey D (2005). *A Brief History of Neo-Liberalism.* Oxford: Open University Press.

Horwitz AV, Wakefield JC (2007). *The Loss of Sadness: how psychiatry transformed normal sorrow into depressive disorder.* Oxford: Oxford University Press.

Illouz E (2007). *Cold Intimacies: the making of emotional capitalism.* Cambridge: Polity.

Johnsen TJ, Friborg O (2015). The effects of Cognitive Behavioural Therapy as an anti-depressive treatment is falling: a meta-analysis. *Psychological Bulletin 14*(4): 747–768.

Jonathan R (1997). *Illusory Freedoms: liberalism and the market.* Oxford: Basil Blackwell.

Jones A (2016). Bosses urged to do more as stress named top health Issue by workers. [Online.] The Independent, 10 October. www.independent.co.uk/life-style/health-and-families/health-news/world-mental-health-day-stress-work-anxiety-depression-bosses-businesses-a7352701.html (accessed 4 February 2018).

Judt T (2005). *Postwar: a history of Europe since 1945.* London: Vintage Books.

Kabat-Zinn J (2001). *Mindfulness Meditation for Everyday Life.* New York, NY: Piatkus.

Layard R (2005). Mental illness is now our biggest social problem. [Online.] *The Guardian*; 14 September. www.theguardian.com/society/2005/sep/14/mentalhealth.socialcare1 (accessed 4 February 2018).

Layard R, Clark DM (2015). *Thrive: the power of psychological therapy*. Harmondsworth: Penguin.

Lynch K (2006). Neo-liberalism and marketisation: the implications for higher education. *European Educational Research Journal 5*(1): 1–17.

Lynch K, Crean M, Moran M (2010). Equality and social justice. The university as a site of struggle. In: Apple M, Ball SJ, Gandin LA (eds). *International Handbook of Sociology of Education*. New York, NY: Routledge (pp296–305).

Lynch K, Grummell B, Devine D (2012). *New Managerialism in Education: commercialization, carelessness and gender*. London: Palgrave-Macmillan.

McInnes B (2011). Nine out of ten people *not* helped by IAPT? *Therapy Today 22*(1): 40.

McVeigh K (2015). Austerity a factor in rising suicide rate among UK men – study. *The Guardian*; 12 November. www.theguardian.com/society/2015/nov/12/austerity-a-factor-in-rising-suicide-rate-among-uk-men-study (accessed 4 February 2018).

Marzillier J, Hall R (2009). The challenge of the Layard initiative. *The Psychologist 22*(6) : 396–399.

Meeks J (2014). *Private Island: why Britain now belongs to someone else*. London: Verso.

Midlands Psychology Group (2017). Psychology as practical biopolitics. In: Pickett J, Jones R, Whitehead M. *Psychological Governance and Public Policy: governing the mind, brain and behaviour.* Abingdon: Routledge (pp75–95).

Millard C (2016). *A History of Self Harm in Britain: a genealogy of cutting and overdosing*. London: Palgrave Macmillan.

Mindfulness All-Party Parliamentary Group (MAPPG) (2015). *Mindful Nation UK*. [Online]. www.themindfulnessinitiative.org.uk/images/reports/Mindfulness-APPG-Report_Mindful-Nation-UK_Oct2015.pdf (accessed 4 February 2018).

Moloney P (2017). 'If the masses have been brainwashed, then they've done the laundry themselves': an interview with William Epstein. *Self and Society* 45(3–4): 342–355.

Moloney P (2016). *Mindfulness: the bottled water of the therapy industry*. In: Purser RE, Forbes D, Burke A (eds). *Handbook of Mindfulness: culture, context and social engagement*. Switzerland: Springer (pp269–292).

Moloney P (2013). *The Therapy Industry: the irresistible rise of the talking cure, and why it doesn't work*. London: Pluto.

Moloney P (2010). How can a chord be weird if it expresses your soul? Some critical reflections on the diagnosis of Aspergers syndrome. *Disability and Society 25*(2): 135–148.

Moloney P, Kelly P (2008). Beck never lived in Birmingham: why CBT may be a less helpful treatment for psychological distress than is often supposed. In: House R, Loewenthal D (eds). *Against and For CBT: towards a constructive dialogue*. Ross-on-Wye: PCCS Books (pp278–288).

Nafstad HE (2002). The neo-liberal ideology and the self-interest paradigm as resistance to change. *Radical Psychology 3*: 1–13.

Newnes C (2014). *Clinical Psychology: a critical examination*. Ross-On-Wye: PCCS Books.

NHS Digital (2016). *Psychological Therapies: annual report on the use of IAPT services, England 2015–2016*. [Online]. NHS Digital. http://digital.nhs.uk/catalogue/PUB22110 (accessed 4 February 2018).

National Institute for Clinical Excellence (2004). Depression: management of depression in primary and secondary care. CG23. London: NICE.

NICE (2017). Depression in adults: treatment and management. Draft for consultation. London: NICE.

NICE (2009). Depression in adults: recognition and management. London: NICE.

NICE (2004). Depression: management of depression in primary and secondary care. CG23. London: NICE.

Orford J (2015). *Addiction, Power and Powerlessness*. London: Sage.

Peters M (2005). The new prudentialism in education: actuarial rationality and the entrepreneurial self. *Educational Theory 55*(2): 123–137.

Pilgrim D (2011). The hegemony of cognitive-behaviour therapy in modern mental health care. *Health Sociology Review 20*(2): 120–132.

Pilgrim D (2008). Reading 'Happiness': CBT and the Layard thesis. *European Journal of Psychotherapy and Counselling 10*(3): 247–260.

Pilgrim D, Bentall R (1999). The medicalisation of misery: a critical realist analysis of the concept depression. *Journal of Mental Health 8*(3): 261–274.

Pollock AM (2005). *NHS plc: the privatisation of our healthcare.* London: Verso.

Power M (1999). *The Audit Society: rituals of verification*. Oxford: Oxford University Press.

Price C (2013). Psychological therapies 'only helping one in ten people', concludes new analysis. [Online]. *Pulse*; 5 November. www.pulsetoday.co.uk/clinical/mental-health/psychological-therapies-only-helping-one-in-ten-people-concludes-new-analysis/20004942.article (accessed 4 February 2018).

Proctor G (2008). CBT: the obscuring of power in the name of science. *European Journal of Psychotherapy & Counselling 10*(3): 231–245.

Richards DA Suckling R (2008). Improving access to psychological therapy: the Doncaster demonstration site organisational model. *Clinical Psychology Forum 189*: 9–16.

Rizq R (2012). The perversion of care: psychological therapies in a time of IAPT. *Psychodynamic Practice 18*(1): 7–24.

Robertson D (2010). *The Philosophy of Cognitive-Behavioural Therapy (CBT): stoic philosophy as rational and cognitive psychotherapy*. London: Karnac Books.

Roemer L, Orisillo SM (2009). *Mindfulness and Acceptance Based Behavioural Therapies in Practice*. New York, NY: Guilford Press.

Rogers A, Pilgrim D (2002). *Mental Health and Inequality*. Basingstoke: Palgrave Macmillan.

Rose N (1996). *Inventing Our Selves: psychology, power and personhood*. Cambridge: Cambridge University Press.

Rose N (1999). *Governing the Soul: the shaping of the private self* (2nd ed). London: Free Association.

Rose N, Miller P (1992). Political power beyond the state: problematics of government. *The British Journal of Sociology 43*(2): 173–205.

Sapolsky RM (2004). *Why Zebras Don't Get Ulcers*. New York, NY: Holt Paperbacks.

Sayer A (2005). *The Moral Significance of Class*. Cambridge: Cambridge University Press.

Seabrook J (2016). *Cut Out: living without welfare*. London: Left Book Club/Pluto.

Segal ZV, Williams JMG, Teasdale JD (2013). *Mindfulness-Based Cognitive Therapy for Depression*. New York, NY: Guilford Press.

Sennett R (2006). *The Culture of New Capitalism*. New Haven/London: Yale University Press.

Sennett R (1999). *The Corrosion of Character: personal consequences of work in the new capitalism.* London: WW Norton & Company.

Shedler J (2015). Where is the evidence for 'evidence-based' therapy? *The Journal of Psychological Therapies in Primary Care 4*: 47–59.

Smail D (2005). *Power, Interest and Psychology: elements of a social materialist understanding of distress.* Ross-on-Wye: PCCS Books.

Smail D (1984). *Illusion and Reality: the meaning of anxiety.* London: Dent.

Sobo S (2009). ADHD and other sins of our children. In: Timimi S, Leo J (eds). *Rethinking ADHD: from brain to culture.* Basingstoke: Palgrave Macmillan (pp360–381).

Stanley S, Longden C (2016). Constructing the mindful subject: reformulating experience through affective-discursive practice in mindfulness-based stress reduction. In: Purser RE, Forbes D, Burke A (eds). *Handbook of Mindfulness: culture, context and social engagement.* Cham: Springer (pp305–322).

Stuckler D, Basu S (2013). *The Body Economic: why austerity kills.* London: Allen Lane.

Throop EA (2009). *Psychotherapy, American Culture, and Social Policy: immoral individualism.* London: Palgrave MacMillan.

Timimi S (2014). Children and young people's improving access to psychological therapies: inspiring innovation or more of the same? *Psychiatric Bulletin 39*(2): 57–60.

Timimi S, Leo J (2009). *Rethinking ADHD: from brain to culture.* Basingstoke: Palgrave Macmillan.

Timimi S, Gardner N, McCabe B (2011). *The Myth of Autism: medicalising men's and boys' social and emotional competence.* Basingstoke: Palgrave Macmillan.

Trades Union Congress (2015). A worker is made ill by work stress every two minutes. *Risks* 725(24 October). www.tuc.org.uk/workplace-issues/health-and-safety/risks-newsletter/risks-2015/tuc-risks-725-24-october-2015 (accessed 4 February 2018)

Verhaeghe P (2014). *What about Me? The struggle for identity in a market-based society.* London: Scribe Publications.

Wampold B, Imel ZE (2015). *The Great Psychotherapy Debate: the evidence for what makes psychotherapy work* (2nd ed). London: Routledge.

Watts J (2016). IAPT and the ideal image. In: Lees J (ed). *The Future of Psychological Therapy: from managed care to transformational practice.* Abingdon: Routledge (pp84–101).

Whitaker R (2010). *Anatomy of an Epidemic: magic bullets, psychiatric drugs and the astonishing rise of mental illness.* New York, NY: Broadway Paperbacks.

Wilkinson RG (2005). *The Impact of Inequality: how to make sick societies healthier.* London: Routledge.

Wilkinson R, Pickett K (2010). *The Spirit Level: why equality is better for everyone.* London: Penguin.

6 The social construction of CBT

Jay Watts

Since the 1980s, a type of psychotherapy called cognitive behavioural therapy (CBT) has become dominant. Like it or loathe it, CBT is now so ubiquitous it is often the only talking therapy available in both public and voluntary health settings (British Psychoanalytic Council/UK Council for Psychotherapy, 2015). It is increasingly spoken about in the media and in living rooms across the country. Yet, when we speak about CBT, when we think of ourselves as 'for' or 'against' it, what are we referring to exactly? For CBT only exists – as we will see – as a political convenience. And maintaining its 'thingness' has consequences.

Doing CBT

To deconstruct CBT, we need to start by exploring how it is constructed in typical prose. Over the past 25 years, CBT has become the treatment of choice in England (Harvey et al, 2004). It has achieved market dominance, developing alongside neoliberal ideology (eg. Watts, 2016). It is cheaper than other therapies, briefer, sellable, and fits brilliantly with today's grand narrative of evidence-based medicine (eg. House & Loewenthal, 2008). The model of psychic change is such that it can, supposedly, be tested through randomised controlled trials (RCTs). RCTS are purported to be the number one type of evidence, the 'gold star' of research (Slade & Priebe, 2001).

There are huge methodological issues with applying RCT design to psychotherapy research (eg. Guy et al, 2011). Given the issues are covered in depth in other chapters, I will limit myself to three brief points. But these points are important, as CBT's relationship to evidence is unique.

An undeniable evidence base

First, CBT is uniquely amenable to RCT design, as its framework includes the notion that problems lie within the individual, and that a treatment can be pre-decided, based on this. The therapist, here, is a technician who applies manualised techniques to the individual for a discrete number of problems – obsessive compulsive disorder, social anxiety, depression, psychosis and so on. This presumption about the categorisability of suffering is not shared by many practitioners, who see it as 'carving nature up at the joints'. For example, someone might be obsessional, but this might serve the function of warding off an otherwise more devastating psychotic decompensation. Something that looks like a symptom may in fact be a solution, or at least a precarious attempt at one. However, the uniqueness of any particular client or any particular therapist, and what they might co-construct, has less importance in CBT than other models of therapy. Thus, CBT's relative success in generating RCT evidence is as much a product of goodness-of-fit between ideology and research design as actual evidence. There are, as the saying goes, other forms of evidence available.

Second, there are huge economic gains in playing the evidence-based game as if it were unproblematic. CBT's relationship to RCTs means it is the primary (and for some conditions, the only) psychological therapy recommended by the National Institute for Health and Care Excellence (NICE), the government-sponsored arbiter of best clinical practice across all the health disciplines. This has led to huge shifts in the entire terrain of therapy in the UK today. We now have a 'new workforce' of CBT practitioners numbering tens of thousands (eg. Watts, 2016). This land-grab has come at the cost of more long-term relational therapies offered by more highly trained, and thus more expensive, psychologists and psychotherapists.

Last, RCTs and, indeed, the NICE guidelines for treatment of anxiety and depression (2009, 2017) reference CBT as if it were one thing. Yet, as we shall see, there are a huge number of approaches, with vastly contradictory epistemologies and techniques, that come under the CBT umbrella. By presenting these very different approaches as one, CBT gains power as a brand, as do its proponents. For example, nearly all the new chairs in psychotherapy and nearly all the new courses that have sprung up in universities in the past 10 years have 'CBT' in the title.

This is important, because legitimisation via evidence is crucial to constructing CBT. Consider a standard website describing 'What is CBT?' – that of the British Association for Behavioural & Cognitive Therapies (BABCP, 2012), the lead organisation for CBT in the UK, and arguably in the world. After only two sentences describing what CBT is, sentences we will return to later in this chapter, a sub-heading screams 'CBT works', and then sets out the evidence base, followed by a second sub-heading, 'What can CBT help with?', with details of problems that CBT is supposed to address. It is difficult to emphasise enough how universally this manoeuvre is used, not just to justify CBT but to actually describe it.

Making 'the right choice'

The other common technique is to describe CBT's superiority by inference. Consider a key publication, The Depression Report (Centre for Economic

Performance's Mental Health Policy Group, 2006). 'These new therapies are not endless nor backward-looking treatments,' the opening page declares. No, indeed: 'They are short, forward-looking treatments that enable people to challenge their negative thinking and build on the positive side of their personalities and situations.' The clear implication, with no supporting evidence, is that all other therapies are the obverse. This rhetorical device is powerful, and further pumped with affect-provoking words such as 'exciting', 'initiative' and 'progressive', with the aim to ensure people make what the 'right choices' for their treatment. Who would want to be backward-looking? Who would want to be seen to make the wrong choice?

This emphasis, however, is also related to a problem defining what CBT actually is. Of course, different forms of CBT do not need to share all the same premises. But one expects, needs, a 'family resemblance' of overlapping similarities to justify category inclusion (Wittgenstein, 1973). Before exploring this further, it is important to note, above and beyond these problems, that, even if one accepts RCTS are a valid – the valid – way of assessing the worth of a psychotherapy, the actual evidence base is not as brilliant as suggested.

A deniable evidence base

Consider CBT for Psychosis, which is supposed to be evidence based, according to the BABCP – a claim it backs up by reference to CBT's prominent location in the NICE guidelines. There is, in fact, considerable debate about whether CBT for Psychosis is effective (Kinderman, McKenna & Laws, 2015) and has any differential effect in comparison with 'befriending' (a control arm in many of the big studies). Such evidence suggests that, while CBT may work, its effect is equivalent to any other relational supplement to 'treatment as usual'. Consider also CBT as practised in IAPT. Layard's discourse implies that mental health conditions are like measles – discrete illnesses that can be 'cured' with the 'right treatment' – but, in fact, cure is a distant dream for the five out of six people referred to IAPT who do not recover (eg. Watts, 2016).

The results that both CBT for Psychosis and IAPT actually produce are, of course, off-message. Although there are many researchers and clinicians who wrestle with this and try to improve things, they tend to be strangely silent when it comes to challenging public discourse about the evidence base around CBT (and the content of the websites of the organisations to which they belong). Of course, CBT practitioners are not exceptional in their bias, which for most people is unconscious and unplanned. But what is unique is a lack of thinking about how vested interests might operate to influence how we read and process data, even though such biases are central to human reasoning, according to CBT.

Legitimising assertions

The actual state of the evidence is masked when authority is asserted through inclusion in the NICE guidelines for treating mental disorders. NICE holds the function of a 'third', which is used to bolster a claimed position of neutral objectivity in the relationship between clinicians and the evidence base. Using the NICE guidelines to bolster a claim to objectivity is problematic. NICE guidelines are decided on a voting system, by committees of people who are usually experts in precisely the therapies that reinforce the RCT ideology (see Moncrieff & Timimi, 2013). Further, NICE guidelines are only revised a couple of times a decade, and it is a long, laborious process. They are nearly always out of date by the time they are published. Last, NICE guidelines only include studies of particular conditions (eg. depression, anxiety), using particular models (eg. CBT, psychodynamic therapy); they ignore the substantial data on trans-modality and trans-condition efficacy. Asserting the evidence base as a form of objective legitimisation is thus problematic.

So far we have focused on how CBT is achieved as a thing by assertion and constant reference to the evidence base, and legitimised by reference to outside bodies such as NICE, and by comparison with other therapies that are deemed 'backwards looking'. But what CBT actually is remains unclear. I would like to turn now to the question of whether there is any family resemblance within the CBT family. To explore this, we need to begin with an exploration of what people mean when they refer to CBT.

Which CBT?

Those 'against CBT' tend to evoke an image of Aaron Beck's CBT – a logico-rational enterprise between a therapist and a client, focusing on changing cognition, or thought (Beck Institute, 2016). This is often referred to as second-wave cognitive behavioural therapy, in contrast to the retrospectively named first-wave, behaviourism. While the shift from first-wave to second-wave techniques is storied as 'progressive', a result of CBT's focus on scientific discovery, the reasons for this development are more complex (eg. Rachman, 2014).

As power dynamics within society at large changed in the 1960s and 1970s, horizontalising relationships between expert and client, the 'doing to' and manipulative aspects of behaviourism became less palatable. The addition of the cognitive element, 'C', then, was partially public relations – to be seen to incorporate subjective human experience. For, while Beck has argued the 'C' was necessary to treat depression, which had proved resistance to behaviourism, the 'C' was then also added to effective behavioural treatments for panic and OCD, despite evidence that the addition of cognition made no difference to efficacy (for evidence on behavioural activation, see Ekers, Richards & Gilbody, 2008).

Rather than acknowledge the 'C' was only differentially effective for depression, Beck and other practitioners joined 'C' with 'B' to produce CBT, which was then applied to each and every condition, despite epistemological clashes between behaviourism and cognitive therapy. It was convenient, and it sold. This move was picked up by psychologists. One in particular, Hans Eysenck, was unhappy with psychology's place in the emerging NHS. It was rather looked down on as a profession, focused as it was at that time on assessment and measurement, not treatment (eg. Hall & Pilgrim, 2015). CBT became used as a way to legitimise clinical psychology as a profession that could enter the talking therapy space previously occupied by psychoanalysts and psychotherapists, while claiming a distinct (more valuable) identity through CBT's tie to science, a 'master signifier' of the day (Lacan, 2004).

A typical CBT session

Let's turn now to a standard CBT session. A client is given a 'thought record' (eg. Hundt et al, 2013), and asked to identify the 'hot cognition' that is bothering them. This thought is then rated on the weight of 'evidence for' and 'evidence against' it. Often, this jury-type examination will result in the writing of a new belief. Thus, 'I can't do anything' might be rewritten as, 'I can sometimes do things, but sometimes struggle.' In Beck's model, common problems like social anxiety or depression are seen as linked to dysfunctional ways of thinking and information biases (eg. Beck Institute, 2016).

Someone with anxiety might be seen as having 'danger-oriented beliefs' and prone to 'jumping to conclusions'. Childhood experiences are not up for discussion. Rather, clients are heavily socialised into certain ideas – that their problems can be changed by thinking differently, that emotional difficulties like depression and anxiety can be cured, and that people can be trained to think in non-disordered ways (eg. Richards & Whyte, 2011). Socialisation into these ideas starts with information leaflets, posters and – crucially – the outcome measures that patients are often required to fill in at each and every session. These materials shape the subjectivity of both patient and therapist – that the 'right' goal is symptom reduction rather than understanding, for example (Watts, 2016). The focus here is on creating what Foucault refers to as 'governable subjects' who construct their distress as an individualised problem, a 'private trouble' to be solved by therapeutic means (Giddens, 2013). This forecloses evidence that links such distress to material conditions such as poverty, job insecurity and temporary accommodation (eg. Psychologists Against Austerity, 2015).

The psychocentrism that Becksian CBT propagates pushes responsibility for mental health onto the individual, who must use CBT techniques to restore a balance or less problematic equilibrium. The procedures used to achieve this have, for many, an echo of 'disciplinary power' (eg. Foucault, 1977), of prescribing new 'emotional rules' about which emotions are ok, and to what degree, and imposing self-help techniques, self-observation and table drawing. While this is storied as free choice, or 'collaborative empiricism', to use the CBT terminology, the degree of socialisation into giving the 'right messages' implies the freedom is actually freedom within constraints defined by ideological norms (see Proctor, Chapter 2, this volume). The power relations inherent within this are masked by both an obsession with the idea that CBT is collaborative, and ever-shorter trainings that are now frequently focused just on CBT, and so packed with manuals for specific conditions that reflection outside the tenets of the model is near impossible.

The core notion behind these claims – that CBT works through changing the content of thoughts – has been called into question by practitioners from what has become known as the third-wave of cognitive behavioural therapies (eg. Brown, Gaudiano & Miller, 2011).

A different CBT

For a couple of decades now, there has been considerable unease about whether the logico-rational techniques of thought-challenging are actually what changes things in CBT (eg. Longmore & Worrell, 2007). As a result of this unease, a number of therapies (eg. Kahl, Winter & Schweiger, 2012) started to bubble up in the late 1990s, focusing not on the content of thought but on the individual's relation to it – metacognition – the very process of thinking itself (eg. Dobson, 2013). As well as springing from radically different ideas about the relationship between language and suffering (eg. Hayes, Strosahl & Wilson, 2004), these approaches give the client a very different clinical experience.

In comparison with the Becksian example above, a session might involve the client eating a raisin incredibly slowly, attending to each and every texture and sensation, in order to become present in the moment, or creating and visualising a safe place to provide an anchor point at moments of trauma (eg. Hayes, Strosahl & Wilson, 2004). Rather than see thoughts as dysfunctional or irrational, the emphasis is on changing one's relationship with one's thoughts, defusing their significance and tackling experiential avoidance instead.

These new approaches were initially ridiculed, and their leaders parodied as cultish. The most famous example of this was a 2006 TIME magazine piece on Steve Hayes, the founder of acceptance and commitment therapy (ACT), which ends with the line that ACT will only succeed if it loses 'its icky zealotry and grandiose predictions' (Cloud, 2006). ACT practitioners were initially excluded from CBT conferences. However, they have since been welcomed into the CBT fold, as they have shown that even Becksian CBT might not work by changing the content of thoughts but by producing a space between the self and thoughts. This revelation, along with evidence that approaches that focus simply on behaviour can be just as effective (after Ekers, Richards & Gilbody, 2008), and that the therapeutic relationship itself is the greatest moderator of change (eg. Lambert & Barley, 2001), have seriously dented Becksian claims that it has something unique to offer, and that its theory is coherent with its practice. But they have also given CBT an escape clause.

The grab-all elements of CBT

The humility that you might expect to be engendered by these realisations about what actually produces change has been hindered by a smash-and-grab approach to any new moderator of change, all of which have been co-opted as CBT. Examples of approaches that have been sucked into the CBT vortex include attachment theory (from psychoanalysis – eg. Taylor et al, 2014), mindfulness (from Eastern wisdom traditions – eg. Teasdale et al, 2000), and compassion (from Plato and, well, everyone – eg. Gilbert, 2009). Practitioners using these other approaches – which have no family resemblance to Becksian thinking – are often complicit in placing their therapies under the umbrella of CBT because there are vested interests in doing this: it brings money, grants, faculty position, shared membership of what CBT apologist Richard Layard evangelically frames as a 'forward-looking' and 'progressive' movement (Centre for Economic Performance's Mental Health Policy Group, 2006). A typical example of this is the popular philosophers who claim, when it is in their interests, that the Stoics got there first (eg. Robertson, 2010), but become part of CBT when there are books to sell or grants to be won (eg. Sadler, 2017). Yet joining this discourse community has consequences.

As one of many possible examples, the radical possibility for mindfulness to exist as an alternative, leftist antidote to suffering – equally effective as CBT (Freeman & Freeman, 2015) but with more community-focused ideology (eg. Rothberg, 2006) – is lost by its subsuming as a form of CBT (for example, mindfulness-based cognitive therapy is 95% the same as mindfulness-based stress reduction, a package that does not belong to psychology (eg. Diggins, 2012)). In this transaction, CBT as a brand gets to position itself as 'cutting edge', although the explanations for change given to the majority of its clients, and evangelised to the public, no longer fit the science. It also gets to boost its membership with new recruits, eager to belong and pay heavy, lucrative membership fees.

Inclusion as shield

Such politicking provides a useful shield to criticisms, with few willing to challenge CBT's dominance. For example, in a special edition of The Psychologist focused on critiquing CBT, authors felt the need to state that they were 'careful not to eschew CBT in itself, which has much to commend it' (Hall & Marzillier, 2009: 396). By conflating a number of vastly divergent approaches with strikingly different ideas of what it means to be human and to suffer and calling them CBT, its proponents can de-legitimise critics by claiming that they do not know 'modern CBT' (Dummett, 2010). CBT, we hear, is no longer about adapting individuals to reality; that is 'based on outdated understandings' – a powerful way to shut down dissent. Yes, techniques from ACT, for example, can be more radical. But this response negates the actuality – that, for all the seeming variation, the overwhelming majority of CBTs still follow Becksian principles of normalisation, fitting a governmental agenda of producing docile working subjects who contribute to the economy and shut up (eg. Watts, 2016).

We know this because the overwhelming majority of what is categorised as CBT is offered by psychological wellbeing practitioners (PWPs) in Improving

Access to Psychological Therapies (IAPT) services. The manuals that they use are available to evidence this (eg. Richards & Whyte, 2011). The price of locating newer therapies with very different ideas and promising research findings under the CBT mantle, despite the lack of family resemblance, is thus that it props up normalising therapies that transmit an individualistic, neoliberal agenda. This meta-narrative, and its shaping effects, is continuously associated with poor mental health by service users (eg. Psychologists Against Austerity, 2015). Just as worrying, the normative focus and emphasis on learning techniques to make emotions more manageable mean that only those who are comparatively well off have access to genuine talking, exploratory therapies, in the private sector. This may be convenient for the government – talking, after all, can be dangerous – but it is an epistemic injustice to those whose lives go untold.

It is useful here to pause and see how CBT uses its smash-and-grab approach to shield itself from criticism. Dummett (2010) provides a useful table on common misperceptions of CBT and the BABCP's response (Dummett, 2010). These echo the defences of CBT one hears in the public realm. Let's take a few examples.

One of the misperceptions is that 'CBT is always a brief form of therapy'. The BABCP response is: 'the duration and frequency of therapy follow from the formulation.' This is wishful thinking. In fact, staff in IAPT and secondary services nearly always have to work to a pre-designated number of sessions, based on what their problem is supposed to be (depression, anxiety, and so on). Clinicians can occasionally argue for an extension, based on a formulation, but this has to be absolutely exceptional or a clinician's competence is called into question (eg. Watts, 2016). Given clinicians' wish to be seen as competent, and the mortgages and cash flow that rely on job stability, most IAPT workers and psychological therapists swallow their objections to having to see desperately in-need clients for a shorter time than desired (eg. Cooke & Watts, 2016).

Another 'misperception' is that 'CBT does not address unconscious processes or take into account past experiences'. The BABCP response, according to Dummett, is that 'formulation of causative, precipitating and maintaining factors encompassing past experience and explicit exploration of unconscious material are fundamental'. Here, we see once more the idea that CBT can do everything. But there is a chasm between discourse and reality. CBT does include references to the causes of distress, in the form of a box on a formulation that is occasionally alluded to as an explainer, but it is constantly blocked as something to explore in depth, despite evidence that CBT clients are often desperate to talk about what has happened to them (eg. Griffiths et al, 2013). Only a small teaspoon of CBT, as practised in the NHS, looks more seriously at childhood (for example, schema-focused therapy), but here too the unconscious and the lure, say, of the death drive are not taken in any way seriously.

The scant attention given to childhood in most CBTs, the brief acknowledgment, works for some – fantastic. But for those who need and would be helped by having this pain born witness to, the 'look-we-do-this-too' reaction shuts down the possibility, both practically and at the level of thinking. For example, a CBT practitioner can, and often will, say that they explore childhood experiences, like bullying and sexual abuse. But, in effect, this often consists of a session at most of listening and empathising before the agenda is set to using this outpouring to make sense of present day cognitions, which can now be altered as trauma has been tagged as a past event no longer of threat. This produces a discursive trap, a double bind, for patients who want and need a space to process trauma in depth, yet are shut down when informed that CBT does this – if that has failed, there is nothing else.

Claiming to be able to do everything, and publicising itself as such, makes dissent more and more difficult. How can a client choose not to have a CBT, for example, because they want to focus on childhood trauma, if the powerful message is 'CBT does this too?'

Depoliticising distress

Consider in more detail mindfulness, which now has an evidence base equal to Becksian CBT (eg. Sundquist et al, 2014). Co-opting meditation as a CBT to be offered as a treatment option by the state, alongside outcome measures communicating that the goal is functional relationships, happiness and work, individualises pain. This is a different political act to supporting meditation's expansion into the community – a growth that nearly always leads to a focus on compassion and radical social action (eg. Rothberg, 2006) — as community is one of the only ways to ensure daily practice is continued after the initial high that comes with doing something new. This is one of many examples of how the interests of CBT and government are now closely intertwined, and how framing everything as CBT is a political act.

The search for family resemblance

But surely there must be a missing commonality? If we look closely at the literature, some studies refer to CBT as an 'umbrella' of techniques (eg. Dobson, 2009). Of course, the concept of an umbrella certainly implies a commonality, a family resemblance at least. Yet each and every attempt to locate this is problematic. A focus on cognition and behaviour? Find me a talking therapy that does not attempt to alter thinking and behaviour through speech. Evidence base? Why, psychodynamic and systemic family approaches also play the evidence-base game nowadays (eg. Shedler, 2012; Von Sydow et al, 2010). Goal-directed and present-focused? But many of the newer CBTs spend a lot of time focusing on childhood (eg. Taylor, Bee & Haddock, 2017), and many therapies that are based on the present and goal-directed are not CBT (eg. O'Connell, 2005).

As these attempts at commonality fail, we are sold a shared history, a development from first-wave behaviourism to second-wave (predominantly Becksian) CBT, and then third-wave, often metacognitively focused, therapies. Yet this history-telling, when it occurs, constructs a linear, progressive narrative (eg. Rachman, 2014) that just does not fit with the facts.

Although the metaphor of waves implies these things come from the same sea, the manufacturing of the story of CBT in this way is a politicised choice. Other ways of story-telling are available to us. For example, one could see Becksian therapy as just as much about earlier psychoanalysis as earlier behaviourism. Beck, after all, was responding to his frustration in his early career as a psychoanalyst, and it is perhaps not coincidental that the great proponent of Becksian CBT in the UK, Richard Layard, grew up in a household where both parents were qualified Jungian analysts (Wikipedia, 2016). The metacognitive therapies cluster as much with the story of meditation, rooted in the caves of Tibet (eg. Newharbinger, 2015), as with Pavlov's original experiments with dogs (eg. Rachman, 2014).

Beyond CBT

However, the most persuasive re-storying of CBT – for me, at least – springs from putting aside therapy brands and considering how therapeutic practice actually advances. The most celebrated CBT theorists in the new wave of therapies draw not from science but from their own experience of pain. The founder of ACT, Steve Hayes, developed his techniques from his own destabilising panic attacks (Cloud, 2006), while the originator of dialectical behaviour therapy, Marsha Linehan, draws from her experiences as a psychiatric inpatient (Carey, 2011). These sufferers found some solace in ways of living that bubbled up from their own profound experience of pain, and which they modified from Eastern wisdom traditions.

Theory? Research? Packaging? Those came later. It was precisely their rejection of contemporary brands that allowed these clinicians to discover something new. Thus, therapeutic change comes from looking inside to generate evidence – not from trying to impose ideas from outside. The more attached we become to brands, the more we insist on stamping them on therapists and the client's experience of therapy, the less we allow clients to follow the great therapeutic innovators and create therapy anew for themselves. Practice and theory have produced some ideas that can help – that control may be the problem, not the solution (Hayes, Strosahl & Wilson, 2004); that avoiding experience leads to squashed lives (eg. Kashdan et al, 2006); that childhood sets the template for how we live (eg. Luborsky & Barrett, 2011). These belong, however, not to CBT but to human experience.

References

BABCP (2012). *What is CBT?* [Online.] www.babcp.com/Public/What-is-CBT.aspx (accessed 19 December 2016).

Beck Institute (2016). *What is CBT (Cognitive Behavior Therapy)?* [Online.] www.beckinstitute.org/get-informed/cbt-faqs (accessed 21 December 2016).

British Psychoanalytic Council/ UK Council for Psychotherapy (2015). *Addressing the Deterioration in Public Psychotherapy Provision*. London: BPC/UKCP.

Brown L, Gaudiano B, Miller I (2011). Investigating the similarities and differences between practitioners of second- and third-wave cognitive-behavioral therapies. *Behavior Modification 35*(2): 187–200.

Carey B (2011). Expert on Mental Illness Reveals her own Fight. [Online.] *New York Times*; 23 June. www.nytimes.com/2011/06/23/health/23lives.html?_r=1&pagewanted=all& (accessed 4 February 2017).

Centre for Economic Performance's Mental Health Policy Group (2006). *The Depression Report: a new deal for depression and anxiety disorders*. London: London School of Economics.

Cloud J (2006). The third wave of therapy. [Online.] *TIME* (February). www.livskompass.se/wp-content/uploads/2013/02/Cloud-2006-Happiness-is-not-normal-Hayes.pdf (accessed 7 February 2018).

Cooke A, Watts J (2016). We're not surprised half our psychologist colleagues are depressed. [Online.] *The Guardian*; 17 February. www.theguardian.com/healthcare-network/2016/feb/17/were-not-surprised-half-our-psychologist-colleagues-are-depressed (accessed 9 February 2017).

Diggins N (2012). *The Difference Between MBCT & MBSR*. [Online.] Mindfulness for Wellbeing. http://mindfulnessforwellbeing.co.uk/mindfulness-brighton-mbct-for-reducing-stress-depression-and-anxiety/difference-mbct-mbsr (accessed 4 February 2017).

Dobson KS (2013). The science of CBT: toward a metacognitive model of change? *Behavior Therapy 44*(2): 224–227.

Dobson KS (2009). *Handbook of Cognitive-Behavioral Therapies* (3rd ed). New York: Guilford Press.

Dummett N (2010). Cognitive–behavioural therapy with children, young people and families: from individual to systemic therapy. *Advances in Psychiatric Treatment 16*(1): 23–36.

Ekers D, Richards D, Gilbody S (2008). A meta-analysis of randomized trials of behavioural treatment of depression. *Psychological Medicine 38*(5): 611–623.

Foucault M (1977). *Discipline and Punish: the birth of the prison* (2nd ed). New York, NY: Knopf Doubleday Publishing Group.

Freeman D, Freeman J (2015). New study shows mindfulness therapy can be as effective as antidepressants. [Online.] *The Guardian*; 21 April. www.theguardian.com/science/blog/2015/apr/21/could-mindfulness-therapy-be-an-alternative-to-antidepressants (accessed 4 February 2017).

Giddens A (2013). *The Transformation of Intimacy: sexuality, love, and eroticism in modern societies*. Chichester: Wiley.

Gilbert P (2009). Introducing compassion-focused therapy. *Advances in Psychiatric Treatment 15*(3): 199-208.

Griffiths S, Foster J, Steen S, Pietroni P (2013). *Mental Health's Market Experiment: commissioning psychological therapies through Any Qualified Provider*. Chester: Centre for Psychological Therapies in Primary Care, University of Chester.

Guy A, Thomas R, Stephenson S, Loewenthal D (2011). *NICE under Scrutiny: the impact of the National Institute for Health and Clinical Excellence guidelines on the provision of psychotherapy in the UK*. London: UKCP Research Unit/Research Centre for Therapeutic Education, Roehampton University. www.easewellbeing.co.uk/downloads/nice%20report%20ukcp.pdf (accessed 7 February 2017).

Hall J, Marzillier (2009). Alternative ways of working. *The Psychologist 22*(5): 406–408.

Hall J, Pilgrim D (2015). *Clinical Psychology in Britain: historical perspectives.* Leicester: British Psychological Society.

Harvey A, Watkins E, Mansell W, Shafran R (2004). *Cognitive Behavioural Processes Across Psychological Disorders: a transdiagnostic approach to research and treatment.* New York, NY: Oxford University Press.

Hayes SC, Strosahl KD, Wilson KG (2004). *Acceptance and Commitment Therapy: an experiential approach to behavior change.* New York, NY: Guilford Press.

House R, Loewenthal D (eds) (2008). *Against and for CBT: towards a constructive dialogue?* Ross-on-Wye: PCCS Books.

Hundt NE, Mignogna J, Underhill C, Cully JA (2013). The relationship between use of CBT skills and depression treatment outcome: a theoretical and methodological review of the literature. *Behavior Therapy 44*(1): 12–26.

Kahl K, Winter L, Schweiger U (2012). The third wave of cognitive behavioural therapies: what is new and what is effective? *Current Opinion in Psychiatry 25*(6): 522–528.

Kashdan TB, Barrios V, Forsyth JP, Steger MF (2006). Experiential avoidance as a generalized psychological vulnerability: comparisons with coping and emotion regulation strategies. *Behaviour Research and Therapy 44*(9): 1301–1320.

Kinderman P, McKenna P, Laws KR (2015). Are psychological therapies effective in treating schizophrenia and psychosis? *Progress in Neurology and Psychiatry 19*(1): 17–20.

Lacan J (2004). *The Four Fundamental Concepts of Psycho-Analysis.* London: Karnac Books.

Lambert MJ, Barley DE (2001). Research summary of the therapeutic relationship and psychotherapy outcome. *Psychotherapy: Theory, Research, Practice, Training 38*(4): 357–361.

Longmore RJ, Worrell M (2007). Do we need to challenge thoughts in cognitive behavior therapy? *Clinical Psychology Review 27*(2): 173–187.

Luborky L, Barrett MS (2011). The core conflictual relationship theme: a basic case formulation method. In: Eells TD (ed). *Handbook of Psychotherapy Case Formulation* (2nd ed). New York, NY: Guilford Press (pp105–135).

Moncrieff J, Timimi S (2013). The social and cultural construction of psychiatric knowledge: an analysis of NICE guidelines on depression and ADHD. *Anthropology & Medicine 20*(1): 59–71.

Newharbinger (2015). *ACT and Compassion: a Q&A with Dennis Tirch PhD, & Laura Silberstein PsyD.* [Blog.] www.newharbinger.com/blog/act-and-compassion-qa-dennis-tirch-phd-laura-silberstein-psyd (accessed 4 February 2017).

NICE (2017). Depression in adults: treatment and management. Draft for consultation. London: NICE.

NICE (2009). Depression in adults: recognition and management. London: NICE.

O'Connell B (2005). *Solution-focused Therapy* (2nd ed). London: Sage.

Psychologists Against Austerity (2015). *The Psychological Impact of Austerity: a briefing paper.* [Online.] https://psychagainstausterity.files.wordpress.com/2015/03/paa-briefing-paper.pdf (accessed 4 February 2017).

Rachman S (2014). The evolution of behaviour therapy and cognitive behaviour therapy. *Behaviour Research and Therapy 64*: 1–8.

Richards D, Whyte M (2011) *Reach Out: national programme student materials to support the delivery of training for psychological wellbeing practitioners delivering low intensity interventions* (3rd ed). London:

Rethink/National Mental Health Development Unit.

Robertson D (2010). *The Philosophy of Cognitive-Behavioural Therapy (CBT): stoic philosophy as rational and cognitive psychotherapy*. London: Karnac Books.

Rothberg D (2006). *The Engaged Spiritual Life: a Buddhist approach to transforming ourselves and the world.* Boston, MA: Beacon Press.

Sadler G (2017). Stoic Week 2016: report part 3 (of 4) – impact on well-being by Tim LeBon. [Online.] *Modern Stoicism*, 21 January. http://modernstoicism.com/stoic-week-2016-report-part-3-of-4-impact-on-well-being-by-tim-lebon/ (accessed 4 February 2017).

Shedler J (2012). The efficacy of psychodynamic psychotherapy. In: Levy R, Ablon J, Kächele H (eds). *Psychodynamic Psychotherapy Research: evidence-based practice and practice-based evidence.* Totowa, NJ: Humana Press (pp9-26).

Slade M, Priebe S (2001). Are randomised controlled trials the only gold that glitters? *British Journal of Psychiatry 179*(4): 286–287.

Sundquist J, Lilja Å, Palmér K, Memon AA, Wang X, Johansson LM, Sundquist K (2014). Mindfulness group therapy in primary care patients with depression, anxiety and stress and adjustment disorders: randomised controlled trial. [Online.] *British Journal of Psychiatry 206*(2): 128–135.

Taylor CDJ, Bee P, Haddock G (2017). Does schema therapy change schemas and symptoms? A systematic review across mental health disorders. *Psychology and Psychotherapy: Theory, Research and Practice 90*(3): 456–479.

Taylor P, Rietzschel J, Danquah A, Berry K (2014). Changes in attachment representations during psychological therapy. *Psychotherapy Research 25*(2): 222–238.

Teasdale JD, Segal ZV, Williams JMG, Ridgeway VA, Soulsby JM, Lau MA (2000). Prevention of relapse/recurrence in major depression by mindfulness-based cognitive therapy. *Journal of Consulting and Clinical Psychology 68*(4): 615.

Von Sydow K, Beher S, Schweitzer J, Retzlaff R (2010). The efficacy of systemic therapy with adult patients: a meta-content analysis of 38 randomized controlled trials. *Family process 49*(4): 457–485.

Watts J (2016). IAPT and the ideal image. In: Lees J (ed). *The Future of Psychological Therapy: from managed care to transformational practice*. Abingdon: Routledge (pp84–101).

Wikipedia (2016). *John Layard*. [Online.] https://en.wikipedia.org/wiki/John_Layard (accessed 4 February 2017).

Wittgenstein L (1973). *Philosophical Investigations* (3rd ed). Oxford: Blackwell Publishers.

PARADIGMATIC PERSPECTIVES

7 Behaviour therapy and the ideology of modernity*

Robert L Woolfolk and Frank C Richardson

This chapter presents a critique of behaviour therapy. The moral and epistemological underpinnings of behaviour therapy are analysed from a socio-historical, hermeneutic perspective. The *Weltanschauung* (philosophy, or world-view) of behaviour therapy is shown to be closely linked with the values and patterns of thought characteristic of modernity, and the implications of behaviour therapy's close association with modern ideological positions are discussed.

A lucid and highly regarded textbook on behaviour therapy offers the following definition:

> As an applied science, behavior therapy is simply a collection of principles and techniques about how to change behavior; it says nothing about who should modify what behavior, why, or when' (Wilson & O'Leary, 1980: 285).

Although behaviour therapy has been given many other definitions (Bandura, 1969; Wolpe, 1973), virtually all have conceived of it as a neutral structure, a body of 'objective knowledge' verified by experimental test. Behaviour therapy's self-image is that of an applied science, devoid of any inherent prescriptive thrust or implicit system of values, the essence of which can be accounted for without reference to any cultural or historical context. Work in the philosophy and history of science, however, has undermined seriously the view of science on which behaviour therapy's self-image is based.

Attempts to equate scientific knowledge with that which is empirically verifiable or to identify scientific progress with some inflexible standard of verification have proven lacking (Bartley, 1962; Burtt, 1964; Weimer, 1979). The

* The original version of this chapter first appeared in the *American Psychologist* 1984; 39(7): 777–786.

form and content of scientific knowledge are strongly influenced by socio-political factors, as well as those related to the attitudes and sensibilities of the community of scientists (Feyerabend, 1975; Kuhn, 1970a, 1970b; Polanyi, 1966). Because their subject matter bears so directly on, and is influenced by, the human self-image, the social sciences and systems of psychotherapy are even more limited in their ability to remain independent of cultural influence (Buss, 1975; London, 1964; Lowe, 1976; Sampson, 1978, 1981).

The notion that all knowledge arises out of a social context and that, hence, a complete account of any system of thought must encompass its cultural and ideological foundations has its roots in the philosophies of Hegel and Marx and has found a strong expression in recent times in three related intellectual movements: the sociology of knowledge, critical theory, and hermeneutic philosophy. Our analysis of behaviour therapy draws on all three of these sources.

The sociology of knowledge (Berger & Luckman, 1966; Mannheim, 1936; Scheler, 1960) takes the perspective that knowledge is one among the many and varied products of culture. Thinkers in this tradition seek to elucidate the relationship between the nature of a given society and the *Weltanschauungen* to which it gives rise, as well as the processes by which definitions of 'reality' are socially constructed. Critical theory (Habermas, 1972, 1973; Horkheimer, 1972) has been engaged in the critique of contemporary patterns of intellectual activity and of modern social institutions.

One of the main concerns of thinkers in this tradition has been to trace the connection between, on the one hand, intellectual and social forms of fragmentation and alienation in modern society, and on the other, the increasing rationalisation (in the Weberian sense) of the relations of social life in a technically managed society. The interpretive or hermeneutic approach to the study of human society and action (Gadamer, 1975; Ricoeur, 1981; Taylor, 1971) holds that any scientific account of human activity is, of necessity, epistemologically embedded within a world of intersubjective cultural meanings that are constitutive of the conceptual categories within which the science operates. From this perspective, no social science can ever truly stand outside or transcend the social practices and institutions that have served to constitute it in the first place.

From the perspectives of the sociology of knowledge, critical theory and hermeneutics, behaviour therapy is a more interesting and complex phenomenon than it purports to be. In addition to being a scientific account of the alteration of emotional and behavioural problems, behaviour therapy is also an intellectual movement, a set of social practices and a system of thought. In each of these guises, it contains not only theoretical and technological aspects but also a prescriptive, ideological component: a favoured mode of thinking and implicit criteria for making judgments that guide behaviour therapists in their activities and also represent a vision of reality underlying the activities that justify and support them. Our approach to behaviour therapy will not be to examine it as a body of techniques and a supporting theory to be compared on the dimensions of technical efficacy or theoretical elegance with some other therapeutic school, such as psychoanalysis. Indeed, to do so would leave unexamined those tacit, epistemological biases and value commitments that must be encompassed by any fundamental critique.

Rather, we will show how behaviour therapy is implicitly predicated on modern epistemological and ethical assumptions. We will also demonstrate how its scientific technological sensibility is reflected in both its immense and estimable achievements as well as in what appear to be very serious limitations in its capacity to address some aspects of the human situation that are basic to the conduct of psychotherapy in the contemporary world. Our explication of the ideological underpinnings of behaviour therapy is closely related to an analysis of modernity and modern modes of thought.

Modernity

Modernity refers to the total condition of culture in those societies that have been transformed by science and the application of scientific technology. What is involved in modernisation is a 'total' transformation of a traditional or pre-modern society into the types of technology and associated social organisation that characterise the 'advanced', economically prosperous, and relatively politically stable nations of the western world. (Moore, 1963: 89)

Along with the application of scientific technology to the means of production within a society come inevitable changes in the world-view of its people (Berger, 1977). This modernisation of the consciousness of pre-modern cultures is a reliable, patterned phenomenon that has been occurring in western societies since the advent of the Industrial Revolution (Nelson, 1981). Such changes of outlook begin in the intellectual elites and extend to the population at large, as education, the absorption of individuals into modern, technocratically managed institutions, and the proliferation of media become more widespread (Parsons, 1971).

The world-view of modernity is dominated by science and scientific technology and the modes of thought peculiar to them (Gehlen, 1980). It is rooted in the ideal of progress, a faith in the power of human abilities to be equal to any problem, the quest for certitude, and a devaluation of the traditional past (Shils, 1981). The cognitive style of modern consciousness tends toward the pragmatic and the rational. The focus of evaluation shifts from the ends of activity to its means and their efficiency, as technique and technical considerations achieve paramount importance. Utility emerges as a generally agreed-upon value (Ellul, 1964). The aims of prediction and control, and a style of planning and decision-making in which emotional and aesthetic considerations are subservient to the rational and pragmatic are the essential features of modern organisational direction, whether those organisations be communist bureaucracies or capitalist industrial corporations (Berger, Berger & Kellner, 1973). Science becomes the ultimate source of knowledge and the model for all forms of intellectual activity (Hayek, 1952; Winner, 1977).

Modernisation, whether it be of society or of methods of psychotherapy, always cuts two ways. Within society, the same forces that boldly advance human freedom and opportunity also erode those traditional belief systems that confer meaning on experience and do damage to those social institutions that sustain emotional security, thus creating the heretofore novel human predicaments of loss of meaning, isolation and alienation (Baumer, 1977). There is a 'dark side' to modernity chronicled thoroughly by sociologists from Weber to Berger: the 'disenchantment' of the world, the loss of community, the end of a self-evident moral structure and of a meaningful relationship between individual and cosmos.

The 'modern consciousness' of the industrialised west is a world-view beset with dilemmas and malaises not found in primitive and traditional views of reality (Levi-Strauss, 1966). So, too, the world-view of behaviour therapy, even in its most complex and sophisticated contemporary variations – for example, cognitive behaviour therapy – partakes so fully of the modern perspective on life and living that it is consequently subject to both the advantages and disadvantages of the modern outlook. In this respect, behaviour therapy is not unique among systems of therapy, many of which have 'modern' thrusts (Bergin, 1980), but is rather a purer and more extreme embodiment of the chief strains of modernity.

The behavioural *Weltanschauung*

Behaviour therapy is a quintessential modern set of activities: the application of a scientifically derived technology to the alteration of behaviour. It is, in addition, a system of thought that adopts a radically scientific and technological perspective on human contact and on the enterprise of behaviour change. Behaviour therapy, in its theory and clinical practice, exemplifies both modern modes of thinking and the values of the modern technological society. The close affinity of the *Weltanschauung* of behaviour therapy and that of modernity can be seen clearly by examining the presence in behaviour therapy of four distinct but interrelated aspects of modernity: technicism, rationality, amorality, and humanism.

Technicism

Although virtually every other system of therapy is partially composed of therapeutic activities that could be properly regarded as techniques, none has sought more self-consciously than behaviour therapy to function as pure 'psychotechnology'. No other has sought to characterise itself almost entirely in terms of relationships between sets of explicit therapeutic aims and specific methods thought reliably to achieve those aims as 'an empirically based technology of behaviour change' (Kazdin & Wilson, 1978: 178).

Most other systems carry what is, from a technological vantage point, some excess baggage: a) methods of treatment that lack power, directness, and immediacy; b) a theory of human functioning that contains rather obvious prescriptive components and, hence, a moral thrust, or c) a prizing of certain forms of understanding or experiencing simply for their own sake, apart from any measurable, correlated changes in behaviour that might ensue.

From its inception, behaviour therapy adopted that most modern of sensibilities that has been variously termed the *technological attitude* (Berger & Kellner, 1981), or *technocratic consciousness* (Gouldner, 1976). From the very beginning, behaviour therapy avoided the sins of inactivity characteristic of the early insight therapies and placed its emphasis on the refinement of technique and on the achievement of measurable results (Kazdin, 1978). Perhaps the most distinctive feature of behaviour therapy's reformulation of psychotherapy theory and practice was its pragmatic temper, its insistence on the demonstrable utility of therapeutic activity, and its attempt to characterise that activity as a body of techniques with specific effects.

The goal of technology is the predictable, rational direction or control of events (Winner, 1977). Not surprisingly, the concept of control is crucial to behaviour therapy and permeates its literature. Krasner (1962) wrote that the fundamental aim of behaviour therapy research was that of devising 'techniques of behavior control' (p103). In their classic book, Goldfried and Davison (1976: 9) state: 'To begin with, the very fact that the client has sought help is an open admission that he has been unable to adequately control certain aspects of his own life.' Similarly, Lazarus (1976) identified the 'control' of unpleasant emotions as an important goal of multi-modal behaviour therapy. Those methods involving the self-administration of behavioural procedures, termed *self-control,* further attest to the technological attitude of the behaviour therapist. Here the therapist seeks to train the client to manipulate both self and environment so as to systematically regulate affect, cognition and behaviour. Clients are taught, in essence, how to engineer their own actions and feelings by the use of specific techniques. Krasner (1982) has suggested that all behaviour therapy procedures might be properly viewed as methods of self-control.

The technological orientation of behaviour therapy has without question enabled it to supply useful methodological and theoretical correctives to the field of psychotherapy and has greatly expanded the range of available therapeutic procedures. Successful technologies, however, carry with them a number of potential drawbacks. One unhappy effect of the proliferation of technology and technological thinking within contemporary society has been to drive out other forms of thinking, often resulting in a triumph of form over content, means over ends, methodology over theory (Barrett, 1978; Stanley, 1978). The ascendance of methodological and technical concerns can divert our attention from those troublesome questions that address the value of the goals achieved by the technology, or that ask upon what basis such goals are to be determined.

Rationality

Max Weber (1958) spoke of the pre-modern world appearing as an 'enchanted garden' to its inhabitants. He observed that, in contrast, 'the fate of our times is characterised by rationalisation and intellectualisation and, above all, by the "disenchantment of the world"' (p155). In a similar vein, Habermas (1973) has written that modern technological society prizes rationality above all other values:

> Because this value [rationality] can be legitimized by pointing to the process of scientific investigation and its technical application and does not have to be justified in terms of pure commitment alone, it has a preferential status as against all other values. (pp270–271)

Rationality can be thought of as the cognitive framework within which all forms of modern technological activity are constituted. It involves 'the imposition of strict means–end criteria … the exclusion of all that is purely traditional, charismatic, or ritualistic; all, in short, that is not directly related to the means necessary to efficient realization of a given end' (Nisbet, 1976: 111).

Those patterns of thought and action that accompany the application of technology are in close harmony with the values linked to the Apollonian sensibility (Berger, Berger & Kellner, 1973; Gehlen, 1980). The Apollonian–Dionysian continuum was first introduced by Nietzsche (1956) and was subsequently employed as a tool of cultural analysis by anthropologists (eg. Benedict, 1934). The Apollonian emphasises balance, restraint, order, reason and sobriety. The Dionysian, on the other hand, values extremism, intensity of experience, spontaneity, emotionality and passion.

The attitude of behaviour therapy toward emotion bespeaks its valuing of the rational, its Apollonian sensibility. The behaviour therapist does not 'work with' affect in any manner analogous to that of more traditional psychotherapy (Messer & Winokur, 1980). Helping clients 'get in touch with', develop or explore feelings is not a high priority in behaviour therapy. Even in those instances in which emotion is purposefully aroused, such as in flooding or implosive therapy, the aim is the extinction rather than the exploration or cultivation of emotional responsiveness or sensitivity (Wilson & Evans, 1977). Mahoney (1980) suggested that then-current cognitive behaviour therapists took an overly narrow view of emotion and has written critically of their 'strong and pervasive assumption' that feelings are phenomena to be 'averted, regulated, or otherwise controlled' (p167).

The behaviour therapy of the 1980s clearly emphasised rationality and logic over intuitive and emotional functions, perhaps to an even greater degree than in its precognitive days (Messer & Winokur, 1984). The cognitive revolution in behaviour therapy (Mahoney & Arnkoff, 1978; Meichenbaum, 1977) saw the rapid assimilation of therapies that stress reason, 'logical' thinking, and rational problem-solving. Among these consequent therapeutic inductees were rational-emotive therapy (Ellis & Grieger, 1977), cognitive therapy (Beck, 1976), and problem-solving therapy (D'Zurilla & Goldfried, 1971).

Many of the methods of behaviour therapy require of patients a rather advanced level of maturity, rationality or ego strength, call it what you will. The ability of clients to achieve clarity about what they want, to trust and collaborate with the therapist, and then to act rationally on the basis of that information are all presupposed by behavioural interventions, especially those procedures labelled *instigation therapy* by Kanfer and Phillips (1966), which involve implementation of specific suggestions by the clients in their daily environments. Gurman and Knudson (1978) have suggested that, in behavioural marital therapy, it is assumed (often incorrectly) that the spouses are two 'rational' adults 'in large part, directly open to the therapist's suggestions and counsel on how to achieve behavioral change... in their own rational self-interest' (p125). Yet numerous clients seemingly do not enter therapy able to function at such mature levels. In fact, deficits in 'maturity' may be the chief problem. In some clients, the capacities to act rationally on their own behalf must first be developed. How best to do so is a question to which many systems of psychotherapy have proposed many different answers, all of which involve clinical and theoretical incorporation of the irrational, emotion-driven aspects of life.

Both the limited power of the 'reason-based' methods of cognitive behaviour therapy to modify irrational feelings and actions, and the shortcomings of the theories of emotion upon which such methods are predicated have been underscored by a number of eminent behaviour therapists (Bandura, 1977; Rachman, 1981). In developing its own answer to the dilemmas posed by the resistance, lack of motivation, and seeming self-destructiveness manifested by many clients in therapy, modern behaviour therapy will probably need to achieve some improved formulation of the capricious and evanescent realm of affect (Pervin, 1981). Here it may find its Apollonian sensibility to be a hindrance.

Amorality

Amorality, when described as a dimension of modern consciousness, refers to the modern separation of fact and value and the removal of 'the good' from the objective order of things (Smith, 1982). This aspect of modernity is related to secularisation, the ascendance of science, and the proliferation of technical reason (Habermas, 1973). Within a technological society, the real, objective external reality of the world is constituted exclusively by empirically derived 'facts'. Morality comes to be viewed as subjective and relative (Adams, 1975; MacIntyre, 1981). Consistent with this axiological stance of modernity, behaviour therapists have tended to be ethical sceptics and relativists (Erwin, 1978; Kitchener, 1980). Behaviour therapy has also sought a clear demarcation between the realms of fact and value and has attempted to include within its purview only those propositions that could be verified by empirical test.

When contrasted with the theoretical foundations of other approaches, the clinical theory that underlies behaviour therapy is less normative. Two related developments in the history of behaviour therapy help to explain this lack of evaluative content.

The goals of traditional psychotherapy were provided in large measure by theories of personality that supplied some definition of what people ought to be and a picture of optimal human functioning. Numerous commentators have demonstrated the evaluative character of traditional personology (Hogan, 1975; Rieff, 1966; Sampson, 1977), revealing such constructs as 'sublimation', 'social interest', and 'self-actualisation' to be moral terms operating in disguise, and serving a clear prescriptive function within their respective approaches.

But the kind of personality theory that infused earlier systems of psychotherapy with prescriptive thrust was antithetical to the behavioural approach. In its first years, behaviour therapy favoured explanations of behavioural dysfunction derived from conditioning theory, and emphasised the external, observable determinants of behaviour. Mischel's (1968) critique of classical personology and psychodiagnosis was widely read and was so frequently cited by behaviour therapists that it came to be regarded as a basic text in the field. Behaviour therapy rejected trait-based conceptions of human behaviour (Craighead, Kazdin & Mahoney, 1981) in favour of a complex 'cognitive social learning theory' (Bandura, 1977; Mischel, 1973) that is neutral with respect to what would constitute a personal ideal or ideal person.

The inherent ethical thrust of behaviour therapy's clinical theory was also limited by what has frequently been cited as a defining characteristic of the approach (Kazdin, 1978) – that is, its opposition to the medical or disease model of psychological dysfunction. Here again, behaviour therapy divested itself of a system of global, evaluative labels that defines what kinds of persons are in need of therapeutic attention, and in what direction their behaviour ought to be changed. The amorality of behavioural clinical theory is entirely consistent with the proclivities of behaviour therapy toward objectivity and facticity. This kind of amorality, however, can serve a higher metamorality. The aspiration to a value-free clinical theory, one that minimally constrains possible therapeutic directions, is entirely consistent with the modern 'formal' virtues of freedom, tolerance, and equality (Stanley, 1978) and with an ideology that emphasises democratic humanism.

Humanism

One of the odd ironies that emerged from the early literature critical of behavioural approaches (eg. Wheelis, 1973) was the suggestion that behaviour therapy is antithetical to humanistic viewpoints. In the 1980s there were at least two versions of humanism reflected in contemporary psychology. The humanistic psychology of Rogers, Perls and Maslow espoused a kind of 'romantic' humanism in its emphasis on cultivation of the passions, aesthetic and emotional sensitivity and creativity. Behaviour therapy, on the other hand, was imbued with a 'classical' humanism. In fact, no other system of psychotherapy can lay such a direct and legitimate claim to the humanistic tradition of the Enlightenment. This is the tradition that, without reservation, commits its allegiance to the primacy of science and reason in intellectual affairs, opposes all irrational authority and arbitrary privilege, and dedicates itself to the active enhancement of human liberty (Brinton, 1963). 1980s humanistic psychology, with its emphasis on feeling and spontaneity, was certainly antagonistic to the rationality of behaviour therapy, just as the Romantic movement of the 19th century was opposed to the Enlightenment's subordination of other human capacities to the dictates of reason. Both behaviour therapy and humanistic psychology, however, reflect what is common to all forms of humanism: a dedication to the promotion of human freedom and happiness (Lamont, 1982).

The early years of behaviour therapy are appropriately viewed as a kind of psychotherapeutic reformation. The flavour of this reformation is found in such classic works as Bandura's (1969) *Principles of Behavior Modification,* Ullmann and Krasner's (1965) *Case Studies in Behavior Modification,* and Lazarus's (1971) *Behavior Therapy and Beyond.* Behaviour therapy was a vigorous, polemical reform movement that sought to hold the feet of dogmatic therapeutic creeds to the fire of empirical test, to challenge irrational authority, and to unleash human capacities for exploration, achievement and self-determination. Early behaviour therapy supplied powerful theoretical and methodological correctives to the field of psychotherapy by its introduction of alternative models of human functioning, and its insistence on rigorous evaluation of therapeutic methods.

But behaviour therapy also provided an ethical as well as a scientific corrective to the field of psychotherapy. It was a social movement with an ideological agenda. The ethical motives of its founders, when inferred from their writings, seem clear:

> A behavioral approach to the formulation and treatment of people called abnormal… can only end in the realm called humanism... It is to be hoped that giving up concepts of demons and diseases leads to more accurate observation and more effective responses. The object is to give people not charity but dignity, not tolerance but respect. To the extent that a person can do this, he is a little closer to the realities of his existence, a little freer of his intellectual limitations, a little more a human being. (Ullmann & Krasner, 1969/1975: 599)

Even so rigorous and precise a thinker as Bandura, who was always careful to separate the realms of fact and value, showed in himself a bit of the reformer when he spoke out against the potential abuses of traditional psychotherapy:

> More serious from an ethical standpoint is the unilateral redefinition of goals by which psychotherapists often impose insight objectives (which mainly

> involve subtle belief conversions) upon persons desiring changes in their behavioral functioning... behavioral approaches hold much greater promise than traditional methods for the advancement of self-determination and the fulfillment of human capabilities. (Bandura, 1969: 112)

The ethical spirit of behaviour therapy was iconoclastic, egalitarian and radically pragmatic. These values functioned as an antithesis to the pronounced strain of scholasticism, indifference to scientific self-scrutiny and conformity that, at that time, ran through medical psychiatry, much of psychoanalysis, and the mental health movement in general (Franks & Rosenbaum, 1983; Szasz, 1978).

Early behavioural models were advanced in the spirit of reform, within that philosophical context that presupposes that science and hence human abilities are capable of transforming the human situation. Time has left largely unaltered both the humanistic purposes and the faith in science that were characteristic of the first days of behaviour therapy. In his presidential address to the Association for Advancement of Behavior Therapy, David Barlow (1980) stated:

> If nothing else behavior therapy is a true, humanistic approach to behavioral and emotional problems... [and] at the core of the philosophy of humanism is a supreme faith in human reason and the methods of science to confront and solve the many problems that humans face and to rearrange the world so that human life will prosper. (p316)

Psychotherapy as technology: limitations and anomalies

Values and psychotechnology

Wilson and O'Leary (1980) provided a concise and illustrative statement on the place of values within the behavioural approach:

> Selecting effective techniques with which to change behaviour is an empirical question in which the therapist is presumably an expert; choosing therapeutic objectives is a matter of value judgement and ought to be determined primarily by the client. (p285)

The position on values stated here is not unique to these authors but is also found in Bandura (1969) and other major sources on behaviour therapy. When this position is pressed to its logical limits, however, certain anomalies emerge.

According to the behavioural view, the therapist ascertains the client's goals and then facilitates the realisation of those objectives. Of course, the therapist and client must engage in some kind of communication for the therapeutic aims to emerge. But if behaviour therapy is, as it claims, 'nothing more than an applied science', several questions come to mind.

Are there scientifically documented techniques of goal assessment? If not, then what procedures are being employed by the behaviour therapist in this sphere of activity? Is the behavioural clinician then thought to be operating outside the bounds of science? What about the statement that the therapeutic objectives ought to be determined by the client? Is this statement itself considered a value judgement, or a proposition of science? Suppose the client wants the therapist to choose the objectives: what then? Because it is necessary for the behaviour therapist to get involved in some way in a discussion of objectives with the client, if this dialogue does not derive from controlled laboratory studies, then this important part of behaviour therapy is without empirical basis. We have in the behavioural literature thousands of studies of therapeutic technique and a growing literature on behavioural assessment, but certainly up to the mid-1980s, virtually no attention to what therapists are doing when they assist the client in specifying exactly what it is that the client wants to achieve in therapy. It is, in fact, inconceivable that a programme of laboratory research could dictate a total course of action for the therapist. The propositions of science take the logical form of material implication: if A, then B. In its most elegant and useful configuration, science is made up of testable, falsifiable propositions that specify *predictive* relationships among variables or events (Popper, 1962).

Research can tell us only *which* techniques will achieve *what* therapeutic objectives, or the achievement of *which* objectives is related to *what* life outcomes. But knowledge of this kind is insufficient to account for the conduct of behaviour therapy. The structure of scientific knowledge is such that it describes contingent relations among phenomena. Science can tell us only what events will follow other events. Hence, research can never generate the goals of therapy. Yet the therapist cannot act in the absence of a clear sense of which therapeutic objectives or what life outcomes to promote. The therapist requires a starting point, some basis upon which to make the first move, some rule that channels his or her attention and behaviour. These primary directives of any system of psychotherapy derive fundamentally not from research but from an ethical ideal, some vision of what is good and proper in human affairs. Any system of thought, when it enters the realm of application, requires bases for the decisions and choices necessary to that application and, therefore, some value position. Hence, behaviour therapy must necessarily contain propositions that do not derive from empirical research. The fundamental premise of clinical behaviour therapy is that the client shall decide the goals of therapy. This directive, upon which clinical behaviour therapy is predicated, is not a scientific proposition but an ethical axiom, one that is related closely to its modern democratic, humanistic ideological underpinnings described earlier.

We must, however, question a viewpoint that requires that clinical activity be so subservient to the avowed preferences of the client. Perhaps the first years of behaviour therapy, with their redoubtable successes, led early practitioners astray and convinced them, wrongly, that all human difficulties can be treated as straightforwardly as simple phobias, given a proper behavioural assessment. Yet clients do not always know what they want, much less what ails them, in the initial stages of therapy. Presenting complaints are often only tangentially related to the client's fundamental problems (Woolfolk & Lazarus, 1979).

Along with various critics of behaviour therapy (Gurman & Knudson, 1978; Messer & Winokur, 1980), we see in the behavioural literature an unfortunate tendency to take client behaviour dogmatically at face value, as though to do anything else would constitute an implicit endorsement of the kinds of psychoanalytic mystification that assumes nothing the client says is ever what it seems to be on the surface.

What we find missing in contemporary behaviour therapy is not only the absence of any locus of evaluation external to the therapeutic direction prescribed by the client, but also a failure to allow for any basis for such an evaluation. It has been apparent to poets, philosophers and psychotherapists throughout the ages that an individual's aims in life are often functionally related to that individual's suffering. Inappropriate goals, fantastic goals, or conflict among goals are at the root of many problems of living. The great difficulty for behaviour therapists is in remaining faithful to their system while simultaneously managing to encompass client aims within a therapeutic dialectic, to challenge the client's goals, or to view certain of the objectives that people bring into therapy as manifestations or outright causes of their difficulties. Thus, behaviour therapy contains few concepts that allow the therapist to take any perspective on the client that is external to the client's frame of reference. Freud, at least, could, within his system, unabashedly advocate the ability to love and the ability to work as universal criteria of competence in living. The behaviour therapist has no analogous pronouncement to make. In the absence of such normative concepts as health and sickness, growth and stagnation, which in other systems transcend the preferences of the individual, the behaviour therapist has fewer categories with which to evaluate client behaviour.

Thus, without an independent, therapeutic compass of this sort, the behaviour therapist is always thrown back on the preferences of the individual. One might, in fact, argue that this is a principal ideological vector of behaviour therapy: to dispense with perspectives that limit the rights of individuals to pursue self-chosen goals in the most expedient manner science can produce.

Meaning and purpose

Throughout its short history, behaviour therapy not only has aspired to the ideals of science but also has sought to exclude from its province all that was not or could not be science. Hence, it falls prey to the difficulties that the modern scientific-technological perspective has in encompassing some essential aspects of the contemporary human dilemma.

Behaviour therapy seems especially limited in addressing those concerns and discontents that have come to be seen by sociologists and philosophers as inevitable accompaniments of modernity.

A chief discontent relates to what is lost in the transition from pre-modern forms of social organisation to modern society. With the advent of modernity, those institutions that once provided a sense of meaningful identity and belonging – the church, the community, and the family – were weakened, and the ties of individuals to them were diminished (Berger & Kellner, 1981).

Such entities as religion, art and ethics, once possessed of an authority equal or superior to that of science, have become debased epistemological currencies. They have lost their status as constituents of an objective external reality, been made relative, and have been reduced to subjective elements in the inner lives of individuals (Heller, 1959). The loss of community, the failure of modern institutions to provide durable social support for so many, the relativisation of standards of conduct, and the inability of modern consciousness to fashion some intersubjective consensus on metaphysical questions have led to considerable psychosocial stress (Garfield, 1979) and philosophical disorientation (Smith, 1982).

Modernity has accomplished many far-reaching transformations, but it has not fundamentally changed the finitude, fragility and mortality of the human condition. What it has accomplished is seriously to weaken those definitions of reality that previously made the human condition easier to bear (Berger, Berger & Kellner, 1973: 185).

As Frankl (1969) and numerous philosophers from Kierkegaard (1962) to Sartre (1956) have attested, there are inherent difficulties in any attempt to fashion a meaningful understanding of existence in terms of the moral and epistemological categories provided by scientific culture. Nor is a 'sense of meaning' a philosophical frill, an intellectual luxury with import only for those consumed by too much zeal for understanding the ultimate nature of things. Concluding his analysis of an impressive epidemiological database, Antonovsky (1979) argued that some aspects of physical health and the maintenance of tolerable levels of psychological stress depend upon what he termed a *sense of coherence*. As Antonovsky defined it, a sense of coherence requires that one's coping activities occur within a personally meaningful context of community, tradition, or cosmos that both sets a limit to personal control and makes 'affectively comprehensible' the many uncontrollable and tragic aspects of human life. In related research that has confirmed the wisdom of sociologists and existential psychologists, Kobasa and her colleagues (Kobasa, 1979; Kobasa, Maddi & Courington, 1981; Kobasa, Maddi & Puccetti, 1982) have shown that the capacity to tolerate life-stress is greatly impaired by alienation, lack of purpose and the absence of commitment. Behaviour therapy has a difficult time conceptualising and doing justice to questions of meaning and purpose. As we have seen, science and the technology that flows from it are capable of generating means for the achievement of preordained ends, but not the ends themselves. This is because the structure of knowledge within behaviour therapy allows it to illuminate only the relationship between means and ends. It cannot adumbrate the wisdom, appropriateness, or desirability of ends except in relation to some standard (some other end) that is generated independently of orthodox behaviour therapy procedure. Behaviour therapy, as it is presently constituted, is unable to further the search for meaning because success in this endeavour necessitates the discovery or creation of the goals and standards that supply purpose and meaning – the determination of what is worth doing at all, rather than the most effective means of doing it.

As one might imagine, behaviour therapists have written sparingly on this topic of 'existential questions'. Kanfer and Saslow (1969) have essentially advocated an abdication by behaviour therapy of responsibility for addressing issues involving 'dissatisfactions with or uncertainties' about 'self-attitudes, or a loss of meaning or purpose' and a reliance upon 'clergymen, teachers, counsellors, work supervisors, even neighbors and friends' (p429).

Ullmann and Krasner (1975) have quite correctly pointed out that some self-reports of *angst* mask more conventional clinical problems that are amenable to straightforward behavioural intervention. But not all existential quandaries can be explained away. And those that cannot do not admit of technical answers. About all behaviour therapy can offer here is some technique to control the emotional and behavioural impact of an absence of meaning. And although such palliatives have their place, one doubts that the simple elimination or control of the negative affect and cognitions emanating from our modern existential predicament is either an effective or a worthy solution. Among behavioural clinicians, Goldfried and Davison (1976) manifest the clearest understanding of this point, and characterise the handling of existential concerns as a major shortcoming of behaviour therapy.

Coda: an uncritical postscript

The aim of this writing has been critical. We have sought to uncover the ideological foundations of behaviour therapy and subject them to critical scrutiny. We see in this work neither an endorsement nor a repudiation of behaviour therapy, but rather a delineation of the distinctive features of its assumptive world as they emerge through the critical process.

We have found problems with the approach that seem inextricably bound up with essential features of modern consciousness and contemporary Western culture. As we have mentioned earlier, behaviour therapy is not alone among systems of psychotherapy in reflecting modern ideological positions. Behaviour therapy is, perhaps, simply the most literal translation into therapy practice of certain facets of modernity. A comparative study of contemporary therapeutic ideologies is, however, a topic for another writing. We are satisfied here to take one step towards developing a model of inquiry for understanding the embeddedness of systems of psychotherapy within history and culture.

A hermeneutic analysis of psychotherapy allows us to take an alternative, somewhat more distal perspective – one not so thoroughly informed by the same assumptions as the object of scrutiny. Knowledge so derived is of both intrinsic interest and practical import. It is vital that we frame our understanding of psychotherapy in social and historical terms because the relation between psychotherapy and culture is one of reciprocal influence.

Systems of psychotherapy not only reflect culture but shape culture as well. If modern men and women are indeed self-defining animals, as Charles Taylor (1975) has suggested, then the values and human image implicit in psychotherapies come to be consequential components in that process of self-definition.

Coda 2008: CBT revisited…

A paper upon which the original article 'Behavior therapy and the ideology of modernity' (Woolfolk & Richardson, 1984) was based was presented at the annual meeting of the Association for the Advancement of Behavior Therapy in the autumn of 1982. In the piece, we presented a critique of the behaviour therapy of the early 1980s, examining its sociocultural context and revealing its philosophical underpinnings. Much change has occurred in the culture of the mental health professions during the period in which behaviour therapy evolved into cognitive behaviour therapy (CBT), and the target of our critique is in many ways different from the behaviour therapy of the mid-20th century.

The predecessors of the current CBT establishment, the early behaviour therapists, were committed to empirical testing of therapeutic interventions. They saw themselves as scientists, not artists; less as healthcare providers or healers, and more as behavioural engineers or as educators. In its first years, behaviour therapy was theory-driven, committed to testing explanations of maladaptive behaviour that were derived from conditioning theory, and to a doctrinaire emphasis upon outcomes that were objective and observable. Mischel's (1968) critique of classical personology and psychodiagnosis was widely read, and so frequently cited by behaviour therapists that it came to be regarded as a basic text in the field. Behaviour therapy rejected person-centred, trait-based conceptions of human psychology in favour of a complex 'social learning theory' (Bandura, 1977) that was idiographic in sensibility and focused on discrete behaviour in particular contexts. Rejection of the medical or disease model of psychopathology, including traditional psychiatric diagnostic categories, was so central to behaviour therapy that it was frequently cited as a defining characteristic of the approach (Kazdin, 1978). Behaviour therapists contrasted their system with the more manifestly value-laden therapies of psychoanalysis and humanistic psychotherapy, presenting it as a value-free psychotechnology.

How did the pioneer researchers of the early days of behaviour therapy become members of the scientific healthcare establishment and bed-fellows with the pharmaceutical industry and various other advocates of evidence-based medicine? How did they come to abjure their commitments to observable behavioural outcome measures to embrace DSM and ICD diagnoses, which are, in practice, little more than assessor-guided patient self-reports: that is, based on data derived from structured clinical interviews? No one can say with certainty how the behaviour therapy movement evolved into an advocacy group for today's diagnosis-driven, empirically supported treatments, but the factors involved represent a complicated sociocultural evolution.

First, there was common cause with those psychiatrists who authored *DSM-III*. The biological revolution in psychiatry did what research on psychotherapy could never have done – put a stake in the heart of psychoanalysis. The enemy of my enemy is my friend. Most biological psychiatrists had little use for Freud; those who did, put their loyalties aside in pursuit of the holy grail of a psychiatry that would resemble somatic medicine. *DSM-III*, stripped of its psychoanalytic theoretical underpinnings (and almost all theory of any kind), was substantially more palatable to behaviour therapists than were the two earlier versions of the document. But neither *DSM-III* nor any of its successors takes a behavioural, situationist, or idiographic approach to psychopathology. Behaviour therapy's original metatheoretical commitment to the potentially infinite variety and ultimate uniqueness of each individual patient's learning history was replaced with the medicalised, Procrustean categorical nosology of the *DSM*s and *ICD*s.

Biological psychiatry researchers, apparently, also found a way to live with CBT. It really wasn't that difficult, once *DSM-III* became orthodoxy. The methods of cognitive behaviour therapy were conceived as psychotechnology, standardised in manuals, and in their method of administration could be viewed as analogous to drug treatment and, therefore, amenable to inclusion in randomised controlled trials (RCTs). As the biopsychiatry revolution unfolded, and the pharmaceutical industry earned billions, and invested billions more, in developing and testing psychotropic drugs, RCTs – the state of the art for approval by the US Food and Drug Administration (FDA) for many decades – also became the gold standard for evaluating the efficacy of psychotherapy. The US National Institute of Health funded numerous RCTs evaluating psychosocial treatments for psychopathology, sometimes in tandem with pharmacological interventions. Standardised CBT techniques easily fit into the methodological mould of the RCT and were readily assimilated into the culture of contemporary biomedical research and evidence-based medicine. All was copasetic.

Of course, along the way something was lost. The atheoretical stance of each *DSM*, along with the emergence of the 'horse race', or 'Coke versus Pepsi' comparative outcome study, produced another change in the culture of therapy efficacy studies. These studies became increasingly unmoored from theoretical formulations about the nature of psychopathology and from hypotheses about the fundamental mechanisms of therapeutic change. Pretensions to the status of applied science were widespread, but CBT research had, in fact, devolved into something that, although still empirical, was not science. Psychotherapy efficacy research had morphed into something much more straightforward and compatible with the industrial culture that it seemed, inevitably, to emulate. It had become little more than product testing.

Ensuing events justified the concerns of those who perceived an intellectual poverty and a failure of theoretical advance at the heart of the CBT establishment.

Things were also a bit discouraging on the practical front. There was a lack of clear-cut winners in the various therapy Derbies, as well as much evidence for the importance of 'common factors' and investigator allegiance effects. That very redoubtable medical-style research that had yielded various life-saving medicines seemed, in this case, to result mostly in review after review filled with meta-analyses signifying nothing, save that almost all psychotherapy produces some benefit for patients.

There is a place in psychotherapy research for something like simple product testing, just to get a pragmatic read on the impact of interventions. But this kind of activity can hardly be the mainstay of our efforts at intellectual advance, given that we are relatively ignorant about the active ingredients of our interventions, as well as the mechanisms through which they produce their effects. The absence of viable theory, the lack of compelling research findings, and the role that extra-scientific sociocultural forces play in the process invite us to do just what contributors to this book encourage – namely, try to identify and rethink the conceptual and sociocultural underpinnings of our work, and of the larger enterprises and institutions of which that work is a part. One way to proceed in this rethinking is to attempt to come to grips with the socio-historical context in which psychotherapy occurs, and with the various disguised ideologies that may underlie it (Richardson, Fowers & Guigon, 1999; Woolfolk, 1998; Woolfolk & Murphy, 2004; see also Brazier and Lees, Chapters 8 and 9 respectively, in this volume).

By the 1990s, some within the CBT movement had raised objections to the emphasis in CBT on modifying and manipulating cognition and behaviour and a view of the passions as entities to be regulated and controlled. The so-called 'third wave' of behaviour therapy (Hayes, Strosahl & Wilson, 1999; Linehan, 1993), and its articulation of rationales for Buddhist-like attitudes of acceptance toward aversive emotional experiences, are quite compatible with the pleading that we made years ago for behaviour therapists to question their view of psychotherapy as pure technique, to discard their Apollonian rationalistic sensibilities, and to understand that, frequently, one's experience should not be so much a target for modification as a process to be observed, savoured, or endured.

Some years ago, in similar fashion, we called for behaviour therapists to seek and adopt in their work a richer appreciation of life – the kind that is found in the humanities. In our view, human flourishing is not equivalent to, nor inevitably results from, the elimination of diagnosable mental disorder. So, today CBT is no longer a renegade, revolutionary movement. It has traded its commitments to ruthless empiricism and anti-medicalisation for a comfortable place inside the big tent of the medical-industrial complex. Today's CBT is highly compatible with the contemporary *zeitgeist*. Neuroscience, behavioural genetics, cognitive science, the medicalisation of problems of living and 'happiness economics' are all highly consonant with the technicism, rationality, mechanism, philosophical materialism and alleged value neutrality of CBT – features that we identified many years ago.

We have several kinds of concerns with the scientism that underlies CBT, biological psychiatry, cognitive neuroscience and related endeavours. The first of these might be termed practical and is related to a marketing mentality that has developed within CBT circles. Although CBT has achieved a kind of cultural ascendancy, especially within the UK, the evidence for the superiority of CBT over other approaches to psychotherapy seems scanty, at best, as several contributors to this volume argue. CBT's coup has been achieved, not by a disinterested review of evidence, but by factors that can be more appropriately characterised as political or sociological. As the American Civil War general Nathan Bedford Forest might have put it, at the dawn of the new era of evidence-based medicine, CBT arrived first, and was armed with the most data. Although we ourselves have been contributors to the CBT literature and believe that many CBT techniques – for example, exposure therapy for phobic behaviour – are sound and very clinically valuable, we believe that CBT has been oversold to the public, and that claims of its efficacy have been widely overstated.

There is a strong analogy with the history of second-generation antidepressants, where, after 25 years of ballyhoo, expectations are finally coming into accord with reality – a less optimistic reality than was promised by early proselytising and drug company marketing. Another related problem that has to do with CBT's rapid rise, and its rather impudent disdain for other pre-existing forms of therapy, is that we may be witnessing the erosion of the psychotherapeutic know-how and the clinical wisdom accumulated over the last century.

Virtually all of the CBT founders and pioneers (for example, Ellis, Beck, Lazarus) were initially trained in the methods and stylistics of some form of traditional psychotherapy. We were fortunate to know those founders personally, and to observe their clinical work. Such folk took for granted basic competency in forming and maintaining salutary therapeutic relationships. They tended to function as teachers, as problem-solvers who manifested a profound appreciation for the uniqueness of each individual they treated. They brought compassion, humour, artistry and wisdom derived from life experience into the therapeutic arena.

As training in CBT has come to be removed further and further from the influence of those tacit principles and human qualities of the founders of CBT, there has been (in our humble, personal opinions) a decline in, and a disdain for, the kind of judgment that results from viewing patients as extremely complex purposive creatures rather than as repositories of mental disorders. The transformation of psychotherapy from therapeutic dialogue to application of quasi-medical technology, either through the process of trainee selection or due to the effects of the training itself, has produced a generation of therapists who prefer to paint by the numbers, and who search for simple problems that can putatively be remedied by the straightforward application of explicit techniques. Fortunately, such therapists, so ruthlessly disciplined by their scientistic orthodoxies, are unlikely to be prey to such follies as past-life regression or the recovery of repressed memories. But, to many nuances of the therapeutic situation, they are too often tone deaf; in their ministrations, they too often are a bit ham-handed.

Alfred North Whitehead famously attributed his philosophical disagreements with Bertrand Russell to the inevitable conflict between a 'simple-minded' intellect (Russell's) and a 'muddle-headed' approach to thought (his own). Somewhat analogously, the evolution of psychotherapy from the old-time religion of psychoanalysis to the Brave New World of CBT suggests a traversing of the distance between the Scylla of the muddleheaded to the Charybdis of the simple-minded. Much of our critique of the 1980s suggested that early behaviour therapists made the error of over-simplifying the world, partially as a result of the laudable effort to avoid the intellectual perils of psychoanalysis and similar forms of thought. Although the CBT of today differs in some ways from the behaviour therapy of the middle of the previous century, it retains its simple-minded sensibility, with all the advantages and disadvantages of a simplistic world-view.

CBT circa 2018

This addendum builds on the Coda 2008 above and presumes familiarity with its contents. Many recent developments have impacted the world of CBT. Ironically, some of the most important of these developments have had little to do with dynamisms within mainstream CBT, or with the results of psychotherapy treatment outcome studies.

It should be recalled that CBT positioned itself as a component of 'evidence-based medicine', or the array of 'empirically supported treatments' for psychopathology. Traditionally, in order to make the claim that a psychiatric treatment is empirically supported, several things typically have to occur: 1) patients with a DSM or ICD diagnosis must be identified; 2) a treatment must be standardised (manualised in the case of psychosocial treatments); 3) the standardised treatment must be tested (preferably against a placebo or comparator treatment) in a randomised controlled trial (RCT).

Following the norms of evidenced-based medicine, many CBT treatments were consistently found in RCTs to have effects superior to placebos, and frequently to achieve results comparable with those of psychoactive medications, especially in studies of depression. CBT has received widespread acceptance as a treatment by the health insurance industry in the US. Current guidelines issued by the UK's National Institute for Health and Care Excellence (NICE) have established CBT as a frontline treatment to be used before resorting to pharmacotherapy, both for non-severe anxiety and non-severe depression (NICE, 2009, 2017).

Over the past decade, CBT researchers in the US and Canada have tended to identify with the 'clinical psychological science' movement, represented by the Association for Psychological Science (APS) and its sister organisation the Psychological Clinical Science Accreditation System. These emerged as self-styled purveyors of true scientific rigour in psychotherapy and clinical training, respectively. APS functions as a rival organisation to the American Psychological Association (APA), which is viewed by many in the CBT movement as too ecumenical and accepting of the idea that therapies may prove their worth in the arena of clinical practice without being subjected to standardisation and validation via the RCT.

During the last few years, many of the assumptions upon which CBT and the clinical psychological science movement were based have been undermined as both the logical structure and empirical findings of published RCTs have come under fire. The evidence base underlying CBT began to be undermined over the last decade, as critiques of the published literature and the release of unpublished studies made it clear that the efficacy of antidepressant drugs was actually rather weak and had been overstated by early published studies (Woolfolk, 2015). Given that one of the proudest achievements of the CBT movement was to demonstrate comparable efficacy to these drugs, the scientific downgrading of drug therapy inevitably implied a similar weakening of efficacy claims of comparably effective treatments. In a consistent development, a recent meta-analysis of 70 studies conducted between 1977 and 2014 suggests that CBT is currently half as effective in treating depression than it appeared to be in early reports (Johnsen & Friborg, 2015).

The efficacy claims of CBT also were made somewhat turbid by the disavowal of *DSM* by the National Institute of Mental Health in the US and the movement of that influential agency toward replacing the *DSM*'s atheoretical, symptom-cluster approach with a classification system putatively underlain by basic scientific knowledge, the Research Domain Criteria (Insel, 2013). Much of the research documenting the efficacy of CBT was structured by the diagnostic criteria of the *DSM*s, which, if fundamentally flawed, also raised some doubts about the status of research on which they were based. At the very least, the idea of 'specific validated treatments for specific discrete disorders' was somewhat undermined by the validity issues plaguing the diagnostic nosologies used in the research. Such authorities as David Barlow (Barlow, Allen & Choate, 2004) began to speak about transdiagnostic treatment, suggesting a revival of the old concept of 'neurosis' and broad-spectrum effects for CBT techniques. Although manualising or producing a standardised set of CBT treatments proved to be feasible, adherence to the standard treatment was not always achievable and, more important, not always associated with positive outcomes. Some research indicated that overly rigid adherence to treatment guidelines was less effective therapeutically, suggesting some role for generic clinical competence. When CBT was compared with other forms of psychotherapy in meta-analyses, its effect sizes tended to be no different from other psychotherapy approaches (Wampold, 2015).

The utility of attempting to directly change dysfunctional cognitions via disputation or dialogic discussion (cognitive restructuring) has been a pillar of CBT, and was fundamental to its originators, such as Albert Ellis and Aaron Beck. But some studies began to show that the direct attack on cognition might be of little benefit to patients, in that cognitive restructuring apparently was not the active ingredient in the CBT treatment package (Woolfolk, 2015). A very popular outgrowth of CBT, acceptance and commitment therapy (ACT) (Hayes et al, 2011), is predicated on the view that it is very difficult or ineffective to attempt to change thinking by disputation. This contemporary approach advocates awareness and acceptance of dysfunctional cognitions and is based on the concept of mindfulness derived from Buddhism. So compelling and popular has been this 'third wave' approach that established thinkers in the CBT camp have bemoaned that Beck's approach to cognition is losing its standing in the field and even now is sometimes referred to as passé or 'counter-therapeutic' (Leahy, 2007).

CBT has been evolving rapidly, creating a conceptual tent big enough to hold both Beck and the Buddha. Given that it was the first psychotherapy to receive extensive empirical support, it achieved rather rapid scientific authority that spread to the culture at large as older forms of psychotherapy, such as psychoanalysis, began to lose favour. As more research is conducted on other therapeutic approaches, the early scientific warrant of CBT may be shared with other forms of psychotherapy. Claims of its superiority to other forms of therapy, once widely promulgated by CBT adherents, currently inspire much scepticism.

References

Adams EM (1975). *Philosophy and the Modern Mind: a philosophical critique of modern western civilization.* Chapel Hill, NC: University of North Carolina Press.

Antonovsky A (1979). *Health, Stress and Coping.* San Francisco, CA: Jossey-Bass.

Bandura A (1977). *Social Learning Theory.* Englewood Cliffs, NJ: Prentice-Hall.

Bandura A (1969). *Principles of Behavior Modification.* New York, NY: Holt, Rinehart & Winston.

Barlow D (1980). Behavior therapy: the next decade. *Behavior Therapy 11*: 315–328.

Barlow DH, Allen LB, Choate ML (2004). Toward a unified treatment for emotional disorders. *Behaviour and Research Therapy 35*: 205–230.

Barrett W (1978). *The Illusion of Technique.* Garden City, NY: Anchor Press/Doubleday.

Bartley WW (1962). *The Retreat to Commitment.* New York, NY: AA Knopf.

Baumer FL (1977). *Modern European Thought: continuity and change in ideas 1600–1950.* New York, NY: Macmillan.

Beck AT (1976). *Cognitive Therapy and the Emotional Disorders.* New York, NY: International Universities Press.

Benedict R (1934). *Patterns of Culture.* Boston, MA: Houghton Mifflin.

Berger PL (1977). *Facing up to Modernity.* New York, NY: Basic Books.

Berger PL, Kellner H (1981). *Sociology Reinterpreted.* Garden City, NY: Anchor Press/Doubleday.

Berger PL, Luckman T (1966). *The Social Construction of Reality.* Garden City, NY: Doubleday.

Berger PL, Berger B, Kellner H (1973). *The Homeless Mind.* New York, NY: Random House.

Bergin AE (1980). Psychotherapy and religious values. *Journal of Consulting and Clinical Psychology 48*: 95–105.

Brinton C (1963). *The Shaping of Modern Thought.* Englewood Cliffs, NJ: Prentice-Hall.

Burtt EA (1964). *The Metaphysical Foundations of Modern Science*. London: Routledge & Kegan Paul.

Buss AR (1975). The emerging field of the sociology of psychological knowledge. *American Psychologist 30*: 988–1002.

Craighead WE, Kazdin AE, Mahoney MJ (1981). *Behavior Modification: principles, issues and applications*. Boston, MA: Houghton Mifflin.

D'Zurilla TJ, Goldfried MR (1971). Problem solving and behavior modification. *Journal of Abnormal Psychology 78*: 107–126.

Ellis A, Grieger R (eds) (1977). *Handbook of Rational-Emotive Therapy*. New York, NY: Springer.

Ellul J (1964). *The Technological Society*. New York, NY: Random House.

Erwin E (1978). *Behavior Therapy: scientific, philosophical and moral foundations*. Cambridge: Cambridge University Press.

Feyerabend P (1975). *Against Method: toward an anarchist theory of knowledge*. London: New Left Books.

Frankl VE (1969). *The Will to Meaning*. New York, NY: New American Library.

Franks CM, Rosenbaum M (1983). Behavior therapy: overview and personal reflections. In: Rosenbaum M, Franks CM, Jaffe Y (eds). *Perspectives on Behavior Therapy in the Eighties*. New York, NY: Springer (pp3–16).

Gadamer H (1975). *Truth and Method*. New York, NY: Crossroad.

Garfield CA (ed) (1979). *Stress and Survival: the emotional realities of life-threatening Illness*. St Louis, MO: CV Mosby.

Gehlen A (1980). *Man in the Age of Technology*. New York, NY: Columbia University Press.

Goldfried MR, Davison GC (1976). *Clinical Behavior Therapy*. New York, NY: Holt, Rinehart, & Winston.

Gouldner AW (1976). *The Dialectic of Ideology and Technology*. New York, NY: Seabury Press.

Gurman AS, Knudson RM (1978). Behavioral marriage therapy: I: A psychodynamic– systems analysis and critique. *Family Process 17*: 121–138.

Habermas J (1973). *Theory and Practice*. Boston, MA: Beacon Press.

Habermas J (1972). *Knowledge and Human Interests*. Boston, MA: Beacon Press.

Hayek FA (1952). *The Counter-Revolution of Science*. Glencoe, IL: Free Press.

Hayes SC, Strosahl KD, Wilson KG (1999). *Acceptance and Commitment Therapy: an experiential approach to behavior change*. New York, NY: Guilford Press.

Hayes SC, Villatte M, Levin M, Hildebrandt M (2011). Open, aware, and active: contextual approaches as an emerging trend in the behavioral and cognitive therapies. *Annual Review of Clinical Psychology 7*: 141–168.

Heller E (1959). *The Disinherited Mind*. New York, NY: Meridian.

Hogan R (1975). Theoretical egocentrism and the problem of compliance. *American Psychologist 30*: 533–540.

Horkheimer M (1972). *Critical Theory*. New York, NY: The Seabury Press.

Insel T (2013). *Director's blog: transforming diagnosis*. [Online.] National Institute of Mental Health; 29 April. www.nimh.nih.gov/about/director/2013/transforming-diagnosis.shtml (accessed 15 October 2013).

Johnsen TJ, Friborg O (2015). The effects of cognitive behavioral therapy as an anti-depressive treatment is falling: a meta-analysis. *Psychological Bulletin 141*: 747–768.

Kanfer FH, Phillips JS (1966). Behavior therapy: panacea for all ills or a passing fancy? *Archives of General Psychiatry 15*: 114–128.

Kanfer FH, Saslow G (1969). Behavioral diagnosis. In: Franks CM (ed). *Behavior Therapy: appraisal and status*. New York, NY: McGraw-Hill (pp417–444).

Kazdin AE (1978). *History of Behavior Modification: experimental foundations of contemporary research*. Baltimore, MD: University Park Press.

Kazdin AE, Wilson GT (1978). *Evaluation of Behavior Therapy: issues, evidence, and research strategies*. Cambridge, MA: Ballinger.

Kierkegaard S (1962). *The Present Age*. New York, NY: Harper & Row.

Kitchener RF (1980). Ethical relativism and behavior therapy. *Journal of Consulting and Clinical Psychology 48*: 1–7.

Kobasa SC (1979.) Stressful life events, personality and health: an inquiry into hardiness. *Journal of Personality and Social Psychology 37*: 1–11.

Kobasa SC, Maddi SR, Courington S (1981). Personality and constitution as mediators in the stress–illness relationship. *Journal of Health and Social Behavior 22*: 368–378.

Kobasa SC, Maddi SR, Puccetti MC (1982). Personality and exercise as buffers in the stress-illness relationship. *Journal of Behavioral Medicine 5*: 391–404.

Krasner L (1982). Behavior therapy: on roots, contexts, and growth. In: Wilson GT, Franks CM (eds). *Contemporary Behavior Therapy*. New York, NY: Guilford Press.

Krasner L (1962). The therapist as a social reinforcement machine. In: Strupp HH, Luborsky L (eds). *Research in Psychotherapy: vol 2*. Washington, DC: American Psychological Association (pp61–94).

Kuhn TS (1970a). Reflections on my critics. In: Lakatos I, Musgrove A (eds). *Criticism and the Growth of Knowledge*. Cambridge: Cambridge University Press (pp231–278).

Kuhn TS (1970b). *The Structure of Scientific Revolutions* (2nd ed). Chicago, IL: University of Chicago Press.

Lamont C (1982). *The Philosophy of Humanism*. New York, NY: Frederick Ungar.

Lazarus AA (1976). *Multimodal Behavior Therapy*. New York, NY: Springer.

Lazarus AA (1971). *Behavior Therapy and Beyond*. New York, NY: McGraw-Hill.

Leahy RL (2007). Emotion and psychotherapy. *Clinical Psychology: science and Practice 14*: 353–357.

Levi-Strauss C (1966). *The Savage Mind*. Chicago, IL: University of Chicago Press.

Linehan MM (1993). *Cognitive-Behavioral Treatment of Borderline Personality Disorder*. New York, NY: Guilford Press.

London P (1964.) *The Modes and Morals of Psychotherapy*. New York, NY: Holt, Rinehart & Winston.

Lowe CM (1976). *Value Orientations in Counseling and Psychotherapy: the meanings of mental health* (2nd ed). Cranston, RI: Carroll Press.

Maclntyre A (1981). *After Virtue: a study in moral theory*. Notre Dame, IN: University of Notre Dame Press.

Mahoney MJ (1980). Psychotherapy and the structure of personal revolutions. In: Mahoney MJ (ed). *Psychotherapy Process*. New York, NY: Plenum (pp157–180).

Mahoney MJ, Arnkoff DB (1978). Cognitive and self-control therapies. In: Garfield SL, Bergin AE (eds). *Handbook of Psychotherapy and Behavior Change* (2nd ed). New York, NY: Wiley (pp689–721).

Mannheim K (1936). *Ideology and Utopia*. New York, NY: Harcourt, Brace & World.

Meichenbaum DH (1977). *Cognitive Behavior Modification: an integrative approach*. New York, NY: Plenum.

Messer SB, Winokur M (1984). Ways of knowing and visions of reality in psychoanalytic and behavior therapy. In: Arkowitz H, Messer SB (eds). *Psychoanalytic Therapy and Behavior Therapy: is integration possible?* New York, NY: Plenum (pp63–100).

Messer SB, Winokur M (1980). Some limits to the integration of psychoanalytic and behavior therapy. *American Psychologist 35*: 818–827.

Mischel W (1973). Toward a cognitive social learning reconceptualization of personality. *Psychological Review 80*: 252–283.

Mischel W (1968). *Personality and Assessment*. New York, NY: Wiley.

Moore WE (1963). *Social Change*. Englewood Cliffs, NJ: Prentice-Hall.

Nelson B (1981). *On the Roads to Modernity*. Huff TE (ed). Totowa, NJ: Rowman & Littlefield.

NICE (National Institute for Health & Care Excellence) (2017). Depression in adults: treatment and management. NICE guideline. Draft for consultation, July 2017. London: NICE.

NICE (National Institute for Health & Care Excellence) (2009). Depression in adults: recognition and management. CG90. London: NICE.

Nietzsche F (1956). *The Birth of Tragedy and the Genealogy of Morals*. Garden City, NY: Doubleday/Anchor.

Nisbet R (1976). *Sociology as an Art Form*. London: Oxford University Press.

Parsons T (1971). *The System of Modern Societies*. Englewood Cliffs, NJ: Prentice-Hall.

Pervin LA (1981). *Conceptual and applied limitations of behavior therapy: a dynamic systems perspective*. Paper presented at the meeting of the Association for Advancement of Behavior Therapy, November; Toronto, Canada.

Polanyi M (1966). *The Tacit Dimension*. Garden City, NY: Doubleday.

Popper KR (1962). *The Logic of Scientific Discovery*. London: Hutchinson.

Rachman S (1981). The primacy of affect: some theoretical implications. *Behaviour Research and Therapy 19*: 279–290.

Richardson F, Fowers B, Guignon C (1999). *Re-envisioning Psychology: moral dimensions of theory and practice*. San Francisco, CA: Jossey-Bass.

Ricoeur P (1981). *Hermeneutics and the Human Sciences*. Thompson JB (ed). Cambridge: Cambridge University Press.

Rieff P (1966). *The Triumph of the Therapeutic*. New York, NY: Harper & Row.

Sampson EE (1981). Cognitive psychology as ideology. *American Psychologist 36*: 730–743.

Sampson EE (1978). Scientific paradigms and social values: wanted – a scientific revolution. *Journal of Personality and Social Psychology 36*: 1332–1343.

Sampson EE (1977). Psychology and the American ideal. *Journal of Personality and Social Psychology 35*: 767–782.

Sartre J (1956). *Being and Nothingness*. New York, NY: Philosophical Library.

Scheler M (1960). *Die Wissenformen und die Gesellschaft*. Bern: Francke.

Shils EA (1981). *Tradition*. Chicago IL: University of Chicago Press.

Smith H (1982). *Beyond the Post-Modern Mind*. New York, NY: Crossroad.

Stanley M (1978). *The Technological Conscience: survival and dignity in an age of expertise*. New York, NY: Free Press.

Szasz T (1978). *The Myth of Psychotherapy*. New York, NY: Anchor.

Taylor C (1975). *Hegel*. Cambridge: Cambridge University Press.

Taylor C (1971). Interpretation and the sciences of man. *Review of Metaphysics 25*: 3–51.

Ullmann LP, Krasner L (1969/1975). *A Psychological Approach to Abnormal Behavior* (2nd ed). Englewood Cliffs, NJ: Prentice-Hall.

Ullmann LP, Krasner L (eds) (1965). *Case Studies in Behavior Modification*. New York, NY: Holt.

Wampold BE (2015). The good, the bad, and the ugly: a 50-year perspective on the outcome problem. *Psychotherapy 50*: 16–24.

Weber M (1958). *From Max Weber: essays in sociology*. Gerth HH, Mills CW (eds). New York, NY: Oxford University Press.

Weimer WB (1979.) *Notes on the Methodology of Scientific Research*. Hillsdale, NJ: Erlbaum.

Wheelis A (1973). *How People Change*. New York, NY: Harper & Row.

Wilson GT, Evans I (1977). The therapist–client relationship in behavior therapy. In: Gurman AS, Razin AM (eds). *The Therapist's Contribution to Effective Psychotherapy: an empirical approach*. New York, NY: Pergamon Press (pp203–243).

Wilson GT, O'Leary KD (1980). *Principles of Behavior Therapy*. Englewood Cliffs, NJ: Prentice-Hall.

Winner L (1977). *Autonomous Technology: technics-out-of-control as a theme in political thought*. Cambridge, MA: MIT Press.

Wolpe J (1973). *The Practice of Behavior Therapy* (2nd ed). New York, NY: Pergamon Press.

Woolfolk RL (2015). *The Value of Psychotherapy: the talking cure in an age of clinical science*. New York, NY: Guilford Press.

Woolfolk RL (1998). *The Cure of Souls: science, values and psychotherapy*. San Francisco, CA: Jossey-Bass.

Woolfolk RL, Lazarus AA (1979). Between laboratory and clinic: paving the two-way Street. *Cognitive Therapy and Research 3*: 239–244.

Woolfolk RL, Murphy D (2004). Axiological foundations of psychotherapy. *Journal of Psychotherapy Integration 14*: 168–191.

Woolfolk RL, Richardson FC (1984). Behavior therapy and the ideology of modernity. *American Psychologist 39*: 777–786. Reprinted in Miller DB (ed) (1993). *The Restoration of Dialogue: readings in the philosophy of clinical psychology*. Washington, DC: American Psychological Association.

8 CBT: a historico-cultural perspective

David Brazier

Once all Europe, more or less, had one God. That God's gospel had spread across the whole continent, largely by persuasion. The impetus of conversion had been accelerated by the moral force of martyrdom – the evident willingness of adherents to die for their cause without aggressing against others. The doctrine of turning the other cheek had a compelling moral power, demonstrating on the one hand an unconditionality of love, faith and acceptance, and on the other a spirit of duty and self-sacrifice triumphing over sinful nature. These two formed, as it were, the yin and yang of the Christian way. Together, they made a dynamic revolutionary force, but it is difficult to stand on two legs without constant forward momentum. To build a civilisation, a third prop is required. This third leg came from the classical world that Christianity displaced yet incorporated.

The triumph of the new religion was consolidated when its leading theorists showed skill in appropriating prime elements of pagan philosophy – Augustine incorporating Plato; Thomas Aquinas, Aristotle and all and sundry borrowing from the Stoics. In the Middle Ages, further learning was incorporated from India via the Islamic world, and algebra and algorithm became two of the very few Arabic words to find a way into the English language. Christianity catered for the heart and for the shadow sides of human nature, but it had to import from elsewhere a repertoire for catering for the head. Here, therefore, we find the origins of a metaphysic of science and materialism that the early Christian thinkers integrated with varying degrees of success into the dominant theistic paradigm. Thus, Europe acquired a culture in which three ideals held sway, the two wings of the Christian formula being supplemented by the precursors of natural science. Here were planted the seeds of later crises that still reverberate today.

Our culture's value system thus rests upon a tripod of supporting pillars: faith, duty and empiricism, or, alternatively, love, guilt and rationalism. We could also call these traditions the Romantic, the Conservative and the Puritan, or Utilitarian. The medieval period knit them into a single fabric.

Time passed, and some of the original ideals became tarnished. The gospel originally spread by peaceful means came to be defended by martial ones. The turning of the cheek was displaced by the Inquisition and the stake. The Albigensian 'heretics', who arguably embodied many of the original ideals better than their persecutors, were nonetheless exterminated in the name of the all-merciful God. The cruel exigencies of power and state did not completely obliterate the original ideals, but moral decay sapped the foundations. Eventually it was the practice of indulgences, of selling salvation for money, that provoked the great schism, led by Luther, that would expose the fundamentally weakened condition of Christendom.

Nonetheless, the real damage was not immediately fully apparent. People quarrelled, but they quarrelled about the nature and wishes of the God whose ultimate position, as yet, still seemed unassailable. Great thinkers like Descartes and Newton believed themselves to be exploring and revealing the creations of the God, and thereby further glorifying his holy name. They little realised their work would later be looked back upon as the beginning of secular philosophy. In the Age of Reason, initially, Reason was thought of as that of God in Everyman. Reason was the crowning glory that God had bestowed on humans as his ultimate mark of favour. Reason and soul were almost synonymous; they were what distinguished us from the beasts.

By a slow insidious process, however, Reason itself gradually became God, displacing the former God, and since Reason was housed in the human breast, humankind itself started to take on the divine mantle. Humankind dispensed God's functions – justice, healing, favour, education, punishment, pardon, and, eventually, even the healing of souls. However, culture does not change abruptly. Even in the post-theistic age, the same fundamental ideals continued to hold sway, often under new names.

In the Age of Reason, Kant took up the cause of duty, appealing now not to God, but to a 'categorical imperative'; Hegel built on the Romantic heritage with its roots in faith and love, and foresaw a dialectic of spirit carrying us ever upward, while Bentham hoisted the banner of utility. The same strands were being carried forward under new insignia. Arguably they were trading upon, and perhaps running down, the capital built up during the theistic age. Certainly, it appears that they were rationalising and seeking a ground other than God for the ideals that had long held sway. First there was the hope, expressed by Rousseau's company, that Reason itself could provide a sound, Godless foundation. This hope proved illusory. Reason proved capable of rationalising anything. The French Revolution provoked hope, then revulsion as the blood flowed. Without any metaphysic as an anchor, the ship of civilisation was adrift in a manner that seemed alternately exciting and alarming, but the philosophies that arose to steady it were by now totally novel, though they owed their popularity and acceptance to the fact that they remained familiar currency, with a new stamp.

Reaching the 20th century, we saw these processes gone further, but still in continuity with the old pattern. The momentum of cruelty had by now built up into a massive tide, evident in two of the most destructive wars in human history, and a multitude of lesser ones. In the 'post-war' period, there was never a year in which there was not serious warfare going on somewhere, and some of those wars, like the Iraq–Iran conflict, caused casualties running to millions of dead, not to mention the maimed, displaced and bereaved. As the century drew to a close, we saw the emergence of 'ethnic cleansing' and genocide, and the greatest tide of displaced people that the world has seen in supposedly peaceful times. As the new century opened, we even saw torture coming back onto the political agenda of the supposedly most civilised countries.

How have the foundational ideals of our culture fared through this gradual erosion of standards and mounting ruthlessness? Who is caring for our souls now, and how are they to do so? In the psychology field, the three basic ideals are still clearly represented, now rivalrous with each other and unintegrated. Carrying forward the romantic tradition of unconditional positive regard, universal empathy and faith in limitless human potential, we have the humanistic-psychology movement and its various offshoots, including transpersonal psychology. The banner of duty and sinful nature is now carried by the diversity of psychoanalytic schools, each discerning our perversities and pointing out our duty. Utilitarian ideals gave us, first, behaviourism – an extreme of puritan minimalism in which nothing that happened 'inside' the person was to be given any consideration at all – and then broadened into a range of 'cognitive' or 'rational' approaches. Proponents of the behavioural approaches saw anything else as unscientific. The most extreme Pavlovian form of this approach found favour in the Soviet domain, which is not surprising since the whole Soviet phenomenon can be seen as having been an experiment in making Puritan Utilitarianism the guiding principle of a whole society.

While the Soviet experiment continued, behaviourism remained relatively eclipsed in the West by the representatives of the other two legs of our cultural tripod. With the experiment in scientific society going on elsewhere, the romantic and conservative tendencies could prosper. Humanistic psychology burgeoned, and psychoanalysis flourished not just as therapies, but as widespread cultural influences affecting every avenue of life. For a time, it seemed as though the Romantic movement would triumph over all, as the 'permissive society' seemed to be overturning centuries of tradition, and even that bastion, the Catholic Church, had its 'Vatican II'. Then, as the costs of permissiveness surfaced, there was a swing 'back to basics' and a reinstatement of conservative duties. Throughout this time, 'scientific' behaviourism remained only a significant undertone.

With the fall of the Soviet Union, however, the dynamics changed. The third leg of the tripod was no longer associated with the enemy and, in a mere decade or two, the greater part of the measures that 'the Free World' was taught to regard as anathema in the Soviet way of doing things became business as normal in our own backyard. We now imprisoned 'suspects' without trial, more or less indefinitely, with no compunction; surveillance of public spaces, comprehensive secret-police activity, and severe restrictions on migration all became 'necessary'.

In this climate, it is not surprising that the utilitarian, 'scientific' branch of psychology suddenly found favour. Non-directiveness was out. It is now legitimate and desirable to tell people how they should think and to re-programme them. If they are sad, it is because they have unrealistic thoughts. If they cannot work, they need to be cognitively restructured. This is in their own best interests, and in any case, where is the evidence that any other approach can achieve patient conformity to desired targets so systematically? Cognitive behaviour therapy is inevitably the treatment of choice when the state sees its duty is to ensure public 'happiness' by the most utilitarian and scientific approaches available. Puritan, utilitarian rationalism now has its day.

The operatives of the system are not of malign intent. Most sincerely wish only to relieve the suffering of their patients by approved and proven means. They may get caught up in professional rivalries or institutional politics from time to time, but that is endemic in the system, and it is the system that we are commenting upon here, rather than the individuals occupying the various niches within it, each doing their best to survive, prosper and help others within the frame available from their spot on the social landscape.

In the present cultural climate, one has to reckon with the spirit of the times but not be seduced into thinking that 'twill ever be so. When we take a step back and try to get a longer-term historical perspective, it is possible to see this as simply the latest phase in a game that has been running for a very long time. It is like the weaving of a three-strand plait. As the plait extends, each strand takes its turn to go over the other two. In due course, we shall see a cultural reaction and a change of fashion. The present bubble will burst or will get subverted. It is possible that the burgeoning interest in 'mindfulness' may prove to be the Trojan horse in the cognitive camp and will let out a bellyful of humanists once again. We shall see.

Time and again in the past, at least since the Chinese Legalists 2,000 years ago, there have been periodic Brave New Worlds in which scientific mind-control aims to solve all human ills. However, when the rationalist aspect of our civilisation becomes dominant, the heart and the shadow of human nature cannot abide them for long, so this tide too will turn – perhaps even now, it is on the point of doing so. When it does, people will think something unprecedented has occurred and all of history is being overthrown, but in all probability, it will simply be that it is the turn of one of the other two strands to take precedence. An age of hope will dawn. The spirit of love and faith will rise again.

We shall have to see whether it is the Romantic or the Classicalist turn next, but a real discontinuity in the bigger project is unlikely. What we need to be more deeply concerned about is the fact that the extension of this threefold plait has not diminished the longer-term trend of mounting cruelty. Planet Earth is getting full. If we cannot find a way of living together in greater harmony, then nature will assuredly solve the problem by exacting a substantial cull of our numbers. The real challenge to psychology lies not in the domain of how many patients suffering from such and such a defined depressive syndrome, or such and such an anxiety category can be made to sustain more than x per cent improvement on tabulated performance indicators for more than two years; it lies in the area of what can actually change our inhumanity to one another on a societal and global scale.

As long as we are all accomplices to acts of gross iniquity carried out on our behalf by officials employed by executives that we have elected for the purpose, we are not going to throw off our basic delusions, nor be healed of our collective sickness, and it is that collective sickness that exacts the greatest toll. It is to that collective sickness that the roots of so much individual anguish should really be traced. It is society that is sick and that needs spiritual care.

Psychologies come and go; professional rivalries are perennial. The game is, however, powered by larger forces. For the moment, we are in an ephemeral mini Age of Reason, and we must all reckon with it. Even the Romantics must make what they do look 'scientific' and conduct 'research' to demonstrate the effectiveness of such contrivances as 'mindfulness-based stress reduction' or advance their cause under such banners as 'emotional intelligence' or 'optimism training'. Analysts must come up with 'treatment protocols' and 'replicable procedures' in order to stay in the game. Much of this is either cynical window dressing or a strategy to sneak what one really wants, and believes in, into the citadels of utilitarian dogmatism. Most of it fails. Many are, therefore, content for the present to remain in the wilderness, gathering spiritual strength or enduring their winter of discontent.

It is important, however, not to waste wilderness years. When the tide turns, there will be a need for creativity – but creativity can already be going on. In the psychological world, the conservative tendency has unfortunately got exceedingly bogged down, stifling itself in a pursuit of respectability, regulation, institutes, complaints procedures and professionalism. The utilitarian rationalists are dominant and cock-a-hoop, but, in the nature of things, their reign will not last indefinitely. It is, therefore, vitally important that the carriers of what I have here called 'the romantic tendency' be now preparing themselves for the opportunity when it comes, but it is also important that we all gain some sense of perspective.

When a movement loses favour, it has to return to its roots, and the roots of the romantic are in the spiritual-existential. It is not surprising, therefore, that one of the few areas where creativity is at present going on in the psychotherapy world is at the psychology–spirituality interface, and that interest in existential approaches, loosely defined, is increasing and becoming a haven for those who once would have followed such figures as Carl Rogers or Abraham Maslow. The mindfulness phenomenon can also be seen in this light as a mushrooming development on the border between the rational-cognitive domain and the spiritual. Spirituality must have in view not merely the salvation of the individual but the raising of the whole human race to new levels of harmony, insight, peace and co-operation. This grander agenda should arrest our attention. It is on our ability to address it that we will be judged when the hour comes.

Those who have espoused human potentiality, self-actualisation, personal growth and so forth in the past must now learn to strive for goals of wider scope than the kind of super-individualism that once inspired us briefly, but then turned sour as it fell before the ridicule directed at the 'me generation'.

Rationalism has reigned not only in psychology but also in the political domain. This now appears to be changing. The rise of conservative forces in many parts of the world speaks of the emergence of a different value system, less rational and more familial, less ambitious and more defensive. This is changing the atmosphere within which psychology operates. It may well provide a set of conditions within which greater understanding of the darker, hidden forces of the psyche comes to be seen as having added relevance.

At the same time, those who hold a more spiritual or humanistic outlook will be challenged to expand their vision. Beyond even the humanistic, we must now think at the whole ecological level. Not only is it too narrow to think of the individual, it is too narrow to think only of the species. The vision we need must turn back a tidal wave that is already threateningly close to our shore.

A turn toward the romantic side of our culture would be welcome, no doubt, but real healing requires more. Somehow, the plait has become too unravelled. We need to seek a higher-level integration so that the three dimensions can work together. Should we not be addressing the real problems facing our times and deriving our work with individuals from that greater perspective, rather than either being sucked into the ubiquitous gulag of 'spin' and mind manipulation on the one hand, or, on the other, narrowly focusing on symptom-specific local remedies?

The individual in treatment needs to know that the treatment he or she receives is a subset of a philosophy that is wholesome for humankind. Let us by all means remember better times, when human potential was not a dirty term, but let us also learn from our failure to address the really big issue, which is the long-term ascendancy of cruelty in a world where every century sees an ever larger proportion of the human race destroyed by violent means, and where the advance of technology that could make life easy inexorably seems to make it more brutal and the wealth divide more extreme. The question for psychology, as for several other human science disciplines today, is not which school of practice shall prevail in public institutions and in the treatment of individual casualties, but where we will find a genuinely integrative approach that can harmonise the three dimensions of our culture and enable us to live at peace with each other and with the planet.

9 Cognitive behaviour therapy and evidence-based practice: past, present and future*

John Lees

In this chapter, I look at the fact that cognitive behaviour therapy and evidence-based practice are currently favoured by the British government and healthcare authorities, and that this is a cause for anxiety and concern among some therapists. I argue for developing an approach to current debates about these approaches to clinical practice in the counselling and psychotherapy profession, based on the principles of the evolution of consciousness. In particular, I take the view that our understanding of such developments can be transformed if we adopt a broader evolutionary perspective.

Cognitive behaviour therapy (CBT) has featured prominently in counselling and psychotherapy discourses by virtue of the fact that it has been put forward as the most efficacious method of treatment for some presenting problems, thereby giving it priority over other therapy approaches. One reason for this growing interest in CBT in recent years is the move toward standardised treatments in this profession, based in particular on the principles of evidence-based practice (EBP). In this chapter, therefore, I will discuss the current ascendancy of CBT and EBP and will explore some of their common characteristics. I will focus in particular on their underlying ontological and epistemological assumptions, their evolution and development, and the principles underpinning their methodology.

In relation to CBT, I will look at its 'pure' underlying principles, as opposed to its 'applied' form. In a Platonic sense, I will be examining its basic guiding Idea. Two potential problems in my approach will also be mentioned. First, CBT practitioners often deviate from the pure form. They may adopt a 'person-centred' orientation, exercise a certain degree of flexibility in response to client need, and

* An earlier version of this chapter appeared in the *European Journal of Psychotherapy and Counselling* 2008; 10(3): 187–196.

encourage 'client ownership of discovery over dramatic therapeutic interventions' (Salkovskis, 1996: 538). Second, concentrating on its pure form can easily involve adopting a caricatured view of what actually happens in practice – for instance, seeing it as a process of applying pre-defined techniques and procedures by an expert and detached scientist-practitioner.

My rationale for concentrating on the underlying philosophical principles of CBT and EBP and a broader evolutionary perspective arises out of my view, along with the late Petruska Clarkson, that the therapy profession has reached a sufficient degree of maturity to be able to begin to reflect on itself in order to 'consider meta-theoretical issues' (Clarkson, 2000: 308). It has, she argues, reached a stage in its development where it has the potential to develop 'an openness to explore the philosophical assumptions, value commitments and ideological bases of even our firmest "scientific" findings'. In order to do this, I will, first, establish the historical framework for looking at CBT and EBT – in particular the notion of the evolution of consciousness, emphasised, for instance, in the work of Rudolf Steiner. Building on this temporal and evolutionary perspective, I will then look anew at the meaning and significance of their ascendancy at this particular moment in time. In conclusion, I will broaden my perspective to include the future, as well as the past and present.

The historical framework

The development of CBT – and, indeed, other therapies – is usually regarded as having taken place over a relatively short period of 100 years or so, since the beginnings of depth psychology; that is, since the work of Freud towards the end of the 19th century. In fact, CBT has been viewed as being a reaction to the work of Freud and psychoanalysis generally. Joseph (2001: 88), for instance, sees behavioural therapy as a reaction to psychoanalysis, and refers to Eysenck's (1952) seminal critique of therapy, and of psychoanalysis especially, based on his meta-analysis of therapeutic outcomes, as an important stimulus to the development of behavioural psychology as a therapy. Furthermore, the pioneers of cognitive therapy, Aaron Beck and Albert Ellis, both had personal experience of psychoanalysis and had found it wanting, thereby stimulating them to develop their own therapeutic approaches based on what they saw as more rational, efficacious and researchable methods of treatment (see, for instance, Salkovskis, 1996: 535).

However, some advocates of cognitive therapy take a longer-term view of its origins. Ross (1999) and Ellis (Shostrom, 1965) see it as containing elements of the Greco-Roman philosophy of Stoicism, in as much as it resembles the Stoic insight that 'people are not emotionally disturbed so much by events as by their beliefs about them' (Ross, 1999: 75). I will also take a longer-term view of the origins of CBT, and will thus develop my argument on the basis of a broad historical perspective. However, my approach is different to that of Ross and Ellis: they simply compare cognitive therapy with a particular way of thinking in Ancient

Greece. In contrast, I will adopt a shorter timescale – namely, the last 400 years or so; but, more importantly, I will view its development in the light of the evolution of consciousness, as mentioned earlier. In particular, I will argue that CBT is a product of the development of Enlightenment science since the beginning of the 17th century.

EBP is generally viewed as having developed over an even shorter period of time than CBT. It was first introduced into clinical discourse in 1992 by the Evidence-Based Medical Working Group (1992). They referred to a 'new paradigm' and encouraged clinicians to use the research literature 'more effectively' in order to apply research findings to their everyday clinical practice, by analysing and critically appraising the aspects of the methods and results sections of research studies that are relevant to the clinical problem, and then using any relevant findings to help to address it. It is thus viewed as being both a pragmatic and a relatively new movement. But I will, again, adopt a different perspective, arguing that, as is the case with CBT, it is useful to view it as emerging over a longer timescale, once again beginning with the origins of contemporary science at the beginning of the 17th century, and, as in the case of CBT, I will examine it from the viewpoint of the evolution of consciousness.

Looking at these two approaches to clinical practice from a narrow, historical point of view may give the impression that their current dominance in healthcare practice will result in those practitioners who work with other approaches eventually being overwhelmed and swept away – at least in the NHS. For instance, as early as the mid-1990s, the EBP movement was already beginning to have an impact on healthcare policy and was tending to favour CBT clinical methods over and above other therapies. In 1996, the National Health Service (NHS) in Britain reviewed psychological therapies and recommended that they should be evidence-based (Parry & Richardson, 1996). The same review also remarked that CBT had a significant advantage over other approaches, particularly with regard to the treatment of those problems that feature prominently in most counselling services – namely, depression and anxiety – because of its efficacy research-orientated nature (Parry, 2004).

Then, in 2005, the National Institute for Health and Care Excellence (NICE), the British government's advisory body on healthcare, explicitly stated that cognitive behaviour therapy is the most efficacious treatment for anxiety and depression (NICE, 2004; Bower, 2005). It recommended that mild depression can be treated with counselling, but that the only variants of talking therapies suitable for more severe depression are CBT, interpersonal therapy and couple-focused therapy, thereby eliminating from the picture the work of the vast majority of therapy practitioners (Hughes, 2005). In the case of anxiety, the situation is even more depressing for those therapists who do not work with CBT methods. Here, just CBT, pharmacology or self-help are recommended (Lawrence, 2005).

These recommendations pertain today, broadly unchanged, in the draft guidelines published by NICE in 2017 (NICE, 2017) – the final version is awaited as this volume goes to press. For people with 'less severe depression', CBT remains the first-choice therapy, with behavioural activation, followed by interpersonal therapy if CBT doesn't help or is not acceptable to the client, and counselling if they have 'significant psychosocial, relationship or employment problems'.

The government-funded Improved Access to Psychological Therapies (IAPT) programme follows the NICE guidelines, also recommending the use of CBT as the primary approach to psychological therapy, although a number of other therapies may also be offered by IAPT services. Overall, these developments have provoked a considerable amount of debate and anxiety among practitioners (see, for example, Proctor, 2015).

The picture begins to change, however, if we adopt the notion of the evolution of consciousness, based on the work of Rudolf Steiner. Steiner speaks about this in many places (for instance, Steiner, 1904, 1909, 1911, 1923), expressing the essence of his view in the following way:

> The present age is, however, one that is peculiarly prejudiced in its thought about the evolution of man and of mankind. It is commonly believed that, as regards his life of soul and spirit, man has always been essentially the same as he is today throughout the whole of the time that we call history… [I]n forming such a conception, we do not take the trouble to observe the important differences that exist in the soul-constitution of a man of the present-time, as compared even with that of a relatively not very far distant past… [and then] if we go over to the ancient Oriental world… there is a disposition of soul utterly different from that of the man of today. (Steiner, 1923: 7–8)

In this statement Steiner is referring to the fact that human beings experience qualitatively different states of consciousness at different times in history. Indeed, the activities arising out of Steiner's work adopt these principles in a practical way. For instance, Steiner (Waldorf) schools adopt the view that the growth of the child emulates the evolution of consciousness. Thus, when the child is experiencing a state of consciousness resembling that of Ancient India, the Steiner curriculum suggests that the children are taught about the myths, stories and events of Ancient India. I thus agree with Welburn that Steiner's thought, and the practical applications arising out of it, comprise a 'most thorough-going response' to 'the possibilities of an evolutionary kind of thinking', and that, in terms of professional life, this viewpoint has the potential to inform the way we think about different theories and paradigms by virtue of the fact that it enables us to look at them in a new light: to view them in the light of 'the growing, changing being of Man' (Welburn, 2004: 48). In other words, we can approach our understanding of the world – and the theories and paradigms that are generated at any one moment in time – from the perspective of the ongoing changes in human consciousness.

Steiner's approach to the evolution of consciousness can be linked to a typical central European way of thinking that was developed by Romantic and idealistic philosophers in the 18th and 19th centuries, who took the view that there are radical differences in how we view the world in different historical periods (Gidley, 2007: 118). The knowledge we generated in the past is not the knowledge we generate today and will be different again in the future. Consequently, we begin to see current developments in therapy practice, including the current privileging of CBT and EBP, as historical moments corresponding to humanity's stage of development, and its current possibilities of knowledge generation and their practical application. Once we begin to see them in this way, we realise that, in due course, they will be superseded by other ways of thinking.

In the next section, I will explore the origins of CBT and EBP from the perspective of the evolution of consciousness. My aim in doing this is to deepen our understanding of these two phenomena, cast some light on the reasons for their popularity, and look at both the usefulness and dangers of their underlying approach to clinical practice. I will argue that, by understanding them in the light of this broader historical perspective, we will be more able to assess their place within current healthcare discourse in a balanced and informed way.

From the past to the present

In looking at CBT and EBP from a historical perspective, as discussed earlier, I take the view that they are both quintessential products of scientific Enlightenment thinking – in particular, that they are characterised by two key aspects of the scientific method: namely, the experimental model and rationality. One of the first people to espouse the use of the experimental method in research was Sir Francis Bacon in the 16th century. As Davy (1985: 36) has remarked, his ideas 'define and describe the modern scientific method – and above all, emphasise the importance of impartial observation and experiment'. Moreover, the notion of rationalistic epistemology, which complements the experimental method, was developed by such people as his contemporary René Descartes, who has been referred to as 'the father of modern philosophy' (Ferré, 1998: 1), but could equally be called the 'father of modern epistemology'. Descartes was not an experimenter, but he was aware of the development of the experimental method and provided the philosophical and theoretical basis for it: 'He was always more concerned with general principles of method than with the detailed work of observation' (Lindsay, 1912: xi).

Descartes' work, above all else, incorporated two principles that dominate our way of thinking about the world today. First, he postulated that our capacity to know about the world is enhanced if it is based on mathematical reasoning, and that, in order to acquire knowledge about the world, we need to use 'the clear vision of the intellect'. He consequently argued for a theory of knowledge that is based on logic and reason (Lynch, 1996), or what he called 'intuition' (Lindsay, 1912: xiv). Second, Descartes developed the notion of the split between mind and body, self and world – so-called Cartesian dualism: that is to say, he took the view that we can only know the world if we disconnect and detach ourselves from it. In summary, in order to know the world, we need to exercise our capacity for logical thinking within the framework of a strict method that distances us from our experience: 'Method is needed so to arrange the objects of our inquiry that we may be able thus to intuit them' (Lindsay, 1912: xv).

There is no doubt that these Enlightenment principles – experimentalism, logic, dualism and detachment – dominate our consciousness, and thus our relationship to the world today. Furthermore, along with Steiner, I take the view that this has been necessary in order to contribute to the development of our individuality and our capacity for self-consciousness. However, like Steiner, I also believe that we are now developing new possibilities in our consciousness. Indeed, I have argued elsewhere that much of the thinking in the psychotherapeutic professions over the last 100 years has been attempting to break away from these basic Enlightenment principles (Lees, 2008). For example, many variants of psychotherapeutic thinking encourage us to overcome dualistic states of mind by focusing on the fact that there are moments in our experience when we are in non-dualistic (or monistic) states of mind: that is to say, when we make a strong connection with other people as a result of our capacity for empathy, or as a result of the experience of countertransference phenomena.

Steiner alludes to these new possibilities of consciousness in his fundamental book *The Philosophy of Freedom* (Steiner, 1894), when he refers to our sense that we are both 'estranged' from the world and 'within' it: 'Here we are no longer merely *I*; here is something which is more than *I*' (p26). We can refer to this new state of consciousness as a form of dynamic dualism (or dynamic monism), in which we are constantly moving between dualistic states of mind, when we feel separated from each other and the world, and monistic states of mind, when we feel linked and interconnected with the world and with each other. The important issue, therefore, is whether psychotherapy responds to these new possibilities arising out of the evolution of consciousness or reinforces the dualism of the Enlightenment.

In my view, CBT and EBP, if applied in a pure way, tend to do the latter. The reinforcement of Enlightenment thinking in CBT and EBP can also be demonstrated by using, following Steiner, the metaphor of a building (1914: 67). There are two aspects to this. First, they both adopt a clear experimental methodology that involves defining the field within which the therapy is going to take place, and which is also based on the epistemological principles I have outlined. In the case of CBT, this may involve using a descriptive diagnostic tool such as *DSM-5*, or an evaluation tool such as Beck's depression inventory. This may require identifying an ailment (such as depression) on the basis of a clear definition, measuring its severity by using, say, the Beck inventory, and establishing the boundaries of the clinical field by eliminating other variables using the same principles as the experimental method. By evaluating the problem in this way, the therapist clarifies the task in hand and what needs to be done in a logical systematic manner, just as a builder identifies what needs to be done in regard to constructing a building.

The therapist then devises appropriate interventions to address the problem that has been defined and delineated. In terms of the building metaphor, s/he tries to determine how the construction is to be undertaken. This, in turn, will involve choosing appropriate materials and adopting an appropriate building technique, just as a therapist operationalises these principles by adopting a particular technique for addressing the problem that has been defined. Overall, the problem is diagnosed, the treatment applied, and the progress evaluated in a systematic way, using logic and reason. This contrasts with the new possibilities of consciousness – what I have referred to as dynamic dualism – where actions tend to be more intuitive and based on the needs of each individual situation (see House and Bohart's Chapter 19, this volume).

Second, as well as adopting clearly defined methods, a building also adopts a plan based on a particular ontological and epistemological position (post-modernist, modernist, or whatever). Similarly, CBT and EBP follow a definite 'plan' that incorporates a particular philosophical outlook or belief – in this case, as discussed, a belief in Cartesian dualism, the reliability of logical thought processes, and a clearly defined experimental method, whether this is at first obvious or not. Their underlying beliefs also suggest a high degree of scepticism and doubt about the emerging possibilities of human consciousness, including a reliance on direct experience and the use of our sensing, feeling and intuiting capacities in our therapeutic work, whereas the techniques of the psychodynamic and humanistic schools incorporate these qualities. As such, CBT and EBP exemplify the Cartesian notion of 'radical doubt' (Ferré, 1998: 1). But, whereas Descartes' doubt was directed towards medieval Christian views, CBT and EBP doubt the possibilities of consciousness open to us today – the use of our direct sensory experience of the world and working with interconnectedness and intersubjectivity gained as a result of the development of non-dualistic, monistic states of mind.

EBP is, in a sense, the quintessence of the above principles – experimentalism, systematisation and applying specific techniques – and the underlying belief in dualism, logic and doubt in intuitive capacities. It also illustrates the historical Enlightenment basis of this approach and these principles very well. Even though its EBMWG 'founders' view it as a relatively 'new paradigm for medical practice', discovered in 1992, from a historical perspective, this is not actually the case. The basic principles of EBP – the notion of meta-analysis of research into clinical outcomes and then applying such research findings in practice – were actually 'invented' by Bacon in a visionary work of imagination called *New Atlantis: a work unfinished*, which he wrote just before his death in 1626. This fragment, in my view, articulates precisely the principles of EBP. Bacon spoke of how, in the mythical Salomon's House, people were allotted various tasks. For instance, it was the job of the 'compilers' to look 'into the experiments of their fellows and cast about how to draw out of them things of use and practice for man's life'. So they were, in the language of EBP, concerned with gathering the findings of research studies and putting them together in such a way as to be useful for practical application, such as in clinical practice. It is interesting to think that these notions were first created out of Bacon's visionary consciousness almost 400 years ago, and not just discovered for the first time in 1992. So, EBP is not as new as it seems to be and, of course, does not explicitly recognise the possibilities of clinical practice, such as using countertransference and other intersubjective practices that have been emerging as a result of the changes in consciousness during the 20th and 21st centuries.

As demonstrated throughout this volume, the dominant scientific-rationalistic Baconian–Cartesian paradigm that underpins CBT and EBP has been challenged by many ways of thinking over the ages, including Romanticism, critical theory, new-paradigm science, human-inquiry research, postmodernism and linguistics, and, as I have discussed, the thinking and practice of psychotherapy itself. However, it remains remarkably resilient and untouched by these critiques – in spite of the fact that the possibilities inherent in our consciousness are moving on. Consequently, it still remains the dominant paradigm within the healthcare professions and within society at large, including within our educational systems.

However, it is my view that it can now be superseded by the new possibilities inherent in our consciousness. In short, in order to work through the many crises facing human beings and the planet in general, we need to develop ways of being and create institutions that help us to establish a different relationship with the world around us, and thereby overcome the malign effects of dualistic states of mind (such as our individual potential for destructiveness, the exploitation of the environment, the increased destructiveness of humankind generally, and social disintegration). In the final section of this chapter, I will look at the future: namely, where we go from here.

The future

While taking the view that CBT and EBT are products of contemporary Western scientific thinking, and so, to some degree, are inevitable developments in our current age, the essential issue is how we can move on from this way of thinking. The first step is to realise that these are ways of viewing the human being that have been socially constructed in the past. The danger is then that they will become problematic if their hegemony is perpetuated beyond its time. Such a state of affairs would contribute to cramping our development, moulding us within a limited frame, and perpetuating the destructive effects of scientism. In fact, I am reminded of Erich Fromm's prophetic notion that:

> In the nineteenth century the problem was that *God is dead*; in the twentieth century the problem is that *man is dead*. In the nineteenth century inhumanity meant cruelty; in the twentieth century it means schizoid self-alienation. The danger of the past was that men became slaves. The danger of the future is that men may become robots. (Fromm, 1956: 360; emphases in original)

This is similar to Steiner's notion of the 'abolition of the soul'. Steiner cites materialistic theories of history and certain aspects of the modern scientific outlook as reasons for this:

> This outlook – I am speaking not of the positive achievements of the scientific '*Weltanschauung*' – which accepts only the reality of the corporeal and regards everything pertaining to the soul as an epiphenomenon, a superstructure on what is corporeal... is the direct consequence [of previous historical developments]. (Steiner, 1917: 28)

In other words, logical, systematised – one could say mathematical – thinking has many advantages but also carries many dangers. It can seriously inhibit, and even blunt, our human potential. Fortunately, there are many other developments today that do not fit into such a narrow scientific paradigm and are trying to move beyond it. I have already mentioned some of them – Romanticism, critical theory, new-paradigm science, human-inquiry research, postmodernism, linguistics and therapy. In the present time, we could now add phenomenology, the transpersonal movement, environmentalism, feminism, the development of therapies arising out of the needs of minority and marginalised groups, the growth of alternative therapies, Steiner's anthroposophy, and many other spiritual movements.

The present, postmodern age seems to me to be ripe for building on these developments, and for developing a humane approach to science as a whole, and to therapy in particular, born out of our changing consciousness. As Gidley writes, there are many signs that 'human consciousness is evolving beyond materialistic instrumental rationality to more integral, more spiritual' states of consciousness (2007: 118), and the way in which we are beginning to understand our experience is becoming more diverse and subtle: we are beginning to value 'complex, dialectical, non-dualistic stances' (p121). In a broader sense, we are living in an age where there is a movement 'toward the potential integration of post-formal notions of cognition with love, reverence and spiritual development' (p122).

The future of the therapy profession, and indeed of the human race, will, in my view, be dependent on whether we can respond to the new possibilities of our consciousness while recognising the limitations of, but always looking for new ways of working with, the thinking we have inherited from the past.

References

Bower P (2005). Counselling for depression: the evidence for. *Healthcare Counselling and Psychotherapy Journal* 5(2): 16–17.

Clarkson P (2000). Eclectic, integrative and integrating psychotherapy, or beyond schoolism. In: Palmer S, Woolfe R (eds). *Integrative and Eclectic Counselling and Psychotherapy*. London: Sage (pp305–314).

Davy J (1985). *Hope, Evolution, Change*. Stroud: Hawthorn Press.

Evidence-Based Medical Working Group (1992). Evidence-based medicine: a new approach to teaching the practice of medicine. *Journal of the American Medical Association (JAMA) 268*: 2420–2425.

Eysenck H (1952). The effects of psychotherapy: an evaluation. *Journal of Consulting Psychology 16*: 319–324.

Ferré F (1998/1963). *Knowing and Value*. New York, NY: State University of New York Press.

Fromm E (1956). *The Sane Society*. London: Routledge & Kegan Paul.

Gidley JM (2007). Educational imperatives in the evolution of consciousness: the integral visions of Rudolf Steiner and Ken Wilber. *International Journal of Children's Spirituality 12*(2): 117–135.

Hughes I (2005). NICE in practice: some thoughts on delivering the new guideline on depression. *Counselling and Psychotherapy Journal 16*(3): 8–11.

Joseph S (2001). *Psychopathology and Therapeutic Approaches*. Basingstoke: Palgrave.

Lawrence S (2005). Anxiety guidelines: why counselling doesn't get a look in. *Counselling and Psychotherapy Journal 16*(2): 34–37.

Lees J (2008). The epistemological basis and scope of psychotherapy research. Unpublished paper. Available from the author.

Lindsay AD (1912). Introduction. In: Descartes R. *Discourse on Method* (J Veitch trans). London: Dent.

Lynch G (1996). What is truth? A philosophical introduction to counselling research. *Counselling 7*(2): 144–149.

NICE (2017). *Depression in adults: treatment and management*. NICE guideline. Draft for consultation, July 2017. London: NICE.

NICE (2004). *Depression: management of depression in primary and secondary care*. Clinical guideline CG23. London: NICE.

Parry G, Richardson S (1996). *NHS Psychotherapy Services in England: review of strategic policy*. Leeds: NHS Executive.

Parry G (2004). Why should counsellors care about research? *Counselling and Psychotherapy Journal 15*(6): 20–21.

Proctor G (2015). The NHS in 2015. *Therapy Today 26*(9): 18-25.

Ross P (1999). Focusing the work: a cognitive-behavioural approach. In: Lees J, Vaspe A (eds). *Clinical Counselling in Further and Higher Education*. London: Routledge (pp75–86).

Salkovskis PM (1996). Cognitive therapy and Aaron T Beck. In: Salkovskis PM (ed). *Frontiers of Cognitive Therapy*. New York, NY: Guilford Press (pp531–540).

Shostrom E (ed) (1965). *Three Approaches to Psychotherapy*. Orange, CA: Psychological Films.

Steiner R (1923/1977). *World History in the Light of Anthroposophy*. London: Rudolf Steiner Press.

Steiner R (1917/1972). *Building Stones for an Understanding of the Mystery of Golgotha*. London: Rudolf Steiner Press.

Steiner R (1914/1973. *The Riddles of Philosophy*. Spring Valley, NV: Anthroposophic Press.

Steiner R (1911/1982). *Occult History*. London: Rudolf Steiner Press.

Steiner R (1909/1963). *Occult Science*. London: Rudolf Steiner Press.

Steiner R (1904/1981). *Cosmic Memory*. San Francisco, CA: Harper & Row Publishers.

Steiner R (1894/1992). *The Philosophy of Freedom*. London: Rudolf Steiner Press.

Welburn A (2004). *Rudolf Steiner's Philosophy*. Edinburgh: Floris Books.

10 Cognitive therapy, Cartesianism, and the moral order*

Patrick Bracken and Philip Thomas

Over the last 30–40 years, cognitive therapy (CBT) has emerged as a popular intervention for a range of psychiatric problems, including anxiety, depression, obsessive compulsive disorder and post-traumatic conditions, as well as the symptoms of psychosis. Its political profile rose considerably following the intervention of economist Professor Lord Richard Layard, who first presented his idea for a national CBT therapy service in a paper presented to a prime ministerial strategy seminar on mental health on 20 January, 2005. Layard argued, on economic grounds, that the British government should make a substantial investment in therapists trained in CBT to reduce the numbers of people unable to work because of depression.

This report was very influential, and its proponents are still making the case that CBT is the key to transforming the lives of hundreds of thousands of people (Clark et al, 2016). As a therapy, CBT appears 'clear' in its concepts, is efficient and effective, and is relatively easy to learn. Its popularity – understandable in a culture that places a high value on efficiency – may also have something to do with its capacity to define its operations, and, purportedly, to measure and quantify its benefits 'scientifically'. In this respect, it differs from other forms of psychotherapy. However, like any form of therapy, CBT makes certain assumptions about the nature of the self and its relationships to others, and to the world in general. Aaron Beck, one of its originators, writes that CBT techniques 'are utilised within the framework of the cognitive model of psychopathology, and we do not believe that the therapy can be applied effectively without knowledge of the theory' (Beck et al, 1979: 4).

---

* An earlier version of this chapter appeared in the *European Journal of Psychotherapy 1999; Counselling and Health*, 2(3): 1999: 325–344.

CBT, therefore, is just one element in a particular approach to psychology and psychopathology. It is premised on the 'cognitive model' of mind, and understands disorders of mind to be caused by 'dysfunctional beliefs' and 'faulty information processing.' This involves a very particular philosophy of mind, which, in turn, has metaphysical and epistemological orientations. The model is not therefore 'value neutral', but involves a specific orientation toward the problems of suffering and healing. Beneath its scientific self-understanding, there is a *moral agenda* inherent in the cognitive framework, which we wish to unearth in this chapter.

Our position is not that CBT, and cognitive models of mind and mental disorder, are fallacious. However, we maintain that the discourse of cognitivism works only on the back of highly challengeable assumptions. We will examine the philosophy of mind that underlies cognitivism, and demonstrate its origins in the philosophy of René Descartes. We then use philosopher Charles Taylor's work to reveal some of the ethical assumptions hidden within this discourse, and we point to some clinical implications stemming from our analysis.

What is the cognitivist approach to mind and its disorders?

Cognitivism assumes an underlying structure to mentation, based on the biological organisation of the brain, but a separate, non-biological set of concepts is required in order to fully grasp it. In this framework, it is logical to treat the brain and the mind as separate realms, so the project of cognitivism concerns an exploration of the structures and the underlying basic elements of the mind. A fundamental assumption is that the elements of psychological life can be characterised in causal terms, so that hypotheses can be generated and then used to predict behaviour under different circumstances. As Harré and Gillett point out (1994: 14), the information-processing model offered the possibility of psychology becoming fully scientific, in the realist sense, with its theories comprising hypotheses about information-processing mechanisms. Behaviour-describing predictions could be deduced from these hypotheses, with speech, emotional display, the evincing of attitudes, problem-solving and so on all being, in principle, comprehensible.

As cognitivism gained influence, more areas of psychology adopted this framework, including Piagetian developmental psychology, social psychology and Kelly's personal construct theory (Kelly, 1955), as formulations based on unconscious drives and traits faded. Chomsky's (1959) critique of Skinner's behavioural account of language led ultimately to the new field of psycholinguistics, mapping grammar directly on to the mind, presaging in turn artificial intelligence (AI) models of mind. Although formulated in different terminologies, the basic proposition remains the same, with the concept of unconscious 'schemas' being especially popular:

All knowledge and experience is packaged in schemas. Schemas are the ghost in the machine, the intelligence that guides information as it flows through the mind (Goleman, 1985: 75).

In our own field of clinical psychiatry, the notion that human beings operate with unconscious models or schemas has been variously used, but it was in relation to 'depression' that CBT first achieved prominence, and through which we can really grasp the significance of schemas. Beck's theory of depression has influenced thought in many areas, including the treatment of voices (eg. Chadwick & Birchwood, 1994). Beck's model proposes that faulty or dysfunctional assumptions are laid down as cognitive schemata in childhood. These are subsequently activated by critical incidents in adulthood, and a meshing between the particular incident and the dysfunctional assumptions brings about a complex of 'negative automatic thoughts'. Beck proposes that these distorted, negative, dysfunctional and unhelpful thoughts underlie the clinical state of depression. He writes:

> In brief, the theory postulates that the depressed or depression-prone individual has certain idiosyncratic patterns (schemas) which may become activated whether by specific stresses impinging on specific vulnerabilities, or by overwhelming nonspecific stresses. When the cognitive patterns are activated, they tend to dominate the individual's thinking and to produce the affective and motivational phenomena associated with depression. (Beck, 1972: 129–130)

Thus, in this view, depression is not simply an affective disturbance but, rather, involves a specific disorder of thinking, of cognition, with the patient's cognitions being out of step with the surrounding culture in a distorted way, and requiring a special form of psychotherapeutic intervention.

In contrast to dynamic approaches, CBT does not involve any significant exploration of the past, focusing instead on the 'here and now'. It does not theorise about the therapeutic relationship in terms of unconscious forces, or transference and countertransference. It involves the therapist 'training' the patient to examine his/her thoughts in a systematic, logical, rational and 'non-distorted' way. The patient, in turn, is involved in 'homework' and 'exercises' between sessions. The therapist's job is thus to help patients confront their cognitive distortions by motivating them to do their homework. CBT believes at root in the importance and benefits of systematic reflection upon the contents of consciousness. By turning 'inwards', the patient is urged to bring reason to bear upon the internal workings of the mind. However, this 'turning inwards' remains unproblematised, as does the position of the therapist who is judging which beliefs are realistic and which distorted.

Beck emphasises the importance of the patient learning how to 'self-question' effectively:

> … the patient begins to incorporate many of the therapeutic techniques of the therapist. For example, patients frequently find themselves spontaneously assuming the role of the therapist in questioning some of their conclusions or

> predictions … Such self-questioning plays a major role in the generalization of cognitive techniques from the interview to external situations. (Beck et al, 1979: 4–5)

In other words, the patient begins to think like the therapist and incorporates the therapist's view of what is reasonable, logical and sensible. We noted earlier that CBT is not independent of the 'cognitive theory of mind'. Therefore, the therapist is effectively training the patient to accept this particular model of mind. This, in turn, raises a number of fundamental ethical issues, which necessitates some understanding of the historical and cultural origins of cognitivism.

The emergence of the cognitivist framework

Cognitive approaches embody the central assumptions of what has been called the 'Enlightenment project'. Although a complex multi-faceted cultural process, the European Enlightenment privileged the importance of reason in human affairs. Finding a path to true knowledge and certainty became the major concern of many Enlightenment thinkers, and epistemology became the central concern of philosophy. A guiding theme was the quest to replace religious revelation and ancient pronouncements with reason and science as the path to truth.

The Enlightenment involved a dramatic reorientation of intellectual life – a movement from 'darkness' to 'light'. Modern man was to look to the future, rather than the past, and to find in his own reason the path to this future. Philosophy was to have a vital role, for it was through a critical philosophy that both the potential and the limits of reason could be defined. Reason would therefore have to give up its preoccupation with what had already been said and handed down in tradition. Kant expresses this forcefully in his declaration that:

> Enlightenment is man's emergence from his self-incurred immaturity. Immaturity is the inability to use one's understanding without the guidance of another. This immaturity is called 'self-incurred' if its cause is not lack of understanding but lack of resolution and courage to use it without the guidance of another. The motto of Enlightenment is therefore *Sapere aude*! Have courage to use your own understanding! (Kant, 1784)

The other major theme emerging from the European Enlightenment concerned the human self and its depths. European thinkers became preoccupied with the 'inner voice' and the structures of subjectivity. In Kant's philosophy, structures of subjectivity become almost the entire subject matter of philosophy. This turning inwards can be seen in the phenomenology of Edmund Husserl, and of course, in the psychoanalysis of Freud.

Foucault (1967) has pointed out that the disciplines of psychology and psychiatry became possible only in a cultural framework substantially influenced by these Enlightenment and post-Enlightenment preoccupations. These disciplines represented a search for causal, scientific accounts of the mind and its disorders. They needed theories of the self and behaviour that would explain human actions and so allow for rational, technical interventions to be made. As Jerome Levin writes:

> In premodern conceptualisations, the self… [derived] its stability from its relationship with God, but now something else was required as a cement. The old verities were no longer certain, and the unity of the self, itself, was now problematical. (Levin, 1992: 16)

While the search for true knowledge and certainty dominated philosophy up to the 19th century, views differed as to how this quest should be pursued. Empiricists like Hobbes, Locke and Hume thought that the senses and empirical observation were the only path to certainty. Rationalist philosophers like Descartes, Spinoza and Leibniz, by contrast, proposed that reason and reflection were the source of true knowledge. Empiricist philosophies of science, dominant in the 19th and first half of the 20th centuries, emphasised the primary importance of perception, observation and data gathering, albeit acknowledging the essential role of reason in the form of induction and deduction. Behaviourism, in many ways a direct descendant of this empiricist tradition, relegated mental processes to a minor role in influencing human action. It refused to engage with the 'inner voice', the internal aspects of mind, and, in its most radical form, completely denied the existence of mental states. The advent of cognitive models and therapies challenged this view, and represented a fundamental shift in psychology toward an acceptance not only of the mind's existence, but also of the central premises of rationalism: the primacy of thought over sensation and the experiential world. In the cognitivist framework, then, inner mental processes come to have a central and dominant role in directing human action.

There are many reasons for the emergence of the 'cognitive revolution' in psychology (Harré & Gillett, 1994), including mounting dissatisfaction with behaviourism's limitations and the emergence of the computer as a Western cultural icon. It has recently become popular not only to think of the mind as being like a computer, but to propose that it *is* in some sense a computer (Churchland & Sejnowski, 1992). As psychology became concerned to explain the mind in terms of causal mechanisms, it found a natural ally in various versions of rule-following formulae that were to be found in the developing world of AI. In fact, the assumptions underlying AI and cognitivist psychology are essentially the same. If it is possible, in principle, to account for different aspects of human thought and behaviour in terms of rule-following formulae, then it should also be possible, in principle, to build machines that operate on the basis of these formulae, replicating human intelligence and behaviour. Both developments assume that the human mind works in the same way as computers.

What philosophy of mind is involved in cognitivism?

Theoretical and practical developments in AI and cognitive psychology have gained substantial support from contemporary developments in philosophy of mind. Philosophers like Jerry Fodor argue for a computational view of thought, a fairly dominant position in current philosophy of mind (Crane, 1995). By the mid-1990s, Lyons (1995: lviii) could write that functionalism, as this philosophy had come to be called, had become 'something approaching an orthodoxy over the last 10 years'.

Functionalists draw on the dualism implicit in the computer model to argue the case for a separate mental realm. Just as computer software cannot be fully accounted for by reference to hardware alone, so too, mental states cannot be reductively explained through an account of brain states alone. Mentation has its own elements and structures that cannot be explained in the language of physics, chemistry and neurophysiology. In his book *Mind, Language and Reality*, philosopher Hilary Putnam outlines the basic case of functionalism:

> According to functionalism, the behaviour of, say, a computing machine is not explained by the physics and chemistry of the computing machine. It is explained by the machine's program. Of course, that program is realized in a particular physics and chemistry, and could, perhaps, be deduced from that physics and chemistry. But that does not make the program a physical or chemical property of the machine: it is an abstract property of the machine. Similarly, I believe that the psychological properties of human beings are not physical and chemical properties of human beings, although they may be realised by physical and chemical properties of human beings. (Putnam, 1975: xiii)

In addition to its assertion of mind–brain dualism, functionalism also makes assertions about the nature of thinking. In this view, representational mental states, such as beliefs, desires, memories and aspirations, are related to one another in a computational way. They are processed in a rule-governed way, as are the representational states of a computer. Fodor calls this the 'Representational Theory of Mind'. He writes:

> At the heart of this theory is the postulation of a language of thought: an infinite set of 'mental representations' which function both as the immediate objects of propositional attitudes and as the domains of mental processes. (Fodor, 1995: 258)

He goes on to spell out what the notion of 'propositional attitude' means for him:

> To believe that such and such is to have a mental symbol that means such and such tokened in your head in a certain way; it's to have such a token 'in your belief box'... Correspondingly, to hope that such and such is to have a

> token of that same mental symbol tokened in your head, but in a different way; it's to have it tokened 'in your hope box'.

Furthermore, this theory of mind involves the claim that, 'Mental processes are causal sequences of tokenings of mental representations' (Fodor, 1995: 258).

In this framework, it makes perfect sense to explore the mind by using physical-scientific methods. With the elements of mind causally connected, hypothesis development and testing can occur, just as in physics or biology. Functionalism as a theory of mind incorporates assumptions that have a long heritage in Western philosophy. With many stemming from the work of Descartes, and some derived from the philosophy of empiricists like Locke, functionalism has become subsumed under the heading of 'Cartesianism' (Dreyfus, 1991). Functionalism, as proposed by Fodor and others, then, essentially amounts to a form of Cartesianism that makes use of the computer metaphor.

A fundamental tenet of Cartesianism is the idea of a separate mental realm, or mind, within which the outside world is somehow represented, and with such representations being interrelated in a way that can be formally described and analysed. The central philosophical problem for Descartes was the question of certainty: how can we be certain that our internal representations provide an accurate account of the external world? He proposed a method of systematic reflection on the contents of the mind, thereby separating what was clear and accurate from what was uncertain and vague. By systematically doubting everything that was unclear, he argued, we could reflexively reach a situation of certainty, which for him was guaranteed by God. Certainty was reached by turning away from the world and looking inwards to examine our own thoughts in isolation, without reference to what they represented in the outside world.

While God was the ultimate guarantor of truth and certainty, his presence was not essential for Descartes' confidence in our ability to look inwards, clarify our thoughts, and separate the clear from the unclear. As long as we adhere to the representational theory of thought, then, even in the absence of a divine guarantor of truth, systematic reflexivity will render us better able to account for our thoughts. A central tenet of Cartesianism is, therefore, a belief in the importance of reflexive clarity, and thus our ability to define and map the ways in which our internal representations are ordered and related.

In addition, Cartesianism operates on a fundamental distinction between the 'inner' world of the mind and the 'outer' world with which it is in contact. Thought becomes the inner functioning of a 'thinking substance' or subject (*subjectum*). This subject is in contact with an outside world, and has knowledge of it through sensation and through the representations it has of it. Thus, the mind stands outside of the world and has a relation to it. Mind becomes something conceivable apart from and separate to this relation.

It is this separation, elaborated in terms of the inner and the outer, that gives sense to the representational theory of mind and thought. It also provides the source for the project of phenomenology, at least as developed by Husserl and his followers.

Husserl's orientation towards the Cartesian project is overtly positive (the title of one of his major works is *Cartesian Meditations*). His fundamental method of enquiry, which he called 'phenomenological reduction', involved setting aside, or 'bracketing', of the existence of an outside world in order to focus in a clear and unbiased way on the phenomena of consciousness and experience. His aim was to reach what he called the 'transcendental standpoint', to be achieved by a series of 'reductions', which were operations performed on everyday experience to isolate the 'pure' consciousness that is obscured if it is not separated from the natural world.

Like Descartes, Husserl was attempting to elaborate a method of investigation into the experiential world that was reliable and foundational. Sass writes:

> Like Descartes' method of doubt, Husserl's approach can be called a kind of 'foundationalism': an attempt to discover a realm of indubitable and transparent meanings or experiential entities that can provide a firm basis on which to build valid knowledge about human existence. (Sass, 1989: 443)

Cartesianism, therefore, provides an account of the self and thought that has been articulated in different ways through different philosophies. In many ways, it has come to be taken as 'commonsense', and through functionalism and phenomenology has come to be an orthodoxy in modern psychology and psychiatry. With reference to the latter, the Cartesian perspective involves a number of orientating assumptions, summarised here:

1. an endorsement of 'methodological individualism' and a belief in the possibility and importance of detached reflection upon the contents of mind
2. an acceptance that the mind is something internal and separate to the world that is external to it
3. a belief in the causal nature of psychological events and a reliance on positivism to guide research and theory formation.

Many cognitivists insist that their understanding of the mind involves a rejection of Descartes' ontological dualism. Mind is a material entity, not a spiritual one. In a Cartesian idiom, it manifests the property of 'extension' – it can be measured. By asserting the computational nature of mind and by using the computer analogy, they feel confident that they have overcome the major difficulties involved in Cartesian dualism. We have no difficulty with the idea that cognitivism involves a materialist understanding of human reality. However, it should be clear from the previous discussion that this move does not free cognitivism from the other assumptions of the Cartesian understanding of mind. In particular, the three assumptions listed above all remain central to the cognitivist framework.

Cartesianism and the moral order

Although this approach to mind has become something of an orthodoxy, the moral framework it assumes has remained hidden. When this is revealed, the limitations of the cognitivist paradigm come clearly to light. In a series of influential writings, philosopher Charles Taylor has argued strongly that modern notions of self, individuality and agency are historically contingent – thereby problematising what routinely seem like self-evident facts in Western modernity. It is, indeed, difficult for us even to imagine other ways of thinking about our selves beyond the ways given to us by this culture. In his book *Sources of the Self: the making of the modern identity*, for example, Taylor (1989) traces the origins of our modern notions about self, highlighting the particular sense of a moral order established around this. Modern ideas about good and bad, right and wrong are often predicated on a certain concept of the individual self, and how this self relates to the wider order of the natural world and the universe at large. Taylor explores what he calls the 'background picture' lying behind our moral and spiritual intuitions – or our 'moral ontology' (Taylor, 1989: 8).

Taylor's investigation of the moral ontology of modernity leads directly to modern notions of human agency, and how these in turn are influenced by modern ideas about the mind and epistemology. He argues that a Cartesian approach to mind and the self, which he calls the 'epistemological tradition', is inextricably bound up with modern ideas about morality and spirituality. He uses this connection to explain the ease with which computer models of thinking have become established in Western societies. The concept of AI is closely allied to a philosophy of functionalism. Empirically, such models have had only limited success: AI has not lived up to its original aspirations and is, at least in its traditional form (described by John Haugeland as Good Old-Fashioned AI, or GOFAI), an example of what Imré Lakatos called a 'degenerating research program' (Dreyfus, 1994). However, the computer model of thought is still widely accepted, and functionalism remains one of the dominant positions in modern philosophy of mind. It has already been noted that cognitivism is of growing importance in psychology and psychiatry. This contradiction leads Taylor to assert that:

> ... the great difficulties that the computer simulations have encountered… don't seem to have dimmed the enthusiasm of real believers in the model. It is as though they had been vouchsafed some revelation a priori that it must all be done by formal calculi. Now this revelation, I submit, comes from the depth of our modern culture and the epistemological model anchored in it, whose strength is based not just on its affinity to mechanistic science but also on its congruence to the powerful ideal of reflexive, self-given certainty. For this has to be understood as something like a moral ideal. (Taylor, 1997: 6)

In other words, our acceptance of cognitivism, and of computer models of mind and thinking, cannot be explained by the empirical success of these approaches alone. Instead, it appears to be driven by other cultural aspirations and ideals as well. Taylor's moral ideal relates to our cultural concern with autonomy and freedom. In the modern sense, a free agent is one who is able to rely on his/her own judgments, who can gaze in at his/her own needs and desires, and who can seek fulfillment of the latter in the outside world. A free agent is one who can stand back from the world and be responsible according to one's own agenda. Thus, our very notion of freedom involves a distinction between inside and outside and a calculating self-reflexivity.

According to Taylor, there are three aspects of this modern view of the self that are particularly bound up with the Cartesian, or epistemological, tradition:

> The first is the picture of the subject as ideally disengaged, that is free and rational to the extent that he has fully distinguished himself from the natural and social worlds, so that his identity is no longer to be defined in terms of what lies outside him in these worlds. The second, which flows from this, is a punctual view of the self, ideally ready as free and rational to treat these worlds – and even some features of his own character – instrumentally, as subject to change and reorganising in order the better to secure the welfare of himself and others. The third is the social consequence of the first two: an atomistic construal of society as constituted by, or ultimately to be explained in terms of, individual, purposes. (Taylor, 1997: 6)

He maintains that to challenge one tradition automatically brings us into conflict with the other. The epistemological tradition gives support to the moral order of modernity and its ideals of disengaged rationalistic agency. In turn, this order gives support to the apparent clarity and naturalness of the Cartesian account of self and thought, and these traditions stand together in 'a complex relation of mutual support' (p8).

In the technologies of psychiatry and psychotherapy, this mutuality becomes explicit in the credence our culture gives to analysis of the self. For example, the word 'insight' is a powerful metaphor of this inwardly directed gaze in search of self-awareness and self-understanding. Reflecting upon oneself in a detached and 'objective' manner has become a moral imperative. Analysing one's desires, motives and aspirations through either cognitive forms of therapy or psychodynamic approaches is widely accepted as a 'good' way to deal with anxiety, depression and, more recently, psychosis. In a wider field, the concept of 'counselling' has penetrated every aspect of personal and social life. However, it is CBT that has a specific agenda of bringing a rational ordering to the world of unconscious 'scripts' and 'schemas', with the apparent objective of ridding ourselves of anxiety and despair through the Cartesian ideal of self-reflexivity. The end result of therapy is a self that is more self-aware and detached; a self that can monitor itself in a rational way and detect emerging difficulties; a self that has loosened the bonds of dependency; a self that is more 'free' in every way.

CBT for voices

It may be easier to understand the implications of the critique developed in this chapter if we examine recent work describing CBT for people who hear voices. The origin of Chadwick and Birchwood's technique is deeply influenced by Aaron Beck:

> ... the belief that a voice comes from a powerful and vengeful spirit may make the person terrified of the voice and comply with its commands to harm others; however, if the same voice were construed as self-generated, the behaviour and affect might be quite different. This cognitive formulation of voices was inspired by Beck's cognitive model of depression (eg. Beck et al, 1979). (Chadwick & Birchwood, 1994: 190–191)

Chadwick and Birchwood thus propose that distress associated with voices may be reduced by changing the subject's beliefs about the voices. They point to empirical evidence from interviews with voice-hearers that suggests that beliefs about voices' identities (whether they are malevolent or benevolent) determine how people respond to them. Their subjects engaged with positive voices, and they resisted malevolent ones. This observation establishes a rationale for the intervention:

> The cognitive treatment approach to hallucinations involves the *elucidation and challenging of the core beliefs that individuals have about their voices*. The weakening or loss of these beliefs is predicted to ease distress and facilitate a wider range of more adaptive coping strategies.' (Chadwick & Birchwood, 1994: 195; emphasis added)

Therapy consists of three stages. In the opening phase, the therapist engages the voice-hearer and establishes rapport. Education is an important component, and a tone of what is described as 'collaborative empiricism' (Beck et al, 1979) is established. The second stage involves disputing the subject's beliefs about voices, using two techniques drawn from CBT – hypothetical contradiction and verbal challenge. The former 'measures' the voice-hearer's willingness to accept evidence that challenges their beliefs by considering their responses to hypothetical contradictory evidence. A verbal challenge is then used to challenge the subject's beliefs directly:

> The next stage in therapy is to question the beliefs directly. This involves first *pointing out examples of inconsistency and irrationality, and then, offering an alternative explanation of events*: namely that the voices might be self-

> generated and that the beliefs are an attempt to make sense of them. (Chadwick & Birchwood, 1994: 196, emphasis added)

Finally, the therapist tries to test the subject's beliefs about voices by setting up situations in which the subject can discover that, for example, control can be exerted over the voices.

There are several ways in which our critique is relevant to this work. First is the importance attached in getting the subject to agree that voices are self-generated. The assumption here is that voices arise through faulty internal mental mechanisms. Cognitive science has expended much effort in seeking to establish the nature of these internal faults, although their nature varies (see, for example, Bentall & Slade, 1985; Frith, 1992). As far as therapy is concerned, the subject has to be persuaded that the voices are located internally, even though, in many cases, the subject's perception is that they are located externally. This is important: subjects then have to be convinced by the therapist that their beliefs about voices are erroneous, and that, if the correct beliefs can be established, then distress will be reduced. Thus, the therapist has an important moral role: that of an arbiter, or judge, as to what might be rational or irrational beliefs for subjects to hold about voices.

There are serious difficulties with this position. The cognitivist insistence that voices are internally generated endorses the strong separation of 'inner mind' from 'external world' discussed earlier. As we have seen, this derives from a particular philosophical and cultural tradition and cannot be regarded as simply reflecting the objectively true nature of reality. In practice, this separation generates a therapeutic situation where little attention is paid to the subject's social reality and the possibility that links may exist between the voices and events that have occurred in this reality. This is important, because there is evidence that links hearing voices to trauma such as sexual abuse (eg. Longden, Madill & Waterman, 2011; Read, Bentall & Fosse, 2009) and personal experiences of racism (Karlsen et al, 2005). It also disregards the view that voices can be seen to have *metaphorical* significance for subjects, and that the understanding of this metaphorical significance – in other words, relating the identity and content of voices to past experience – is important in helping the person to cope (Davies, Leudar & Thomas, 1999; Romme et al, 1992).

CBT thus fails to contextualise the subject's voices and disregards the possibility of understanding voices in terms of experience. This problem is compounded by the therapist's attempts to convince subjects that their beliefs about voices are wrong. For example, someone who has been abused in childhood may hear the voice of the devil telling them they are evil. The voice may share pragmatic features of the abuser (Leudar et al, 1997), which suggests that the identity of the voice (devil) is aligned with the abuser. From the voice-hearer's position as an abused person, it is quite true to say that the voice represents the devil. Most people would agree that abuse is evil. If we attempt to persuade the subject that they are not really hearing the devil, and the voice comes from within, we are denying that aspect of the subject's reality that signifies the abuse. Some would regard such an act as itself abusive. This demonstrates one of the fundamental difficulties within cognitivism as a clinical discourse: *its preoccupation with interiority means that there is a systematic neglect of the external social world.*

Cognitivism undermines the possibility of understanding voices, or, for that matter, any other aspect of human experience, within shared human contexts. To be fair, some cognitivists are aware of these shortcomings, and have become increasingly aware of them since we wrote the original version of this chapter. A subject in a study by Haddock and colleagues (1993) found it extremely difficult to accept that his voices were internally generated. The authors noted, though, that his voices were largely understandable in terms of the depressing social and material circumstances in which he was living at the time.

While cognitive behaviour therapy remains the main psychological intervention for people who hear voices and experience psychosis, it is important to recognise that, in recent years, therapists increasingly use CBT in conjunction with other forms of therapy that engage with contexts of adversity, such as trauma and abuse. (Cooke, 2017)

Implications

CBT and other forms of self-reflective therapy endorse the two traditions described by Taylor, offering each other mutual support: namely, Cartesian notions of self and thought and a moral order based on individualism and atomism. Such theories and therapies are at home in a culture that strongly values and privileges the 'ideally disengaged' subject.

The first issue here concerns the extent to which such a view of self and agency can be regarded as universal – a question that can be answered only by reference to the literature of social anthropology. Our treatment of the issue here will not be extensive, and we will simply point to a few examples that make the point. The anthropologist Clifford Geertz defines the issue at stake:

> The Western conception of the person as a bounded, unique, more or less integrated motivational and cognitive universe, a dynamic centre of awareness, emotion, judgement, and action organised into a distinctive whole and set contrastively both against other such wholes and against a social and natural background, is, however incorrigible it may seem to us, a rather peculiar idea within the context of the world's cultures. (Geertz, 1975: 48)

Arthur Kleinman has conducted extensive research on the problem of depression in Chinese and American patients. In his book, *Rethinking Psychiatry*, he writes:

> Psychiatry in the West is strongly influenced by implicit Western cultural values about the nature of the self and its pathologies which emphasise a

> deep, hidden private self. In contrast… the Chinese view the self, to a large degree, as consensual – a sociocentrically oriented personality that is much more attentive to the demands of a particular situation and key relationships than to what is deeply private… Social context, not personal depth, is the indigenous measure of validity. (Kleinman, 1988: 98)

Laurence Kirmayer (1988) points out that in Japan autonomy in interpersonal relationships is much less valued than in the West. For the Japanese, the moral value of the self is expressed through an idiom of social connectedness, rather than personal achievement. Kirmayer contrasts what he calls the 'sociosomatic' origins of distress in Japan with the more familiar psychosomatic framework developed in the West. Shweder and Bourne (1982) also distinguish two different approaches to the individual–social relationship: the 'egocentric contractual' and the 'sociocentric organic'. Societies endorsing the former as an ideal tend to emphasise the intrapsychic, promoting reflection on the self and its desires and cognitions. Sociocentric societies have much less focus on the psychological realm; instead, there is an orientation toward individual integration with the natural, supernatural, and social worlds. This differentiation is now generally accepted in social anthropology, and is also increasingly accepted by mainstream transcultural psychiatrists (eg. Leff, 1988).

Thus, the disengaged self, a basic assumption of Western psychiatry and psychology, is not a recognised notion in many world cultures. In multi-cultural modern Europe, the promotion of CBT as an answer to distress entails promoting a particular view of the self – with major implications for many ethnic minority communities struggling to maintain a sense of their own identity and ways of life. Because CBT is presented as a 'scientific' enterprise, devoid of value orientations, these implications often remain unseen. The foregoing analysis therefore raises profound problems for the 'exporting' of therapies based on cognitivism to other parts of the world (Bracken & Petty, 1998).

The second issue can be formulated as a question: is the moral order predicated on the philosophy of mind implicit in cognitivism the sort of order to which we should aspire? Nikolas Rose has developed a sustained Foucauldian analysis of how psychology and psychotherapeutics have now penetrated into everyday life. He points to the political dimension of these developments, arguing that we are now substantially governed, ironically, through our own individual quests for freedom and self-expression:

> Psychotherapeutics is linked at a profound level to the socio-political obligations of the modern self. The self it seeks to liberate or restore is the entity able to steer its individual path through life by means of the act of personal decision and the assumption of personal responsibility. It is the self freed from all moral obligations but the obligation to construct a life of its own choosing, a life in which it realises itself… [T]he norm of autonomy

> secretes, as its inevitable accompaniment, a constant and intense self-scrutiny, a continual evaluation of our personal experiences, emotions, and feelings in relation to images of satisfaction, the necessity to narrativise our lives in a vocabulary of interiority. The self that is liberated is obliged to live its life tied to the project of its own identity. (Rose, 1989: 253–254)

Cognitive therapy, then, locates the problems of anxiety, depression and psychosis firmly in the interior, with the 'irrational' network of faulty schemata and dysfunctional beliefs giving rise to these problems allegedly being ordered by the exercise of reason alone. Distress can then be neutralised by looking within. Moreover, CBT enthusiastically asserts the value of this move toward self-scrutiny. In doing so, it not only connects the individual to the 'sociopolitical obligations of the modern self', but also works to devalue any contextualising understanding of distress. In a thoughtful, philosophical appraisal of CBT, Richard Gipps argues that this form of therapeutic approach incorporates a sort of 'alienated' form of human subjectivity. He writes:

> Mind becomes a domain of inner states and processes rather than a matter of how we are embedded in our intentional worlds. The self will no longer speak *from* its attitudes, but will rather be reduced to speaking *about* them.' (Gipps, 2013: 1260).

To grapple with the fact that we are always and everywhere, first and foremost, embedded beings, we will need to turn in a different direction philosophically. Two of the greatest philosophers of the 20th century, Martin Heidegger and Ludwig Wittgenstein, both argued for a very different understanding of human reality, attaching particular importance to understanding, in terms of background (or social) context. This influence is now being felt in, for example, new phenomenological approaches (Csordas, 1994), the 'discursive turn' within psychology (Harré & Gillett, 1994), and latterly in a newly emerging 'post-existential' cosmology (Loewenthal, Chapter 14, this volume). While not without difficulties themselves, such approaches at least make it possible to lay open the moral assumptions and values that underpin cognitivism.

References

Beck AT (1972). *The Diagnosis and Management of Depression*. Philadelphia, PA: University of Pennsylvania Press.

Beck AT, Rush AJ, Shaw BF, Emerry G (1979). *COgnitive Therapy of Depression*. New York, NY: Guilford Press.

Bentall RP, Slade PD (1985). Reality testing and auditory hallucinations: a signal detection hypothesis. *British Journal of Clinical Psychology 24:* 159–169.

Bracken P, Petty C (1998). *Rethinking the Trauma of War*. London: Free Association Books.

Chadwick P, Birchwood M (1994). The omnipotence of voices: a cognitive approach to auditory hallucinations. *British Journal of Psychiatry 164*: 190–201.

Chomsky N (1959). Review of BF Skinner's *Verbal Behaviour. Language* 35: 26–58.

Churchland P, Sejnowski T (1992.) *The Computational Brain.* Cambridge, MA: MIT Press.

Clark AE, Flèche S, Layard R, Powdthavee N, Ward G (2016). *The Origins of Happiness: evidence and policy implications.* [Blog.] VOX, 12 December. http://voxeu.org/article/origins-happiness (accessed 2 February 2018).

Cooke A (ed) (2017). *Understanding Psychosis and Schizophrenia* (revised ed). [Online.] Leicester: British Psychological Society Division of Clinical Psychology. www.bps.org.uk/system/files/userfiles/Division%20of%20Clinical%20Psychology/public/CAT-1657.pdf (accessed 22 July 2017).

Crane T (1995). *The Mechanical Mind.* London: Penguin.

Csordas T (1994). Words from the Holy People: a case study in cultural phenomenology. In: Csordas T (ed). *Embodiment and Experience: the existential ground of culture and self.* Cambridge, MA: Cambridge University Press (pp269–290).

Davies P, Leudar I, Thomas P (1999). Dialogical engagement with voices: a single case study. *British Journal of Medical Psychology 72*: 179–187.

Dreyfus H (1991). *Being-in-the-World: a commentary on Heidegger's* Being and Time. Cambridge, MA: MIT Press.

Dreyfus H (1994). *What Computers Still Can't Do: a critique of artificial reason.* Cambridge, MA: MIT Press.

Fodor J (1995). The persistence of attitudes. In: Lyons W (ed). *Modern Philosophy of Mind.*

London: Everyman (pp240–271).

Foucault M (1967). *Madness and Civilization: a history of insanity in the age of reason* (R Howard trans). London: Tavistock.

Frith C (1992). *The Cognitive Neuropsychology of Schizophrenia.* London: Lawrence Erlbaum.

Geertz C (1975). On the nature of anthropological understanding. *American Scientist 63*: 48.

Gipps R (2013). Cognitive behaviour therapy: a philosophical appraisal. In: Fulford KWM, Davies M, Gipps R, Graham G, Stanghellini G, Thornton T (eds). *The Oxford Handbook of Philosophy and Psychiatry.* Oxford: Oxford University Press (pp1245–1263).

Goleman D (1985). *Vital Lies, Simple Truths: the psychology of self-deception.* New York, NY: Simon & Schuster.

Haddock G, Bentall RP, Slade PD (1993). Psychological treatment of chronic auditory hallucinations: Two case studies. *Behavioural and Cognitive Psychotherapy 21*: 335–346.

Harré R, Gillett G (1994). *The Discursive Mind.* Thousand Oaks, CA: Sage.

Kant I (1784). *What is enlightenment?* Available at: http://library.standrews-de.org/lists/CourseGuides/religion/rs-vi/oppressed/kant_what_is_enlightenment.pdf (accessed 14 February 2018).

Karlsen S, Nazroo J, McKenzie K, Bhui K, Weich S (2005). Racism, psychosis and common mental disorder among ethnic minority groups in England. [Online.] *Psychological Medicine 35:* 1795–1803.

Kelly GA (1955). *The Psychology of Personal Constructs*. New York, NY: Norton.

Kirmayer LJ (1988). Mind and body as metaphors: hidden values in biomedicine. In: Lock M, Gordon D (eds). *Biomedicine Examined*. Dordrecht: Kluwer Academic (pp57–93).

Kleinman A (1988). *Rethinking Psychiatry: from cultural category to personal experience*. New York, NY: The Free Press.

Layard R (2005). *Mental Health: Britain's biggest social problem*. Paper presented at the No10 Strategy Unit Seminar on Mental Health on 20th January 2005. [Online.] London: Centre for Economic Performance, London School of Economics. http://cep.lse.ac.uk/textonly/research/mentalhealth/RL414d.pdf (accessed 8 August 2008).

Leff J (1988). *Psychiatry around the Globe*. London: Royal College of Psychiatrists.

Leudar I, Thomas P, McNally D, Glinski A (1997). What voices can do with words: pragmatics of verbal hallucinations. *Psychological Medicine 2*: 885–898.

Levin JD (1992). *Theories of the Self*. Washington, DC: Hemisphere.

Longden E, Madill A, Waterman M (2011). Dissociation, trauma, and the role of lived experience: toward a new conceptualization of voice hearing. *Psychological Bulletin 138:* 28–76.

Lyons W (1995). Introduction. In: Lyons W (ed). *Modern Philosophy of Mind*. London: Everyman (pp xlv –lxviii).

Putnam H (1975). *Mind, Language and Reality: philosophical papers, vol 2*. Cambridge: Cambridge University Press.

Read J, Bentall RP, Fosse R (2009). Time to abandon the bio-bio-bio model of psychosis: exploring the epigenetic and psychological mechanisms by which adverse life events lead to psychotic symptoms. *Epidemiologia e Psichiatria Sociale 18*(4): 299–310.

Romme M, Honig A, Noordhoorn E, Escher A (1992). Coping with voices: an emancipatory approach. *British Journal of Psychiatry 161*: 99–103.

Rose N (1989). *Governing the Soul*. London: Routledge.

Sass L (1989). Humanism, hermeneutics, and humanistic psychoanalysis: differing conceptions of subjectivity. *Psychoanalysis and Contemporary Theory 12*: 433–504.

Shweder RA, Bourne EJ (1982). Does the concept of the person vary cross-culturally? In: Marsella AJ, White GM (eds). *Cultural Conceptions of Mental Health and Therapy*. Dordrecht: Reidel (pp97–137).

Taylor C (1997). *Philosophical Arguments*. Cambridge, MA: Harvard University Press.

Taylor C (1989). *Sources of the Self: the making of the modern identity*. Cambridge, MA: Harvard University Press.

CLINICAL PERSPECTIVES

11 Psychoanalysis and cognitive behaviour therapy: rival paradigms or common ground?*

Jane Milton

Over the last 20 years, CBT has become the dominant form of psychotherapy available in the public sector, with psychoanalytic psychotherapy and counselling pushed to the very margins. The old psychotherapy departments, headed mostly by psychoanalytically trained psychiatrists and often staffed by honorary psychotherapists in training, who received skilled supervision in return for their free services to local people, have been all but obliterated. Similarly, experienced psychodynamic counsellors and psychotherapists working in general practice have often been replaced with newly trained IAPT therapists. Such has been the effect of complex political, cultural and economic changes, not least the IAPT programme – the letters ironically standing for 'Improving Access to Psychological Therapies'. At the same time, psychoanalytic psychotherapy is in increasing demand in the private sector and psychoanalysis remains an evolving and flourishing discipline, both in theory and in practice.

In this paper, I often use the term 'psychoanalysis' to refer to the psychoanalytic approach, but it should be noted that, strictly speaking, psychoanalysis implies treatment four or five times weekly, while the more commonly encountered practice of psychoanalytic psychotherapy is less intensive work using the same basic approach. The former allows detailed study of the mind, which then can act as a seedbed for discoveries that can be applied more generally (see Milton, Polmear & Fabricius, 2011).

This chapter will not attempt to cover the philosophical and political issues, which are ably addressed in other chapters, but will concentrate on comparing the

---

* An earlier version of this chapter appeared in the *International Journal of Psychoanalysis* 2001; 82(3): 431–447. It was originally presented at a conference of the same title organised by the Association for Psychoanalytic Psychotherapy in the NHS on 3 March 2000 at St Anne's College, Oxford.

psychoanalytic and cognitive paradigms. How do they differ? Has anything, in fact, been lost by the systematic dismantling of the psychoanalytic frame of reference in the public sector? Is any loss partially remedied by the combination or integration in practice of the two forms of treatment?

In comparing the two clinical paradigms, I suggest that CBT practitioners are rediscovering the same phenomena that psychoanalysts earlier encountered and have changed their practice accordingly. These rediscovered phenomena concern unconscious processes, the complexity of the internal world and the intrinsic difficulties of psychic change. I suggest that early psychoanalysis was itself more 'cognitive' and had to evolve to meet similar challenges. We may find that CBT technique continues to become more 'analytic'. Accompanying this, I think it is even possible that the need for longer and more complex training of therapists, including the necessity of personal training therapy, will be discovered.

In relation to the patient, the therapeutic stance of the therapist in CBT is a socially ordinary one (Milton, Polmear & Fabricius, 2011), which makes intuitive sense. The psychoanalytic stance is much harder to swallow and is maintained against the resistance of both the analyst and the patient. I suggest that there is a constant tendency for 'decomposition', or collapse, into something simpler during psychoanalytic work. The analyst is pushed constantly from without and from within, either into being more 'cognitive', or into a simpler counselling stance. The advantage of the striving for analytic neutrality is that more disturbance becomes available in the room, within the therapeutic relationship itself, to be worked with and potentially transformed. CBT is less disturbing and intrusive. It is important that, although it forfeits potential therapeutic power, CBT is acceptable to some patients in a way that psychoanalytic therapy is not, protecting privacy and defences that the individual has good reasons for wishing to preserve.

Paradoxically, the stance of the CBT therapist (which I suggest is nearest to that of a 'personal trainer') is ultimately more paternalistic than that of the psychoanalytic 'participant observer'. The latter has no recommendations about how to think but aims simply to understand and to introduce the patient to him or herself as fully as possible. Any perception that the analyst is wiser or more knowledgeable about life than the patient is analysed, along with other feelings and thoughts about the analyst, ultimately leading to greater freedom.

In practice, 'integration' of analytic and cognitive methods produces something more cognitive than analytic. Once cognitive or behavioural parameters are introduced by the therapist, I argue that a true analytic stance essentially ceases to exist – the analytic paradigm again collapses into the cognitive one, with a loss of potential therapeutic power. This is worth exploring, in view of the current enthusiasm for 'integrated' treatments, of which 'cognitive analytic therapy' (CAT) is an example.

One oft-quoted argument for offering CBT, rather than psychoanalytic treatments, to patients in the public sector is that there is more empirical research evidence for its efficacy – an issue several chapters address in detail in this book.

On the surface, it also appears cheaper, as it is brief and needs less training to apply. This alleged superior efficacy of CBT is, however, questionable empirically, and I will look briefly at the outcome research field in this connection.

History of the split from psychoanalysis

Aaron T Beck, a central figure in the development of CBT, started his professional career as a psychoanalyst, graduating from the Philadelphia Psychoanalytic Institute in 1956. He became disillusioned and impatient with the psychoanalytic culture in which he found himself – in his view, it was unfocused, rested on dubious theoretical foundations, and was insufficiently located in the patient's current reality. It is worth noting that psychoanalysis was very much the dominant, authoritative culture in psychiatry at that time in the US – a situation radically different from that in the UK or in the rest of the world, then or now. To the dismay of Freud himself, psychoanalysis in the US in the early days became, not an independent lay discipline, as it is in the UK, but, as Freud described it, 'a handmaid of psychiatry' (Freud, 1961), ruled by an almost exclusively male, medical hegemony (see Hale 1995). This robbed it, I think, of its essential subversiveness, and gave rise to the stereotype of the 'fatherly shrink'. Beck might well have found the relatively active, here-and-now-based object relations approach of modern British (and much American) psychoanalysis more to his taste.

Beck, in opposition to the establishment model in which he found himself, elaborated a 'cognitive theory' of depression, from which he derived a brief therapeutic approach. Beck's biographer, Weishaar (1993), notes that he is open about having developed his theory and technique not just through his clinical experience but, as Freud did, through introspection and analysis of his own neurotic problems.

Born in 1921, the youngest of five siblings, Beck had, according to family mythology, 'cured' his mother by being born. Elizabeth Beck had been depressed since the loss of her first child, a son, in infancy, followed later by the death of a young daughter in the 1919 influenza epidemic. Described as a powerful matriarchal figure, overshadowing the quieter father, she remained an explosive person, whose unpredictable and irrational moods the young Aaron found disturbing. She is described as having been 'over-protective' of her youngest son, who spent months in hospital with a life-threatening illness at the age of eight. Beck is said to have systematically desensitised himself to a serious 'blood/injury phobia' during his medical training, treating his fears of heights, tunnels, public speaking, and 'abandonment' with similar sorts of behavioural and cognitive strategies. He is also described as curing himself of 'moderate depression'.

Weishaar relates how, in the decade following his qualification as an analyst, Beck carried out empirical research into depression. One of his experiments involved a card-sorting test. The fact that depressed subjects did not react negatively to success in the task showed, Beck thought, that they did not have a need to suffer, and went towards disproving the psychoanalytic theory that depression was due to 'inverted hostility'. Many might question this as a research paradigm for psychoanalytic concepts, isolated as it is from the context of a close interpersonal relationship. However, I think it illustrates how great the conceptual differences sometimes are between practitioners of the two treatments, which can lead to major difficulties in communication.

Beck began to develop a cognitive theory, and from that a cognitive therapy (CT) for depression. He was influenced by Kelly's (1955) personal-construct theory, and by the idea that the patient could become his or her own 'scientist' of the mind. He was also influenced by the ideas of the psychoanalysts Adler, Horney and Stack-Sullivan. Beck communicated with Albert Ellis, who was independently developing rational-emotive therapy, which shares some, but not all, of its features with cognitive therapy (Ellis, 1980). Beck, together with Ellis and Donald Meichenbaum (see, for example, Meichenbaum, 1985), is regarded as one of the 'founding fathers' of cognitive behaviour therapy (CBT), an umbrella term that covers this broad therapeutic approach, and which, in the UK at least, is now used more or less synonymously with CT.

Early theories underpinning CBT were relatively simple, with little emphasis on the precise mechanism of symptom causality: things had been 'mislearnt' through childhood experience. The emphasis was rather on the way in which symptoms were currently maintained and underpinned by 'negative cognitions', which were in turn generated by maladaptive internal 'schemas' – deep, cognitive structures that organise experience and behaviour. Beck believed that discovering and challenging negative cognitions was a simpler, shorter path to change than psychoanalysis, and made more theoretical sense. He saw himself as shifting away from the 'motivational' psychoanalytic model to an 'information-processing' one – he directed attention away from 'why' and towards 'how' distressed psychological functioning operates.

The basic cognitive behaviour paradigm

In its classical form (Beck et al, 1979; Hawton et al, 1989; Moorey, 1991), CBT is a short-term, structured, problem-solving method by which a patient is trained to recognise and modify the maladaptive, conscious thinking and beliefs that are, it is argued, maintaining his or her problems and distress. This treatment/training is done first by educating the patient in the cognitive model of emotion, often with the help of written material. The therapist then helps the patient to recognise negative automatic thoughts and encourages him or her to use a process of logical challenging and reality-testing of thoughts, both in the session and in between-session homework.

A vital feature of CBT is the sympathetic, collaborative therapeutic relationship, in which the therapist tries to be an inspiring and imaginative trainer in self-help skills. The therapist encourages the patient to become a scientific observer of him/herself and his or her thoughts and to start to question the logical basis on which beliefs – for example, beliefs about being unlovable, or a failure – are held. Sessions are structured and directive, with the patient and therapist focusing general complaints down onto specific negative cognitions, which can then lead to experimental tasks to be carried out, and the outcomes monitored. For example, a depressed patient might be found to have core beliefs that no one is interested in her, and that everyone else is having a better life. These core beliefs are found to generate day-to-day thoughts like 'No one talks to me at parties', and 'Other people have much more interesting jobs'. Such beliefs can be specifically tested out, through discussion in sessions (often through a sort of Socratic dialogue) and then through carefully planned homework involving observations and, possibly, behavioural tasks.

The usual practice is to offer between 10 and 20 sessions of treatment, with follow-up refresher sessions. Training required for the therapist is relatively brief, not requiring, for example, any personal therapy. Beck, however, stresses that it is far from enough for the therapist simply to learn a set of techniques – he/she needs to have an overall 'cognitive conceptualization', and to have well-developed interpersonal skills and sensitivity. Weishaar (1993) notes that Beck's treatment manual for depression fails to capture the heart of his own empathic therapeutic style, as seen on videotapes.

Developments in CBT for personality disorders

When CBT therapists inevitably found themselves working with people suffering from personality disorders, their early formulations and treatment strategies proved insufficient. The work became more experiential and emotive, and concentrated more on the therapeutic relationship. Cognitive theory began to evolve into something less mechanistic and more 'constructivist' – concerned with how the patient constructs reality (Beck, 1991). A number of authors (eg. Power, 1991) referred to a 'psychoanalytic drift' in the practice of cognitive therapy, just as there had been a 'cognitive drift' in the practice of behaviour therapy. Something a bit more 'object-related' also seeped into schema theory, via a flourishing of interest among cognitive theorists (eg. Liotti, 1991) in Bowlby's ideas about attachment. According to Weishaar (1993: 125), active debate ensued among cognitive theorists as to 'whether clinical deficits were cognitive or interpersonal in nature'.

However, notwithstanding this apparent 'analytic drift', I differ from Bateman (2000) and believe that the cognitive clinical paradigm remains fundamentally different from the psychoanalytic one. An examination of the way 'second-wave' CBT therapists modified their technique will, I hope illustrate, this. Beck (eg. Beck & Freeman, 1990) suggested modifications to standard CBT technique when working with patients with a personality disorder diagnosis. This included careful attention to the relationship between patient and therapist, which, if not addressed, could lead to losing the patient prematurely, or the therapy getting stuck. The patient (we are told), for example, will not want to mention his or her troubling negative thoughts about the therapist, and instead will go silent, or show in other ways that something is being resisted, like pausing, clenching their fists, stammering, or changing the subject. To quote Beck: 'When questioned the patient may say, "It's not important, it's nothing". The therapist should press the patient nonetheless' (Beck & Freeman, 1990: 65). This is reminiscent of Freud's early 'pressure technique', around the turn of the 20th century, when he would insist that the patient tell him what was in their mind, however much they would prefer not to. Freud describes (Breuer & Freud, 1895) how it is often the most significant things that are withheld from the physician, although the patient insists that they are insignificant.

Using a wealth of case examples, Beck describes how treatments have to be longer, and sometimes more frequent than once a week. His therapeutic optimism is more guarded than before, and he discusses the difficulty of researching these longer-term, more complex treatments using the controlled trial format, suggesting that one should value single case studies and clinical experience more. He talks about the importance of getting to know about the patient's total life, exploring their childhood, and not just focusing down too much, or too prematurely, on cognitions and tasks. He emphasises the importance of here-and-now affective experience and the use of experiential techniques. Beck says that it may be useful for the patient to re-experience relationship difficulties in relation to the therapist – that this may be 'grist for the mill' (Beck & Freeman, 1990: 107).

Psychoanalysts would most certainly agree with this latter point. In fact, it is a hallmark of psychoanalytic technique. However, unlike the psychoanalyst, the cognitive therapist is supposed swiftly to challenge these 'negative transference' phenomena, in order to re-establish a benign working relationship. (Interestingly, Freud tried also in the early years of psychoanalysis to explain to his patients that their transference misperceptions of him were simply 'false connections' that were no longer relevant.) Beck says that one should 'be in the role of friend and advisor', 'draw on one's own life experience and wisdom' in order to 'propose solutions' and 'educate the patient regarding the nature of intimate relationships' and become a 'role model' for the patient (Beck & Freeman, 1990: 66).

Although the psychoanalyst may also at times be perceived as a role model by the patient in the transference, one tries as an analyst to analyse rather than accept this sacrifice of the patient's autonomy. Beck surely claims unwarranted superiority over patients in knowing how a life should be lived. Illustrating the simple 'deficit' model assumed in CBT, which requires the therapist to be a sort of teacher of life-skills, Beck states:

> This process of re-education is particularly important in treating patients with borderline personality disorder, whose own personality deficits may have prevented them from acquiring and consolidating many of the basic skills of self-control and stable relations with others. (Beck & Freeman, 1990: 66)

In this same book, Beck refers frequently to disappointment, frustration and other negative feelings that will be induced in the therapist by these difficult patients. He emphasises the importance of supervision in such cases, and also refers now and again to the idea of the therapist dealing with his or her negative feelings and impulses toward the patient by keeping a 'dysfunctional thought record' of their own.

The abstract from a recent article by a CBT therapist (Cartwright et al, 2015) includes the statement:

> There is evidence that [CBT] therapists' countertransference responses can affect the therapeutic relationship. There is also evidence that trainee therapists can experience difficulty understanding and managing countertransference. This evidence suggests the need for greater focus on countertransference in the training of professionals, such as psychologists, for whom therapy is a core activity. However, little is currently known about the best way of providing such training... This pilot study examined clinical psychology trainees' responses to a teaching and learning method for conceptualising and managing countertransference... the majority of participants who completed the post intervention questionnaire reported that training increased awareness of or the ability to conceptualise countertransference. They reported strategies for managing countertransference, although they were less confident in this area. (Cartwright et al, 2015: 148)

The conceptual gap between psychoanalysis and CBT seems perhaps at its greatest in this quotation. I can imagine no effective method of helping students with countertransference other than an experiential one: personal psychotherapy.

Later additions – 'third-wave' CBT

As discussed in detail in many other chapters in this book, CBT treatment has in the last 15 years or so been radically altered by the addition of 'mindfulness' techniques. These originate from a completely different frame of reference, that of Zen Buddhism, although the link is rarely made explicit in the CBT literature. Govrin (2016) describes the necessity of – and strain involved in – the incorporation of such seemingly 'alien' practices into therapies that need rejuvenating. Variations on mindfulness based cognitive therapy (MBCT) are, among others, acceptance and commitment therapy (ACT), compassionate mind therapy (CMT) and cognitive-based compassion training (CBCT). Essentially, the emphasis in these 'third-wave' versions of CBT is to learn to become aware of and to accept one's negative feelings and thoughts in a compassionate way, and to then re-evaluate them and live with them more productively, rather than trying to avoid or eliminate them. This 'third wave' has led currently to great variations in technique among CBT practitioners. Some still work in a relatively 'classical' way, and others espouse techniques that are much more 'mindful'.

The issue of lengthening CBT treatments

CBT evolved as a short-term treatment, and the short, focused training of CBT therapists is in accordance with this. In my view, great caution should be exercised about cognitive therapy that is continued outside this standard short-term frame. I do not here include follow-up sessions and 'refresher' courses of CBT, CAT or other similar therapy, which are already built into the standard frame. However, I am aware of patients who have been seen over many years by cognitive therapists. The patient will become attached and feel dependent, as in any prolonged relationship, but tools will not be available, as they are in psychoanalytic psychotherapy, to work through these phenomena. In particular, the therapist will not have the tools to deal with his or her countertransference and his or her tendency to enact the patient's unconscious expectations. Such therapies, even if they do not end with boundary violations of one sort or another, can become very stuck and repetitive, and limit the patient's freedom.

Comparing the psychoanalytic and CBT paradigms

Contemporary psychoanalytic conceptualisation and clinical technique in the UK, as I have mentioned, mostly differ from that of 1950s Philadelphia. I will lay out the basics of this contemporary psychoanalytic clinical paradigm in order to contrast it with the cognitive one. I approach this from the traditional 'positivist' paradigm, rather than an intersubjective 'constructivist' one – that is, I see the primary object of study and discovery as being the inner world of the patient. Thus, I see the analyst as doing his or her best, with an extensively trained, although inevitably imperfect and biased, observing instrument – namely, his or her mind – to strive towards understanding the internal world of the other.

It goes without saying that both CBT and psychoanalytic therapy need a therapist who is humane, sensitive and empathic. However, the position that the therapist takes in relation to the patient is very different in the two ways of working. Unlike the more socially ordinary 'personal trainer' stance of the CBT therapist, the psychoanalytic stance is counter-intuitive and less socially acceptable, and so much harder to swallow for both analyst and patient. The therapist offers close, empathic attention, but does not direct, leaving the agenda to the patient's free associations. Instead, he or she becomes involved with the patient as participant-observer in an unfolding relationship. The aim is to understand the patient as fully as possible, from an empathic and non-judgmental position, and to help the patient to come to know him or herself.

The analyst often has powerful wishes to respond naturally to the patient, to explain and to reassure, rather than to observe and analyse. Giving way to such natural impulses relieves the analyst – it enables him or her to feel comfortable. In particular, it spares the analyst the moral reproach intrinsic in being the negative-transference figure (Milton, 2000). The paradox is that, if the analyst responds 'naturally', far from becoming more 'real', he or she, by fitting in with the patient's pressures, remains the predictable figure of the patient's inner world. The patient is then left, externally and internally, with this familiar, relatively weak figure (Feldman, 1993). Collapse of the analytic stance has removed the potential for the analyst to become a truly surprising and new object (Baker, 1993). This is a new object for internalisation, who can bear and reflect on the patient's misperceptions (transference projections), rather than quickly disowning them by becoming a superficially 'reassuring' figure.

The idea of analytic neutrality does not refer to coldness, but to a personal unobtrusiveness that allows the analyst to become clothed in whatever the patient needs to bring. By reducing the extraneous 'noise' from one's own personality, a clearer field is provided for locating this. 'Live' emotional experiencing is allowed to occur, which can be sometimes fraught, anxiety-provoking, or painful for analyst, patient, or both. However, allowing the full expression of distorted 'internal object relationships' (a concept related to an idea of internal templates or schemas, but a more dynamic one) in a live way introduces the potential for them to be explored and gradually altered by experience. Change promoted by psychoanalytic work is relatively independent of the conscious aspects of insight but involves change to unconscious structures. This is ambitious, which is why it takes a long time.

The analytic stance will frequently be lost and have to be refound, as the analyst is subtly pulled into fulfilling the patient's unconscious scripts (Joseph, 1985; Sandler, 1976). There will be constant invitations, which the analyst will at times unwittingly partly accept, to become more prescriptive, or educational, more partisan, more emotionally reactive, and so on. It is as if the patient tries all the time to get the analyst to be a different sort of therapist – whether this is more of a humanistic counsellor, a guru, a teacher, or, which I think is quite common, the patient unconsciously nudges the analyst into providing a weak version of cognitive therapy. All these therapies, with the one exception of psychoanalytic therapy, use therapeutic stances that come more naturally because they are specialised forms of ordinary social contact. So, it is always a hard task, against the grain, for the analyst to observe the collapse of the analytic stance, work it through in the countertransference, and re-establish its counter-intuitiveness and complexity again.

In classical CBT, broadly speaking, the set-up is such that the patient and therapist talk together about a disturbed patient they mostly only hear reported. They try to think, with the sensible patient in the room, of ways to help him or her feel, and be, more reasonable. The rational part of the self is strengthened, in order to get on top of the disturbance. This maintains, even strengthens, a division in the personality between rational and irrational, conscious and unconscious. Analytic conditions, by contrast, allow disturbed aspects of the patient to come right into the room, with all their passion and irrationality. These, importantly, include hateful and destructive aspects of human nature, which I think are poorly theorised and addressed in cognitive theory and practice. The patient is able to project, challenge, disrupt, complain, and involve the analyst in myriad ways in the psychic drama. Primitive and disturbing unconscious phantasies, involving both body and mind, may come to light.

The analyst, then, has the advantage of a much greater range of orientations to the patient, and aspects of the patient, than does the cognitive therapist. Linked to this, an important, but particularly intrusive feature of psychoanalysis is the analyst's frequent occupation of an observing 'third position' in relation to what happens in the therapeutic relationship. This triangularity can arouse the primitive feelings of 'oedipal exclusion', which Britton (1989, 1998) describes. The analyst's reflective, independently thinking mind can seem an infuriatingly private, superior place, where an excluding sort of 'mental intercourse' takes place between parents. The 'other room', from which one, by definition, is always excluded, may, for many people, become idealised in a way that empties their own life of meaning, and halts the process of separation and independence. This deep sense of 'oedipal exclusion' may be linked to both childhood deprivations and/or to a particular difficulty with tolerating separateness and difference.

It is easier and more comfortable to flatten this triangle, to discuss things that are already visible from a shared position, or to get together to discuss as if it were someone else. The 'collaborative colleague' stance of CBT, together with a setting that does not invite live manifestation of disturbance, can avoid triangularity almost completely. At times, the psychoanalyst takes the risk of precipitating the patient's narcissistic indignation, or even rage, by speaking openly about things he or she sees that the patient cannot see, or half-sees and wants to keep hidden. Although this is uncomfortable for both, it means narcissistic parts of the personality are activated and may become gradually modified and integrated.

Returning now to the hypothetical depressed patient mentioned earlier, who comes for help feeling no one is interested in her and that other people are having better lives, a psychoanalyst with whom she consults will not actively encourage her to challenge and test this belief outside the room but will accept it as her real experience. A neutral, unstructured setting will be provided in which the patient will view the analyst through the lens of her pre-existing internal template. That is, she will soon experience the analyst as uninterested, involved in his or her own thoughts, and speaking from a superior and privileged position. The analyst will find him or herself the main target of this patient's miserable resentment. The nature and source of this resentment will gradually become clear through its re-experiencing, this time in relation to another who gives their whole attention and tries to help make sense of what is being re-experienced.

The patient's bitter misery may (to take an example) prove to be linked to feelings that she was never properly loved or understood by her parents; that perhaps another sibling was preferred, or perhaps that she was used to contain the needs of a self-absorbed parent, ill themselves. An experience of being deeply understood is helpful. It is also often helpful for the patient to recognise, through painfully re-experiencing these issues in a live relationship, that she is merely sacrificing her own peace of mind by continually reproaching and punishing the parents inside. Such recognition can gradually allow the patient to mourn what is past and finally let go of it. Although the practice of meditation or mindfulness can also help with letting go of miserable thoughts, the deep, unconscious structures that are driving them are harder to address in this way, meaning that the 'mindfulness' exercise has to be repeated over and over again.

When a psychoanalytical psychotherapist finds him or herself becoming logical, reasonable and 'cognitive' with a patient, I think this is due to an unconscious short-circuiting, which avoids a painful but necessary bit of emotional experiencing for both patient and analyst. One might ask oneself at this point whether there is a wish to be seen as a good, blameless object – in which case, it is worth wondering what form the bad object would take at this point that would feel so unbearable. It might also be that there is a larger picture in the transference and countertransference that is being missed. I will illustrate this latter possibility with the case of Mr A.

MR A

A 45-year-old man who was still living with his parents, working in a clerical job far below his capabilities, Mr A came to analysis for help to move on. He intermittently would come to a session in a particularly thinking and constructive mood, wanting help with a particular plan for change – such as learning to drive, applying for a new job, buying his own flat, and so on. I would observe myself feeling encouraged and pleased for him, because he really was miserably stuck. I would then notice I was joining him in trying to analyse his difficulties with these tasks, linking things in, when I could, with the transference relationship and troublesome past relationships. In subsequent sessions, Mr A would become very anxious and doubtful about the change. He would start to spin it out – he would have a form to fill in but leave it at work or lose it; he would tell me in great detail about why a necessary phone call had had to be put off, and so on, and I would find myself experiencing the frustration of every stage of the postponement. He would still seem to want help with his fears. The nature of the scene-setting, followed by the delays, was such that I was often left with a very strong sense of thwarted desire.

At first, I would find myself full of sensible and practical ideas and strategies for helping Mr A to challenge his fears, and (with a guilty sideways look toward my own analytic superego) I would slip into making interpretations that were really disguised practical suggestions, such as: 'It is interesting that you don't seem to feel that you could…' At this stage, we would enter, as I came to see, a 'cognitive' mode that was ultimately unproductive. Mr A would passively seem to accept my barely disguised cognitive and behavioural suggestions but continue to let the project slide. As Mr A became flatter and more passive, I would find myself more and more lively. I would now, perhaps, analyse his resistance in terms of his rebellious attitude to me, or to his disowning and projection of his mind into me, or perhaps in terms of his internal conflict.

Nothing would happen – that is, Mr A would still report to me flatly or hopelessly, or sometimes (as I came to notice) a tinge triumphantly, that he had still not done anything about the project. I would sometimes feel pushed beyond endurance at this stage. If I could not contain my countertransference, I would hear myself making a rather sharp and impatient interpretation about Mr A's passivity or wishes to thwart me. In response, he would become either very weak and demoralised, or subtly excited and mocking. He began to tell me about dreams in which someone was pursued or intimidated by gangsters or con men – it was often unclear which side he was on in these dreams.

By repeatedly working through these situations with Mr A, I came to understand a complex internal situation in which he was both trapped by, and took revenge upon, a monstrous internal figure that was partly a version of a very abusive stepmother. I came to see my 'cognitive' impulses as part of a larger picture in which we, as an analytic couple, enacted a sadomasochistic scenario that both trapped Mr A and also fulfilled a wish and need for a timeless infantile-like dependence on a carer of some sort. In phantasy, he seemed to have lodged himself inside me, projecting his active mind in a very wholesale way. Movement could only occur at times when I could get outside the situation, see the whole picture, and interpret it in a non-retaliatory way in which Mr A could become really interested and concerned about. This work used to test my analytic capacity to the full, but it eventually enabled Mr A to experience his own mind more fully. This meant him having to face and mourn his own situation, internal and external, and experience his rage, guilt, sadness and, ultimately, his own freedom and considerable strength, through which he was able to make radical changes in his life.

Modes of learning in psychotherapy

We know that both psychoanalysis and CBT involve learning. The main sort of learning hoped for in psychoanalysis is learning from emotional experience. CBT therapists also hope that their patients will learn from experience. The whole point of homework experiments is that the patient can test out distorted preconceptions outside the session. The analytic patient can, however, learn something quite subtle and complex through understanding, containment, repeated experiment, and sustained experience within the therapeutic relationship. For example, in Mr A's case, they can learn that giving up a dependent, sadomasochistic way of relating involves both some loss and a new sort of loneliness, but also a new freedom and independence of thought and action.

Implicit in classical CBT is the belief that, if one pays attention to modifying the patient's conscious distortions of reality, or 'dysfunctional assumptions', over a brief period, the deeper structures generating such assumptions will dissipate, or become far less powerful. The implicit view of human nature is that the application of reason and the right external conditions are sufficient for healing. Psychoanalysts are more sanguine about this. A patient, Ms B, may be encouraged to find, as a result of a courageous homework exercise, that her actual family are pleased about her applying for promotion at work. However, after a short remission, she remains plagued and seriously inhibited in her life by a nightmarishly caricatured inner maternal figure who is weak, ill and reproachful if her daughter leaves her own depression and self-doubt behind – it feels at a deep level as if she is 'abandoning' the mother. Another patient, Mr C, has a near-psychotic fear that sexual intercourse will somehow damage either himself or the woman. There is no chance of his experimenting in reality to disprove this. However, experience of his thoughts and feelings in relation to his female analyst reveals how his childhood fury at being neglected by his mother and left out of his parents' smugly exclusive relationship leads to a hitherto unconscious phantasy of violent intrusion into his mother's body.

Although, on the one hand, we are programmed from birth to learn about the world as much as possible, there are, on the other hand, formidable psychological barriers to knowledge. It is difficult to bear the knowledge of what we have lost, or never had, the harm that has been done to us, or the damage we may have done to others or to our own lives over many years of psychological disability.

Also, learning certain fundamental truths about self and others is a complex process – both sought after but also desperately hated and resisted (Money-Kyrle, 1968). It is hard to give up feeling omnipotent, the centre of the universe, to know instead that we are dependent on others and the product of a couple who came together outside our control and have minds that are separate and different from ours.

These factors that make learning so difficult will mean certain patients will simply not be able to tolerate the sort of knowing and understanding that psychoanalysis offers. They will neither want it nor be accessible to it. In such cases, it would be arrogant (as well as pointless) for a psychoanalytic therapist to attempt to impose such treatment. A patient must be free to choose a collaborative, less ambitious and more directly educational approach that will not threaten needed defences. In a good assessment, one will hopefully be able to gauge how much intrusion a patient welcomes or is prepared to tolerate.

'Integration' of psychoanalytic and cognitive therapies

A number of psychotherapists believe that you can combine the advantages of different techniques without losing therapeutic power. Thus, for example, 'cognitive-analytic therapy' (CAT) (Ryle, 1990) is a brief, flexible approach where the patient is encouraged to think about themselves and their relationships and to formulate and monitor, with the therapist, what is habitually going wrong. The CAT therapist may use classical CBT approaches, such as encouraging the patient to keep a symptom diary and make homework experiments, while at the same time interpreting transference phenomena as they arise. The patient's resistances to diary-keeping and other tasks often (for example) quickly provide material for work in the transference. CAT sessions are less structured than classical CBT sessions, and unconscious as well as conscious meanings are sought. There is, as in CBT, reading matter for the patient, and emphasis on early collaborative written formulation of the problems. The formulations can be referred back to when problems arise in the transference relationship or when external difficulties are discussed. Another writing task is that both patient and therapist are supposed to write each other 'goodbye letters' expressing their views about the therapy as it comes to an end.

Ryle (1995) describes CAT as a very useful and safe first intervention for patients referred for NHS outpatient psychotherapy. He regards the transference as a 'hardy plant', arising whatever one does and certainly not requiring the therapist to be inactive. He regards the collaborative stance of CAT as less potentially dangerous than psychoanalysis, which he sees as placing the patient in quite a powerless position (Ryle, 1994). I agree with Ryle that bad psychoanalysis has more potential for harm than bad CAT. This is because conditions are created such that the 'hardy plant' of transference (which, I agree, is ubiquitous in any relationship, therapeutic or not) can flourish in a fuller, often more disturbing way, much as the pot plants of colder climes are also the bushes and trees of the Tropics. In addition, just as many plants will not even germinate outside the Tropics, there will be important aspects of the transference and countertransference that will not come to light at all in the setting of CBT or CAT. I think CBT and so called 'integrated approaches' have a fundamental similarity to each other and are different from a psychoanalytic approach. The therapist's active assertion of the benign colleague/teacher stance in CAT, as in CBT, and the structured nature of the work, help to limit the patient's regression and the nature and intensity of the transference. This makes them, on the whole, safer therapies for relatively unskilled therapists to perform.

I think the same factors in CAT and CBT that limit the potential for harm and abuse to the patient also limit the potential power for good of the treatments. However, CAT, like CBT, may be more accessible and user friendly on initial contact. I think another linked and important limitation of both CAT and CBT, as compared with the analytic approach, is the therapist's non-neutral alignment in CAT and CBT with the ideal of 'progress'. However gently they are expressed, the introduction of explicit tasks places implicit pressure and expectation on the patient, from the outset, to conform and to improve. I think this both makes good CBT and CAT more paternalistic than good analysis and introduces a subtle moral restrictiveness through its very reasonableness and friendliness.

Empirical research comparing psychoanalytic and cognitive therapies

Professional rivalries and external pressures mean that something of a horse-race mentality can enter into the empirical comparison of outcome in cognitive and psychoanalytic treatments. There are indications that clinicians of different temperaments tend to be drawn toward the different modalities (Arthur, 2000), making it difficult for each to appreciate both the value of the other's way of working and the limitations of their own.

CBT as a brief, focused therapy lends itself well to the randomised controlled trial (RCT) format, which has been repeatedly and enthusiastically undertaken, albeit often not with typical outpatient populations (Enright, 1999). Outcome measures are usually in the form of simple symptom scores, and follow-up periods are usually short. When attempts are made to fit psychoanalytic psychotherapy into the extremely atypical (for a psychoanalytic modality) 16-session format suited to CBT, most psychoanalysts would not predict very much change, as there is no opportunity for vital working through. Thus, one might expect the efficacy of very brief psychoanalytic psychotherapy to resemble that of CBT and other brief therapies, rather than exceed it. This is borne out in the relatively few good quality comparative trials of CBT and brief psychoanalytic psychotherapy – there is essentially no difference in outcome (Crits-Cristoph, 1992; Luborsky et al, 1999). The famous 'dodo bird verdict' is based essentially on the study of short-term therapy, which, when applied by skilled exponents of different methodologies, tends to show the same significant, but modest, efficacy. It is not surprising that any brief therapy practised professionally yields similar, modest results.

One study attempting to link process and outcome in brief cognitive and dynamic therapies has suggested, interestingly, that it is the more typically 'dynamic' elements of therapy that are important (Jones & Pulos, 1993). These authors expected to find that cognitive therapy worked via cognitive procedures and dynamic therapy through dynamic ones. Instead, they observed that 'evocation of affect', 'bringing troublesome feelings into awareness', and 'integrating current difficulties with previous life experience, using the therapist–patient relationship as a change agent' (Jones & Pulos, 1993: 315) all predicted improvement in both therapies. This was in contrast to the more typically 'cognitive' procedures of 'control of negative affect through the use of intellect and rationality' and 'encouragement, support and reassurance from therapists', which were not predictive of positive outcome.

Jones and Pulos suggest that all such treatments work via the provision of a unique, safe context within which relationships with the self and the world can be explored. They are aided by privileging emotional experience over rationality, and by emphasis on developmental history. According to this study, at least, when cognitive therapists take a 'rationalist' approach, in which affect is conceptualised and treated as the expression of irrational and unrealistic beliefs, and when they view their role as one of imparting technical instruction and guidance, the therapy appears to be less successful. CBT, as we have seen, has in fact already evolved in response to such findings, and is often rather different today.

Another study comparing process in 'dynamic-interpersonal' and cognitive behaviour therapies (Wiser & Goldfried, 1996) looked specifically at the types of interventions made in sections of sessions that the experienced therapists themselves deemed change-promoting for their patients. Again, these researchers noted an unexpected tendency in the cognitive therapists toward both using and valuing more 'dynamic' techniques, suggesting again that this is part of the recent shift in CBT toward a more interpersonal focus.

There is a growing body of empirical research on typical-length, public-sector psychoanalytic psychotherapy in adults and children (eg. Bateman & Fonagy, 1999; Guthrie et al, 1999; Moran et al, 1991; Sandahl et al, 1998), with emerging evidence that these comparatively lengthy, more ambitious treatments may offer important additional benefit. The most recent and striking in this regard is the Tavistock Adult Depression Study (TADS) (Fonagy et al, 2015). The 129 patients recruited into this well-designed and ambitious trial suffered from treatment-resistant depression that had failed to respond to various treatments, often over many years. They were randomly allocated either to 18 months of weekly psychoanalytic psychotherapy or to treatment as usual according to UK national guidelines. Differences in remission from depression were small and not significant at the end of the treatment. However, the striking finding was that, over the follow-up period of 42 months, improvement took hold in the treated group, and steadily increased on the multiple measures, leaving the control group behind. This 'sleeper effect' is an important finding that should prompt a change in current NICE recommendations for the treatment of depression.

Full psychoanalysis itself requires four or five sessions weekly over some years; one often sees radical changes in the patient's relationships, work capacity and creative fulfilment, over and above 'symptom relief'. Such outcome criteria are difficult and complex to measure, although progress is being made in this area of 'objective measurement of the subjective' (Barber & Crits-Cristoph, 1993; Hobson & Patrick, 1998; Luborsky, Crits-Cristoph & Mellon, 1986).

When we research outcome in these longer-term and intensive psychoanalytic treatments, the 'gold standard' RCT format, which works reasonably well for relatively short-term therapy, poses huge logistical problems, and may be quite inappropriate (Galatzer-Levy, 1995; Gunderson & Gabbard, 1999). We are dealing with a complex interpersonal process involving multiple variables. Controls may become impossible to achieve, and randomisation is a questionable activity in comparative trials where patients show marked preferences or aptitudes for different ways of working. The dearth of RCT evidence for the efficacy of full psychoanalysis is a function of the huge difficulties involved in researching typical psychoanalytic treatments in this way and is often falsely equated with 'evidence against' (Parry & Richardson, 1996). Leuzinger-Boeleber and colleagues have demonstrated how good empirical outcome research can nevertheless be done in such situations (Leuzinger-Boeleber & Target, 2002, Leuzinger-Boeleber et al, 2003).

Together with studies of psychoanalysis itself, the hardest of all to research, evidence begins to emerge that these lengthy, more ambitious treatments may indeed offer important additional benefit. Fonagy and colleagues (1999) have collected and critically reviewed 55 studies of psychoanalytic outcome. Although they expose many methodological limitations in the data, these authors adopt overall what they term a 'cautiously optimistic' attitude to psychoanalytic outcome, given the evidence available. Key provisional findings (which are fully referenced in the work itself) include the following:

1. Intensive psychoanalytic treatment is generally more effective than psychoanalytic psychotherapy; the difference sometimes only becomes evident years after treatment has ended, and this applies particularly to the more severe disorders.
2. Longer-term treatment has a better outcome, as does completed analysis.
3. There are findings that suggest psychoanalysis and psychoanalytic psychotherapy are cost-beneficial and perhaps even cost-effective, and that psychoanalysis can lead to a reduction in other healthcare use and expenditure, although one study suggests an increase.
4. Psychoanalytic treatment appears to improve capacity to work and reduce borderline personality disorder symptomatology and may be an effective treatment for severe psychosomatic disorder.

Summary and conclusions

I have tried to show how I see the CBT paradigm as useful but less complex than the psychoanalytic one and limited in its explanatory power and in terms of the change its therapeutic application can be expected to achieve. Its far less intrusive and threatening nature will, however, make it more acceptable for a number of patients. I have also tried to show how there is a strong attraction towards working in a 'cognitive' way for both psychoanalyst and patient, and that the inherent tension and complexity of the analytic stance is constantly on the brink of decomposing, or collapsing, sometimes resulting in a weak version of cognitive therapy taking place. However, if the tension of psychoanalytic work can be borne by both patient and analyst, the reward can be experiential, emotional learning by the patient, which is likely to be deeper and more enduring.

I have also suggested that, because psychoanalysts and cognitive behaviour therapists share the same field of study, they are increasingly going to discover the same clinical phenomena; indeed, they are now doing so, although they may then approach these phenomena in fundamentally different ways. It is important, I think, that the shared endeavour is recognised, to relieve the misery of psychic suffering, and also the differences, which will have important implications for which patients are treated, in what way, and with what aims. It is unfortunate that clinicians from the two groups are currently often pushed by external economic pressures to compete with one another in the public sector, which exacerbates the innate rivalries that are bound to exist between practitioners of two such very different sorts of treatment.

The selected empirical evidence I have quoted gives some interesting indications as to shared therapeutic factors in brief psychodynamic and cognitive therapies. In the relatively few instances in which comparative studies have been carried out, there is found to be essentially no difference in outcome. We might, in fact, be rather impressed that psychodynamic therapy does as well as CBT under such circumstances. The claims I made earlier in the chapter about psychoanalysis as a method facilitating deep and lasting change certainly need substantiating empirically, rather than simply asserting, and we are not yet able to do this with confidence and in detail. However, research evidence from the last few decades is beginning to confirm analysts' expectations that intensive and long-term psychoanalytic treatments have something substantial to offer over and above what brief treatments, whichever the modality used, can provide.

References

Arthur A (2000). The personality and cognitive–epistemological traits of cognitive-behavioural and psychoanalytic psychotherapists. *British Journal of Medical Psychology 73*: 243–257.

Baker R (1993). The patient's discovery of the psychoanalyst as a new object. *International Journal of Psycho-Analysis 74*: 1223–1233.

Barber JP, Crits-Cristoph P (1993). Advances in measures of psychodynamic formulations. *Journal of Consulting and Clinical Psychology 61*: 574–585.

Bateman A (2000). Integration in psychotherapy: an evolving reality in personality disorder. *British Journal of Psychotherapy 17*: 147–156.

Bateman A, Fonagy P (1999). The effectiveness of partial hospitalisation in the treatment of borderline personality disorder - randomised controlled trial. *American Journal of Psychiatry 156*: 1563–1569.

Beck A (1991). Cognitive therapy as the integrative therapy: comments on Alford and Norcross. *Journal of Therapy Integration 1*: 191–198.

Beck A, Freeman A (1990). *Cognitive Therapy of Personality Disorders*. New York, NY: Guilford Press.

Beck A, Rush AJ, Shaw BF, Emery G (1979). *Cognitive Therapy of Depression*. New York, NY: Wiley.

Breuer J, Freud S (1895). Studies on hysteria. In James Strachey (ed). *The Standard Edition of the Complete Psychological Works of Sigmund Freud, vol 2*. London: Hogarth Press (pp1–335).

Britton R (1998). *Belief and Imagination*. London: Routledge.

Britton R (1989). The missing link: parental sexuality in the Oedipus complex. In: Britton R, Feldman M, O'Shaughnessy E, Steiner J. *The Oedipus Complex Today: clinical implications*. London: Karnac (pp83–101).

Cartwright C, Rhodes P, King R, Shires A (2015). A pilot study of a method for teaching clinical psychology trainees to conceptualise and manage countertransference. *Australian Psychologist 50*: 148–156.

Crits-Cristoph P (1992). The efficacy of brief dynamic psychotherapy: a meta-analysis. *American Journal Psychiatry 149*: 151–158.

Ellis A (1980). Rational-emotive therapy and cognitive behaviour therapy: similarities and differences. *Cognitive Therapy and Research 4*: 325–340.

Enright S (1999). Cognitive-behavioural therapy - an overview. *CPD Bulletin of Psychiatry 1*: 78–83.

Feldman M (1993). The dynamics of reassurance. *International Journal of Psycho-Analysis 74*: 275–285.

Fonagy P, Kächele H, Krause R, Jones E, Perron R (1999). *An open-door review of outcome studies in psychoanalysis.* London: International Psychoanalytical Association.

Fonagy P, Rost F, Carlyle J, McPherson S, Thomas R, Pasco Fearon R, Goldberg D, Taylor D (2015). Pragmatic randomised controlled trial of long term psychoanalytic psychotherapy for treatment-resistant depression: the Tavistock Adult Depression Study (TADS). *World Psychiatry 14*(3): 312–321.

Freud S (1961). Letter from Freud to Jeliffe, 9 February 1939. In: Freud E (ed). *Letters of Sigmund Freud 1873–1939.* London: Hogarth Press.

Galatzer-Levy R (1995). Discussion: the rewards of research. In: Shapiro T, Emde R (eds). *Research in Psychoanalysis: process, development, outcome.* Madison, CT: International Universities Press.

Govrin A (2016). Blurring the threat of 'otherness': integration by conversion in psychoanalysis and CBT. *Journal of Psychotherapy Integration 26*: 78–90.

Gunderson J, Gabbard G (1999). Making the case for psychoanalytic therapies. *Journal of the American Psychoanalytic Association 47*: 679–739.

Guthrie E, Moorey J, Margison F, Barker H, Palmer S, McGrath G, Tomenson B, Creed F (1999). Cost-effectiveness of brief psychodynamic–interpersonal therapy in high utilizers of psychiatric services. *Archives of General Psychiatry 56*: 519–526.

Hale N (1995). *The Rise and Crisis of Psychoanalysis in the US.* New York, NY: Oxford University Press.

Hawton K. Salkovskis PM, Kirk J, Clark DM (1989). *Cognitive Behaviour Therapy for Psychiatric Problems.* New York, NY: Oxford University Press.

Hobson P, Patrick M (1998). Objectivity in psychoanalytic judgements. *British Journal of Psychiatry 173*: 172–177.

Jones E, Pulos S (1993). Comparing the process in psychodynamic and cognitive-behavioural therapies. *Journal of Consulting and Clinical Psychology 61*: 306–316.

Joseph B (1985). Transference: the total situation. *International Journal of Psycho-Analysis 66*: 447–454.

Kelly G (1955). *The Psychology of Personal Constructs.* New York, NY: Norton.

Leuzinger-Boeleber M, Target M (eds) (2002). *Outcomes of Psychoanalytic Treatment: perspectives for therapists and researchers.* London: Whurr.

Leuzinger-Boeleber M, Stuhr U, Ruger B, Beutel M (2003). How to study the quality of psychoanalytic treatments and their long-term effects on patients' well-being: a representative, multi-perspective, follow-up study. *International Journal of Psychoanalysis 84*: 263–290.

Liotti G (1991). Patterns of attachments and the assessment of interpersonal schemata: understanding and changing difficult patient–therapist relationships in cognitive psychotherapy. *Journal of Cognitive Psychotherapy 5*: 105–114.

Luborsky L, Crits-Cristoph P, Mellon J (1986). The advent of objective measures of the transference concept. *Journal of Consulting and Clinical Psychology 54*: 39–47.

Luborsky L, Diguer L, Luborsky E, Schmidt KA (1999). The efficacy of dynamic versus other psychotherapies: is it true that 'everyone has won and all must have prizes'? – an update. In: Janovsky DS (ed). *Psychotherapy: indications and outcomes.* Washington, DC: American Psychiatric Press.

Meichenbaum D (1985). *Stress Inoculation Training.* New York, NY: Pergamon.

Milton J (2000). Psychoanalysis and the moral high ground. *International Journal of Psycho-Analysis 81*: 1101–1115.

Milton J, Polmear C, Fabricius J (2011). *A Short Introduction to Psychoanalysis.* London: Sage.

Money-Kyrle R (1968). Cognitive development. *International Journal of Psycho-Analysis 49*: 691–698.

Moorey S (1991). Cognitive behaviour therapy. *Hospital Update* September: 726–732.

Moran G, Fonagy P, Kurtz A, Bolton A, Brook C (1991). A controlled study of the psychoanalytic treatment of brittle diabetes. *Journal of the American Academy of Child Psychiatry 30*: 926–935.

Parry G, Richardson A (1996). *NHS Psychotherapy Services in England: a review of strategic policy*. London: Department of Health.

Power M (1991). Cognitive science and behavioural psychotherapy: where behaviour was, there shall cognition be? *Behavioural Psychotherapy 19*: 20–41.

Ryle A (1990). *Cognitive Analytical Therapy*. Chichester: Wiley.

Ryle A (1994). Psychoanalysis and cognitive analytic therapy. *British Journal of Psychotherapy 10*: 402–404.

Ryle A (1995). Psychoanalysis, cognitive-analytic therapy, mind and self. *British Journal of Psychotherapy 11*: 568–574.

Sandahl, C, Herlitz, K, Ahlin G, Rönnberg S (1998). Time-limited group therapy for moderately alcohol-dependent patients: a randomised controlled trial. *Psychotherapy Research 8*: 361–378.

Sandler J (1976). Countertransference and role-responsiveness. *International Review of Psycho-Analysis 3*: 43–47.

Weishaar M (1993). *Aaron T Beck*. London: Sage.

Wiser S, Goldfried M (1996). Verbal interventions in significant psychodynamic-interpersonal and cognitive-behavioural therapy sessions. *Psychotherapy Research 6*: 309–319.

12 Person-centred therapy – a cognitive and behavioural therapy*

Keith Tudor

In the first edition of this book, this chapter had two parts: the first on research, and the second on behaviour and cognition in person-centred therapy (PCT). Discussing research from a person-centred perspective, I took issue with the conceptual and methodological bias of the UK's National Institute for Health and Clinical Excellence (NICE); noted the extensive research regarding the therapeutic relationship and client factors, both of which support person-centred approaches to research about therapy; and argued for the need for practice-based evidence and alternative methodologies in psychotherapy outcome research (see Bohart and House's Chapter 18 and Lees' Chapter 9 in this edition; also Tudor, 2018).

As these arguments have been well made and, by now, are well known, for this edition I have replaced the part on research with a discussion about some of the differences between PCT and cognitive behavioural therapy (CBT). In many ways, this discussion follows on from the previous one, as it elaborates some of the underlying differences on which research methodology – as well as research bias – is based. Essentially and effectively, as a *process-oriented* form of therapy, PCT has a different ontology, epistemology and methodology to that of CBT.

Despite the fact that, for over a quarter of a century we have been 'beyond Schoolism' (Clarkson, 1989), and in an era of pluralism (Samuels, 1989), and, for this decade, have been discussing post-professionalism (see House, 2010), counselling psychologists, counsellors, and psychotherapists still tend to be educated or trained in one therapeutic orientation or modality. Moreover, the names of some of these modalities of or approaches to therapy (a generic term I use to encompass counselling, counselling psychology and psychotherapy) indicate a certain territory and, with this, imply a certain exclusive occupation of that territory: person-centred therapists centre on the person; transactional

* This chapter is based on work previously published in Tudor & Worrall, 2006.

analysts analyse transactions; relational psychotherapists work relationally, and so on – and cognitive behavioural therapists focus on cognition and behaviour, as if other therapists do not.

So, as a counterpoint to the apparent dominance of CBT in and over cognition and behaviour, in the second part of the chapter, I elaborate the behavioural and cognitive aspects of PCT. I do so partly because, I suggest, they are not terribly well known even among person-centred therapists, or particularly emphasised in person-centred training, let alone familiar to other educators or trainers – or politicians.

Person-centred therapy, a process-centred therapy

> '... too many therapists think they can make something happen. Personally, I like much better the approach of an agriculturalist or a farmer or a gardener: I can't make corn grow, but I can provide the right soil and plant it in the right area and see that it gets enough water; I can nurture it so that exciting things happen. I think that's the nature of therapy. It's so unfortunate that we've so long followed a medical model and not a growth model. A growth model is much more appropriate to most people, to most situations. (Rogers, in Rogers & Russell, 2002: 259)

In this statement, made in an interview conducted in the last year of his life, Rogers, in effect, summarises his methodology and method: based on a growth model of the person. This is significant in that it therefore follows that the therapist is more of an agriculturalist, farmer or gardener, supporting the inherent direction of the actualising organism, than an interpreter, director, teacher, trainer or detective who tells the client what to do or think, or that what they are doing or thinking is wrong. The metaphors we use for people (clients or patients) and practice matter, as they reveal our ontological assumptions and presuppositions about the essence of things.

Broadly, PCT is based on an ontology represented by its root metaphor of the person as an organism that cannot be understood outside its social and cultural context, and one that, as far as human nature is concerned, has an inherent pro-social direction (see Tudor & Worrall, 2006). In person-centred psychology, the concept of the organism is prior to that of the self (which, generally, is not reified, as it is in other branches of psychology). PCT is based on an epistemology that privileges experiential and personal knowledge or knowing and, therefore, what the person or subject (whether an individual or a group, tribe, or organisation etc) experiences and knows about themselves, others and the world. From this (ontology and methodology), it follows that the method or practice of PCT is supportive of the fact that the organism tends to actualise (hence the non-directive attitude on the part of the therapist), and, in the spirit of the agriculturalist, farmer, or gardener, that the client has the right conditions for growth (and hence the necessary and sufficient conditions for therapeutic change).

Influenced by Otto Rank and Jessie Taft, the origins of these conditions can be traced back to Rogers' own work in the early 1940s, and, based on his early research, the six therapeutic conditions: contact; client incongruence; therapist genuineness, unconditional positive regard and empathy, and the client's reception/perception of the therapist's conditions or qualities (Rogers, 1957, 1959). They have continued to be researched, and, as practice-based theory and evidence, were the precursor to what is generally referred to now as 'common factors research', although the language of 'conditions' has changed to 'relational variables'.

Fundamentally, PCT is about supporting the inherent tendency of the organism to actualise – a perspective that requires an acknowledgement, as Sanders (2009: 1) puts it, 'that the only useful expertise in therapy consists of the ability to get out of the way of the client's healing process and [to] accompany them'. This is the philosophical stance and psychological posture of the person-centred approach to and in therapy, and thereby is different from more interventionist approaches.

All this is encapsulated in the view that PCT is a *process-oriented therapy*: it is interested in the client's process, and in the process (ie. the relationship between client and therapist). In his major formulation of theory in the client-centred framework, Rogers (1959) places process at the heart of his theory of therapy. Building on the experiential and constructive nature of the human organism, he proposed a theory of therapy based on a two-part formulation: 1) *if* certain conditions (independent variables) exist, *then* a process (the dependent variable) will occur, following which, 2) *if* this process (now independent variable) occurs, *then* certain personality and behavioural changes (dependent variables) will occur.

Rogers' (1957, 1959) theory of the six necessary and sufficient conditions for change are well known (for a contemporary, relational re-conceptualisation of which, see Tudor, 2011), but his theory of the process of therapy is perhaps less widely disseminated. In his 1959 formulation, he describes 12 aspects of this, which include the client's increasing freedom in expressing feelings, increasing extensionality in perceptions, increasing reference to incongruity between certain experiences and self-concept, and so on. In a paper written later than the 1959 chapter but published a year earlier, Rogers (1958/1967a) describes seven stages of process – from fixity to fluidity – with regard to seven aspects of experience: the individual's feelings, the manner of their experiencing, their congruence, communication, and constructs, their relationship to the problems, and their manner of relating (for a detailed summary of which, see Tudor, 2006). Even when Rogers describes outcomes in personality and behaviour, they are predominantly *process* outcomes:

- *being* more congruent, open to experience, and less defensive; more realistic and objective; more effective in problem-solving; less vulnerable to threat; less tense and anxious
- having an increased degree of positive self-regard, and values that are determined by an organismic valuing *process*

- perceiving the loci of evaluation of choice as residing within her or himself; feeling that her or his behaviour is more within their control, and perceiving others more realistically and accurately
- feeling more confident and self-directing
- experiencing more acceptance of others, and
- owning her or his behaviour.

In his original chapter, Rogers (1959) cites some 34 studies that support these outcomes, and this theory of process.

The attention and priority given to process in PCT is very different from the focus of CBT. Despite an increased interest in the therapeutic relationship in CBT, its ontology is essentially based on realism, its view of human nature on determinism, its epistemology on positivism, its methodology on nomothetic (or legislative) approaches, and its method on a practice (or treatment) that is primarily solution-focused, linear, instrumental and manualised. This is very different from approaches that see a problem as an initial mystery (Heidegger, 1930/1993), and not so much a problem to be solved but, as Mølbak (2012: 463) puts it, 'a question to be further pursued through curiosity and inquiry'. Indeed, the third force of humanistic psychology (in which client-centred therapists such as Rogers were very influential) was founded precisely to offer an alternative to the dominance of psychoanalysis and of behaviourism (see Tudor, 2013), and person-centred theory and its therapy were central in providing alternative views about human nature, the therapeutic relationship, and the role both of therapist and client.

Mølbak (2012) draws some differences between the 'rational/planning approach to therapy' and a process-oriented approach, which I compare in Table 1.

Table 1. Comparative assumptions of rational/planning and process-oriented approaches to therapy (based on Mølbak, 2012: 464)

The rational/planning approach to therapy	A process-oriented approach
That we can define a client's problem in advance 'through a diagnostic interview, psychological testing, [and/] or a rational collaborative discussion with the client'	That 'the objective of therapy is to discover what the problem is rather than to provide a solution to a problem that has been defined at the beginning of therapy'
That 'therapy is a linear process in which goals can be determined in advance and will remain steady throughout the course of therapy'	That 'the process of therapy transforms goals rather than leads to the realisation in some progressive and linear way'

That 'the therapist is in control of the therapeutic process and is able to direct treatment in a rational goal-oriented manner'	That 'the therapist is most therapeutic, not when he plans out and administers universal interventions, but when he responds to what emerges in the moment and contextual and well-timed manner'

It is all too easy to link the empiricism and pragmatism of cognitive behavioural therapy to an agenda of social adaptation, social control and managerialism. One obvious example of this in the UK has been the Layard thesis (Layard, 2006), which (in its briefest essence) proposes that, following six sessions of CBT, depressed clients will be happier, therefore able to return to economic productivity, no longer claim social benefits, and thereby save the gGovernment money. Layard's proposition was based entirely on an economic argument, not on any substantive assessment of the relative benefits of different approaches to therapy. The consequences of this, and of the UK government's Improving Access to Psychological Therapies (IAPT) (note the plural) programme – which has actually resulted in people having less access to psychological therapies other than CBT – is well documented, and others in this volume consider the politics of CBT in greater detail (see Guilfoyle, Chapter 1, and Proctor, Chapter 2).

Despite compelling evidence that other forms of therapies (often categorised as reflective and supportive) are equally effective in facilitating change and 'treating' various 'conditions' (sometimes referred to as 'the dodo bird verdict'), CBT still tends to be favoured by national governments. In trying to make sense of this wilful bias, it is hard to look beyond the politics of CBT – that it is more concerned to help people adapt and conform to social norms than to discover and explore the nature of the underlying desires.

One change in this picture since the first edition of this book has been the decision of the Swedish government (which had invested heavily in CBT) in 2012 to break this monopoly and fund other therapeutic approaches. Commenting on the report from the Swedish National Audit Office, one newspaper headline put it thus: 'The one-sided focus on CBT is damaging Swedish mental health' (Miller, 2012).

Behaviour and cognition in person-centred theory and therapy

Having argued that PCT and CBT are different forms of therapy, due to their different ontologies, epistemologies and methodologies, this is not to say that PCT does not have a theory of behaviour or of cognition. Just as each school, orientation or modality has its theory of human development, health and psychopathology and the nature and process of change etc, so too it has a theory about the origins and place of behaviour and of thinking, and of how this changes. Unfortunately, the term 'cognitive behaviour therapy' (CBT) and the identity 'cognitive behaviour therapist' imply – or can be taken to mean – that only cognitive behaviour therapists do CBT, and that CBT is the exclusive territory of cognitive behaviour therapists. In response to this, in this part of the chapter, I detail the theory of behaviour and cognition in person-centred psychology.

Person-centred therapy is based on organismic psychology that represents a holistic approach to human beings and to life (see Tudor & Worrall, 2006). This means that our behaviour and cognition, as well as our affect and other aspects and qualities, are features of a whole organism/person, and inextricably linked. In 1970 Rogers wrote a paper titled 'Bringing together the cognitive and the affective-experiential' (which he published two years later (Rogers, 1972)). When asked by Russell whether the therapist's approach should be emotional rather than cognitive, Rogers replied that it is both emotional and cognitive (Rogers & Russell, 2002). From a holistic perspective, the separation of behaviour and cognition is a conceptual abstraction; I separate them here only in order to elaborate Rogers' and person-centred thinking about behaviour and cognition.

Behaviour in person-centred psychology

In his book, *Client-Centred Therapy*, Rogers (1951) expounds his theory of personality and behaviour in a number of propositions, five of which explicitly refer to behaviour, while many others describe the behavioural actions of the human organism:

> Behavior is basically the goal-directed attempt of the organism to satisfy its needs as experienced, in the field as perceived [Proposition V]… Emotion accompanies and in general facilitates such goal-directed behavior [Proposition VI]… The best vantage point for understanding behavior is from the internal frame of reference of the individual her/himself [Proposition VII]… Most of the ways of behaving which are adopted by the organism are those which are consistent with the concept of self [Proposition XII]… Behavior may, in some instances, be brought about by organic experiences and needs which have not been symbolized. Such behavior may be inconsistent with the structure of the self, [and thus] is not 'owned' by the individual [Proposition III]. (pp:491–509)

There are a number of implications that follow from these propositions:

- that behaviour is the expression of the organism that tends to actualise – that is, to maintain, enhance and reproduce itself
- that behaviour is inextricably linked to needs – that is, it is needs-driven and goal-directed, even when those needs are difficult to ascertain or understand and the goal is not known or perceived, and all behaviour is enacted in order to meet a present need, although past experience, and our understanding of that experience, may modify the present meaning given to experience

- that behaviour is a reaction to the environmental field, *as perceived*. Evans and Zarate (1999: 160) state that:

  > Every kind of behaviour results from the way our minds interact with our environment, and the mind results from the interaction of the environment with our genes. Different environments will lead the mind to develop differently and change the way in which the mind causes behaviour.

- that all needs have what Rogers refers to as 'a basic relatedness' (Rogers, 1951: 491), and spring from and refer to the human organism's tendency to actualise. Individual behaviour is, thus, dialogic, in that it cannot be understood without being symbolised and, at least initially, a baby cannot symbolise on her or his own. She or he needs the 'abstract', empathic, and symbolising attitude of another. As Goldstein (1934/1995: 19) puts it: 'Thus the behaviour of the infant is not at all an expression of his concrete capacity alone *but also of the abstract attitude of someone else*. Thus, normal behaviour in infancy becomes comprehensible as the result of the activity of two persons' (my emphasis)
- that, in pursuing the satisfaction of needs, the organism *is* its behaviour at any one moment – an implication that provides further support for the importance of the interchange between organism and environment and the inseparability of the holistic mind/body organism/environment from its behaviour. It is this final implication that is the most radical and controversial. If behaviour is an organismic attempt to satisfy current need, then a person *is* her or his behaviour, whether that is loving, hating, generous, jealous, aggressive, or even violent. This has huge implications, especially for those humanistic psychologists, therapists and trainers who seek to separate the person from her or his behaviour, as in the instruction, 'Criticise the behaviour, not the person.' From an organismic and holistic perspective, this separation is artificial, unhelpful and misses the point. It is artificial in that it is the person who is behaving in the way which is being criticised. It is unhelpful in that the separation doesn't work: when faced with criticism, most people do take it personally – because it *is* personal! The attempt to separate behaviour from the person misses the point: faced with cruelty, oppression, nastiness or evil in the world, the issue is how to respond to, deal with and work with people who are, *at that moment when they do something cruel*, themselves cruel.

It is, therefore, unrealistic to suggest that, in some way, everyone is 'in essence' simply 'good'. Human organisms are more complex and life is more complicated than that. Such liberalism about ontology (the essence of things) sets up a false idealism about human nature and life itself. Finally, the attempt to claim a comforting 'niceness' about an essence of human nature does not allow for entropy, or disorder, alongside syntropy, or unity. Equally, it is simplistic and naïve to offer unconditional positive regard for the person but not for her or his behaviour. This constitutes an untenable dichotomy, in that a person's behaviour is an intimate and accurate expression of who she is as a person in the moment of her behaving. Elsewhere, Tudor and Worrall (2006) offer a solution to this dichotomy, and argue that:

> It makes more sense to say that we hold unconditional positive regard for the fact that a person tends to actualise, and to see that she or he is tending to actualise whatever she, he or others may think of the behavioural manifestations of that tendency. (p74)

In a paper written a few years after his 1951 paper on personality and behaviour, Rogers (1957/1967b: 194–195) concludes his view of 'the good life' and the 'fully functioning person' with the following lines, which describe a tension between organismic functioning and consciousness:

> Man's behaviour is exquisitely rational, moving with subtle and ordered complexity toward the goals his organism is endeavoring to achieve. The tragedy for most of us is that our defenses keep us from being aware of this rationality, so that consciously we are moving in one direction, while organismically we are moving in another.

Following Goldstein, Rogers distinguishes between defensive and disorganised behaviours. The distinction is based on a description of a gradual process from discrepancy, threat and defence to a distinct point at which a person's process of defence no longer holds. This experience and the concept of disorganisation includes many of the more 'irrational' and 'acute' psychotic behaviours. Rogers argues both that this is a more fundamental classification than the neurotic–psychotic one, and that it avoids the concepts of neurosis and psychosis being viewed as entities in themselves.

Rogers' ideas about behaviour are clearly different from those of behavioural psychologists such as BF Skinner, with whom he had a number of encounters or dialogues (in 1956, 1960 and 1962) (see Kirschenbaum & Henderson, 1990; Nye, 2000). While Rogers acknowledges that objective, quantitative approaches to the study of human behaviour are important means of obtaining certain knowledge, he places more emphasis on subjective knowledge (knowing oneself) and on empathic, intersubjective knowledge (knowing the subjective states of the other), and thus represents a different view of scientific knowledge (Rogers, 1985). He also represents a different view from that of behaviourism regarding the 'control' of human behaviour (Rogers & Skinner, 1956; see also Nye, 2000), and different views of 'reality' (Rogers, 1974/1980). For further reading on the distinctions between person-centred psychology and behaviourism and behavioural methods see Rice (1984) and Nye (2000).

Cognition in person-centred psychology

While there has been an emphasis on feeling and emotion, and, specifically, the reflecting of feeling in client- and person-centred therapy, which may be traced back to Rogers' early work (Rogers, 1942), Rogers and other subsequent theorists have also addressed cognition. This is evident in Rogers' (1951) book *Client-Centered Therapy,* in which he describes defences, including distortion, and in his major formulation of client-centred theory (Rogers, 1959), when he discusses cognition in terms of perceptions, constructs, self-concept and intensionality. Here I summarise these concepts and discuss the cognitive strand of person-centred psychology.

Distortion

Rogers (1951) describes distortion as a defence mechanism by which an experience that is incongruent with or threatening to a person's self-concept is not admitted to awareness, but, rather, transformed into something more acceptable to the person's concept of her- or himself. Thorne (1996: 128) offers a good example:

> ... perceptual distortion takes place whenever an incongruent experience is allowed into conscious awareness but only in a form that is in harmony with the person's current self-concept. The virtuous man, for instance, might permit himself to experience hostility but would distort this as a justifiable reaction to wickedness in others: for him his hostility would be rationalized into righteous indignation.

Perceptions

Rogers (1959: 199) defines a perception as 'a hypothesis or prognosis for action which comes into being in awareness when stimuli impinge on the organism'. As such, perception is almost synonymous with awareness, but is a more specific term that relates to the importance of the usually external stimulus.

Constructs

A construct is a certain idea, the basis on which a prediction about the world is made. It is a term that Rogers borrowed from George Kelly (Kelly, 1955) and used in his process conception of psychotherapy, one element of which is the concept of constructs, which Rogers (1958/1967a: 157) refers to as 'the cognitive maps of experience'. Rogers sees the seven stages of his process conception as describing a movement from construing experience in rigid ways to developing constructions that are modifiable by each new experience (see Rogers, 1958/1967a; Tudor & Worrall, 2006).

Self-concept

According to Rogers (1951: 136–7) a self-concept is:

> ... an organized configuration of perceptions of the self which are admissible to awareness, it is composed of such elements as the perceptions of one's characteristics and abilities; the percepts and concepts of the self in relation to the environment; the value qualities which are perceived as associated with experiences and objects; and goals and ideals which are perceived as having positive or negative value.

In person-centred psychology, the term 'self-concept' is mainly used synonymously with self and self-structure. However, 'self-concept' is also used to refer to a person's view of herself or himself, as distinct from his or her self-structure, which is used more precisely to refer to the internalised view someone has of herself or himself that derives from another. Rogers also discusses the defence mechanism of distortion – that is, the distortion of perception. This is similar to Beck's (1967) concept of 'cognitive distortion'.

In his 1959 paper, Rogers describes the process of breakdown and disorganisation of the personality in terms of the tension between the concept of self, with its distorted perceptions and experiences that are not accurately symbolised. He also describes the process of reorganisation, which includes the creation of conditions under which experiences, including threatening ones, are accurately symbolised.

Rogers drew his ideas on the self-concept from Victor Charles Raimy, one of his students, whose doctoral thesis on the subject, 'The self-concept as a factor in counselling and personality organization', was published in 1971. In a subsequent work, Raimy (1975: xi) defined self-concept as 'composed of more or less organized notions, beliefs and convictions that constitute an individual's knowledge of himself and that influence his relationships with others'. Raimy also developed 'the misconception hypothesis', which proposes that psychological disturbances are the result of faulty beliefs or convictions, and that:

> ... if those ideas or conceptions of a client or patient which are relevant to his psychological problems can be changed in the direction of greater accuracy where his reality is concerned, his maladjustments are likely to be eliminated' (Raimy, 1975: 7).

Commenting on Raimy's work, Patterson (1986) identifies a number of diagnostic clusters that are, or involve, cognitive misconceptions – see Table 2.

Table 2. Diagnostic clusters and cognitive misconceptions (based on Patterson, 1986)

Diagnostic cluster	**Cognitive misconceptions**
Paranoid cluster	Delusions involving failure of reality testing; disordered content of thought; delusions of persecution, and ideas of reference
Depressive neurotics	Being hopeless, helpless, or worthless; that they will never recover and are not 'normal'
Obsessive neurotics	That they have to be punctual, orderly, conscientious and reliable
Hysterical personalities	That they are effective (only) when flirtatious, seductive, vivacious and/or dramatic, and that they cannot tolerate frustration and disappointment
Phobia reactions	That the feared object is dangerous; that they will probably collapse when the feared object is present, and that they cannot overcome their fear reaction to the object
Phrenophobia	The false belief that there is something wrong with one's mind
Being special (narcissism)	That they must control others; that they are superior to others; that they should not compromise; that they suffer from more frustrations than others do; that they must strive to be perfect, and that others cannot be trusted

Raimy's approach is based on the view that one of the goals of most therapies is to help the client recognise and change such misconceptions, and that one of the major 'contentions' of therapy is that such misconceptions can be changed by evidence or information presented by the therapist, by means of:

- client self-examination
- therapist explanation, through reflection of feelings, asking questions, and making suggestions and exhortations
- self-demonstrations, whereby the client, through reflecting on either real or imagined situations, can observe her or his own misconceptions, and
- vicariation or modelling.

While many person-centred practitioners would find some of Raimy's – and Patterson's – somewhat pejorative language ('faulty beliefs' and 'maladjustments') a long way away from some of the traditional or classical – and, indeed, contemporary – person-centred principles and thinking, it is interesting that the concept of the 'self-concept' has been developed in a way that offers a precise understanding of cognitive processes. Cartwright and Graham (1984) developed this cognitive approach to self-concept in their work on and research into self-concept and identity as overlapping portions of a cognitive structure of self. They base their argument on cognitive theory, and elaborate Rogers' (1951) model of personality to include concepts, categories, instance categories, and perceived social images.

Intensionality

Originally taken from general semantics (in which the word refers to the meaning or way in which we think/perceive in relation to an external object), Rogers uses the term in a particular way to describe the specific types of behaviour of an incongruent individual who, as he (Rogers, 1959: 205) described it, tends 'to see experience in absolute and unconditional terms, to overgeneralise, to be dominated by concept or belief, to fail to anchor his reactions in space or time, to confuse fact and evaluation, to rely upon abstractions rather than reality-testing'. Intensionality is a term that encompasses the characteristics of the behaviour – and cognition – of the individual who is in a defensive state. It, together with other terms – defence, defensiveness, distortion, and denial – describes the organism's response to threat. Neither intensionality nor its opposite, extensionality, are much used in person-centred psychology, although Cornelius-White (2007) has, more recently, discussed extensionality as an aspect of congruence.

Cognition in person-centred thinking since Rogers

It is clear, then, that there is a distinct cognitive strand in the history and literature of client-centred therapy.

According to Lietaer (1990), the emergence and later consolidation of four strands or 'factions' within client-centred therapy (CCT) can be discerned following the termination of the Wisconsin project. One of these was a group around David Wexler and Laura Rice, who chose cognitive learning psychology as a theoretical framework for their development of CCT, whereby they recast client-centred concepts of growth and actualisation in a framework drawn from cognitive and information-processing psychology.

This shift is represented in a volume edited by Wexler and Rice in 1974, *Innovations in Client-Centered Therapy*. In his own contribution to this volume, Wexler (1974) critiqued Rogers' theorising on self-actualisation and experiencing and argued that a cognitive view helps explain the process of change in the moment-to-moment interaction between client and therapist. In the same volume, Zimring (1974) also took a cognitive view of CCT, arguing that both the practice of CCT and the cognitive framework in scientific psychology emphasise the knowing rather than the known. According to Zimring, the goal of CCT is an increase in the client's experiential organisation. He asserts that 'the therapist achieves this goal through an interaction involving joint processing of the client's experience. The therapist works both at the same time level with and slightly ahead of the client's ability to organize, thus facilitating his processing' (p136).

In a subsequent volume on CCT and the person-centred approach, Rice (1984) distinguishes CCT from cognitive behaviour approaches in which cognitive structures are examined and compared with 'reality' in a way that makes cognitive behaviour therapy a kind of 'learning lab'. Rice compares this kind of CBT with therapies at the other end of a conceptual continuum that focus on, and even encourage, the client's expression of strong affect and impulses. Rice views good CCT as somewhere in the middle of this continuum as, according to her (p183), it involves 'the resolution of a series of cognitive-affective reprocessing tasks'. While Rice does identify a series of these tasks, she distances herself from cognitive behaviour methods used to effect change. Although she does not name it, her reluctance is presumably to do with wanting to maintain a non-directive attitude or an identification with non-directive therapy.

Rice's conceptualisation of therapeutic change in terms of cognitive theory comprises four phases:

1. *Positioning for exploration* – in which the client describes a particular experience that is problematic and a reaction that she or he views as problematic in that she or he considers it to be peculiar, unreasonable, exaggerated, or inappropriate.
2. *Exploring the two sides* – an exploration of the client's inner reaction and perceptual processing, involving:

   > ... the discovery of a *meaning bridge* between the quality of one's affective reaction and the idiosyncratic, subjective nature of one's construal of salient elements of the stimulus situation – that is, one's reaction is seen to fit the stimulus situation as construed. (Rice, 1984: 193)

3. *Recognition and exploration of self-schemas* – which represents an explicit attempt to understand and re-evaluate the relatively enduring clusters of cognitive and affective structures by which we assimilate input and organise output. (Some writers and clinicians, including Rice (1974), consider that the word 'scheme' is a more accurate translation of Piaget's term *schème* than 'schema'.)
4. *Awareness of new options* – viewed in the light of 'loosening and reorganized self-schemas' (Rice, 1984: 201).

This structured approach is similar to the description of therapeutic work offered by those associated with the experiential faction, or tribe, of person-centred and experiential therapies (see, for instance, Leijssen & Elliott, 2008).

While there is no sense of a strong cognitive 'faction' within the person-centred approach or within the World Association of Person-Centred and Experiential Psychotherapy and Counselling (www.pce-world.org), there have been a number of more recent articles on cognition. One paper on the relationship between emotions and cognitions (Tausch, 1988/2002) includes an analysis of Rogers' interactions with a client, 'Gloria' (Rogers, 1965), in which the author suggests that, in 67% of his responses, Rogers attends more to the client's cognitions than emotions – responses that seem to have had a parallel effect on the client. Comparing Rogers' responses to those of two other therapists, Tausch observes:

> *Carl Rogers' empathic understanding of the client's cognition ... seems to be an appropriate and helpful therapeutic approach,* since it avoids the disadvantages that arise with the exclusive attention to cognitions or emotions only. (Tausch, 2002: 139, original emphasis).

Other articles on cognition focus on a cognitive perspective on borderline personality development (Bohart, 1990); focusing and cognitive functions (Iberg, 1990); cognitive processes as a cause of psychotherapeutic change (Zimring, 1990); the importance of empathy in cognitive restructuring (Vanaerschot, 1993); incongruence and social cognition (Hoyer, 1996); cognition patterns in a client-centred therapy session in the context of a schizophrenic client process (Trytten, 2003); reflecting cognitions (Tausch, 2007), and cognition as a component of schema or schemes (Behr, 2009a, 2009b).

However, while theories of cognition and behaviour are part of person-centred psychology, PCT has a different emphasis to its cognitive behavioural counterpart, and it is this that I have elaborated in the second part of the chapter.

We're all cognitive behavioural therapists now

In the first part of this chapter, I noted the basis of PCT as a process-oriented therapy and drew some distinctions between this and CBT as an outcome-focused therapy. I would argue that such a directive therapy, as distinct from reflective and supportive therapies, is not only instrumental, but somewhat narrow and short term in its focus and its ambition. In contrast, process-oriented therapy has, as Mølbak (2012: 483) acknowledges, 'a revolutionary potential that does not fit with managerial society'. Whatever one's analysis, the point here is to be clear that the differences between therapies reflect and represent very real differences in the philosophical assumptions and values that underpin these various approaches – and that the bias in favour of CBT is a political and economic one, and not one based on and in evidence, whether empirical or pragmatic.

In his foreword to the first edition of this book, Stephen Palmer understandably defended CBT against criticisms, but suggested that these come from a perception of CBT as a threat or challenge, and ended by extolling

CBT: 'Its common-sense, pragmatic approach will continue to have wide appeal, regardless of how it is viewed within the counselling and psychotherapy professions' (Palmer, 2008: vi). These are quite remarkable statements: the first, an *ad hominem* argument, discounts any research- or practice-based critique of CBT, and the second both extols pragmatism and empiricism over any other philosophical traditions and discounts the genuine concerns that many of us in the counselling and psychotherapy professions have about the unwarranted claims made about and on behalf of CBT, and the philosophical and therapeutic differences we have with CBT.

In the second part of the chapter, I detailed the cognitive and behavioural aspects of person-centred theory, psychology and therapy. If people – clients themselves, commissioners, referrers, policy-makers and politicians – want therapists to focus on clients' cognition and behaviour, then person-centred and other therapists can do that. We can play the game and 'deliver' the required outcomes – or, more accurately, we can translate the client's outcomes into the language of the current dominant discourse. Given that the evidence from comparative and meta-studies suggests a certain equivalence of therapeutic effectiveness across theoretical orientations, and on the basis of promoting client/patient choice and *increased* access to a choice of psychological therapies in the public sector, some of this detail, and the research instruments and measures that lie behind them, can contribute to the argument in favour of sharing conceptual and clinical space rather than claiming, colonising, and then defending therapeutic territory. We can then engage in debates about brief, short-term, or time-limited therapy (see Tudor, 2008). We should be under no illusion, however, that we are on a level playing field. Despite therapeutic equivalence, and despite well-argued criticisms of CBT, it is still favoured by governments. The fact that, ultimately, politicians fund CBT is not to do with the lack of PCT theory regarding cognition behaviour, or research evidence that shows the efficacy of other approaches to therapy; it is more to do with research bias (in favour of empirical methodology and empirically-supported treatments), and political influence and expediency, for a critique of which see Tudor (2010) and other chapters in this volume.

In conclusion, I have a hope, some suggestions and a strategy. Rather than simply discounting colleagues with whom they disagree, I hope theoreticians and practitioners will develop more open-mindedness, as well as greater intellectual rigour in debate. Rather than simply claiming the empirical high ground, I suggest that therapy researchers need to be more impartial and open to diverse and multiple methodologies, 'evidence' and methods. Rather than remaining uncritically allegiant to a particular school/orientation/modality of therapy, I suggest that therapists need to be more open to pluralism and to understanding the strengths of different approaches, as well as the weaknesses of their own. Finally, and perhaps most ambitiously, rather than operating on the basis of short-term economic thinking, I suggest that politicians need to be more honest about the ideological and economic basis of their policies, take a long-term view about health and social health care, and promote improving access to psychological *therapies* (plural), rather than restricting access to one favoured form of therapy.

My strategy (until this hope is fulfilled) is to claim and reclaim what is ours, including the psychology of the whole person, from the compartmentalisation of CBT. Of course, most therapists don't 'do' cognitive and behavioural therapy using CBT techniques, and in that sense, they are not 'cognitive behaviour therapists'. However, in the sense that all therapists work with cognition and behaviour, *we are all cognitive and behavioural therapists*. This is an important point and strategy if we are to break the monopoly of CBT, and monopoly of cognitive behavioural therapists on CBT, and assert the efficacy of other therapies with regard to cognition and behaviour.

References

Beck AT (1967). *Depression: clinical, experimental and theoretical aspects*. New York, NY: Harper & Row.

Behr M (2009a). Constructing emotions and accommodating schemas: a model of self-exploration, symbolization, and development. *Person-Centered & Experiential Psychotherapies 8*(1): 44–62.

Behr M (2009b). Schemas, self, and personality change. *Person-Centered & Experiential Psychotherapies 8*(3): 233–242.

Bohart AC (1990). A cognitive client-centered perspective on borderline personality development. In: Lietaer, Rombauts J, Van Balen R (eds). *Client-Centered and Experiential Psychotherapy in the Nineties*. Leuven: Leuven University Press (pp599–621).

Cartwright DS, Graham MJ (1984). Self-concept and identity: overlapping portions of a cognitive structure of self. In: Levant RS, Shlien JM (eds). *Client-Centered Therapy and the Person-Centered Approach*. New York, NY: Praeger (pp108–130).

Clarkson P (1989). Beyond schoolism. *Changes 16*(1) : 1–11.

Cornelius-White JHD (2007). Congruence as extensionality. *Person-Centered & Experiential Psychotherapies* 6(3): 196–204.

Evans D, Zarate O (1999). *Introducing Evolutionary Psychology*. Cambridge: Icon Books.

Goldstein K (1934/1995). *The Organism*. New York, NY: Zone Books.

Heidegger M (1930/1993). On the essence of truth. In: Krell DF (ed). *Martin Heidegger: basic writings*. San Francisco, CA: HarperCollins (pp115–138).

House R (2010). *In, Against and Beyond Therapy: critical essays towards a 'post-professional' era*. Ross-on-Wye: PCCS Books.

Hoyer J (1996). Incongruence and social cognition. In: Esser U, Pabst H, Speierer G-W (eds). *The Power of the Person-Centered Approach: new challenges–perspectives–answers*. Köln: GwG (pp3–22).

Iberg JR (1990). Ms C's focusing and cognitive functions. In: Lietaer G, Rombauts J, Van Balen R (eds). *Client-Centered and Experiential Therapy in the Nineties*. Leuven: Leuven University Press (pp173–203).

Kelly GA (1955). *The Psychology of Personal Constructs, vol 1*. New York, NY: WW Norton.

Kirschenbaum H, Henderson VL (eds) (1990). *Carl Rogers: dialogues*. London: Constable.

Layard R (2006). *Happiness: lessons from a new science*. London: Penguin Books.

Leijssen M, Elliott R (2008). Integrative experiential psychotherapy in brief. In: Tudor K (ed). *Brief Person-Centred Therapies*. London: Sage (pp31–46).

Lietaer G (1990). The client-centered approach after the Wisconsin project: a personal view on its evolution. In: Lietaer G, Rombauts J, Van Balen R (eds). *Client-Centered and Experiential Therapy in the Nineties*. Leuven: Leuven University Press (pp19–45).

Miller SD (2012). *Revolution in Swedish Mental Health Practice: the cognitive behavioral therapy monopoly gives way*. [Blog.] www.scottdmiller.com/revolution-in-swedish-mental-health-practice-the-cognitive-behavioral-therapy-monopoly-gives-way (accessed 3 February 2018).

Mølbak RL (2012). Cultivating the therapeutic moment: from planning to receptivity in therapeutic practice. *Journal of Humanistic Psychology 53*(4): 461–488.

Nye RD (2000). *Three Psychologies: perspectives from Freud, Skinner, and Rogers* (6th ed). Belmont, CA: Wadsworth/Thomson.

Palmer S (2008). Foreword: polemics and cognitive behaviour therapy. In: House R, Loewenthal D (eds). *Against and For CBT: towards a constructive dialogue?* Ross-on-Wye: PCCS Books (ppv–vi).

Patterson CH (1986). *Theories of Counseling and Psychotherapy*. New York, NY: Harper Collins.

Raimy V (1975). *Misunderstandings of the Self: cognitive psychotherapy and the misconception hypothesis*. San Francisco, CA: Jossey-Bass.

Raimy V (1971). *The Self-Concept as a Factor in Counselling and Personality Organization*. Columbus, OH: Ohio State University.

Rice LN (1984). Client tasks in client-centered therapy. In: Levant RF, Shlien J (eds). *Client-Centered Therapy and the Person-Centered Approach: new directions in theory, research and practice*. New York, NY: Praeger (pp182–202).

Rice LN (1974). The evocative function of the therapist. In: Wexler DA, Rice LN (eds). *Innovations in Client-Centered Therapy*. New York, NY: Wiley (pp289–311).

Rogers CR (1985). Toward a more human science of the person. *Journal of Humanistic Psychology 25*(4): 7–24.

Rogers CR (1974/1980). Do we need 'a' reality? In: Rogers CR. *A Way of Being*. Boston, MA: Houghton Mifflin (pp96–108).

Rogers CR (1972). Bringing together ideas and feelings in learning. *Learning Today 5*: 32–43.

Rogers CR (1965). *Three Approaches to Psychotherapy* (E Shostrom producer). [Film.] Santa Ana, CA: Psychological Films.

Rogers CR (1959). A theory of therapy, personality and interpersonal relationships, as developed in the client-centred framework. In: Koch S (ed). *Psychology: a study of a science. Vol 3: formulation of the person and the social context*. New York, NY: McGraw-Hill (pp184–256).

Rogers CR (1958/1967a). A process conception of psychotherapy. In: Rogers CR. *On Becoming a Person*. London: Constable (pp125–159).

Rogers CR (1957/1967b). A therapist's view of the good life: the fully functioning person. In: Rogers CR. *On Becoming a Person*. London: Constable (pp183–196).

Rogers CR (1957). The necessary and sufficient conditions of therapeutic personality change. *Journal of Consulting Psychology 21*: 95–103.

Rogers CR (1951). *Client-Centered Therapy*. London: Constable.

Rogers CR (1942). *Counseling and Psychotherapy: newer concepts in practice*. Boston, MA: Houghton Mifflin.

Rogers CR, Russell DE (2002). *Carl Rogers the Quiet Revolutionary: an oral history.* Roseville, CA: Penmarin Books.

Rogers CR, Skinner BF (1956). Some issues concerning the control of human behavior: a symposium. *Science 124*: 1057–1066.

Samuels A (1989). Analysis and pluralism: the politics of psyche. *Journal of Analytical Psychology 34*(1): 33–51.

Sanders P (2009). Person-centered challenges to traditional psychological health care systems. *Person-Centered and Experiential Psychotherapies 8*(1): 1–17.

Tausch R (2007). Promoting health: challenges for person-centered communication in psychotherapy, counseling and human relationships in daily life. *Person-Centered & Experiential Psychotherapies 6*(1): 1–13.

Tausch R (1988/2002). The relationship between emotions and cognitions: implications for therapist empathy. In: Cain D (ed). *Classics in the Person-Centered Approach.* Ross-on-Wye: PCCS Books (pp134–142).

Thorne B (2003/1992). *Carl Rogers* (2nd ed). London: Sage.

Thorne B (1996). Person-centred therapy. In: Dryden W (ed). *Handbook of Individual Therapy.* London: Sage (pp121–146).

Trytten JD (2003). *Schizophrenic Client Process: phase and cognition patterns in a client-centered therapy session.* Unpublished PhD thesis. Chicago, IL: Argosy University.

Tudor K (2018). *Psychotherapy: a critical examination.* Monmouth: PCCS Books.

Tudor K (2013). From humanism to humanistic psychology and back again. *Self & Society: an International Journal for Humanistic Psychology 40*(1): 35–41.

Tudor K (2011). Rogers' therapeutic conditions: a relational conceptualization. *Person-Centered & Experiential Psychotherapies 10*(3): 165–180.

Tudor K (2010). Being in process, being in context: a person-centred perspective on happiness. In: Loewenthal D, House R (eds). *Critically Engaging CBT.* Milton Keynes: Open University Press (pp84–97).

Tudor K (ed) (2008). *Brief Person-Centred Therapies.* London: Sage.

Tudor K (2006). Appendix 3: a process conception of development and psychotherapy. In: Tudor K, Worrall M. *Person-Centred Therapy: a clinical philosophy.* London: Routledge (pp259–262).

Tudor K (2000). The case of the lost conditions. *Counselling 11*(1): 33–37.

Tudor K, Worrall M (2006). *Person-Centred Therapy: a clinical philosophy.* London: Routledge.

Vanaerschot G (1993). Empathy as releasing several micro-processes in the client. In: Brazier D (ed). *Beyond Carl Rogers.* London: Constable (pp47–71).

Wexler DA (1974). A cognitive theory of experiencing, self-actualization and therapeutic process. In: Wexler DA, Rice LN (eds). *Innovations in Client-Centered Therapy.* New York, NY: Wiley (pp49–116).

Wexler DA, Rice LN (eds) (1974). *Innovations in Client-Centered Therapy.* New York, NY: Wiley.

Zimring F (1990). Cognitive processes as a cause of psychotherapeutic change. In: Lietaer G, Rombauts J, Van Balen R (eds). *Client-Centered and Experiential Therapy in the Nineties.* Leuven: Leuven University Press (pp361–380).

Zimring F (1974). A cognitive theory of experiencing, self-actualization and therapeutic process. In: Wexler DA, Rice LN (eds). *Innovations in Client-Centered Therapy.* New York, NY: Wiley (pp49–116).

13 Cognitive behaviour therapy: from rationalism to constructivism?*

David A Winter

Treatment guidelines indicate that the treatment of choice for most psychological problems is cognitive behaviour therapy. This chapter suggests that there are alternative constructions of the evidence base from which such guidelines are drawn, and reviews another relevant evidence base, in this case concerning the relationship between clients' and therapists' philosophical beliefs, personal styles and treatment preferences. It draws a distinction between rationalism and constructivism, which is illustrated by approaches to the 'resistant' client and discusses possible constructivist trends in cognitive behaviour therapy.

With at least 500 psychological therapies available (Karasu, 1986), the choices faced by clinicians, clients and healthservice commissioners in selecting a therapeutic approach would appear to be bewildering. However, relief is provided from making such complex decisions by guidelines and reviews indicating that the treatment of choice for most psychological ills (Chambless et al, 1998; National Institute for Health and Clinical/Care Excellence, 2004, 2009, 2017; Roth & Fonagy, 2005), not to mention economic ones (Centre for Economic Performance's Mental Health Policy Group, 2006), is cognitive behaviour therapy.

Such assertions, generally framed within a discourse of evidence-based practice and empirical support, may appear rooted in scientific considerations. However, the situation is not quite so simple, since therapies differ not only in terms of technical features but also in underlying philosophical assumptions, which may be at least as relevant to treatment selection as is scientific evidence concerning therapeutic efficacy.

* An earlier version of this chapter appeared in the *European Journal of Psychotherapy and Counselling 2008; 10*(3): 221–230.

This chapter will review an alternative evidence base, which concerns the relationship between philosophical beliefs and clients' and therapists' preferences for different therapies, as well as the practice of, and clients' response to, these therapies. It will also indicate that the more familiar evidence base concerning the outcome of cognitive behaviour and other therapies is open to alternative constructions, which call into question the treatment guidelines that have been derived from it. Finally, the chapter will consider the implications for this debate of the increasing diversification of cognitive behaviour therapies.

Philosophical beliefs, personal styles, and therapeutic preferences

A research programme that commenced in the 1960s has provided consistent evidence that, whether they are staff or clients, people's preferences for different treatments for psychological problems reflect their 'personal styles' (Caine, Wijesinghe & Winter, 1981/2014; Caine & Winter, 1993). Two dimensions of personal style that are of particular relevance are inner- versus outer-directedness – a focus on subjective concerns or on the external world – and radicalism versus conservatism. People who preferred, chose to practise, were allocated to, or improved in more structured, directive therapies (such as behaviour therapy) were found to be more outer-directed and conservative than those who preferred, practised, were allocated to, or improved in less directive, more interpersonally focused approaches (such as group-analytic therapy).

A related body of research concerns the epistemological positions characterising different therapies. Schacht and Black (1985) found behaviour therapists to have an empirical 'epistemic style' (concerned with the correspondence of beliefs with observations), in contrast to the predominantly metaphorical style (concerned with symbolic representations and the ability to generalise from beliefs) of psychoanalytic therapists. Arthur (2000), as well as confirming the difference between these therapists on the metaphorical style dimension, showed cognitive behaviour therapists to be characterised by the objectivist worldview described as mechanism, in contrast to the organicism, or subjectivist worldview, of psychoanalytic psychotherapists. Neimeyer and colleagues (1993) also found that people prefer therapeutic approaches that match their epistemic styles.

Another distinction is between rationalist and constructivist epistemological positions – essentially, whether people are viewed as passively perceiving an independently existing real world or actively constructing their realities. It has been found that rational emotive therapists are more rationalist and less constructivist than personal construct psychotherapists (Neimeyer & Morton, 1997), and that therapists' epistemological positions are reflected in their personal characteristics, therapeutic styles and choice of interventions, with rationalists being more likely to use cognitive behavioural techniques (Neimeyer et al, 2006). A further indication of the rationalist position of cognitive behaviour therapists was provided by Winter and colleagues (2006), who, comparing them with psychotherapists of eight other orientations, found them to be more rationalist than all except hypnotherapists. They were also more outer-directed than all other therapists, and more likely to construe therapy in technical terms.

Philosophical beliefs in practice

Psychotherapists' philosophical beliefs would be expected to be reflected in their therapeutic practice, and distinctions between rationalist and constructivist therapies have been delineated in this regard (Mahoney, 1988). Fundamental to these distinctions is rationalist therapists' primary concern with the validity of the client's view of the world, and hence with the correction of 'cognitive errors', as opposed to constructivist therapists' primary concern with the viability of this view.

There is some evidence of distinctive features of constructivist and rationalist therapies. Vasco (1994) found that the therapeutic practice of constructivist psychologists was characterised by low levels of structure, directiveness, focus on current issues and confrontation regarding resistance. Viney (1994) demonstrated that personal construct and client-centred therapy sessions showed greater acknowledgement of clients' emotional distress than did rational emotive therapy sessions, which tended to regard it as indicating irrationality. Winter and Watson (1999) found that, compared with cognitive therapy sessions, personal construct psychotherapy sessions were characterised by a less negative therapist attitude, greater therapist exploration and client participation, greater use of less structured response modes and less use of directive responses, and greater use by the client of complex levels of perceptual processing. The two types of therapist also held different views of the therapeutic relationship.

It is in their approach to the client who is considered resistant to therapy that differences in practice between therapists of different orientations often come into the sharpest focus. The difference between rationalist and constructivist therapists may be framed in terms of Liotti's (1989) distinction between pedagogical and exploratory approaches. The former is nowhere more vividly presented than in Albert Ellis' (1980) remark that resistance may be due to 'the therapist's engaging in... therapy in a namby-pamby, passive way instead of vigorously getting after clients' (p256). Compare this, and the battlefield metaphors often used by rationalist therapists in describing work with resistant clients, with Mahoney's (1988) description of the constructivist view:

> ... that resistance to core psychological change is a natural and healthy expression of an individual's attempt to protect and perpetuate his systemic integrity... For the constructivist therapist, then, resistance to change is not the enemy in counselling. It is not something to be 'overcome', but a healthy self-protective process that is to be respected and worked *with* rather than *against.* (p306, original emphases)

Rationalist therapists' approach to resistance may be illustrated by the following extract from a session focusing on a client's failure to comply with homework strategies suggested by her cognitive behaviour therapist to tackle her trichotillomania (Watson & Winter, 2000):

Therapist (T): So, did you manage to wear the gloves while you were driving?

Client (C): No, I didn't.

T: Any problem with that?

C: To be quite honest I didn't really think about it because I'm always in a rush…

T: Right, I see, but I think that would be a very good way of stopping that when you're driving.

C: Mm.

T: Because to overcome this problem you have to have a strategy, otherwise nothing is going to change for you… Have you been breathing?

C: Yeah sometimes... But I can't see how doing all this wearing gloves and breathing and so forth is going to stop me hair pulling, because it won't.

T: I know about these problems and there's a whole range of things that one needs to do together to get a grip on these problems, because the problem is very difficult and therefore you need a sledgehammer to crack it, it's a very evasive problem and you can't have half-hearted attempts at dealing with it.

It was perhaps unsurprising that the client dropped out of therapy after this session. In contrast, a constructivist approach is illustrated by a session with a client who did not comply obediently with the instructions of fixed-role therapy (Kelly, 1955) requiring him to take on a new role. Rather than fully adopting this role, a character named Barry, he held a conversation between Barry and his angry self, whom he named Billy (Winter, 2008). The client, who had previously been through the mill of cognitive behaviour and other approaches to therapy, recounted this to the therapist, and the following interaction ensued:

C: ... I don't know where that quite leaves us with it because there's been some moderate benefit at least in the short term, but I'm aware that it isn't doing as you had intended.

T: It doesn't need to be.

C: [laughs] Say it again.

T: It doesn't need to be done in a very prescriptive way. A conversation, albeit a short one, between Barry and Billy might be.

C: [laughs] Well, perhaps that's the other novelty of a personal construct approach, because if it's fair to characterize a personal construct approach as a cognitive approach… other cognitive approaches are extraordinarily directive.

T: Which is why I would say that it isn't a cognitive approach.

C: [laughs] ...once again I've sabotaged the therapy, which has been the accusation in the past, resistance, not wanting to do as you're told, all these kind of things.

T: It could be looked at in that way, but it could also be seen that you've done something quite novel, which seems to have had some effect.

A constructivist approach such as this to the 'resistant' client may be less likely to lead to therapeutic casualties than the 'ballistic' (Stiles, Honos-Webb & Surko, 1996), invalidating approach demonstrated in the first example (Winter, 1997).

Therapeutic outcome

Lists of 'evidence-based' or 'empirically supported' therapies are dominated by cognitive behavioural approaches. However, the evidence on which such lists are based is open to alternative constructions, and different interpretations of research findings in this area have been apparent at least since Eysenck's (1952) assertions concerning the ineffectiveness of psychotherapy. While early meta-analyses of outcome research did indicate some superiority of cognitive behavioural over other approaches, such differences could be attributed to features of research design favouring cognitive behaviour therapy. More generally, the very criteria for what constitutes an empirically supported therapy (Chambless et al, 1998), emphasising quantitative, randomised controlled trials of manualised therapies for clients with specific diagnoses, may be considered biased toward cognitive behavioural approaches, and to lead to the 'empirical violation' of humanistic and constructivist therapies (Bohart, O'Hara & Leitner, 1998; Bohart & House, Chapter 18, and House & Bohart, Chapter 19, this volume). As Slife has asked:

> Is it merely coincidental that the therapies that match the values of objectivist science are those that are most scientifically supported?... Is it merely coincidental that cognitive behavioural therapy has virtually the same epistemological assumptions (values) as traditional science (ie. a wedding of empiricism and rationalism). The positive empirical evaluations of this therapy may be the result of systematic bias rather than efficacy without such bias. (Slife, 2004: 51–52)

Roth and Fonagy (2005) concede this point in the second edition of their influential book, *What Works for Whom?*, where, commenting on research on personal construct psychotherapy (PCT), they remark that 'what is available is philosophically at variance with a conventional review such as this one. This latter point could be used to argue that the absence of reports of evidence for PCT in this book reflects our selection bias rather than a real absence of evidence' (p492).

Meta-analyses have, indeed, suggested that this form of therapy is at least as effective as other approaches, including cognitive behaviour therapy (Metcalfe, Winter & Viney, 2007; Viney, Metcalfe & Winter, 2005). However, given its founder, George Kelly, rejected the labelling of personal construct psychology as cognitive (1969), it is ironic that, when evidence for personal construct psychotherapy *has* been included in reviews of the psychotherapy research literature, this has been in sections devoted to cognitive behaviour therapy (Carr, 2009; Cooper, 2008).

Even when the focus is on comparative outcome studies conducted according to traditional scientific method, which might be expected to favour cognitive behaviour therapy, recent meta-analyses have indicated little or no difference between therapies (Wampold, 2001). Furthermore, there is little or no evidence for the effects of specific ingredients of therapy, leading Wampold to conclude that 'the ingredients of the most conspicuous treatment on the landscape, cognitive-behavioral treatment, are apparently not responsible for the benefits of this treatment' (pp147–148). Similarly, in their review of the evidence base for cognitive and cognitive behaviour therapies, Hollon and Beck (2013) note that: 'For many disorders, the extent to which the underlying mechanisms of change are cognitive in nature remains unclear' (p425).

Some authors, viewing the research evidence for the superiority of cognitive behaviour therapy as at best modest, and noting the methodological deficiencies of various of the studies concerned, have questioned the basis for the generally strong recommendations for this form of therapy in treatment guidelines such as those produced in the UK by the National Institute for Health and Care Excellence (NICE) (Jauhar et al, 2014; Jauhar, McKenna & Laws, 2016; Taylor & Perera, 2015). As I have argued elsewhere, such recommendations may be 'based less on a balanced review of the evidence base than on the allegiances of members of the Guideline Development Group or political considerations, such as support of current National Health Service (NHS) policies and initiatives' (Winter, 2010: 6). This conclusion is consistent with analyses of some NICE guidelines that have indicated that higher effect sizes may have been necessary for a non-cognitive behaviour therapy to be recommended in them than for a cognitive behaviour therapy (Coghill, 2015; Kramo, Winter & Sullivan, 2017). It is also supported by a study of determinants of group judgments in clinical guideline development, which provided evidence that participants were more likely to accept evidence if this was consistent with their current practice, and that there may have been a halo effect for cognitive behaviour therapy, whereby its perceived effectiveness with some conditions led to assumptions that it would be similarly effective for others (Raine et al, 2004).

Varieties of cognitive behaviour therapy

Cognitive behaviour therapy has diversified considerably over the last half century. The 'first wave' of empirically based behaviour therapies was succeeded, during the 'cognitive revolution', by a 'second wave' of therapies that, while incorporating attention to cognitions, were still essentially mechanistic (Hayes, 2004). The more recent 'third wave' of cognitive behaviour therapies, regarded as contextualist (viewing events within their total context) and more concerned with process than with content, are so varied that one wonders at what point the cognitive behaviour label becomes so permeable as to be no longer useful. They include dialectical behaviour therapy (Linehan, 1993), mindfulness-based cognitive therapy (Segal, Williams & Teasdale, 2002), and acceptance and commitment therapy (Hayes, Strosahl & Wilson, 1999). As Watson (2005) indicated, cognitive behaviour therapy is 'no longer about correcting cognitive errors', unlike the rationalist therapies which she had previously differentiated from personal construct psychotherapy. Nevertheless, there is some evidence that at least one 'third-wave' approach, dialectical behaviour therapy, differs from personal construct psychotherapy in ways that are not inconsistent with her earlier study (Winter et al, 2003).

Nor is it easy to accept the claims of leading cognitive 'second-wave' therapists, such as Beck (Weishar, 1993) and Ellis (1990), that their approaches are constructivist. Indeed, Ellis' (1990: 118) assertion that rational emotive therapy 'is not only nonrationalist but... is in several important respects more constructivist and more process-oriented than just about all of the other cognitive therapies' perhaps only goes to prove his thesis that all of us, even rational emotive therapists, are prone to irrationality.

Conclusions

Psychological therapies differ markedly in their underlying philosophical assumptions, and people, whether clients, therapists, health commissioners, or policy makers, tend to favour approaches with assumptions matching their own beliefs and 'personal styles'. These beliefs are also likely to influence constructions placed on the 'evidence base' for psychological therapies, including those of guideline developers. For example, since 'the science of economics has largely endorsed empiricism and the operationalization of nonmaterialist constructs', as well as hedonism (Slife, 2004: 54), it is not surprising that an economic reading of this evidence base might view cognitive behaviour therapies as a panacea.

This was graphically demonstrated in England by the government's initial commitment of £300 million to improve access to predominantly cognitive behaviour psychological therapies, on the basis of a report by an economist, who has also authored a book on happiness (Layard, 2005; see also Pilgrim's Chapter 3, this volume). The language used by the UK Secretary of State for Health when introducing this initiative clearly reflected the rationalist philosophy on which it was based: 'Successful psychological therapies ensure that the *right number* of people are offered a choice of the *right services* at the *right time* with the *right results*' (Hewitt, 2007: 2, emphasis in original). Whether the subsequent results of the programme[1] may be considered any more *right* than those of one based on any other form of therapy depends upon your view of a reported reliable recovery rate of 46% (NHS Digital, 2016).

Although there is little doubt that cognitive behavioural approaches are effective with some problems, it can no longer be confidently asserted (admittedly in this particular reader's view of the 'evidence') that these therapies are generally more effective than any other, or that their effects are due to their specific cognitive behavioural ingredients (see Bohart & House, Chapter 18, and House & Bohart, Chapter 19, this volume). Rather than being accepted uncritically, the research evidence, and the guidelines presented as based on interpretations of this evidence, should be subjected to just as much scrutiny as in another field of therapy where there are clear vested interests, the pharmaceutical industry (Goldacre, 2012).

In addition, the diversification of cognitive behaviour therapies, while perhaps to be welcomed in making them more contextualist and constructivist and less likely to subject the resistant client to a 'ballistic' approach, might also be viewed as rendering them so indistinct that it prompts the question, when is such a therapy no longer cognitive behavioural? Given the overwhelming support for cognitive behaviour therapies by health service funders, and the slick marketing of such therapies, it is perhaps understandable that even those who develop what are presented as radical new approaches may be loath to discard the cognitive behaviour label. For example, O'Connor (2015) has presented a framework based on phenomenological and constructionist concepts and methods, albeit not fully exploiting the potential of all of these methods (Winter, 2015), which he regards as having 'far-reaching implications since it views all behaviour, activity, thought and feeling as a creative process' (p3). However, this framework is described as 'a constructionist clinical psychology for cognitive behaviour therapy', rather than a truly alternative approach. Furthermore, as we have seen, even those approaches that do clearly differentiate themselves from cognitive behaviour therapy, such as personal construct psychotherapy, may nevertheless be subsumed under the cognitive behavioural umbrella if they are seen to be effective. This perhaps indicates a view, reportedly expressed by Beck (Beutler, personal communication), that 'If it works, it's CBT'.

1. The Improving Access to Psychological Therapies programme has now, with further funding, been expanded from adult services to those for children and adolescents and incorporates some NICE-recommended non-cognitive behavioural approaches, although the first-choice therapy offered is still CBT.

References

Arthur AR (2000). The personality and cognitive-epistemological traits of cognitive behavioural and psychoanalytic psychotherapists. *British Journal of Medical Psychology 73*: 243–257.

Bohart AC, O'Hara M, Leitner LM (1998). Empirically violated treatments: disenfranchisement of humanistic and other psychotherapies. *Psychotherapy Research 8*: 1–57.

Caine TM, Winter DA (1993). Personal styles and universal polarities: implications for therapeutic practice. *Therapeutic Communities 14*: 91–102.

Caine TM, Wijesinghe OBA, Winter DA (1981). *Personal Styles in Neurosis: implications for small group psychotherapy and behaviour therapy*. London: Routledge & Kegan Paul.

Carr A (2009). *What Works with Children, Adolescents, and Adults? A review of research on the effectiveness of psychotherapy.* London: Routledge.

Centre for Economic Performance's Mental Health Policy Group (2006). *The Depression Report: a new deal for depression and anxiety disorders*. London: London School of Economics.

Chambless DL, Baker MJ, Baucom DH, Beutler LE, Calhoun KS, Crits-Christoph P, Daiuto A, DeRubeis R, Detweiler J, Haaga DAF, Johnson SB, McCurry S, Mueser KT, Pope KS, Sanderson WC, Shoham V, Stickle T, Williams DA, Woody SR (1998). Update on empirically validated therapies II. *The Clinical Psychologist 51*: 3–16.

Coghill D (2015). Are NICE guidelines losing their impartiality? *British Journal of Psychiatry 207*: 271.

Cooper M (2008). *Essential Research Findings in Counselling and Psychotherapy: the facts are friendly.* London: Sage.

Ellis A (1990). Is rational-emotive therapy (RET) 'rationalist' or constructivist? In: Ellis A, Dryden W (eds). *The Essential Albert Ellis: seminal writings on psychotherapy*. New York, NY: Springer (pp26–32).

Ellis A (1980). Treatment of erectile dysfunction. In: Leiblum SR, Pervin LA (eds). *Principles and Practice of Sex Therapy.* London: Tavistock (pp235–261).

Eysenck HJ (1952). The effects of psychotherapy: an evaluation. *Journal of Consulting Psychology 16*: 319–324.

Goldacre B (2012). *Bad Pharma: how drug companies mislead doctors and harm patients.* London: HarperCollins.

Hayes SC (2004). Acceptance and commitment therapy, relational frame theory, and the third wave of behavioral and cognitive therapies. *Behavior Therapy 35*: 639–665.

Hayes SC, Strosahl KD, Wilson KG (1999). *Acceptance and Commitment Therapy: an experiential approach to behavior change.* New York, NY: Guilford Press.

Hewitt P (2007). Foreword. In: CSIP Choice and Access Team. *Commissioning a Brighter Future: improving access to psychological therapies.* London: Department of Health (p2).

Hollon SD, Beck AT (2013). Cognitive and cognitive-behavioral therapies. In: Lambert MJ (ed). *Bergin and Garfield's Handbook of Psychotherapy and Behavior Change (6th ed).* Hoboken, NJ: Wiley (pp393–442).

Jauhar S, McKenna PJ, Laws KR (2016). NICE guidelines on psychological treatments for bipolar disorder: searching for the evidence. *Lancet Psychiatry 3*: 386–388.

Jauhar S, McKenna PJ, Radua J, Fung E, Salvador R, Laws KR (2014). Cognitive-behavioural therapy for the symptoms of schizophrenia: systematic review and meta-analysis with examination of potential bias. *British Journal of Psychiatry 204*: 20–29.

Karasu TB (1986). The psychotherapies: benefits and limitations. *American Journal of Psychotherapy 40*: 324–343.

Kelly GA (1969). The therapeutic relationship. In: Maher B (ed). *Clinical Psychology and Personality: the selected papers of George Kelly.* New York, NY: Wiley (pp216–223).

Kelly GA (1955). *The Psychology of Personal Constructs.* New York, NY: Norton.

Kramo K, Winter DA, Sullivan K (in preparation). Exploring the strength of the evidence in NICE depression guidelines for cognitive-behavioural versus other psychotherapies.

Layard R (2005). *Happiness: lessons from a new science.* London: Allen Lane.

Linehan MM (1993). *Cognitive-Behavioral Treatment of Borderline Personality Disorder.* New York, NY: Guilford Press.

Liotti G (1989). Resistance to change in cognitive psychotherapy: theoretical remarks from a constructivist point of view. In: Dryden W, Trower P (eds). *Cognitive Psychotherapy: stasis and change.* London: Cassell (pp28–56).

Mahoney MJ (1988). Constructive metatheory II: implications for psychotherapy. *International Journal of Personal Construct Psychology 1*: 299–315.

Metcalfe C, Winter DA, Viney LL (2007). The effectiveness of personal construct psychotherapy in clinical practice: a systematic review and meta-analysis. *Psychotherapy Research 17:* 431–442.

National Institute for Health and Care Excellence (2017). Depression in adults: treatment and management. Draft for consultation. London: NICE.

National Institute for Health and Clinical Excellence (2009). Depression in adults: recognition and management. London: NICE.

National Institute for Health and Clinical Excellence (2004). Depression: management of depression in primary and secondary care. CG23. London: NICE.

Neimeyer GJ, Morton RJ (1997). Personal epistemologies and preferences for rationalist versus constructivist psychotherapies. *Journal of Constructivist Psychology 10*: 109–123.

Neimeyer GJ, Lee J, Aksoy G, Phillip D (2006). Epistemic styles among seasoned psychotherapists: some practical implications. In: Raskin J, Bridges S (eds). *Studies in Meaning, vol 3.* New York, NY: Pace University Press (pp31–54).

Neimeyer GJ, Prichard S, Lyddon WJ, Sherrard PAD (1993). The role of epistemic style in counselling preference and orientation. *Journal of Counseling and Development 71*: 515–523.

NHS Digital (2016). *Psychological Therapies: annual report on the use of IAPT services, England 2015–2016.* [Online]. NHS Digital. http://digital.nhs.uk/catalogue/PUB22110 (accessed 4 February 2018).

O'Connor KP (2015). *A Constructionist Clinical Psychology for Cognitive Behaviour Therapy.* Hove: Routledge.

Raine R, Sanderson C, Hutchings A, Carter S, Larkin K, Black N (2004). An experimental study of determinants of group judgments in clinical guideline development. *The Lancet 364*: 429–437.

Roth A, Fonagy P (2005). *What Works for Whom? A Critical Review of Psychotherapy Research.* New York, NY: Guilford Press.

Schacht TE, Black DA (1985). Epistemological commitments of behavioural and psychoanalytic therapists. *Professional Psychology: Research and Practice 16*: 316–323.

Segal ZV, Williams JMG, Teasdale JD (2002). *Mindfulness-Based Cognitive Therapy for Depression: a new approach to preventing relapse.* New York, NY: Guilford Press.

Slife BD (2004). Theoretical challenges to therapy practice and research: the constraint of naturalism. In: Lambert MJ (ed). *Bergin and Garfield's Handbook of Psychotherapy and Behavior Change* (5th ed). New York, NY: Wiley (pp44–83).

Stiles WB, Honos-Webb L, Surko M (1996). *Responsiveness as a Challenge to Process Research.* Paper presented at 27th Annual Meeting of Society for Psychotherapy Research, Amelia Island, Florida.

Taylor M, Perera U (2015). NICE CG178 Psychosis and Schizophrenia in Adults: treatment and management – an evidence-based guideline? *British Journal of Psychiatry 206*: 357–359.

Vasco AB (1994). Correlates of constructivism among Portuguese therapists. *Journal of Constructivist Psychology 7*: 1–16.

Viney LL (1994). Sequences of emotional distress expressed by clients and acknowledged by therapists: are they associated more with some therapist than others? *British Journal of Clinical Psychology 33*: 469–481.

Viney LL, Metcalfe C, Winter DA (2005). The effectiveness of personal construct psychotherapy: a meta-analysis. In: Winter DA, Viney LL (eds). *Personal Construct Psychotherapy: advances in theory, practice and research.* London: Whurr (pp347–364).

Wampold BE (2001). *The Great Psychotherapy Debate: models, methods, and findings.* Mahwah, NJ: Erlbaum.

Watson S (2005). *Personal Construct Therapy and the Cognitive Therapies Revisited: how different are they in the 21st century?* Paper presented at the 16th International Congress of Personal Construct Psychology, Columbus, Ohio.

Watson S, Winter DA (2000). What works for whom but shouldn't and what doesn't work for whom but should? *European Journal of Psychotherapy, Counselling and Health 3*: 245–261.

Weishar ME (1993). *Aaron T Beck.* London: Sage.

Winter DA (2015). Towards a less mechanistic cognitive behaviour therapy. *PsycCRITIQUES 60*(46): 3.

Winter DA (2010). Allegiance revisited. *European Journal of Psychotherapy and Counselling 12*: 3–9.

Winter DA (2008). Personal construct psychotherapy in a National Health Service setting: does survival mean selling out? In: Raskin JD, Bridges SK (eds). *Studies in Meaning 3: constructivist psychotherapy in the real world.* New York, NY: Pace University Press (pp229–252).

Winter DA (1997). Everybody has still won but what about the booby prizes? *British Psychological Society Psychotherapy Section Newsletter 21*: 1–15.

Winter DA, Watson S (1999). Personal construct psychotherapy and the cognitive therapies: different in theory but can they be differentiated in practice? *Journal of Constructivist Psychology 12*: 1–22.

Winter DA, Tschudi F, Gilbert N (2006). Psychotherapists 'personal styles', construing and theoretical orientations. In: Loewenthal D, Winter DA (eds). *What is Psychotherapeutic Research?* London: Karnac.

Winter DA, Watson S, Gillman-Smith I, Gilbert N, Acton T (2003). Border crossing: a personal construct psychotherapy approach for clients with a diagnosis of borderline personality disorder. In: Chiari G, Nuzzo ML (eds). *Psychological Constructivism and the Social World.* Milan: FrancoAngeli (pp342–352).

14 Post-existentialism as a reaction to CBT?

Del Loewenthal

The purpose of this chapter is to describe a place for exploring notions of wellbeing at the start of the 21st century that are in contrast to the increasing cultural dominance of cognitive behaviour therapy (CBT). While post-existentialism can be held as an alternative to CBT, it is of course far more than this. An attempt is made to offer such an alternative place, where we might still be able to think about how alienated we are through valuing existential notions such as experience and meaning, while questioning other dimensions such as existentialism's inferred narcissism and the place it has come to take up with regards to – for example – psychoanalysis and the political.

The chapter describes an approach that is being developed, in part as a reaction to CBT, where existentialism and phenomenology are critically revisited and, as a result, post-existentialism is offered in terms of its implications for practice. It is argued that post-existentialism also has significant implications for our cultural practices in general, including the current interest in 'wellbeing', enabling the psychological therapies to have a quite different emphasis to that provided by CBT.

It is considered by many that the German philosopher Heidegger (1962) is a – if not *the* – foremost writer on the subject of being. Heidegger is associated with existentialism, and in many ways post-existentialism implies a combination of both Heideggerian and some post-Heideggerian approaches. One feature of key importance to post-existentialism is that we *start with* considering such notions of being, rather than attempting to add them afterwards to a technique that is based on more rational assumptions about what it means to be human, as some more recent CBT theorists have done. This chapter is part of work-in-progress at the Research Centre for Therapeutic Education at Roehampton University, London, where we are re-looking at existentialism in a post-Heideggerian era, with particular reference to the psychological therapeutic practices of counselling and psychotherapy as a psychotherapeutic training (see www.safpac.co.uk, and also, for example, Loewenthal, 2011, 2016).

The changing nature of escapism

In keeping with the post-existential, including something of the phenomenological, I would like to start by describing an experience I had while preparing this chapter. I was visiting a Canadian university, and, on my first evening, on returning to my hotel, I switched on the TV. The first programme focused on a section of road where, one by one, people in cars picked up other people, and forced them to carry out various sexual acts that you did not see in close-up; you did see, subsequently, in detail, these victims being horrendously beaten up. I changed channels to an evangelical preacher entrancing his audience. The next time I watched TV, it was a programme advertising sleeping tablets, which showed beautiful people waking up in beautiful houses to the background of sweet music and the enticing voice-over saying, 'This could be addictive.' As someone who watches very little TV, I still feel traumatised by the first programme.

I am not suggesting that this is only a North American problem: on returning to London, I went into a bar where there were at least two TV programmes and two different sound systems on concurrently. I assume that this entertainment is provided in order to anaesthetise the clients, in the name of relaxation. Is the dose of these different stimuli (as with the evangelical preacher, medication and simultaneous entertainments) having to be continually increased in order for people not to think? Is CBT, when it becomes the main state-approved approach to improving our wellbeing, a logical development of this need to take our mind off those thoughts that might otherwise come to us – thoughts that are individually and culturally too much?

In a previous era, many spoke of alienation, and existentialists spoke of self-estrangement: Heidegger (1962), for example, with 'the crowd', and Sartre (1943/1956) in terms of 'bad faith'. However, it would appear, as in the Canadian examples above, that new ways have been established for dealing with our increasing alienation that include no longer naming it as such. Thus, such ways of reduced awareness – what I have termed 'escape motivation' (whether it be of death, nothingness, oneself, others, or the world) – and which organisations including the state can use to manipulate us (Loewenthal, 2002), are no longer in our everyday vocabulary. Perversely, it is as if the better the escape, the better our level of so called 'wellbeing'.

For example, it is as if the more CBT and its equivalents can help to take our minds off our problems, the better off we will be. CBT may well be helpful to individuals, but when adopted as *the* main mode of 'treatment' by a society, then the implications are that we cannot allow thoughts to come to us, individually and collectively, and we will not therefore be able to 'come to our senses'. As Letiche has commented: 'Doubt not… catastrophe is inevitable' (Letiche, 1990: 238). There would be, for example, no point in worrying about our and others' responsibilities for how we are – indeed, such concepts as alienation are, in an age of happiness (Layard, 2006; Seligman, 2002), not only unnecessary but counterproductive.

Developments in the UK

In the UK, the so-called 'British school of existentialism' (Van Deurzen, 1997/2006, 2001; Spinelli, 1989, 2007), which has done so much to put existentialism on our map, initially favoured Boss over Binswanger (Cooper, 2003), as they were influenced by Heidegger working with Boss, whereas Binswanger had said that he had misunderstood Heidegger, although the misunderstanding was a fruitful one (Friedman, 1991: 414, 426). However, what then seems to have developed is a reaction to the psychoanalytic influences on Boss. While what I am calling the 'post-existential' would not want to get caught up in Freud's (and particularly his later) universalising, meaning-making schemas, it would also not wish to ignore the writings of psychoanalysis, in that, for example, our past can unknowingly influence the present, and we will always be subject to something 'life-giving' in ourselves that we are not in control of. It is therefore considered unhelpful to attempt to deny this in therapy.

In some ways, the work of RD Laing (1967, 1969, 1990) would come close to one attempt to keep open (with failings) what is being termed here a post-existential approach. There are those at the Philadelphia Association, which Laing founded, who continue this tradition (Cooper, 1990; Gordon & Mayo, 2004), registering their students as psychoanalytical psychotherapists. Here, psychoanalysis is considered together with philosophy. The Roehampton University programme, with which the term 'post-existential' is primarily associated (Loewenthal, 2007), is also influenced by Laing. (I, for one, trained at the Philadelphia Association.) However, there are significant differences in that, for example, at Roehampton, phenomenology is initially explored with an emphasis on practice, through Carl Rogers, and then existentialism, followed by a phenomenological reading of Freud. What happened to phenomenology is then followed through those who might be labelled 'postmodern', such as Lacan, Derrida, Levinas and French feminists like Kristeva, Cixous and Irigaray, before examining the implications of all this for carrying out 'relational research'. Previous descriptions of this learning process have been given in terms of theory (Loewenthal & Snell, 2003), research (Loewenthal, 2007), and training (Loewenthal & Snell, 2008).

At Roehampton, with post-existentialism and 'post-phenomenology' as the particular focus, the psychotherapy students are registered as integrative, and the counselling psychology students take relational approaches as their major model, and contrast this with CBT. Thus, besides its relationship with psychoanalysis, our post-existential training may have a greater emphasis on starting with the experiential and exploring what is meant by research than most other UK trainings in existentialism. There is also less enthusiasm for incorporating the existential with the cognitive (Spinelli & Worrell, 2009).

Research and the post-existential

Does this increasing need to escape from what Aristotle called the 'what is' also apply to what we regard as research? 'Positive psychology', together with positivism and, as already mentioned, techniques such as cognitive behaviour therapy, are increasingly dominating our culture. Indeed, are rarely questioned contemporary approaches such as 'evidence-based practice' the only way we can think about things in order to ensure that thoughts do not come to us? It seems that, if those supporting a particular therapeutic approach can afford randomised controlled trials, it cannot then be said that this therapeutic approach is better or worse than another (Seligman, 1995), and the research methods currently in fashion seem not to be able to allow for all the significant variables, such as the characteristics of the therapists (or 'therapist factors') – not to mention their supervisors. Also, what is presented is so often not scientific – for example, Rogerians suddenly have 'treatment goals' (Elliott, 2002), and Freud is also being manualised (for example, Allen & Fonagy, 2006), perhaps in the hope of ensuring public funding.

A prominent researcher said to me, when I asked what the evidence-based research she had successfully carried out for her modality had to do with truth and justice: 'Not a lot about truth but it is justice, as my approach has been accepted.' Of course, selective watering-down is, in some ways, not new; it happened to Freud and Rogers, and also to the founding fathers of psychology, like Wilhelm Wundt and William James. Indeed, Wundt (1904) insisted that psychology should be not only about the experimental (of which he is regarded as the founder), but also about the historical and the cultural (a point that will be developed later with regard to Foucault). However, as with positivistic research, which is meant to come up with rules of thumb as an aid, the measurement instead becomes the goal, and in this case the treatment goal, thus fundamentally altering the very essence of the original endeavour. Essentially what has happened is that the measuring tool now determines the therapy, even though Physis or Phusis is what comes from itself. Yet, increasingly, it seems too difficult for most people to be able to hear what is coming from themselves or from others. It is as if we are now so alienated that we are unable to explore our alienation.

Practice, the post-existential, and the training of psychological therapists

The previous discussion with regard to, for example, science has particular implications for the development of practitioners. While existentialism can be seen as healing various dualisms – for example, subject vs object, mind vs body, reason vs passion, fact vs value (Cooper, 1990) – neither existentialism nor post-existentialism can, or should, give a primacy to the scientific/technical over the soul. It is vital that the soul comes first. There are, of course, many ways of facilitating the development of post-existential practitioners, but such programmes may, in their different ways, need to start with what is increasingly termed 'relational practice', and find a way to consider science, not as technique or positivism, but as including the experimental with the cultural and social, while recognising that the soul can never be incorporated, even by the latter.

Post-existential approaches are likely to attempt to start with practice, and explore what it might mean to be human, while accepting that we will never fully understand. Indeed, at times it may be necessary to consider the writings of those like Merleau-Ponty (1962), who suggests that mystery (not to be confused with mystification) sometimes defines the very thing itself, and Levinas (1989), who warns us of the potential violence of attempting to know. Theories including the psychoanalytic and the postmodern can then come to mind on a case-by-case basis, as implication rather than application. There is, therefore, an important distinction to be made here from the work of those like Askay and Farquhar (2006), who, in contrast to the post-existential, first take psychoanalysis and then examine the existential-phenomenological.

Questions of definition

One way of looking at the Greek roots of existentialism is that it is about something that is both astonishing and ever changing (Heaton, 1990). Yet, has existentialism got stuck in the nostalgia of the 1950s and 1960s, thus no longer forever changing? What, then, would we need to re-look at? There is also the question of definition in a post-postmodern era. Locating post-existentialism with some aspects both of existentialism and of postmodernism raises the question as to the appropriateness of universalising definitions.

Rather, the attempt here is to locate an approach that is broadly defined and forever open to new possibilities (but not all possibilities). In fact, existentialism was never clearly defined. It appears to be a term used by the French philosopher Marcel (1948) to describe the work of those like Sartre (1943) and De Beauvoir (1972), even though they initially disagreed with being labelled in this way. Heidegger is thought of as probably the most important thinker on existentialism, particularly for psychotherapy. Both Heidegger (1962) and, before him, Kierkegaard (1941, 1980) saw our being as always in the process of becoming, and, as such, it fundamentally questioned technical categorisation. (Besides Heidegger and Kierkegaard, Nietzsche (1883/1933, 1974) can also be seen as an important influence in the development of existentialism.)

In some ways, the method of existentialism might be seen as phenomenology, but again, there has never been agreement about its definition. Husserl's (1983) idea of 'to the things themselves' is grounded in the notion of intentionality, which others, like Sartre, were not at one with. It was, however, Foucault (1974) who, while initially a strong adherent, criticised phenomenology in the light of developments in structural linguistics. But would it not be possible to take, for example, Merleau-Ponty's notion of phenomenology as to do with what emerges in 'the between', and then also consider the implications of Saussure and others for helping us make sense of our being-in-the-world? In fact, it may be even more important to consider what is being suggested in this chapter as not only being post-existential, but in particular post-phenomenological.

What we will then have for post-existentialism is some aspects of existentialism in terms of experience and meaning, together with something from post-phenomenology in what emerges in the between, while at the same time allowing to come to mind the developments that have been termed post-modern, without getting stuck in them.

Further differences of post-existentialism from existentialism and postmodernism

The post-existential would challenge existentialism, particularly in terms of questions of choice, politics, psychoanalysis, and feminism. Sartre's 'I am my choices' has been taken by many to be about the development of autonomy – for some, to the extent that one could almost decide what one wanted to be. The post-existential might be more about finding ourselves taking a certain place where we will have some agency but never full agency: we will always be *subject to*. What we might be subject to can be explored in various ways – for example, heteronomy and ethics (Levinas), an unconscious (Freud), writing and difference (Derrida), and language (Lacan).

From a post-existential perspective, we might look at the implications of an aspect of one of these authors for our practice without being fully caught up by a Levinasian, Freudian, Lacanian, or Derridean mode of thought (see Loewenthal, 2006). Indeed, Derrida (1990) acknowledged this in showing us how we are always caught up in a way of looking. So we would end up being destructured, but not to the extent that this makes communication impossible and destabilisation too much to take. In some ways, it would appear that postmodern ideas on their own have also become too much for people to take, and what we seem to have done is culturally return to the straightjacket of the positivistic. The post-existential might therefore be seen to lie somewhere between the existential and the post-postmodern.

Other important difference between post-existentialism and existentialism would include greater political awareness. In some ways, it seems too easy for existentialists to be fascists or royalists, and for psychotherapists to say that they are not interested in the political. Feminism, as developed by those like Cixous (1975), Irigaray (1977, 1990), and Kristeva (1986), can provide important insights for the post-existential, and some understanding of Lacan would be necessary to reach these important cultural developments.

Approaching, post-phenomenologically, the individual with the historical/cultural

Foucault became interested in power and knowledge and the political status of psychiatry as science. To question, through post-existentialism, issues such as wellbeing, power and knowledge, and the political nature of psychology as science, would be, in some ways, similar to how Foucault and some existentialists questioned the political status of psychiatry as science. In this, at least a primacy would be given to first thinking of what is termed 'mental illness' as not like a physical illness but more to do with relations with others. Yet there would be vitally important distinctions.

Foucault's (1974) abandonment of his early interest in phenomenology was, as Hoeller (1986) points out, because he took up Husserl's notion of transcendental phenomenology, which does not really allow for the historical and cultural. Yet Heidegger, with his *dasein* as being in the historical/cultural world with others, enables phenomenology to be released from Husserl's attempts to show a pure subjectivity, and thus 'a universal doctrine of the structures of individual subjectivity and intersubjectivity' (Hoeller, 1986: 7). Binswanger, Boss and Laing further developed this opening up of phenomenology for psychotherapy. Thus, if we could perhaps both be attentive to what emerges in the between of client and therapist and be aware of what is regarded culturally and historically as common sense, we could have an interest in how our clients, and those around them, have brought and bring pressures on each other. This meeting, which could include the implications for the present of the client's history and the history of the culture, without being caught up in a potentially totalising Foucauldian genealogical approach, would be an example of post-phenomenology, and might also be closer to what those like Wilhelm Wundt saw as psychology.

CBT vs post-existentialism in practice

It is suggested here that the underlying assumptions behind CBT are fundamentally different to those behind post-existentialism. If we take the often-quoted scenario where a client speaks of six colleagues, five of whom cheerfully say 'good morning', and one who appears to ignore this particular client, it would appear that there is far less likelihood that the therapist who is influenced by post-existentialism, as opposed to CBT, will focus on the five colleagues who have been pleasant, or will wonder with the client whether perhaps the one who ignored him was preoccupied with something completely different. There is also a greater likelihood that the post-existential, rather than CBT, therapist will be influenced by, for example, Kierkegaard's (1944) education by dread, rather than attempting to shore up the client with positive thinking, which some would consider to be part of a systematic attempt to govern through developing a climate of false security, and by notions of Lacan (1977), such as that we will never know what the other person thinks, and it is only through allowing a gap, with all its associated anxieties, that desire will emerge. Not only is it important for the individual to be able to doubt, if thoughtfulness is to be enabled to flourish; it is also particularly true for us as a society, otherwise it is more likely that catastrophe will be inevitable.

Conclusion

Post-existentialism can therefore be seen, on the one hand, to be attempting to find a place between existentialism and post-postmodernism, enabling us to take from the existential and the postmodern that which can be helpful to us in exploring our existence at the start of the 21st century. Another dimension of post-existentialism is to find a place between natural and social science, although starting with notions of existence is to imply starting with the human soul (Plato, in Cushman, 2001) and the historical and cultural aspects of social (rather than starting with the natural) sciences. With this emerges the possibilities of a political viewpoint that, unlike CBT, could engage with various notions of democracy, as well as an unconscious, coming more from those like Kierkegaard (1941, 1980) and Nietzsche (1883, 1974). I do not see this changing with the advent of third-wave CBT (for example, Gilbert 2009); rather, as argued by Kelly and Moloney in this volume (Chapter 5), these approaches are still a way of using technology instead of the soul, albeit in the name of the soul.

I would like to emphasise, again, however, that in developing post-existentialism in part as a reaction to CBT, I am not doubting the integrity of people who are cognitive behaviour therapists, nor that some clients will benefit more from CBT. Nor am I questioning that, in terms of conventional costings, it can be more cost effective (but see the conclusion to the first edition of this volume). There is, however, the danger of any approach, including that of post-existentialism, being a totalising move, and, while there have been dangers of this previously with both psychoanalysis and humanism, CBT (despite the unheard protestations of some of its adherents) appears particularly susceptible to being used in this way.

I have previously attempted to explore some of these dimensions – initially through how individuals and structures in society conspire to produce a form of alienating escape motivation (Loewenthal, 2002). More recently, I have been interested in exploring how postmodernism has emerged from phenomenology (Loewenthal & Snell, 2003), with particular reference to Levinas as a post-existential philosopher (Loewenthal, 2007). There are, of course, others who are developing interesting ideas that have some similarities with what I have described here. For example, there are those who are considering some of Wittgenstein's ideas to question the very nature of how we use theory (Heaton, 2000; House, 2008); with regard to research, Heideggerian ideas are becoming increasingly in evidence – for example Polkinghorne (2000) and Rennie (2007). Certainly, what these approaches do have in common is a concern with the humanness of the human, which is different from a managerialism based on very narrow notions of so-called evidence, with which CBT has come to fit so well. The danger is that, rather than being useful for the specific, we are making CBT culturally dominant in a way that we can no longer recognise ourselves and are too frightened by any possibility of doing so.

References

Allen JG, Fonagy P (2006). *The Handbook of Mentalization-based Treatment*. Oxford: Blackwell.

Askay R, Farquhar J (2006). *Apprehending the Inaccessible: Freudian psychoanalysis and existential phenomenology*. Evanston, Ill: Northwestern University Press.

Cixous H (1991/1975). The laugh of the Medusa. In: Warhol RR, Herndl DP (eds). *Feminisms: an anthology of literary theory and criticism*. New Brunswick, NJ: Rutgers University Press (pp331–349).

Cooper DE (1990). *Existentialism: a reconstruction*. London: Blackwell Publishing.

Cooper M (2003). *Existential Therapies*. London: Sage.

Cushman R (2001). *Therapeia: Plato's conception of philosophy*. Piscataway, NJ: Transaction Publishers.

De Beauvoir S (1972/1949) *The Second Sex* (HM Parshley trans). London: Penguin.

Derrida J (1990). *Resistances to Psychoanalysis*. Stanford, CA: Stanford University Press.

Elliott R (2002). Hermeneutic single-case efficacy design. *Psychotherapy Research 12*(1): 1–21.

Foucault M (1974/1954). *The Psychological Dimensions of Mental Illness* (AM Sheridan-Smith trans). New York, NY: Harper & Row.

Friedman M (1991). *The Worlds of Existentialism: a critical reader*. New York, NY: Humanity.

Gilbert P (2009). Moving beyond cognitive behaviour therapy. *The Psychologist 22*(5): 400–403.

Gordon J, Mayo R (eds) (2004). *In Between Philosophy and Psychotherapy: essays from the Philadelphia Association*. London: Whurr Publications.

Heaton J (2000). *Wittgenstein and Psychoanalysis*. New York, NY: Totem Books.

Heaton J (1990). What is existential analysis? *Journal of Existential Analysis 1*(1): 1–5.

Heidegger M (1962/1927). *Being and Time* (J Macquarrie, ES Robinson trans). London: Harper & Row.

Hoeller K (1986). Editor's foreword: dream and existence. *Review of Existential Psychology and Psychiatry* (special issue) *23*(1–2): 7–17.

House R (2008). Therapy's modernist 'regime of truth': from scientistic 'theory-mindedness' towards the subtle and the mysterious. *Philosophical Practice 3*(3): 343–352.

Husserl E (1983). *Ideas Pertaining to a Pure Phenomenology and to a Phenomenological Philosophy* (F Kersten trans.) The Hague: Nijhoff.

Irigaray L (1977). *Ce Sexe Qui N'en Est Pas Un*. Paris: Editions de Minuit.

Irigaray L (1990/1993). *Je, Tu, Nous: towards a culture of difference* (A Martin trans). London: Routledge.

Kierkegaard S (1844/1980). *The Concept of Anxiety* (R Thomte trans). Princeton, NJ: Princeton University Press.

Kierkegaard S (1848/1944). *The Concept of Dread* (W Lowrie trans). Princeton, NJ: Princeton University Press.

Kierkegaard S (1855/1941). *The Sickness unto Death* (W Lowrie trans). Princeton, NJ: Princeton University Press.

Kristeva J (1986). *The Kristeva Reader* (T Moi ed). Oxford: Blackwell.

Lacan J (1977). *Ecrits: selected writings* (A Sheridan trans). London: Routledge.

Laing R (1990). *The Divided Self: an existential study in sanity and madness.* London: Penguin.

Laing R (1969). *Self and Others* (2nd ed). London: Routledge.

Laing RD (1967). *The Politics of Experience.* London: Tavistock Publications.

Layard R (2006). *Happiness: lessons from a new science.* London: Penguin.

Letiche H (1990). Five postmodern aphorisms for trainers. *Management Education and Development* 21(3): 229–240.

Levinas E (1984/1989). Ethics as first philosophy. In: Hands S (ed). *The Levinas Reader.* Oxford: Blackwell (pp75–87).

Loewenthal D (2016). *Existential Psychotherapy and Counselling after Postmodernism: the selected works of Del Loewenthal.* London: Routledge.

Loewenthal D (2011). *Post-existentialism and the Psychological Therapies: towards a therapy without foundations.* London: Karnac.

Loewenthal D (2007). *Case Studies in Relational Research.* Basingstoke: Palgrave Macmillan.

Loewenthal D (2006). Counselling as a practice of ethics: some implications for therapeutic education. *Philosophical Practice 2*(3): 143–151.

Loewenthal D (2002). Involvement and emotional labour. *Soundings 20*: 151–162.

Loewenthal D, Snell R (2008). The learning community and emotional learning in a university-based training of counsellors and psychotherapists. *International Journal for the Advancement of Counselling 30*: 38–51.

Loewenthal D, Snell R (2003). *Postmodernism for Psychotherapists.* London: Routledge.

Marcel G (1948). *The Philosophy of Existence.* London: Harvil Press.

Merleau-Ponty M (1962). *The Phenomenology of Perception* (C Smith trans). London: Routledge & Kegan Paul.

Nietzsche F (1882/1974). *The Gay Science.* (W Kaufman trans). New York, NY: Vintage Books.

Nietzsche F (1883/1933). *Thus Spoke Zarathustra* (A Tille trans). New York, NY: Dutton.

Polkinghorne D (2000). Psychological inquiry and the pragmatic and hermeneutic traditions. *Theory and Psychology 10*(4): 453–479.

Rennie D (2007). Methodical hermeneutics and humanistic psychology. *The Humanistic Psychologist 35*(1): 1–14.

Sartre J-P (1956/1943). *Being and Nothingness: an essay on phenomenological ontology* (H Barnes trans). New York, NY: Philosophical Library.

Seligman MEP (2002). *Authentic Happiness: using the new positive psychology to realize your potential for lasting fulfillment.* New York, NY: Free Press.

Seligman MEP (1995). The effectiveness of psychotherapy: the consumer reports study. *American Psychologist 50*(12): 965–974.

Spinelli E (2007). *Practicing Existential Psychotherapy: the relational world.* London: Sage.

Spinelli E (1989). *The Interpreted World: an introduction to phenomenological psychology*. London: Sage.

Spinelli E, Worrell M (2009). *Existentially Focused Cognitive Behavioural Therapy*. New York, NY: Wiley.

Van Deurzen E (1997/2006). *Everyday Mysteries: existential dimensions of psychotherapy* (2nd ed). London: Routledge.

Van Deurzen E (2001). *Existential Counselling and Psychotherapy in Practice*. London: Sage Publications.

Wundt W (1874/1904). *Principles of Physiological Psychology* (EB Tichener trans). London: Allen.

15 Considering the dialogic potentials of cognitive therapy

Tom Strong, Mishka Lysack, Olga Sutherland and Konstantinos Chondros

> The possibility of dialogue has not been ended by those who plan continually for monologue to be followed by cheers of acceptance. (Billig, 1996: 109)

Cognitive therapy, along with so many other recent cultural developments, has been a site of diversity and hybridity – more a family of theoretically affiliated approaches to therapy than a singular method (eg. Dobson, 2001; Mansell, 2008; McMain et al, 2015). What has been hybrid about cognitive behavioural therapy (CBT) is its evolving inclusion of new theoretical and clinical ideas, such as Ellis' (1993) integration of constructivist ideas, or the adoption of mindfulness-based practices from various Buddhist traditions (Fennell & Segal, 2011; Segal, William & Teasdale, 2012). In this chapter, we consider CBT as a dialogic practice, where language use in clinical conversation is its focal activity and bring a discourse analysis and social constructionist view to our discussion. We share our concerns for non-dialogic variants of practice, and in particular for technologising CBT into a cultural prescription and examine conversational practices that show some of CBT's therapeutic aims being met.

We write from a preference for a collaboratively practised CBT that conversationally mobilises the expertise and resourcefulness of both clients and therapists. For us, therapy is a dialogue occurring at the nexus of many dialogues in which clients and therapists are already engaged. This extends to how we regard 'cognition', since we see it as inseparable from these dialogues (Billig, 1996; Ford, 2012). Consistent with these different dialogues in which we find ourselves are different ways of understanding and orienting to experience, and to each other. CBT is one such dialogue: one in which client and therapist could refract meanings and other ways of talking in which they are also engaged and could beneficially talk from.

Given our preference for dialogue, we are concerned about where CBT has been and could be taken. CBT, practised monologically, could be seen as an ideological instrument for holding others to particular understandings of reality, or particular ways of engaging with it (see Bakhtin, 1984; Eagleton, 1991). Variations on this theme come up when practice is reduced to scripts for therapists and clients, or to cultural prescriptions for self-conduct (Layard, 2005). It also comes up in ways that CBT might be used with clients – 'administered', 'implemented' – as if therapy was about doing something to a merely receptive client. Closer to our dialogic views are practices in the CBT literature that speak to actively engaging clients in *co*-developing preferred and viable ways of understanding and acting.

We will say more about how we position ourselves within CBT's therapeutic approaches in ways we think are useful for its continued development and hybridisation. We elaborate on what we mean by 'dialogical' practice, relating this to the meaning-making of both clients and therapists, particularly in how they make sense of and respond to each other in clinical interviews. Seeing cognition, discourse and dialogue as related, we share how relationships between them can generatively inform the practice of CBT. In the other direction, we further articulate our concerns about and objections to reducing the practice of CBT to narrow cultural and therapeutic prescriptions. We aim to add to the debates about CBT with our focus on resourceful and collaborative dialogues with clients.

Positioning ourselves and CBT

> We can't use our minds at full capacity unless we have some idea of how much what we think we're thinking is really thought, and how much is familiar words running along their own familiar tracks. Nearly everyone does enough talking, at least, to become fairly fluent in his own language, and at that point there's always the danger of automatic fluency, turning on a tap and letting a lot of platitudinous bumble emerge. The best check on this so far discovered is some knowledge of other languages, where at least the bumble has to fit into a different set of grammatical grooves. (Frye, 1962: 50)

Our position with respect to CBT is that it involves particular kinds of conversations: the kinds that develop 'their own familiar tracks', as Frye suggests above. So, we will link our intentions to some possibly unfamiliar tracks for readers and relate these to the conversations we aim to have with clients. Each of us has been fortunate to work with the renowned family therapist Karl Tomm. Tomm (as cited in Godard, 2006; also see Strong et al, 2008) has conceptualised such conversations in terms of the intentions held by therapists as they work with clients – interactions he classifies in four ethical quadrants, as seen in Figure 1.

Figure 1. Karl Tomm's grid of ethical postures as delineated by two continua (axes)

Closing space, or decreasing options

Manipulation	Confrontation
Separate, professional knowledge, Hierarchical relationship	Shared knowledge, Collaborative relationship
Succorance	Empowerment

Opening space, or increasing options

The figure is delineated by two continua. The vertical axis refers to the degree to which therapists promote options of practice that restrict or increase client options on the matter of clinical interest. This extends to how therapists might hold clients to their particular therapeutic initiatives or conceptualisations, or, conversely, 'open space for' client initiatives and conceptualisations. The horizontal axis reflects the degree to which therapists make their knowledge shared, transparent and contestable, and the degree to which decisions about therapy's goals, procedures and interventions are shared or expertly prescribed by the therapist. Tomm's quadrants thus make explicit the choices therapists can make in how they 'position' themselves with clients in terms of their use of professional knowledge in therapeutic conversations. We locate our approach to CBT primarily in the lower 'Empowerment' quadrant, and see our expertise as focused on collaboratively eliciting and mobilising clients' expertise in addressing their presenting concerns (Anderson, 1997; Anderson & Gehart, 2007; Strong, 2002). We focus our expertise on hosting generative therapeutic conversations where decisions about the interview's conduct and progress are made transparently and mutually.

CBT practised from this 'position' requires improvising skill in responsive therapists who open themselves and the therapeutic process to client direction. In our dialogic and constructionist view of CBT, the interview is a construction (or deconstruction) zone, collaboratively constructed and maintained (Strong, 2004, 2010). CBT's primary focus is the meanings and ways of thinking clients bring to therapy, find their inadequacies, or fit in this construction zone. For us, however, thinking and meaning are linked to language, as the primary means by which people not only represent their experiences but influence them as well. We borrow from Wittgenstein (1958), for whom the aptness of language was a paramount concern, and from narrative therapists, for whom there can be 'better' discourses or stories for experience (Freedman & Combs, 1996; Malinen, Cooper & Thomas, 2012; White & Epston, 1990). CBT, as we envision it, is a collaborative and critically informed search – not for better thinking, but for more viable language (in clients' eyes) to articulate ways forward where clients have been experiencing concerns.

Thought as dialogue and discourse

We agree with writers who see thoughts as extensions of dialogue (Beck, 1976; Edwards, 1995; Maranhão, 1986), and find it odd that thoughts could be seen as being apart from dialogue when they are discussed as a part *of* dialogue. We agree with writers such as Vygotsky (1978) that any 'intra'-mental representation or activity begins 'inter'-mentally – between people. Cognition in this sense is a representational activity sustained in dialogue. But, there is another dimension brought out by writers such as Michael Billig (1996, 1999), for whom this activity remains rhetorical, not merely representational. By this we refer to the way that thoughts are partly developed in anticipation of how they might be received in the interactions. Billig (1999) used the example of repression to illustrate how a repressive style of talking or interacting parallels the internal dynamics (ie. way of thinking) associated with that style of talking. This is a significant shift away from locating maladaptive thinking in particular constructs or evaluations made by the individual. Rhetorically, the same style of participating in dialogue that preceded a particular thought or way of thinking could sustain it in later dialogues. For us, therefore, *how* conversations occur are as important, if not more important, for therapeutic dialogue than *what* gets discussed in such dialogues.

What therapy can offer is a dialogue outside the hurly-burly of habitual, everyday conversation – a break from the kinds of conversations where others hold us to particular accounts and ways of interacting (Shotter, 1993). Therapists can offer proxy dialogues for those conversations, where therapy's outcomes can hopefully be talked into being, while exploring possibilities seemingly unavailable to clients in their everyday interactions. Practised this way, therapy hinges on a question: how can we have a dialogue that is different from the ones you have been having with yourself and others, on the matter that brought you to therapy? A therapeutic conversation that occurs in new ways – ways different from one's prior internal and external dialogues – affords possibilities for new mental connections (Wittgenstein, 1958) and new ways of thinking, at the same time. Therapy can help clients overcome their stalled projects in dialogue, where lines of talk or inquiry lack a satisfactory resolution until helpful dialogue facilitates this. Not surprisingly, internal dialogue can sometimes be seen as 'unspeakable dilemmas' (Griffith & Griffith, 1994), because of how others are expected to receive what is said. Our CBT reverses Vygotsky's inter- to intra-mental trajectory, by eliciting the not-yet-said aloud, or by welcoming efforts to talk beyond previous dialogic impasses that got similarly stuck internally.

We are, of course, not alone in seeing cognition as inner dialogue. However, such inner dialogues are often portrayed as eccentric projects hived off from real-world interaction. That doesn't square with our sense of dialogue, or how individuals create and convey understandings via the discourses accessible to them. Emotional life thus finds its meanings and performances in particular discourses, or 'language games' (Wittgenstein, 1958), or in what Harré (1986, 2009) termed 'emotionologies'. The notion that a construct or schema could be extracted, collaboratively evaluated or re-construed, and 'therapeutically' replaced in unchanged patterns or dialogues in clients' lives comes up short for us. Thoughts are contextually linked to the inner and outer dialogues, where they find their currency. Thus, therapy is a dialogue to transform such contexts.

From monologic to dialogic interaction in CBT

There is little doubt that CBT's attention to inner 'talk' and careful use of questions assists clients to construct useful knowledges and actions for making changes in their lives. How this talking occurs merits consideration. Meichenbaum (1996) distinguishes 'rationalist' and 'constructive' perspectives taken up within CBT (Ellis, 1993; Wessler, 1992). Bruner (1990; Monteagudo, 2011) highlights these differences by contrasting computational knowledges and narrative knowledges. Therapy focused on thought as rationally computed positions both client and therapist differently from therapy focused on client story-making. Sampson's (1981) concerns relate to the former stance: cognitive psychology has tended towards subjectivism in granting 'primacy to the structures and processes of the knowing subject' (p730), and towards individualism for centring on the individual knower, apart from relationship. Such a view of cognition breaks it into discrete components and mechanisms located *in* individuals. Instead, Sampson (1993) highlights a relational and social character to human knowing that arises in and from interactions between people in social and cultural contexts, culminating in an emergence of individuals' unique perspectives or '*voices*' (Bruner, 1990: 77).

Monologue and dialogue

Bakhtin's (1984, 1986; Lysack, 2002, 2008) distinction between monologue and dialogue has helped us distinguish differences between *hierarchical* and *collaborative* forms of therapeutic interaction. Bakhtin (1984) outlined the main characteristics of a monologic orientation: '... monologue manages without the other, and therefore to some degree materialises all reality… [and] pretends to be the ultimate word' (pp293–294). However, in relationships oriented by dialogue, human consciousness, life and relationships combine to construct a shared dialogic space: 'The single adequate form for *verbally expressing* authentic human life is the *open-ended dialogue*. Life by its very nature is dialogic. To live means to participate in dialogue' (p293; emphasis in original). The distinction between monologue and dialogue relates to an accompanying ethics (Bakhtin, 1984; Larner, 2015). It is 'one thing to be in relation to a dead thing, to voiceless material that can be molded and formed as one wishes, and another thing to be active *in relation to someone else's living, autonomous consciousness*' (p285; emphasis in original). Consistent with a view that knowledge is relational and transactional, Bakhtin also wrote: 'Truth is not born, nor is it to be found inside the head of an individual person; it is born *between people* collectively searching for truth, in the process of their dialogic interaction' (p110; emphasis in original). For Bakhtin, dialogue is where and how a person is 'constructed.'

Dialogic relationship and emergence of voice

A dialogical perspective also entails an awareness of the co-presence of voices within language and conversation. This occurs between people *and* within the inner speech of one's consciousness, which points to other voices, and to other consciousnesses. For Bakhtin, these voices are not content simply to co-exist alongside of one another but gravitate to an intense interanimation with one another in what he calls a 'microdialogue', where '[t]hey hear each other constantly, call back and forth to each other, and are reflected in one another' (1984: 75).

Like others (Hermans, Kempen & van Loon, 1992; Hermans & Kempen, 1993; Paré & Lysack, 2004), Penn and Frankfurt (1994) explored therapeutic possibilities of clients shifting from monologue to dialogue in their inner conversations:

> Frequently, clients… tell their first stories as though they were monologues: single-voiced, absolute and closed... Unlike the monologue, dialogical conversation is many-voiced. It listens to others and is open, inviting, relative, and endless because it is future-oriented. It awaits an answer. (p223)

We have also found that clients can be dominated by negative inner 'voices', initially experiencing these voices to the exclusion of others. Penn and Frankfurt suggest that, in struggling with problems we construct:

> ... an internal monologue that is often experienced as a negative, self-accusing voice: 'You're hopeless, you've failed, you're incompetent, unlovable,' and so on. However, given the ability to reply to ourselves, we can create a balance of power, so to speak, through the discovery or invention of our other voices – more positive, confident, even ecstatic voices – that can converse with our negative monologue. (p218)

Similarly, Meichenbaum (1996) found that clients suffering post-raumatic stress disorder (PTSD) from the effects of abuse described themselves as 'spoiled goods', 'damaged property' or 'useless'. He suggests a client 'may inadvertently reproduce the "voice" of the perpetrator, as in the case of victims of domestic violence. She needs to develop her own voice' (p135). For Penn and Frankfurt (1994), this is where a beneficial plurality of voices can come into contact and engage with each other interactively, in what might be called a 'dialogic space' (p222).

Such ideas inform our participation in therapy as a dialogic interaction that can generate multiple perspectives while expanding on existing meanings with other possible meanings through responsive dialogue between client and therapist (Lysack, 2005; Paré & Lysack, 2004; Strong, 2003). Therapy can enact a polyphony of voices that Bakhtin saw as crucial to a dialogic orientation. We share Meichenbaum's (1996) view when he suggested that therapists working with clients 'should not do the thinking for them, nor put words in their mouths' (p140).

Cognitive modification as dialogical accomplishment

One of the significant contributions of CBT has been its focus on 'commonsense psychology', or on people's attempts to define their problems in their own terms (Beck, 1976; Ellis, 1962; Meichenbaum, 1977). Proponents of behaviourist or bio-psychiatric approaches have too often dismissed as irrelevant the value of exploring clients' judgments and understandings of their problems. CBT practitioners make people's routine meaning-making a primary target of investigation and intervention. But many CBT practitioners adopt a correspondence theory of truth and evaluate clients' appraisals of events and experiences by comparing them with what they claim is their objective perception of reality (Lyddon, 1995). Such therapists assess and challenge the 'incorrect meanings' implicit in clients' reports (Beck, 1976: 95).

In contrast to an 'objectivist' approach, social constructionists (Berger & Luckmann, 1967; Gergen, 2015) focus on meaning as it arises in social interaction. Similarly, discursive psychologists (eg. Tileagă & Stokoe, 2015 and other discursive scholars (eg. Antaki & Jahoda, 2010; Auburn, 2010; Kondratyuk & Peräkylä, 2011; Weiste & Peräkylä, 2013) attend to how thoughts, attitudes, memories, proposals for action, and other phenomena that CBT practitioners deem relevant are social performances that must be 'brought off', or accomplished, in interaction, and have interactional contexts and consequences. For example, Ekberg and LeCouteur (2015) examined how clients responded to therapists' proposals (eg. to exercise more, to talk to a family member about something) in CBT sessions. It was noted that clients resisted therapists' proposals by implicitly claiming superior knowledge of their personal experience or family circumstances. In other words, they claimed that they could not follow the therapists' proposals because they knew something that the therapists did not (for example, they had already tried exercising, and it did not work). The attention here, and in other interactional analyses of CBT, is on sequences of actions and discourse as constructing psychological phenomena.

Constructionist and critical movements in psychology focus on how socio-cultural, family and (inter)personal circumstances occasion particular meanings (cognitions), and how prior meaning shapes such circumstances (Gergen, 2015; Prilleltensky & Nelson, 2002). Some CBT writers also warn against considering cognition, affect and behaviour apart from contexts that shape and sustain them (Alexander et al, 1996; Baucom et al, 1996; Linehan, 1993; Neimeyer & Cabanillas, 2004; Safran & Segal, 1990). Critically-oriented CBT practitioners attend to factors that shape (or constrain) how clients come to cognise themselves and their life situations, aiming to minimise power differentials in the therapeutic relationship (Doherty, 1995; Dunst, Trivette & Deal, 1988; McWhirter, 1994; Safran & Muran, 2000). Instead they promote a dialogic context where clients' problematic meanings and experiences are welcomed, then collaboratively formulated, evaluated and modified.

Consistent with some approaches to CBT (eg. Hayes et al, 2006; Meichenbaum, 1977), constructionists propose that cognition is derived, created and maintained in and through interpersonal processes, across the lifespan. A common assumption among CBT practitioners is that clients' experiences and appraisals of them are not observable by others and are relatively stable. According to Beck (1976: 26), social constructionists 'externalize' clients' 'internal communication system'. Clients' rationality is not internally 'pre-packaged'. Instead, the reality clients utter has many possible articulations for understanding and describing that reality, some of which are formulated and unpacked in the back-and-forth of clients' communication with others, including therapists.

Viewing clients' voiced cognitions as emergent in and through the interactions of therapist and client challenges traditional conceptions of the therapist as a neutral and objective elicitor and describer of intrapsychic reality. From our perspective, therapists co-articulate clients' cognitive material, and neither can objectively 'discover' that material (Fourie, 2012; Guidano & Liotti, 1983; Lyddon, 1995; Mahoney, 1988; Safran & Segal, 1990). While clients are conceived of as active and purposeful interpreters of events and circumstances, their constructions of reality will overlap in some ways and differ in others from those of the therapist (Neimeyer, 1993, 2009). Collaborative and dialogically oriented cognitive-behavioural therapists are often pragmatists who recognise that the value and utility of the client's cognitions are established and evaluated conjointly by the client and therapist as they talk (Dattilio & Hanna, 2012; Neimeyer, 2002). They propose to view cognitive-behavioural intervention as a relational act (Bannink, 2014; Safran & Muran, 2000; Safran & Segal, 1990) of meaning construction and negotiation. They join clients in their unique ways of construing their lives and experiences and expand collaboratively on those ways by encouraging clients step into, or 'try on', alternative meanings and experiential descriptions (Strong, 2000).

CBT as ideology?

> Human beings have largely conquered nature, but they have to still conquer themselves. (Layard, 2006: 9)

It may seem a heavy-handed criticism, but some see therapists as being ideological in how their notions and ways of practising can become complicit with dominant cultural aims and norms (Foucault, 1990; Rose, 1990). Typically, one associates therapy with expanding one's possibilities for freedom and happiness, not hitching these to some restrictive practice of ideas. Feminists (Brown, 1994, 2013; Bruns & Kaschak, 2010; Miller, 1976) and 'radical' psychiatrists (Laing, 1967; Szasz, 1970) have long taken issue with therapy 'helping' clients adjust to unjust realities. Linking such realities to practised ideologies, however, is a move that makes some uncomfortable, and to others suggests activism (Gergen, 2000). Quite a literature has developed examining therapists' power vis-à-vis that of the client (eg. Proctor, 2002, 2008; Spong, 2012), particularly in how therapy's dialogues often tilt asymmetrically towards therapist control of the interview and its content (eg. Antaki, 2001; Davis, 1986). But the reality-ideology critique, extended to the practice of therapy, has some important implications for the practice of CBT.

In his book *Happiness*, Richard Layard (2006), an economist, invites readers to find their happiness internally. He also argues that depression is of greater concern than poverty (p181), and that CBT has potential to enhance inner control for overcoming moodiness and attaining happiness. Two streams of critique converge for us here (Foucault, 1990; House, 2003; Newman & Holzman, 1997), because therapy can – intentionally or inadvertently – become a quintessential activity in upholding particular moral and cultural orders. CBT's 'realist' approaches can position therapists as expert 'arbiters of correct subjectivity' (Rose, 1990), as if there were correct ways of understanding reality or conducting oneself in it. Our other concern is with turning inward, when addressing what is outward and unjust might be a client preference. At worst, therapists can ignore the external realities of clients' lives, 'helping' them, instead, cope *internally* with their thoughts and feelings.

Within the CBT spectrum, we recognise a range of approaches and opinions on the kinds of concerns we have been raising. Within constructivist CBT circles, one finds construals of reality with no focus on correctly articulating it (as if this could be adjudicated by a knowing therapist). So, the dialogical empiricism we see in Beck's practice of Socratic questioning (Clark & Egan, 2015; DeRubeis, Tang & Beck, 2002) can fit here as a means to contest problematic linguistic constructions, while searching for *viable* and fitting constructions of reality (Parker, 1998). Realists would see things differently, inviting clients to dispute distortions or maladaptive beliefs, so who decides what is (or whether one has) a distortion or maladaptive belief is therefore of no small concern to us. Within more behaviourally focused CBT approaches, one finds problem-solving and skill-developing approaches to addressing client-defined realities (eg. Goldfried, 1995). The client-centred challenge is in tailor-making skills and problem-solving strategies to address client circumstance.

CBT practices of 'self-management', however, are where our Foucaultian concerns and Layard's cultural prescription for happiness collide. Foucault (1994) partly focused his later career on 'biopower' and 'technologies of the self'. These notions refer to living 'correctly' or 'appropriately', denoting how correctness, or appropriateness, has specific personal requirements in differing historico-cultural contexts. These are moral requirements as much as they are prescriptions for proper living. Once embedded in psychological discourse, they take on a prescribed and presumed scientific correctness (Cushman, 1995; Danziger, 1997), not unlike the moral correctness one associates with religious practices of confession followed by spiritual direction (Foucault, 1990). CBT's practices of 'self-management' (eg. Hudson et al, 2016; Rokke & Rehm, 2001) focus on 'self-instruction', 'self-monitoring', and 'self-control'. The problem here is with the word 'self'. From Foucault's (1994) perspective, extended to considering CBT 'self-management practices', this involves taking on CBT in apprenticing oneself to its practices of 'self-subjectification', and policing or disciplining oneself accordingly. Said another way, this is how one learns to be a person on CBT's terms. Ideology can creep into CBT in insidious ways, even though the intentions behind Layard's prescriptions of CBT are obviously meant to be helpful. The practices and philosophy of certain approaches to CBT, applied as a personal technology for self-conduct, can be seen as a kind of ideology. Where things can get problematically ideological is when, in a sense, clients are instructed to ignore certain features of their realities that can't be remedied with thought modification (eg. poverty), or to use forms of 'self-monitoring' and 'self-control' that preclude other avenues to happiness and contentment.

Coda

Wittgenstein writes: 'For words only have meaning in the stream of life' (1988: aphorism 687). Our aim here has been to share our dialogic and discursive views on CBT, since it has become a dominant and pluralistic presence. We identify with some aspects of CBT's pluralism more strongly than with others and admire its creative hybridity in incorporating research and theoretical developments. Particularly dear to us have been the growing efforts to collaborate with clients in aspects of practice formerly deemed the therapists' prerogatives. In this regard, we have shared our ideas and concerns from social constructionist theory, dialogue theory and discursive research, to further discussion on potential new hybrids of CBT. For us, it is fundamentally important to locate the practice of CBT as dialogic, as an activity that takes place in 'streams' of respectful and generative dialogues. We extend this to our thinking about our part in dialogues that might further the practice of CBT in ways we have described.

References

Alexander JF, Jameson PB, Newell RM, Gunderson D (1996). Changing cognitive schemas. In: Dobson KS, Craig KD (eds). *Advances in Cognitive-Behavioral Therapy.* London: Sage (pp174–192).

Anderson H (1997). *Conversation, Language and Possibilities.* New York, NY: Basic Books.

Anderson H, Gehart, DR (eds) (2007). *Collaborative Therapy: relationships and conversations that make a difference.* New York, NY: Routledge.

Antaki C (2001). 'D'you like a drink then do you?' Dissembling language and the construction of an impoverished life. *Journal of Language and Social Psychology. 20*(1–2): 196–213.

Antaki C, Jahoda A (2010). Psychotherapists' practices in keeping a session 'on-track' in the face of clients' 'off-track talk. *Communication and Medicine 7*(1): 11–21.

Auburn T (2010). Cognitive distortions as social practices: an examination of cognitive distortions in sex offender treatment from a discursive psychology perspective. *Psychology, Crime & Law 16*(1–2): 103–123.

Bakhtin M (1986) *Speech Genres and other Late Essays.* Austin, TX: University of Texas Press.

Bakhtin M (1984). *Problems of Dostoevsky's Poetics.* Minneapolis, MN: University of Minnesota Press.

Bannink FP (2014). Positive CBT: from reducing distress to building success. *Journal of Contemporary Psychotherapy 44*(1): 1–8.

Baucom DH, Epstein N, Raskin LA, Burnett CK (1996). Understanding and treating marital distress from a cognitive-behavioral orientation. In: Dobson KS, Craig KD (eds). *Advances in Cognitive-Behavioral Therapy*. London: Sage (pp210–236).

Beck AT (1976). *Cognitive Therapy and the Emotional Disorders.* New York, NY: International Universities Press.

Berger P, Luckmann T (1967). *The Social Construction of Reality.* New York, NY: Doubleday.

Billig M (1999). *Freudian Repression: conversation creating the unconscious.* Cambridge: Cambridge University Press.

Billig M (1996). *Arguing and Thinking* (2nd ed, revised). Cambridge: Cambridge University Press.

Brown LS (2013). Feminist therapy as a path to friendship with women. *Women & Therapy, 36*(1–2): 11–22.

Brown LS (1994). *Subversive Dialogues: theory in feminist therapy.* New York, NY: Basic Books.

Bruner J (1990). *Acts of Meaning.* Cambridge, MA: Harvard University Press.

Bruns CM, Kaschak E (2010). Feminisms: feminist therapies in the 21st century. *Women & Therapy 34*(1–2): 1–5. doi: 10.1080/02703149.2011.532447

Clark GI, Egan SJ (2015). The Socratic method in cognitive behavioural therapy: a narrative review. *Cognitive Therapy & Research 39*(6): 863–879. doi: 10.1007/s10608-015-9707-3

Cushman P (1995). *Constructing the Self, Constructing America: a cultural history of psychotherapy.* Cambridge, MA: Perseus Publishing.

Danziger K (1997). *Naming the Mind: how psychology found its language.* London: Sage.

Dattilio FM, Hanna MA (2012). Collaboration in cognitive-behavioral therapy. *Journal of Clinical Psychology 68*(2): 146–158. doi: 10.1002/jclp.21831

Davis K (1986). The process of problem (re)formulation in psychotherapy. *Sociology of Health and Illness 8*(1): 44–74.

DeRubeis RJ, Tang TZ, Beck, AT (2002). Cognitive therapy. In: Dobson KS (ed). *The Handbook of Cognitive Behavioral Therapies* (2nd ed). New York, NY: Guilford Press(pp246–294).

Dobson KS (ed) (2001). *The Handbook of Cognitive Behavioral Therapies* (2nd ed). New York, NY: Guilford Press.

Doherty WJ (1995). *Soul Searching: why psychotherapy must promote moral responsibility.* New York, NY: Basic Books.

Dunst CJ, Trivette CM, Deal G (1988). *Enabling and Empowering Families: principles and guidelines for practise.* Cambridge, MA: Brookline Books.

Eagleton T (1991). *Ideology: an introduction.* London: Verso.

Edwards D (1995). Two to tango: script formulations, dispositions and rhetorical asymmetry in relationship trouble talk. *Research on Language and Social Interaction 28*(4): 319–350.

Ekberg K, LeCouteur A (2015). Clients' resistance to therapists' proposals: managing epistemic and deontic status. *Journal of Pragmatics 90*: 12–25.

Ellis A (1993). Constructivism and rational-emotive therapy: a critique of Richard Wessler's critique. *Psychotherapy 30*(3): 531–532.

Ellis A (1962). *Reason and Emotion in Psychotherapy.* New York, NY: Lyle Stuart.

Fennell M, Segal Z (2011). Mindfulness-based cognitive therapy: culture clash or creative fusion? *Contemporary Buddhism 12*(1): 125–142.

Ford M J (2012). A dialogic account of sense-making in scientific argumentation and reasoning. *Cognition and Instruction 30*(3): 207– 245.

Foucault M (1994). *Ethics: subjectivity and truth. Essential works of Michel Foucault 1954–1984*, vol I (P Rabinow ed). New York, NY: The New Press.

Foucault M (1990). *The History of Sexuality: an introduction* (vol 1). New York, NY: Vintage.

Fourie DP (2012). Where is the dialogue? A social constructionist view of empirically supported treatments. *South African Journal of Psychology 42*(1): 127–137.

Freedman J, Combs G (1996). *Narrative Therapy: the social construction of preferred realities.* New York, NY: Norton.

Frye N (1962). *The Educated Imagination.* Concord, MA: House of Anansi Press.

Gergen K (2000). From identity to relational politics. In: Holzman L, Morss J (eds). *Postmodern Psychologies, Societal Practise, and Political Life.* New York, NY: Routledge (pp130–150).

Gergen K (2015). *An Invitation to Social Construction* (3rd ed). Thousand Oaks, CA: Sage.

Godard G (2006). *Love, Violence and Consciousness: ethical postures for therapist positioning.* A final project submitted for the Master of Counselling degree. Calgary AB: University of Calgary, Campus Alberta Applied Psychology Counselling Initiative.

Goldfried MR (1995). *From Cognitive Behavior Therapy to Psychotherapy Integration.* New York, NY: Springer.

Griffith J, Griffith M (1994). *The Body Speaks.* New York, NY: Basic Books.

Guidano VF, Liotti G (1983). *Cognitive Processes and Emotional Disorders.* New York, NY: Guilford Press.

Harré R (2009). Emotions as cognitive-affective-somatic hybrids. *Emotion Review 1*(4): 294–301.

Harré R (ed) (1986). *The Social Construction of Emotions.* Oxford: Blackwell.

Hayes SC, Luoma JB, Bond FW, Masuda A, Lillis J (2006). Acceptance and commitment therapy: model, process and outcomes. *Behaviour Research and Therapy 44*(1): 1–25.

Hermans H, Kempen H (1993). *The Dialogical Self: meaning as movement*. San Diego, CA: Academic Press.

Hermans H, Kempen H, van Loon R (1992). The dialogical self: beyond individualism and rationalism. *American Psychologist 47*(1): 23–33.

House R (2003). *Therapy Beyond Modernity: transcending profession-centered therapy*. London: Karnac.

Hudson JL, Moss-Morris R, Game D, Carroll A, Chilcot J (2016). Improving distress in dialysis (iDiD): a tailored CBT self-management treatment for patients undergoing dialysis. *Journal of Renal Care 42*(4): 223–238.

Kondratyuk N, Peräkylä A (2011). Therapeutic work with the present moment: a comparative conversation analysis of existential and cognitive therapies. *Psychotherapy Research 21*(3): 316–330. doi: 10.1080/10503307.2011.570934

Laing RD (1967). *The Politics of Experience and the Bird of Paradise*. Baltimore, MD: Penguin.

Larner G (2015). Dialogical ethics: imagining the other. *Australian and New Zealand Journal of Family Therapy 36*(1): 155–166. doi: 10.1002/anzf.1093

Layard R (2006). *Happiness: lessons from a new science*. London: Penguin Books.

Linehan MM (1993). *Cognitive-Behavioral Treatment of Borderline Personality Disorder.* New York, NY: Guilford Press.

Lyddon WJ (1995). Cognitive therapy and theories of knowing: a social constructionist view. *Journal of Counseling and Development 73*(6): 579–585.

Lysack M (2002). From monologue to dialogue in families: internalized other interviewing and Lysack M (2008). Relational mindfulness and dialogic space in family therapy. In: Hick S, Bien T (eds). *Mindfulness and the Therapeutic Relationship.* New York, NY: Guilford Press (pp141–158).

Lysack M (2005). Empowerment as an ethical and relational stance: some ideas for a framework for responsive practises. *Canadian Social Work Review 22*(1): 31–51.

Mahoney MJ (1988). Constructive metatheory: basic features and historical foundations. *International Journal of Personal Construct Psychology 1*(1): 1–35.

Malinen T, Cooper ST, Thomas FN (eds) (2012). *Masters of Narrative and Collaborative Therapies: the voices of Andersen, Anderson and White*. New York, NY: Routledge.

Mansell W (2008). The seven c's of CBT: a consideration of the future challenges for cognitive behaviour therapy. *Behavioural and Cognitive Psychotherapy 36*(6): 641–649.

Maranhão T (1986). *Therapeutic Discourse and Socratic Dialogue.* Madison, WI: University of Wisconsin Press.

McMain S, Newman MG, Segal ZV, DeRubeis RJ (2015). Cognitive behavioral therapy: current status and future research directions. *Psychotherapy Research 25*(3): 321–329.

McWhirter EH (1994). *Counseling for Empowerment.* Alexandria, VA: American Counseling Association.

Meichenbaum D (1996). Cognitive-behavioral treatment of posttraumatic stress disorder from a narrative constructivist perspective: a conversation with Donald Meichenbaum. In: Hoyt M (ed). *Constructive Therapies: vol 2.* New York, NY: Guilford Press (pp124–147).

Meichenbaum D (1977). *Cognitive Behavioral Modification.* New York, NY: Plenum.

Miller JB (1976). *Toward a New Psychology of Women.* Boston, MA: Beacon.

Monteagudo JG (2011). Jerome Bruner and the challenges of the narrative turn: then and now. *Narrative Inquiry 21*(2): 295–302.

Neimeyer RA (2009). *Constructivist Psychotherapy: distinctive features.* New York, NY: Routledge.

Neimeyer RA (2002). The relational co-construction of selves: a postmodern perspective. *Journal of Contemporary Psychotherapy 32*(1): 51–59.

Neimeyer RA (1993). An appraisal of constructivist psychotherapies. *Journal of Consulting and Clinical Psychology 61*(2): 221–234.

Neimeyer RA, Cabanillas WE (2004). Epistemology and psychotherapy: a constructivist conversation. In: Raskin JD, Bridges SK (eds). *Studies in Meaning 2: bridging the personal and social in constructivist psychology.* New York, NY: Pace University Press (pp69–83).

Newman F, Holzman L (1997). *The End of Knowing.* New York, NY: Routledge.

Paré D, Lysack M (2004). The willow and the oak: from monologue to dialogue in the scaffolding of therapeutic conversations. *Journal of Systemic Therapies 23*(1): 6–20.

Parker I (ed) (1998). *Social Constructionism, Discourse and Realism.* London: Sage.

Penn P, Frankfurt M (1994). Creating a participant text: writing, multiple voices, narrative multiplicity. *Family Process 33*: 217–231.

Prilleltensky I, Nelson G (2002). *Doing Psychology Critically: making a difference in diverse settings.* New York, NY: Palgrave Macmillan.

Proctor G (2008). CBT: the obscuring of power in the name of science. *European Journal of Psychotherapy & Counselling 10*(3): 231–245.

Proctor G (2002). *The Dynamics of Power in Counselling and Psychotherapy.* Ross-on-Wye: PCCS Books.

Rokke PD, Rehm LP (2001). Self-management therapies. In: Dobson KS (ed). *The Handbook of Cognitive Behavioral Therapies* (2nd ed). New York, NY: Guilford Press (pp173–210).

Rose N (1990). *Governing the Soul: the shaping of the private self.* New York, NY: Routledge.

Safran JD, Muran JC (2000). *Negotiating the Therapeutic Alliance: a relational treatment guide.* New York, NY: Guilford Press.

Safran JD, Segal ZV (1990). *Cognitive Therapy: an interpersonal process perspective.* New York, NY: Basic Books.

Sampson E (1993). Identity politics: challenges to psychology's understanding. *American Psychologist 48*(12): 1219–1230.

Sampson E (1981). Cognitive psychology as ideology. *American Psychologist 36*(7): 730–743.

Segal ZV, Williams JMG, Teasdale JD (2012). *Mindfulness-Based Cognitive Therapy for Depression* (2nd ed). New York, NY: Guilford Press.

Shotter J (1993). *Conversational Realities.* London, UK: Sage.

Spong S (2012). Validity, vision and vocalization: social responsibility arguments and power-sensitised counselling. *Psychotherapy and Politics International 10*(1): 69–75.

Strong T (2000). Six orienting ideas for collaborative counselors. *European Journal of Psychotherapy, Counseling, and Health 3*(1): 25–42.

Strong T (2010). Staying in dialogue with CBT. *European Journal of Psychotherapy & Counselling 12*(3): 243–256.

Strong T (2004). Ethical 'construction zones' in psychology's big tent. *International Journal of Critical Psychology 11*: 131–152.

Strong T (2003). Dialogue in therapy's 'borderzone'. *Journal of Constructivist Psychology 15*(4): 245–262.

Strong T (2002). Collaborative 'expertise' after the discursive turn. *The Journal of Psychotherapy Integration 12*(2): 218–232.

Strong T, Sutherland O, Couture S, Godard G, Hope T (2008). Karl Tomm's collaborative approaches to counselling. *Canadian Journal of Counselling 42*(3). [Online]. http://cjc-rcc.ucalgary.ca/cjc/index.php/rcc/article/view/443/149 (accessed 3 February 2018).

Szasz TS (1970). *The Manufacture of Madness*. New York, NY: Delta.

Tileagă C & Stokoe E (Eds) (2015). *Discursive Psychology: Classic and contemporary issues*. London: Routledge.

Vygotsky LS (1978). *The Collected Works of LS Vygotsky, vol 1: problems of general psychology*. New York, NY: Plenum Books.

Weiste E, Peräkylä A (2013). A comparative conversation analytic study of formulations in psychoanalysis and cognitive psychology. *Research on Language and Social Interaction 46*(4): 299.

Wessler RL (1992). Constructivism and rational-emotive therapy: a critique. *Psychotherapy 29*(4): 620–625.

White M, Epston D (1990). *Narrative Means to Therapeutic Ends*. New York, NY: Norton.

Wittgenstein L (1988). *Remarks on the Philosophy of Psychology*, vol II (GH von Wright, H Nyman eds; CG Luckhardt, MAE Aue trans). Chicago, IL: University of Chicago Press.

Wittgenstein L (1958). *Philosophical Investigations* (3rd ed). Anscombe G (trans). New York, NY: MacMillan.

EPISTEMOLOGICAL AND RESEARCH PERSPECTIVES

16 Thinking thoughtfully about cognitive behaviour therapy

John D Kaye

> In the varied topography of professional practice, there is a hard, high ground, which overlooks a swamp. On the high ground, manageable problems lend themselves to solution through the use of research-based theory and technique. In the swampy lowlands, problems are messy and confusing and incapable of technical solution… in the swamp lie the problems of greatest human concern. (Schön, 1992: 54)

> We are shaped by the tools and instruments we use. (Vygotsky, 2012)

> Suffer us not to mock ourselves with falsehood
> Teach us to care and not to care
> Teach us to sit still. (Eliot, 1930)

Among mental health professionals, cognitive behaviour therapy (CBT) is widely prescribed for the treatment of what are viewed as psychological problems or diagnosed as disorders, such as, *inter alia*, anxiety or depression. This chapter is concerned with the limits placed on the conceptualisation of the behavioural and emotional problems people experience, their mental and emotional distress, and the limits placed on both therapists and consultees[1] by working solely within the prescriptive limits of the paradigm governing CBT.

Recent decades have witnessed an increasing realisation in Australia of the prevalence of high rates of depression in the community, inadequate treatment opportunities, and the associated social, familial and economic costs to the

1. I use the word *'consultee'* throughout this chapter rather than 'client' or 'patient'. People experiencing psychological distress *consult* us for help and I find the word 'client' too mercenary and the word 'patient' too medicalised, carrying the connotation of illness, defectiveness or deficiency.

community. As a result of this awareness, together with pressing concern and representations to the Federal Minister of Health on the part of health and welfare bodies, including the Australian Psychological Society, the Australian government in 2006 legislated for the Better Outcomes in Mental Health Care programme. Under this initiative, patients referred by their GP were able to claim, under Australia's universal Medicare system, a rebate for psychological services, including psychotherapy provided by registered psychologists.

Managed by the Department of Health and administered by the Department of Human Services, the programme is policed by the Australian Health Practitioner Regulation Agency (AHPRA). Its brief is to manage and improve the treatment of mental disorders in the community. Its role mandates the development and maintenance of what are claimed to be established and bureaucratically established skill sets, standards and competencies. AHPRA thus has a socio-cultural regulatory role and, as such, a role in the maintenance of social order. In the pantheon of psychotherapeutic methods, CBT has achieved accredited status by virtue of its claim that its treatment programmes have a scientific base, are evidence based and that its practitioners are scientist practitioners.

Thus, given its claim to be the most validated psychotherapeutic modality in the research literature (or, rather, given its claims to be evidence based), it has gained the status as the 'treatment of choice' for conditions such as depression, anxiety, obsessional-compulsive disorder and social phobia.

At the same time, as a discipline concerned with mental health, it is inevitable that CBT is itself imbued with socially regulative concepts. Loewenthal (2016) argues that psychological therapies have unwittingly become agents of the state – reducing the choice that is being offered to patients and clients. With its normalising focus and stress on psychological and behavioural adjustment, CBT can be seen as acting to maintain the interests of society and its economic system. Put simply by Parker (2014): 'The neo-liberal state governs the health of its citizens in such a way as to ensure that they are ready to work to some degree.' The socioeconomic role played by the helping professions, including CBT practitioners, is forensically analysed by Parker in Parker and Ravelli (2008) and Parker (2014; 2015).

Not only can CBT be viewed as performing a culturally regulative role, but its own research tradition and cultural positioning act as crucial determinants of its philosophy and practices. Inscribed as it is by modernist socio-cultural and medicalised prescriptions of what constitutes normality, it cannot but be regulative and its interventive techniques reproductive of the socially normative and medically accepted view of the well-adjusted person. In practice, this governs its very conceptualisation of psychological distress, the therapeutic interaction, its mode of enquiry, assessment of the 'problem', goal of intervention and verbal interaction with the consultee. The model thus determines and places limits on the conceptualisation of both the problem and the approach taken toward its amelioration. To explore this requires an examination of CBT's rhetorical structuring and governing paradigm.

My aim in this chapter, therefore, is not simply to engage in a detailed deconstruction of the paradigm governing CBT, as this is fully addressed elsewhere in this book. Nor is it critically to deconstruct the 'scientist-practitioner' model that forms the foundation of most clinical master's and doctoral degrees in Australia, and to which most practising psychologists pay lip service while also employing methods drawn from other schools of therapy (for example, solution-focused therapy, systemic family therapy, collaborative therapy, narrative therapy) when confronted with the exigencies of practice. Rather my aim is to:

- critique some of the governing paradigm's limits and consequences
- question the privileged status granted to CBT, and
- briefly consider therapeutic developments drawing on constructs from outside CBT's governing paradigm – for example, mindfulness-based cognitive behaviour therapy (MBCT) and acceptance and commitment therapy (ACT), as these have been incorporated under the CBT banner and have enriched its practice.

On the rhetorical construction of the scientist practitioner model and CBT

In advocating for psychology's rightful place as a preferred provider of psychotherapeutic treatment and in establishing its scientific credentials, the Australian Psychological Society (APS) has sought to construct a base of scientific credibility on a foundation of positivist and empiricist views of what constitutes scientific knowledge and, within that frame, legitimate scientific research.

Its advocatory role in employing legitimating rhetoric, drawing on the authority of science as the underpinning of the much-vaunted 'scientist-practitioner' model, cannot be underestimated. Its rhetoric has certainly proved invaluable in establishing psychology's stake in the provision of therapeutic services, its presence in the marketplace and its reputation for accountability. In turn, the acceptance by the mainstream profession of the scientist-practitioner model, and the nature of the evidence supporting the efficacy of CBT, is obdurately maintained, in spite of consistent critique of its governing positivist paradigm (Gergen, 1985, 1987; Hoffman, 1993; John, 1987, 1998; Kaye, 2003; Martin, 1989); in spite of critiques of the nature of the evidence cited in support of CBT (Bohart, 2002; Wampold, 2001), and in spite of evidence from meta-analytic studies of therapeutic efficacy citing outcome equivalence across all therapies (Ahn & Wampold, 2001; Luborsky, Singer & Luborsky, 1975; Smith & Glass, 1997; Cuijpers et al, 2008).

That is, despite differing theoretical orientations between schools of therapy, research has not yielded demonstrable differences in effective outcomes. Thus, currently, there is no conclusive evidence of differential effects between therapies, despite consistent research efforts to establish primacy of the medical model-based CBT approaches.

This being so, it can be said with reasonable certainty that the primacy granted CBT by its proponents is based more on obstinate belief in its governing scientistic paradigm and its accompanying legitimising rhetoric, rather than on hard evidence – a somewhat savage irony for a discipline that prides itself on being empirically supported. The privileged status granted to the category 'CBT', while definable in terms of a set of attributes and methods (eg. Beck 1972, 1976; Greenberger & Padesky, 1995; Wells, 1997) is the result of a particular form of rhetorical advocacy on the part of behavioural scientists with interests to serve and a stake to protect. As John (1987: 227) puts it:

> … what is ultimately to be resolved is who is to be authorised or legitimated to adjudicate claims for inclusion in the category and how this is to be justified. The definition of the term is a political, rather than an empirical matter, and the meaning accorded to it can only be grasped in relation to the wider social historical context in which it is embedded.

To quote John further:

> That is, the portrayal or representation of psychotherapy as an applied science serves an ideological function of legitimating particular claims concerning the nature of psychotherapy and in doing so of advancing and securing political objectives, amongst which are the social and economic interests of various groups of psychologists. (1987: 283)

If psychology's mission is to generate knowledge about human behaviour and to apply this knowledge to the promotion of human welfare, the question then arises whether the specification of CBT as the authorised treatment modality, to the exclusion of other therapies, necessarily benefits the people who approach us for help in overcoming the full range of psychological/emotional dilemmas, relationship problems and problems in living. What is considered to be evidence-based practice mandates only those therapies that use a particular set of methodologies established and assessed by randomised controlled trials and aimed at specific disorders (Chambless & Ollendick, 2001). The research methodology in many studies uses experimental manipulations under control conditions vastly different to those in 'real-life' clinical situations – conditions that meta-analyses have shown to be effective. In this sense, the evidence favouring empirically supported treatments can be construed as evidence *biased* – biased against other forms not similarly tested. Attention focuses on methodological critique rather than on outcome, as a way of discrediting the efficacy of therapies outside the parameters set by the empirically supported treatments (EST) lobby (Westen, Novotny & Thompson-Brenner, 2004). In this sense, a pro-EST, politically driven ideology militates against the acceptance of such therapies.

A further question arises then of the *ethic* of authorising CBT at the expense of other therapies when a) therapeutic modalities emerging from other traditions such as the post-foundational turn to language have been shown to produce positive outcomes, and b) there are problems in restricting practice to CBT techniques. To address this issue, it is necessary to discuss the role of paradigms.

On paradigms and paradigmatic astigmatism: a brief critique

All psychotherapies are governed by a paradigm – a disciplinary narrative consisting of a set of interlinked propositions undergirded by presuppositions, which together constitute the boundaries of its knowledge domain and which direct its practice. As I have written elsewhere (Kaye, 2005), these presuppositions produce and sustain what Foucault (1980) labels 'truth effects' and function as a necessary part of the 'regime of truth' (Parker, 1995) that is at work:

> They are constructed assumptions that shape our view of phenomena and, within the parameters of the paradigm, are held to be true – impervious to criticism and inviolable. The paradigm also mandates rules of procedure governing sanctioned research and practice to which members of the discipline are constrained to adhere. In turn, it guides the assumptions made by the practitioner, the questions he or she might ask, and the interpretations made. Unfortunately, just as the presuppositions and rules that govern a model (in this case one such as the 'scientist-practitioner' and its offspring, mainstream CBT) define its boundaries, so they also constitute limits. (Kaye, 2005: 180)

In the case of psychotherapy, these limits disqualify phenomena that, from the viewpoints of alternative paradigms, are crucial to the understanding of human experience – or, indeed, those core anxieties and profound, deeply embodied experiential and existential fears that so trouble people. They also exclude consideration of the socio-cultural networks of ideas, values and practices by which people are positioned – let alone the interactional nature of the problems people experience in their relationships. In this regard, it is crucial to understand that problems do not necessarily reside *within* the individual, they are the product of the relationship between people and how they interact around issues and are thus not simply attributable to any one person. According to the Emergent Principle (Checkland, 1988), relational problems are an emergent – with the inter-relatedness of units in a system giving rise to new qualities that are a function of that very relatedness. Bearing this in mind, any problem assessment that focuses solely on individual characteristics, cognitions, or construals is of necessity limited and misleading.

However, the paradigm that informs cognitive behaviour therapy is predominantly essentialist and focused on the individual. That is, it assumes:

1. an underlying cause or basis of pathology
2. the location of this cause within individuals, their behaviour and cognitions
3. the diagnosability of the problem
4. its treatability via a specifically designed set of techniques.

As Prilleltensky and Nelson (2002) put it:

> The focus of diagnosis is on the occurrence of various signs and symptoms (thoughts, emotions and behaviours) that are presumed to reflect an underlying diagnostic condition, as defined in the *Diagnostic and Statistical Manual* of the American Psychiatric Association.

As I have argued elsewhere:

> Implicit in these suppositions are the concepts of normality and abnormality, the normatively good or bad and the presumption of a true root cause that can be objectively established, known and remediated. Within this frame, therapy can be seen as an instrumental practice consisting of the treatment of what is judged to be mental disorder and abnormal or dysfunctional behaviour. Therapists working within these parameters seek to bring about a restructuring or reprogramming of behaviour… against some criterion of the normal, the deviant, the well-adjusted, the problematic and the non-problematic. (Kaye, 2003: 227).

The implicit injunction in this, and other convention-driven therapeutic models, is to bring about change in the person – their thinking, their emotions, their behaviour, their relationships. It is subtractive in that it strives to take away some aspects of the troubled person's cogito/emotional repertoire, and in this sense, it is oppositional – it pits the therapist against the consultee. And how often do we hear from our frustrated colleagues: 'Oh that impossible, rigid, resistant Mr or Ms X' – totally unaware of how they may unwittingly have triggered the so-called resistance. It is only too easy to blame the client.

On despotic therapy

Diagnostic and therapeutic intervention in the frame described above involves the translation of the consultee's story into the therapist's frame of reference and engages them actively in reinterpreting their narrative within that frame. This has several troubling implications. As Loewenthal (2015) asserts: 'To completely adopt a Lacanian (or any other school of therapy) is a totalising move that greatly increases the act of doing violence to the client.' Furthermore, this process is potentially prejudicial to the consultee's interests. It is a totalising move that, according to

Loewenthal, acts to encompass the individual completely in the theoretical frame-ups of the practitioner.

In translating a client's account of experience into the concepts governing their model, clinicians impose their theoretical structure on the client's account, such that the person's views are perceived through the monocular funnel of the therapist's theoretical lens and rendered secondary – a form of hegemonic psychological colonisation. Put another way, the act is despotic: it reduces the other's experience to a subset of a diagnostic system, rather than seeking to search for an *understanding* of what the troubled person is experiencing and how this relates to their distress.

The translation, too, circumscribes the possible ways in which the problem can be helpfully construed. In order to bring about change (itself a problematic ambition), the therapist's construction (carrying authority and power as it does) can be inadvertently oppositional in that it contests the consultee's version of construing their experience and events in their life, thus subtly undermining them – hardly a therapeutic move. In turn, the nature of the questions asked and processes set in motion by the questions, the mode of questioning and the therapist interventions themselves help forge the causal link to the conclusion drawn by the practitioner. As Spence (1982: 29) puts it:

> [The therapist] is constantly making decisions about the form and status of the patient's material. Specific listening conventions… help to guide these decisions. If, for example, the analyst assumes that contiguity indicates causality, then he will hear a sequence of disconnected statements as a causal chain… If he assumes that the transference predominates and that the patient is always talking, in more or less disguised fashion, about the analyst, then he will hear the material in that way and make some kind of ongoing evaluation of the state of the transference.

In this way, therapists, guided by the categories mandated by their theory, *produce* what is taken to be the problem, and may well devise ingenious solutions to the wrong problem. Seeking to establish the nature of the problem can be pathologising in a further way. Berg and De Shazer (1993: 8), writing about 'problem talk', put it this way:

> As we listen to people describe their problems and search for an explanation, 'fact' piles up upon 'fact' and the problem becomes heavier and heavier. The whole situation can quickly become overwhelming, complicated and perhaps even hopeless… Such problem-talk, talking more about what is not working is doing more of the same of something that has not worked… Simply, the more clients and therapists talk about so-called facts the greater the problem they jointly construct.

This, together with the assumption of a problem residing in the individual, as well as its expression in a language of deficit or deficiency, can indeed prove iatrogenic, leading the consultee directly into what Gergen (1991) has called a 'spiral of infirmity'. In this interaction, the therapist is positioned as the knowing expert while the client, implicitly informed of his or her deficiency, is given a lesson in inferiority, defectiveness or deficiency. Truly *a despotic act*. In this respect, therapists are only too often unaware of the power and influence exercised by their language.

If I might briefly allow myself an anecdote from my practice, James (not his real name), for many sessions, sat with an inexpressive, straight face as we discussed his experience, his hurt childhood and his difficulty in forming relationships. One day, discussing when he first sought psychological help, he told me how his GP had diagnosed depression and referred him to a psychologist. Sitting in the psychologist's office for the first time, anxious, not sure what to expect and with a strained smile on his face, this vulnerable and confused young man was jolted when the psychologist leaned forward with furrowed brow and, staring directly at him, said: 'I've got your diagnosis. You have smiling depression.' For three years, until he arrived in my rooms, James refused to smile. To him, it proved he was depressed.

In other words, not only can the relational frame influence the client's wellbeing, but the therapist's words can be pathologising. The words used by the therapist in conveying an assessment or diagnosis can be taken in by the client in such a way that the 'problem' becomes internalised as a central part of the person's identity. Alternatively, where those personal constructs fused to a person's sense of psychological survival are threatened or disconfirmed by the therapist's 'socratic' questioning, it can trigger severe existential anxiety.

A final problem with the individualisation of distress is that it can divert attention from the socio-cultural siting of a consultee's problem, subtly imputing personal responsibility and thereby unjustly enjoining him or her to adjust to the unjust – unemployment for example, redundancy, marginalisation or discrimination.

Modernist therapy as regulative practice

The majority of mainstream cognitive behaviour therapies draw on socio-culturally derived or disciplinary discourses that embody what constitutes 'normality' or 'abnormality', adjustment or maladjustment. Given also their assumed value neutrality, they tend to be blind to the broad cultural conditions that govern their precepts and practices. In this way, they are unknowingly infused with ideologically saturated 'regimes of truth' that specify particular power relations between consultant and consultee and govern the nature of the interaction.

The process is vested with particular techniques of discursive regulation or practices of power that, in turn, produce, maintain and reproduce particular rules and practices, including specific 'technologies' of self.

In this light, modernist CBT therapies may be seen as socially regulative, in that they may position their subjects to become complicit in their own subjugation by being recruited into conforming to particular specifications of personhood carried in dominant assumptions of normality and the moral codes governing exemplary being – discursive formations that problematised their experience in the first place. As Rose (1990) asserts, therapy may well co-opt people into engaging in practices or technologies of the self in which they attempt to discipline, govern or change themselves in relation to mandated specifications of personhood, while attention is drawn away from socially oppressive structures and practices.

If, as a socially sanctioned disciplinary technology, modernist CBT psychotherapy does unreflectively reproduce dominant discourses and mechanisms of control while masking inegalitarian regimes of truth, if the practice implicates the subjects of the discipline in their own subjection (Foucault, 1979, 1988), it thereby exercises limiting and subjugating effects. Its very instantiation of self-examination draws attention to the personal while excluding attention to discursive positioning, thereby immuring people within essentialist identities that constrain change.

Within the above frame, mainstream CBT may be construed as an ideologically infused practice that a) supports the social order; b) may serve as an instrument of social control preserving the dominant culture, and c) maintains inequitable social conditions and arrangements that may be constitutive of the problems people experience (White, 1991). In this view, such treatments may unwittingly act to perpetuate the causes of the problem they seek to treat by confirming and normalising oppressive or problematising social beliefs, norms and mores.

From first-order to second-order CBT

Traditional, or what I call first-order CBT seeks to alter what is seen to be maladaptive behaviour by modifying its underpinnings in the form of associated thoughts and assumptions presumed to be 'dysfunctional'. It acts on people's accounts of their problem through the narrow lens of cognitive theory. Among the ranks of CBT's true believers are some practitioners who have become aware of problems with this approach, both conceptually and in practice. I will reiterate the conceptual issues and, in relation to these, will outline therapeutic developments, the central axioms of which are separating the problem from the person, acceptance of a 'not-knowing' and 'client-as -expert' stance, and an attitude of therapist curiosity – a wanting to know, to understand.

In conventional CBT, 'more of the same' problem-talk is seen as being part of the problem, and as acting to maintain and even intensify it (Hayes & Batten, 1999) – something that strategic and solution-focused therapies, emerging as they do from an alternative, non-linear, post-foundational paradigm, have argued for some years. Second, there is empirically established evidence of resistance to CBT's emphasis on change (Linehan, 1993) – especially, I believe, where embodied, emotion-saturated core beliefs that are central to a person's sense of psychological safety are threatened. This is likely to trigger defence or resistance, engaging the protagonists in a counter-therapeutic battle for control of the 'symptom'.

Symptoms, symptomatic behaviour, and their thought associations have a function – they can serve a protective purpose, for example, or, in the consultee's mind, are the only way of dealing with anxieties and shame, or life circumstances and occurrences seen as intolerable or threatening. Put another way, they are emotionally clung to as central to the person's sense of self-preservation, wellbeing and, indeed, their very sense of existential being. In this sense, *they are functional rather than dysfunctional,* and stubbornly defended against intrusion.

Insistence on change invites resistance. And, unfortunately, where the therapist acts unwittingly to induce change, this can lead to its opposite – problem maintenance, in which the person persists in the pattern of thinking and acting that reinforces the problem.

In contrast to this model of therapy with its embodied *professional as expert stance* is an approach that I label 'second order'. It is an approach that not only helps people to resolve the problem that brought them into therapy but furnishes them with a perspective that enables them to deal effectively with the existential and emotional challenges with which living confronts us. The central axiom of this orientation to therapy is to defocus from the problem. Instead of focusing on questioning or contesting the cognitive and emotional constituents of the so-called problem, it, seemingly paradoxically, takes the focus off the so-called problem. This is achieved predominantly by viewing therapy as a process of creating new meanings and possibilities via a collaborative, shared exploration of experience (Anderson, 1997) and by, as it were, separating the person from the problem. Let me briefly elaborate.

Psychotherapy as shared exploration of experience is governed by a philosophy centred in a 'not-knowing', 'client-as-expert' position (Goolishian & Anderson, 1987), with the consultee seen as the expert on their own experience. Anderson describes it as follows:

> Knowing – the delusion of understanding or the security of methodology – decreases the possibility of seeing and increase our deafness to the unexpected, the unsaid and the not yet said... Not-knowing refers to a therapist's position – an attitude and belief that a therapist does not have access to privileged information, can never fully understand another person, always needs to be in a state of being informed by the other. (1997: 134)

This therapist stance emerges from the knowledge that we cannot gain direct, uninterpreted access to another's experience, and is informed by a philosophy that values a readiness to seek to be open to the other's experience and interactively enable him/her to explore and expand their understanding via a non-judgmental therapist interest and facilitative questioning in a context of shared enquiry

(Anderson & Goolishian, 1998). This therapist stance is informed by an attitude of curiosity (Cecchin, 1998) and a willingness to work from and stay with not-knowing (Lowenthal, 2016) – perspectives that enable a non-judgmental openness in conjointly exploring the other's experience towards the uncovering or creation of new understanding. TS Eliot captures it well in East Coker (1943):

> In order to arrive at what you do not know
> You must go by a way which is the way of ignorance.

This philosophic therapist stance enables a process of shared collaborative enquiry. As Harlene Anderson puts it (1997: 118):

> Psychotherapy (as shared enquiry) is a process of forming, saying, and expanding the unsaid and the yet-to-be-said – the development, through dialogue, of new meanings, themes, narratives and histories from which new self-descriptions may arise.

In Loewenthal's view, as I understand it, new meaning emerges from the interaction between therapist and consultee, from their verbal interchange – the therapist in this sense becoming a co-constructor of the understandings created by the interchange.

The question then arises of how this co-construction becomes transformative of the consultee's experience in such a way that it acts to enable them to gain better or enhanced self-understanding. The answer lies in the fact that interaction in the context of this mode of interested enquiry involves an exploratory re-narration. The narration of experience in this elaborative mode of enquiry prompts *a thinking about, a reflection on, a re-visioning* that is (potentially) healing. It places the person *meta* to their construction of experience. *Reflective re-telling, of necessity, involves a re-experiencing that is at the same time a re-visioning, a re-cognising.* In this way, it constitutes a dynamic that positions the speaker *outside – a viewer of the original experience and thus outside it, rather than as the still-immersed, engulfed subject.*

This constitutes a profound, if subtle, shift in the perspective or stance the person takes toward their existentially lived experience. It is a double shift, from the ongoing hurt and distress in which the person was engulfed on entering therapy to the lived memory of it via the re-telling, the re-cognising – one that opens up a new perspective.

Overlapping with the above is a technique (and, indeed, one that may be construed as at least congruent with CBT, even though emerging from a different paradigm) that also places consultees *meta* to their experience by separating the problem from the person, thereby creating psychological distance from it. This technique no longer treats the problem as some dysfunctional way of thinking or 'negative' cognition within the person that needs to be corrected. As Dallos (2011) describes it:

> Rather than seeing the problem as some fundamental quality inherent in, or an essential part of, the person, it is portrayed instead as an externally driven, temporary, unwelcome and transient state that has entered into the person's life.

Prime amongst these techniques is that of externalisation, developed by Michael White (1991, 1995), whereby the problem that has oppressed the person is personified as external to them. Distance from the troubling experience is created by giving it its own 'personality' and voice.

CBT reconsidered

Some understanding of the limits of traditional CBT, together with a shift from a focus on dysfunctional thoughts to a focus on thinking as an active process, has led to a move from first-order to *second-order* CBT – a move from a focus on the *category* of problem ('dysfunctional thoughts/dysfunctional behaviour/ intersection') to a focus on the *superordinate-class* 'thinking'. In practice, this is operationalised by having the consultee engage in what Hackman and colleagues (2011) and Bennett-Levy (2015) call behavioural experiments, many of which are visualisations or activities that place people in the position of being active observers of their thoughts, feelings or actions – again, a meta-position, distancing the person from their troubled experience rather than their remaining positioned by or engulfed in it.

A further second-order therapeutic method, Mindfulness-integrated CBT (MiCBT), has been developed by Bruno Cayoun (2011). Incorporating the concepts of neuroplasticity and neurotransmission, the technique addresses the process of cognito/affective thought formation itself, rather than challenging negative beliefs or unhelpful thinking styles. The central modality consists of the inclusion of a visualisation technique during a mindful induction.

During a mindful meditation, the troubled person is invited to create and focus on a visual representation or image of his/her sensations, in elaborate detail. The aim of this intervention is to have the person direct their attention away from their troubling ideation to the image they have constructed, thus disrupting the automatic reciprocal fusion between sensory arousal and their distressed interpretive cognitions. The process thus acts as a circuit breaker, bypassing immersion in distress and establishing a new neural pathway.

Similarly, MBCT (Segal, Williams & Teasdale, 2002), mindful compassion (Gilbert & Choden, 2013) and ACT (Hayes & Batten, 1999) have adopted an approach in which the attention is not on acting to modify thoughts considered dysfunctional, but, rather, on the superordinate concept of how they are maintained. In essence, this constitutes a shift in paradigm. Both approaches *defocus* from the problem – the link between thinking and feeling – to how feelings are maintained (for example, by experiential avoidance), and both focus on acceptance of whatever is experienced. Acceptance of experience is central to the contemporary integration of mindfulness into psychotherapy. It is an experiential approach, using awareness exercises with an emphasis on the development of a non-judgmental, curious, receptive attitude towards their experience on the part of the consultee. In this way, it fosters self-acceptance, as against rejection/avoidance of experience, with the core aim being:

> ... to help participants develop a different way of relating to sensations, thoughts, and feelings – specifically, mindful acceptance and acknowledgement of unwanted feelings and thoughts, rather than habitual, automatic, preprogrammed routines that tend to perpetuate difficulties. (Segal, Williams & Teasdale, 2002: 86)

The approach is not crudely to work to overcome negative thoughts (first-order) but to attend to these with interest and comfort, and for this sense to spread to a general sense of wellbeing as an embodied counter to negative or depressive ideation. In this, it is apparent that there is a similarity not only to exposure approaches but to Victor Frankl's paradoxical intention, the paradoxical methods used by the Mental Research Institute (MRI) school at Palo Alto, and the Gestalt focus on awareness-raising in the here and now. Mindfulness seeks to enable a different stance toward troubling issues and emotions: the ability to adopt a state of reflective awareness toward feelings, as opposed to one of non-reflective awareness in which one is engulfed by them. Central to mindful acceptance is that it releases one from the hopeless attempt to control feelings, others and events in our lives. It is a relinquishing of the illusion of control – the attempt at which anchors one in anxiety, depression, anger, frustration and hurt.

In this way, *radical acceptance is transformative*, as it brings one to no longer dispute the reality of the inevitability of troubling events in the course of our lives. In turn, for ACT, 'seeing thoughts and feelings as the problem is itself part of the problem, and solutions based on this analysis are also part of the problem' (Hayes & Batten, 1999: 2). In common with MBCT, ACT seeks to counteract coping strategies that focus on avoidance of experience, and to develop the willingness to remain in touch with private experiences construed as negative. Beyond this, ACT has a characteristic focus on language and the meanings people attribute to their experience, differentiating between what people take to be 'givens' and pragmatic truth, and how we become fused with the meanings socially given to particular experiences. Thus, according to Hayes and Batten (1999: 1): 'One of the core elements of ACT is undermining this type of cognitive fusion by altering the normal verbal context provided by the social/verbal community.' From this it is clear that ACT's guiding principles are consistent with both the turn to language in the social sciences and the constructivist and social constructionist concepts that our realities are socially constructed and language-constituted. Thus, the constructs that govern people's experience, and indeed our psychological practices, are just that – constructs, and not invariant truths.

It should be clear, finally, that CBT, given these theoretical developments based on constructs outside its original governing paradigm and its use of techniques drawing from therapeutic models inconsistent with that paradigm, is not a homogeneous, static entity. The field known as CBT has undergone a process of transformation in which one or more of its parameters have been altered. Thus, it is no longer restricted to the set of procedures so proudly touted as the one, uniquely evidence-based method of therapy, even while its enhanced intervention repertoire is still conveniently gathered under the rubric 'CBT' for public consumption and the benefit of the industry. It is ironic that what could simply be called mindfulness therapy still seeks the security and respectability conferred by the 'CBT' acronym.

Finally, one can only applaud those innovators who have had the courage to step outside the limited view of therapy and the impoverished conceptualisation of human ways of being imposed by traditional cognitive behaviour thinking, with its narrow concept of the cognition/behaviour nexus. This model can no longer claim to be to be *the* preferred method of choice. The contemporary contextual therapies (such as MBCT and ACT), with their enriched but still systematic approach to therapy, offer expanded possibilities, and the ability creatively to confront life's more profound existential and emotional challenges, problems of spiritual emptiness, or the sense of meaninglessness and disconnection that afflict so many – Schön's swamplands. This can only be to the benefit of consumers – those who come to us for help and deserve better than the rigid methodologies imposed by the unimaginative guardians of the original CBT faith.

References

Ahn H, Wampold BE (2001). Where, oh where are the specific ingredients? A meta-analysis of component studies in counselling and psychotherapy. *Journal of Counselling Psychology 48*(3): 251–257.

Anderson H (1997). *Conversation, Language, and Possibilities: a postmodern approach to therapy.* New York, NY: Basic Books

Anderson H, Goolishian H (1998). Human systems as linguistic systems: evolving ideas about the implications for theory and practice. *Family Process 27*: 371–393.

Beck AT (1972). *Depression: causes and treatment.* Philadelphia, PA: University of Pennsylvania Press.

Beck AT (1976). *Cognitive Therapy and the Emotional Disorders.* New York, NY: International Universities Press.

Bennett-Levy J, Thwaites R, Haaroff B, Perry H (2015). *Experiencing CBT Inside Out: a self-practice/self-reflective workbook for therapists.* New York, NY: Guildford Press.

Berg IK, de Shazer S (1993). Making numbers talk: language in therapy. In: Friedman S (ed). *The New Language of Change.* New York, NY: Guilford Press (pp5–24).

Bohart A (2002). A passionate critique of empirically supported treatments and the provision of an alternative paradigm. In: Watson JC, Goodman RN, Warner MS (eds). *Client-Centered and Experiential Psychotherapy in the 21st Century: advances in theory, research and practice.* Ross-on-Wye: PCCS Books (pp258–277).

Cayoun BA (2011). Mindfulness-Integrated CBT: principles and practice. Chichester: Wiley-Blackwell.

Chambless D, Ollendick T (2001). Empirically supported psychological interventions: controversies and evidence. *Annual Review of Psychology 52*: 685–716.

Cecchin B (1987). Hypothesizing, circularity and neutrality revisited: an invitation to curiosity. *Family Process 26*(4): 405–413

Checkland P (1988). *Systems Thinking, Systems Practice*. Chichester: Wiley.

Cuijpers P, van Straten A, Andersson G, van Oppen P (2008). Psychotherapy for depression in adults: a meta-analysis of comparative outcome studies. *Journal of Consulting and Clinical Psychology 76*(6): 909–922.

Dallos R (2011). *Attachment Narrative Therapy: integrating systemic, narrative and attachment approaches*. Maidenhead: Open University Press.

Eliot TS (1943). East Coker. In: Eliot TS. *The Four Quartets*. New York: Harcourt.

Eliot TS (1930). *Ash Wednesday: six poems*. London: Faber & Faber.

Foucault M (1988). *The Care of the Self: the history of sexuality, vol 3*. London: Allen Lane.

Foucault M (1980). *Power/Knowledge: selected interviews and other writings (1972-1977)*. Brighton: Harvester Press.

Foucault M (1979). *Discipline and Punish: the birth of the prison*. Middlesex: Peregrine Books.

Gergen KJ (1991). *The Saturated Self: dilemmas in identity in contemporary life*. New York, NY: Basic Books.

Gergen KJ (1987). The language of psychological understanding. In: Stam HJ, Rogers TB, Gergen KJ (eds). *The Analysis of Psychological Theory*. Washington, DC: Hemisphere (pp115–129).

Gergen KJ (1985). The social constructionist movement in modern psychology. *American Psychologist 90*: 266–275.

Gilbert P, Choden (2013). *Mindful Compassion: using the power of mindfulness and compassion to transform our lives*. London: Constable & Robinson Ltd.

Goolishian H, Anderson H (1987). Language systems and therapy: an evolving idea. *Psychotherapy 24*(3S): 529–538.

Greenberger D, Padesky CA (1995). *Mind over Mood: change how you feel by changing the way you think*. New York, NY: Guilford Press.

Hackman A, Bennett-Levy J, Holmes EA (2011). *Oxford Guide to Imagery in Cognitive Therapy*. New York, NY: Oxford University Press.

Hayes SC, Batten SV (1999). Acceptance and commitment therapy. *European Psychology 1*(1): 2–9.

Hoffman L (1993). *Exchanging Voices: a collaborative approach to family therapy*. London: Karnac Books.

John ID (1987). The social construction of psychotherapy and psychological practice. *Australian Psychologist 22(*3): 275–289.

John ID (1998). The scientist-practitioner model: a critical examination. *Australian Psychologist 33*(1): 24–30.

Kaye JD (2003). Psy no more: toward a non-iatrogenic psychotherapy. In: Bates Y, House R (eds). *Ethically Challenged Professions: enabling innovation and diversity in psychotherapy and counselling*. Ross-on-Wye: PCCS Books (pp226–242).

Kaye JD (2005). Reconstituting psychology's paradigm: toward a reformulated disciplinary practice. In: Gülerce A, Hofmeister A, Staeuble I, Saunders G, Kaye J (eds). *Contemporary Theorising in Psychology: global perspective*. Concord, ON: Captus Press (pp179–188).

Linehan MM (1993). *Cognitive Behavioural Treatment of Borderline Personality Disorder*. New York, NY: Guilford Press.

Loewenthal D (2016). *Existential Psychotherapy and Counselling after Postmodernism*. London: Routledge.

Loewenthal D (2015). *Critical Psychotherapy, Psychoanalysis and Counselling*. London: Palgrave.

Luborsky L, Singer B, Luborsky L (1975). Comparative studies of psychotherapies. *Archives of General Psychiatry 32*: 995–1008.

Martin PR (1989). The scientist-practitioner model and clinical psychology: time for a change? *Australian Psychologist 24*: 71–92.

Parker I (2015). Towards critical psychotherapy and counselling: what can we learn from critical psychology (and political economy)? In: Loewenthal D. *Critical Psychotherapy, Psychoanalysis and Counselling*. London: Palgrave (pp41–52).

Parker I (2014). Managing neoliberalism and the strong state in higher education: psychology today. *Qualitative Research in Psychology 11*(3): 250– 264.

Parker I, Revelli S (eds) (2008). *Psychoanalytic Practice and State Regulation*. London: Karnac Books.

Parker I, Georgaca E, Harper D, McLaughlin T, Stowell-Smith M (1995). *Deconstructing Psychopathology*. London: Sage.

Prilleltensky I, Nelson G (2002). *Doing Psychology Critically*. Basingstoke: Palgrave Macmillan.

Rose N (1990). Psychology as a social science. In: Parker I, Shotter J (eds). *Deconstructing Social Psychology*. London: Routledge (pp103–115).

Schön D (1992). The crisis of professional knowledge and the pursuit of an epistemology of Practice. *Journal of Interprofessional Care 6*(1): 49–63.

Segal Z, Williams J, Teasdale J (2002). *Mindfulness-based Cognitive Therapy for Depression: a new approach to preventing a relapse*. New York, NY: Guilford Press.

Smith ML, Glass GV (1997). Meta-analysis of psychotherapy outcome studies. *American Psychologist 32*: 752–760.

Spence D (1982). *Narrative Truth and Historical Truth*. New York, NY: WW Norton & Co.

Vygotsky L (2012). *Thought and Language*. Cambridge, MA: MIT Press.

Wampold B (2001). *The Great Psychotherapy Debate: models, methods and findings*. Mahwah, NJ: Erlbaum.

Wells A (1997). *Cognitive Therapy of Anxiety Disorders*. Chichester: Wiley.

Westen D, Novotny CM, Thompson-Brenner H (2004). The empirical status of empirically supported psychotherapies: assumptions, findings and reporting. I: Controlled clinical trials. *Psychological Bulletin 130*(4): 631–663.

White 1995. Re-Authoring Lives. Adelaide: Dulwich Centre.

White M (1991). Deconstruction and therapy. *Dulwich Centre Newsletter 3*: 21–40.

White M, Epston D (1990). *Narrative Means to Therapeutic Ends*. London: WW Norton & Co.

17 CBT and empirically validated therapies: infiltrating codes of ethics*

Christy Bryceland and Henderikus J Stam

Codes of ethics have begun to refer to preferences that interventions be 'empirically supported'. The movement toward empirically supported treatments (ESTs) is based on a medical model of intervention using randomised controlled trials as the prime method. Cognitive behavioural therapies are the most prominent of the ESTs, and threaten to dominate the field of psychotherapy by virtue of their easily measurable and limited outcomes. Alternative practices are at risk of being considered unethical within this framework because their practitioners are unlikely to conduct the kind of outcome research that is considered necessary to demonstrate efficacy. In this chapter, we consider the symbiotic relationship of CBT in supporting the dominance of ESTs.

Professions are normally defined by their use of a publicly recognised and expert body of knowledge and skills, their control of a labour market based on credentials obtained through specialised training programmes typically associated with universities, and autonomy in the workplace, including evaluative autonomy, along with a public service ideal (eg. Freidson, 1999). Professional autonomy is today increasingly threatened by the interventions of state agencies and by marketplace considerations. For example, the organisational settings in which professionals find themselves have become vastly more complex in recent decades, making the control of professional work no longer the exclusive purview of peers and professional organisations, but instead nesting it with professional managers of employing organisations (eg. Leicht & Fennell, 1997). As Miller and Magruder (1999) have put it, psychotherapy has gone through a 'metamorphosis… from a decentralized, fee-for-service cottage industry, to a massive market-driven, largely for-profit, health care system' (pxv).

* This chapter is a revised and shortened version of a paper that originally appeared in the *Journal of Constructivist Psychology* 2005; 18: 131–155.

Threats to autonomy are among the most serious recent threats for professionals. This is largely because professionals' work is based on 'theoretically based discretionary specialization' (Freidson, 1999: 119). In addition to the complexity of organisational settings in which professionals are employed, consumer pressure can also place demands on a profession. More likely, however, it is managerial and bureaucratic pressure to contain costs and limit potentially unlimited services that most directly restrains professionals. In the health and service professions, these constraints have come in the form of guidelines, or other forms of prescriptive advice to limit variation in diagnostic and therapeutic practice and to develop so-called 'standards of care'.

Evidence-based medicine was the first to demand that practice should not be dominated 'by opinion (possibly ill-informed) and by consensus formed in poorly understood ways by "experts". [Instead] the idea is to shift the centre of gravity of health care decision making towards an explicit consideration and incorporation of research evidence' (Sheldon, 1997: vi). As Berg and colleagues (2000) have noted, there is an implicit tension in the demand for 'objectivity' wherein the enhancement of the scientific status of the discipline may in fact lead to a reduction in the autonomy of the professional, at the same time as the increasing transparency of the decision-making process makes it more vulnerable to scrutiny and to interference by outsiders, particularly managers. This dilemma is also clearly visible in the psychotherapeutic domain, as the push to use only treatments with empirical support gains momentum (eg. Blease, Lilienfeld & Kelley, 2016). This issue has been widely discussed on both sides of the Atlantic, and will continue to be worked out in local as well as national and international contexts.

This chapter specifically addresses the role played by codes of ethics in these debates, and their use to support empirically validated therapies. Recent discussion on the use of codes of ethics clearly reflects differing moral views on what constitutes proper, effective and ethical practice. More importantly, this has implications for therapies that are not cognitive-behavioural, such as psychodynamic and constructivist approaches. We will argue that it is a misuse of codes of ethics to co-opt them into debates that are essentially professional and bureaucratic, but are not primarily about proper or ethical conduct in the field of therapy.

Psychology associations and evidence-based practice

Psychological associations such as those in the UK, US and Canada have become more outspoken regarding the need for psychologists to provide interventions that have empirically supported efficacy. Psychologists in the UK led the move toward empirically based psychological treatments, within a larger movement known initially as 'evidence-based medicine' (EBM; Sackett et al, 1997).

In 1993, the American Psychological Association's (APA) Division 12 (Clinical Psychology) developed a taskforce to define, identify and disseminate information about empirically-supported interventions. The taskforce (Task

Force on Promotion and Dissemination of Psychological Procedures, 1993) made controversial recommendations that the APA develop and maintain a list of empirically validated treatments for distribution, and that training programmes include training in these treatments. The task force also had, as an initial goal, that the criteria be used to develop practice guidelines for government, professionals, managed-care organisations and mental health insurers. However, political pressure from within the APA led Division 12 to renounce this goal (Chambless et al, 1996). Despite the controversy, particularly over the development and use of an empirically supported treatment list, the group issued the first of a series of reports in 1995, identifying a number of psychological interventions as 'empirically validated'. Later, these became known as 'empirically supported treatments' (ESTs). The APA Committee on Accreditation decided in 1996 to include training in ESTs as part of the guidelines for accreditation of doctoral and internship training programmes. Division 12 has continued to maintain its website of ESTs to the present day (APA Division 12, 2016).

In 2005, an APA Presidential Task Force published its own report on evidence-based practice (APA Presidential Task Force, 2005) that supported ESTs, although with some qualifications. They included the demand that 'clinical decisions should be made in collaboration with the patient, based on the best clinically relevant evidence, and with consideration for the probable costs, benefits, and available resources and options' (p285). References to 'clinical expertise' as a moderator of EBPs suggested a certain hesitancy not found in the APA Division 12 recommendations. Not surprisingly, however, the overall thrust of the document was in support of the EST movement.

The Clinical Section of the Canadian Psychological Association (CPA) has also entered the debate. In a key paper, published in 1999, a CPA task force recommended that the section explicitly endorse the APA Division 12 work on ESTs, encouraged the CPA as a whole to endorse the Division 12 list, and recommended that CPA accreditation require mandatory training in ESTs for accreditation of doctoral programmes and internships in clinical psychology (Hunsley et al, 1999). In addition, the task force recommended that CPA work with provincial regulatory bodies to require knowledge of and training in empirically supported treatments as part of the assessment of suitability to independently provide health services to the public.

Then, in 2011, the CPA established another taskforce on evidence-based practice (Canadian Psychological Association, 2012). The report of this task force is careful about avoiding a narrow definition of 'evidence', and recognises that strict demands for evidence may marginalise certain kinds of therapy. Although the authors of the report cite an earlier version of this paper (Bryceland & Stam, 2005), they nonetheless recommended expansion of the CPA Code of Ethics to include explicit mention of evidence-based treatment options (see below).

In the UK, the National Institute for Health and Clinical Excellence (NICE) is responsible for producing clinical practice guidelines that provide 'national guidance on promoting good health and preventing and treating ill health'. Their guidelines include treatments for mental health and behavioural disorders, such as anxiety, depression, eating disorders and schizophrenia. Many of these guidelines specify CBT as the psychological treatment of choice, and go so far as to suggest the necessary number of sessions required (eg. NICE, 2009). In 2006, Richard Layard based his economic arguments for the cost-effectiveness of a national Improving Access to Psychological Therapies service for the treatment of anxiety and depression on the NICE guidelines, and, in his report to the then government, recommended that these services should provide 'predominantly' CBT (Layard, 2006).

Critiques of the empirically-supported treatment movement

Critics have noted that empirically supported treatment, as it has been defined by APA's Division 12 Task Force (2016), encompasses a narrow field of practice and leaves much outside its scope. The vast majority of interventions listed fall within the domain of CBT. It has also been argued that the EST list systematically discriminates against certain classes of research, treatment and patients, including non-English-language research and the treatment of people from ethnic minorities and children, as well as psychodynamic and experiential approaches that have different assumptions about the nature of treatment, its possibility of manualisation, and research design (Elliott, 1998). The criteria whereby treatments are selected for the list have also been criticised as too restrictive, because they limit empirical support to a particular kind of research trial, based on the methodology used in drug trials. Some authors make a distinction between empirically supported treatments and evidence-based practice (eg. Castelnuovo, 2010; Goldfried, 2013) – the latter allows one to cast a 'wider empirical net' than ESTs. Furthermore, these authors note that measures of clinical efficacy are not the same as measures of effectiveness of therapy.

The criteria have also been criticised for focusing on therapy technique and manualisation, and downplaying more important research findings, such as the general equivalence of most treatments (sometimes referred to as the 'dodo bird verdict' – see, for example, Luborksy et al, 2002), or the importance of client and therapist variables. Henry (1998), for example, is critical of the EST movement for tacitly ignoring 'the vast bulk of empirical psychotherapy and psychopathology research' (p128). There is great variation in the degree to which different theoretical approaches to psychotherapy embrace conceptions of disorder and treatment. The Division 12 criteria only apply to a very narrow conception of psychotherapy: models that fall outside this conception are not considered to have 'empirical support', despite the fact that, in many cases, they have large bodies of supporting empirical evidence. Critics contend that the EST movement is deeply embedded in the concern for professional autonomy on the one hand, and controlling other, non-EST therapies on the other (eg. Elkins, 2009).

Reactions from therapies marginalised by the EST movement

The implications of the EST movement have not gone unnoticed by those who adhere to theoretical perspectives that are essentially marginalised by it, such as psychodynamic, systemic, humanistic and postmodern therapeutic practitioners and theorists. Bohart and colleagues (1998) argue that the APA Division 12 Task Force criteria for ESTs could 'disenfranchise therapies that do not share [their] assumptions about the nature of psychotherapy and will stifle psychological research' (p141; see also Bohart & House, Chapter 18, this volume). Their primary critique of the Division 12 criteria is their basis in a 'medical-like meta-model of psychotherapy', designed to appeal to the market forces of managed care. Such a model is 'inappropriate for therapies whose primary focus is not to cure disorder', such as humanistic, constructivist and feminist approaches (p141). They criticise the Division 12 criteria on grounds that they are driven by what the authors consider to be 'obviously financial and territorial' considerations (p142).

Bohart and colleagues (1998) also articulate the fear that Division 12's EST list, with its implication that unlisted treatments are either 'experimental' or not empirically supported, will be used to 'expose persons practicing from alternative theories to the possibility of malpractice suits' (p141). Henry (1998) highlighted a related concern, stating that, as the EST list becomes entrenched and taken up by managed care, 'it would be reasonable from the standpoint of a consumer or a third-party payer to increasingly look askance at therapies that were not on the list' (p130).

Likewise, Elkins (2009) has argued that ESTs of the sort approved by Division 12 of the APA will mark the end of the humanistic tradition in psychology, as well as other, more traditional psychotherapies, such as psychodynamic therapies. Wampold had already begun to make this case in 2001 and has since developed the argument further (Wampold & Imel, 2015).

'Ethics' and empirically-supported treatment

Is there legitimacy to the fears that EST lists and criteria will become regulatory tools, used to de-legitimate particular therapies by either disciplinary or financial means? One sign that positions are becoming entrenched is that the language of ethics is being recruited to the debate about empirically supported treatments. Proponents of ESTs have begun to argue that the use of empirically supported or evidence-based treatments constitutes ethical practice, and that, by implication, practising a therapy that does not have empirical support is unethical. It is important to recognise the gravity of this move. One of the features of professions is a service ethic. Professions provide a public service, based on specialised education and training. In return, professions are largely self-governing – a privilege upheld by codes of ethics and professional conduct that impose sanctions for misconduct. The prescriptive use of particular forms of therapy has not traditionally been part of these codes.

This may change, however. For example, in a special issue of *Canadian Psychology* covering the debate on empirically supported treatment, Morin wrote: 'Practitioners have an ethical responsibility to use EST, whenever such treatment is available' (1999: 314). Similarly, the authors of the CPA Task Force report on ESTs (Hunsley et al, 1999) declared:

> It is an ethical requirement that Canadian psychologists keep informed of relevant knowledge and progress in their areas… that health services be based on sound scientific evidence should, therefore, not only pose no threat to the practices of psychologists, it should be warmly embraced by psychologists. (p316)

A similar argument was repeated in the CPA Task Force report on evidence-based practice (Canadian Psychological Association, 2012: 75). This recommended that Standard I.17 of the Canadian Code of Ethics be expanded to read:

> I.17 Recognize that informed consent is the result of a process of reaching an agreement to work collaboratively, rather than of simply having a consent form signed. *This includes ensuring those receiving services from psychologists are apprised of available evidence-based treatment options and the psychologists' ability to provide those services effectively and efficiently.* (Italics in original)

Australian psychologist Gavin Andrews (2000) argues that:

> ... any clinician, asked by a client what other treatments there are for their 'disorder', would be ethically obliged to mention treatments listed as supported by Type 1 [supported by at least two rigorous randomized controlled trials showing superiority to placebo or another treatment] evidence before offering advice about the treatment to be preferred. (p265)

At the moment, these claims still remain at the level of rhetorical flourish. Indeed, 'sound, scientific evidence' is a contestable phrase, and is entirely non-threatening in the context of a broad interpretation of what is meant by 'scientific'. Nor is the notion of 'empirical status' particularly problematic, so long as we understand by it that empirical content is always theory laden. It is the conflation of these notions with specific lists generated around narrow considerations of psychotherapy that signals the appropriation of the language of ethics to the debate, and Andrews is a very clear example in this regard. The problematic assumption is that 'mechanical objectivity', or the agreement to follow certain rules and methods for the collection and evaluation of evidence, can solve problems of a broader disciplinary and judgmental nature.

The language of 'empirical support' has appeared in more recent code revisions for a number of psychological associations and regulatory bodies. It is not known if references to empirical support in these documents are intended to specify empirically supported treatment as defined by the APA Division 12 Task Force; more important may be whether these ethical principles will come to be interpreted in a manner that reflects the Division 12 criteria.

The 2002 and subsequent revisions of the APA code to the present day do not explicitly use the language of 'empirical support', but they include a number of points that increase the emphasis on science or research-based evidence for the practice of both assessment and therapy. With regard to the delivery of therapy, for example, the current (2017) version notes:

> When obtaining informed consent for treatment for which generally recognized techniques and procedures have not been established, psychologists inform their clients/patients of the developing nature of the treatment, the potential risks involved, alternative treatments that may be available, and the voluntary nature of their participation. (APA, 2017: 10.01(b)).

The Code of Ethics of the British Psychological Society (2009) similarly does not explicitly use the language of empirical support. Whereas the previous code (BPS, 2000) required that psychologists 'value and have respect for all relevant evidence and the limits of such evidence when giving psychological advice or expressing a professional opinion', (BPS, 2000: 5), the new code requires only that psychologists 'Remain abreast of scientific, ethical, and legal innovations germane to their professional activities' (BPS, 2009: 16).

The Canadian Code of Ethics for Psychologists also contains revisions to reflect greater emphasis on the ethics of evidence-based practice, and actually incorporates the language of empirical support, recommending that psychologists choose interventions with 'reasonable theoretical or empirically-supported efficacy' (CPA, 2000: 18). In 2017, the code was revised and now mentions the importance of providing services based on the 'best available evidence', which is defined as 'the evidence that is the most trustworthy and valid according to a hierarchy of evidence (ie. a hierarchy that ranks evidence from strongest to weakest), and which is appropriate to the services being delivered' (CPA, 2017: 9). The new code, however, does not contain the exact recommended changes by the CPA evidence-based task force mentioned above. Instead I.17 now reads:

> Recognize that obtaining informed consent is a process that involves taking time to establish an appropriate trusting relationship and to reach an agreement to work collaboratively and may need to be obtained more than once (eg. if significant new information becomes available).

The New Zealand Code of Ethics for Psychologists (2002) was modelled on the Canadian Code. Like the Canadian Code, it contains a clause that refers to expectations for competence in terms of 'scientifically derived' knowledge (p16).

Codes of ethics do not necessarily serve a role as regulatory documents that specify disciplinary action; in fact, they are often presented as educational and aspirational documents. However, a number of codes of conduct developed by the provincial regulatory bodies in Canada have also come to reflect the language of empirical support. These codes use language such as 'empirical foundation of intervention', and demand that registrants be familiar with reliability, validity, standardisation and outcome research for their techniques, and be trained in their proper application (eg. College of Psychologists of British Columbia, 2014; College of Psychologists of Ontario, 2009). These codes of conduct are where disciplinary 'teeth' may be found. The encroachment of the EST language on these codes may give real grounds for fear of disciplinary action by those who practise therapies labelled as 'experimental' by the APA Division 12 and for those that practise therapies that are not on the EST list at all.

While there is clearly variation in the degree to which codes discuss or even suggest the need for empirical support for interventions, there is a trend within these codes to emphasise psychologists' responsibility to base their practices on scientific evidence. We believe that it is reasonable and just to expect psychologists to be knowledgeable about questions of evidence, outcome studies, reliability, validity, and so on. Moreover, what is meant by terms such as 'science', 'research', or 'evidence' in these codes is open to interpretation. However, could such terms come to be interpreted to reflect the narrow demands of the EST movement, as defined by APA's Division 12 Task Force? Or will codes move toward mandating that psychologists inform their clients whether the therapy they provide has empirical support, or one step further, mandate the practice of empirically supported treatment?

Codes of ethics and psychotherapy's professionalisation agenda

Disciplinary measures are not the only concerns related to these semantic shifts in codes of ethics and conduct. A number of theorists have argued that codes of ethics play a central role in the professionalisation of groups and the development of their political power. Dunbar (1998) has argued that the professionalisation goals of codes of ethics include the marketing of psychology, establishing the exclusive rights of psychologists to certain areas of practice, and influencing public policy and decision-making. Codes of ethics are important indicators and legitimators of professional autonomy and self-governance.

From the perspective of professionalisation, the worries about the incorporation of the language of ESTs in codes of ethics may reflect more than a worry about certain practices themselves becoming labelled unethical and vulnerable to disciplinary action. Viewing codes of ethics as tools of professionalisation, it becomes apparent that they also serve to designate professional boundaries. The inclusion of the language of empirical support in codes of ethics may serve a number of purposes for the psychology profession, including that of laying claim to particular technologies as the domain of psychologists and underscoring psychologists' unique role as 'scientist-practitioners' or 'clinical scientists' who base their interventions in a particular kind of empirical support. Henry (1998) argued that the political agenda of the EST movement includes the promotion of the survival of professional psychology and academic research in psychology. Including the practice of ESTs in codes of conduct would serve to further this political agenda by legitimising the EST agenda within the regulatory mechanisms of the psychology profession. A number of authors have continued to pursue this agenda in recent years (eg. Baker, McFall & Shoham, 2016; Blease, Lilienfeld & Kelley, 2016).

The infiltration of ESTs: narrowing the field

The inclusion of ESTs in codes of ethics is not based on considerations that necessarily address issues of moral hazard or protect the public interest. Instead, they bring concerns with quantification, legitimation, and bureaucratic efficiency, together with mechanical objectivity and the limits of human judgment, into the centre of the client–therapist relationship. We do not argue that these considerations should not be of concern or debated – quite the contrary. They should, in fact, be discussed for what they are: historically specific disputes concerning the nature and function of therapy, the relationship between therapist and client, and arguments about what constitutes the best form of therapy for what kinds of problems. We also believe that psychotherapists should be accountable and knowledgeable, and up to date in their use of techniques in so far as they are relevant to their practice. But efficiency in technique is not the same as psychotherapy, and accountability is not the same as being current in the research, as some commentaries have argued.

Conclusion

Our argument against the inclusion of ESTs in codes of ethics rests not on their inherent instability as scientific and rational indicators (that is a debate going on elsewhere), nor primarily on their political uses to strengthen psychology as a discipline (a question worthy of further discussion in its own right), nor their bureaucratic uses in managed care organisations (where they serve to enhance efficiency and ultimately reduce costs). Instead, we feel that ESTs may become confused with the ends of therapy, and, by finding their way into the language of ethics, have already pushed the debate in a direction inimical to the aims of psychotherapy. Particularly by potentially foreclosing 'other' therapies, they threaten the very enterprise of therapy itself by promising technique above what is, after all, a moral vocation. Moreover, those 'other' therapies are precisely those that are not cognitive and behavioural. Their demise would greatly restrict the discourse of therapy, if not our conceptual resources. More likely, they will create two classes of therapists: scientists and non-scientists. Those considered non-scientist will certainly go by other titles, but the social and professional implications for them could be serious.

References

American Psychological Association (APA) (2017). *Ethical Principles of Psychologists and Code of Conduct.* Washington, DC: American Psychological Association.

APA Division 12 (2016). *Psychological Treatments.* [Online.] www.div12.org/psychological-treatments/treatments/ (accessed 4 February 2018).

APA Presidential Task Force (2005). Report of the 2005 Presidential Task Force on Evidence-Based Practice. Washington, DC: American Psychological Association.

Andrews G (2000). A focus on empirically supported outcomes: a commentary on search for empirically supported treatments. *Clinical Psychology: Science and Practice 7*: 264–268.

Baker TB, McFall RM, Shoham V (2008). Current status and future prospects of clinical psychology: toward a scientifically principled approach to mental and behavioral health care. *Psychological Science in the Public Interest 9*: 67–103.

Berg M, Horstman K, Plass S, van Heusden M (2000). Guidelines, professionals and the production of objectivity: standardisation and the professionalism of insurance medicine. *Sociology of Health & Illness 22*: 765–791.

Blease CR, Lilienfeld SO, Kelley JM (2016). Evidence-based practice and psychological treatments: the imperatives of informed consent. [Online]. *Frontiers in Psychology 7.* doi.org/10.3389/fpsyg.2016.01170 (accessed 4 February 2018).

Bohart A, O'Hara M, Leitner L (1998), Empirically violated treatments: disenfranchisement of humanistic and other psychotherapies. *Psychotherapy Research 8*: 141–157.

British Psychological Society (2009). *Code of Ethics and Conduct: guidance published by the Ethics Committee of the British Psychological Society.* Leicester: British Psychological Society.

British Psychological Society (2000). *A Code of Conduct for Psychologists.* Leicester: British Psychological Society.

Bryceland C, Stam HJ (2005). Empirical validation and professional codes of ethics: description or prescription? *Journal of Constructivist Psychology 18*: 131–156.

Canadian Psychological Association (2017). *Canadian Code of Ethics for Psychologists* (4th ed). Ottawa, ON: Canadian Psychological Association.

Canadian Psychological Association (2012). Evidence-based practice of psychological treatments: a Canadian perspective. Ottawa: Canadian Psychological Association (pp1–84).

Canadian Psychological Association (2000). *Canadian Code of Ethics for Psychologists* (3rd ed). Ottawa, ON: Canadian Psychological Association.

Castelnuovo G (2010). Empirically supported treatments in psychotherapy: towards an evidence-based or evidence-biased psychology in clinical settings? *Frontiers in Psychology 1*(27). doi: 10.3389/fpsyg.2010.00027

Chambless D, Sanderson W, Shoham V, Bennett Johnson S, Pope KS, Crits-Christoph P et al (1996). An update on empirically validated therapies. *The Clinical Psychologist 49*: 5–18.

College of Psychologists of British Columbia (2014). *CPBC Code of Conduct.* [Online]. www.collegeofpsychologists.bc.ca/docs/10.CPBCCodeofConduct.pdf (accessed 11 February 2018).

College of Psychologists of Ontario (2009). *Standards of Professional Conduct.* [Online]. www.cpo.on.ca/WorkArea/DownloadAsset.aspx?id=335 (accessed 20 January 2017).

Dunbar J (1998). A critical history of CPA's various codes of ethics for psychologists (1939-1986). *Canadian Psychology 39*: 177–186.

Elkins D (2009). *Humanistic Psychology: a clinical manifesto – a critique of clinical psychology and the need for progressive alternatives.* Colorado Springs, CO: University of the Rockies Press.

Elliott R (1998). Editor's introduction: a guide to the empirically supported treatments controversy. *Psychotherapy Research 8*: 115–125.

Freidson E (1999). Theory of professionalism: method and substance. *International Review of Sociology 9*: 117–129.

Goldfried MR (2013). What should we expect from psychotherapy? *Clinical Psychology Review 33*: 862–869.

Henry WP (1998). Science, politics, and the politics of science: the use and misuse of empirically validated treatment research. *Psychotherapy Research 8*: 126–140.

Hunsley J, Dobson KS, Johnston C, Mikail SF (1999). The science and practice of empirically supported treatments. *Canadian Psychology 40*: 316–319.

Layard R (2006). *The case for psychological treatment centres.* [Online.] British Medical Journal 332: 1030 (accessed 4 February 2018).

Leicht KT, Fennell ML (1997). The changing organizational context of professional work. *Annual Review of Sociology 23*: 215–231.

Luborsky L, Rosenthal R, Diguer L, Andrusyna TP, Berman JS, Levitt JT, Seligman DA, Krause ED (2002). The Dodo bird verdict is alive and well – mostly. *Clinical Psychology: Science and Practice 9*(1): 2–12.

Miller NE, Magruder KM (1999). Introduction. In: Miller NE, Magruder KM (eds). *Cost-effectiveness of Psychotherapy.* New York, NY: Oxford University Press (ppxv–xxx).

Morin C (1999). Empirically supported psychological treatments: a natural extension of the scientist-practitioner paradigm. *Canadian Psychology 40*: 312–315.

New Zealand Psychological Society (2002). *Code of Ethics for Psychologists Working in Aotearoa/New Zealand.* Auckland, NZ: New Zealand Psychological Society.

National Institute for Health and Care Excellence (NICE) (2009). *Depression in Adults: recognition and management.* London: NICE.

Sackett D, Richardson W, Rosenberg W, Haynes R (1997). *Evidence-Based Medicine.* New York, NY: Churchill Livingstone.

Sheldon T (1997). Introduction. In: Grayson L (ed) *Evidence-Based Medicine.* London: British Library (ppvii–xi).

Task Force on Promotion and Dissemination of Psychological Procedures (1993). *A Report to the Division 12 Board.* Washington, DC: American Psychological Association.

Wampold BE, Imel ZE (2015). *The Great Psychotherapy Debate: the evidence of what makes psychotherapy work* (2nd ed). New York, NY: Routledge.

18 Empirically supported/validated treatments as modernist ideology, part 1: the dodo, manualisation and the paradigm question*

Arthur C Bohart and Richard House

For philosopher of science Kuhn (1977), it is commonly difficult for those speaking from different paradigms or 'world-views' to understand one another, not least because of the incommensurable and often unarticulated assumptions from which each speaks and thinks. Rather like Ludwig Wittgenstein's lion: 'Even if a lion could speak, we could not understand him [because we don't know how he structures his world]' (Wittgenstein, 1958/1973: 223). What we will term the 'empirically supported/validated treatments' (ESVT) approach, like any and every research approach, necessarily entails a paradigm underpinned by assumptions about what psychotherapy, and research into it, are concerned with. From within its own internal logic, the ESVT approach seems so self-evidently rational that its advocates have difficulty grasping any objections to it. More specifically, its proponents commonly fail to recognise the paradigmatic or ontological level from which objections to their approach are being raised; attempts are almost invariably made to assimilate and deal with those objections from within their own paradigm. Not that those of us who subscribe to an alternative paradigm are immune from this very same process, of course. So, it may be that ESVTers feel misunderstood by us, too. In this chapter, we present one view of what the ESVT paradigm looks like, and how it is experienced, from the different paradigmatic standpoint we share.

When confronted with objections, ESVT proponents sometimes claim that their opponents' motivation is to advance what they (the ESVT advocates) view

---

* This chapter is a substantial elaboration of Arthur C Bohart's chapter entitled 'A passionate critique of empirically supported treatments and the provision of an alternative paradigm', first published in Watson JC, Goldman RN, Warner MS (eds) (2002). *Client-Centered and Experiential Psychotherapy in the Twenty-First Century: advances in theory, research, and practice*. Ross-on-Wye: PCCS Books (pp258–277).

as 'unscientific' practice. They define 'science' in terms of proceduralised, often manualised, clinical practice, with randomised controlled clinical trial (RCT) methodology seen as the 'gold standard' – as *the* valid route to scientifically legitimate practice.

Alternatively, ESVTers sometimes maintain that any objections can be dealt with from within their own paradigm. However, the ways in which issues are framed, and even thought about, is different in different paradigms. While it may be true that, in some cases, analogues of some therapeutic approaches can be created within the ESVT paradigm, it does not follow from this that their real spirit or essence can be captured within, or effectively represented by, such analogues.

It is not at all wise to prematurely impose a unitary paradigm or 'regime of truth' onto a field, especially when that paradigm has not been consensually arrived at, has been created by a minority of people in a narrowly circumscribed part of the field, and is disputed by many professionals and academics in that field.

Furthermore, as we will see both in this and our next chapter, and in the rest of this book, the impetus for the development of ESVT standards, with their accompanying ideology, is arguably far more economic, political and driven by vested interests than it is genuinely scientific (Beutler, 1998; Hubble, Duncan & Miller, 1999). Thus, those of us subscribing in a principled way to different paradigmatic assumptions view attempts to entrench ESVT assumptions as *the* (only) route to legitimate practice as a hegemonic attempt to impose on both science and practice what is to us, at least in part, an alien and epistemologically unsustainable world-view.

A few words about the notion of a 'paradigm'. The term commonly denotes a set of background assumptions about whatever 'reality' is being studied (including a theory of what exists, and what it might mean to say that something 'exists') – a way of conceptualising the world that underlies, informs, and to some extent determines specific theories and practices. According to Kuhn (1970), our routine procedural paradigms substantially control the ways in which we study the world during periods between what he termed 'scientific revolutions'. A paradigm can therefore both constrain and constructively influence the kinds of theories that are developed, how research is conceived and carried out (House, 2010a), and what is to be considered as legitimate research-based knowledge.

In psychotherapy, for example, a 'paradigm' might refer to a model of what the process of providing help consists of – for example, therapy as 'treatment' for a 'psychopathological disorder' (the so-called 'medical-model' paradigm – eg. Aho, 2008), contrasted with therapy as interpersonal encounter, intersubjective dialogue, and/or consultation or co-operative inquiry.

Another key issue is the underlying metaphysical model influencing both practice and research. Thus, we could counterpose a 'modernist', Newtonian view of the universe, with its goal of increasing control over dependent variables by specifying and manipulating independent variables. This could be contrasted with, say, a more 'postmodern' systemic cosmology, where we can never totally predict or control the phenomena being studied, and where 'science' is acknowledged and respected as one kind of knowledge, but without it necessarily determining or dominating practice.

In what follows, we will first examine the so-called dodo bird verdict in psychotherapy, and its paradigmatic significance. We will then outline the implicit but unarticulated logic of the paradigm underlying the ESVT approach, along with the implicit logic of an alternative plausible paradigm. We maintain there are paradigms that are, at the very least, as plausible as an ESVT-driven one, one of which we here loosely term a 'relational meta-paradigm'. We believe that the latter can convincingly be argued to underlie, and make sense of, psychotherapy experience and practice, of which the ESVT criteria seem to make at best only limited sense. The research and practice of psychotherapy, we argue, need to remain open to a rich diversity of alternative paradigms (House & Totton, 1997) until, through the slow, steady accumulation of results and by emerging common consent, one or another paradigm begins to take prominence. Finally, we maintain that there exist 'evidence-based' and demonstrably effective ways of practising therapy that do not depend on the ESVT world-view. We look in particular at the manualisation issue and that of RCT methodology, about which significant reservations have already been expressed in the literature (eg. Persons & Silberschatz, 1998).

Although we make comparatively limited direct reference to CBT *per se*, it should be clear that many, if not most, of our arguments are of direct relevance to the CBT phenomenon, given its current place as modernity's paradigm-crowning modality, and its inextricable intertwining with questions of 'evidence-based practice', RCT research methodology, and so on. In fact, at present in the US, CBT is enshrined at a number of mainstream research universities as the only practice allowed, with other approaches, such as psychodynamic, dismissed as 'unscientific' (Levendorsky & Hopwood, 2017). This is happening despite considerable evidence for the effectiveness of psychodynamic and humanistic/experiential approaches, from studies done within the ESVT paradigm (see, for example, Lambert, 2013; Shedler, 2010).

For two writers from different continents to co-author a chapter that they can both stand by, in what is such a controversial area as contesting psychotherapy paradigms, is a challenging yet enlightening experience. While we may have some differences in terms of nuance, emphasis or detail, what is more notable is that we have quite effortlessly found extensive common ground on which we can stand together – which, in turn, reaffirms our confidence in the paradigmatic challenges and alternatives that we offer in both this and the following chapter.

The dodo: an example of a paradigm clash

The dodo bird verdict refers to the contention that the extant research supports the conclusion that all bona fide approaches to psychotherapy work equally well for almost all presenting problems (eg. Budd & Hughes, 2009; Luborsky et al, 2002).

The term comes from Lewis Carroll's book, *Alice in Wonderland*, in which a 'caucus race' takes place. The dodo is the judge, and he concludes that, 'All have won and all must have prizes.'

The dodo bird verdict, that all therapies are for the most part equally effective, beautifully illustrates the difference between competing psychotherapy paradigms. For the purposes of this discussion, we set aside for a moment the methodological complication that it might not be meaningful to speak of distinctive approaches or modalities *per se*. This assumes that comparison between what are assumed *from the outset* to be distinct modalities is a legitimate object of study, and/or a more valid comparative metric than is, for example, differences in level of experience, or whether the practitioner has had a personal therapy, or whether s/he holds any spiritual world-view – and so on. The dDodo bird verdict certainly illustrates very clearly the phenomenon of *incommensurable psychotherapy paradigms*.

For ESVT proponents, the dodo bird verdict, if true, would be catastrophic. First, there would be little or no point in developing and studying different treatments for different labelled 'disorders'. Second, the ESVT paradigm is a quintessentially 'technological' view of therapy – assuming that it is the technical aspects of therapy that are the primary cause of therapeutic change. The 'scientific' ESVT approach aspires to develop and test specific technologies, which are then proceduralised, even manualised, for the various 'disorders'. Under this approach, even 'the therapeutic relationship' itself is commonly treated as a kind of 'thingified', manipulable 'variable', to be studied and then differentially 'delivered' for different 'disorders'. It comes as little surprise, therefore, that ESVT advocates maintain that the dodo bird verdict is 'flawed' (eg. Lampropoulos, 2000), or that it has been superseded (Task Force on Promotion and Dissemination of Psychological Procedures, 1995).

A plausible alternative paradigm might conceive of therapy as a fundamentally interpersonal/dialogical process, perhaps using technical interventions that have some significance, but are always of secondary, or even incidental, importance – merely the vehicle through which 'the relational' manifests. Advocates of 'relational' paradigms can easily accept the dodo bird verdict, not being in the least surprised that different modalities, often using very different (or no) therapeutic 'techniques', may have only minimal (and often unpredictable) differential treatment effects.

The question of who is 'winner of the race' is unlikely to be resolved until – if ever – one therapy paradigm prevails or predominates. In our view, from any dispassionate standpoint, the evidence from which the dodo bird verdict derives is so compelling that, were its conclusions in accord with 'mainstream' beliefs and theories, it would surely long ago have been accepted as a major finding, and then built upon (Bohart & Tallman, 1999; Wampold & Imel, 2015). What is arguably the existence of what we might term 'paradigmatic hegemony' is surely clear in paradigm-bound assertions like that of Lampropoulos (2000): that therapists should not be allowed to rely exclusively on the therapeutic relationship, powerful placebos and other ill-defined 'common factors' (eg. van Kalmthout, Schaap &

Wojciechowski, 1985; Frank, 1989), which, he argues, seem to be major assumptions shared by most opponents of ESVTs.

The opposite of the dodo bird verdict, that differential treatment effects have been scientifically demonstrated, has been equally strongly challenged. Wampold and Imel (2015), for example, point out that the number of such findings does not exceed what one would expect by chance, and findings of 'experimenter allegiance effects' (eg. Berman & Reich, 2010; Loewenthal, 2010) cast further doubt on differential treatment findings. We maintain, and seek to show in this and the next chapter, that those practitioners who pursue a different therapeutic approach from the medical model differential-treatment one, and rely on more 'postmodern' notions like 'ill-defined' or 'non-specific' common factors, are at least as defensible and legitimate in their practice as those whose work is ESVT driven.

A non-believer perspective on the ESVT paradigm

In its underlying logic, the ESVT paradigm is a particular model concerning the nature of psychotherapy, which is underpinned, in turn, by a more general metaphysical position that necessarily entails implicit and interconnected assumptions about reality, science, knowledge and truth. Mainstream psychotherapy practice is routinely viewed through an analogy to the medical model (eg. Aho, 2002; Bohart & Tallman, 1999; Hansen, 2007; House, 1996; Stiles & Shapiro, 1989), with a central focus on *treatment*, which is viewed as analogous to drug treatment, and which seeks to 'correct' abnormal, so-called psychopathology (Parker et al, 1995; House, 2001, 2010b), just as drugs are supposed to correct or cure 'pathology'. From this, modernist view, it is believed that the treatment *qua treatment* is somehow *applied to* the problem or 'disorder' in a causal way, in order to eradicate it. As in mainstream allopathic medicine, it is further assumed that, the more specifically tailored and customised the treatment is to the 'disorder', the more likely it is to be effective. It is taken as axiomatic that differential treatment must *by definition* be more effective than so-called 'non-specific' treatment, with research then becoming a matter of demonstrating differential treatment effects – preferably via 'gold standard' RCTs. Within this world-view, therapy therefore becomes a technological enterprise, with, at worst, therapists viewed as '"behavioral engineers" rather than storytellers or moral guides' (Johnson & Sandage, 1999: 4).

A central sequela of a treatment-driven approach is that treatments must necessarily be described with as much specificity as possible, with above all, a need for a standardisable application for all identified and diagnosed 'cases' – with the predictable concomitant: explicit procedure specification or manualisation. Some ESVTers have even implied that such specificity is the ideal. If a manual were 'merely' a general statement of therapeutic principles that could be operationalised by different practitioners in different ways and contexts, then it would, of course, be impossible to research specific 'treatments' (although, recently, to be fair, there are those who have argued that manuals can be principle based – eg. Bargenquast

& Schweitzer, 2014). This highlights a key issue so often neglected in the literature – namely, the many individuals within the 'professionalised' therapy field (House, 2003) with a powerful vested interest in the medical-model world-view and its accompanying 'treatment' ideology.

The metaphor of a procedure- or manual-driven therapy implies an approach in which the practitioner follows imported, externally generated rules that do not emerge from the specificity and arguable uniqueness of a therapeutic encounter and are reasonably specific and amenable to 'protocolisation'. A manual is effectively a set of rules and prescriptions for action, a 'how-to' or rule book of operating procedures. Many practitioners, and we are among them, view this guiding metaphor as strongly contradicting widespread viewpoints, intuitions and practices in the field about the nature of therapeutic experience, and how therapy can be most appropriately conducted and researched.

The metaphysics of the ESVT paradigm and its relation to research

The ESVT research paradigm is based on conventional natural-scientific experimental logic, which many in the field believe to be quite inappropriate for therapy work. The essence of the approach is as follows. First, an attempt is made at the outset to specify a so-called independent variable, with other variables allegedly controlled or 'held constant'. Standardised measures of the dependent variable are used so that one can claim to have demonstrated a so-called linear causal relationship between the independent and dependent variables.

Such a procedure entails a whole host of highly questionable ontological assumptions, with an underpinning and routinely implicit linear-causal, mechanistic view of how psychotherapy – and the universe – works. In stark contrast, Stiles and colleagues (1998), for example, refer to what they call 'a responsive view' of therapy as an *ongoing intersubjective experience*, where issues and experiences emerge and change, often in response to what has gone before, and in quite unpredictable, unspecifiable ways. From this viewpoint, the therapeutic encounter is therefore *invented*, at least in part, as therapist and client respond to emerging and co-created contingencies that could not in principle have been specified or predicted at the outset.

Randomised controlled trial (RCT) methodology

In the ESVT paradigm, the randomised controlled trial (RCT) methodology is routinely seen as the 'method of choice' to which all research should aspire. Because the RCT is the widely recognised 'gold standard' in medicine, it is also assumed *a priori* to be the gold standard in psychotherapy research (eg. Persons, in Persons & Silberschatz, 1998; Cooper, 2011; but see Rogers, Maidman & House, 2011) – arguably, a glaring example of the colonising hegemony of a positivistic, control-orientated modernity that assumes its one-size-fits-all methodologies to be universally applicable to all dimensions of reality.

Yet the RCT approach to research may well not be a particularly valid or useful tool for the study of complex ecological systems (eg. DeGreene, 1991): for example, 'Group designs, in which patients are randomly assigned to treatment conditions, simply do not generalise to how we practice clinically' (Goldfried & Wolfe, 1996: 1015). There is, indeed, a long list of objections that, taken together, constitute a devastating 'case against' the embracing of RCT methodology in psychotherapeutic research. RCT methodology is open to a range of compelling challenges that have never been satisfactorily refuted (House & Loewenthal, 2008; cf. Hemmings, Chapter 23, this volume) – not least, that:

1. it hides, through the comparison of means, what actually happens to *individuals* in the research trial – with the consequence, for example, that there may well be people in both groups who are worse off after 'treatment'
2. it ignores the different responses of different individuals to the same treatment, so that, as Heron has argued, it simply 'cannot help with the everyday question, "What is the treatment of choice for this individual patient?"' (Goldfried & Wolfe, 1996: 198)
3. it routinely ignores the powerful effect of the mind on the body (assuming we accept that ontological distinction), and the latent, subtle, and often mysterious phenomenon of self-healing
4. it assumes unquestioningly the validity of its univariate approach, which separates out the single treatment variable from all other influences in order to assess its causal impact (as if real, lived life were remotely like that; see Hall, 1993: 193)
5. it objectifies suffering as a 'thingified' process, inappropriately reifying 'external' causal influence and ignoring subjective illness categories experienced and made sense of by the client, and ignoring too the meaning or tacit intentionality of the illness, where suffering is often a necessary route to deep change, that should be allowed and worked with, rather than focusing on removing it – see also Woolfolk, 2002; Wilson, 2009)
6. it ignores the possibility that its so-called 'statements of fact' (including variable specification and measurement) may be unavoidably theory and value laden and can only be formulated *within a pre-existing (and therefore self-fulfilling) set of theoretical/metaphysical assumptions*, which can then so easily become a circular proving of what was assumed to exist at the outset (see Parker et al, 1995).

In drug-dominated, allopathic scientific medicine, with its cause-and-effect materialist cosmology, the 'independent variable' is allegedly controlled as tightly as possible, primarily in order to identify the medication's 'active ingredients'. In uncritically mimicking a procedure that is even open to challenge within natural-science methodology, psychotherapy research duly proceeds to conduct dismantling studies that claim to identify active 'operative ingredients'. Moreover, the unquestioned underpinning assumption that the best way to practise therapy is to discover general nomothetic laws and then treat individual cases as specific instances of these general laws or categories (Schön, 1983) never seems to be even acknowledged by ESVT proponents, let alone opened up to critical reflection.

The 'treatment', then, is the independent variable, which is applied to the 'dependent variable', *the client* (or the client's 'disorder'), the goal being to 'operationalise' the treatment clearly and unambiguously. The more precisely the independent variable can be operationalised, the better for plotting predictable, specifiable linear-causal relationships between it and the dependent variable, or so the thinking goes.

As already mentioned, ESVTers routinely criticise 'ill-defined' or 'non-specific' common factors, such as 'the relationship' dimension, presumably because the latter cannot be specified as a series of unambiguously definable, measurable and controllable therapist strategies. In short, a kind of epistemologically naïve, 1930s logical positivism seems to dominate the research consciousness of the ESVT tendency, as they dismiss as meaningless concepts that cannot be easily operationalised within their positivistic cosmology. Yet if, as many practitioners believe, it is precisely these difficult-to-define 'imponderables' that are *most* important in many a healing and change experience (see our Chapter 19, this volume), then to embrace a methodology that systematically rules them out of account, and which instead privileges only that which is measurable and controllable, may well be to do a kind of methodological *violence* to the reality we are interrogating, and certainly radically to misrepresent it – and in what is, ironically, a most unbefitting *un*scientific way.

We can predict that, in this positivistic instrumental universe, any findings that 'the relationship' plays an important role in therapeutic change will likely lead to a fundamentally misguided attempt to 'technologise' the relational – which in turn betrays a fundamental misunderstanding of what we might call 'the efficacy of the relational'. For, at worst, it too will then be studied so that it can be 'manipulated' as a form of 'treatment' – and the intangible '*healing through relationship*' experience will inevitably be lost. In such circumstances, if such healing still manages somehow to occur, it will be *in spite of*, rather than because of, any positivistic atomising of 'the relationship' that is attempted.

We view ESVT proponents as inhabiting a modernist, mechanistic, linearly determined world, where near-perfect predictability and control are at least in principle achievable. Underlying this world-view appears to be a traditional Newtonian cosmology of the universe as a giant clockwork mechanism. A clock can of course be dismantled, and how each part contributes to the operation of the whole can be accurately specified. Using a simple additive model of main effects and interactions, ultimately the whole clock can be known theoretically, and its workings predicted and controlled without remainder or unaccounted-for 'noise'. Further, because it is a completely deterministic universe, as discussed earlier, the goal of research is to establish the independent variable's *control* over the dependent variable. In sum, in this cosmology the client becomes truly a 'dependent variable' (a *live* dependent variable, to be sure) on which the independent variable is then operating to bring about its effects.

Intimations of an alternative paradigm

A paradigm very different from that just described can be derived from two (and by no means only two) prominent therapeutic approaches: client- or person-centred therapy, and the so-called 'constructive' therapies (for example, strategic/solution-focused therapy and its descendants). Existential-phenomenological and postmodern therapy approaches would be other examples. As with the ESVT paradigm, we can distinguish both a practice level and an underlying philosophical or metaphysical level.

The nature of therapy: practice level

Taking client-centred therapy and strategic therapy as exemplars, they share some common assumptions. Both adopt a holistic attitude: the therapist *as person* is working with a whole person in order to help the latter remove obstacles to living what, for them, is a more fulfilling life. This contrasts markedly with an approach in which a 'treatment' is being applied to 'dysfunctional' *parts* or aspects of the person (egos, schemas, conditioned responses etc). Second, the therapist relies on clients' own capacities for self-healing (Bohart & Tallman, 1996, 1999), and works within the client's frame of reference. The client's own creative 'generativity' is an integral part of this process, and insights and solutions emerge from and are co-created by the therapist and client interrelating, rather than being dictated *a priori* by a 'cookbook' list of treatments matched to problems, conditions or diagnoses. Third, the practitioner is guided by a set of *broad relational principles*, which can be, and routinely are, embodied or actualised by different practitioners in relation with different clients in different ways. The resulting therapy experience will therefore often look very different from one therapist–client pair to another, while still being principle-guided.

Moreover, therapy is generally not really a *treatment* in the medical-model sense of that term. In contrast to the idea that the therapist is 'treating' a 'disorder', therapy becomes a co-created dialogue between two (or more) intelligent, living, embodied beings. The guiding metaphor for this approach is therefore *conversation* and *dialogue* (eg. Anderson, 1997), and therapy is no longer seen as a medical-like treatment. To try to proceduralise or manualise a co-created and inherently unpredictable dialogue is contrary to what both intuition and rational argument suggest genuine, authentic dialogue might consist of. The metaphor of manualisation and procedural specification is therefore fundamentally antithetical to the guiding metaphor of this alternative approach.

Since, in this cosmology, successful therapy relies crucially on clients' active, creative intelligence, interventions become things therapist *and* client use to fashion therapeutic movement or 'solutions' (Bohart & Tallman, 1999). Contrary to the ESVT paradigm explored earlier, it is neither helpful nor accurate to conceptualise these 'ways of being' as 'independent variables' that operate on 'dependent variables' (clients) in order to give rise to therapeutic 'effects'.

Furthermore, if we accept the psychodynamic view that a significant aspect of human consciousness is not, and never can be, amenable to conscious awareness, and if the therapeutic change process itself occurs, at least in part, beyond conscious awareness and articulation, then to assume through our conceptualisations and methodologies that all that matters *is* available to conscious awareness will necessarily mis-specify, and quite possibly grossly distort, what is actually happening therapeutically in any change process. It would then follow that not only will any modelling or theorising arising from such highly partial research procedures necessarily be inadequate, but we will have no way of finding out through empirical science just how inadequate it is. In our view, that some psychoanalytic practitioners have attempted to manualise psychodynamic therapy (eg. Lemma et al, 2011; House, 2012) does not detract from this key point.

We might also observe in passing that psychodynamic thinking is likely to have much of interest to say about the motivation underpinning and driving the wish to make the nature of the therapeutic process consciously explicit and controllable in its entirety, but such an important discussion is beyond the scope of this chapter. In the kind of alternative paradigm we are proposing here, then, solutions are in no way 'applied' to clients. From a systemic perspective, for example, two clients with what is notionally 'the same' problem (for instance, 'depression') may differ considerably in how the problem was generated, how it is maintained, how it is self-defined and experienced and how it interacts with their life spaces (Kleinman, 1988). Solutions, or paths to progress, will therefore accordingly vary, and it would most certainly do a kind of violence to this paradigm's core ethos to apply a standardised solution or protocol to them. Rather, solutions *emerge* out of an intelligent inter-relational dialogue, and are in that sense emergent and necessarily idiosyncratic, even unique.

With client-centred therapy in particular, it is the 'being' of the therapist and client in indissoluble relationship that is assumed to be therapeutic, and not specific 'therapist operations', skills, or programmatic interventions. This kind of view is very difficult to understand from a modernist paradigmatic position, which claims that only what is definable and measurable has meaning and effectivity – or even can be said to exist. There may be, and probably is, a potentially *infinite* set of different ways in which therapists could embody and actualise the relational qualities of warmth, empathy and genuineness with different clients. Therapy 'works' through the authentic inter-relational *presence* of the therapist, rather than through specific technological or skill-based operations. It is very difficult to imagine, for example, how one could measure, specify, control or manualise authenticity, or 'being yourself' in therapy. Yet there does now seem to be some empirical support for a view of therapy that values authenticity (eg. Elliott, Greenberg & Lietaer,

2013). Finally, both person-centred and constructive-therapy approaches place *responsiveness* first. That is, they rely on moment-to-moment phenomenological sensitivity to the subtlety and complexity of the emerging process, and on their ability to respond appropriately from unique moment to unique moment (see our Chapter 19 in this volume).

Kinds of interventions, then, emerge out of the dialogue with the client, with the therapist effectively using the resources in/of the moment. A client's difficulty or problem would not therefore be treated merely as an instance of a more generalised category of 'disorder'; nor would a standardised 'treatment' be applied to the client for a given 'disorder'. Indeed, a completely different kind of intervention (or interventions) might have been co-created with different clients who were describing *the same* 'symptoms' or 'disorder', depending on the client and her or his life, how client and therapist met and what they co-created together, and on the particular therapeutic experience that their unique meeting generated. Further still, a different therapist working with the same client might have productively used an entirely different approach or interventions, while still being faithful to general strategic principles – and still being effective. Viewed from within such a paradigmatic world-view, then, the very project of generalisation-driven proceduralisation or manualisation is quite literally nonsensical and fundamentally wrong-headed – and it is exceedingly difficult, if not impossible, to imagine how the kinds of approaches described above could be proceduralised in any meaningful sense. To quote Rosenbaum (1994: 248):

> Therapy requires a constant, ongoing process where the therapist adjusts to the client, and the client adjusts to this adjustment. This makes the manualising of therapy precisely the wrong strategy for psychotherapy research.

Some attempts have, of course, been made to manualise client-centred therapy (eg. Greenberg & Watson, 1998; Sanders & Hill, 2014). What they create is an excellent analogue of client-centred therapy mapped into a different intellectual universe, but they certainly do not fully represent client-centred therapy as we understand it. In sum, the very idea of following a pre-decided procedure or a manual is antithetical to the fundamental nature of client-centred therapy.

The alternative paradigm we are describing here has *subtlety* and *discernment* at its core – along the kind of lines written about by educationalists Max van Manen, Rudolf Steiner and Robert Sardello (see van Manen, 1986; Sardello, 2002; see our Chapter 19, this volume). On this view, to call what therapists do in their work 'interventions' fundamentally misrepresents it in ways that distort the human, experienced meaning of it for both therapist and client. Therapists do not typically do or say something deliberately in order to 'intervene'; rather, for example, they will often be genuinely interested and curious, or will be a witness and respond from that experience – albeit in a way that pays attention to the therapeutic helping context in which the experience is unfolding. Yet this perspective is certainly *not* a recipe for an undisciplined '*anything* that is experiential, goes' (see Norcross, 1999: xviii).

In sum, it seems to us particularly absurd to think of many therapists all trying to 'provide' the same 'intervention' in a standardised fashion, when arguably what is so clearly healing about a given unique, contextual experience is its natural and unspecifiable spontaneity and human quality. This may sound rather like a straw-man caricature – but we are merely describing the logical implications stemming from the world-view entailed in the ESVT paradigm. In terms of research implications, all this is to argue that we would do well to come up with meaningful ways to study client-centred therapy phenomenologically in its 'natural setting' (see van Manen, 1997), rather than distort its nature by manualising it to fit into a paradigm whose very nature is really alien and even procedurally 'violent' to it.

The nature of therapy: metaphysical level

At the metaphysical or philosophical level, there are two key aspects to the alternative paradigm we are propounding.

The nature of professional practice and the 'uniqueness' assumption

First, psychotherapy is conceived of, above all, as *a practice*. The kinds of knowledge and the way knowledge is used within a given practice are different from the goals of acquiring scientific or theoretical knowledge (Schön, 1983). The goal of conventional 'scientific knowledge' is the nomothetic one of formulating general laws, while the goal of practice is the idiographic one of focusing on the unique, particular individual case or situation.

The approach to practice described above is highly compatible with what a number of writers have described as the real nature of professional practice across all professions (eg. Bourdieu, 1990; Schön, 1983; Sundararajan, 2002). In any walk of life or profession, practice is fundamentally different from the approach to practice implied by the ESVT approach. The manualisation mentality is an instance of what Schön, Habermas (eg. 1972), the Frankfurt School of Theodor Adorno and others have called 'technical rationality', being an example of the traditional way in which science is to be applied to practice. However, based on Schön's studies of practitioners in a variety of professions, it does not represent how expert professionals actually practise – even, tellingly, professionals who use conventional scientific knowledge, such as architects and engineers. The manualisation and procedure-fixated approach (and ESVT in general) is also an example of what Nadler and colleagues (1995), in their studies of how professionals creatively solve problems in business, call the 'traditional' problem-solving model, and does not represent how creative business professionals actually develop effective solutions to problems.

According to Schön, Nadler and colleagues, and others, effective and successful professionals treat each new problem or case as unique. In stark contrast, the proceduralist manualisation approach starts out from an (often implicit, unarticulated) *assumption of similarity* (for example, 'This case is merely an instance of a more general category'), and only embraces uniqueness when the manual fails. In real life, however, one case is rarely, at the very least, sufficiently like another to lead to the mechanistic generalisation of a thought-replacing rule from one case to another. In some sense, manualised generalising may sometimes work, or *appear* to work (which is different), but in all cases it is flexible, open discernment and the judgment of the practitioner that transcends and supersedes the application of any such rules.

To use the language of positivism for a moment, uniqueness exists in the real world because each individual case is a complex combination of many different 'variables', with 'more variables – kinds of possible moves, norms, and interrelationships of these – than can be represented in a finite model' (Schön, 1983: 79). To quote DeGreene (1991, quoted in Nadler, Hibino & Farrell, 1995: 89): 'The concept of clearly definable and correlatable independent, intervening and dependent variables may be completely inappropriate in a dynamic, mutually causal world.' Phenomena in the real world are characterised by '... complexity, uncertainty, [and] instability' (Schön, 1983: 39), and, for Robert Sternberg (1987, quoted in Nadler, Hibino & Farrell, 1995: 273), 'Real problems are often poorly structured and hard to define.'

In medical practice, for example, patient care is seldom a simple matter of prescribing precise treatments for distinct, unambiguously definable disease states. Rather, patients typically present as 'polysymptomatic', their complaints often being vague, and of an emotionally tinged (or sometimes drenched) nature. Neat, clearly identifiable syndromes/diseases often fail to emerge from the review of symptoms (eg. Sobel, 1995). Indeed, doctors use hunch and intuition far more often than 'medical science' cares to acknowledge (Scovern, 1999: 287) – with 'the art of the healer' and/or culturally sanctioned or legitimated healing practices (Frank, 1973) perhaps being far more significant and efficacious than the 'objective' diagnoses of the scientist-practitioner. Schön refers to an ophthalmologist (more of a 'scientist' than a psychotherapist, one might plausibly assume) who says: 'In 80 or 85 percent of the cases, the patient's complaints and symptoms do not fall into familiar categories of diagnosis and treatment' (1983: 64).

The uniqueness assumption therefore means that the practitioner focuses on the particulars of each individual case, rather than the distracting wild goose chase of how a given case fits into a general category (Schön, 1983). Both general principles and prior knowledge are, of course, significant and can be drawn on to help understand the unique case but are not privileged over and do not override the necessity of dealing with the uniqueness.

Thus, Schön maintains that, '[The practitioner] is not dependent on the categories of established theory and technique, but constructs a new theory of the unique case' (1983: 68). Actual solution-finding in real-life situations therefore involves a complex and normally quite unpredictable blend of nomothetic knowledge, the use of prior exemplars, intuition (however we might try to define it – see Atkinson & Claxton, 2000; our Chapter 19 in this volume), and considerable tacit knowledge (Polanyi, 1966) gained through experience – all applied to understanding each unique case. In addition, practice involves an ongoing, experimental, self-correcting *dialogue* with the situation itself. Through such a dialogue, solutions (if appropriate) are frequently forged that are, at the least, creative modifications of old solutions, and, at best, often entirely new ones that are discovered through that dialogue (or emergence). Moreover, such emerging co-creativity often *is* the essence of the therapy – a phenomenon that again would appear quite nonsensical from a narrow ESVT perspective.

Schön also refers to something akin to the so-called 'law of unintended consequences', noting that:

> Because of this complexity, the designer's moves tend, happily or unhappily, to produce consequences other than those intended. When this happens, the designer may take account of the unintended changes he has made… by forming new appreciations and understandings and by making new moves. He shapes the situation… the situation 'talks back', and he responds. (1983: 79)

Such a description of practice is compatible with our earlier description of practice in (for example) client-centred and strategic/solution-focused therapy. In this alternate paradigm, then, the therapist treats each case as unique – meaning that each case is its own unique blend of what is similar to other cases, and what is different. Any response or solution that emerges is developed through a process of ongoing experimentation and discerning *judgment* by the professional and client, wherein prior knowledge and ideas are tested, modified and so on, until responses, new ways forward or solutions are developed.

Standardised nomothetic knowledge is one possible aspect of what might be used to develop an approach or a solution with an individual client. ESVT- and RCT-based information would then be just one source of information that can be factored into the professional's and client's decision-making process, but there would certainly be no automatic assumption that, just because a particular treatment has been procedurally manualised and found through an RCT to 'work' for a given 'disorder', that this is what the professional and client would necessarily use in this particular instance. Given that the description of practice presented here is compatible with how Schön (1983) and others have found that practitioners *in general* function, this seems an entirely reasonable way to conceptualise a way of practice, notwithstanding its being antithetical to programmatic manualisation. Accordingly, if we wish really to learn how to be effective practitioners, it would be counterproductive, and potentially disastrous, to force both research and practice into a mould that does not represent and do justice to real, effective practice.

Conclusions

In what is the first part of this two-chapter essay (part 2 follows next, in Chapter 19), we have looked in some depth at the question of contested paradigms in psychotherapy, through the media of the troublesome (for some) dodo bird verdict, the issue of common or 'non-specific' factors, the ontological and methodological shortcomings of positivistic approaches to research, and the mentality and practice of clinical 'manualisation'. As made clear in a number of chapters in this volume, CBT is very much a creature of 'modernity' and all that goes with the modernist world-view or paradigm. As such, if it can be demonstrated that the epistemological and ontological assumptions of a modernist cosmology itself, and certainly as applied to psychotherapy experience, are open to severe and arguably devastating challenge – not least from incommensurable paradigms that are, at the very least, as legitimate as modernist ones – then it follows from this that we can by no means take at anything like face value the hegemonic claims of 'scientific' superiority that routinely emanate from the ESVT tendency in general, and from some in the CBT practitioner-field in particular.

In our next chapter, we consider further the fascinating phenomenon of what has been termed 'the intuitive practitioner' (Atkinson & Claxton, 2000) as just one example of the kinds of key relational qualities that the positivist research mentality finds extremely difficult, if not impossible, to encompass. In the process, we also look to reclaim for alternative, post-modern therapy paradigms the 'empirically supported treatment' label that has been quite unjustifiably colonised and annexed by the modernist ESVT tendency in the psychotherapy field.

References

Aho K (2008). Medicalizing mental health: a phenomenological alternative. *Journal of Medical Humanities 29*: 243–259.

Anderson H (1997). *Conversation, Language and Possibilities: a postmodern approach to therapy*. New York, NY: Basic Books.

Atkinson T, Claxton G (eds) (2000). *The Intuitive Practitioner: on the value of not always knowing what one is doing*. Milton Keynes: Open University Press.

Bargenquast R, Schweitzer R (2014). Metacognitive narrative psychotherapy for people diagnosed with schizophrenia: an outline of a principle-based treatment manual. *Psychosis: Psychological, Social and Integrative Approaches 6*: 155–165.

Berman JS, Reich CM (2010). Investigator allegiance and the evaluation of psychotherapy outcome research. *European Journal of Psychotherapy and Counselling 12*: 11–21.

Beutler LE (1998). Identifying empirically supported treatments: what if we don't? *Journal of Consulting and Clinical Psychology 66*: 113–120.

Bohart AC, Tallman KA (1996). The active client: therapy as self-help. *Journal of Humanistic Psychology 36*(3): 7–30.

Bohart A, Tallman K (1999). *How Clients Make Therapy Work: the process of active self-healing*. Washington, DC: American Psychological Association.

Bourdieu P (1990). *The Logic of Practice* (R Nice trans). Stanford, CA: Stanford University Press.

Budd R, Hughes I (2009). The Dodo bird verdict – controversial, inevitable and important: a commentary on 30 years of meta-analyses. *Clinical Psychology and Psychotherapy 16*: 510–522.

Cooper M (2011). Meeting the demand for evidence-based practice. *Therapy Today 22*(4): 10–16.

DeGreene KB (1991). Rigidity and fragility of large sociotechnical systems: advanced information technology, the dominant coalition, and paradigm shift at the end of the 20th century. *Behavioral Science 36*: 64–79.

Elliott R, Greenberg LS, Lietaer G (2013). Research on humanistic-experiential psychotherapies. In: Lambert MJ (ed). Bergin and Garfield's *Handbook of Psychotherapy and Behavior Change* (6th ed). New York, NY: John Wiley & Sons.

Frank JD (1989). Non-specific aspects of treatment: the view of a psychotherapist. In: Shepherd M, Sartorius N (eds). *Non-Specific Aspects of Treatment*. Toronto: Hans Huber Publishers (pp95–114).

Frank JD (1973). *Persuasion and Healing*. Baltimore, MD: John Hopkins University Press.

Goldfried MR, Wolfe BE (1996). Psychotherapy practice and research: repairing a strained alliance. *American Psychologist 51*: 1007–1016.

Greenberg LS, Watson J (1998). Experiential therapy of depression: differential effects of client-centered relationship conditions and process-experiential interventions. *Psychotherapy Research 8*: 210–224.

Habermas J (1972). *Knowledge and Human Interests*. London: Heinemann.

Hall J (1993). *The Reluctant Adult: an exploration of choice*. Bridport: Prism Press.

Hansen JT (2007). Should counseling be considered a health care profession? Critical thoughts on the transition to a health care ideology. *Journal of Counseling and Development 85*: 286–293.

Heron J (1996). *Co-operative Inquiry: research into the human condition*. London: Sage.

House R (2012). General practice counselling amidst the 'audit culture': history, dynamics and subversion of/in the hypermodern National Health Service. *Psychodynamic Practice: Individuals, Groups and Organisations 18*: 51–70.

House R (2010a). 'Psy' research beyond late-modernity: towards praxis-congruent research. *Psychotherapy and Politics International 8*: 13–20.

House R (2010b). *In, Against and Beyond Therapy*. Ross-on-Wye: PCCS Books.

House R (2003). *Therapy Beyond Modernity: deconstructing and transcending profession-centred therapy*. London: Karnac Books.

House R (2001). Psychopathology, psychosis and the Kundalini: postmodern perspectives on unusual subjective experience. In: Clarke I (ed). *Psychosis and Spirituality: exploring the new frontier*. London: Whurr (pp107–125). (Plus composite references retrievable from the Critical Psychiatry website at www.uea.ac.uk/~wp276/article.htm (accessed 4 February 2018).

House R (1996). Counselling in general practice: a plea for ideological engagement. *Counselling 7*(1): 40–44.

House R, Loewenthal D (2008). Editorial. Special issue on 'CBT in Question'. *European Journal of Psychotherapy and Counselling 10*(3): 181–186.

House R, Totton N (1997). *Implausible Professions: arguments for pluralism and autonomy in psychotherapy and counselling*. Ross-on-Wye: PCCS Books.

Hubble MA, Duncan BL, Miller SD (eds) (1999). *The Heart and Soul of Change: what works in therapy*. Washington, DC: American Psychological Association.

Johnson EL, Sandage SJ (1999). A postmodern reconstruction of psychotherapy: orienteering, religion and the healing of the soul. *Psychotherapy: Theory, Research, Practice, Training 36*: 1–15.

Kleinman A (1988). *The Illness Narratives: suffering, healing and the human condition*. New York, NY: Basic Books.

Kuhn TS (1977) *The Essential Tension: selected studies in scientific tradition and change*. Chicago, IL: University of Chicago Press.

Kuhn TS (1970). *The Structure of Scientific Revolutions* (2nd ed). Chicago, IL: University of Chicago Press.

Lambert MJ (ed) (2013). Bergin and Garfield's *Handbook of Psychotherapy and Behavior Change* (6th ed). New York, NY: John Wiley.

Lampropoulos GK (2000). A re-examination of the empirically supported treatments critiques. *Psychotherapy Research 10*: 474–487.

Lemma A, Target M, Fonagy P (2011). The development of a brief psychodynamic protocol for depression: Dynamic Interpersonal Therapy (DIT). *Psychoanalytic Psychotherapy 24*: 329–347.

Levendorsky AA, Hopwood CJ (2017). A clinical science approach to training first year clinicians to navigate therapeutic relationships. *Journal of Psychotherapy Integration 27*: 153–171.

Loewenthal D (2010). Introduction to Special Issue on 'Researcher Allegiance in the Psychological Therapies'. *European Journal of Psychotherapy and Counselling 12*: 1.

Luborsky L, Rosenthal R, Diguer L, Andrusyna TP, Berman JS, Levitt JT et al (2002). The dodo bird verdict is alive and well – mostly. *Clinical Psychology: Science and Practice 9*(1): 2–12.

Nadler G, Hibino S, Farrell J (1995). *Creative Solution Finding: the triumph of breakthrough thinking over conventional problem solving*. Rocklin, CA: Prima Publishing.

Norcross JC (ed) (2011). *Psychotherapy Relationships that Work: evidence-based responsiveness*. New York, NY: Oxford University Press.

Norcross JC (1999). Foreword. In: Hubble MA, Duncan BL, Miller SD (eds). *The Heart and Soul of Change: what works in therapy*. Washington, DC: American Psychological Association (ppxvii–xix).

Parker I, Georgaca E, Harper D, McLaughlin T (1995). *Deconstructing Psychopathology*. London: Sage.

Persons JB, Silberschatz G (1998). Are results of randomized controlled trials useful to psychotherapists? *Journal of Consulting and Clinical Psychology 66*: 126–135.

Polanyi M (1966). *The Tacit Dimension*. New York, NY: Doubleday.

Rogers A, Maidman J, House R (2011). The bad faith of evidence-based practice: beyond counsels of despair. *Therapy Today 22*(6): 26–29.

Rosenbaum R (1994). Single-session therapies: intrinsic integration? *Journal of Psychotherapy Integration 4*: 229–252.

Sanders P, Hill A (2014). *Counselling for Depression: a person-centred and experiential approach to practice*. London: Sage.

Sardello R (2002). *The Power of Soul: living the twelve virtues*. Charlottesville, VA: Hampton Roads Publishing Co.

Schön DA (1983). *The Reflective Practitioner: how professionals think in action*. New York, NY: Basic Books.

Scovern AW (1999). From placebo to alliance: the role of common factors in medicine. In: Hubble MA, Duncan BL, Miller SD (eds). *The Heart and Soul of Change: what works in therapy*. Washington, DC: American Psychological Association (pp259–296).

Shedler J (2010). The efficacy of psychodynamic psychotherapy. *American Psychologist 65*: 98–109.

Sobel DS (1995). Rethinking medicine: improving health outcomes with cost-effective psychosocial interventions. *Psychosomatic Medicine 57*: 234–244.

Stiles WB, Shapiro DA (1989). Abuse of the drug metaphor in psychotherapy process outcome research. *Clinical Psychology Review 9*: 521–544.

Stiles WB, Honos-Webb L, Surko M (1998) Responsiveness in psychotherapy. *Clinical Psychology: Science and Practice 5*: 439–458.

Sundararajan L (2002). Humanistic psychotherapy and the scientist-practitioner debate: an 'embodied' perspective. *Journal of Humanistic Psychology 42*(2): 34–47.

Task Force on Promotion and Dissemination of Psychological Procedures, Division of Clinical Psychology of the American Psychological Association (1995). Training and dissemination of empirically validated psychological treatments: report and recommendations. *The Clinical Psychologist 48*: 3–23.

van Kalmthout MA, Schaap C, Wojciechowski FL (eds) (1985). *Common Factors in Psychotherapy*. Lisse: Swets & Zeitlinger.

van Manen M (1997). *Researching Lived Experience: human science for an action sensitive pedagogy* (2nd ed). New York, NY: SUNY Press.

van Manen M (1986). *The Tone of Teaching*. Richmond Hill, Ontario: Scholastic/TAB Publications.

Wampold BE, Imel ZE (2015). *The Great Psychotherapy Debate: the evidence for what makes psychotherapy work* (2nd ed). New York, NY: Routledge.

Wilson EG (2009). *Against Happiness: in praise of melancholy*. New York, NY: Farrar Straus Giroux.

Wittgenstein L (1973/1958). *Philosophical Investigations* (GEM Anscombe trans). Oxford: Wiley-Blackwell.

Woolfolk RL (2002). The power of negative thinking: truth, melancholia, and the tragic sense of life. *Journal of Theoretical and Philosophical Psychology 22*: 19–26.

19 Empirically supported/validated treatments as modernist ideology, part 2: alternative perspectives on research and practice*

Richard House and Arthur C Bohart

> What is most tangible has the least meaning and it is perverse then to identify the tangible with the real. (Polanyi, 1966)

In Chapter 18 we looked in some depth at how CBT is just a part of a wider paradigmatic world-view that we can (rather inadequately) term 'modernity' (eg. Toulmin, 1990). A strong theme that comes out of that discussion is that, as Brazier and Lees make clear in their chapters 8 and 9 in this volume, *not* to attempt to locate therapeutic practices and their assumptive philosophies within the evolution of ideas and human consciousness is a major (and telling) omission. For, if we fail to seek, and gain, some kind of philosophical purchase on just what is entailed in the assumptive world-views and practices to which we implicitly or explicitly adhere, then this can, at worst, lead to a kind of uncritically damaging, *paradigm-bound 'acting-out'*, which will tend to be self-reinforcing and 'status-quo preserving' – that is, generating an inherently conservative 'status quo theory', to use the term coined by theorist of postmodernity, David Harvey (1973). This is surely the very antithesis of the kind of critical, deconstructive thinking that is arguably the way in which human consciousness can and does healthily evolve (Tarnas, 1996).

In this chapter we will look more closely at the kinds of phenomena that could be argued to be central in an alternative paradigmatic world-view and its associated research undertaking, paying special attention to issues like subtlety,

* This chapter is a substantial elaboration of Arthur C Bohart's chapter entitled 'A passionate critique of empirically supported treatments and the provision of an alternative paradigm', which first appeared in Watson JC, Goldman RN, Warner MS (eds). *Client-Centered and Experiential Psychotherapy in the Twenty-First Century: advances in theory, research and practice.* Ross-on-Wye: PCCS Books, 2002 (pp258–277).

intuition, discernment and 'the tacit' in human relational experience (Polanyi, 1966) – *phenomenological* qualities *par excellence* that rarely if ever figure in the kinds of scientistic research that regrettably dominate our field and in modernist therapy practices.

The role of science

The realisation that therapy is the *practice* of a professional activity leads us to view the role of science in a different way. In a practice-view of what therapists are doing in their work, the practice itself is not, nor can it ever be, we maintain, mechanistically scientific. Artists and artisans use science inventively and unpredictably to solve real-life problems in ways that simply cannot be specified at the outset (eg. Lawrence, 2005), and any such knowledge is certainly not 'manualistically' applied.

It is interesting and illuminating to imagine a thought-experiment world in which an alternative paradigm such as the one we are advocating here were routinely accepted, and in which no one might even think of doing empirically supported/validated treatments (ESVTs). For a start, they would ask very different research questions – for example, they might want to know about the principles of change involved in helping, and how expert practitioners blend tacit and explicit knowledge to co-create ways of being with, or making productive decisions with, individual clients. Or they might inquire into whether there is any causal connection between the kinds of experiential practices undertaken by therapy trainees and their capacity for intuitive relating and tacit knowing.

Alternatively again, they might be interested in questions concerning sensitivity to individual cases, or they might be interested in how practitioners learn from, and adjust to, ongoing feedback they receive in therapy sessions. Such knowledge would certainly not then be proceduralised or manualised, because it would be understood that *practice knowledge* is different from (but includes) more conventional scientific knowledge (Schön, 1983; Sundararajan, 2002). This is the kind of research that would tend to be pursued, then, not writing theory-based treatment manuals and then engaging in RCTs to test these manuals for so-called 'standardised disorders'.

In short, research would tend to investigate *principles and processes of change*, and even the spiritual aspects of change, in so far as they are researchable (eg. Steiner, 1918/1989; Heron, 1998). What would be useful to practitioners, for example, might be to study the tacit-knowing processes used by successful practitioners to discover whether they can be explicitly improved upon or deepened. Beginning attempts have already been made in this regard. We can say, for instance, with some degree of scientific backing, that therapists who are a) adept at facilitating the formation of a good therapeutic alliance; b) adept at dialoguing with the client, empathically listening, and taking the client's frame of reference centrally into account (Duncan, Hubble & Miller, 1997; Norcross, 2011); c) adept at supporting client involvement (Bohart & Tallman, 1999) and mobilising their hope and optimism (Duncan, Hubble & Miller, 1997; Greenberg, 1999; Snyder, Michael & Cheavens, 1999); d) are adept at fostering the developing of insight, development of new perspectives, and clarification of the problem (Grawe, 1997); e) allow or foster problem actuation in the learning environment of therapy (Grawe, 1997), and f) provide the opportunity for mastery experiences (Grawe, 1997) will be more likely to be effective and successful.

In this sense, practitioners who work with these kinds of experiences could legitimately be said to be practising therapy in an 'empirically supported' fashion, although they do not necessarily practise (RCT-endorsed) empirically supported *treatments*. If it turns out that these are indeed the kinds of qualities that are more important than standardised treatment packages for specific 'disorders', then the whole modernist ESVT approach (see our previous chapter 18) may well turn out to have been an unfortunate and highly wasteful distraction – a mystifying detour that has actually taken us *further away from* a truly 'scientific' understanding (broadly defined) of therapy and relational experience.

The nature of the human relational experience

At a deeper level still, our alternative paradigm is arguably far more compatible with a postmodern, non-deterministic, post-foundational view of the universe (House, 2003) than it is with 19th century Newtonian mechanics. Postmodernism is in fact not an 'ism', or any kind of thing, but rather a key transitional moment in the evolution of ideas and human consciousness – a moment that denotes both an important disillusionment with the objectivist Enlightenment project of modernity, and a liminal potential space that presages something that is as yet unknown and undefined (and may, of course, remain intrinsically so, as 'knowing' and 'definition' themselves are increasingly problematised – see, for example, Clarke, 2005; Hart, Nelson & Puhakka, 1997). Not only, then, is there the question of the place of the transpersonal and the spiritual in forms of knowing (see, for example, Baruss, 1996; Heron, 1998; Clarke, 2005; Hart, Nelson & Puhakka, 1997, 2000), but, even at the level of modernist science, there is a degree of indeterminacy in the universe, and reality will never be known with 100% predictability – *not* because we simply don't possess the computational capacity to learn everything (a purely practical problem), but because of the very nature of knowing itself. Complete predictability is not even in principle possible.

Our alternative paradigmatic approach has some affinity with a systems view that is, in turn, compatible with Stiles and colleagues' (1998) notion of responsiveness. The two complex, intersubjective 'systems' that are therapist and client influence one another and psychically interpenetrate in a multitude of different and often unspecifiable ways: verbally, non-verbally, emotionally, bodily, cognitively, perceptually, behaviourally, and even, some might argue, spiritually or transpersonally. These multiple paths of influence cross and re-cross in dynamic, circular, non-linearly causal ways. On this kind of view, *a 'meeting of persons' is a complex, indissolubly holistic phenomenon that simply cannot be dismantled into component, linear-causal parts.* There are just far too many ways in which two individuals can 'meet' and psychically interpenetrate, and 'meeting' even within the 'system' of the same two individuals can vary from moment to moment, as these two systems themselves change, mutually influence one another, and evolve.

Talking about 'meeting' or encounter in this way may seem too 'ill-defined' and wishy-washy to ESVT advocates, who perhaps demand that the therapy process be fully specified and articulated, but that is because its very nature is that of a complex, interlocking, shifting phenomenon, not reducible to easily specified behaviours or their combinations. What is easily forgotten is that the label of 'wishy-washiness' is nothing more than a paradigm-bound belief underpinned by a modernist ideological mentality that ontologically assumes (typically in an unexamined way) that 'reality' is necessarily relatively sharply and easily definable and capturable. As critics of logical positivism have relentlessly pointed out, it is also a move of faulty logic to assume that what cannot be measured and accurately specified therefore doesn't exist or can safely be treated as if it doesn't. Thus, because of what we believe to be the mutual, ongoing reciprocal influence of the dynamic system that constitutes a therapeutic meeting or encounter, we maintain that an operationalisable 'independent variable' cannot sustainably exist in psychotherapy research.

Again, procedure-fixated manualisation may offer some kind of reassuring illusion that such a variable is validly specifiable, but within our paradigm, this is merely an illusion – albeit, perhaps, a comforting one for some. When complex systems interpenetrate, it is both philosophically incoherent in principle and impossible in practice to chart simple linear-causal relationships between input from one system to another. Therapeutic interventions simply do not map in a one-to-one fashion into client effects, but rather set up perturbations in complex ecological systems where, at best, all we will ever be able to expect are partial, incomplete, and therefore *quite possibly misleading* correlations between inputs and ultimate outputs. Predictability may sometimes be possible, but it is inherently imperfect and probabilistic.

Further, and to add to the complexity, because of the systemic nature of the co-creating intersubjective meeting, along with the phenomenon of emergence, the very meaning of any intervention shifts and changes as an ongoing function of its place in that evolving complex system. Because we realise that we can never have perfect predictability, and that there is no necessary standard solution for a given problem, we need to just try things out, trusting our phenomenological experience and intuition, experimenting, self-correcting, and so on. This in turn leads us to operating *intelligently*, and it then becomes important, in practice and in research, to *consult* with the system being worked with (see Heron, 1996).

Thus, one works *with* the system, not *on* the system. The systems involved must therefore be viewed as self-correcting – both therapist and client. The process is inherently *discovery oriented*, including creative generation of new insights and solutions through processes of dialoguing with the challenge or problem, and then reflexively correcting in an ongoing way. Ultimately, each approach or solution will be unique to that system's intersubjective nature, and unfolding, sometimes in very obvious ways, sometimes in relatively subtle ways. This also implies that there is no one solution to any given problem: many different solutions may 'fit' a given problem (equifinality) – if, indeed, we are even to speak the discourse of 'problems'. Thus, this approach is much more based on metaphors of *responsiveness* and *resonance*. Moreover, responsiveness and resonance are primary, and not additions or bolts-on to a standardised format. As argued in our previous chapter, the client is not a 'dependent variable' to be operated on by an 'independent variable'.

Tacit knowledge and role of the therapy practitioner

In Chapter 18 we referred in passing to the issue of tacit knowledge. Effective practitioners do not practise by following set procedures or manuals but learn how to use their intuition appropriately to transcend any rules. Internalised 'rules' become progressively irrelevant because, through practice, practitioners progressively acquire a much more subtle and differentiated *tacit knowledge* of the terrain of practice than can ever, *in principle*, be expressed in explicit rules or procedures. Once again, therefore, we can see how a procedure-fixated manualisation approach fundamentally misrepresents what *actually happens* in therapy practice. We should note in passing that it is also unlikely that actual therapy practice in any ESVT research project is, in reality, guided by manualisation either. Rather, it is guided by the considerable tacit learning that has occurred through training, and then through ongoing practice supervised by experienced practitioners. One of us (ACB) has personally observed Leslie Greenberg train therapists for his manualised research studies, and it was clear that he was using considerable tacit, fine-grained understanding to explain subtleties that went well beyond any descriptions in the training manual.

On this view, then, pre-decided procedures or manuals merely give *an illusion* of the comforting specificity (understandably) sought after by researchers, but are actually nothing more than 'pretend pseudo-science' – a grand, scientific emperor with no clothes on. It is also quite illusory to believe that the immense degree of tacit knowledge often *mysteriously* conveyed by experienced practitioners in their tutoring process could ever be specified well enough in manuals to render practice as 'scientific' as those who advocate ESVTs seem to be pursuing (Schön, 1983) – and, if we accept the phenomenon of unconscious processes, then this merely reinforces our conclusion here. Notwithstanding any manualisation, it will be expected that effective practitioners will practise differently, as they do in all other professions. The same melody played by two different musicians, or conducted by two different conductors, is always different. It is the player him or herself who really matters, and not the technical, procedural content of what is played, to anything like the same extent.

We therefore support the radical conclusion that, in the real world of actual therapy practice, there is no standardised 'treatment' that is being applied, *even in the case of manualised therapies.* In the paradigm favoured here, a starting assumption is that each practitioner–client pair will generate its own unique ways of working effectively. Different practitioners will embody practice principles in different ways, and in all cases of practice, the role of the practitioner is crucial. Put somewhat differently, one might say that *diversity* (House & Totton, 1997), rather than *standardisation,* rules – however much the attempt is made to shoe-horn the subtleties and complexities of therapeutic experiencing into a measurable, predictable metric. Or, as Moen (1991: 6) evocatively puts it: 'Selective analysis of general properties is not a substitute for the aesthetic intuition of a concrete and particular presence.'

Subtlety, intuition and therapeutic experience

In the kind of alternative, 'transmodern' paradigm we are exploring here, and in our previous chapter, the phenomenon of *subtlety* and its experiential handmaiden, the virtue of *discernment* (Sardello, 2002), can be seen as key aspects of a therapeutic experience that a modernist, ESVT (and CBT-orientated) worldview would find exceedingly difficult, if not impossible, to encompass. The *Concise Oxford Dictionary* defines 'subtle' thus: 'pervasive or elusive owing to tenuity; evasive, mysterious, hard to grasp or trace; making fine distinctions, having delicate perception; acute; ingenious, elaborate, clever; crafty, cunning.' This is a useful starting point – though the very nature of subtlety perhaps renders any attempt at a dictionary definition less than satisfactory.

Subtlety, then, is a quality of a kind of human consciousness that is tragically absent from the technocratic *Zeitgeist* of 'modernity' that still dominates modern consciousness. It is a telling commentary on the prevailing paradigmatic *Zeitgeist* that *The Subtlety of Emotions* (Ben-Ze'ev, 2000) seems to be one of a very small number of books that explicitly addresses the question of subtlety.

In his voluminous writings, educationalist and spiritual polymath Rudolf Steiner (whose work Lees discusses in Chapter 9) repeatedly emphasised how modern, materialistic natural science is incapable of the kind of subtle insight with which an alternative paradigm for psychotherapy is explicitly concerned (see *Self and Society*, 2017). In April 1924, for example, he wrote: '… the kind of intimate observation that reveals fine and delicate changes in man's soul or his bodily structure does not evolve out of scientific ideas' (1968: 28), and: 'The interests of this materialistic conception of the world… have developed in the educationist a terrible indifference to the more intimate and delicate impulses in the soul of the human being who is to be educated' (1926: 18) – with the result that 'materialistic thought is unpractical when the need is to enter into life in a living way' (1938: 60).

The educationalist and phenomenologist Max van Manen also explicitly addresses what we might call, after Steiner, the 'intangibles' or 'imponderables' in his writings on pedagogy. Van Manen was Professor of Education at the University of Alberta when he wrote a number of deeply insightful books on 'pedagogical subtlety' – the kind of subtleties that are notably absent, or at best neglected, in mainstream education (see Brown, 1992; van Manen, 1986, 1991).

Van Manen was also founding editor of the journal *Phenomenological Pedagogy*, and his contributions are deeply influenced by hermeneutical-phenomenological thinking (where 'hermeneutics' refers to 'the process of describing the "essence" of something' (Brown, 1992: 47)). His two major studies, *The Tone of Teaching* (1986) and *The Tact of Teaching* (1991), are veritable goldmines of wisdom and insight on the 'soul-subtleties' of teaching as practice and experience, and his seminal text, *Researching Lived Experience: human science for an action sensitive pedagogy* (1990) gives us a glimpse of what research might begin to look like within a 'postfoundationalist' alternative paradigm. Rather than setting out manipulatively to control the world (as the technocratic objectivist does), the sensitive phenomenologist offers the possibility of in-touch contact with, and full participation in, the 'life-world'. In short, the approach privileges sensitivity, openness to existential experience, and a commitment to inquire into lived, revealed meaning, and to illuminate 'contextualised humanity' (Brown, 1992: 49–51, and throughout).

The Tone of Teaching is full of wisdom about an attuned pedagogy's intangible subtleties. Van Manen writes, for example, that '"Atmosphere"... is a vaporlike sphere which envelops and affects everything... *Mood is a way of knowing* and being in the world... Atmosphere is a complex phenomenon... the way human beings experience the world' (van Manen, 1986: 31, 32; emphasis added). Van Manen also pays attention to the critical question of 'presence'. Within the field of counselling and psychotherapy, *presence* refers to the Buberian I–Thouness of the therapeutic relationship (eg. Robbins, 1997; Friedman, 2002) – the capacity to relate in a relatively undefended, open, projection-minimising way that encourages real human contact, intimacy and genuine encounter. Just as the teacher's presence with and for the children in her charge is a vital aspect of their pedagogical identity, so it can be argued that a *passionate presence* (Natiello, 2001), or encountering the other at *relational depth* (Mearns & Cooper, 2005), constitutes a core dimension of what we might call 'transmodern' therapy practice from the kind of paradigmatic stance we are attempting to articulate.

Here is van Manen on presence – with the words 'therapist' and 'client' substituted for his terms, 'teacher' and 'child' (with our apologies to Max):

> The most important aspect of our living hope is a way of being with [clients]. It is not what we say and do, first of all, but a way of being present to the [client]... When a [therapist] fails to be what ostensibly he or she *does*, then the [therapist] is really an absence... We may be physically present to [clients] while something essential is absent in our presence. (1986: 27, 43; original emphasis)

Sardello (2002: 118) is surely referring to something very similar when he writes of 'a letting-be-present of the soul-being of the other in radical proximity to our own soul-being'. Buber wrote similarly about what he called 'contact' (a term also used, incidentally, in Gestalt psychotherapy): '... through his mere existence, only he must be a really existing man and he must be really present to his pupils; *he educates through contact*' (Buber, 1990/1967: 102; emphasis added).

Van Manen proceeds to make an even more subtle link between atmosphere and presence: '... atmosphere is also the way a teacher [therapist] is present to children [clients], and the way children [clients] are present to themselves and to the teacher [therapist]' (1986: 36). Certainly, 'pedagogic thoughtfulness and tact are not simply a set of external skills to be acquired in a workshop' (1986: 50), and '[a] professional can act first because his or her body has been readied by thoughtfulness' (1986: 53).

Many of the critical arguments about the toxic instrumentalism of hyper-modern educational practices can also be applied to the realm of the psychological therapies, or what Samuels (2013) terms 'state therapy' (2013: x). Van Manen, again, has a strongly non-instrumental approach to teacher competency that is very different from the current mainstream ideology:

> Methods or techniques of teaching cannot be adequately described by external knowledge… Teacher competency has more to do with pedagogical tactfulness, having a sensitivity to what is best for each child [client], having a sense of each child's [client's] life and his or her deep preoccupation. (1986: 49, 46)

Van Manen is also not afraid to enter the political arena: '… the "administrative" and "technological" have so penetrated the very lifeblood of our existence that parents and teachers are in danger of forgetting a certain other type of understanding' (1986: 29). And here is Rudolf Steiner speaking prophetically around a century ago about what we recognise today as the modernist 'audit culture' in education and the damage it perpetrates:

> The state imposes terrible learning goals and terrible standards, the worst imaginable, but people will imagine them to be the best. Today's policies and political activity treat people like pawns. More than ever before, attempts will be made to use people like cogs in a wheel. People will be handled like puppets on a string. Things like institutions of learning will be created incompetently and with the greatest arrogance…. We have a difficult struggle ahead of us... (Steiner, 1996: 29–30)

In sum, 'teaching [or therapy] is much more than the dutiful execution of technical acts' (Brown, 1992: 56); it involves an improvisational thoughtfulness requiring 'the corporeal being of the person, an active sensitivity toward the subjectivity of the other' (van Manen, quoted in Brown, 1992).

Towards the intuitive practitioner: beyond 'competencies', towards being

Generalisable knowledge about teaching and learning will never fully reflect or be reflected in the individual cognitive framework of practitioners (Atkinson & Claxton, 2000: 4).

The role of intuition (however we might attempt to define what it consists in) within the professions – most notably in teaching – has been recognised in an important book, tellingly titled *The Intuitive Practitioner: on the value of not always knowing what one is doing* (Atkinson & Claxton, 2000). Although focusing primarily on education, we maintain that this edited collection has great relevance to the work of psychotherapy and counselling as well. It starts from the observation that, for much of the time, experienced professionals are unable to account for and explain what they are doing, or, indeed, tell us what they 'know'. Yet, within the prevailing 'audit-culture' values (Power, 1997) of the crass, positivistic specification of measurable so-called 'competencies' rooted in a politically correct and typically unquestioned accountability culture (see Strathern, 2000), professional development and practice are routinely discussed as if conscious understanding and specification are not only unproblematic to deliver but are of central relevance and importance. *The Intuitive Practitioner* addresses the relationship between rational or explicit ways of knowing and learning, on the one hand, and inarticulate, intuitive, or implicit ones on the other – embracing what is a seeming paradox and exploring the dynamic relationship that exists between reason and intuition within the realm of professional practice. The book's contributors delve deeply and revealingly into the much-neglected nature of intuition and illustrate the crucial role that it plays in the exercising and development of professional decision-making and judgment.

The book fundamentally questions the 'modernist' tendency to 'fetishise' the conscious and the declarative, and to interpret reflection solely in terms of conscious articulation, and strongly asserts the value of forms of reflection that are not necessarily possible to articulate. We should note in passing that it has considerable relevance to therapy training in its offering of diverse practical lessons for the initial training and continuing professional development of educators that takes full account of the import of the intuitive.

The chapter by Broadfoot (2000) is especially pertinent to our current concerns in our two chapters in this volume. Broadfoot opens up the question of the effect of what we might term 'assessment-mindedness' (House, 1996a) on intuitive capacity. There are important parallels here with so-called 'evidence-based practice' and the associated near-obsession with the need for certain kinds of research in the therapy world. It is virtually unheard of for anyone to challenge *the very idea* of 'research' (as currently conceived as hypothesis-testing quantification) in our field, but that is precisely what we are going to do here (for a further articulation, see House, 2008). First, we think it is important to be aware of the *emotional dynamics* that may well be driving, at least in part, the field's current obsession with research, accountability and 'evidence-based practice' – rooted in part, one of us (RH) suggests, in a culturally pervasive and essentially unprocessed anxiety to do with loss of control, a phantasy of powerlessness, and cultural and spiritual anomie – an anxiety, moreover, of which therapy practitioners would normally be expected to be particularly aware and able to contain, and certainly not to 'act out'. Yet, in the field's largely uncritical embracing of the 'audit culture', the New Managerialism, and the New Public Management (King & Moutsou, 2010; House, 2008a; Power, 1997), the grave concern is that we are unawarely colluding with these pernicious cultural forces in our obsession with accountability, efficacy and 'scientific evidence' cast in a positivistic mould.

It is important not to assume, of course, that, merely because a process may be anxiety- and unconsciously driven, that this *de facto* renders it necessarily invalid. However, it certainly does cast considerable doubt on the essentially uncritical way in which research- and efficacy-mindedness have been embraced by the field with virtually no critical debate as to their relevance and appropriateness in our peculiar field (for a very notable exception, see King & Moutsou, 2010). One might reasonably ask why it is that, to date, there has been comparatively little engagement with these crucial issues in the therapy world.

Might it be that there is some kind of insidious process operating in modern culture such that we all end up '*thinking like a state*' (Scott, 1999) – with all of the deadly limiting and distorting consequences of that surreptitious mentality? Broadfoot puts it thus:

> ... assessment is... so central to the discourse of contemporary culture that [quoting Wittgenstein] we find ourselves in a 'linguistic prison'; we have been 'bewitched' by the concepts of... assessment ... to such an extent that even what we are able to think is constrained by the boundaries of that conceptual language. (2000: 207)

There is also an important story that needs to be told here about what might be termed 'the neoliberal psyche' (Robinson & House, in preparation) and its insistent imperatives, but this is beyond the scope of the present discussion (for illuminating viewpoints, see McGuigan, 2014; Verhaeghe, 2014; Sloan; 1995; Levin, 1987).

These are surely the kinds of questions that culturally, critically and *politically* engaged psychotherapeutic thinking at its most incisive is very best placed to address. To the extent that we don't do it, the therapy field could be in for very big trouble indeed. After all, the 'audit culture' and its accompanying ideology are systematically saturating every aspect of public and, increasingly, private life, and therapy is by no means immune from these arguably toxic developments (House, 2012). With the current obsession with 'evidence-based practice', for example, the very notion of 'evidence' itself is routinely taken for granted and uncritically assumed to be unproblematic (see House, 2010). There are at last some welcome signs that the audit culture and its control-obsessed, managerialist ideology are beginning to fall apart at the seams. Yet, should not the insight afforded by a psychotherapeutic ethos and sensibility have led to a forensically critical, deconstructive spotlight being shone upon the way in which the audit culture has been infecting the therapy world in all manner of ways? We are thinking particularly of the CBT (and in some cases the happiness) agenda (see Pilgrim's Chapter 3, this volume) and the extraordinarily naïve 'outcomes' claims that have been made for the superiority of CBT-type approaches over other modalities, which are at the very least problematic (see various chapters in this volume; see also Atkinson, 2014; Ali et al, 2017).

Just as there has been a kind of 'trance induction' (Postle, 2007) involved in the seemingly inexorable move toward the state regulation of the psychological therapies in Britain (eg. Postle & House, 2009), a similar kind of trance induction has arguably been active in the case of the audit culture within therapy, with erstwhile critically minded practitioners seemingly taking the notion of 'evidence' and 'evidence-based practice', and the underlying dynamics driving these preoccupations, as unproblematic givens.

The other important point to make here is the impact of 'audit-mindedness' (House, 1996a) on the very subtle practitioner qualities that we are discussing here. For if, as we strongly believe, qualities like subtlety, discernment and intuitive capacity are key common-factor 'ingredients' of effective practitionership, and if those very qualities are not only *not* amenable to the positivistic 'violence' that is 'variable specification' and all that goes with it (see our previous chapter 18 in this volume), but are actually *adversely affected by* such an 'evidence-based' mentality, then it may well be that the very act of importing a 'politically correct' preoccupation with accountability into our work substantially compromises it (eg. Strathern, 2000). It may even end up with the grotesque outcome that our anxiety-driven need to somehow guarantee the efficacy of our work and the armamentarium of procedures that we adopt to prove it actually do far more net damage to the quality of therapy work than any improvements brought about by the assessment and accountability regime itself.

We also surely have enough experience by now to know that virtually all technocratic intrusions into human systems generate all manner of normally unconscious 'material' around power (see Guilfoyle's and Proctor's Chapters 1 and 2, this volume; see also Hook, 2010; Parker, 2007), and routinely precipitate quite unpredictable side-effects that commonly do more net harm than the pre-existing shortcomings that the interventions were supposed to address. Crassly positivistic and technocratic conceptions of service evaluation – what Kilroy and colleagues (2004: 1) refer to as 'the reduction of (qualitative) thought to (quantitative) product, (critical) education to (utilitarian) skill-set' – are surely singularly inappropriate means of evaluating efficacy in the peculiarly unique and idiosyncratic field of psychotherapeutic help. As Broadfoot has it: '... attempts to pretend that a human being's achievements, or even more, their potential, can be unambiguously measured are doomed from the outset' (2000: 215). Again, within the field of education, Fendler (1998: 57) develops the kind of critique that has been notably missing in the mainstream therapy world. Below, we reproduce an aspect of her incisive critique, again substituting therapy for education terms (as precisely the same arguments apply in both fields):

> Now there is a reversal; the goals and outcomes are being stipulated at the outset, and the procedures are being developed post hoc. The 'nature' of the [client's experience] is stipulated in advance, based on objective criteria, usually statistical analysis. Because the outcome drives the procedure (rather than vice versa), there is no longer the theoretical possibility of unexpected results; there is no longer the theoretical possibility of becoming unique in the process of becoming ['treated']... In this new system, evaluation of [psychotherapeutic] policy reform is limited to an evaluation of the degree to which any given procedure yields the predetermined results... (Fendler, 1998: 57)

What our field should surely be embracing is the most radical thinking in relevant and associated fields (eg. Trifonas, 2004; Strathern, 2000; Apple, 2005; Geyer, 2012; Shore & Wright, 2015), rather than uncritically mimicking the worst features of the 'surveillance culture' and the soulless technocracies of 'high modernity'. The kinds of epistemological and methodological critiques that will be necessary are at last beginning to be made within the field (eg. House, 2010), but we find ourselves asking, where have they been all these years? Might it be the case, for example, that some process commonly occurs whereby we are all in some sense infantilised by statist thinking, and haven't yet found a mature position to adopt in relation to overweening, control-oriented state intrusion into human experience, and into life itself? And might this be especially so in the post 9/11 cultural milieu of acute and often largely unprocessed anxiety, which may well have triggered all manner of unconscious phantasies?

These are the kinds of questions to which analytic and psychotherapeutic thinking might have a significant contribution to make, if we are not to sleepwalk into a thoroughgoing 'surveillance society', shamefully aided and abetted by Samuel's (2013: x) uncritical 'state therapy'. To follow Samuels' important work in this respect (eg. Samuels, 2001; 2015), as the anxiety-saturated 'audit culture' proceeds to penetrate every aspect of public and private life, these are also questions that will surely manifest in the consulting room itself, and with which politically committed and aware practitioners surely cannot fail to engage, with their clients and patients. There are also interesting institutional questions about the extent to which a *radical countercultural space* can be preserved in a psychotherapy field that becomes increasingly professionalised and subject to the all-pervasive audit culture – the kind of space that the UK-based activist group The Alliance for Counselling and Psychotherapy is currently holding (see House et al, 2015; https://allianceblogs.wordpress.com).

Over a decade ago, Spinelli provocatively wrote: '[T]here exists precious little about therapy that we can say with any certainty... therapists really don't know what they're doing – even if they insist upon pretending... they are "experts"' (Spinelli, 1996: 56, 59). We strongly concur with this view, which paradoxically further entails that the more we are able to admit to our 'ignorance' – albeit it in a 'disciplined' way, perhaps – then the more likely we are to discover the requisite abilities and capacities really to help our clients in a sensitive and effective way.

Discussion

At the risk of oversimplification, we can say that the main 'culprits' in the ESVT paradigm ultimately reduce to two tendencies: first, the underlying mechanistic assumptions upon which the ESVT paradigm appears to be based, which erroneously presume that greater and greater specificity will lead to better and better predictability and control (the modernist 'more is more' syndrome), based on the research model wherein an independent variable is manipulated to influence and 'control' the dependent variable; and second, the misguided metaphorical identification of psychotherapy with a medical-model, drug/treatment/cure ideology (eg. House, 1996b; Stiles & Shapiro, 1989; Elkins, 2009). In regard to the former, the ESVT paradigm can be argued to be based on a traditional Newtonian, billiard-ball view of the universe, in which it is in principle conceivable (if not actually possible) to know everything in a conscious, specifiable way (or, at least, what is most important and efficacious), so that one can predict and control everything – or at least everything that really matters. From this paradigmatic vantage point, science is only imperfect because we haven't yet discovered and identified pretty much everything – while in principle, perfect (or at least good-enough) predictability is assumed to be possible.

In contrast, we maintain that, in a complex, systemic, non-linear view of the universe, more compatible with postmodern, New Paradigm thinking, one will never, even in principle, be able to know with any degree of certainty how 'A' affects 'B' (assuming this to be the causal-deterministic way we presume to chop up the universe), certainly where complex systems are involved. In other words, even within in its own terms, the linear-deterministic approach is quite inadequate for producing the kind of knowledge to which it claims to aspire and which it assumes to be achievable.

Thus, simple input–output models of research, while perhaps useful as 'rough cuts', are positively misleading in understanding the complex nature of the phenomena involved (or more accurately, perhaps, they *may well* be – but, crucially, we have no way from within the positivist world-view to ascertain the extent of this misleadingness). When two complex non-linear systems 'bump up' against one another, one can perhaps hope for research to show an increase in the probability that input 'A' may increase the probability of effect 'B', but the idea that one can successively dismantle and disaggregate the phenomenal 'whole' and move closer and closer to complete mechanistic predictability is unrealistic and ontologically unsustainable. In sum, then, we can say that pro-ESVT advocates live in a modernist universe, while those sceptical of the ESVT ideology, like us, inhabit one that is more post- or transmodern – however, we might attempt a *definition-which-is-not-one* of the philosophically challenging postmodern mentality.

The second culprit appears to be the medical-model 'drug metaphor'. In medicine, when a new drug comes along, RCTs are carried out to test its effects. However, when any remotely competent medical doctor encounters a patient with a problem, in practice she or he does not mechanistically simply apply the drug and do nothing else. The drug, which has been validated in a drug trial, is used as a *part* of treatment (and, of course, we are ignoring here the crucially important question of the placebo effect (Shepherd & Sartorius, 1989; Peters, 2001; Kirsch, 2009)). Note that *the whole course* of treatment is not in itself manualised or pre-decided. In contrast, because the whole course of a psychotherapy experience (for example, a treatment for a 'difficulty of living' – *à la* Peck (1993)) is made analogous to a drug, in the psychotherapy domain, those who want to adopt the drug metaphor make the quite unwarranted jump of manualising or proceduralising the whole course of treatment.

Looked at from the kind of paradigmatic perspective adopted in this and the previous chapter 18, it is a form of scientific hegemony, and an epistemologically naïve and unsustainable position, to suggest that all research should be carried out within the ESVT paradigm. Anyone who claims that it should is either uncritically caught up either in the 'ideology of modernity' (see Woolfolk & Richardson, Chapter 7 this volume), or in parochial vested interests or configurations of institutional power (see Guilfoyle, Chapter 1, this volume).

It is equally a form of hegemony, and again a scientifically unsustainable position, to argue that practice should be based on therapies that meet ESVT criteria, or, by extension, to argue that it is unethical if one does not use an RCT-supported therapy where appropriate (eg. Persons, in Persons & Silberschatz, 1998; Bryceland & Stam, Chapter 17, this volume).

ESVTers would no doubt raise objections to what we have argued here. First, it might be objected that the 'ideal-typical' picture we have painted of contesting paradigms in psychotherapy is oversimplified to the point of caricature, and that, as a consequence, our critiques have a 'straw man' quality that bears little relation to what actually happens in the world of therapy practice. We would certainly be committing precisely the error we attribute to the modernist mentality if we were to assert a dichotomous, mutually excluding categorisation of therapy approaches into 'modernist' and 'postmodernist' ones. Not least, we are *all* in some quite unavoidable sense creatures of 'modernity', and it is simply impossible to excuse ourselves completely from modernity's culturally pervasive influences and effects.

However, we do maintain that the epistemological tendencies that we have identified and elaborated on in this and the previous chapter do have a very real and demonstrably tangible presence and effectivity in modern therapeutic practice, and we base this on our own personal experience of both practising as therapists and reflecting deeply on this peculiar work we do. We maintain, further, that if any coherent sense is to be made of the efficacy controversies that currently beset our field, then a full engagement with the *level and nature of argument* developed in these chapters is an essential necessary condition if any progress towards insight and understanding is to be made.

ESVTers might propose a head-to-head test of a manualised, empirically supported treatment versus therapy carried out from within the alternative paradigm propounded here. But this simply won't do, for the troubling question would then be: which set of research criteria from which paradigm would be used to answer the question? – or, in other words, how do we decide which paradigmatic criteria should be given precedence in order to provide an allegedly 'objective' answer to the question? Of course, we are entering the thorny and highly contested philosophical field of relativism here, which is a discussion well beyond the scope of this chapter. Yet we can see the kinds of difficult and complex philosophical and epistemological arguments that need to be engaged with in order adequately to address the efficacy question in the therapy field – and to date, ESVTers have, tellingly, shown no inclination to enter and engage with them.

It is highly likely that the framing of such a question in a way that would satisfy advocates of the ESVT approach would not satisfy advocates of the alternative, postmodern paradigm – and, of course, vice versa. Moreover, and based on what we know about therapy research, the most likely outcome would be the dodo bird verdict. And even if one approach could somehow be shown to be superior to the other, advocates of whichever approach had 'lost' would argue that the test wasn't fair.

Surely a far better way to proceed is for researchers from different paradigms to pursue their varying ends, and, somewhere down the road, the slow, steady accumulation of results will decide the issue – with a Kuhnian paradigm shift perhaps being the outcome (Kuhn, 1970), should postmodernist approaches prevail in the broad sweep of the evolution of ideas and human consciousness (see Lees Chapter 9, this volume). So, let us allow the rich diversity of therapy approaches to flourish, and let us dare to trust the paradigmatic outcome.

Finally, and in relation to this book, what are the implications of our arguments for CBT and its continuing and seeming hegemony in the therapy world, driven as it is by complex cultural and political-economic forces (eg. Pilgrim, Chapter 3, this volume), and the overriding 'ideology of modernity' (see Woolfolk & Richardson, Chapter 7 this volume)? Briefly, we maintain – with no little irony – that the detailed arguments developed in this and the previous chapter cast considerable doubt on, if not constitute a devastating undermining of, the allegedly *scientific* legitimacy that is routinely and uncritically claimed for CBT by some of its proponents.

We maintain that, at the very least, philosophers and theorists of CBT urgently need to construct a coherent, philosophically informed and defensible *metaphysical underpinning* for its theory and practice – for it seems clear from the epistemological arguments and paradigmatic critiques presented in this book in general, and in our own two chapters in particular, that, as yet, no one in the field seems to have attempted to construct a meta-theory that is able to make a coherent and sustainable case against them. Until such an attempt is made, it seems to us that, at the very least, a far greater degree of modesty is called for from those who aspire to entrench CBT as *the* therapy of choice across the therapeutic realm. As Woolfolk and Richardson (Chapter 7) articulated so clearly some 35 years ago, what is at stake in all this is a veritable Kuhnian 'paradigm war' between the forces of modernity and post- or transmodernity. We maintain that it is impossible to understand the precipitate rise of CBT without locating it within such a cultural and paradigmatic world-view (see Lees Chapter 9, this volume).

Conclusion

> The need to recoup the loss of depth and particularity is urgent if we are not to treat fellow human beings as abstract objects or lapse into anaesthetic and destructive indifference to the natural environment. (Moen, 1991: 6)

A 'transmodern' world-view calls forth, then, the imperative to move far beyond therapy as merely a *technology* and a medical-model 'diagnosis-and-treatment' model of care, as envisaged in the world of cognitively biased CBT and positivistic evidence-based practice, to embrace what is an uncomfortable reality for many – that therapy as a healing practice entails many practitioner qualities that are *in principle* beyond rational 'modernist' specification. So, a number of writers in diverse fields well beyond therapy have argued (see Michael Polanyi's (1966) notion of 'tacit knowledge' and Donald Schön's (1983) 'reflective practitioner', for example). As Frank put it nearly three decades ago, in a typically insightful comment: '[P]sychotherapy transpires in the realm of meaning... [I]n contrast to facts, meanings cannot be confirmed or disconfirmed by the objective criteria of the scientific method' (Frank, 1989: 144).

In their excellent anthology, *The Intuitive Practitioner*, we find Atkinson and Claxton (2000) arguing that there is a great value in 'not always knowing what one is doing', and that *intuition* is often the key to effective and successful practitionership in the human caring vocations. Such radical counter-cultural perspectives on therapy in the 21st century clearly have major implications for the becoming of therapy practitioners and for the kinds of training experiences that might be most effective and enabling (House, 2007, 2008b) – and, of course, for the practice of psychotherapy research itself.

References

Ali S, Rhodes L, Moreea O, McMillan D, Gilbody S, Leach C et al (2017). How durable is the effect of low intensity CBT for depression and anxiety? Remission and relapse in a longitudinal cohort study. *Behaviour Research and Therapy 94*: 1–8.

Apple MW (2005). Education, markets, and an audit culture. *Critical Quarterly 47*: 11–29.

Atkinson P (2014). The sorry state of NHS provision of psychological therapy. [Online]. *Free Psychotherapy Network*.https://freepsychotherapynetwork.com/2014/03/09/the-sorry-story-of-state-provision-of-psychological-therapy (accessed 3 February 2018).

Atkinson T, Claxton G (eds) (2000). *The Intuitive Practitioner: on the value of not always knowing what one is doing*. Buckingham: Open University Press.

Baruss I (1996). *Authentic Knowing: convergence of science and spiritual aspiration*. West Lafayette, IN: Purdue University Press.

Ben-Ze'ev A (2000). *The Subtlety of Emotions*. Cambridge, MA: MIT Press.

Bohart A, Tallman K (1999). *How Clients Make Therapy Work: the process of active self-healing*. Washington, DC: American Psychological Association.

Broadfoot P (2000). Assessment and intuition. In: Atkinson T, Claxton G (eds). *The Intuitive Practitioner: on the value of not always knowing what one is doing*. Milton Keynes: Open University Press (pp199–219).

Brown RK (1992). Max van Manen and pedagogical human science research. In: Pinar WF, Reynolds WM (eds). *Understanding Curriculum as Phenomenological and Deconstructed Text*. New York, NY: Teachers College Press (pp44–63).

Buber M (1990/1967). *A Believing Humanism: my testament 1902–1965*. Atlantic Highlands, NJ: Humanities Press International.

Clarke C (ed) (2005). *Ways of Knowing: science and mysticism today*. Exeter: Imprint Academic.

Duncan BL, Hubble MA, Miller SD (1997). *Psychotherapy with 'Impossible' Cases: the efficient treatment of therapy veterans*. New York, NY: Norton.

Elkins DN (2009). The medical model in psychotherapy: its limitations and failures. *Journal of Humanistic Psychology 49*: 66–84.

Fendler L (1998). What is it impossible to think? A genealogy of the educated subject. In: Popkewitz TS, Brennan M (eds). *Foucault's Challenge: discourse, knowledge and power in education*. New York, NY: Teachers College Press (pp39–63).

Frank JD (1989). Non-specific aspects of treatment: the view of a psychotherapist. In: Shepherd M, Sartorius N (eds). *Non-Specific Aspects of Treatment*. Toronto, ON: Hans Huber Publishers (pp95–114).

Friedman M (2002). Martin Buber and dialogical psychotherapy. *Journal of Humanistic Psychology 42*: 7–36.

Geyer R (2012). Can complexity move UK policy beyond 'evidence-based policy making' and the 'audit culture'? Applying a 'complexity cascade' to education and health policy. *Political Studies 60*: 20–43.

Grawe K (1997). Research-informed psychotherapy. *Psychotherapy Research 7*: 1–20.

Greenberg RP (1999). Common psychosocial factors in psychiatric drug therapy. In: Hubble MA, Duncan BL, Miller SD (eds). *The Heart and Soul of Change: what works in therapy*. Washington, DC: American Psychological Association (pp297–328).

Hart T, Nelson P, Puhakka K (eds) (1997). *Spiritual Knowing: alternative epistemic perspectives*. Carrollton, GA: State University of West Georgia.

Hart T, Nelson P, Puhakka K (eds) (2000). *Transpersonal Knowing: exploring the horizon of consciousness.* Studies in Social Sciences, vol 34. Albany, NY: State University of New York Press.

Harvey D (1973). *Social Justice and the City.* London: Arnold.

Heron J (1998). *Sacred Science: person-centred inquiry into the spiritual and the subtle.* Ross-on-Wye: PCCS Books.

Heron J (1996). *Co-operative Inquiry: research into the human condition.* London: Sage.

Hook D (2010). *Foucault, Psychology and the Analytics of Power.* Basingstoke: Palgrave Macmillan.

House R (2012). General practice counselling amidst the 'audit culture': history, dynamics and subversion of/in the hypermodern National Health Service. *Psychodynamic Practice: Individuals, Groups and Organisations 18*: 51–70.

House R (2010). 'Psy' research beyond late-modernity: towards praxis-congruent research. *Psychotherapy and Politics International 8*: 13–20.

House R (2008a). The dance of psychotherapy and politics. *Psychotherapy and Politics International* 6(2): 98–109.

House R (2008b). Training and education for therapy practitionership: 'trans-modern' perspectives. *Counselling Psychology Quarterly 21*: 1–10.

House R (2007). The be-coming of a therapist: experiential learning, self-education and the personal/professional nexus. *British Journal of Guidance and Counselling 35*: 427–440.

House R (2003). *Therapy Beyond Modernity: deconstructing and transcending profession-centred therapy.* London: Karnac Books.

House R (1996a). 'Audit-mindedness' in counselling: some underlying dynamics. *British Journal of Guidance and Counselling 24*(2): 277–283.

House R (1996b). General practice counselling: a plea for ideological engagement. *Counselling* 7(1): 40–44.

House R, 441 others (2015). Austerity and a malign benefits regime are profoundly damaging mental health. Letter to the editor. *The Guardian*; 17 April. goo.gl/ppyt54.

House R, Totton N (eds) (1997). *Implausible Professions: arguments for pluralism and autonomy in psychotherapy and counselling.* Ross-on-Wye: PCCS Books.

Kilroy P, Bailey R, Chare N (2004). Editorial sounding: auditing culture. *Parallax 31 10*(2): 1–2.

King L, Moutsou C (eds) (2010). *Rethinking Audit Cultures: a critical look at evidence-based practice in psychotherapy and beyond.* Ross-on-Wye: PCCS Books.

Kirsch I (2009). *The Emperor's New Drugs: exploding the antidepressant myth.* London: The Bodley Head.

Kuhn TS (1970). *The Structure of Scientific Revolutions* (2nd ed). Chicago, IL: University of Chicago Press.

Lawrence RL (2005). *Artistic Ways of Knowing: expanded opportunities for teaching and learning.* San Francisco, CA: Jossey-Bass.

Levin DM (ed) (1987). *Pathologies of the Modern Self: postmodern studies on narcissism, schizophrenia and depression.* New York, NY: New York University Press.

McGuigan M (2014). *Neoliberal Culture.* Basingstoke: Palgrave Macmillan.

Mearns D, Cooper M (2005). *Working at Relational Depth in Counselling and Psychotherapy.* London: Sage.

Moen MK (1991). Introduction. In: den Ouden B, Moen M (eds). *The Presence of Feeling in Thought.* New York, NY: Peter Lang (pp1–9).

Norcross JC (ed) (2011). *Psychotherapy relationships that work: evidence-based responsiveness.* New York, NY: Oxford University Press.

Natiello P (2001). *The Person-Centred Approach: a passionate presence.* Ross-on-Wye: PCCS Books.

Parker I (2007). *Revolution in Psychology: alienation to emancipation.* London: Pluto.

Peck MS (1993). Salvation and suffering: the ambiguity of pain and disease. *Human Potential* 15(17): 24–26.

Persons JB, Silberschatz G (1998). Are results of randomized controlled trials useful to psychotherapists? *Journal of Consulting and Clinical Psychology 66*: 126–135.

Peters D (ed) (2001). *Understanding the Placebo Effect in Complementary Medicine: theory, practice and research.* Edinburgh: Harcourt Publishers.

Polanyi M (1966). *The Tacit Dimension.* New York, NY: Doubleday.

Postle D (2007). *Regulating the Psychological Therapies: from taxonomy to taxidermy.* Ross-on-Wye: PCCS Books.

Postle D, House R (eds) (2009). *Compliance? Ambivalence? Rejection? Nine Papers Challenging HPC Regulation.* London: Wentworth Learning Resources.

Power M (1997). *The Audit Society: rituals of verification.* Oxford: Oxford University Press.

Robbins A (1997). *Therapeutic Presence: bridging expression and form.* London: Jessica Kingsley.

Robinson G, House R (eds) (in preparation). *The Neoliberal Psyche: subjectivity and experience in/and late Capitalism.*

Samuels A (2015). *Passions, Persons, Psychotherapy, Politics: the selected works of Andrew Samuels.* Hove: Routledge.

Samuels A (2013). Foreword. In: House R, Kalisch D, Maidman J (eds). *The Future of Humanistic Psychology.* Ross-on-Wye: PCCS Books (pp ix–xiv).

Samuels A (2001), *Politics on the Couch: citizenship and the internal life.* London: Karnac.

Sardello R (2002). *The Power of Soul: living the twelve virtues.* Charlottesville, VA: Hampton Roads Publishing Co.

Schön DA (1983). *The Reflective Practitioner: how professionals think in action.* New York, NY: Basic Books.

Scott JC (1999). *Seeing Like a State: how certain schemes to improve the human condition have failed.* New Haven, CT: Yale University Press.

Self & Society (2017). Special issue: Rudolf Steiner and the Psychological Therapies. Self & Society 45(1).

Shepherd M, Sartorius N (eds) (1989). *Non-Specific Aspects of Treatment.* Toronto, ON: Hans Huber Publishers.

Shore C, Wright S (2015). Governing by numbers: audit culture, rankings and the new world order. *Social Anthropology 23*: 22–28.

Sloan T (1995). *Damaged Life: the crisis of the modern psyche.* London: Routledge.

Snyder CR, Michael ST, Cheavens JS (1999). Hope as a psychotherapeutic foundation of common factors, placebos, and expectancies. In: Hubble MA, Duncan BL, Miller SD (eds). *The Heart and Soul of Change: what works in therapy.* Washington, DC: American Psychological Association (pp179–200).

Spinelli E (1996). Do therapists know what they're doing? In: James I, Palmer S (eds). *Professional Therapeutic Titles: myths and realities.* Division of Counselling Psychology; Occasional Paper 2. Leicester: British Psychological Society (pp55–61).

Steiner R (1968). *The Roots of Education*. London: Rudolf Steiner Press.

Steiner R (1938). *The Education of the Child in the Light of Anthroposophy*. London: Rudolf Steiner Press/ New York: Anthroposophic Press.

Steiner R (1926). *The Essentials of Education: five lectures delivered by R Steiner during the Educational Conference at the Waldorf School, Stuttgart, April 1924*. London: Anthroposophical Publishing Co.

Steiner R (1918/1989). *Knowledge of the Higher Worlds: how is it achieved?* London: Rudolf Steiner Press.

Stiles WB, Shapiro DA (1989). Abuse of the drug metaphor in psychotherapy process outcome research. *Clinical Psychology Review 9:* 521–544.

Stiles WB, Honos-Webb L, Surko M (1998). Responsiveness in psychotherapy. *Clinical Psychology: Science and Practice 5*: 439–458.

Strathern M (ed) (2000). *Audit Cultures: anthropological studies in accountability, ethics and the academy*. EASA series. London: Routledge.

Sundararajan L (2002). Humanistic psychotherapy and the scientist-practitioner debate: an 'embodied' perspective. *Journal of Humanistic Psychology 42*(2): 34–47.

Tarnas R (1996). *The Passion of the Western Mind: understanding the ideas that have shaped our world view*. London: Pimlico.

Toulmin S (1990). *Cosmopolis: the hidden agenda of modernity*. New York, NY: Free Press.

Trifonas PP (2004). Auditing education: deconstruction and the archiving of knowledge as curriculum. *Parallax 31 10*(2): 37–49.

van Manen M (1991). *The Tact of Teaching: the meaning of pedagogical thoughtfulness*. New York, NY: SUNY Press.

van Manen M (1990). *Researching Lived Experience: human science for an action sensitive pedagogy*. Albany, NY: SUNY Press.

van Manen M (1986). *The Tone of Teaching*. Richmond Hill, ON: TAB Publishers.

Verhaeghe P (2014). *What About Me? The struggle for identity in a market-based society*. London: Scribe.

20 Where is the magic in cognitive therapy? A philo/psychological investigation

Fred Newman

> Effective therapy often seems magical.
> (Kenneth Gergen, 2006: 28)

Is cognitive therapy an effort to analyse common sense and to show how and when commonsensical thinking can go astray and lead to emotional disorders? Or is cognitive therapy an effort to make use of common sense in dealing with those emotional disorders? Or is cognitive therapy an effort to do both of those and more?

Aaron Beck's seminal work on cognitive therapy (1979) begins its very first chapter, 'Common Sense and Beyond', with a quotation from the distinguished British philosopher Alfred North Whitehead, addressing a meeting of the British Association for the Advancement of Science:

> Science is rooted in what I have just called the whole apparatus of common sense thought. That is the datum from which it starts, and to which it must recur... You may polish up common sense, you may contradict it in detail, you may surprise it. But ultimately your whole task is to satisfy it. (1916: 6)

There is, of course, a colossal irony here. For one of Whitehead's great intellectual contributions (albeit a very early one) was *Principia Mathematica* (written in collaboration with Sir Bertrand Russell, also a philosopher). *Principia* was a monumental effort to show that all of mathematics could be reduced to logic (in particular, to mathematical logic, provided that mathematical logic included, as supposed by Russell and Whitehead, the unassailable concept of a set: Russell and Whitehead's assumption being that nothing could be more *intuitively* obvious than the notion of a collection of things or a group, which is what they and almost everyone else meant by a set). Yet, starting with Frege, through Gödel and beyond, this commonsensical notion of a set appeared to introduce paradoxes which rendered implausible the reductionistic projects of Russell and Whitehead, and dozens of other mathematical logicians.

What if anything does common sense have to do with science?

Whitehead's observations seem commonsensically sound, yet serious efforts to deconstruct and analyse science and the scientific method (a project that consumed the minds of many philosophers in the first half of the 20th century) yield distinctly uncommonsensical (and unacceptable) results. This came as a surprise to some, but by no means to all, for the historical and mathematical roots of science, complex as they may be, are arguably as much in magic (somewhat broadly interpreted) as they are in common sense (see, for example, Styers (2004), or, pertaining to the medical sciences, Thorndike (1941)).

Pythagoras seemed to have gained genuine insight by exploring magical numerological connections. And when Newton wasn't downstairs 'wowing' the Royal Academy, he was apparently upstairs exploring ancient alchemic relationships. And even today, if common sense alone could do it, what need for the most interesting esoteric elements that make up modern science, from quanta to quarks to string theory?

The first half of the 20th century was marked by many philosophers serving as the self-appointed handmaidens of science, attempting to articulate a logical and empiricist model of science that would be rigorous and unassailable. Logical positivism was its name; worldwide was its fame; Vienna was its home and – while he himself denied it adamantly – the early writings of Ludwig Wittgenstein were its inspiration. But that project (especially in the US) had come crumbling down to the ground rather forcefully by the 1950s, with the appearance of WVO Quine's 'Two Dogmas of Empiricism' (1951), and 'meta-ironically' with Wittgenstein's posthumous publication *Philosophical Investigations* (1953).

Quine's American revolution

Quine, at once a first-rate logician, a philosopher of science and also situated at Harvard, fully in the tradition of American psychological pragmatism (from William James to CI Lewis), summed up almost half a century of positivistic self-criticism in his revolutionary essay. What he showed with remarkable eloquence was that logical empiricism, which purported to be in some version or another the model for all of science (including mathematics), was itself a methodology that rested firmly yet fatuously on two dogmas. The first, the so-called (dogma of the) distinction between analytical propositions and so-called synthetic propositions, went back at least to Kant.

The distinction claimed that there were basically two kinds of scientific propositions that could be articulated. One kind, the analytical, was definitional in character (in many cases mathematical) and was true (or false) by virtue of the language and definitions employed (Euclidean geometry was the best example). The other, the synthetic, was true or false by virtue of its relationship to empirically verifiable conditions (direct observation is the paradigm here). These two radically different kinds of propositions, the analytic and synthetic, constituted what most people accepted as the terrain of science, if not the broader terrain of knowledge. What Quine showed was that the commonsensical notion that these two kinds of propositions were clear and distinct (from each other) was not at all clear and distinct. The second and related dogma of empiricism, the dogma of reductionism, was a critique of the commonsensical belief that complex propositions – be they analytic or synthetic – could be reduced to the smallest elements of which they consisted, and that this process made visible the significance of the more complex proposition.

Finally, in the last sections of his essay, Quine lays down guidelines for the creation of a science (or a conception of science) free of dogmas. His student, Thomas Kuhn, more a sociologist than a philosopher, and many, many others advanced this conception. Quine's and Kuhn's (1970) work shaped a new philosophical foundation of philosophy of science, though whether they have anything to do with, or impact at all on, science as practised is difficult to say. Yet, beginning in the 1960s, in *both* the Anglo-American tradition and the continental-existential tradition, there has been a persistent reconsideration of what science is, of what common sense is, and of whether these two have anything to do with each other. Some have considered these explorations a component of an intellectual movement known as 'postmodernism'. Others have taken great pains to distinguish their research from that appellation. Yet what is most interesting to me is the extent to which contemporary science and contemporary philosophers of science and others move along parallel tracks while seemingly oblivious of each other.

Most relevant to this chapter, the evolution, practice and influence of cognitive therapy grow abundantly, while philosophers of psychology seriously question and advance the concept of cognition itself. (It is as if Lewis and Clark insisted that there be two different trails because they did not walk in each other's precise footsteps.)

Turn, turn, turn

The cognitive turn, the linguistic turn and the postmodern turn are obviously inter-related. How is not the least bit clear to many, and probably excessively clear to some. To me, all seem a reaction to the arrogant and radical 'deductiveness' of a great deal of 19th and early 20th century thought, be it positivistic or idealistic or Marxist – they are all modernist. Many, if not most, reactions come from those quite familiar with the approaches they are unraveling. So it is with Quine and Kuhn, and many of those who pursued their work; so, of course, with Wittgenstein who, in his *Philosophical Investigations*, was in fact deconstructing his own earlier work in the *Tractatus* (1921); so it is with the therapeutic cognitivists who grew up under the influence of Freudian analytical theory, behavioural theory, and neuropsychological theories. (So it is with me, as an orthodox Marxist-turned-postmodern Marxist.) Indeed, Beck's somewhat *defensive* beginning (pardon the therapeutics), which over-connects, in my opinion, science and common sense, reveals his concern to reassure the world that a return to cognition as both a subject and a mode of study is not to be seen as any kind of rejection of science.

From a broader perspective of the 'turns of the century', such defensiveness was (and remains) unnecessary, of course. For not only was consciousness, in one form or another, from radical existentialism to Quine and Gödel (who was, after all, a self-identified Platonist), coming back into fashion, but theoreticians as well as practitioners in all these fields were beginning to violate the constraining and narrow-minded prohibitions of late 19th and early 20th century positivistic thought.

These successful revolutions (or turns, if you like) in physics, mathematics, psychiatry, philosophy (particularly philosophy of science), linguistics etc essentially occurred (as I have said) simultaneously, without very much of an awareness of each other, and eventually resulted in overstatements, to the detriment of each of the particular revolutions. By the way, the intellectual revolutions of this period (which have been vastly more successful than the much more publicised and deadly, on-the-ground revolutions of the same period) have yet to be synthesised, or, in the minds of some, correctly characterised or labelled. It is not within the scope of this chapter to do so (or even want to), but the critique being offered of cognitive therapy is that *it has, in general, gone way too far in an effort to preserve a scientific character that science no longer has.* And so, while it is a most significant advance in psychotherapeutics (as well as in psychotherapeutic theory), it has done so at the expense of taking the magic out of science and, thereby, for their purposes, out of the examination of consciousness and, therefore (and this concerns me most), out of therapy, where magic is what makes it work. Some have gone to other extremes, characterising consciousness in such a way as to make it incomprehensible (or, at least, barely recognisable as consciousness). The failing and irony of the cognitive therapy movement is its *excessive* comprehensibility, particularly in light of the revolutionary world, the ever-turning, anti-positivist world, into which it was born.

This formulation might well seem to many like philosophical claptrap, so abstract as to be of no value to anyone. So, let me put it another way: less precise, but more to the point. Cognitive behaviour therapy is overly decidable (in Gödel's sense of the word (Nagel, Newman & Hofstadter, 2001); it is thereby insufficiently magical (in my sense of the word) and, finally, cognitive behaviour therapy is insufficiently political in the broadest sense of the word. It is *unrelentingly* apolitical. And this is a serious flaw. For not only is all science magical and virtuously undecidable (Newman, 2003); all science is political. And the three are related. For it is a proper combination of magic (properly understood) and politics (properly understood) and undecidability (properly understood) that relates science, and indeed all thought, to the world and, thereby, to the lives of people.

Politics properly understood

I have spent a lifetime writing about and, more importantly, trying to perform 'politics properly understood'. It is, first and foremost, an *activity*: a collective, humanistic, creative building of new things – large and small, *mental* and *physical*. Science should not be performed in the service of partisan politics; nor should it be carried out in the name of ideologically driven politics. It must 'serve the people'. While I have worked hard for almost four decades to create projects that do just that, I have never been able to put into words this humanistic ideal. Perhaps the closest I have come is in my psychological plays (mainly comedies), written for and performed at several meetings of the American Psychological Association (APA). Others have expressed the humanism of psychology better than I – none better, in my view, than Dr Martin Luther King Jr in the following statement, made on 25 April 1957 at the Conference on Christian Faith and Human Relations, Nashville:

> There are certain technical words in the vocabulary of every academic discipline which tend to become stereotypes and clichés. Psychologists have a word which is probably used more frequently than any other word in modern psychology. It is the word 'maladjusted'. This word is the ringing cry of the new child psychology. Now in a sense all of us must live the well-adjusted life in order to avoid neurotic and schizophrenic personalities. But there are some things in our social system to which I am proud to be maladjusted and to which I suggest that you too ought to be maladjusted. I never intend to adjust myself to the viciousness of mob-rule. I never intend to adjust myself to the evils of segregation and the crippling effects of discrimination. I never intend to adjust myself to the tragic inequalities of an economic system which takes necessities from the many to give luxuries to the few. I never intend to become adjusted to the madness of militarism and the self-defeating method of physical violence. I call upon you to be maladjusted. The challenge to you is to be maladjusted – as maladjusted as the prophet Amos, who in the midst of the injustices of his day, could cry out in words that echo across the centuries, 'Let judgment run down like waters and righteousness like a mighty stream'; as maladjusted as Lincoln, who had the vision to see that this nation could not survive half slave and half free; as maladjusted as Jefferson, who in the midst of an age amazingly adjusted to slavery could cry out, in words lifted to cosmic proportions, 'All men are created equal, and are endowed by their creator with certain unalienable rights, that among these are Life, Liberty and the pursuit of Happiness.' As maladjusted as Jesus, who dared to dream a dream of the Fatherhood of God and the brotherhood of men. The world is in desperate need of such maladjustment. (King, 1992)

What Dr King is saying, with his usual extraordinary eloquence, is that psychology must never become so scientific as to abandon its humanism. I could not agree more. Moreover, if 'scientific' is properly (contemporaneously) understood, it need not.

Adding Wittgenstein to Quine

Although it is a decade-and-a-half since it appeared on the bookshelves of the world, John R Searle's *The Rediscovery of the Mind* (1992) still amazes and delightfully confuses those of us, like me, who began a philosophical career in the dying moments of logical positivism. My first philosophical trick was to point a finger at my imaginary debating opponent, while not quite screaming, 'That's a category mistake you've made,' and then laughing ever so quietly under my breath. This admonition came, of course, from Gilbert Ryle. His famous, though, as it turned out, faddish, book, *The Concept of Mind* (1949), certainly did not envision a rediscovery of mind four decades later.

Ryle's work, a British combination of AJ Ayerian-style logical positivism in its death knell and the later Wittgenstein in its birth moment, was designed to celebrate the human intellectual capacity finally to get rid of mind. 'Mind' itself was a category mistake, according to my reading of Ryle, or at a minimum it was a result of centuries of category mistakes. It was ultimately indistinguishable from Hegel's Absolute and Heidegger's Nothingness. It was *unverifiable*, invoking the positivist cross to the devil of meaninglessness. But even as Ryle and his friends at Cambridge and Oxford were playing with this new idea, Quine at Cambridge, Massachusetts was pragmatising the entire issue, and showing in some way that the concept of science (or at least its foundations) suffered as much from metaphysicality as the most boring existentialist on the Left Bank of the Seine. Forty years later, which philosophically speaking is a drop in the historical bucket, John Searle, knowing a good deal of all of this tradition and even something of neuropsychology, authored *The Rediscovery of the Mind* (1992).[1] Searle, known for his contributions to philosophy of mind and consciousness, rejects dualism, and seems, to me, more comfortable with paradoxicality. He considers language (and the ontological commitments of our discourse) carefully – although not with Quine's logicality and pragmatism. (Searle, as I recall a student of JL Austin, is more an ordinary-language realist.)

Searle (Kreisler, 1999) locates the mind–body problem in the obsolete vocabulary and false assumptions that philosophers and psychologists accept, and with which they perpetuate dualism:

> We've inherited this vocabulary that makes it look as if *mental* and *physical* name different realms... I'm fighting against that... The way I solve [the

---

1. More recent publications of Searle's include *Mind: a brief introduction* (2005) and *Freedom and Neurobiology: reflections on free will, language and political power* (2006).

> mind–body problem] is to get rid of the traditional categories. Forget about Descartes' categories of *res existence* and *res cogitance,* that is, the extended reality of the material and the thinking reality of the mental. (p2)[2]

Searle's own view, which he terms 'biological naturalism', asserts that 'the brain is the only thing in there, and the brain causes consciousness' (Searle, 1992: 248). What is most critical here is that, in Searle's conception of causation (at least, psychological causation), there is no dualistic cause–effect divide; consciousness is not an effect separate from the processes producing it.

Holding to dualism, no matter how sublimated, frequently forces philosophers and cognitive scientists alike to posit ontological units that violate common sense (such as it is) and ordinary experience (ontological subjectivity) – units such as mental rules and patterns and unconscious mental phenomena. Some kind of mental content to mental processes is then conjured up (magically and/or pseudo-scientifically) in order to 'make intelligible' the relationship between the dualisms – mind–body, cognition–behaviour, and so on. (In psychotherapeutics, witness the *DSM-IV* (Newman & Gergen, 1999).) It is an error, Searle says (seemingly in a partial rejection of Hume), to assume that, if a patterned or meaningful relationship can be said to exist between entities or events, then the process producing that relationship must be equally patterned or meaningful. If a person thinks of B when seeing A, which resembles B, we should not (but too many do) assume there is either any content or a particular form to the mental process that results in relating A and B. We are not following any mental rules when we think of B; there is no extra mental logic needed to account for the phenomenon in question.

In sum, Searle's point is that there is no mind–body problem. Indeed, there is no mind–body distinction. So we should stop talking as if there is one and move on to the best we have at the moment – neuropsychology. The mind is rediscovered in this interesting relationship between the brain and conscious thought, and consciousness, like mind, has (to vary the use of Ryle's extraordinary metaphor) 'no ghosts in its machinery' (Ryle, 1949: 15–16). The brain produces thoughts that are transmitted to others via behaviour, most especially linguistic behaviour, which stimulates other brains to produce other thoughts, and so on. No mystery. A little magic, but no mystery.

Donald Davidson: the making of a conservative

Another of Quine's students, perhaps his most brilliant (in the name of full disclosure, he was my mentor and tennis partner at Stanford University in the

2. Richard Rorty's (1979) dismissal of the concept of truth on the grounds that he is no longer interested in it may sound like Searle's dismissal of mind–body, but they are quite different. For Searle is accepting the magicality of science, while Rorty is simply defending the failure of pragmatism to understand truth.

early 1960s) takes it upon himself to rehabilitate some of the critical conceptions that, for example, Rorty and Searle are justifiably, if not rigorously, abandoning. In particular, Donald Davidson (1980) seeks to reintroduce into the ontology of philosophical thought some notion of truth (a weak one), some conception of cause (a strong one), and an idea of deducibility that goes back at least to Hempel (a logical positivist), and perhaps to Plato and Aristotle (Greeks). Davidson's conservatism is formidable if not, to me, ultimately convincing.

After his work on decision theory (done early in his career), Davidson published little for many years, focusing his attention on brilliant teaching. When he returned to publishing in 1963, with his seminal essay 'Actions, Reasons and Causes' (Davidson, 1980), his mission appeared to be to salvage from the critical writings of the many anti-positivists, pro-late Wittgensteinian critical authors of the period those key concepts we, the people, would be *lost without.* Indeed, his real mission, it seems to me, was to salvage philosophy itself. Wittgenstein, on his death-bed, had left it on its death-bed.

Davidson's brilliant analyses of various features of mental activities (intentional acts, desires, wilful acts etc), contained as they are in separate and discrete essays written over an extended period, make it difficult to see his overall perspective. But it is there. And for me, it became more apparent in viewing a dialogue that Philosophy International (PI), from the London School of Economics (LSE), produced of him and Quine in their later years before a group of its scholars and students (Davidson & Quine, 1997).

Much of what Davidson pursues in this discussion with his former teacher is what he calls a third dogma of empiricism, which Quine (claims Davidson) overlooked (indeed, committed). Davidson, who in the LSE discussion claimed he had spent half a century trying to convince 'Vann' of his 'missing dogma', focused not on Quine's critical analysis in the first half of 'Two Dogmas' (which most agree is analytically valid), but rather on Quine's efforts in the final sections to metaphorically characterise a dogma-free sense of science.

There, Quine invokes a CI Lewis-like 'buzzing, blooming confusion' (a flux) upon which varying conceptual frameworks from the gods of Homer to modern science somehow impose order. But Davidson insists that this formulation (the idea of a flux), while perhaps useful in certain ways, invokes a third empiricistic dogma: namely, the dogma of the flux. Davidson says, correctly it seems to me, that there is no flux: that whatever the ordering mechanisms may be – gods, nature, particles, or quanta – the world appears to us and is, ontologically speaking, 'already ordered'. It is a fiction and a dogma to suppose that we humans must order a flux of subjective experience (sense datum, phenomenological experience, or whatever). I can recall Davidson, himself a radical naturalist, approvingly teaching in his epistemology class about a little-known medieval theologian (Bishop Butler), who is said to have said, 'Everything is what it is and not another thing!'

Lewis, Quine's teacher and very much a Kantian *and* a Humean (a modernist), apparently felt a pragmatic need to include in his ontology a 'buzzing, blooming confusion' to justify the function of whatever conceptual apparatus history (and geography) – ie. culture – happens to provide us with. Quine, according to Davidson, uncritically carries on this tradition (dating back at least to Plato), but it is as much a dogma of empiricism (deriving from its idealistic roots) as either the analytic/synthetic distinction or reductionism. It is classical Davidson, for the rejection of 'the flux' is not ultimately ontological, it is epistemological; the human capacity, if you will, to *connect* the 'flux' and the 'conceptual framework' would itself require a connector, and so on and so on. No, says Davidson, the *connection* must be as fundamental as the *connected* and, moreover, it *must* be causal. For even as Davidson is cleaning out the flux, he is constructing the broom, *connecting* all of his writings on these matters by saying in his introduction to *Essays on Actions and Event* (the first collection of his essays):

> All the essays in this book have been published elsewhere, and each was designed to be more or less free standing. But though composed over a baker's dozen of years, they are unified in theme and general thesis. The theme is the role of causal concepts in the description and explanation of human action. The thesis is that the ordinary notion of cause that enters in to scientific or commonsense accounts of non-psychological affairs is essential also to the understanding of what it is to act with a reason, to have a certain intention in acting, to be an agent, to act counter to one's own best judgment, or to act freely. Cause is the cement of the universe; the concept of cause is what holds together our picture of the universe, a picture that would otherwise disintegrate into a diptych of the mental and the physical. (1980: xi)

And so we more clearly discover Davidson's philosophical conservatism. He is, ultimately, an *anti-disintegrationist*, a rehabilitationist. For all his radical analysis of particular mental acts, he must ultimately pull everything together. He is a systematic philosopher defending philosophy for philosophy's sake. The use of the Wittgensteinian idea (developmental in my view) of employing philosophy to escape the limits of philosophy is turned (reacted to) by Davidson into using philosophy to clean up the mess made by philosophy. And then what? Presumably, wait passively for the next mess. I, of course, do not favour disintegration or rehabilitation; I favour development and, thereby, growth. Davidson seems to feel it is essential constantly to clarify philosophy, while I feel – deriving from Wittgenstein, Marx, and Vygotsky – that humankind must build a new world, not make up fantastical categories to explain or interpret or 'cement' the old one. We don't have to hold, and therapy must not seek to hold, the world together– ie. we neither need the flux nor the cement, we need to develop.[3]

3. 'The philosophers have only *interpreted* the world, in various ways; the point, however, is to *change it*' (Marx, 1845: 15; emphasis added).

Philosophy goes therapeutic

Davidson's assault on Wittgenstein is equally a serious and formidable defence of the roots of modernism. Not only is it reactionary, it is a reaction formation (pardon the therapeutics again), and, indeed, it does not stand alone. For the reaction to the postmodern assault has been powerful and, arguably, somewhat successful, although exposing (Newman & Holzman, 1997).[4] Certainly in psychology, postmodern thinking and ideas are still relegated to the fringe, while neuropsychology in its modernist guise dominates. All the more reason why cognitive behaviour therapy (and, more generally, all forms of therapy) must take a political stand. In some ways, the point of this chapter is to give therapy, a very critical component of psychology, a theoretical basis for 'going postmodern'. Cognitive behaviour therapy, the dominant therapeutic form, must lead the way.

What is social therapy?

Social therapy is, to my way of thinking, a cognitive behaviour form of therapy. It is, after all, about helping people understand better (though not necessarily cognitively) and thereby do better (as in performing better). But it endeavours to return the necessary magic to therapy by insisting on its revolutionary nature. 'Revolution', as used here, does not mean an ideologically driven (determined) set of views imposed on people in as traditionally an authoritarian a manner as the market will bear. Nor is it an appeal to some highly abstract spirit best understood by studying the history of the world's varied religions. Rather, it is a conceptual revolution we seek: not a new therapy, but a new way of looking at therapy and, thereby, of practising it. It is a practice of method shaped by activity theorists going back at least to Vygotsky and Marx (Newman & Holzman, 1993). Its tools (and results) are an updated, indeed postmodernised, dialectic, greatly influenced by Wittgenstein and other relatively contemporary philosophers of mind. As well, it relies a good deal on the concept/activity of performance and has taken much from contemporary theatre and dramaturgy (Holzman & Mendez, 2003; Newman & Holzman, 2006).

But, for all that, it remains a cognitive behaviour therapy. Hopefully, it is a positive advance, but as with all positive advances, it is to some extent a critique of what came before.

What is that critique?

Let us go back to the beginning of our remarks. Cognitive therapy, we are told, is scientific, in that it is based on common sense. But Gödel, Wittgenstein,

4. 'In response to the postmodernist "attitude", they [the scientists] have given up objectivity, empirically based findings, and logical argumentation in favor of hyperbole, emotional outbursts, and arguments *ad hominem*' (Newman & Holzman, 1997: 1).

Einstein, Heisenberg and others have taught us that common sense is often less than commonsensical. The view of science invoked by the theoreticians and practitioners of traditional cognitive behaviour therapy is based on an ignorance or misunderstanding of contemporary thinking about the philosophy of mind, and, more generally, the philosophy of science. By way of summing up my own brief account of that history – a revolutionary turn from modernism to a sometimes muddled postmodernism – let us consider a final and critical element in Davidson's defence of modernism.

More on me 'n Donald

My earliest discussions on these matters with Donald Davidson came early in the 1960s, while I was still a graduate student and he was justifiably identified as the genius of Stanford's philosophy department, just about to set out to conquer the philosophical world. He did. Meanwhile, I sought to turn my intellectual efforts to radical organising and psychology. I did not presume that Davidson and I would run into each other again. But we have.

My PhD dissertation, written under the direct supervision of Daniel Bennett, a brilliant young Wittgensteinian at the time and, ironically, a former student and then a colleague of Davidson, was a study of the concept of explanation in history. And an analytical consideration of such matters required a reading of Carl Hempel's 'The function of general laws in history' (1942). Davidson, a friend of Hempel, very much admired some of the positions that Hempel took in his important essay and, naturally, to begin with (this is the first law of graduate school), so did I. But as I proceeded in studying what was then contemporary philosophy of history, reading Scriven, Dray and others, I grew more and more wary of Hempel's logical-positivist position.

Davidson and I, sadly, parted ways before anything resembling a deepening of that discussion happened. But, in my own mind, I have been having it with Donald ever since. It is something like Donald's discussion with 'Vann' on 'the flux'. In many of my imaginary discussions, I say to Donald: 'But look, Carl Hempel was a highly dedicated empiricist and yet he speaks of the function of general laws in history. But there are no general laws in history.' Perhaps a rare historian seeks to speculate on the existence of such a law, but in almost 100 per cent of historical writings, there are no such laws to be found. How odd, then, that Hempel, a confirmed radical empiricist, is seeking to discover the function of the non-existent laws. Perhaps Hempel's essay might have been called 'Why there should be' or 'How there could be' general laws in history. But not 'The function of general laws in history'.

Many years ago, Scriven made something very close to this point (Scriven, 1958). I, of course, do not know Davidson's response to my imaginary polemic, since we never had it. But in my reconsideration of Davidson's lifelong defence of modernism, I see what he found attractive in Hempel's almost bizarrely entitled paper, for the most essential claim in Hempel's view is that there must be a connection between what is explained and its explanation (in Hempel's Latin, the '*explanans*' and the '*explanandum*'). For, in the final analysis, while causality might be the cement, connectedness (in Hempel's case, deducibility) is the justification for the logical positivist and, indeed, for the modernist, and eventually for the early scientist's claim that everything must be connected. But if and when everything is connected, we lose the magic (or, more accurately put, we lose the space for the magic) that is necessary for human development. Surely therapists must be sensitive to this.

Vygotsky speaks to the child's learning-developing process in such language as the child growing 'a head taller than him/[her]self' (Vygotsky, 1978: 102). Some may write this off as metaphor; I do not. I think it points to an essential feature of growth. And it is equally applicable to cognitive growth and to emotive growth, and to grown-ups, as well as to the child.

In my view, Davidson betrays the depth of his commitment to modernism by his dogmatic defence of *connectedness*. There are, it seems to me, two major arguments against *connectedness*. The first is that there is no need for *connectedness,* because everything is connected. This argument is something like (bears a family resemblance to) Davidson's argument against the flux/conceptual framework picture. The second argument is that everything *isn't* connected. Why? Because there must be room for development.

Cognitive behaviour therapy (indeed, all therapy) requires a theoretical basis to move in a postmodern direction. Modernist science and the demand for everything being 'connected' costs us the space for magic – not tricks and games, but the real magic of real science. It is not only that cognitive behaviour therapy's argument that science and scientific psychology is commonsensical eliminates the magic; that framework also adds to people's neuroses. For in eliminating the 'space for magic' – a concept critical for understanding human development, it seems to me – we eliminate the possibility of cure. Vygotsky's idea of performing a head taller than one's self is based on the notion of performing what one is becoming. Is Vygotsky suggesting that one literally grows a second head, making one a 'head taller'? In social therapy – once again a cognitive behaviour therapy, but primarily a group therapy – the second head is the creating of the group. And both from the personal or individual point of view and from the broader social point of view, it is the creating of the group that is the revolutionary activity necessary for further human development.

Dialectics and performance (social therapy, part 2)

Aristotle, who knew a great deal about both ethics and logic (indeed, a case could be made that he invented both), noted, famously, that the conclusion of a practical syllogism was an *action*, not another proposition. It is within that overall spirit that, several thousand years later, in what is now a *postmodern* period, as opposed to a *pre*-modern period, we consider the relationship between dialectics and performance. Aristotle set in motion an extraordinary conversation (actually several) that ran its course throughout the entire history of modernist thought, for it was never apparent how propositional thinking could lead to action, any more than it was apparent how mental activity could produce physical activity. The mind and the body, which obviously work together, seem, conceptually, to keep getting in each other's way.

For the pre-modernist, God was allowed to solve this puzzle, as well as all other problems. But modernism's rejection of God re-raised the problem and, roughly speaking, starting with Descartes, the mind–body issue has dominated epistemology/psychology. The writings of Searle, Rorty, Davidson and others represent, to me, the best of late modernism's efforts to solve the Aristotelian problem. But postmodernism both requires and makes possible a new way of looking at this whole matter. And the location of such discussions requires stepping outside of the cognitive sciences and into the therapeutic arts, for, although therapeutics are very much a product of cognitive thinking (witness Freud and many other things as well), they are, in practice, most fundamentally an art form. Such is the case with social therapy.

An anti-dichotomist (a postmodernist) point of view such as mine would hardly permit a rock-hard differentiation between art and science. On the other hand, these two central phenomena in Western history have very different cultural histories and, as such, play very different roles in the life of the society – most significantly, in the lives of the masses of the society. Ask two people – ordinary citizens – one of whom is off to an art exhibition and the other to a science show, what their expectations are.

Psychotherapeutics may not be Western society's only art/science crossover phenomenon (witness poker playing), but it is surely one of the most important. Attempting to deconstruct a phenomenon so large and so ontologically and methodologically confused is not only daunting; it provides no obvious starting point. We leave ourselves open to the charge that we are fundamentally mixing apples and oranges – and, of course, we are at least doing that.

All those authors whom we have considered (Ryle, Wittgenstein, Quine, Rorty, Searle, Davidson and hundreds of others) have all recognised these issues and attempted to evolve a method for even considering the mind–body relationship. Aristotle's several-thousand-year-old provocation about the practical syllogism seems bolder to me than all the others. I seek a postmodern version of his pre-modern audacity.

Of course, I'm mixing apples and oranges (postmodernism is a fruit cocktail). Sentence NAD (not a definition):

> Within a performatory (as opposed to a cognitive) modality (community), we (social therapy/ social therapists) seek to help create a pointless dialectical (a mixture of Plato's and Marx's) group conversation (a conversation

> oriented toward discovery/creation) in order to generate a new game (a Wittgensteinian game) that completes (in a Vygotskian sense) the thinking, and is itself (by magic, aka art) a performance (though more activity than an action).

That might well be the most complex sentence I have ever intentionally created. I normally prefer simple sentences. I am very much scientific in my orientation, and this has been the case all of my intellectual, and perhaps my pre-intellectual, life. What is the essence of that posture, of that attitude? Well, I've always felt very close to the hardness of the subject matter of science; the effort to account for or explain that unbelievably complex body of knowledge by the simplest of means, namely science has always been my ideal. But when Carl Hempel, and many others, started to speak of the general laws in history (when there are no such things), a philosopher of science like myself, with a modicum of intelligence and a reputable PhD, had to put his foot down… even if it meant taking on the most intelligent man I had ever met in my life – namely, Donald Davidson.

And so, some 50 years ago, I began that process for a variety of reasons, in a variety of ways, which, at its most fundamental level, involved taking on philosophy itself. For science, which in some ways emerged as a challenge to philosophy, had itself gone too far. It was insisting that its methodology, probably the most brilliant in all of Western thought, had somehow gained the privilege of applying itself to everything in Western thought. The next thing I knew, I was a practising therapist. And, as such, I was introduced to *DSM-IV*. The authors of *DSM-IV* make Carl Hempel look very modest indeed, for, although he spoke as if they existed, Hempel did not make up any historical laws. *DSM-IV*, while it does not quite make up laws of psychology – more precisely, laws of emotionality – comes very close to doing so. It is something of a *Poor Richard's Almanac*[5] of mental disturbances designed apparently for therapists of all stripes to identify what is mentally wrong with a client, and to explain to the client what is wrong with her or him.

Gergen and I considered it in our paper on diagnosis (1999), which we speak of as 'The Rage to Order' – it might as well be called the 'Rage to *Connect*'. These pseudo-laws (perhaps they should be called pre-laws) are surely not scientific. Even the psychiatrists who authored *DSM-IV* would agree with that. But in relatively ordinary language they as much insist upon a connectedness as laws of optics.

The pseudo laws suggested by *DSM-IV* are perhaps not a bad bunch of cracker-barrel ideas in relatively ordinary language about emotional pain within our culture. But even cracker barrels have a history. And even *Poor Richard's* suggestions as to weather conditions 10 years hence can, in the minds and hands of some, turn into certainties, or at least serious predictions. With the weather, this rarely turns into a serious problem. With therapy, it does. For believing that something might well be

5. *Poor Richard's Almanack* was written and published by the US statesman Benjamin Franklin, under the pseudonym 'Poor Richard'. It appeared annually from 1732 to 1758.

a proper description of your disturbing emotional state is quite different to being certain it is. You may say it is up to the therapist to make this very distinction, but the codification of these connections into a very official sounding book called *DSM-IV*, together with the rules and regulations, often equally misleading, of the American Psychiatric Association, make it quite difficult for all but the most self-assured therapists to do so.

Finally, I discovered a relatively small band of scientifically-trained academics and clinicians who are sympathetic to these concerns (Ken Gergen, Mary Gergen, Sheila McNamee, John Shotter, Tom Strong, Andy Lock, Lynn Hoffman, Harlene Anderson, Ian Parker, Erica Burman and others), and I am encouraged to articulate my strong view that it is science (and hard-nosed philosophy of science) that stimulates the growth of postmodernism, and not fuzzy-headed thinking by inebriated Frenchmen, à la Sokol.[6]

Were there no space constraints in this volume, I would lend some completion to this somewhat rambling chapter by unpacking the Sentence NAD:

> Within a performatory (as opposed to a cognitive) modality (community), we (social therapy/social therapists) seek to help create a pointless dialectical (a mixture of Plato's and Marx's) group conversation (a conversation oriented toward discovery/creation) in order to generate a new game (a Wittgensteinian game) which completes (in a Vygotskian sense) the thinking, and is itself (by magic, aka art) a performance (though more activity than an action).

I hope to do so in a subsequent article.

Acknowledgements

Many thanks to Dr Lois Holzman, my lifelong collaborator, for teaching me virtually all that I know about psychology. Thanks to my Developmental Philosophy Class, held every Saturday afternoon at the East Side Institute in New York City, for their patience and assistance. Thanks to Kim Svoboda and Jacqueline Salit for their assistance in reading and writing this chapter.

6. In *Beyond the Hoax: science, philosophy and culture* (2008), Alan Sokol continues *ad infinitum* to do little but berate those poor hung-over Frenchmen.

References

Beck AT (1979). *Cognitive Therapy and the Emotional Disorders.* New York, NY: Penguin Press.

Davidson D (1980). Actions, reasons, and causes. In: Davidson D. *Essays on Actions and Events.* Oxford: Clarendon Press (pp3–19).

Davidson D, Quine WVO (1997). *In Conversation: Donald Davidson – the Quine discussion.* [Video.] London School of Economics: Philosophy International.

Gergen KJ (2006). *Therapeutic Realities: collaboration, oppression and relational flow.* Chagrin Falls, OH: Taos Institute Publications.

Hempel CG (1942). The function of general laws in history. *Journal of Philosophy 39(*2): 35– 48.

Holzman L, Mendez R (2003). *Psychological Investigations: a clinician's guide to social therapy.* New York/ London: Brunner-Routledge.

Hood [Holzman] L, Newman F (1979). *The Practice of Method: an introduction to the foundations of social therapy.* New York, NY: Institute for Social Therapy and Research.

King ML Jr (1992). The role of the church in facing the nation's chief moral dilemma. In: King ML Jr, Carson C, Holloran P, Luker R, Russell PA. *The Papers of Martin Luther King Jr Volume IV: symbol of the movement, January 1957–December 1958.* Berkeley, CA: University of California Press (pp184–91). www.stanford.edu/ group/King/publications/papers/vol4/570425.002-The_Role_of_the_Church_in_Facing_the_Nations_Chief_Moral_Dilemma.htm. (accessed August 2008).

Kreisler H (1999). *Philosophy and the Habits of Critical Thinking.* Conversation with John R Searle, Mills Professor of Philosophy, UC Berkeley. [Online]. Conversations with History. Institute of International Studies, UC Berkeley. https://conversations.berkeley.edu (accessed 3 February 2018).

Kuhn TS (1970). *The Structure of Scientific Revolutions.* Chicago, IL: University of Chicago Press.

Marx K (1845/1969). XI Theses on Feuerbach. In: *Marx/Engels Selected Works, Vol One.* Moscow: Progress Publishers (pp13–15).

Nagel E, Newman JR, Hofstadter DR (eds) (2001). *Gödel's Proof.* New York, NY: New York University Press.

Newman F (2003). Undecidable emotions (What is social therapy? And how is it revolutionary?) *Journal of Constructivist Psychology 16*(3): 215–232.

Newman F, Holzman L (1996/2006). *Unscientific Psychology: a cultural-performatory approach to understanding human life.* Lincoln, NE: iUniverse Inc.

Newman F, Gergen K (1999). Diagnosis: the human cost of the rage to order. In: Holzman L (ed). *Performing Psychology: a postmodern culture of the mind.* New York, NY & London: Routledge (pp73–86).

Newman F, Holzman L (1997). *The End of Knowing: a new developmental way of learning.* New York/ London: Routledge.

Newman F, Holzman L (1993). *Lev Vygotsky: revolutionary scientist.* New York, NY/London: Routledge.

Quine WVO (1951). Two dogmas of empiricism. *Philosophical Review 60*: 20–43. Reprinted in: Quine WVO (1953). *From a Logical Point of View.* Cambridge, MA: Harvard University Press.

Rorty R (1979). *Philosophy and the Mirror of Nature.* Pinceton, NJ: Pinceton University Press.

Ryle G (1949). *The Concept of Mind.* Chicago, IL: University of Chicago Press.

Scriven M (1958). Definitions, explanations, and theories. In: Feigl H, Maxwell G, Scriven M (eds). *Concepts, Theories, and the Mind-Body Problem: Minnesota studies in the philosophy of science*, vol 2. Minneapolis, MN: University of Minnesota Press (pp99–175).

Searle JR (2006). *Freedom and Neurobiology: reflections on free will, language and political power.* New York, NY: Columbia University Press.

Searle JR (2005). *Mind: a brief introduction*. New York, NY: Oxford University Press.

Searle JR (1992). *The Rediscovery of the Mind*. Cambridge, MA: MIT Press.

Sokol J (2008). *Beyond the Hoax: science, philosophy and culture*. New York, NY: Oxford University Press.

Styers R (2004). *Making Magic: religion, magic and science*. New York, NY: Oxford University Press.

Thorndike L (1941). *A History of Magic and Experimental Science*. New York, NY: Columbia University Press.

Vygotsky LS (1978). *Mind in Society*. Cambridge, MA: Harvard University Press.

Whitehead AN (1916). The organization of thought. *Science 44(*1134): 409–419. (The text of his address to the British Association for the Advancement of Science meeting in Newcastle-on-Tyne, September 1916.)

Wittgenstein L (1953). *Philosophical Investigations*. Oxford: Blackwell.

Wittgenstein L (1921). Logisch-philosophische abhandlung [Tractatus Logico-Philosophicus]. *Annalen der Naturphilosophische* 14(3/4).

CBT PERSPECTIVES AND RESPONSES

21 What is CBT *really* and how can we enhance the impact of effective psychotherapies such as CBT?*

Warren Mansell

In preparation for this new edition, I read the revised manuscripts for the chapters in this book. I can't easily express my degree of disappointment that none of these new chapters had replied to my chapter in the first edition. This was the case even though I had made it easy by breaking down every chapter into its problematic claim about CBT and an alternative, evidenced repost to each. So, how far are we 'towards a constructive dialogue' after 10 years? Not very far at all. On the positive side, it has made my job of revising my chapter easier, but in lieu of making any counter-replies, I will expand at the end of this chapter on what a therapy 'beyond' CBT should look like, building on my work elsewhere (eg. Alsawy et al, 2014; Mansell, 2008a).

At its core, CBT focuses on how we attend, interpret, reason, reflect and make sense of inner and outer events. It is a journey into personal meaning-making at the edge of mind and objective experience. It emerged from ego-analytic psychotherapy in the 1950s and 1960s, rooted itself in academic psychology, and began the slow process of scientific investigation during the 1970s (Padesky, 2004).

One way to clarify CBT is to emphasise its focus on conscious mental processes. While it acknowledges that unconscious processing clearly exists, it proposes that the most effective method of engaging with a client and facilitating change is to help them become aware of their conscious experience of meaning-making. Beck (1976) contrasts cognitive therapy with psychoanalysis, which emphasises the therapist's interpretations of the client's unconscious motivations; with early behaviour therapy, which takes the measurement of observable behaviour as the only source of valid

* This chapter is an extended version of a chapter from the *European Journal of Psychotherapy and Counselling 2008; 10*(3).

data, and with neuropsychiatry, which locates the source of the client's problems within a disordered neurochemical process. According to Beck (1976), all three approaches ignore the validity of the client's own reports. CBT therapists have to listen very carefully to what clients are saying, because this is the information they use and share with the client to try to understand their lives better, and to work with them on improving their lives, in line with the clients' own goals.

Yet, contemporary CBT is not quite the same as Beck's early cognitive therapy. CBT is often perceived as a single, knowable entity, but this is not the case. It evolves through the reciprocal interplay of theory, research and clinical observation (Salkovskis, 2002).

It is often claimed that the only scientific support for CBT is from randomised controlled trials. Again, this is not the case. The scientific support for CBT derives from a convergent range of diverse methodologies, including case studies (eg. Visser & Bouman, 1992), case series (eg. Watkins et al, 2007), experimental manipulations (eg. Browning, Holmes & Harmer, 2010), statistical modeling (eg. Stahl, Rimes & Chalder, 2014), diaries (eg. Clark et al, 1999), qualitative interviews with service users (Knowles et al, 2014), practice-based evaluations (eg. Gillespie et al, 2002), and, last but not least, randomised controlled trials, including their systematic reviews and meta-analyses (eg. Tolin, 2010).

Figure 1 provides a simplified illustration of the historical and theoretical origins of CBT. This diagram illustrates both the diversity of CBT's origins and the diversity of contemporary directions for CBT. It has always had diverse influences. There is an emerging consensus that we are in the process of a 'third wave' of CBT that builds on the first (cognitive therapy and behavioural therapy) and second waves. While the second and some of the first waves are clearly still present and practised daily, the third-wave approaches represent a range of advances that have incorporated diverse theoretical and philosophical approaches. Clearly, CBT is not a stand-alone treatment; it is embedded within a wide system of knowledge and discourse. This is reflected in current definitions. At present, the UK professional association for CBT practitioners defines CBT as follows:

> The term 'Cognitive-Behavioural Therapy' (CBT) is variously used to refer to behaviour therapy, cognitive therapy, and to therapy based on the pragmatic combination of principles of behavioural and cognitive theories. (BABCP, 2008).

Maybe most importantly, how would you know that you were having a CBT session? Admittedly there are no absolute criteria, but in general you would expect:

- to be working together, collaboratively, with the therapist, in an equal, power-sharing arrangement
- to be able to talk about your current problems and set your own goals for the therapy

Figure 1. A simplified diagram of the development of contemporary CBT. Unbroken lines represent strong influences; dotted lines represent mild influences. Theoretical influences are printed in italics. All other labels refer to forms of CBT.

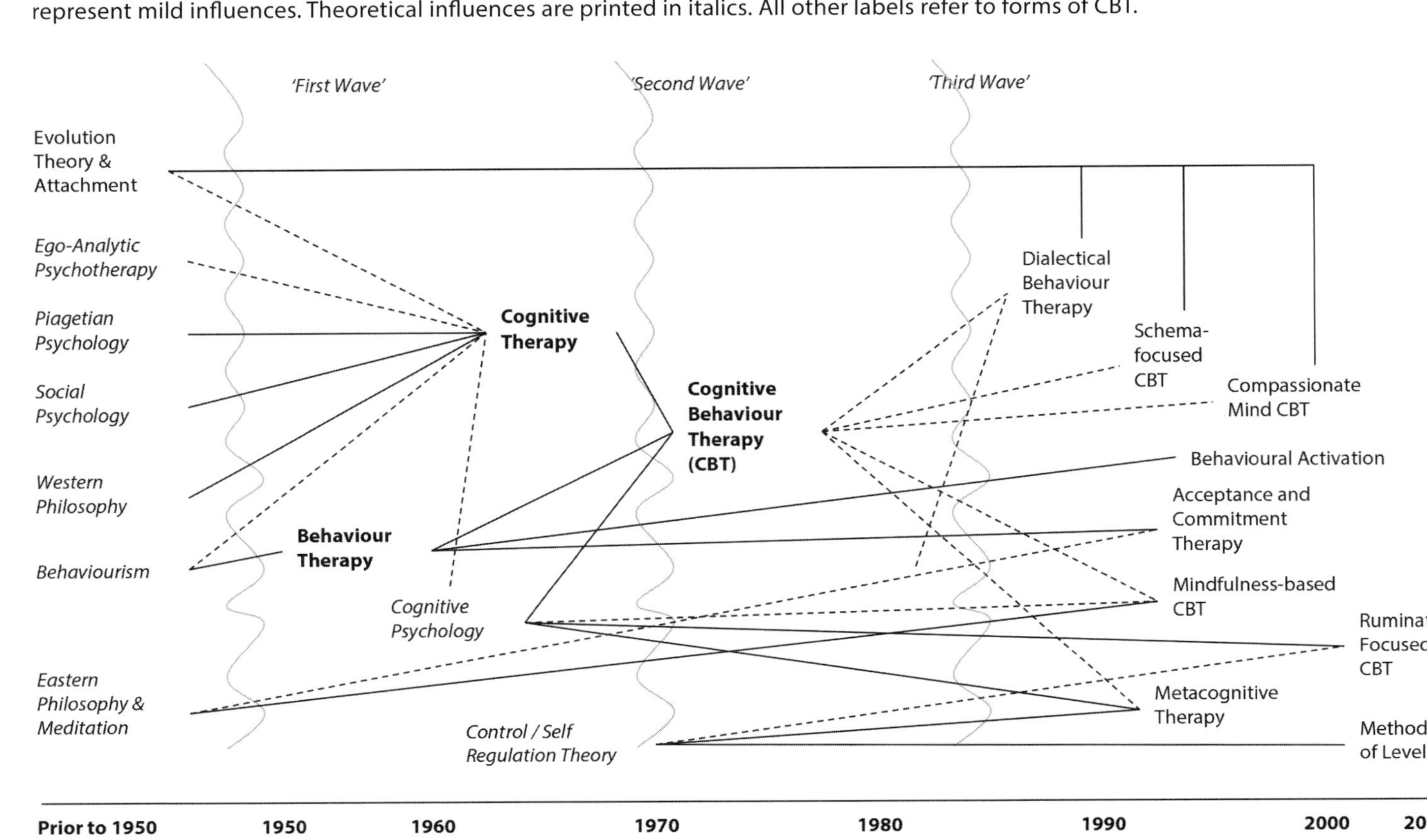

- to be asked questions about your current and recent thoughts, feelings, memories, mental imagery, behaviours, environment and social experiences
- to work with the therapist to produce a map, or 'formulation', for how these factors might combine negatively to contribute to problems, or positively to help you recover and improve your quality of life
- to test out new ways of thinking and behaving to see if they are helpful
- to be able to manage independently or fully recover after the therapy, and to be offered the opportunity to return for 'booster' sessions in the future.

In the preceding chapters, you will have read many critical chapters on CBT. I must admit that I shuddered at how many of them have misrepresented CBT. Therefore, I urge you to read the original sources that explain CBT, rather than take at face value the accounts that are provided here. If at all possible, get a chance to see an experienced and well-trained CBT therapist at work, either live or on video. That's how you will know what it involves.

Despite my shock at how CBT is described in the chapters, I do resonate with many of the reasoned concerns about where the field of psychological therapy is heading. I felt simultaneously frustrated by their inaccurate rendering of the therapy that I practise and research, and yet humbled and impressed by the breadth of scope and vision they achieved through considering the societal and philosophical context of psychotherapy. In keeping with these conflicted judgments, I would first like to briefly clarify the misrepresentation of CBT in these chapters and update the readers on the generally accepted view of the principles and context of CBT. Next, I will move on to tackle the more important question of how we are all to pursue both quality and quantity within the current expansion of evidence-based psychological therapies.

The straw man and the authoritarian archetype of CBT

Across the chapters as a whole, as I read further, I felt that I began to visualise an extreme characterisation of CBT. The image generated in my mind was of a CBT therapist who is controlling, over-rational, medicalising and only concerned with using techniques and seeking evidence in the services of a power-hungry and oppressive Western state. My first thought was that this is a 'straw man', often employed to beef up an argument. Then I realised that this image resonated with a cultural myth within our society that is just as much a Western social construction as the power structure that the chapters described. This person is the rigid, authoritarian and punitive leader. I recognised this figure from a dozen Dickens stories, from Big Brother in George Orwell's *1984* right up to 'The Man' in *School of Rock*, and a couple of po-faced penguins in *Happy Feet*. Then I thought of those traits again to get a better picture – controlling, ruled by logic, a pawn of the state – and the image came to mind – it was the Enforcement Droid (ED-209) from *Robocop*. I could imagine his emotionless commands: 'You have 20 seconds to comply with cognitive restructuring!' I am not surprised that these chapters had such a critical tone. Any self-respecting person would run for the door rather than spend more than a second with such a fear-provoking and uncompromising individual.

I began to think, is this really the face of CBT? Or is it some pervasive Jungian archetype that is being mistaken for CBT? Alternatively, is it the critical inner mentality that we try to understand and challenge in CBT itself (Gilbert, 2005)? Suffice to say, I do not recognise Enforcement Droids in any of my colleagues and friends who are CBT therapists; nor do I even tend to see any of these worrying properties in isolation. Why not? One possibility is that I do not mix with the kinds of CBT therapists who fit this description, yet they do exist. A second, overlapping possibility is that there is a cultural view of CBT that spreads through the health services, academia and the public, independently of CBT therapists. A third possibility is that I have learned about CBT later than the authors of these papers, and so am unfamiliar with the early, rigid origins of the approach that surely must have plagued the 1970s and 1980s. But this explanation does not fit with my reading of the primary sources of this period, which do not reflect this aversive image. The explanation I favour is that the principles and practice of CBT guard against this grotesque abstraction, and in fact encourage the opposite traits in a CBT therapist: an approachable, emotional attuned, empowering, real person, who understands the reciprocal relationship between theory, research and practice and has only the concerns of the client at heart. For this reason, I particularly like the chapter by Strong, Lysack, Sutherland and Chondros (Chapter 15) on the dialogic potentials of cognitive therapy. They point to the potential value of CBT as an empowering psychotherapy that provides open space for clients to develop personal meaning in their life and share knowledge within a collaborative relationship.

It is important to acknowledge that the (mis)representation of CBT in the chapters varies widely, from almost none to extreme. Rather than write any more on this issue, a reference and two tables will suffice. Here, Table 1 summarises several of the properties of CBT that are suggested in the chapters and contrasts them with the documented properties of CBT within the Cognitive Therapy Rating Scale (Blackburn et al, 2001; Young & Beck, 1980). This scale is currently accepted internationally as the means to assess the competence of cognitive behaviour therapists (Kazantis, 2003). Thus, if the scale is being used as it was designed, then CBT therapists will emerge as truly collaborative, client-centred, formulation-led practitioners who facilitate clients' own, alternative perspectives and empower them to take control of their lives. This fits with the evidence. In a range of studies, CBT patients rate their therapists higher than psychodynamic therapists on various relationship variables (eg. interpersonal skills, accurate empathy, support), and their level of 'active listening' is equivalent to insight-oriented therapists (see Keijsers, Schaap & Hoogduin, 2000). CBT therapists are active, empathic people who enable clients to solve challenging life problems.

Table 1. Key suggested characteristics of CBT compared with the established characteristics and their systematic assessment during CBT training.

Suggested characteristic of CBT	**Chapter author**	**Established feature of CBT**	**Indicator of a high level of therapist competence on the Cognitive Therapy Rating Scale (Blackburn et al, 2001; Young & Beck, 1980)**
Rationalist; cold and logical; the therapist models 'correct' thinking or guides to the 'right' solution	Winter, Proctor, Bracken & Thomas, some aspects of Strong et al.	Constructivist; clients consider multiple perspectives and are helped to form their own solutions	'The cognitive therapist often uses exploration and questioning to help patients see new perspectives.' 'Therapist was especially adept at using guided discovery during the session to explore problems and help patient draw his/her own conclusions.' 'The cognitive therapist should display optimal levels of warmth, concern, confidence genuineness, and professionalism.'
The therapist controls the session	Winter, Proctor, Kaye, Tudor	The balance of the control dynamic but generally equal or client-centred	'Collaboration seemed excellent; therapist encouraged patient as much as possible to take an active role during the session (eg. by offering choices) so they could function as a "team".'
Technique-driven	Winter, Bohart, some aspects of Milton	Formulation-driven and particularly attuned to the interpersonal processes in the session. Techniques are used within this context.	'Therapist seemed to understand the patient's "internal reality" thoroughly and was adept at communicating this understanding through appropriate verbal and non-verbal responses to the patient (eg. the tone of the therapist's response conveyed a sympathetic understanding of the patient's "message"). Excellent listening and empathic skills.'

Table 2. Suggested contexts of CBT compared with the perspectives within the mainstream CBT literature.

Suggested context of CBT in chapter	**Reference**	**Alternative perspective on the context of CBT**	**Examples of references**
Superficial relationship with cognitive theory	Pilgrim	Ongoing, reciprocal relationship with cognitive theory	Brewin (1988)
Based on Cartesian dualism	Lees, Bracken & Thomas, Kelly & Moloney	Based on a monistic, integrative model of human functioning	Beck, Emery & Greenberg (1986); Gilbert (2002)
Justification largely based on evidence from RCTs	Lees, Bohart; Bryceland & Stam	Justified and developed through reciprocal links between theory, research and practice	Salkovskis (2002)
Pathologises distress as a disease entity	Pilgrim, Bohart	Based on a continuum model of psychological distress	Beck (1976); Morrison (2001); Mansell, Morrison, Reid, Lowens, Tai (2007)
Requires a diagnosis	Lees	Does not require a diagnosis	Ellis (1962); Harvey, Watkins, Mansell & Shafran (2004); Mansell (2008b)
Considers only outcomes based on symptoms of psychiatric illnesses; a form of psychiatric treatment	Lees, Pilgrim	Considers impact on overall quality of life and seeks opinions from service users as to appropriate outcome measures	Knight, Wykes & Hayward (2006)

Table 2. continued…

Complicit with contemporary power arrangements	Guilfoyle, Bracken & Thomas, Kaye, Moloney & Kelly	Radical, innovative, and questions and transforms existing power structures	Padesky (2004)
Therapist has the power, and takes control of factors such as number of sessions	Winter, Proctor	Therapist strives to balance power and help client determine key components of the therapy such as number, length and frequency of sessions	Giesen-Bloo J, van Dyck R, Spinhoven P, et al (2006)
Often ignores the role of interpersonal processes and the social context	Strong et al, Tudor, Milton, Bracken & Thomas, Woolfolk & Richardson, Moloney & Kelly	Interpersonal processes have a reciprocal relationship with intrapersonal processes; social context forms part of the cognitive formulation	Strong et al (this volume); Gilbert (2005)
CBT claims to always be superior in efficacy to other forms of psychological therapy	Guilfoyle, Bohart, Kaye, Moloney & Kelly	CBT has a substantially wider, more consistent evidence base than other therapies, but it is accepted that its relative efficacy varies across studies	Veale (2008)
Does not typically involve bringing unconscious material into awareness and integrating life experiences	Milton	Negative automatic thoughts occur fleetingly until brought into awareness; counterproductive avoidance strategies push distressing material outside awareness; cognitive formulation incorporates life experience including trauma	Beck (1976); Ehlers & Clark (2000)

Table 2 summarises the contexts of CBT that are suggested by some of the chapters. In each case, they are contrasted with perspectives from mainstream clinicians and researchers within the CBT field. Clearly, everyone does not speak with exactly the same voice, but these chapters would be deemed generally acceptable and consistent with CBT as it is theorised and practised. Thus, it would seem quite possible to characterise CBT as a radical, innovative, socially aware and scientifically grounded discipline of psychotherapy that questions received dogma about the nature of psychological distress, works to challenge rigid power arrangements within society, and yet takes a measured view of its strengths and limitations.

For the rest of this chapter, I would like to focus on the points of agreement I have with some of the authors and the important implications for the future of psychological therapies.

Taking stock of the broader perspective on psychotherapy

Putting the chilling chimera of CBT Enforcement Droid-209 to one side, the chapters have a refreshing interpersonal and societal angle on the process of training, practising, evaluating and disseminating effective psychological therapies. They also address critical philosophical and scientific issues that may help us to understand where psychological therapy is heading. I will comment on a number of the key themes that they introduce.

Interpersonal processes are important and are closely related to intrapersonal (cognitive) processes

Several of the chapters emphasise the importance of social context and interpersonal factors. The chapter by Strong and colleagues makes a strong case that our internal dialogue is shaped by our interactions with others. They are concerned that there may be a shift to seeing psychotherapy as focused on establishing objective truth and ignoring the reality of clients' lives, which are potentially rich with social interaction. Bracken and Thomas (Chapter 10) are also very concerned that CBT ignores the social reality of people's lives in its focus on internal mental processes, as are Kelly and Moloney, in Chapter 5. Similarly, in Chapter 18, Arthur Bohart and Richard House note the importance of interpersonal processes in therapy – the moment-to-moment sensitivity during therapy and the therapist's ability to respond in that moment, and Keith Tudor (Chapter 12) emphasises the key importance of the 'other' in therapy and in everyday life within a person-centred perspective.

In CBT, therapist trainers also have a concern that CBT therapists maintain their attention to the social context, both within and outside the session. For this reason, in CBT, therapists are encouraged to help their clients challenge the pervasive cultural beliefs that are counterproductive for them (for example, 'I must be thin'; 'I must earn lots of money'), and provided with the opportunity, often through imagery work and role play, to explore and rehearse opportunities to assert themselves and achieve their goals in real life, often in harsh or poverty-stricken environments (eg. Kellogg & Young, 2006). CBT is not seen as a replacement for good public health schemes and social planning – it is merely what the health service provides to the individual to allow them to cope with their situation, given the circumstances, along with any other necessary support from other organisations, and any more radical changes afoot in the culture.

In addition, a significant amount of the training process for CBT involves building up the interpersonal skills that a therapist needs to maintain a good, collaborative relationship with the client. From a theoretical perspective, the importance of interpersonal processes is also actively pursued (eg. Gilbert & Leahy, 2007). Since the inception of the new, large-scale training schemes, there have been assurances that these essential features of CBT can be maintained (Holland, 2008). For my part, I have worked with IAPT services that use training and supervision to focus on the importance of maintaining a collaborative therapeutic relationship.

Controlled trials are contextualised and offer only one source of scientific support

It was encouraging to see that John Lees, in Chapter 9, immediately recognises that CBT is in practice person-centred and incorporates flexibility in response to client need. However, he is concerned that the decisions about how to decide on the investment in a particular psychological therapy are based almost entirely on the apparent evidence base, over and above the consideration of the context of how that evidence base is constructed and defined. He makes an excellent case that how we define evidence now is likely to change in the future, as the philosophy of our culture and our outlook change. Arthur Bohart and Richard House (Chapter 18) make several similar points in their chapter, and Bryceland and Stam (Chapter 17) explore the ethical dimensions of the apparent over-emphasis on evidence-based treatment.

In CBT, we have many of the same concerns as Lees, Bohart and House, and Bryceland and Stam. It is possible to hide behind that shiny veneer of an evidence base without scrutinising one's own practice and being a true science-practitioner. Yet, without the dynamic interface of theory, research and practice and the drive of innovation, CBT would not be as well developed as it is today (Salkovskis, 2002). There is a concern that CBT will become freeze-dried in a certain image, in order to match the requirements of the health system as a whole, rather than to continue its propensity to evolve and adapt.

I chime with Bohart and House in stating that the best evidence for a therapy is contextual: within one's own practice with one's own patients (Margison et al, 2000; Miller, Duncan & Hubble, 2004; Mansell, 2008a). Therefore, a normal part of the development of a new form of CBT is to establish its effectiveness in a variety of practice settings (eg. Gillespie et al, 2002). In CBT, we need to monitor not just the apparent competence of therapists and their grasp of the core theory underlying their work, but also their personal impact on the outcomes that matter to their clients. To do this, we need to continue to evaluate the therapy and examine its correspondence with theory, rather than to assume its efficacy, and continuously change it. Thus, while it is appropriate to allow certain evidence-based psychotherapies, like CBT, to be accredited by the health system, we need space for innovators who adapt and devise their own approaches from a firm cultural and scientific foundation.

Psychological therapy is a way of thinking and relating to other people and is not a stand-alone intervention

David Pilgrim (Chapter 2), along with Kelly and Moloney, is concerned that, as a culture, we are cultivating a desire for happiness through consumerism but failing to address the real causes of distress. According to Pilgrim, while Richard Layard has ostensibly attempted to counter this trend, the process has been compromised by a number of factors, including a limited understanding of social factors and an overemphasis on the medicalisation of distress.

In CBT, there are similar concerns. There is a concern that service users, managers and health professionals will see CBT as a stand-alone treatment within a system that does not necessarily adhere to its principles. But this is not possible to sustain. The equal relationship that therapists and clients have in CBT impacts on the clients' expectations of how they relate to other health professionals, and the multidisciplinary working of the contemporary health system necessitates a negotiated debate about how to work with service users. On the positive side, it is possible that the increasing prevalence of psychological therapists in these teams will help facilitate an approach of collaboration and service user choice that is beneficial to the systems themselves (Kinderman & Tai, 2007).

Psychological therapy needs to challenge existing counterproductive power structures

A valuable point to take from Michael Guilfoyle's chapter (1) is a concern that psychological therapy can become complicit with existing power structures in society that are themselves toxic to mental health. John Kaye takes a similar stance in his chapter (16), as do Paul Kelly and Paul Moloney.

In CBT we are aware of this uneasy alliance. On the one hand, it is fruitful to think that CBT can help people to return to work, as that is what most of our clients wish to do. On the other hand, if this evidence were to be taken to justify the maintenance of an increasingly work-oriented society, then it would not fit with the aims of CBT, which is essentially to help facilitate our clients' to achieve a good quality of life, as they choose to define it.

Similarly, it can be very fruitful when CBT is promoted within psychiatry to widen access to effective psychological therapy. Yet, in contrast to most practitioners in psychiatry, the CBT therapist strives (unsuccessfully at times, of course) to maintain an equal balance of power in the relationship and to refute notions of being 'the expert' in the role. Enabling recovery during CBT often necessitates questioning assumptions that many in the psychiatric profession make about the lifelong nature of mental health problems and dependence on medication as a treatment.

As a whole, it appears that people involved in CBT embrace the fact that the therapy has become recognised and recommended by key organisations, but most of us would not wish this to be at the cost of losing the central principles of the therapy and its agenda for empowering all individuals to recover from mental health problems through what they have learned during the therapy.

Control, purpose, meaning and needs

Perhaps the most valuable contributions from this book relate to theories of human functioning, and in particular how psychological therapy addresses the fact that human beings are purposeful agents who have their own needs, who want to be in control of their lives and to imbue them with personal meaning. For example, Gillian Proctor (Chapter 2) emphasises the importance of gaining a 'sense of control' in one's life. Where there are power imbalances within therapy, the client's sense of control is compromised.

There is an interest in how to quantify and assess shifts in personal meaning and sense of purpose in CBT (Brown et al, 2008). In practice, the CBT therapist strives to maintain a collaborative relationship, to use the therapy in service of the client's own needs (via a client-driven goal list and agenda at the start of each session), and to explore the development of meaning within thoughts, behaviours, emotions and the social context. As CBT becomes more available and more widely disseminated, it is important that new trainees can fully grasp the notion of collaborative goal-setting – the standard, while not always achieved, is a true balance in power, where clients can express themselves freely by stating their own goals for therapy, and take control of their lives outside the session. In the future, the equal balance of control aimed for in CBT is likely to expand to wider areas, such as patient choice over the number, frequency and duration of sessions (Carey, 2005).

Woolfolk and Richardson (Chapter 7) take issue with the assumption that a behaviour therapy (and presumably CBT), as it is currently *theorised*, can genuinely help individuals to consider and pursue their own goals. They cite at least two reasons – that the methods of helping clients elicit goals are not part of the theory or empirical evidence upon which behaviour therapy relies, and that a linear model of events predicting further events will not provide the appropriate approach for such an intervention. This is an important issue for psychological therapies – they need to use a theory that explains the whole process of therapy, not simply one component that is presumed to be core, such as 'distorted thinking' or 'unconscious conflict'. What's more, we need a theoretical approach that incorporates and explains the role of features such as how clients set goals and how they derive and maintain purposeful values in their life.

Keith Tudor, in his chapter, articulates Carl Rogers' (1951) theory of personality and behaviour, which fulfils some of these requirements. Rogers (1951) stated:

'Behaviour is basically the goal-directed attempt of the organism to satisfy its needs as experienced, in the field as perceived.' Tudor explains that we may therefore understand behaviour as the best a client can do in any given moment, given their perception of their inner and outer environment. Rogers (1951) articulated several important premises of this kind, yet he did not produce a working theory. To be more specific, Rogers' theory was a set of verbal propositions regarding the nature of the self, behaviour, perception and reality. He did not attempt to construct a model or diagram of the components that could actually *function* in order to simulate how such relationships could work in practice.

Interestingly, in 1973, Carl Rogers endorsed a theoretical framework that was highly consistent with his premises, *Behavior: the control of perception* (Powers, 1973/2005): 'Here is a profound and original book with which every psychologist – indeed every behavioural scientist – should be acquainted,' commented Rogers. The basic premise of this book was the same as Rogers – that behaviour is the control of perception. Yet Powers, with a background in engineering, provided a sophisticated mechanistic framework for how human functioning is managed and orchestrated from this first principle, through networks of hierarchical control systems. Computer simulations are available that provide some of the best evidence for its validity (Powers, 2008).

The theory described in Powers' 1973 book, perceptual control theory (PCT), has had a wide influence, and it would not be accurate to align it exclusively to either a person-centred approach or, indeed, any other therapeutic approach. Yet, it has contributed to some of the most recent advances in CBT. For example, it has been used to reframe and extend existing CBT approaches (Alsawy et al, 2015; Mansell, 2005; Mansell et al, 2007), has influenced new therapies through its influence on theories of self-regulation (Watkins, 2008), and has directly led to a new form of cognitive therapy –Method of Levels (MoL) (Carey, 2008; Mansell, Carey & Tai, 2012). Nevertheless, in the broad family of CBT therapies, PCT-related innovations form just a small part of the eclectic mix.

Psychotherapies must balance the need to embrace diversity with the need for parsimony and coherence

In line with the kind of innovations stated above, David A Winter's chapter (13) draws appropriate attention to the shift from a rationalist to a constructive approach within CBT. Whatever the debate concerning the exact starting point, degree and timescale of this shift, it is surely to be welcomed and maintained. Winter also points to the high degree of diversity within contemporary CBT, to include mindfulness, acceptance and commitment therapies and interpersonal approaches such as compassionate-mind-based CBT. John Kaye also reviews these progressions in CBT and is aware that CBT is not a homogenous, static entity. Paul Kelly and Paul Moloney acknowledge this diversity too.

The heterogeneity of CBT is a two-edged sword. The open, scientific and pragmatic approach of CBT therapists has perhaps encouraged this eclecticism, and, on the one hand, it provides us with a wide range of different styles of CBT for new trainees to select. On the other hand, it has placed a strain on the boundaries of how CBT is defined, as Winter suggests. One potential solution is for researchers involved in CBT and other psychotherapies to alter their research approach. Instead of using methodologies and statistics that use a competitive mode of comparing therapies, we need to explore commonalities across different therapies, and then try to identify the mechanisms for change – cognitive, behavioural, emotional, interpersonal or otherwise – that are tapped by different approaches (Mansell, 2008b). This concurs with Arthur Bohart and Richard House's take on the importance of moment-to-moment sensitivity in therapy, and Jane Milton's emphasis (Chapter 11) on evocation of affect and the development of personal coherence. Ultimately, we need a consensual theoretical framework that explains the importance of these core features of effective psychological therapy.

Summary and conclusions

Although targeted at CBT, I would suggest that the key themes of these chapters provide important points for any widely accessible form of psychological therapy. Namely, an effective and acceptable psychotherapy:

- needs to consider the person in their social context and their immediate interpersonal interactions, because of the close relationship with inner mental processes
- must be based on more than the standardised evidence base, because it needs to match the needs of the clients at whom it is targeted when put into practice in a particular context
- is likely to be at odds with a purely medical model of mental 'illness' and so needs to develop ways to accommodate to, or transform, its health service context
- needs to consistently monitor the process of control, sense of purpose and the balance of power during therapy so that clients can gain a perception of control in their lives
- needs a coherent theoretical model to guide its core principles that evolves in a dynamic way in response to new evidence or new ways of thinking about that evidence.

Taking the family of CBT therapies as a whole, I see that they are tackling the above issues directly, in tandem with the popularisation and dissemination of the therapy. This process of evolution is likely to be a rocky one, as the desire for immediate accessibility is pitched against the need to adhere to these, and other, key principles. There is an emerging acceptance that CBT, as it is currently practised, will not exist in the future – it constantly changes, in response to new research (Veale, 2008). There will need to be shifts in the nature of CBT and related psychotherapies during this process, and the evolving solution will lie in identifying commonalities, rather than differences, across approaches, and placing them within a coherent and clear scientific framework. In order to manage this, CBT clinicians and researchers will need to communicate and collaborate with a range of professions, including non-CBT psychotherapists, to form a coherent account of how to help manage psychological distress and facilitate people's quality of life and wellbeing. This book can be one step on the way, if we agree to leave the straw (or metal?) man on the sidelines, and take psychotherapy forward together.

Addendum: beyond CBT from 2018

In the 10 years since the first edition of this book, I, Sara Tai, Tim Carey, and an increasing number of researchers and clinicians, such as Vyv Huddy, Filippo Varese, Doug Turkington, Timothy Bird, Rebecca Kelly, Sally Higginson and Robert Griffiths, have been disseminating and evaluating MoL therapy. We have long recognised the limitations of traditional CBT, as well as the limitations of other psychotherapies. Instead of focusing our energies on criticising these therapies, we have spent our time building up the scientific and practical basis of MoL. What have we learned in this period? Here are what we regard as some of the features of this form of psychotherapy, which goes beyond the critiques stated in this book.

- Clients need to book their own appointments and determine their own schedules of frequency, duration and length of therapy (Carey, Tai & Stiles, 2013). Clearly this goes beyond usual practice, where clients are offered a fixed number of sessions and informed of these by their therapist. Not only does client-led appointment scheduling allow the therapist to adapt the provision of therapy to the individual, but the efficiencies of working in this way are huge, with greatly reduced non-attendance and shorter waiting times. Owing to its accessibility, MoL has been used with first-episode psychosis patients, high school pupils, psychiatric inpatient wards, in prisons and even on Death Row.
- Therapy needs to be as simple as possible, but not too simple – the principle of parsimony. Our work with MoL reveals that an effective therapy can involve short, frequent questions from the therapist to serve two goals – to talk about a problem, and to catch the client's background thoughts about the problem. Our research shows that the client experience of being in control and talking freely are tightly related to whether they feel therapy is helpful, and this effect is over and above elements of the therapeutic approach or the therapeutic relationship (Cocklin et al, 2017). In the absence of such a rule, therapies become awash with dozens of specific techniques, each of which then need

to be learned, making their training (and their scientific evaluation) highly inefficient.

- Every element of a therapy, including appointment-setting, and how and why a therapist asks a question, needs to be accountable to a single, robust, scientific theory. When one makes an 'eclectic' use of more than one theory, it introduces uncertainty as to how one might possibly combine them. By maintaining a tight link between one theory and practice, training can be made more efficient and effective. We use perceptual control theory because it can be used as a framework to answer these clinical questions, it has a robust research base (Mansell & Carey, 2015), and it crystallises the principles that we regard as most important to therapy: namely, control, conflict and reorganisation (Carey, Mansell & Tai, 2015).

Owing to the highly innovative nature of MoL, we would not consider it to be merely an example of a CBT. It has no greater affiliation with CBT than with any other school of psychotherapy. Indeed, it was first practised by a medical physicist, Bill Powers, who was trying to bring insights from engineering to develop a novel psychological theory. As such, it is not only beyond CBT, but beyond the alternative psychotherapies that are traditionally available. We wait to see whether its merits, in terms of its client-led nature, efficiency and scientific rigour, can make a lasting impact on the mental health sphere in this century, beyond that of CBT in the last century.

Acknowledgements

Thank you to Paul Gilbert, Roz Shafran, Tim Carey, David Veale, and Rod Holland for their helpful comments on an earlier version of this chapter.

References

Alsawy S, Mansell W, Carey TA, McEvoy P, Tai SJ (2014). Science and practice of transdiagnostic CBT: a Perceptual Control Theory (PCT) approach. *International Journal of Cognitive Therapy 7*(4): 334–359.

BABCP (2008). *What is CBT?* [Online.] www.babcp.com (accessed 7 August 2008).

Beck AT (1976). *Cognitive Therapy and the Emotional Disorders.* New York, NY: Penguin.

Beck AT, Emery G, Greenberg RL (1985). *Anxiety Disorders and Phobias: a cognitive perspective.* New York, NY: Basic Books.

Blackburn IM, James IA, Milne DL, Baker C, Standart S, Garland A, Reichelt FK (2001). The revised cognitive therapy scale (CTS-R): psychometric properties. *Behavioural and Cognitive Psychotherapy 29*(4): 431–446. Scale available at http://ebbp.org/resources/CTS-R.pdf (accessed 29 January 2018).

Brewin CR (1988). *Cognitive Foundations of Clinical Psychology.* Hove: LEA Associates.

Brown GP, Roach A, Irving L, Joseph K (2008). Personal meaning: a neglected transdiagnostic construct. *International Journal of Cognitive Therapy 1*: 223–236.

Browning M, Holmes EA, Harmer CJ (2010). The modification of attentional bias to emotional information: a review of the techniques, mechanisms, and relevance to emotional disorders. *Cognitive, Affective, & Behavioral Neuroscience 10*(1): 8–20.

Carey TA (2008). Perceptual control theory and the method of levels: further contributions to a transdiagnostic perspective. *International Journal of Cognitive Therapy 1*: 237–255.

Carey TA (2005). Can patients specify treatment parameters? A preliminary investigation. *Clinical Psychology and Psychotherapy 25*: 326–335.

Carey TA, Mansell W, Tai S (2015). *Principles-Based Counselling and Psychotherapy: a method of levels approach.* London: Routledge.

Carey TA, Tai SJ, Stiles WB (2013). Effective and efficient: using patient-led appointment scheduling in routine mental health practice in remote Australia. *Professional Psychology: Research and Practice 44*(6): 405–414.

Clark DM, Salkovskis PM, Hackmann A, Wells A, Ludgate J, Gelder M (1999). Brief cognitive therapy for panic disorder. *Journal of Consulting and Clinical Psychology 67*(4): 583–589.

Cocklin A, Mansell W, Preston C, Emsley R, McEvoy P, Comiskey J, Tai S (2017). Client perceptions of helpfulness in therapy: a novel video-rating methodology for examining process variables at brief intervals during a single session. *Behavioural and Cognitive Psychotherapy 45*(6):647–660.

Ehlers A, Clark DM (2000). A cognitive model of posttraumatic stress disorder. *Behaviour Research and Therapy 38:* 319–345.

Ellis A (1962). *Reason and emotion in psychotherapy.* Secaucus, NJ: Citadel Press.

Giesen-Bloo J, van Dyck R, Spinhoven P, van Tilburg W, Dirksen C, van Asselt T, Nadort M, Arntz A (2006). Outpatient psychotherapy for borderline personality disorder: randomised trial of schema-focused therapy vs transference-focused psychotherapy. *Archives of General Psychiatry 63:* 649–658.

Gilbert P (2008). *Cognitive Behavioural Therapy: a guide to purchasers.* [Online.] www.babcp.com/members/cbt_for_purchasers.htm (access to members only).

Gilbert P (2005). *Compassion: conceptualisations, research and use in psychotherapy.* Hove: Routledge.

Gilbert P (2002). Evolutionary approaches to psychotherapy and cognitive therapy. *Journal of Cognitive Psychotherapy 16:* 263–294.

Gilbert P, Leahy RL (2007). *The Therapeutic Relationship in the Cognitive Behavioural Psychotherapies.* Hove: Routledge.

Gillespie K, Duffy M, Hackmann A, Clark DM (2002). Community-based cognitive therapy in the treatment of post-traumatic stress disorder following the Omagh bomb. *Behaviour Research and Therapy 40*: 345–357.

Harvey AG, Watkins ER, Mansell W, Shafran R.(2004). *Cognitive Behavioural Processes across Psychological Disorders: a transdiagnostic approach to research and treatment.* Oxford: Oxford University Press.

Holland R (2008). Accreditation standards 'to be maintained'. *CBT Today 38:* 3.

Kazantis N (2003). Therapist competence in cognitive-behavioural therapies: review of the contemporary empirical evidence. *Behaviour Change 20*: 1–12.

Keijsers GPJ, Schaap CPDR, Hoogduin CAL (2000). The impact of interpersonal patient and therapist behavior on outcome in cognitive-behavior therapy: a review of empirical studies. *Behavior Modification 24*: 264–297.

Kellogg SH, Young JE (2006). Schema therapy for borderline personality disorder. *Journal of Clinical Psychology 62*(4): 445–458.

Kinderman P, Tai S (2007). Clinical implications of a psychological model of mental disorder. *Behavioural and Cognitive Psychotherapy 35*: 1–14.

Knight MTD, Wykes T, Hayward P (2006). Group treatment of stigmatisation and self-esteem in schizophrenia: a waiting list trial of efficacy. *Behavioural and Cognitive Psychotherapy 35*: 304-318.

Knowles SE, Toms G, Sanders C, Bee P, Lovell K, Rennick-Egglestone S, Coyle D, Kennedy CM, Littlewood E, Kessler D, Gilbody S, Bower P (2014). Qualitative meta-synthesis of user experience of computerised therapy for depression and anxiety. *PLoS One 9*(1): e84323.

Mansell W (2008a). The seven Cs of CBT: a consideration of the future challenges for cognitive behaviour therapy. *Behavioural and Cognitive Psychotherapy 36*: 641–649.

Mansell W (2008b). Keep it simple – the transdiagnostic approach to CBT. *International Journal of Cognitive Therapy 1*: 179–180.

Mansell W (2005). Control theory and psychopathology: an integrative approach. *Psychology and Psychotherapy: Theory, Research and Practice 78*: 141–178.

Mansell W, Carey TA (2015). Perceptual Control Theory: will it lead to a revolution in psychology? *The Psychologist 28*: 896–899.

Mansell W, Carey TA, Tai S (2012). *A Transdiagnostic Approach to CBT Using Method of Levels Therapy: distinctive features.* London: Routledge.

Mansell W, Morrison AP, Reid G, Lowens I, Tai S (2007). The interpretation of and responses to changes in internal states: an integrative cognitive model of mood swings and bipolar disorder. *Behavioural and Cognitive Psychotherapy 35*: 515–540.

Margison FR, Barkham M, Evans C, McGrath G, Clark JM, Audin K, Connell J (2000). Measurement and psychotherapy: evidence-based practice and practice-based evidence. *British Journal of Psychiatry 177*: 123–130.

Miller SD, Duncan BL, Hubble MA (2004). Beyond integration: the triumph of outcome over process in clinical practice. *Psychotherapy in Australia 10*: 2–19.

Morrison AP (2001). The interpretation of intrusions in psychosis: an integrative cognitive approach to hallucinations and delusions. *Behavioural and Cognitive Psychotherapy 29*: 257–276.

Padesky CA (2004). Aaron T Beck: mind, man, and mentor. In: Leahy RL (ed). *Contemporary Cognitive Therapy: theory, research and practice.* New York, NY: Guilford Press (pp3–26).

Powers WT (1973/2005). *Behavior: the control of perception.* New Canaan, CT: Benchmark.

Rogers C (1951). *Client-Centred Counselling.* London: Constable.

Salkovskis PM (2002). Empirically grounded clinical interventions: cognitive-behavioural therapy progresses through a multi-dimensional approach to clinical science. *Behavioural and Cognitive Psychotherapy 30*: 3–10.

Stahl D, Rimes KA, Chalder T (2014). Mechanisms of change underlying the efficacy of cognitive behaviour therapy for chronic fatigue syndrome in a specialist clinic: a mediation analysis. *Psychological Medicine 44*(6): 1331–1344.

Tolin DF (2010). Is cognitive–behavioral therapy more effective than other therapies? A meta-analytic review. *Clinical Psychology Review 30*(6): 710–720.

Veale D (2008). Psychotherapy in dissent. *Therapy Today 19*(1): 4–7.

Visser S, Bouman TK (1992). Cognitive-behavioural approaches in the treatment of hypochondriasis: six single case cross-over studies. *Behaviour Research and Therapy 30*(3): 301–306.

Watkins E (2008). Constructive and unconstructive repetitive thought. *Psychological Bulletin 134:* 163–206.

Watkins E, Scott J, Wingrove J, Rimes K, Bathurst N, Steiner H, Kennell-Webb S, Moulds M, Malliaris Y (2007). Rumination-focused cognitive behaviour therapy for residual depression: a case series. *Behaviour Research and Therapy 45*(9): 2144–2154.

Young JE, Beck AT (1980). *Cognitive Therapy Scale.* Unpublished manuscript. Philadelphia, PA: University of Pennsylvania. Scale available at www.beckinstitute.org/wp-content/uploads/2015/10/CTRS-12-2011_portrait-Cognitive-Therapy-Rating-Scale-1.pdf (accessed 29 January 2018).

22 The case for CBT: a practical perspective from the NHS frontline

Isabel Clarke

In writing a response to the criticisms of CBT in this book, I will first address the broader arena of politics and power in which this debate takes place. I am in agreement with the editorial and a number of the contributors in identifying issues of power and resources as a crucial factor in the current prominence of CBT, but will add my own perspective on this context. I will then explain why and how I ended up as a CBT therapist, as opposed to any other sort of therapist, before tackling the philosophical and scientific substrate of CBT, which is a focus in a number of the chapters. I will not answer the points raised in all the chapters, but hope to cover a representative selection of the arguments.

A number of the contributors have noted that CBT is far from monolithic, and in what I write I am probably only representing my own take on the modality, although I will make clear what this is and how it fits into the wider picture. As a therapist accredited by the BABCP, who has published CBT papers in peer-reviewed journals and presented at BABCP conferences, I do not consider myself a complete outsider.

To begin with, there are a lot of the points made by both the editors and contributors about the current status of CBT with which I can agree. I studied history before coming into psychology in mid-life and need no persuading that power and economics lie at the root of most movements in human affairs. As a fan of Gilbert's (1992) ecological view of human interactions (ie. we are a bunch of primates vying for position in the hierarchy), I have no problem with seeing a very basic power dynamic and struggle for resources behind the language of evidence base. However, I do take issue with Kelly and Moloney's exposition of this power dynamic. They suggest that CBT has been seized upon as a means of maintaining the position of the ruling class by redefining discontent with social conditions as individual pathology. I am not denying that there is an element of that, especially in Layard's thesis (Centre for Economic Performance, 2006) (on which more later), but, having worked in or around the NHS (first as a member of a community health council and then as an employee) since the 1980s, I can identify another and more immediately relevant power dynamic in the rise of CBT and evidence-based therapy. This is the dynamic specifically around health service politics, which centres on the dilemma of how to control the medical establishment. What follows is very much a personal perspective from the shop floor.

The NHS was achieved through Bevan's Faustian pact with the doctors. The introduction of general management in the 1980s was an attempt to temper the medical grip on the system. It was unsuccessful; managers found themselves managing everyone, apart from the doctors. Evidence-based practice and the establishment of the National Institute for Health and Care Excellence (NICE), as it is now called, with its panoply of clinical guidelines, were the next attempt to exert some degree of political control over the medical juggernaut. Until recently, the therapeutic modality embraced by psychiatry was psychodynamic. The promotion of CBT was therefore part of this strategy, but also, as I will argue below, CBT is a more sensible therapy for your average NHS punter than, in particular, the psychoanalytic branch of psychodynamic therapy. Many of the contributors to this book represent other, humanistic, existential and person-centred therapies that are neither psychodynamic nor CBT. I see them as incidental casualties in this particular battle – they have been caught in the crossfire.

The Layard debate

The debate about Layard and his intentions introduces a whole other dimension. I completely agree with Pilgrim and all the other commentators who have pointed out that Layard's idea that CBT will get everyone on incapacity benefit happy and well and back into paid work is implausible. However, my experience of the impact of Layard on the ground is overwhelmingly positive in shifting the emphasis of service provision away from the purely medical (ie. medication and ECT) and towards talking therapy – and this impact has extended beyond primary care and into the arena of serious mental illness, where I work. Layard has successfully argued for a huge injection of resources into talking therapies through the Improving Access to Psychological Therapies (IAPT) programme. No one else has ever achieved that before, to my knowledge, despite the insistent request by service users that they want to be listened to and given a chance to make sense of their situation. Service users often also appreciate being given the tools to take responsibility for and manage their own emotional wellbeing. I appreciate that some may say they should be listened to by people other than CBT therapists. From my perspective, the first priority is the provision of therapy, and I am not sympathetic to anything that might stall this (as I have seen happen as a result of intermodality rivalries in the past).

While welcoming the IAPT programme, I can only agree with the contention of Kelly and Moloney (Chapter 5), Pilgrim (Chapter 3) and other contributors to this book that therapy cannot cure the ills of a sick society or transform the situation of someone ground down by poverty, injustice and a degraded environment. On the other hand, as a therapist, I feel a bit powerless to fix the social malaise of 21st century life. However, I do know how to help the people who are struggling with an adverse social situation to go about it more effectively and stop shooting themselves in the foot. Often people do not want to avail themselves of this help. They may choose instead to anaesthetise themselves with substances, remain in the parallel universe of psychosis, or take one of the other escape routes devised by human ingenuity in the face of an intolerable reality. I can only respect their choice, while remaining aware that each of these solutions carries with it severe consequences for their mental wellbeing and quality of life. So, I continue to offer an alternative to these siren solutions – a more effective engagement with the very real challenges faced by most of the people I see. In this respect, I am in complete agreement with Pilgrim when he argues against therapy being linked to diagnostic categories, as Layard does, and for the importance of deconstructing diagnosis. This is my agenda entirely, as I explain in a number of my writings (eg. Clarke, 2008a).

Choice of therapy modality

To return to the debate between modalities, the choice of which therapy to train in will be influenced by a variety of factors, including individual inclination, chance encounter and the state of the market. However it is reached, it is a major decision, entailing a considerable investment in time, emotional energy, effort, and often money. As a psychologist, I am familiar with the concept of confirmatory bias research (eg. Fischhoff, 1977, 1982) – that once someone has made a decision, they will register information that confirms that decision, and filter out or discount information that supports the rejected options. The greater the cost of the decision, the stronger the confirmatory bias. Choice of therapeutic modality is a decision that reaches to the heart of a person's identity. It is only to be expected that such choices will be defended vigorously.

That is the individual perspective. In the wider social context, there are complex mechanisms that decide how resources should be distributed. In the case of private therapy, the market decides, but the market will be influenced by the wider rhetoric. The looming issue of compulsory accreditation will also reach into the private sector. In the UK, the NHS is the major player in the healthcare stakes, and it is here that the battle for resources is most evident. In 1992, when I started work in a hospital department of psychiatry as a newly qualified clinical psychologist, the bulk of psychotherapy resources was concentrated in the psychodynamic department; of the three psychologists, one was psychodynamic, and the other two were both cognitive analytic therapy (CAT) and CBT trained. All the junior doctors took psychodynamic training cases, and the psychiatrists tended to see this as the modality of choice when referring patients. The shift in resources that has taken place throughout the NHS, from mixed modalities with the weight of medical power supporting psychodynamics towards an emphasis on CBT and other 'evidence-based therapies', can also be seen in that department (where I no longer work). Such a shift in resources cannot be accomplished without pain. It is entirely understandable that the concept of 'evidence base' should be viewed with suspicion as a means to accomplish a coup d'état, and its basis and details questioned by those who have been deposed.

In their editorial to one of the issues of the European Journal of Counselling and Psychotherapy from which many of the chapters in this book have come, House and Loewenthal (2008) make reference to 'vested interest groups whose over-long held privileges are being threatened – or even the envious attacks of the displaced and the superseded in therapy's free market'. These comments reflect this argument.

A personal perspective

So where do I come from? What are my motives for nailing my colours to the CBT mast? A cursory glance at my background might suggest that it was a purely cynical choice on my part. CG Jung has always been one of my heroes, and I have read extensively in the psychoanalytic and psychodynamic literature. My road to clinical psychology was long and winding, taking me through a second degree with the Open University and extensive voluntary work with a mental health theme before I finally arrived at clinical training in my mid-40s. The Samaritans, for whom I was a volunteer for nine years, gave me an essentially person-centred training. I value that induction to the acceptance of the individual and their pain without flinching as a sure foundation for all my subsequent training. Relate gave me an eclectic training with a psychodynamic bias. During my three years of clinical psychology training, as well as learning CBT, I spent one year under the supervision of a consultant psychotherapist learning to practise brief psychodynamic therapy and completed my CAT training at practitioner level when I qualified.

So, with all those options to choose from, why CBT? Is it just because CBT has cornered the resources and I want a job? I see the real answer as residing in my primary motivation throughout those long years of career change and voluntary work that eventually allowed me to practise in the NHS with people with severe mental health problems. It took over 15 years. I would have arrived a whole lot sooner if I had opted for a counselling training and private practice.

My motivation was to understand and to be able to make a difference for people who have suffered severe breakdown and are perhaps left with enduring problems. It started with the major depression of a good friend when we were all in our 20s; my experience as a Samaritan volunteer, of following people into hospital after suicide attempts, strengthened my resolve. I did not like the way people were treated there. It did not seem to respect their humanity or their need to make sense of both their experiences and themselves. I wanted to work to change that. My primary loyalty has always been to those people, and it remains with them. My profession, which I greatly value, and the different therapy modalities, are for me just means to that end.

So, why CBT? The other modalities in which I trained also have much to offer. As a newly trained clinical psychologist, I took seriously the question of how best to help my chosen client group, and in the early 1990s there was no pressure on me to opt for CBT. As the only clinician in my setting working with people who had acquired a diagnosis of psychosis, a new field for therapy at that time, I was resourced to attend any training or conference I could find. In this way, I surveyed the field and concluded that, when it came to psychosis, CBT offered the most collaborative, containing and effective option. Furthermore, the CBT practitioners really were working with psychosis; often, when psychodynamic practitioners talk about psychosis, they are referring to people in transient psychotic states who are sufficiently together to be able to afford to have psychoanalysis several times a week.

Things changed, and I found myself working less with psychosis and more with so-called personality disorders (I prefer the term 'complex trauma'). Once again, I found the explicit and collaborative stance of CBT to be effective with people who were relatively fragmented, and to be respectful of them. The same is true of CAT, and it was purely local politics that caused me to leave CAT. The advent of dialectical behaviour therapy (DBT) has alerted all of us in the field to the importance of introducing the individual to non-harmful ways of dealing with unbearable emotion before embarking on 'exploratory' or 'exposure' work to address the underlying trauma (Linehan, 1993a).

With the development of 'third wave', mindfulness-based CBT approaches, such as Linhehan's DBT and Hayes' acceptance and commitment therapy (Hayes, Strosahl & Wilson, 1999), I am even happier with this choice. These approaches get away from the thought-challenging aspect of CBT, which works for people with mild to moderate difficulties but falters when faced with more intractable problems. Mindfulness seeks to alter the person's relationship to both thought and feeling, as opposed to seeking to alter feeling by altering thought. I have developed my own variant of the third-wave approach that is particularly suited to inpatient and crisis contexts, which is where I now work (Durrant et al, 2007; Clarke & Wilson, 2008).

The evidence base

In explaining why I am a CBT therapist, I have concentrated on individual experience and failed to invoke the mantra of the 'evidence base'. Again, on this subject, I both have sympathy with many of the arguments put forward in this book and will offer some defence of the concept. I have already indicated that I consider the concept of 'evidence base' to have been deployed in the NHS power struggle as polemic. On the other hand, with my wish to hand control to the service user, I have little sympathy with therapies that tend to promote dependency and be mysterious about their operation. If a therapist purports to have some effect on an individual, it should be possible to know what this might be, and to check whether it is occurring, in at least a majority of cases. I agree that randomised controlled trials are more appropriate for medication trials than for therapy. I can personally attest that they are a nightmare to conduct in routine clinical practice, and question how representative some of the bigger trials are of our practice. It is always possible to pick holes in more rough-and-ready, before-and-after measures, but I still think we owe it to our clients to use them, and to publish the results. That has been my practice whenever I have developed the model in new directions (Bradbury & Clarke, 2006; Durrant et al, 2007; Naeem, Clarke & Kingdon, 2009).

Underlying philosophy and science

Perhaps the greatest weight of argument against CBT in this book concerns the philosophical basis of the modality (for example, the chapters by Bracken and Thomas, Brazier, Loewenthal and others), and the psychology of its implied model of the person. A number of the contributors argue that CBT is a purely positivistic approach, which therefore excludes the subjective and relational. Woolfolk and Richardson (Chapter 7) make this point, accusing CBT of being mechanistic. Brazier (Chapter 8) sees CBT as the heir to a tradition starting at the end of the Middle Ages that replaced God with reason. Loewenthal (Chapter 14) compares CBT with existentialism, arguing that, whereas existentialism confronts the individual with the pain of existence, CBT offers a way of escaping this reality.

There are two strands of argument that need distinguishing here. One concerns the positivistic values implicit in insisting on an evidence base, and the other is a comment on the nature of CBT itself. I have covered the evidence base issue above, so will here concentrate on the underlying philosophy of CBT. First, as noted by many of the contributors, this is far from monolithic. A number of the chapters cite the elasticity of CBT and give the third wave as an example of this. The reliance on evaluation and evidence is integral to this. Any new element can become an accepted part of CBT, provided it is shown to be effective. Imagery, compassionate mind and mindfulness are all examples of new approaches that have been introduced and evaluated over the last 10 years. This factor does make it harder to challenge Warren Mansell's 'straw man' epithet (Chapter 21), and it is also irritating to therapies whose techniques have been purloined in this way.

Tom Strong and colleagues (Chapter 15) note the limitations of a modality that is purely intra-psychic, as opposed to inter-psychic, and it is undeniable that CBT concentrates on the individual. They also note the potential for moving towards a more dialogic view. The brief 'Making Friends with Yourself' programme we run in our hospital (Hill, Clarke & Wilson, 2008) would be an example of this. This programme challenges self-critical cognitions by encouraging participants to treat themselves as they would a good friend, using role play with fellow participants. This approach draws on the compassionate mind techniques introduced by Gilbert and others (Gilbert, 2005). My hope is that developments like these will serve to temper the possibly over-individualistic focus of classical CBT.

I am drawn to answer Loewenthal's comparison of CBT with existentialism (to the detriment of CBT), as I have always been attracted by the sense of freedom and moment of choice afforded by the latter. That is precisely where I seek to lead people in therapy – to a place where they can see clearly the vicious circles and redundant patterns of behaviour that keep them trapped and can choose to walk free and make their own future – choices about both how they make sense of things and what they do. Integral to the process are management of state of arousal, so that the problematic affect need not hold sway, and clear-sighted, mindful encounter with that affect.

Loewenthal's charge that CBT is a way of avoiding the real issues is serious, but one that I would suggest perpetuates a common misconception. In my former job, my psychodynamic colleagues would regularly refer on people whom they had assessed as avoidant of their feelings and therefore unable to benefit from their therapy. The reality is that all therapy is at root about creating space to think about, and therefore be able to cope with, feelings. Conventional CBT goes for the thought, the behaviour or state of physical arousal first, as a means of reaching the feeling, as opposed to addressing the affect directly, as I learnt in order to practise brief psychodynamic therapy. The feeling is still the target. After all, the major diagnoses of depression and anxiety are simply another way of labelling troublesome emotions.

That is conventional CBT, but the third wave goes further in addressing emotion. Paradoxically, these approaches are often marketed as being behavioural rather than cognitive, but a cursory examination reveals them to be very different from the examples of behaviourist writing from the 1970s and 1980s cited by Woolfolk. Dialectical behaviour therapy (DBT), for instance, sees emotional dysregulation as lying at the heart of the presentation called 'borderline personality disorder'. The therapy, therefore, teaches skills in regulating and managing emotion. At first sight, this sounds very mechanistic and unlike therapy. I must confess that this was my suspicion when I first heard of it, but I have since become a total convert.

On the issue of teaching skills, I would defend the approach on two counts. First, it really works. Second, time and again, service users find very acceptable the idea of learning a skill, as opposed to being subjected to some mysterious therapy. To return to Loewenthal's point, by encouraging direct engagement with painful emotions through mindful attention and acceptance, DBT and the other third-wave approaches at least cannot be accused of shirking affect. Learning these skills requires the person to confront previously avoided, deep, emotional issues, and putting these skills into practice is inevitably challenging and needs all the support of the group and the therapist to facilitate it.

On the other hand, I can recognise an element of rigidity in more 'old-fashioned' CBT approaches that target 'dysfunctional thinking' and rely more heavily on challenging thoughts. This is particularly a problem where the therapy is delivered by people with inadequate training and supervision. I recognise this as a real danger where there is a perception that anyone can deliver CBT after a brief training and with no specialist supervision – a view beloved of cost-cutting managers. At worst, the therapist is trying to 'fix' people's thoughts in the same way that the doctor uses medication to 'fix' symptoms. This danger is an argument for good, professional control, and the linking of training, practice, ongoing supervision and continuous professional development in the delivery of therapy in the NHS.

This is a problem I encountered when working in tertiary acute and community mental health services. IAPT was set up to avoid this; training and supervision are provided, and practitioners are mandated to deliver therapy of a length and type that have been shown to be efficacious. However, more recently, the demands of commissioners and the pressure of continuous retendering, which favours the lowest bidder, have led to concern about erosion of standards. My employment in an NHS IAPT service has given me first-hand experience of this. Pressure from commissioners to cut number of sessions to below NICE-recommended levels in order to manage waiting lists more cheaply with fewer staff, combined with two re-tendering processes within six years, presumably aimed at securing a more compliant provider, all placed intolerable strain on the organisation. In this instance, the tender was retained and the line against erosion of standards was held, but at personal cost to staff.

BABCP has made strong representations about this danger: for example, in a press release issued in September 2014, headed '"Bullying culture" in NHS mental health services putting vulnerable patients at risk'. This warns:

> Concerned BABCP members working at all levels within NHS mental health services increasingly report that service managers are being forced or are choosing to ignore NICE guidelines in order to meet unrealistic service contracts and funding or misrepresent reductions in waiting lists and mask the impact of draconian cuts in services. With vulnerable patients left unseen or with an incomplete service, this could have serious consequences for their ability to recover. (BABCP, 2014)

The model of the person in CBT

A number of the contributors criticise the implied model of the human being and the operation of the human mind behind CBT. Kelly and Moloney (Chapter 5) point to the evidence that heuristic rather than logical reasoning dominate ordinary human thinking, stating: 'There is no "Cartesian Theatre" of the mind, in which our thoughts might be viewed and then manipulated.' Bracken and Thomas (Chapter 10) argue that CBT is based on a model where disorders of the mind are caused by 'dysfunctional beliefs' and associate this perspective with the Enlightenment. I will first consider the question of beliefs, and then look critically at the current theoretical basis for CBT, with emphasis on my own preferred perspective.

Beliefs, meaning and the sense that people make of their situation do powerfully influence how they feel about it, and approaches based on re-appraising meaning undoubtedly work. As cognitive therapy became applied to more intractable conditions, it ceased to work so consistently. A gap opened up between logical appraisal and emotional conviction: the individual might agree with the reasonable explanation but still be governed by the emotional reaction. DBT characterises this as the gap between 'Emotion Mind' and 'Reasonable Mind' (Linehan, 1993b). Teasdale and Barnard (1993) locate this gap deep in cognitive organisation. Both Linehan and Teasdale have been at the forefront of the third-wave movement in CBT. Both advocate mindfulness in order to bridge the gap.

Teasdale and Barnard have developed a solidly cognitive science-based exposition of cognitive architecture that they call 'Interacting Cognitive Subsystems' (ICS). If I could say that CBT as a whole had embraced this model, I would be able to refute with some confidence the charge of philosophical and scientific incoherence. When the model was first proposed, I was convinced that this was the way forward, and have based my own development of CBT firmly on this foundation (Clarke, 1999). By recognising the modular nature of the brain, and the existence of not one but two higher-order organising systems, ICS neatly explains human fragility, the limitations of our grasp on 'reality' and the tenuous and illusory nature of our control of our situation and sense of self. This is not a model that produces a mechanistic, Cartesian take on the human being. Its subtleties offer a way of explaining spirituality and our persisting sense of the sacred, along with the 'otherness' of psychotic experience (Clarke, 2008b).

Unfortunately, the CBT community as a whole has not adopted ICS. Barnard argues eloquently (Barnard, 2004) that the diverse theoretical models promoted by different factions are partial and poorly supported by basic science, in comparison with ICS. Indeed, more and more papers have been appearing that base their argument on ICS (eg. Duff & Kinderman, 2006; Lun, 2008). To explain this incoherence, I can only return once again to Gilbert's evolutionary argument, cited earlier this chapter: each CBT authority, having made a particular theory their own, hangs onto it as a part of their identity and their claim to eminence in the hierarchy. We are all only human.

Conclusion

In conclusion, I would like to draw a distinction between three issues that can easily become confused in this important debate. One is the position of CBT in comparison or competition with other therapeutic modalities. The other is the expansion of CBT as a means of making talking therapy more widely available, and therefore strengthening the position of therapy as a practical intervention for those in mental distress and one that can stand up to the assumption in mental health circles that medication is the first and usually the only remedy on offer. The third is the debate around the evidence base.

To take the comparison argument first, I have already made clear my position that there are historical factors, independent of the merits of the case, that have led to the extremes of the present situation. Further, I would not defend a monolithic situation where CBT was the only therapy available. In fact, because of its increasing dominance, CBT has extended its range and adopted many of the principles associated with rival modalities, such as recognition of the role of transference and the unconscious (although, for the most part, without using those terms) and the significance of the therapeutic relationship. However, I would argue that, with its open, collaborative and explicit way of operating, CBT is a therapy that is well-suited to people with severe problems that lead to a degree of fragmentation. I do not have sufficient breadth of experience and knowledge to state that it is the only one, but it has proved to work best for me with this client group, and I have observed real dangers with some other approaches. For the wider client group, I would wish to see many modalities flourish.

On the availability of therapy issue, I have no doubts. I have seen inter-modality rivalry restrict the already miserly availability of therapy on the NHS, and I welcome the new climate in which talking therapy is seen as a right and medication and ECT are no longer assumed to be the only options. There are dangers with the current enthusiasm. It suits managers to regard CBT as a simple, technical fix that can be applied by any of their existing staff with minimal training and no extra support or supervision. Qualified CBT therapists like me try hard to stand up against this sort of travesty. It is too early to say where this particular struggle will end – probably in compromise.

Finally, to return to the question of the evidence base. While fully acknowledging the shortcomings of some of the research on which the NICE guidelines, for instance, are based, I would take issue with those who argue that measuring outcomes has no place in the field of therapy. Routine evaluation and taking responsibility for the effects of our interventions is respectful of those we treat. In the private sector, there is a free market. Within the NHS, because access to therapy is so restricted, people generally have to take what they are offered. If diligently collected feedback, supervision and continuous professional development of practitioners ensure that what is offered is good quality, this often produces a better option than the vagaries of the market. Further, the principle of evaluation and development based on evidence has enshrined responsible creativity and flexibility within CBT. At the same time, the tally of evidence-based therapies increases all the time, as more research is conducted and published. This principle holds within itself the seeds of the end of the hegemony of CBT, but in a responsible manner, likely to benefit the end user.

Endword for the new edition

I stand by everything I wrote back in 2008, but I want to add a brief update.

The diagnosis debate

In the section on the evidence-base above, I outline my take on mental health problems – namely, that they arise from the ways that human beings have devised to help them cope with their internal state when this is intolerable. These (eg. drinking alcohol, staying in bed) work well in the short term but prove counterproductive when relied upon in the long term (see Clarke (2009) for more on this). In the years since 2008, I have developed this third-wave, transdiagnostic CBT approach in acute services (Clarke, 2015; Araci & Clarke, 2017). It is now known as Comprehend, Cope and Connect (CCC; Clarke & Nicholls, 2018), and combines individual formulation with the skills training discussed in the context of DBT above. The approach lends itself to the dissemination of psychological thinking and practice throughout a whole team, which centrally addresses the criticisms of the mental health services that prompted me to change career, as I explained above.

In the wider world, the critique of a purely medical approach has grown more incisive and more insistent – without as yet leading to major change. The appearance of *DSM-5* led to a backlash from both the Critical Psychiatry Network (Bracken et al, 2012) and the Division of Clinical Psychology of the BPS (2013). At the same time, evidence has been gathering about the way in which psychoactive medications have been both over-sold (Whitaker, 2010) and mis-sold (Moncrieff, 2008).

This has not led to any marked change in the medical hegemony in services in general. IAPT remains the exception in terms of the shift of resources towards talking therapy, but attempts to extend its reach into severe mental illness appear to have largely stalled without extra money and political will to effect significant transfer of resources. The Open Dialogue initiative (Razzaque & Wood, 2015) is a bold exception. This dialogic and inter-psychic approach, pioneered in Finland, strikes out in a different direction from both CBT and the other modalities represented in this book, and would indeed transform the mental health landscape if widely adopted.

IAPT and me

Since the original edition, there have been changes in IAPT. Significantly, it no longer offers only CBT. Dynamic interpersonal therapy (DIT), interpersonal psychological therapy (IPT), counselling for depression (CfD) and couples therapy have been added as IAPT-accredited, evidence-based therapies. Cognitive analytic therapy (CAT) is also often offered, as well as newer variants of CBT such as compassion-focused therapy (CFT), which are less strictly cognitive. On the negative side, the service has also become more pressured, more tightly controlled by the commissioners and more subject to regular, disruptive, retendering processes, with the subtext of privatising the service, which has happened in a lot of places (the service I work with is still within the NHS, so far). It is worth noting that NHS spending on talking therapies has tripled since the foundation of IAPT. Anecdotally, John Green, who headed up the IAPT service in the Central and North West London NHS Trust at the time of the Grenfell Tower fire, recalled at a conference shortly after that, when another major disaster had occurred in his patch 10 years previously, they had been in no way as good a position to offer support and therapy because IAPT did not then exist and there were far fewer therapists available to be deployed.

Since 2015, I have been employed on a project to introduce CCC in Hampshire IAPT (named italk). In IAPT in general, the tyranny of diagnostic-specific approaches remains (whether CBT or other modalities, as outlined above). CCC is the exception as it introduces individually and collaboratively devised trans-diagnostic formulation to an IAPT service. The project arose out of an audit, conducted by italk, of a patient cohort who made limited recovery with the existing interventions. The strategic health authority funded a project to develop a service for this group. The audit identified the target group as having problems exacerbated by complex trauma (normally characterised by relationship difficulties and chronicity). CCC was adopted, as the approach incorporates consideration of past trauma and relational aspects of therapy into its collaborative formulation and facilitates motivation towards clear treatment protocols for IAPT therapists. I have been employed on a project to pilot this since 2015 (see Clarke & Nicholls 2018). Data collection and publication are in process, but we are not yet in a position to claim an evidence base for its efficacy. If this approach should become more widely available, it will go some way to answering the criticisms of the limitations of CBT therapy as offered by IAPT.

References

Araci D, Clarke I (2017). Investigating the efficacy of a whole team, psychologically informed, acute mental health service approach. *Journal of Mental Health 26*(4):307-311.

BABCP (2014). 'Bullying culture' in NHS mental health services putting vulnerable patients at risk. Press release. [Online.] www.babcp.com/About/Press/Bullying-Culture-in-NHS-Mental-Health-Services-Putting-Vulnerable-Patients-at-Risk.aspx (accessed 3 March 2018).

Barnard PJ (2004). Bridging between basic theory and clinical practice. *Behaviour Research and Therapy 42*: 977–1000.

BPS Division of Clinical Psychology (2013). *Classification of Behaviour and Experience in Relation to Functional Psychiatric Diagnoses: time for a paradigm shift.* Division of Clinical Psychology position statement. Leicester: British Psychological Society.

Bracken P, Thomas P, Timimi S, Asen E, Behr G, Beuster C et al (2012). Psychiatry beyond the current paradigm. *British Journal of Psychiatry 201*(6): 430–434.

Bradbury KE, Clarke I (2006). Cognitive behavioural therapy for anger management: effectiveness in adult mental health services. *Behavioural and Cognitive Psychotherapy 35*: 201–208.

Centre for Economic Performance's Mental Health Policy Group. *The Depression Report.* London: London School of Economics.

Clarke I (2015). The emotion-focused formulation approach: bridging individual and team formulation. *Clinical Psychology Forum 275*(November): 28–33.

Clarke I (2009) Coping with crisis and overwhelming affect: employing coping mechanisms in the acute inpatient context. In: Columbus AM (ed). *Coping Mechanisms: strategies and outcomes. Advances in Psychology Research, vol 63.* Huntington, NY: Nova Science Publishers Inc.

Clarke I (2008a). Pioneering a cross diagnostic approach, founded in cognitive science. In: Clarke I, Wilson H (eds). *Cognitive Behaviour Therapy for Acute Inpatient Mental Health Units: working with clients, staff and the milieu.* Hove: Routledge.

Clarke I (2008b). *Madness, Mystery and the Survival of God.* Winchester: 'O' Books.

Clarke I (ed) (2001). *Psychosis and Spirituality: exploring the new frontier.* Chichester: John Wiley & Sons.

Clarke I (1999). Cognitive therapy and serious mental illness: an interacting cognitive subsystems approach. *Clinical Psychology and Psychotherapy* 6: 375–383.

Clarke I, Nicholls H (2018). *Third Wave CBT Integration for Individuals and Teams: comprehend, cope and connect.* Abingdon: Routledge.

Clarke I, Wilson H (eds) (2008). *Cognitive Behaviour Therapy for Acute Inpatient Mental Health Units: working with clients, staff and the milieu.* Hove: Routledge.

Duff S, Kinderman P (2006). An interacting cognitive subsystems approach to personality disorder. *Clinical Psychology & Psychotherapy 13*: 233–245.

Durrant C, Clarke I, Tolland A, Wilson H (2007). Designing a CBT service for an acute in-patient setting: a pilot evaluation study. *Clinical Psychology and Psychotherapy 14*: 117–125.

Fischhoff B (1982). Debiasing. In: Kahneman D, Slovic P, Tversky A (eds). *Judgment Under Uncertainty: heuristics and biases.* Cambridge: Cambridge University Press (pp422–444).

Fischhoff B (1977). Perceived informativeness of facts. *Journal of Experimental Psychology: human perception and performance* 3: 349–358.

Gilbert P (ed) (2005). *Compassion: conceptualisations, research and use in psychotherapy.* Hove: Routledge.

Gilbert P (1992). *Depression: the evolution of powerlessness.* Hove: Routledge.

Hayes S, Strosahl KD, Wilson KG (1999). *Acceptance and Commitment Therapy.* New York, NY: Guilford Press.

Hill G, Clarke I, Wilson H (2008.) The 'making friends with yourself group' and the 'what is real and what is not group'. In: Clarke I, Wilson H (eds). *Cognitive Behaviour Therapy for Acute Inpatient Mental Health Units: working with clients, staff and the milieu.* London: Routledge.

House R, Loewenthal D. Editorial. *European Journal of Psychotherapy and Counselling* 10(3): 181–186.

Linehan M (1993a). *Cognitive Behavioural Treatment of Borderline Personality Disorder.* New York, NY: Guilford Press.

Linehan M (1993b). *Skills Training Manual for Treating Borderline Personality Disorder.* New York, NY: Guilford Press.

Lun LMW (2008). A cognitive model of peritraumatic dissociation. *Psychology and Psychotherapy: theory, research and practice 81*: 297–307.

Moncrieff J (2008). *The Myth of the Chemical Cure.* Basingstoke: Palgrave MacMillan.

Naeem F, Clarke I, Kingdon D (2009). A randomized controlled trial to assess an anger management group program. *The Cognitive Behaviour Therapist 2*: 20–31.

Razzaque R, Wood L (2015). Open dialogue and its relevance to the NHS: opinions of NHS staff and service users. *Community Mental Health Journal 51*(8):93193–198.

Teasdale JD, Barnard PJ (1993.) *Affect, Cognition and Change: remodelling depressive thought.* Hove: Psychology Press.

Whitaker R (2010). *Anatomy of an Epidemic: magic bullets, psychiatric drugs, and the astonishing rise of mental illness in America.* New York, NY: Crown.

23 A response to the chapters in *Why Not CBT?**

Adrian Hemmings

Having read with interest the chapters in this book, I have a number of comments to make on the specific criticisms of cognitive behaviour therapy (CBT) – namely, the technical nature of CBT, and the notion of collaboration becoming a form of coercion and an expression of power. I reflect on CBT's relationship with powerful institutions, and examine the notion of evidence-based treatment, and particularly the role of randomised controlled trials (RCTs) in effectiveness research. I also examine some of the issues arising from the current social and political context in which CBT lies.

Before I do so, I wish to place these comments in the context of three main areas: current research that examines therapist effects; the Improving Access to Psychological Therapies (IAPT – perhaps more accurately described as IACBT) training, and the notion of CBT being a single entity.

Current research and therapist effects

Let us look first at the current research. The initial thrust of psychotherapy research was centred on the question, 'Does psychotherapy work?' A considerable body of literature attests to the effectiveness of psychotherapy, culminating in a number of meta-analyses that have demonstrated effect sizes comparable to, and in some cases considerably better than, many medical and educational interventions (Lipsey & Wilson, 1993; Robinson, Berman & Neimeyer, 1990; Shapiro & Shapiro, 1982; Wampold et al, 1997).

Since then, the research has changed to investigate the specific ingredients of the therapy that work and, in particular, whether there is a model of therapy that is superior to another. Here, the famous dodo bird effect (see Chapter 18, this volume)

---

* This chapter is an extended version of a paper published in the *European Journal of Psychotherapy and Counselling 2008;* 10(3): 271–279.

has been frustratingly consistent in showing that, when one model of therapy is compared head to head with another, there is little or no difference in outcome (Saxon et al, 2016; Godley et al, 2004; Luborksy et al, 2002; McDonagh et al, 2005; Miller, Wampold & Varhely, 2008; Shapiro et al, 1994; Stiles et al, 2006 ; Pybis et al, 2017), although a more recent meta-analysis showed marginal superiority of CBT for people who present with anxiety or depression (Tolin, 2010).

So, when CBT has been compared with other forms of therapy, there has been little evidence that it is any less or more effective than any other model. In fact, meta-analyses of these comparative studies have shown that the model or technique used in the therapy only accounts for eight per cent of the variance in the positive outcome (Wampold, 2001; Wampold & Imel, 2015; Barlow, 2010). Even in studies using a dismantling design, where specific ingredients that have been posited to be the main 'effective ingredient' have been taken out of the intervention, for instance *exposure*, still no difference in outcome has been found (Jacobson et al, 1996).

Psychotherapy research has now moved on to attempting to identify what it is that is effective in therapy, and, in particular, *who* it is that is effective in therapy. Therapist effects are increasingly becoming more evident, and when studies are comparing two forms of therapy delivered by the same therapists, then between-therapist effects are often considerably larger than between-model effects (Elkin, 1999; Huppert, Bufka & Barlow 2001; Kim, Wampold & Bolt, 2006; Okiishi et al, 2003). In other words, the title of Roth and Fonagy's next book should not be *What Works for Whom?* (Roth & Fonagy, 2005; Saxon et al, 2017), but perhaps *Who Works for Whom?*

In relation to this chapter, the implication is clear: while there may be some specific criticisms of CBT as a model, of equal concern should be CBT that is carried out by an ineffective therapist, just as with any other model of treatment carried out by an ineffective therapist.

Improving access to psychological therapies training

It is the training of therapists in the context of the IAPT that is my next contextual point. CBT focuses on the presenting problem, and positive outcome is couched in terms of symptom reduction. This makes CBT particularly amenable to current research methods that require specificity of treatment and specificity of presenting problem, which is usually placed in a diagnostic category. This notion is explored very eloquently and in much more detail in the chapters by Bohart and House (Chapter 18) and Bryceland and Stam (Chapter 17) in this volume. Their critiques are of empirically supported treatments, or ESTs.

ESTs are particularly prevalent in the US, where much of the funding is provided by insurance companies and where the dictum to the therapist is sometimes 'No EST, no payment'. The basis of an EST is the splitting off of the technique from the person that is delivering it. Perhaps because of this, it can collude with a fantasy that it is technique that is effective, in much the same way that a pill is effective. Carrying this fantasy further is the notion that the technique is all that is required, regardless of the people involved, and there is a consequent minimising of the therapeutic relationship. This too is similar to the belief that what is important is the medication, and who delivers it and to whom are immaterial to the outcome (incidentally, even this is being challenged by therapist-effect research, which has shown that the person prescribing the medication has a sometimes greater effect on outcome than the medication itself in working with people with depression (McKay, Imel & Wampold, 2006). If we take this notion to its logical conclusion, practitioners who deliver the therapy simply need to learn how to deliver it, and there is little acknowledgement of the role of the relationship within which it is delivered.

This brings me to the current training of IAPT high-intensity workers and psychological wellbeing practitioners (PWPs). PWPs will work with people with presenting problems of relatively low complexity, as defined by their GP and a screening instrument, which is usually the PHQ-9 (Kroenke, Spitzer & Williams, 2001) and the GAD-7 (Spitzer et al, 2006). PWPs have 45 days of academic training and four days of supervised practice over two, or sometimes three, semesters. High-intensity workers, who work with people with more complex needs, have a year's training in CBT, comprising two days a week at university and three days a week supervised clinical practice. Unlike training in most other schools of psychotherapy, CBT trainees are not required to have their own therapy (Williams, 2015).

My concern is that, when a potentially potent CBT technique is used simply as a technique, without the sensitivity achieved by a more relational training, it could prove to be destructive, and even dangerous. An example is the 'downward arrow technique', in which a client is invited to consider the implications of automatic thoughts. This technique can rapidly move the client to identify fundamental core beliefs about him or herself which, if not worked with in a safe, contained environment, could prove very distressing for them, and, indeed, for the inexperienced therapist. It is not that this method of working is inherently 'bad'; the potential for harm is in how it can be practised.

Meantime, while more high- and low-intensity workers are being trained, there are approximately 44,000 counsellors and therapists who are members of the British Association for Counselling and Psychotherapy (BACP), some 8,000 psychotherapists in the UK Council for Psychotherapy (UKCP) and 1,500 psychoanalysts in the British Psychoanalytic Council (BPC) (2017 figures) in the UK (many of whom may be members of both or all of the above organisations) who are already trained in models other than CBT, many of whom are employed as general practice counsellors in the NHS (Foster & Murphy, 2005). A large proportion of these counsellors are having to reapply, many unwillingly, for their jobs as high-intensity workers. Currently there seems to be little effort to work alongside these counsellors and offer them training so that they can incorporate CBT techniques into their practice (sometimes referred to as a cognitive behavioural approach (CBA)). The combined effect of this idealising of CBT, the employment of under-trained workers, and the undervaluing of other models is likely to be enormous.

A report by the BPC and UKCP in 2015 identified a reduction in funding and availability of NHS psychotherapy services outside the IAPT programme, leading to counsellor and psychotherapist resignations and redundancies. These professionals have a wealth of experience in working with people and in NHS institutions, as well as a depth of skills that have been built up over many years. IAPT was set up initially to get people who are on incapacity benefit back to work, so, if it renders unemployed those very people who can help this happen, it would be ironic in the extreme.

CBT as a single entity

Some of the criticisms in the book's chapters are levelled at CBT as if it were a monolithic entity. It is not. It is evolving, as David Winter and John Kaye describe in their chapters (Chapters 13 and 16, respectively). Current 'third -wave' forms of CBT are rapidly integrating other theoretical models into their practice, such as Gestalt and object relations in schema therapy (Young, Klosko & Weishaar, 2003), Buddhist mindfulness techniques in mindfulness CBT (Segal, Williams & Teasdale, 2002), relational frame theory in acceptance and commitment therapy (ACT) (Hayes & Spencer, 2005), and the dialogic approach so eloquently described by Strong and colleagues in Chapter 15.

Grant and colleagues (2004: 243) describe CBT as occupying a continuum between two poles:

> One end represents an explicitly technique-focused style, where concern is given to standardised interventions based on experimental and randomised control research methods. At this end sits computerised CBT packages and highly structured, manual intervention protocols that can be disseminated to a wide range of healthcare professionals at relatively low cost. Formulation-based approaches are located at the other end of the continuum, where the richness of individual experiences is celebrated and valued.

They go on to say that there is conflict in the CBT community between the 'technicalists' and the 'formulationists', particularly in relation to personal therapy. The 'technicalists' might dismiss this notion as it is not evidence based, and 'might disparage the notion of personal therapy on the grounds that, unlike their clients they are on the other, non-disordered, side of the fence' (Grant et al, 2004: 243).

Given this continuum, it is easy to see why the criticisms of mechanistic practice, positivist imperialism, rationalism, the use of simplistic diagnostic categorisation, and the collusion with the medical model of mental 'health' can be levelled at the more 'technicalist' end of the spectrum. Having said this, it is also easy simply to view 'technical' as 'bad', and more subtle 'formulations' as 'good'. In my view, there is a place for simple, pragmatic and technical interventions for some people. Not everyone needs complex input, which, in some cases, can pull people into a system that is too complex and possibly self-limiting. CBT practitioners at both ends of the spectrum tend to take people at face value, and do not automatically assume that there is an underlying cause (which, of course, there might be), thus potentially avoiding what O'Hanlon and colleagues (1999) refer to as 'theory countertransference', whereby the therapist's countertransference is to his or her theory of the patient (whether that is a diagnosis or a 'complex'), rather than what is happening in the room. Simple information is sometimes sufficient, and I am reminded of the empowering effects of information offered to someone who has panic attacks. Simple information on what happens in the body when in 'flight or fight' mode offers an alternative explanation to the terrifying thought 'I am having a heart attack'. It is, of course, knowing how, when and, indeed, whether to share this information so that is not an imposed truth that depends so much on the therapist, their training, experience, and their relationship with the client. In the hands of an unsophisticated therapist, these techniques can be at best futile, at worst harmful, reinforcing the client's fundamental notions that they are not good enough. Once more we arrive at therapist effects.

The relationship of CBT with powerful institutions – collaborator or Trojan horse?

Much is made in the chapters by Michael Guilfoyle (Chapter 1) and David Pilgrim (Chapter 3) of the relationship of CBT practitioners with 'powerful institutions', such as the psychiatric community and medicine. The technicalist end of the CBT community spectrum has indeed taken the notion of diagnosis as reality, rather than as, perhaps, a means for the practitioner to manage their anxiety. If we have a diagnosis, then we know what to do, and, of course, something must be done. In some ways, I can see that the reification of what is essentially a process can have some benefits, such as 'naming the beast', universality, and hope (Yalom, 1995). However, the disadvantages (identification with the diagnosis, as in 'I am a depressive', externalisation, reification, medicalisation, passivity, inviting an external locus of control, collusion with pharmaceutical companies…) seem to far outweigh the advantages – a discussion that is outside the remit of this chapter.

There seems to be a view in Guilfoyle's chapter that there has been an almost unethical collaboration with 'the enemy', and that the technicalist end of the CBT community has somehow sold its soul to the devil. I would suggest that this is not the case, and that they genuinely believe in these categorisations, and in the importance of the scientific method in establishing truth. In so doing, they have been taken seriously by the 'powerful institutions'. After all – and this is one aspect of current practice that seems to be absent from the chapters in this book – the overwhelming alternative to psychological therapies is the use of medication for 'mental health' problems. Medication is by far the most common intervention for mental health problems, and up until the recent rise in interest in CBT, it was recommended as the first level intervention. Indeed, it remains, the mainstay in the GP's toolkit.

It is really only since the interest in CBT that psychological therapies have been viewed as a realistic alternative for a large number of people with mild to moderate presenting difficulties. Because of this, psychological therapies will be available to many more patients, and will be used by other clinicians who are much more aware of alternatives to medication, which will go some way toward redressing the imbalance between medication and psychological therapies. David Brazier (Chapter 8) is right when he points out that CBT is very much a product of our time. Perhaps because of this, CBT theorists have used the language that is understood by powerful institutions, in the same way that an effective therapist uses the language of the client. What seems to have happened is that, having been taken seriously, they have been invited into the fold.

However, inside the Trojan horse there are also the formulationists, who are constantly reviewing and critiquing the model, to a point where, as David Winter quite rightly says in his final paragraph (Chapter 13), 'one might ask when such a therapy is no longer cognitive-behavioural'. If this is the case, and I am aware of more than a little Pollyanna idealism, then this could have profound implications for psychotherapy in general. Perhaps the psychotherapy community is reacting as it did when threatened by Eysenck's (1952) broadside on psychotherapy (his finding that not only did psychoanalytic psychotherapy have no benefit for a significant majority of people with what we now call common mental disorders; it had the inverse effect – the more therapy you had, the less likely you were to recover).

The current infatuation with CBT, like most idealisations, is likely to fade when it is noticed that it is not the panacea for all ills. This is already happening – a recent meta-analysis has found that CBT is almost half as effective as it used to be in the treatment of depression (Johnsen & Friborg, 2015). However, this is at the time of writing still being contested (Cristea et al, 2017; Ljótsson et al, 2017), and so the debate continues (Friborg & Johnsen, 2017).

CBT can undoubtedly be used as a pragmatic and sophisticated form of therapy, and one that many people find life changing. It has its limitations, but these can be addressed through collaboration with other forms of therapy. Indeed, useful alternatives are proposed in Del Loewenthal's and Keith Tudor's chapters in this book (Chapters 14 and 12). Perhaps this collaboration could be achieved a little more easily if, as a profession, we move away from the hazards of paradigm zealotry to a more pan-theoretical model of therapy.

This might be difficult, given the understandable potential for envy towards the favoured Son, who is enjoying so much attention. However, if a dialogue can be maintained between the different schools of therapy within the psychotherapy community, this could be a possibility. By doing this, we could, as a profession, explore how different schools of psychological therapy could be integrated into a broader, more complex and viable alternative to medication, rather than battling among ourselves and possibly re-enacting the conditions that bring people to therapy in the first place. After all, the main beneficiary of this conflict is Big Pharma.

Yet the situation in the UK appears to be relatively benign when compared with the French experience reviewed in Robert Snell's Chapter 4.

Randomised controlled trials (RCTS)

I agree with John Lees' criticisms (Chapter 9) of the notion of evidence-based treatment, particularly regarding their reliance on the randomised controlled trial (RCT) in evidencing the effectiveness of psychological treatments. While I can see a use for RCTs in efficacy trials (trials that are carried out in the best and most specific possible conditions, such as type of presenting problem and clinical setting), there are a number of difficulties about their use in effectiveness research (research carried out in the real world, with people who present with multiple problems, and where therapists often adjust their response according to the individual with whom they are working, and often in less than ideal environments) (Hemmings, 2000).

The RCT has come to represent the epitome of good scientific research. It was developed in medicine in order to evaluate physical treatments and was later adopted in psychiatry to test the efficacy of medication for certain psychiatric disorders. However, different commentators have identified several limitations to the use of RCTs in the study of effectiveness.

1. *Representativeness* – the controls required in an RCT, such as specificity of treatment using manuals and the inclusion of disorders that meet stringent research criteria, mean that the patients seen are simply not representative of normal clinical practice (Shapiro et al, 1995).
2. *Feasibility* – RCTs are expensive; they require large amounts of researcher time, and often large numbers of participants in order to achieve the necessary statistical power (Shapiro et al, 1995).
3. *Informativeness* – if these trials take place in the rarefied environment of the efficacy study, how informative are they of real-life practice (Shapiro et al, 1995)? This is of particular concern in relation to the current NICE guideline recommendations, which seem to rely almost entirely on efficacy research on CBT.
4. *Differing assumptions* of the researcher and the model of therapy being used. For example, the assumptions of what constitutes a 'positive outcome' may vary from one form of therapy to another. Some forms of therapy may focus on symptom reduction, while others focus on how the client is functioning in the world.
5. *RCTs' attempt to measure 'technique'* – as I have described earlier, there is considerable emphasis on specificity of treatment, and technique and model account for small percentages of the variance associated with positive outcome.

6. *Entry criteria for an RCT* – The US *Diagnostic and Statistical Manual of Mental Disorders* (*DSM-5*) is often used to classify the disorders being treated. There is considerable debate as to the usefulness of this form of classification (Morey, 1991; Rosenthal, 2008).
7. *Dual diagnosis* is also a problem. Personality disorders (Axis 2) are highly prevalent and have a profound effect on treatment outcome (Das-Munshi et al, 2008; Sullivan, Joyce & Mulder, 1994).
8. *Sample sizes* are hardly ever enough to control for the confounding variables that are present in a clinically representative situation.
9. *Randomisation* – while clients may be randomised, therapists almost never are, and, given the increasing evidence that therapist variables are important (discussed earlier), this again introduces a confound.
10. *Use of placebos and 'double blind' methods* is the staple of pharmaceutical trials, and, while placebos have been attempted in psychotherapy research, it is difficult to imagine therapists delivering a form of therapy that they know is sham.
11. *Client preference* – clients are active participants in therapy, and often choose to have a particular form of therapy. Not getting their preferred choice could introduce confounds.
12. *Practitioner preference* – when a therapy is not blinded and therapists are delivering a form of therapy that they may not prefer, one might wonder about the effects on outcome.

So, the RCT's journey from medicine to psychology has been fraught with difficulties. The RCT would appear to be most useful when the disorder and intervention that are being studied are highly controlled and specific – ie. during the efficacy stage. When the intervention is carried out in a more clinically realistic situation (ie. effectiveness research), the usefulness of such a methodology is considerably reduced. Unfortunately, much of the evidence accepted for evidence-based treatments is from RCTs.

One of the criticisms of CBT is that most of the evidence is based on efficacy research, which is not based on real-world practice. While there is considerable evidence that CBT is effective in the treatment of depression when the client has 'pure' depression, there is little evidence that CBT is effective in the real world of clinical practice.

There are some exceptions to this (Wade, Treat & Stuart, 1998), and attempts are being made to address this by the use of RCTs in more *effectiveness* research, although, given the number of variables that have to be included, this is an onerous task. The debate continues, and is described in a recent paper by Carey and Stiles (2016). It will be interesting to note how this practice-based evidence is managed and disseminated.

Power between therapist and client

Gillian Proctor's excellent analysis of the dangers of the potential abuse of power by the therapist over the client in CBT (Chapter 2) is a cogent warning to practitioners. Her arguments are highly relevant and are of particular concern when CBT is delivered from the technicalist end of the spectrum. Where I part company with Proctor is in the notion that this is largely a problem in CBT. I would argue that these power dynamics are played out in other forms of therapy, from psychodynamic models, where patient resistance is overtly interpreted, to a less overt acceptance of a power imbalance in person-centred therapy. The use and abuse of power within the helping professions has an extensive literature (Guggenbühl-Craig, 1971). In CBT, the notion of *collaboration* is an overt attempt to recognise this imbalance, and the standard mantra of many CBT therapists is, 'I have expertise in the model of CBT but I do not have expertise in you – only you have that.'

Take, for example, the use of behavioural experiments. It is recognised that, if these are imposed on the client as a form of 'homework', then this becomes part of the therapist's agenda and not the client's. If this is the case, then it is possible that the client will use his or her power in a passive way in order to confirm their world-view, or to frustrate the therapist. Once again, I would argue that CBT done badly can have all the power dynamics described, but done well by a competent therapist, the likelihood is reduced. The power imbalance in CBT is recognised by the CBT fraternity and discussed at length in David Kingdon and colleagues' book *CBT Values and Ethics* (2017).

Paul Kelly and Paul Moloney's intriguingly titled chapter (Chapter 5) makes the very relevant contextual point that CBT happens within a social environment. The larger system needs to be addressed, and here we move into the realms of social policy. I agree with this argument, but would point out that *any* form of psychosocial intervention needs to bear this in mind – this criticism cannot be laid solely at the feet of CBT. The development of the 'five areas' approach does at least go some way toward recognising this problem (Wright, Williams & Garland, 2002; Williams, 2012).

Conclusion

CBT has much to offer the psychotherapy community: it is popular with many clients and therapists alike, as well as having a focus on behaviour change, insight and awareness. It also has considerable efficacy research to support it. It is not, however, the only therapy in town. It is important that, in their attempt to be recognised as scientists, CBT theorists do not ignore the research evidence on therapist effects on outcome. It is also important that these effects are recognised in the training of new CBT therapists, and that they are not reduced to simply delivering a set of techniques, which seems so against the spirit of enquiry and curiosity that is prevalent in so much CBT theory.

References

Barlow DH (2010). The dodo bird – again – and again. *The Behavior Therapist 33:* 15–16.

BPC, UKCP (2015). *Addressing the Deterioration in Public Psychotherapy Provision.* London: BPC.

Carey T, Stiles W (2016). Some problems with randomized controlled trials and some viable alternatives. *Clinical Psychology & Psychotherapy 23*(1): 87–95.

Cristea IA, Stefan S, Karyotaki K, David D, Hollon SD, Cuijpers P (2017). The effects of cognitive behavioral therapy are not systematically falling: a revision of Johnsen and Friborg (2015). *Psychological Bulletin 143*(3): 326–340.

Das-Munshi J, Goldberg D, Bebbington P, Bhugra D, Brugha T, Dewey ME, Jenkins R, Stewart R, Prince M (2008). The public health significance of mixed anxiety and depressive disorder: beyond current classification. *British Journal of Psychiatry 192*: 171–172.

Elkin I (1999). A major dilemma in psychotherapy outcomes research: disentangling therapists from therapies. *Clinical Psychology: Science and Practice 6*: 10–32.

Eysenck H (1952). The effects of psychotherapy: an evaluation. *Journal of Consulting and Clinical Psychology 60*: 659–663.

Foster J, Murphy A (2005). *Psychological Therapies in Primary Care: setting up a managed service.* London: Karnac Books.

Friborg O, Johnsen TJ (2017). The effect of cognitive-behavioral therapy as an anti-depressive treatment is falling. Reply to Ljótsson et al (2017) and Cristea et al (2017). *Psychological Bulletin 143* (3): 341–345.

Godley SH, Jones N, Funk R, Ives M, Passetti L (2004). Comparing outcomes of best-practice and research-based outpatient treatment protocols for adolescents. *Journal of Psychoactive Drugs 36*(1): 35–48.

Grant A, Mills J, Mulhern R, Short N (2004). *Cognitive Behavioural Therapy in Mental Health Care.* London: Sage.

Guggenbühl-Craig A (1971). *Power in the Helping Professions.* Dallas, TX: Spring Publications.

Hayes SC, Spencer S (2005). *Get Out of Your Mind and into Your Life: the new acceptance and commitment therapy.* Oakland, CA: New Harbinger Publications.

Hemmings A (2000). Evidence-based practice or practice-based evidence? *British Journal of Guidance and Counselling 28*(2): 233–252.

Huppert JD, Bufka LF, Barlow DH (2001). Therapists, therapist variables, and cognitive-behavioral therapy outcomes in a multicenter trial for panic disorder. *Journal of Consulting and Clinical Psychology 69*: 747–755.

Jacobson NS, Dobson KS, Truax PA, Addis ME, Koerner K, Gollan JK, Gortner E, Prince SE (1996). A component analysis of cognitive-behavioral treatment for depression. *Journal of Consulting and Clinical Psychology 64*: 295–304.

Johnsen TJ, Friborg O (2015). The effects of cognitive behavioral therapy as an anti-depressive treatment is falling: a meta-analysis. *Psychological Bulletin 141*(4): 747–768.

Kim DM, Wampold BE, Bolt DM (2006). Therapist effects and treatment effects in psychotherapy: analysis of the National Institute of Mental Health Treatment of Depression Collaborative Research Program. *Psychotherapy Research 16*(2): 161–172.

Kingdon D, Maguire N, Stalmeisters D, Townen M (2017). *CBT Values and Ethics* (2nd ed). London: Sage.

Kroenke K, Spitzer RL, Williams JB (2001). The PHQ-9: validity of a brief depression severity measure. *Journal of General Internal Medicine 16*(9): 606–613.

Ljótsson B, Hedman E, Mattsson S, Andersson E (2017). The effects of cognitive–behavioral therapy for depression are not falling: a re-analysis of Johnsen and Friborg (2015). *Psychological Bulletin 143*(3): 321–325.

Lipsey MW, Wilson DB (1993). The efficacy of psychological, behavioral, and educational, and behavioral treatment: confirmation from meta-analysis. *American Psychologist 48*(12): 1181–1209.

Luborsky L, Rosenthal R, Diguer L, Andrusyna TP, Berman JS, Levitt JT, Seligman DA, Krause ED (2002). The dodo bird verdict is alive and well – mostly. *Journal of Psychotherapy Integration 12*(1): 32–57.

McDonagh A, Friedman M, McHugo G, Ford J, Sengupta A, Mueser K, Demment CC, Fournier D, Schnurr PP, Descamps M (2005). Randomized trial of cognitive-behavioral therapy for chronic posttraumatic stress disorder in adult female survivors of childhood sexual abuse. *Journal of Consulting and Clinical Psychology 73*(3): 515–524.

McKay KM, Imel ZE, Wampold BE (2006). Psychiatrist effects in the pharmacological treatment of depression. *Journal of Affective Disorders 92*(2–3): 287–290.

Miller SD, Wampold BE, Varhely K (2008). Direct comparisons of treatment modalities for youth disorders: a meta-analysis. *Psychotherapy Research 18*(1): 5–14.

Morey LC (1991). *The Personality Assessment Inventory Professional Manual.* Odessa, Fl: Psychological Assessment Resources.

O'Hanlon W, O'Hanlon S, Bertolino B (1999). *Evolving Possibilities: selected papers of Bill O'Hanlon.* New York, NY: Psychology Press.

Okiishi J, Lambert MJ, Nielsen SL, Ogles BM (2003). Waiting for supershrink: an empirical analysis of therapist effects. *Clinical Psychology and Psychotherapy 10*: 361–373.

Pybis J, Saxon D, Hill A, Barkham M (2017). The comparative effectiveness and efficiency of cognitive behaviour therapy and generic counselling in the treatment of depression: evidence from the 2nd UK National Audit of Psychological Therapies. *BMC Psychiatry 17*(1): 215.

Robinson LA, Berman JS, Neimeyer RA (1990). Psychotherapy for treatment of depression: a comprehensive review of controlled outcome research. *Psychological Bulletin 108*: 30–49.

Rosenthal S (2008). *Class, Health and Health Care.* Victoria, BC: Trafford Publishing.

Roth A, Fonagy P (2005). *What Works for Whom?* (2nd ed). New York, NY: Guilford Press.

Saxon D, Barkham M, Foster A, Parry G (2017). The contribution of therapist effects to patient dropout and deterioration in the psychological therapies. *Clinical Psychology and Psychotherapy 24*(3): 575–588.

Saxon D, Firth N, Barkham M (2016). The relationship between therapist effects and therapy delivery factors: therapy modality, dosage, and non-completion. *Administration and Policy in Mental Health and Mental Health Services Research* 44(5): 705–715.

Segal ZV, Williams JM, Teasdale JD (2002). *Mindfulness-Based Cognitive Therapy for Depression.* New York, NY: Guilford Press.

Shapiro DA, Shapiro D (1982). Meta-analysis of comparative therapy outcome studies: a replication and refinement. *Psychological Bulletin 92*: 581–604.

Shapiro DA, Barkham M, Rees A, Hardy GE, Reynolds S, Startup M (1995). Decisions decisions decisions: determining the effects of treatment and duration on the outcome of psychotherapy for depression. In: Aveline M, Shapiro D (eds). *Research Foundations for Psychotherapy Practice.* Chichester: John Wiley (pp151–174).

Shapiro DA, Barkham M, Rees A, Hardy GE, Reynolds S, Startup M (1994). Effects of treatment duration and severity of depression on the effectiveness of cognitive behavioural and psychodynamic-interpersonal psychotherapy. *Journal of Consulting and Clinical Psychology 62*: 522–534.

Spitzer RL, Kroenke K, Williams JBW, Löwe B (2006). A brief measure for assessing generalized anxiety disorder: the GAD-7. *Archives of Internal Medicine 16*(10):1092–1097.

Stiles WB, Barkham M, Twigg E, Mellor-Clark J, Cooper M (2006). Effectiveness of cognitive behavioural, person-centred and psychodynamic therapies as practiced in UK national health service settings. *Psychological Medicine 26*: 555–556.

Sullivan PF, Joyce PR, Mulder RT (1994). Borderline personality disorder in major depression. *Journal of Nervous and Mental Disease 182*: 177–178.

Tolin D (2010). Is cognitive-behavioral therapy more effective than other therapies? A meta-analytic review. *Clinical Psychology Review 30*(6): 710–720.

Wade WA, Treat TT, Stuart GL (1998). Transporting an empirically supported treatment for panic disorder to a service clinic setting: a benchmarking strategy. *Journal of Consulting and Clinical Psychology 66*: 231–239.

Wampold B (2001). *The Great Psychotherapy Debate*. New York, NY: Lawrence Erlbaum.

Wampold B, Imel Z (2015). How important are the common factors in psychotherapy? An update. World Psychiatry 14(3): 270–277.

Wampold BE, Mondin GW, Moody M, Stich F, Benson K, Ahn H (1997). A meta-analysis of outcome studies comparing bona fide psychotherapies: empirically, 'all must have prizes'. *Psychological Bulletin 122*: 203–215.

Williams C (2015). Improving access to psychological therapies (IAPT) and treatment outcomes: epistemological assumptions and controversies. *Journal of Psychiatric Mental Health Nursing* 5: 344–351.

Willams C (2012). *Overcoming Anxiety, Stress and Panic: a five-areas approach* (3rd ed). Boca Raton, FL: CRC Press.

Wright B, Williams C, Garland A (2002). Using the five areas cognitive-behavioural therapy model with psychiatric patients. *Advances in Psychiatric Treatment 8*(4): 307–315.

Yalom I (1995). *The Theory and Practice of Group Psychotherapy* (4th ed). New York, NY: Basic Books.

Young JE, Klosko JS, Weishaar M (2003). *Schema Therapy: a practitioner's guide*. New York, NY: Guilford Press.

Conclusion to the first edition: contesting therapy paradigms about what it means to be human

Del Loewenthal and Richard House

Concluding a book such as this one is not an easy task. In following such a rich diversity of contributions from both proponents of and sceptics about CBT, we will endeavour to be succinct, economical, and unavoidably selective in our summing-up.

The foremost issue we wish to address in this final chapter is the question of what any dialogue around CBT should be focused on. For us, it is essentially concerned with what it means to be human, and the questions of knowledge and method that arise from this. It is, therefore, these ontological, epistemological and methodological concerns that are, for us, central to the debate about therapy paradigms that has periodically been raised in earlier chapters.

In recent years, the CBT field as whole, and its practitioners in particular, have certainly had to deal with the very complex task of holding and making sense of what are very divergent forces: on the one hand, arguably inappropriate over-idealisation from government, policy-makers and a populace, all perhaps yearning for 'quick-fix' solutions to the challenges of living, and on the other, critical, and sometimes unfairly dismissive, attention from within the therapy world itself.

To what extent do the criticisms levelled at CBT from within the therapy world, and hopefully represented in this book, have any substance? Are, we wonder, the differences alleged to divide CBT and the other therapy modalities more imagined and expedient for *both* 'sides', than is actually the case (assuming that it's *ever* possible to say or to know what is 'actually the case')?

To our knowledge, this book represents the first time that such a rich array of proponents and critics of CBT have entered into anything approaching public dialogue – which in itself is a somewhat sad commentary on our field's capacity to engage with difference, especially when there are issues of power, resources and identity involved. There is also a view in some circles that any such associated, profession-level turmoil is actually connected, at least in part, with what we cannot bear *in ourselves*, and which we therefore displace onto others, with inner-psychological conflict thereby being inappropriately externalised – a process that has perhaps been all too apparent in the psychological therapies which, as such, thereby become the very worst kind of advert for what these same therapies are aspiring to address.

We are hopeful that such questions, as raised by our contributors, can increasingly be faced and reflected on by more psychological therapists – a process that surely needs to happen, and with some urgency, if the unpleasantness of current schisms in the field are to lose at least some of their divisiveness, and take us towards the kind of engaged and constructive, mutually respectful dialogue and tolerance of difference that we think all would agree are important values of our psychotherapeutic work.

It would certainly be possible to write a series of books on the theme of 'against and for…' for all of the various therapy modalities. However, we have focused here on CBT because it has recently become *the* main modality supported by the state – a quite unprecedented development in modern political life, and one that throws up many questions about the legitimate place of the state – if any – in making legally enforced (and therefore necessarily limiting) decisions about the talking therapies in what is (allegedly?) a putatively open democracy. Moreover, state managerialism (Loewenthal, 2008), with its arguably disingenuous discourse of transparency etc (eg. House, 2008), can be understood as a means for creating insecurity and securing a state mechanism of control, and the CBT modality certainly fits this kind of managerialism better than any other. In marked contrast, it should be noted that it is by no means an inevitability that the state will necessarily embrace a managerialist, instrumentalist ideology – for, as Snell points out (Chapter 4), 'in February 2005 the Minister of Health, Philippe Douste-Blazy, publicly declared psychic suffering to be "neither measurable nor open to evaluation", and withdrew the INSERM report from his Ministry's website'. So, the resigned fatalism that seems to have overtaken parts of the British psychoanalytic establishment in the face of the NICE evidence-based juggernaut is perhaps at best premature, and at worst a chronic self-betrayal of psychoanalysis (see Parker & Revelli, 2008).

At least one of us (DL) doesn't have a problem with the view that CBT could be particularly helpful with some clients. However, what is at issue for many, if not most of CBT's critics, is when it becomes *the* dominant mode. For, while it might arguably be appropriate sometimes to help people by taking their mind off the problem, if this approach becomes generalised to society at large, then a catastrophe is almost inevitable. There is also the concern that CBT can be more easily manualised than other approaches (see Bohart & House, Chapter 18), although these have been, and are still in the process of being, dumbed down, with extraordinary claims that even psychoanalysis can be manualised.

It is important to distinguish clearly between, on the one hand, the state and the policy-making uses to which CBT is being put, and, on the other, the sincere good faith of many CBT practitioners on the ground, who have a genuine, principled, and thought-through commitment to their chosen modality, as represented in

Chapters 21–23 of this book. There is, indeed, a rigorous debate unfolding within the CBT modality itself, and there are also many dissenting voices with regard to how CBT is being used by the government through the Improving Access to Psychological Therapies (IAPT) programme, and so on.

More generally, however, perhaps the main concerns that come through in this book are the underlying assumptions about what it means to be human, together with the nature of therapeutic change and psychotherapeutic knowledge itself. In terms of *ontological* questions, there are the assumptions of whether we see people as both good and evil, rational and irrational, free or determined, and it is here that one of the great divides emerges between CBT and other therapy modalities. This is the divide between the holistic and mechanistic approaches, where the former begins with the indissoluble human soul and its resources, and the latter looks consciously to manipulate human experience (most notably, via cognition), in the view that this latter route will necessarily enhance well-being. From existential, post-existential (see Loewenthal, Chapter 14) and postmodern (Loewenthal & Snell, 2003) perspectives, the great danger is that such interventions will have precisely the opposite effect of that intended and will move human subjects even further away from what it means to be human than they already are.

There are, no doubt, many clients who would be very grateful not to have to think about what is troubling them. For some, this requires a working through of what they might dread; for others, it requires a more up-front reformulation. One might say that, for most people, then, the sooner they can stop worrying about what is troubling them, the better. But there is also the argument that we all get through life by the successful repression of unthinkable anxieties. One set of methods would seem to bring to this kind of problem an immediate helping hand. An alternative approach encourages troubling thoughts to be uncovered, in the hope that, as a result of this 'working through', the client will be able to allow thoughts to come to him or her. In some ways, both approaches aspire for the client to be freed up from that which previously constricted them, and there are probably circumstances in which both will have their place.

With regard to *epistemological* questions, a major issue is the place of what Polyani calls 'tacit knowledge' (see House & Bohart, Chapter 19), which may account for why it would appear that the relationship in therapy (and elsewhere) is of vital importance. Thus, the learning that can take place in therapy through the relationship can never be fully described by a set of competencies. Much of what we are discussing was expressed as a parody in the film *Dead Poet's Society* (1989), where a comparison is made with a teaching relationship that is to do with the heart, and all its ecstasies and dangers, as opposed to a deadening one that relies on technique.

More clearly than other approaches, CBT seems to be saying that methods will change as new evidence becomes available (see Mansell, Chapter 21. Initially, this is a very attractive argument, but there is the possible detrimental effect on client and therapist of the removal of personal therapy for the therapist as a training requirement, and then there is a major difficulty with regard to what is accepted as legitimate research. And this is, in turn, part of a cultural trend in which, for example, one might see doctoral theses in universities having an increasingly important quantitative component. Yet this quantification is often a positivistic technique and, at best, poor science.

Some unresolved editors' questions

Having read the chapters in this book closely, we are left with some lingering questions raised by several of the contributors. First, in Chapter 21 and Chapter 23 respectively, both Mansell and Hemmings claim (and other contributors argue similarly) that CBT is not 'a single, knowable entity'. Such a claim is all very well, but if this is the case, then why is the term 'CBT' even used by practitioners who allegedly practise 'it' – and certainly in such an arguably casual and uncritical way across modern culture? This strikes us as rather similar to the unfalsifiability critique of so-called *post-hoc* justification propounded by philosopher of science Karl Popper (1963), in which he convincingly lambasted those theories that insulated themselves from any kind of sustained criticism or refutation, simply by changing one aspect of the theory every time it was undermined ('third-wave' CBT perhaps being a case in point), thereby leaving the main body of the theory untouched *and effectively immune from refutation*. In other words, the chameleon-like nature of CBT allows its proponents to insulate it from any criticism that might stick, because it can always be claimed that *somewhere* in the diverse CBT stable, 'it's not being done like that'. So, in this way, 'CBT' becomes little more than an expedient branding label that conceals far more than it reveals and is used much more for its *political* effects than to accurately represent and correspond to the actual content of the approach.

This seems to us to be a potentially devastating critique. However, it is one that has also previously been levelled at, for example, psychoanalysis, where it has been argued that proponents of this modality put forward the concept of 'defence mechanisms' whenever criticisms have been laid at its door. Also, CBT is probably wrongly suffering from that which has happened in the past – that, when a modality becomes popular, many others jump on to the bandwagon and try quickly to change their approach in order to get in under the wire. Nonetheless, it is perhaps doubly ironic that the very argument adduced by Popper to challenge the scientificity of Freudian psychoanalysis is now eminently quotable against what claims to be the crowning-glory of modern 'scientific' therapy practice – evidence-based CBT. In David Pilgrim's words (Chapter 3), 'CBT is a technology without a true theory' – and, moreover, 'theoretically confused and practically-obsessed'.

A related criticism is that 'third-wave' forms of CBT are (Hemmings, Chapter 23) 'rapidly integrating [or is it *colonising*?] other theoretical models into their practice', such as Gestalt and object relations in schema therapy, Buddhist mindfulness techniques in mindfulness CBT, relational frame theory in ACT, and the dialogic approach described by Strong and colleagues in Chapter 15. This apparent eclecticism would appear to have little if anything to do with theoretical authenticity, and there is the danger of falling into opportunistic exploitation of other approaches that are effectively 'bolted on' as soon as any of the core assumptions of CBT are exposed to concerted challenge.

The difficulty for CBT is that it can then be accused of adopting an unscientific approach when it is a modality that makes such a strong claim to relatively pure scientific credentials. As Winter asks in his final paragraph (Chapter 13), one has every right to ask just when such therapies can no longer be legitimately deemed to be 'cognitive-behavioural'. As Tudor points out (Chapter 12), 'as all therapists work with cognition and behaviour, in this sense we *are* all cognitive and behavioural therapists'. And, he continues, 'this is an argument in favour of sharing conceptual and clinical space rather than claiming territory'. Mansell (Chapter 21) also claims that, 'while it is appropriate to allow certain evidence-based psychotherapies, like CBT, to be accredited by the health system, we need space for innovators who adapt and devise their own approaches from a firm cultural and scientific foundation'. Such a view could be seen to raise as many questions as it answers. Thus, the term 'evidence-based' is used quite uncritically and assumes that what constitutes valid evidence is an unproblematic given, when clearly it is not (see Winter, Chapter 13). Moreover, it is perhaps a naïve view that claims, in the face of the state's uncritical anointing of CBT as *the* therapy of choice, that there will be any space left at all in this brave new therapeutic world for innovation – for the whole history of the way innovation works and flourishes suggests otherwise. Paying lip service to the virtue of innovation is all very well, but if one supports an approach that a government latches on to in an uncritical, totalising way, then such lip service is just that – and at worst, empty aspirations.

There is also the issue raised by Lees (Chapter 9) and Brazier (Chapter 8), that we need to locate therapy practices within the evolution of human consciousness. In the case of CBT, it seems clear that, no matter how it is dressed up in what some would see as a *post-hoc* justificatory way (see earlier), it universally privileges *thinking and cognition* over other ways of being – yet who says that this is invariably, or even remotely, the most fully realised way of being human? As Bracken and Thomas put it (Chapter 10), 'the acceptance of cognitivism, and of computer models of mind and thinking, cannot be explained by the empirical success of these approaches alone. Instead, it appears to be driven by other cultural aspirations and ideals as well'.

Having trained in the 1990s as holistic body psychotherapist, I (RH) have worked with many clients over the years who, in my judgment, have demonstrably suffered chronically from *a surfeit* of thinking, and who have learnt to use thinking as a kind of comforting 'dependency object' that can never in principle succeed in '(re)solving' the problems that are demanded of it (see Winnicott's notion of the 'mind object', where children, from a developmental standpoint, prematurely develop a precocious mind at far too early an age because of a failure of the early nurturing environment – see Corrigan & Gordon, 1995). In such cases, my clinical view is that the introduction of yet more of an emphasis on thinking is *the very last thing* that such clients need on their healing journey – and all my therapy experience has confirmed this. *Yet the kinds of symptoms that are exhibited by such clients are the very ones for which the NICE guidelines would recommend CBT* – ie. yet more emphasis on the cognitive, at the expense of the rest of the client's being. As Bracken and Thomas put it (Chapter 10), 'CT is not independent of the "cognitive theory of mind". Therefore, the therapist is effectively training the patient to accept this particular model of mind.' We have never seen any reference in the CBT literature that shows any awareness of what should surely be a key therapeutic issue – that is, an informed consideration of the possibly iatrogenic nature of a CBT-type 'intervention' with clients for whom more thinking will merely exacerbate their difficulties.

However, both of us consider that the issues of thinking, thoughtfulness, and 'the cognitive' are not at all straightforward – for there are great subtleties and distinctions here that need very careful specification and thinking through in a psychotherapeutic context. Thus, for example, we could in some circumstances be equally critical of humanistic approaches that uncritically privilege the emotional over the cognitive, and there might be a substantial, even a decisive difference between thinking, on the one hand, and allowing thoughts to come to one, on the other.

In Chapter 23, Hemmings suggests that, 'as a profession we move away from potential paradigm zealotry to a more pan-theoretical model of therapy'. He continues, 'if we can maintain a continued dialogue with the formulationist wing of CBT, this could be a possibility. By doing this we could, as a profession, examine how different paradigms of psychological therapy can integrate into a broader more complex and viable alternative to medication'. Some of the otherwise critical chapters in the book are in fact already endeavouring to find some kind of rapprochement with CBT – see, for example, the chapters by Strong et al, Tudor and Newman. However, there is the concern that such moves could be a kind of procedural expediency that places the desire to avoid conflict and schism above paradigmatic authenticity and internal consistency.

Pilgrim's concern with the epistemic fallacy (that is, confusing reality with *what we call* reality) appears to be a strong argument, as is his scepticism about the functions served by diagnostic labelling (with which CBT commonly colludes), for 'we need to understand the variety of interests which maintain categories which are scientifically dubious and are experienced often as stigmatising and unhelpful by their recipients' (Chapter 2; see Parker et al, 1995). Thus, for Pilgrim, a diagnosis of depression 'not only diverts us from socio-political relationships to the diseased person; it renders the latter a passive victim of their putative disease. It thereby risks robbing them of their agency and their opportunity for existential reflection.' He continues: 'This claim of naturalism is premature, as philosophers interrogating psychiatric nomenclature have demonstrated' (see Bracken & Thomas, Chapter

10). For Pilgrim, it is *commercial and professional interests* 'that have shaped premature claims of psychiatric success about categorising misery and madness' – which fits all too cosily with Layard's 'invest[ing] too much faith in the technical fix… impl[ying] that the mechanisms of extreme misery are being increasingly explicated by modern therapeutic technologies, when they are not'.

We are most interested in Michael Guilfoyle's position, where he argues (in Chapter 1) that 'CBT participates in societal networks of power relations', thence suggesting that CBT's 'success and widespread recognition may be a function not of its effectiveness *per se*, but of its comfortable integration with existing cultural and institutional power arrangements'. For Guilfoyle, a 'rationalist ordering of the therapies in accordance with narrow and preconstructed values that correspond with those of society's most powerful institutions' is in great danger of precipitating 'the gradual diminishment of a once rich landscape of therapeutic possibilities'.

From her psychoanalytic perspective, Jane Milton (Chapter 11) refers illuminatingly to 'how great the conceptual differences sometimes are between practitioners of the two treatments [ie. CBT and psychoanalysis], which can lead to major difficulties in communication'. For Milton, 'the cognitive clinical paradigm remains fundamentally different from the psychoanalytic one, and… true rapprochement is more apparent than real' – and she proceeds to offer an examination of the way in which modern CBT therapists tend to modify their technique. Thus, for Milton, any possibility of a common-ground, paradigmatic rapprochement between CBT and psychoanalysis seems very remote. At the level of research, Milton maintains, 'We are dealing with a complex interpersonal process involving multiple variables. Controls may become impossible to achieve and randomisation is a questionable activity in comparative trials where patients show marked preferences or aptitudes for different ways of working.'

We cite her view here just to make the point that claims that a pan-theoretical, trans-paradigmatic common ground between CBT and other approaches certainly cannot be assumed. Strong et al (Chapter 15) usefully raise the issue of the self from a Foucaultian perspective. For them, there is a problem with the term 'self', as CBT can effectively involve 'taking on CBT in apprenticing oneself to its practices of "self-subjectification", and policing or disciplining oneself accordingly. Said another way, *this is how one learns to be a person on CBT's terms*' (emphasis added). For Strong et al, then, 'ideology can creep into CBT in insidious ways, [and] the practices and philosophy of certain approaches to CBT, applied as a personal technology for self-conduct, can be seen as a kind of ideology'. This is of especial concern when clients 'are instructed to ignore certain features of their realities that can't be remedied with thought modification (eg. poverty) or in forms of "self-monitoring" and "self-control" that preclude other avenues to happiness and contentment'.

Finally, we are somewhat surprised by two apparent omissions in this book, hardly referred to by our contributors. The first concerns what many see as the need for personal therapy in the training of psychological therapists, which is not a training requirement for CBT practitioners, thus appearing to make CBT more cost-effective – but only when the accounting system adopted is at the individual level rather than at the level of society as a whole. Thus, with CBT's 'technological' approach, the 'person of the therapist' is not seen as a central 'measuring instrument' of the work, and CBT therapists therefore need to be far less concerned than other practitioners about whether what they are saying is truly *for* the client or is more about their own issues. Many, if not most, therapy approaches would view the lack of such therapist awareness as preventing the therapist from really hearing the client, thereby inhibiting the client from being able to speak of what is really troubling them. This, in turn, may cause ill health in both the client *and* the therapist, and further prevents, perhaps intentionally, our culture from facing up to underlying societal problems, which, if tackled, could reduce the need for therapy, whatever its label.

The second surprising omission is that nowhere in the book is there any discussion of the implicit (and sometimes explicit) *theory of change* and its mechanics, as advocated in CBT. Thus, CBT practice is based on the assumption that cognition and ideation somehow precede, *and can therefore unproblematically be invoked to control*, emotion; yet, on the basis of careful psychological research, this assumption is called into significant question – for, as Zajonc (1980) has quite unambiguously shown, it seems far more likely that *emotions precede thoughts, rather than the other way around*. Thus, Zajonc found that by no means all feelings (or preferences) are based on cognitive processes, but often *precede* them, and affect certainly doesn't appear to require extensive cognitive processing to occur. Given this finding, combined with Damasio's work on holistic perspectives on the brain, thinking and emotion (eg. Damasio, 1994, 2000), it may seem something of a surprise that CBT has managed to continue to maintain its legitimacy, notwithstanding the argument that its theoretical basis for change may be at best challenged, and at worst fundamentally flawed. All this could be seen to confirm the arguments of Guilfoyle (Chapter 1) and others that CBT's cultural ascendancy has far more to do with its implication and manoeuverings within regimes of power and influence than it is to do with any demonstrable *scientific* legitimacy. And it further suggests that CBT's attempt to control emotion via thought may well sometimes perpetrate an even greater 'violence' on human beings than many of us previously intuitively felt to be the case.

A final reflection

This concluding chapter has selectively focused on certain lacunae in the CBT story that particularly strike us, based on ontological, epistemological and methodological concerns. Other writers would no doubt have homed in on different dimensions of the CBT phenomenon, with its various inconsistencies and its alleged weaknesses and strengths. We hope that readers will make their own lists of the strengths and weaknesses of the criticisms of CBT, and that the book's diverse contributions will help them to reach a more informed decision about where the balance of argument lies.

Whatever the shortcomings of this book – and there will undoubtedly be many – we hope that it will make a significant contribution to the emerging debate about the place of CBT within modern therapy culture – and the extent to which CBT's current position of cultural and political ascendancy is based more on science or ideology.

Coda to the first edition

In the first edition of this book, we ended by referring to the (then) preliminary data emerging from the two 'demonstration' IAPT sites in Newham (Newham IAPT, 2007) and Doncaster (Richards & Suckling, 2007), which appeared to bring into question whether the 'success rates' arising from introducing CBT-informed high- and low-intensity therapeutic services were evidence of any greater effectiveness than that achieved by either previous or existing NHS mental health provision. We also observed that it was far from clear from those preliminary data whether the hoped-for resulting return to employment (see Pilgrim's Chapter 3) would actually occur. Those who are sceptical about the ubiquity and uncritical enthusiasm with which CBT has been embraced as a socio-economic 'engineering tool' will derive little comfort from the knowledge that we still don't have that evidence of superior effectiveness, or of the promised employment pay-offs, and IAPT has nevertheless continued its relentless march across the psychological landscape, in England at least, regardless.

References

Corrigan EG, Gordon P-E (eds) (1995). *The Mind Object: precocity and pathology of self-sufficiency.* New York, NY: Jason Aronson.

Damasio AR (1994). *Descartes' Error: emotion, reason, and the human brain.* New York, NY: Putnam.

Damasio AR (2000). *The Feeling of What Happens: body, emotion, and the making of consciousness.* New York, NY: Vintage.

House R (2008). The dance of psychotherapy and politics. *Psychotherapy and Politics International* 6(2): 98–109.

Loewenthal D (2008). Regulation or ethics as the basis of psychoanalytic training. In: Parker I, Revelli S (eds). *Psychoanalytic Practice and State Regulation*, London: Karnac Books (pp.85–93).

Loewenthal D, Snell R (2003). *Postmodernism for Psychotherapists.* London: Routledge.

Newham IAPT (2007). *Newham Improved Access to Psychological Therapies (IAPT): the first year, draft 3.* Newham: NHS Newham Primary Care Trust.

Parker I, Revelli S (eds) (2008). *Psychoanalytic Practice and State Regulation.* London: Karnac Books.

Parker I, Georgaca E, Harper D, McLaughlin T, Stowell-Smith M (1995). *Deconstructing Psychopathology.* London: Sage.

Popper KR (1963). *Conjectures and Refutations.* London: Routledge & Kegan Paul.

Richards D, Suckling R (2007). *Doncaster Improved Access to Psychological Therapies (IAPT) Demonstration Site: annual report.* Doncaster: University of York and IAPT Doncaster.

Zajonc RB (1980). Feelings and thinking: preferences need no inferences. *American Psychologist* 35(2): 151–75.

Conclusion to the second edition: no single therapy should be the only game in town

Del Loewenthal and Gillian Proctor

In summary, there can be seen to be two problems facing the future of the psychological therapies: the nature of psychotherapeutic knowledge, and the need for a preventative psychotherapeutic ethos with attention to socio-political causes of distress. With regard to the former, it would appear that no theories can conclusively and generally account for what might be therapeutic. Instead, we have different cultural practices that endeavour to focus on behaviour, or feelings, or an unconscious, or meaning, and so forth. None would appear to be able to offer sufficient grounds to claim that they provide a foundation for diagnosis and treatment (Loewenthal, 2011) – yet most attempt this. What has happened, though, is that we have a cultural moment where there is a great emphasis on encouraging people, and our society, to take their minds off their problems, rather than attempting to find meaning in difficulties. Hence, while we acknowledge CBT can sometimes be useful, it has frightening consequences for our futures, individually and collectively, if, as seems to have happened, this becomes the dominant approach.

The second issue is that the psychological therapies only attempt to help to close the stable door once the horse has bolted. Our current societies are so structured that vested interests will not allow significant resourcing to bring about the social and economic change that might lead to lessening people's suffering. We desperately need to dwell on providing thoughtful therapies for individuals and communities and, even more so, on whether we can find a way for psychotherapists to feed into re-evaluations at a social and economic level for the prevention of mental illness and promoting the wellbeing of our societies (see for example: Johnstone et al, 2018; House & Loewenthal, 2009; Proctor, 2006).

As Warren Mansell points out in Chapter 21, few of the contributors to this second edition have attempted to respond to the hope that the first edition of this book would lead 'towards a constructive dialogue', as its sub-title expressed. This aspiration has failed. This is probably because, first, as mentioned, there is a fundamental difference between approaches that attempt to find meaning and those that primarily attempt to take our minds off these problems. Second, while third-wave CBT may also have shared interests (see, for example, Isabel Clarke's Chapter 22) with those other therapies that give a primacy to relational aspects (see, for example, Loewenthal & Samuels, 2014), the roots of CBT's fundamental starting point are very different.

We are also in a cultural time where the questioning of and challenges to so-called evidence-based practice, as in this book and elsewhere, to date seems to fall into a vacuum and have very little impact, despite compelling arguments. While not wanting to repeat these arguments in this book, we will nevertheless cite here John Norcross's fascinating finding (2005) that the 'the vast majority of behavior therapists did not choose behavioral treatment for themselves' (p846).

The ability of the mainstream status quo to seemingly absorb these critiques without any change is reminiscent of the situationist descriptions of how resistances are absorbed and neutralised (eg. Debord, 1973). However, despite such criticisms (and we certainly could be critical of other psychotherapeutic approaches too), we wish to make clear that we do not want to demonise CBTers. We regard CBT practitioners as no less potentially well-intentioned than any other practitioners. We also consider that CBT can be helpful for clients who choose this approach, with informed consent, having been provided with information about it and alternative options. However, we find it frightening when CBT becomes the main, if not the only, game in town and when it offers potential for governments to use it as a form of ideological control.

Hence, 10 years after the first edition, we are in that dire situation of which our contributors originally warned us – a place where we have less of a schism in the therapy world and more a domination by CBT: CBT is, essentially, what you are likely to get if you seek therapy from the NHS. In the 2015 IAPT workforce census (NHS England & Health Education England, 2016), 70% of IAPT qualified workers were qualified in CBT. Notwithstanding the argument that what IAPT provides as CBT is not CBT proper, CBT as delivered by IAPT is increasingly how the general public understand talking therapies; other approaches are more rarely offered, or available, other than in private practice.

Yet 'research' has not stood still over the past 10 years. There are, as this book shows, new challenges to CBT's technical approach from, for example, relational perspectives, and from the lack of clarity emerging in the 'third-wave' variation as to what CBT actually is. The profession too is questioning with increasing authority the evidence base on which CBT rests – which research results are cited, and who sets the parameters for the so-called gold standard. Published research trials are being revisited and re-analysed, with very different conclusions, and comparison studies are producing results that are far from in CBT's favour. The dodo bird's infamous verdict still pertains, unchallenged in any serious sense. Yet all this new research is still not acceptable to NICE or the APA, and has yet to exert much meaningful influence on their guidance.

What is clear from this book is that there are some grounds where all the authors meet: all are united in a wish to prioritise the quality of the therapy relationship or the importance of the common factors, as demonstrated by research such as Rosenzweig (1936) and Hubble and colleagues (1999), and to offer something useful to clients in distress, most knowing that no one approach will be best for everyone. We cannot, however, ignore that the client voice is remarkable by its absence from the contents of this book; the client's voice is no more present in the research generally, and certainly in the data published on IAPT services. This, then, is surely a further aspect of what is missing in all these debates, along with the nature of psychotherapeutic knowledge and the central importance of social/economic ideological factors (Loewenthal, 2015).

Throughout the decades, clients have consistently argued that it is the relational qualities of therapy that make the difference (eg. Proctor & Hargate, 2013; Beutler & Harwood, 2002; Luborsky et al, 1985). If clients come to therapy, stay with therapy, and leave therapy continuing to feel better able to manage their own lives, then we are doing right – CBTers have yet to demonstrate convincingly that their ways of working deliver that.

References

Beutler L, Harwood T (2002). What is and can be attributed to the therapeutic relationship? *Journal of Contemporary Psychotherapy 32*(1): 25–33.

Debord G (1973). *The Society of the Spectacle*. London: Rebel Press.

House R, Loewenthal D (2009). *Childhood, Wellbeing and a Therapeutic Ethos*. London: Karnac.

Hubble MA, Duncan BL, Miller SD (eds) (1999). *The Heart and Soul of Change: what works in therapy*. Washington, DC: American Psychological Association.

Johnstone L, Boyle M, with Cromby J, Dillon J, Harper D, Kinderman P, Longden E, Pilgrim D, Read J (2018). *The Power Threat Meaning Framework: overview*. Leicester: British Psychological Society.

Loewenthal D (2011). *Post-Existentialism and the Psychological Therapies: towards a therapy without foundations*. London: Karnac.

Loewenthal D, Samuels A (2014). *Relational Psychotherapy, Psychoanalysis and Counselling*. Hove: Routledge.

Loewenthal D (ed) (2015). *Critical Psychotherapy, Psychoanalysis and Counselling: implications for practice*. Basingstoke: Palgrave Macmillan.

Luborsky L, McLellan AT, Woody GE, O'Brien CP, Auerbach A (1985). Therapist success and its determinants. *Archives of General Psychiatry 42*(6): 602–611.

NHS England, Health Education England (2016). *2015 Adult IAPT Workforce Census Report*. London: NHS England.

Norcross J. (2005) The psychotherapist's own psychotherapy: educating and developing psychologists. *American Psychologist 60*(8): 840–850.

Proctor G (2006). Therapy: opium for the masses or help for those who least need it? In: Proctor G, Cooper

M, Sanders P, Malcolm B (eds). *Politicizing the person-centred approach: an agenda for social change.* Ross-on-Wye: PCCS Books (pp 66–79).

Proctor G, Hargate R (2013). Quantitative and qualitative analysis of a set of goal attainment forms in primary care mental health services. *Counselling and Psychotherapy Research 13*(3): 235–241.

Rosenzweig S (1936). Some implicit common factors in diverse methods of psychotherapy. *American Journal of Autopsychiatry* 6(3): 412–415.

Contributors

Arthur C Bohart is a retired professor emeritus at California State University Dominguez Hills. He was also affiliated with Saybrook University. He is the co-author or co-editor of several books, including *How Clients Make Therapy Work: the process of active self-healing; Empathy Reconsidered: humanity's dark side,* and *Constructive and Destructive Behavior.* His work has focused on experiencing, empathy, the person-centered approach and evidence-based practice in psychotherapy. He considers himself an integrative person-centered therapist.

Pat Bracken is a psychiatrist who has been working for nearly 35 years in the field of mental health. As well as general adult clinical work, he has had experience of service development and management as well as service evaluation, work with refugees, asylum seekers and victims of violence and abuse, critical thinking and philosophy. He was appointed Professor of Philosophy, Diversity and Mental Health at the University of Central Lancashire, UK in 2006. He was one of the founders of the Critical Psychiatry Network.

David Brazier, PhD, MA is an author, psychotherapist, Buddhist, authority on Buddhist psychology and social commentator. He has written a dozen books, including *Beyond Carl Rogers*; *Zen Therapy*; *Love and Its Disappointment,* and *Who Loves Dies Well,* plus many other writings. He has initiated social aid projects in several countries, especially the UK, Bosnia and India. He is retired and lives in France, but continues to write and still lectures internationally from time to time.

Christy Bryceland completed her PhD in clinical psychology at the University of Calgary under the supervision of Henderikus J Stam. She is in full-time clinical practice in Nelson, British Columbia, Canada. Her practice focuses on assessment and treatment of children and young people, especially those with developmental disabilities.

Konstantinos Chondros is a doctoral student in counselling psychology interested in hermeneutic phenomenological inquiry. Currently he is using Gadamer's philosophical hermeneutics to explore queer counselling professionals' experiences of practising social justice with queer clients. His practice interests are in the broader field of human sexuality, and how therapists use postmodern approaches (eg. narrative therapy) to address issues related to gender and sexual diversity.

Isabel Clarke is a consultant clinical psychologist with over 20 years' experience working as a therapist in the NHS with people with complex problems. Her book, co-edited with Hannah Wilson, *Cognitive Behaviour Therapy for Acute Inpatient Mental Health* describes an innovative approach to acute services that she is currently applying in IAPT. Her other books, *Psychosis and Spirituality: consolidating the new paradigm* and *Madness, Mystery and the Survival of God*, explore the themes of spirituality, mental health and being human.

Michael Guilfoyle was a clinical psychologist based in Ireland and an Extraordinary Professor in the Department of Educational Psychology at the University of the Western Cape, South Africa. His primary interest was in exploring therapeutic practices from a narrative and post-structural perspective. His book *The Person in Narrative Therapy: a post-structural, Foucauldian account*, was published in 2014, and he contributed numerous journal articles and book chapters in international publications. He died in 2017.

Adrian Hemmings DPhil is a chartered psychologist and UKCP registered psychotherapist. He has many years' experience as a practitioner in the NHS and third sector organisations. He was a research fellow at the University of Sussex for 12 years and then Professional Head of Psychology for a primary care mental health team and Director of Sussex Alcohol and Substance Use Service. He is a past chair of the BPS Psychotherapy Section. Adrian integrates a cognitive behavioural approach in his work with clients. He is currently collaborating in a study with the Centre for Psychological Therapies in Primary Care, developing a broader model of working in an IAPT service.

Richard House PhD, CPsychol is an educational, mental health and left–green political campaigner-consultant in Stroud, UK. Formerly senior lecturer in early childhood (Winchester) and psychotherapy (Roehampton) and co-editor of *Self and Society* journal, Richard is co-founder of the Independent Practitioners Network and the Alliance for Counselling and Psychotherapy. Author/editor of 12 books, including *In, Against and Beyond Therapy*; *Too Much, Too Soon?*, and *Humanistic Psychology: current trends, future prospects* (co-edited), he is a trained Steiner teacher and childhood campaigner, and has co-ordinated (with Sue Palmer) four international, multiple-signatory press letters on the state of childhood in modern culture.

John D Kaye founded the M(Clinical) Psychology degree and co-founded the Discourse & Rhetoric Unit in the School of Psychology, University of Adelaide. He also co-founded, with Valerie Walkerdine, the Millennium World Conference in Critical Psychology in Sydney, 1999. He is currently in private practice and supervises four interns toward registration as clinical psychologists. Resisting imprisonment in the strait-jacket of the 'scientist practitioner' model, his practice is underpinned by concepts drawn from philosophy, post-foundational theory, post-structuralism, social constructionism, discourse theory, existentialism and literature. John's interests span literature, poetry, theatre, art, social justice – and fine wine.

Paul Kelly trained as a clinical psychologist in Birmingham and was involved in setting up the West Midlands Community and Critical Psychology Interest Group and the Midlands Psychology Group. He was also active in the Irish Mental Health Forum. Since returning to live in Ireland in 2004, he has been working as a psychologist in the Student Health and Counselling Service at University College Dublin. He is interested in understanding the social and material causes of personal distress and how mainstream psychology functions ideologically to reflect and support the status quo.

John Lees is Associate Professor of Psychotherapy and Counselling at the University of Leeds, a counselling and psychotherapy practitioner in private practice in London and Sussex and founder editor of the journal *Psychodynamic Counselling* (now *Psychodynamic Practice*). He has edited a book series, five books – most recently *The Future of Psychological Therapy: from managed care to transformational practice* – and published numerous book chapters and professional articles, many of which have been peer reviewed. He designed and ran an MSc in Therapeutic Counselling and is course leader of a post-qualifying course in anthroposophic psychotherapy.

Del Loewenthal is Director of the Research Centre for Therapeutic Education and Professor of Psychotherapy and Counselling in the Department of Psychology at the University of Roehampton. He is an existential-analytic psychotherapist, chartered counselling psychologist and photographer, and has a small private practice in Wimbledon and Brighton. He is founding Editor-in-Chief of the *European Journal of Psychotherapy and Counselling*. His books include, with Richard House, *Against and for CBT: towards a constructive dialogue?*; *Post-Existentialism and the Psychological Therapies*; *Phototherapy and Therapeutic Photography in a Digital Age*, and with Andrew Samuels, *Relational Psychotherapy, Psychoanalysis and Counselling*; *Critical Psychotherapy, Psychoanalysis and Counselling*, and *Existential Psychotherapy and Counselling after Postmodernism*.

Dr Mishka Lysack began teaching full-time at the University of Calgary in 2006, where he is currently an associate professor in the Faculty of Social Work. He is also an adjunct assistant professor in the Faculty of Medicine, and has taught at a graduate level in the Faculty of Environmental Design since 2008.

Dr Warren Mansell is Reader in Clinical Psychology at the University of Manchester. In 2011, he received the May Davidson Award from the British Psychological Society for the outstanding contribution to the field of clinical psychology, within 10 years of qualifying as a clinical psychologist. He was the co-chair of the Scientific Committee for the Annual Conference for the British Association of Behavioural and Cognitive Psychotherapies 2008–2013. He has authored more than 100 peer-reviewed publications on CBT research and practice. His current interests lie within the development and evaluation of transdiagnostic and trans-theoretical psychological interventions based on perceptual control theory.

Jane Milton works as psychoanalyst in London. In the NHS, she has worked as a consultant psychiatrist in psychotherapy at King's College Hospital and in the adult department of the Tavistock Clinic. She has also been involved in student health at both King's College and the Guildhall School of Music and Drama. When she first came to London in 1987, it was as research assistant to Dr Anthony Ryle, in a CAT study with people with diabetes. She went on to train at the Institute of Psychoanalysis. She is actively involved with the development of psychoanalysis in Eastern Europe, particularly Ukraine. Her books include (with Caroline Polmear and Julia Fabricius) *A Short Introduction to Psychoanalysis.*

Paul Moloney is an NHS counselling psychologist based in an adult learning disabilities service in Shropshire. He teaches on the clinical psychology course at Birmingham University and the University of Stafford and was formerly a lecturer in mental health with the Open University. His main clinical interest is in how the world in which we live shapes our wellbeing and distress. He is a member of the Midlands Psychology Group – a collective of psychologists dedicated to questioning the assumptions of therapeutic psychology – and author of *The Therapy Industry: the irresistible rise of the talking cure and why it doesn't work.*

Fred Newman was co-founder of the East Side Institute for Group and Short-Term Psychotherapy, a psychotherapist, playwright and director. He received his PhD in analytic philosophy and the foundations of mathematics from Stanford University. His writings on psychotherapy, politics, culture and social change include *Performance of a Lifetime: a practical-philosophical guide to the joyous life* and, with Lois Holzman, *Unscientific Psychology* and *The End of Knowing.* He died in 2001.

Stephen Palmer PhD is the Founder Director of the Centre for Stress Management, President of the International Stress Management Association and Vice President of the Society for Dialectical Behaviour Therapy. He is a Visiting Professor at Middlesex University and Adjunct Professor of Coaching Psychology, Aalborg

University. He has written/edited more than 50 books. He is an AEI-approved RE and CBT Supervisor, an AREBT-accredited supervisor and a BABCP-accredited therapist and holds the European Certificate of Counsellor Accreditation. In 2000, the British Psychological Society Division of Counselling Psychology awarded him the Annual Counselling Psychology Award, and in 2008 he received the Lifetime Achievement Award from the BPS Special Group in Coaching Psychology.

David Pilgrim PhD is Honorary Professor of Health and Social Policy at the University of Liverpool and Visiting Professor of Clinical Psychology at the University of Southampton. His publications include *Understanding Mental Health: a critical realist exploration* and *Key Concepts in Mental Health* (4th ed). Others (all with Anne Rogers) include *A Sociology of Mental Health and Illness* (winner of the 2006 BMA Medical Book of the Year Award); *Mental Health Policy in Britain,* and *Mental Health and Inequality.* His most recent book, *Child Sexual Abuse: moral panics and states of denial*, is to be published by Routledge.

Dr Gillian Proctor is a clinical psychologist and independent person-centred therapist. She is Programme Lead for the MA in psychotherapy and counselling at the University of Leeds. Her particular interest are in ethics and politics in therapy. She is the author of two text books, The *Dynamics of Power in Counselling and Psychotherapy* (2nd ed), and *Values and Ethics in Counselling and Psychotherapy.*

Frank C Richardson is Professor of Educational Psychology (Emeritus) at the University of Texas, Austin. He is author or editor of several books, including *Re-envisioning Psychology* and *Critical Thinking about Psychology*, and the author of more than 100 articles and chapters in theoretical psychology and the philosophy of social science. His current interests include topics in psychology and religion. He is a past president of the Society for Theoretical and Philosophical Psychology (Division 24 of the American Psychological Association) and recipient of its Distinguished Lifetime Achievement Award.

Andrew Samuels is Professor of Analytical Psychology at Essex and holds visiting chairs at New York, Roehampton, Macau and Goldsmiths, University of London. He is a former chair of the UK Council for Psychotherapy and one of the two co-founders of Psychotherapists and Counsellors for Social Responsibility. His interests include the tragic fate of 'real' psychotherapy in the public sector and NHS. He works internationally as a political consultant. His many books have been translated into 21 languages and include, most recently, *Relational Psychotherapy, Psychoanalysis and Counselling* (co-edited with Del Loewenthal); *Persons, Passions, Psychotherapy, Politics*; *A New Therapy for Politics?* and *Analysis and Activism*.

Robert Snell is an analytic psychotherapist, a member of the British Psychotherapy Foundation and the British Psychoanalytic Council, and an Honorary Senior

Research Fellow in the Centre for Therapeutic Education at Roehampton University, London. He is the author of *Théophile Gautier: a romantic critic of the visual arts*; co-author with Del Loewenthal of *Postmodernism for Psychotherapists: a critical reader*, and author of *Uncertainties, Mysteries, Doubts: romanticism and the analytic attitude* and *Portraits of the Insane: Theodore Géricault and the subject of psychotherapy.*

Henderikus J Stam is a Professor of Psychology at the University of Calgary, where he teaches courses in the history and theory of psychology as well as clinical psychology. His recent scholarly interests have focused on contemporary theoretical problems in psychology and the historical foundations of 20th century psychology, on which he has published numerous articles and book chapters. Founding editor of *Theory & Psychology* (now Editor Emeritus), he is a former president of the American Psychological Association's Division 26 (Society for the History of Psychology) and Division 24 (Society for Theoretical and Philosophical Psychology).

Tom Strong is a professor, couple and family therapist, and counsellor-educator at the University of Calgary, who researches and writes on the collaborative, critically-informed and practical potentials of discursive approaches to psychotherapy.

Olga Sutherland lists her main areas of research as family therapy and discourse analysis. She uses discursive methods of inquiry (eg. conversation analysis, discursive psychology, membership categorisation analysis) to examine interactions in therapy. She also conducts research in the field of gender and language and explores how the broader socio-cultural context influences wellbeing and how therapists can promote social inclusion and justice.

Philip Thomas worked as a consultant psychiatrist in the NHS for over 20 years. He left clinical practice in 2004 to write. He has published many papers, mostly in peer-reviewed journals, latterly in philosophy and its relevance to madness and society. He is well known for working in alliance with survivors of psychiatry, service users and community groups, nationally and internationally. Until recently, he was chair of Sharing Voices Bradford, a community development project working with black and minority ethnic communities. He was a founder member and, until 2011, co-chair of the Critical Psychiatry Network.

Keith Tudor is Professor of Psychotherapy at Auckland University of Technology, Aotearoa New Zealand, where he is also Head of the School of Public Health & Psychosocial Studies. He has a long association with the person-centred approach (PCA), including as co-director of Temenos (www.temenos.ac.uk), Sheffield, UK for 17 years. He is the author and/or editor of some 80 publications on the PCA, including six books. His most recent book is *Psychotherapy: a critical examination.*

Jay Watts is a clinical psychologist and psychotherapist. She is Honorary Senior Research Fellow at Queen Mary, University of London, and in full-time, independent practice. Jay has held a number of senior academic and NHS posts, including leading early intervention in psychosis and integrative psychotherapy teams, and developing teaching modules as Senior Lecturer in Counselling Psychology at City University. She is on the editorial boards of the *European Journal for Counselling and Psychotherapy* and *Self & Society*. Jay is Foreign Correspondent for Robert Whitaker's activist collective *Mad in America*. She writes regularly for the *Guardian* and *Independent*, and spends an unhealthy amount of time tweeting as @Shrink_at_Large.

David Winter is Professor Emeritus of Clinical Psychology at the University of Hertfordshire. He was previously Programme Director of the university's doctorate in clinical psychology, and spent most of his working life practising as a clinical psychologist and personal construct psychotherapist in the NHS. He has held visiting positions at various universities, including Visiting Professor at the University of Padua, Brotherton Fellow at the University of Melbourne and Visiting Scholar at the University of Wollongong. He is a Fellow of the British Psychological Society, and has written more than 170 publications, primarily on personal construct psychology and psychotherapy research.

Robert L Woolfolk is Professor of Psychology and Philosophy at Rutgers University. He was formerly Professor of Psychology at Princeton University. His work has included empirical investigations of psychopathology and psychotherapy and research on the philosophical foundations of psychology. He served as editor of the *Journal of Theoretical and Philosophical Psychology.* He is the co-author of *Stress, Sanity, and Survival* and *Treating Somatization: a cognitive-behavioral approach*, and is the author of *The Cure of Souls* and *The Value of Psychotherapy: the talking cure in an age of clinical science.*

Name index

G

H

L

M

N

O

P

Q

R

S

T

U

V

W

Y

Z

Subject index

C

F

G

T